The
GOOD HOUSEKEEPING
All-American
COOKBOOK

The GOOD HOUSEKEEPING *All-American* COOKBOOK

HEARST BOOKS · NEW YORK

The Good Housekeeping All-American Cookbook was designed, edited, and produced by Dorling Kindersley Limited

Good Housekeeping

Editor-in-Chief   John Mack Carter

Food Department

Director   Mildred Ying

Associate Director   Susan Deborah Goldsmith

Associates   Ellen H. Connelly
Marianne Zanzarella

Special Consultant   Lucy Wing

Dorling Kindersley Limited

Editorial Director   Amy Carroll

Art Director   Vanessa Pryse

Project Editor   Elizabeth Wolf-Cohen

Designers   Sally Powell
Peter Cross
Helen Claire Young

Editors   Beverly LeBlanc
Heather Maisner
Irene Lyford
Debra Grayson

Published by The Reader's Digest Association, Inc., with permission of Hearst Books, an affiliate of William Morrow & Company, Inc.

Library of Congress Catalog Card Number:

ISBN: 0-688-06333-0

Printed in the United States of America

First Edition

1 2 3 4 5 6 7 8 9 10

Foreword

This special collection of recipes is a celebration of America's great culinary heritage. Many are classic recipes, direct from the pages of Good Housekeeping Magazine; others have been newly developed for this book. All of them, whether traditional or contemporary, have been brought up to date. We've included calorie counts for each one, and made certain that they use the best ingredients, and fewest special utensils. We've also photographed them in attractive settings to provide inspiration for serving.

Each finished dish is shown in the Color Index at the beginning of the book, accompanied by a caption giving its main ingredients, the time needed to prepare it, and the number of servings. In this way, you can browse through the pages selecting the most appropriate dishes for your meals since you'll know at a glance what you need to make them, as well as the time they will take to cook.

Once you've decided, you will find the recipes set out in an easy to follow step-by-step format; many of the recipes are accompanied by a complete set of diagrams. Therefore, even beginning cooks will be able to use the recipes successfully. Of course, it helps to bear the following things in mind: When you prepare a recipe for the first time, read it through carefully to make sure that you have allowed enough preparation time. Before beginning to cook, assemble the utensils needed and measure all the ingredients. Avoid substituting key ingredients, product forms (such as regular or instant) or package sizes, unless the recipe suggests an alternative. Be cautious, too, about doubling or halving any recipe; although some can be increased successfully, many more cannot. For best results, make up the recipe as given and, if a larger quantity is desired, repeat the recipe a second time. Seasonings and spices can be varied safely according to personal taste, but it is always a good idea to follow the recipe directions exactly for the first time.

By following these few tips, and the wealth of diagrams and photographs throughout, we hope that this book will provide all the necessary practical information, plus the inspiration, for you to serve a multitude of memorable meals — not only on special occasions, but every day.

Contents

Introduction 8

How to use this book 14

Color index 15

APPETIZERS 83

Hot appetizers 85
Cold appetizers 89

SOUPS 95

Vegetable soups 97
Hearty soups 100
Chicken and turkey soups 104
Fish soups 106

EGGS AND CHEESE 107

Egg dishes 109
Cheese dishes 114

FISH AND SHELLFISH 117

Clams 119
Crabs 120
Crayfish 121
Lobsters 122
Oysters 123
Scallops 124
Shrimp 124
Mixed shellfish 126
Valentine's Day Party *128*
Easter Lunch *130*
Mother's Day Lunch *132*
Bass 134
Bluefish 134
Catfish 135
Cod 136
Flounder 138
Halibut 139
Red snapper 140
Salmon 141
Sole 142
Swordfish 143
Trout 143
Tuna 144

POULTRY 145

Chicken
  Whole chicken 147
  Cut-up chicken 149
  Chicken legs and thighs 155
  Chicken breasts 156
  Chicken cutlets 158
  Rock cornish hens 159
Turkey 160
Duckling 164
Goose 166
Game 167
Chicken livers 168
Stuffings 169

MEAT 171

Beef 173–187
  Steaks 173
  Roasts 176
Pot roasts 178
Stews and pieces 180
Ground 182
Pork 188–200
  Roasts 188
  Chops and steaks 189
  Tenderloin 191
  Hocks 192
  Stew 193
  Ribs 194
Smoked pork 195–203
  Whole ham 195
Memorial Day Picnic *196*
4th of July Barbecue *198*
Labor Day Clambake *200*
  Canned ham 202
  Ham slices 202
  Ham hocks 203
Lamb 204–207
  Roasts 204
  Chops 205
  Stew and shanks 207
  Shish kabob 207
Veal 208–211
  Roasts 208
  Chops 209
  Cutlets 210
  Stew 211
Variety meats 211–214
  Calf's liver 211
  Sausages 212
  Tongue 214
  Venison 214

BARBECUE 215

Meat
  Steaks 217
  Brisket 217
  Larger cuts 218
  Ribs 219
  Kabobs and chops 220
Poultry 221
Fish 223
Vegetables 225
Fruit 226
Barbecue sauces 226

VEGETABLES 227

Artichokes	229
Asparagus	230
Beans	231
Dried beans	232
Beets	234
Broccoli	234
Carrots	234
Cauliflower	235
Corn	236
Eggplant	237
Mushrooms	238
Onions	238
Peas	239
Peppers	240
Potatoes	242
Squash	245
Sweet potatoes	246
Tomatoes	247
Halloween Party Buffet	*248*
Thanksgiving Day	*250*
Christmas Eve Party	*252*
Mixed vegetables	254
Sauces for vegetables	256

PASTA AND RICE 257

Pasta	259
Sauces for pasta	265
Rice	265

SALADS 269

Green salads	271
Coleslaws	272
Potato salads	273
Bean and grain salads	274
Vegetable salads	276
Molded salads	277
Chef's salads	278
Seafood salads	279
Chicken salads	280
Pasta and rice salads	282
Fruit salads	283
Salad dressings	284

DESSERTS 285

Fruit	287
Molded desserts	293
Puddings	295
Mousses and soufflés	299
Ice-cream desserts	301
Fruit ices	306
Sauces for ice cream	306

PIES 307

Fruit pies	309
Fruit tarts	316
Rich pies	318

CAKES, COOKIES, CANDIES 325

White cakes	327
Yellow cakes	328
Coffeecakes	329
Chocolate cakes	330
Christmas Dinner	*332*
New Year's Eve Supper	*334*
New Year's Day Brunch	*336*
Special occasion cakes	338
Cheesecakes	340
Fruit, spice, and nut cakes	341
Frostings and fillings	344
Brownies	345
Chocolate cookies	346
Spice cookies	347
Sugar cookies	348
Nut and grain cookies	350
Christmas cookies	352
Candies	354

BREADS 355

Grain breads	357
Sweet yeast breads	359
Rolls and buns	361
Biscuits	363
Quick breads	364
Corn breads	366
Muffins	368
Doughnuts	369
Pancakes and waffles	370
Crêpes	371
Sandwiches	372
Pizza	374

PICKLES, PRESERVES, RELISHES 375

Pickles	377
Preserves	379
Relishes	383
Sauces	385

INDEX 386

Our cuisine reflects the country we live in – one that is constantly changing and open to new ideas and customs, yet traditional, too, with an emphasis on the tried and true. Therefore, all-American food embraces both the native turkey and the Italian tortellini; home-grown corn and the imported croissant. The most important factors that shaped our style of cooking are our indigenous produce, the way the native Americans used it, and the culinary contributions of the settlers and immigrants. Early colonists and successive waves of immigrants brought their various cultures, customs, and, of course, their cooking techniques with them. Within our vast melting pot, we can still trace the diverse influences that have given American cooking its distinctive character.

CORN – THE INDIAN'S GIFT

The food that greeted the first arrivals to the New World in the early 1600s was corn, or Indian maize, which numerous Indian tribes had been cultivating for centuries. Corn took the place of the European grains, wheat and barley, which failed to grow in the early settlements. Sometimes corn was eaten three times a day – fresh, dried, or ground into meal. The Indians taught our ancestors to bake primitive kinds of bread called ashcakes, hoe cakes (so called because they were baked on hoes in front of the fire), and corn pone. Corn is still a major part of our diet and is eaten as a vegetable, in cornbreads, puddings, soups and chowders, and salads. Throughout this book you will find a variety of recipes based on this important ingredient.

THE SETTLERS' STAPLES

Between the rows of corn, the Indians planted beans and sometimes squash. They often combined the corn and beans in a stew known as succotash, a dish more popular in the South, although it often appears on tables all over America at Thanksgiving-time. Corn, beans, and squash are still found in soups, stews, and salads, but for the early settlers these were the mainstays of their diet. To these basics, they added freshly caught fish and game. Strange and plentiful seafoods were encountered for the first time: succulent lobsters, clams, oysters, and scallops were there in profusion, and settlers learned how to prepare them from the coastal Indians. Game was so prevalent that pigeons darkened the skies; the Indians simply knocked them from the trees with poles. Bear, squirrel, opposum, and elk, were eaten when available and nuts, roots, fruits, and berries were also gathered as part of the diet. So, from very early on, a variety of ingredients could be combined with the settlers' culinary traditions to create a unique cuisine.

FARM FARE

During the seventeenth and eighteenth centuries, the farm became the basic economic unit. Except for game, fish, and wild birds, which they hunted, families grew what they needed. Once wheat was planted successfully, the colonists made bread. They grew corn, rye, oats, vegetables, salad greens, and herbs; they collected berries and harvested fruits, such as apples, plums, and peaches from the orchard; and they raised poultry, pigs, and cows for eggs, bacon, and milk. As the range of produce widened and the frontier expanded westward, the diet became more varied. Wheat flour production increased in the mid-1800s after the invention of a Swiss steel roller which could grind the flour very fine. After the turn of the century, most wheat flour was processed white by bleaching and removing the wheat germ which also decreased the nutritional value. Today we favor unbleached and whole-wheat flours.

WESTWARD HO!

But there was little refinement among the pioneers and frontiersmen at that time; their only cooking equipment was a kettle, and sometimes a skillet, into which they tossed game and wild vegetables, or pork and peas, or even fried bacon, covering it with rum! Frontiersmen often subsisted on a diet of fish, hard tack (a dehydrated mixture of flour and water which stayed edible for months), sugar, and coffee. Soups were the first convenience foods; they were left simmering on the fire, and leftover meat and vegetables were added daily providing instant meals. The delicacies of the day were beaver tail and buffalo. Buffalo, in fact, provided a means of survival for the early pioneers. In addition to the vast quantities of meat it furnished, the tongue was a specialty, the marrow bones provided "hunter's butter", and the meat was the main ingredient of pemmican or jerky – pounded with fat and pulverized berries, and preserved in natural casings, it was the frontiersman's version of K rations.

LAND OF THE FREE

Much of the food produced in America is the result of a particular soil and climate, but early on, the way it was used depended on the cultural background of its settlers. The bounty of fish and seafood off the harsh New England coast encouraged English settlers to fill their traditional meat pies with lobsters, oysters, or other fish.

As English puddings were impossible to create without wheat flour, corn puddings soon replaced them as a staple in all the thirteen colonies. Beef and beans became synonymous with the Southwest, but were later found in California-style cooking. The cooking of the Midwest was dominated by wheat, corn, and dairy products, although these ingredients were used differently by the various German, Swedish, and Polish homesteaders.

Beginning in the mid-1800s, peaking during the early years of the twentieth century, waves of European immigrants arrived seeking religious freedom and a chance to make a new and better life in a New World. It is easy to understand their wish to create familiar foods which served as an emotional link to their pasts. But they were forced to adapt their Old World dishes to include New World ingredients, and this process created a cuisine with a character all its own. By using local, rather than

Mediterranean seafood, an Italian dish became "cioppino", a typical seafood stew popular in San Francisco. Crawfish found in Louisiana's bayous combined with African okra to transform the French Cajun's bouillabaisse into the gumbo we find there today.

In some areas of our vast country, the influence is more obviously that of one group over another: the Dutch in New York, the Swedes in Minnesota, the Germans in Pennsylvania, the French in Louisiana, the Spanish in Florida and California, and our Mexican neighbors in Texas and New Mexico. Many immigrant contributions are now considered part of our national cuisine – pizza, chow mein, frankfurters, blintzes, and tacos – yet, these dishes are sometimes far removed from their original sources.

AMERICA'S FAVORITE MEAT

Beef was, and still is, the favorite meat in America. Corned or pickled, beef was eaten by generations of early settlers and pioneers who otherwise would have been without meat in winter. Early on, steak was served at coach stops or "porterhouses" and by the 1760s, some cities had "beef steak houses."

Our early desire for beef was met by the successful transportation of Spanish cattle to Texas. They were a hardy breed, raised to withstand heat and lack of water so they could be driven for up to a thousand miles to the railroad centers for distribution. By the 1850s, Chicago was established as a meat-packing center, and by the end of the Civil War, the demand for beef was so high the era of the great cattle drives had begun; the cowboy and westward expansion became symbols of romance and unending destiny. By the 1880s, beef was being shipped abroad and steakhouses were among the most popular restaurants in the big cities. Pioneers heading west brought with them recipes for preparing a variety of meat cuts; roasted sirloins and joints, braised dishes like our Yankee Pot Roast, New England Boiled Dinner, Beef in Beer, and Old Country Short Rib Dinner, and pan-fried steaks and chops.

Despite its foreign-sounding name, the hamburger is a truly American invention. Ground beef patties were eaten by the earliest colonists, but the word hamburger was not common until the 1920s. We include a special feature with original serving suggestions for the versatile hamburger, and traditional recipes as well as a whole range of contemporary meat dishes in our Meat and Barbecue Chapters.

★UNITED STATES

POTATOES

MINN

OREGON

Salt Lake City

Denver

San Francisco

NEVADA

Los Angeles

Santa Fé

NEW MEXICO

HAWAII

The USA covers a vast area stretching from the rocky New England coastline and the sandy beaches of Florida to the spectacular palisades of the West Coast and includes the tropical forests of Hawaii and the Alaskan tundra. Differences in geography and climate have provided American cooking with varied and unique ingredients; Vermont's maple syrup, Georgia's peanuts and peaches, the Midwest's corn, and California's year-round fruits and vegetables have helped create a cuisine of great character. Our fanciful interpretation depicts just some of America's most spectacular natural wonders, resources, and bounty.

HOME BAKED

Every ethnic group brought its own special bread or style of baking when it settled here. While simple breads have always been part of the daily diet, the vast quantity of the breads we eat today has its origins elsewhere. Jewish immigrants brought bagels and bialys — tasty, flat, onion rolls; Scandinavians came with crisp breads and rye breads; the French favored us with their long loaves and croissants; the Italians, Danes, and Germans also brought sweet breads like panettone, Danish pastries, and kolachy; and the English their smoothly rounded Sally Lunn. Sourdough bread, in which the starter, a fermentation of flour, water, and sugar, was substituted for yeast, found lasting fame from the time of the California Gold Rush and is still associated with San Francisco. Pancakes, griddle cakes, baking soda biscuits, muffins, and crackers also evolved from various Old World recipes such as Scotch pancakes and English scones, crumpets, and biscuits. They were easy to prepare and required little cooking time.

Quick breads, cake-like breads made without yeast, were more indigenous. These became more popular in the mid-nineteenth century after the invention of baking powder, a combination of sodium bicarbonate and acid salt which made the dough rise. Commercial production of baking powder, followed by baking soda in the 1870s, freed the cook from laboriously beating dough to give it lightness, and brought about a new range of breads, cakes, cookies, and baked goods that are wholly American in character. A variety of quick breads, from banana to peanut butter, muffins, pancakes, waffles, and blintzes are included in our Bread Chapter, as well as many old favorites among the Cakes and Cookies recipes.

SWEET THINGS

From rural bake sales which raise money for charities to ice cream carts on city street corners, desserts and sweet things are a very important part of American culture. Good homemade desserts are found in the cooking of all nationalities; many of these were transformed by our native ingredients and ingenuity, producing such specialties as Apple Pandowdy, Strawberry-Rhubarb Grunt, and Cranberry-Pear Cobbler. Fresh wild and cultivated berries had been served with cream since the earliest days, and were sweetened with maple syrup, before cane sugar became readily available. Strawberry shortcake, a biscuit-type cake spread with butter, layered with sugar-sprinkled fruit, and topped with whipped cream became popular wherever strawberries grew. Coffee-cakes, a legacy of German immigrants, have developed a particularly American character. The coffee klatch, originally an informal get-together over a cup of coffee, was an important aspect of life in the "old country" and Germans brought this delightful custom here where it took a firm hold. Delicious sweet yeast and non-yeast cakes and breads, sometimes with chocolate, fruit, spices, or nuts are part of this tasty tradition.

Doughnuts and cookies are among our most popular sweet things. Doughnuts may have arrived here with the Pilgrims, who spent several years before 1620 in Holland, where they learned to make these deep-fried snacks before coming to the New World. But it was the Pennsylvania Dutch who introduced the hole in their centers, making them a perfect shape for "dunking" which has become the standard way of eating them. Sprinkled with sugar and cinnamon or stuffed with jelly or cream, they are enjoyed every day across the country. So too are cookies, those sweet flat cakes that arrived with Dutch settlers. Filled with chocolate chip, sugar, spice, butter, and spritz cookies, the cookie jar has become a national symbol. And since their first appearance in the nineteenth century, small dark brownies have rarely left the scene. Sometimes flat, crisp, and cookie-like, other times soft and fudgy, we offer some delicious brownie variations in this book.

Layer cakes have also become a favorite. Their light yet rich texture, many layers, and fluffy or fudgy fillings and frostings are well known and certainly rival the cakes of any other nation. Many arrived here at the turn of the century, but many more have been modified or created this century, enhanced by the advent of baking powder and other technological developments. Angel-Food Cake, Lane Cake, and Devil's Food Cake are uniquely American. We've created a special cake for a Valentine's Day Dessert party, a national excuse for celebrating sweet things.

We also have a special place in our hearts for ice cream. Legend has it that ice cream was made at George Washington's home at Mount Vernon and that Thomas Jefferson brought egg-custard based ice creams back from France. Dolly Madison often served ice cream at the White House, and by the War of 1812, this favorite frozen dessert was being sold commercially in Philadelphia and along the East Coast. Inside is a special feature on some soda fountain specials, as well as some original ice-cream tortes and other desserts and snacks.

A LOVE OF INVENTION

America is an inventive nation and many new processes contributed to the growth of American cookery. Each new labor-saving device or gadget was embraced with energy and enthusiasm – the ice-box gave way to the refrigerator and then to the refrigerator-freezer. Cooking in general became more easily controlled with the invention of better stoves, which affected bread and cake making in particular. By the middle of the twentieth century, with air freight and rail shipping, supermarkets, and technological develoments in canned, ready-prepared, and frozen foods, our diets and tastes became more varied. Kitchens changed to accommodate gas and electric stoves, refrigerators, freezers, and a range of gadgets including toasters, blenders, mixers, food processors, and the all-desirable dishwasher.

EATING HERE, THERE, EVERYWHERE

The most important result of these technological advances was the increase in leisure time. This allowed people to gather together more frequently and more informally. As a nation, we tend to be a casual and relaxed people and this is reflected in both the foods we eat and where, when, and how we eat them. Brunch, a combination of breakfast and lunch became very fashionable in the 1930s. Often accompanied by cocktails like the Bloody Mary or Mimosa, menus can include eggs, pancakes or waffles, sausages, smoked fish, salads, quiches, and endless casserole dishes. We've included a delicious California-style brunch to celebrate New Year's Day.

The cocktail party, a particularly American get-together, was invented in the 1920s during Prohibition when alcoholic drinks were illegal outside the home. The variety of snacks, tidbits, dips, which became very popular in the 1960s, and "finger foods" consumed at these gatherings is endless. Many of our appetizers are suitable for this type of party; the fare can range from light and simple to more substantial offerings and very elegant canapes.

Picnics, barbecues, clambakes, and tailgate parties are other popular forms of casual entertaining. Often the kind of food we enjoy at these occasions is less formal as well. Hamburgers, hot dogs, fried chicken, sandwiches, pizzas and salads, somehow seem more at home in the outdoors, on a back porch, or on a beach. Of course, even sophisticated food can be enjoyed at these occasions; a whole poached fish served cold with an elegant salad followed by an iced dessert on the back porch can create elegant open-air dining. A hamper or cold box packed with delicious cold meats and salads, and maybe a pie or fresh fruit, is an ideal portable meal served on a blanket by the sea, or off the tailgate of a station wagon at a football stadium. Earlier generations set the scene with New England clambakes that celebrated the catch and Western barbecues that glorified meat cooked over an open fire. Even box suppers, where local ladies' most popular special dishes were sold, not only raised money for community charities, but provided a social occasion which remained popular for years.

A RETURN TO BASICS

The casual nature of our eating and entertaining, as well as our love of progress, is probably one of the reasons we have embraced convenience foods more enthusiastically than any other nation. But at the same time, we are appreciative of the foodstuffs and preparation techniques which make American cooking great. In our zeal to exploit our country's bounty to the full, food enthusiasts are constantly adding to our repetoire of recipes by using favorite ingredients in a new way, or discovering new ingredients, or new styles of cooking which derive from older methods. Today's new style of cooking also is concerned with health. Many people are counting calories, reducing their intakes of red meat, fat, and processed foods, and trying to add more fish, poultry, vegetables, and grains to their daily diet and our recipe selection reflects this. Today, as always, Americans enjoy cooking for family and friends and our dining tables are once more a center of domestic life.

How to Use the Book

This book is a collection of favorite American recipes. It includes dishes based on ingredients present when the Pilgrims arrived, up through ones that make use of the latest imported ingredients and eating styles. Above all, it is a collection of American recipes tested in the kitchens of Good Housekeeping. The home economists at Good Housekeeping made certain these dishes were good to eat, easy to prepare, and attractive to serve. We believe you'll agree.

THE COLOR INDEX

Immediately following is the color index – 64 pages of photographs of every recipe in the book. When planning your meal, all you need to do is look through these pages and choose the dishes which suit you and your menu. Captions describe the dish in detail, inform you how many servings it makes and how long it takes to prepare, and directs you to the page where the recipe appears in the book. Once you have chosen your recipe, you can turn directly to the page, and follow our step-by-step directions.

THE RECIPES

Each recipe is set out in an easy-to-read, step-by-step format, and many are fully illustrated. Those recipes which are of special interest historically have a short, concise introduction or interesting anecdote. Where necessary, notes are given on how to garnish the dish and there are cross-references to sauces and/or other recipes that make good accompaniments. The number of servings the dish makes, and the preparation time, should help you plan your meal well in advance. There is also a calorie count for each.

TIP BOXES

Throughout the recipe section there are illustrated tip boxes which provide additional information. Some suggest ways of making the preparation of a dish easier, for example, tips on kneading bread and ways of carving meat. Others show you how to serve a dish to give it a more appealing and original presentation – garnishing with vegetables, decorating a whole cheese, and making heart-shaped tart shells. Still others are concerned with ways of handling special ingredients or types of equipment – preparing tropical fruits and chili peppers and special tools for use with shellfish. More ideas on entertaining are found on the Special Occasion pages.

SPECIAL OCCASIONS

To help you celebrate those great American occasions throughout the year, we have planned our special menus and serving ideas to make your entertaining as successful and trouble-free as possible. We've tried to cover the spectrum of holidays that people enjoy celebrating, and have given them regional themes, such as a Southern-style Easter lunch. The availability of ingredients, however, means they can be cooked anywhere. Each occasion has a menu, composed of recipes from the book. There's an introduction about the history of the holiday, a timetable for preparation, and tips on presentation.

Where useful, a special recipe or serving tip is given: For example, assembling a heart-shaped cake for Valentine's Day and presenting a rack of lamb as a guard of honor for a Mother's Day lunch.

From our New Year's Day Brunch to a New Year's Eve Supper, we're certain you'll enjoy celebrating these holidays with us, your family, and friends.

THE COLOR INDEX

Cold appetizers/Eggs

SHRIMP COCKTAIL WITH TANGY DIP
Plump shrimp served with a catchup-based sauce with horseradish and lemon juice.
6 servings, early in day. Page 89

TOP LEFT: ITALIAN ANTIPASTO PLATTER. Page 94. **COUNTRY PÂTÉ LOAF** Page 91. **MOLDED TUNA PÂTÉ** Page 144. **CHEDDAR CHEESE SPREAD, LIPTAUER CHEESE, BLUE CHEESE SPREAD, HOT PEPPER PECANS** Page 92. **VERMONT CHEDDAR STICKS** Page 93. **DIPS: CHILI-CHEESE, HOT TUNA and ORIENTAL ONION** Page 94.

CHEESE-STUFFED BREAD *Cream cheese and pimento stuffing. 60 slices, 5 hours.* Page 93. **COCKTAIL MEATBALLS** *With chopped gherkins. 40 meatballs, 45 mins.* Page 86

FRESH FRUIT IN ORANGE CUPS
Kiwi fruits, strawberries, and orange segments with brandy in orange shells.
8 servings, day ahead. Page 90

PICKLED EGGS *(left) Hard-cooked eggs with sliced beets and spices, served here with mayonnaise. 12 eggs, day ahead.* **MARBLED EGGS** *(center back) Hot tea is poured over cracked hard-cooked eggs for the marbled effect. 12 eggs, early in day.* **SPICED EGGS** *(right) 12 eggs, early in day.* Page 113. **DEVILED EGGS** *12 egg-halves, 40 mins.* Page 90

Hot appetizers/Cold appetizers

BUFFALO-STYLE CHICKEN WINGS, OVEN-FRIED CHICKEN WINGS, SAUCY CHICKEN WINGS, BAKED CHICKEN WING APPETIZERS Page 85

SCALLOPED OYSTERS (left) Oysters in a half-and-half sauce with crushed cracker topping. 4 servings, 40 mins. **OYSTERS ROCKEFELLER** (top right) Baked oysters with a spinach, bacon, and cheese topping. 6 servings, 30 mins. Page 123. **CLAM FRITTERS** Chopped cherrystone clams with grated onion and eggs served with tartar sauce. 4 servings, 45 mins. Page 119

QUESADOS Flour tortilla sandwiches with sour cream, guacamole, and cheese. 32 pieces, 30 mins. Page 87. **GUACAMOLE** With tortilla chips. 2 cups, 1 hour. Page 91

CHEDDAR-CHEESE FONDUE A bubbling cheese and mustard-flavored fondue to serve with French bread, shrimp, and ham. 4 cups fondue, 30 mins. Page 88

HERBED GOAT CHEESE WITH SUN-DRIED TOMATOES (left) Fresh basil leaves, thinly-sliced green onions, and the tomatoes over thinly sliced cheese. 12 servings, 30 mins. Page 92. **FIRST COURSE AVOCADO SALAD** A spicy chili-tomato sauce with catchup, grated onion, and hot-pepper sauce served with avocado and salami slices. 4 servings, 1 hour. Page 91

Hot appetizers/Cold appetizers

MARINATED MUSSELS ON THE HALF SHELL *With slivered red peppers. 36 mussels, early in day.* Page 89. **OYSTERS ON HALF-SHELL** *16 oysters, 15 mins.* Page 123

BACK TO FRONT: STUFFED MUSHROOMS Page 88. **BRIE AND SMOKED SALMON TORTILLA TRIANGLES** Page 86. **PIG IN A BLANKET** *32 pieces, 2½ hours.* Page 87. **SAUSAGE-MUENSTER MELTS** *48 pieces, 1 hour.* Page 86. **HAM AND CHEESE CUPS** *36 cups, 1½ hours.* Page 86

FRESH COOKED CRAB *Crab meat served with Creamy Cocktail Sauce, made with chili sauce and mayonnaise. 6 servings, early in day.* Page 120

CRAB CLAWS WITH SPICY RED-PEPPER DIP *Alaska Snow crab cocktail claws with zesty pepper dip with capers and basil. 20 pieces, 1¼ hours.* Page 89

FRIED ARTICHOKE HEARTS AND ZUCCHINI *Vegetable pieces coated with beer batter and fried, then served with a Tomato-Basil Dip. 4 servings, 40 mins.* Page 88

Vegetable

CREAMY CALIFORNIA ARTICHOKE *(left) Artichokes puréed with potatoes, heavy cream, and chicken broth. 8 cups, 2 hours.* **CREAM OF FRESH TOMATO** *(center) Puréed tomatoes, onion, celery, and cream. 5 cups, 45 mins.* **CREAM OF MUSHROOM** *A creamy mushroom purée with chicken-flavor bouillon and cream. 7 cups, 45 mins.* Page 98

VICHYSSOISE
Leeks and potatoes simmered in chicken-flavor bouillon, then blended with cream. Serve chilled. 7 cups, 50 mins. Page 99

CORN CHOWDER
Potatoes, celery, green pepper, and frozen whole-kernel corn simmered together. 9 cups, 45 mins. Page 97

CHILLED CUCUMBER SOUP
Chopped cucumber simmered in chicken broth with green onions, then chilled and puréed. 5¼ cups, 4 hours. Page 99

VELVETY PUMPKIN BISQUE
Canned pumpkin puréed with chicken-flavor bouillon, then blended with half-and-half. 5 cups, 30 mins. Page 97

ONION SOUP GRATINÉ
Sliced onions simmered in condensed beef broth. Top with sliced French bread and melted Swiss cheese. 7½ cups, 40 mins. Page 97

CHILLED WATERCRESS SOUP
Fresh watercress blended with chicken-flavor bouillon and a potato, then mixed with half-and-half. 5⅔ cups, 2½ hours. Page 99

Vegetable/Hearty

GAZPACHO
Spanish in origin, this puréed tomato soup with hot-pepper sauce and garlic is served well chilled with a selection of diced cucumber, chopped onion, diced green peppers, and crisp croutons. 7 cups, 2½ hours. Page 100

BARLEY, BEEF, AND VEGETABLE
Beef shanks, simmered with celery, carrots, mushrooms, barley, and broccoli. 16 cups, 2½ hours. Page 102

BLACK BEAN SOUP
Sherry is added to this bean, celery, ham, and carrot soup. Top with chopped hard-cooked eggs. 10½ cups, 3½ hours. Page 100

CREAM OF PEANUT SOUP
Peanut butter adds flavor and thickness to this rich soup garnished with chopped peanuts. 8 cups, 30 mins, Page 102

BEET AND VEGETABLE SOUP
Shredded beets give this soup its distinctive color. Serve hot or cold with sour cream. 14 cups, 1½ hours. Page 102

CHUNKY LAMB AND BEAN SOUP
White pea (navy) beans, frozen Italian green beans, and carrots are added to lamb shanks in beef bouillon. 14 cups, 3½ hours. Page 101

PHILADELPHIA PEPPER POT
This soup combines fresh honeycomb tripe, salt pork, veal knuckles, and vegetables with heavy cream. 12 cups, 4½ hours. Page 102

MINESTRONE
White and red kidney beans simmered in beef broth with macaroni and vegetables. Serve with Parmesan cheese. 12 cups, 1¾ hours. Page 101

LENTIL AND FRANKFURTER SOUP
Sliced frankfurters, lentils, peppers, a carrot, and an onion are simmered in chicken-flavor bouillon cubes in this family-style soup. 14 cups, 2 hours. Page 101

OYSTER SOUP
An elegant soup; shucked oysters are cooked in a thickened mixture of milk and half-and-half with Worcestershire. 12 cups, 30 mins. Page 106

CHICKEN-ESCAROLE SOUP
Chunky chicken pieces simmered in broth with vegetables and escarole, a member of the chicory family. 12 cups, 1½ hours. Page 104

PENNSYLVANIA DUTCH CHICKEN AND CORN SOUP
Slowly simmering a broiler-fryer produces a richly-flavored broth for the base of this chunky soup made with frozen whole-kernel corn and broccoli. Small dumplings are added just before serving. 12 cups, 2 hours. Page 104

MULLIGATAWNY
Curry powder gives this chicken, carrot, and celery soup its distinctive flavor. Serve with hot rice. 8 cups, 1½ hours. Page 104

Chicken and turkey/Fish/Hearty

CREOLE TURKEY SOUP
Leftover turkey and frozen cut okra seasoned with hot-pepper sauce, rice, green pepper, and celery. 14 cups, 2 hours. Page 105

HEARTY SPLIT PEA SOUP
Ground pork meatballs are added to the split peas with carrots, celery, onions, and potatoes. 13 cups, 2 hours. Page 103

MANHATTAN CLAM CHOWDER *(front) Hard-shell clams and tomatoes are the classic ingredients in this soup with bacon and diced onions, carrots, celery, potatoes, and parsley. 14 cups, 1½ hours.* **NEW ENGLAND CLAM CHOWDER** *Potatoes thicken this traditional soup made with hard-shell clams, salt pork, flour, milk, and seasonings. 10 cups, 30 mins. Page 106*

LOUISIANA GUMBO
Frozen okra, oysters in the shell, shrimp, and Alaska King crab are combined in a hot-pepper tomato sauce. Serve with hot cooked rice for an authentic touch to this traditional Southern-style dish. 14 cups, 2 hours. Page 106

CHICKEN AND RICE SOUP
Watercress adds extra flavor to this hearty chicken, celery, carrot, and onion soup with rice. 12 cups, 1½ hours. Page 105

23

Egg dishes/Cheese dishes

GOLDEN BUCK
A Cheddar-cheese-and-beer sauce tops poached eggs and tomato slices on toast. 4 servings, 40 mins. Page 115

CORNED BEEF HASH AND EGGS *(top) A skillet dish with baked eggs. 4 servings, 45 mins. Page 110.* **RANCH-STYLE EGGS** *(left) Fried eggs on tortillas with a hot tomato sauce, sour cream, and avocado slices. 4 servings, 45 mins. Page 111.* **WESTERN SCRAMBLED EGGS** *With green pepper, grated onion, and ham. 6 servings, 30 mins. Page 110.*

COUNTRY EGG BAKE
Eggs baked on a bed of vegetables with garbanzo beans and Cheddar cheese. 6 servings, 1½ hours. Page 109

EGGS BENEDICT
Bacon roses, cooked peppers, and poached eggs on English muffins with Hollandaise Sauce. 4 servings, 50 mins. Page 109

ZESTY MEXICAN EGGS AND BEANS *(left) Eggs baked with tomatoes and kidney beans flavored with chili and served with shredded lettuce and corn chips. 4 servings, 30 mins. Page 109.* **CHEESY TORTILLA BAKE** *Green chilies, tomatoes, and spices with scrambled eggs and topped with tortilla strips. 8 servings, 1 hour. Page 115*

SKILLET PEPPERS AND EGGS
*Sautéed pepper strips with onions and basil top an "egg pancake",
served here with tomato slices and green onion. 2 servings,
30 mins. Page 112*

**TOMATO-SAUSAGE
SCRAMBLE** *Sausage
chunks and tomatoes scrambled
with eggs. 8 servings, 30 mins. Page 110*

WELSH RABBIT
*A velvety sauce with Cheddar cheese,
Worcestershire, and mustard over
toast. 6 servings, 20 mins. Page 115*

HAM AND ONION FRITTATA
*Sautéed potatoes and green onions cooked
with eggs until set, then topped with diced
ham. 8 servings, 50 mins. Page 112*

PARTY CREAMY EGGS *(back) Ideal for a brunch, cream-cheese scrambled eggs served with
crisp bacon slices, smoked salmon, mushrooms, and seasoned avocados with pimento slices.
8 servings, 1½ hours. Page 111.* **SHRIMP CREOLE OMELET** *With chopped shrimp filling and
a tangy tomato sauce topping. 1 main-dish serving, 30 mins. Page 112*

25

Cheese dishes/Egg dishes/Soufflés

EGG-AND-SPINACH CASSEROLE
Eggs baked on a bed of chopped spinach and topped with a Cheddar cheese sauce.
4 servings, 1 hour. Page 110

WILD RICE AND CHICKEN SOUFFLÉ
Beaten egg whites lighten this baked dish with chicken pieces and cooked wild rice.
8 servings, 1½ hours. Page 116

BROCCOLI QUICHE WITH WHOLE-WHEAT CRUST (top) *Broccoli with cottage and Swiss cheeses. 6 servings, 40 mins.* **NO-CRUST ARTICHOKE QUICHE** (left) *Muenster cheese with artichoke hearts. 6 servings, 40 mins.* **ASPARAGUS QUICHE** *A rich and creamy Swiss-cheese and fresh asparagus filling. 6 servings. 1½ hours. Page 114.*

HERB AND CHEESE SOUFFLÉ
Parsley, thyme, and Cheddar cheese. 6 servings, 1¼ hours. Page 116

ROLLED MUSHROOM OMELET
A creamy mushroom and Swiss-cheese mixture fills this puffy omelet rolled jelly-roll style served on a platter with crisp bacon slices. 8 servings, 1 hour. Page 113

Clams/Crayfish/Oysters/Crabs

STEAMED SOFT-SHELL CLAMS
Clams in their shells with a flavorful broth, chopped parsley, and melted butter. 3 servings, 1 hour. Page 119

FAMILY CLAMBAKE
Littleneck clams, bluefish, lobsters, chicken, and corn make a complete meal served with melted butter and a tasty Yogurt-Watercress Sauce. 6 servings, 1½ hours. Page 119

CRAYFISH ETOUFFEE
A creole dish of crayfish tails, onion, celery, green pepper, and spices, then served with rice. 4 servings, 1¾ hours. Page 121

DEVILED CRAB
Individual portions of crab meat baked with a mixture of chopped parsley, mustard, lemon juice, Worcestershire, and hot-pepper sauce, topped with bread crumbs and garnished with lemon and parsley. 4 servings, 45 mins. Page 121.

HANGTOWN FRY
Breaded and fried oysters in a set scrambled egg mixture with crumbled bacon. 4 servings, 35 mins. Page 123

Lobsters/Crabs/Scallops

LOBSTER À L'AMERICAINE
A splash of brandy and white wine added to lobster pieces in tomato sauce. 4 servings, 1½ hours. Page 122

LOBSTER THERMIDOR
An elegant dish of lobster meat mixed in a sherry and half-and-half flavored sauce, then broiled in the lobster shell with Cheddar cheese. Served here with dill-flavored rice, garnished with lemon wedges and parsley sprigs. 4 servings, early in day. Page 122

PAN-FRIED SCALLOPS
Tender scallops coated with dried bread crumbs, then fried and served on toast points. 3 servings, 15 mins. Page 124

PAN-FRIED SOFT-SHELL CRABS
Flavored with parsley, lemon juice, and Worcestershire, then served with toast. 4 servings, ½ hour. Page 120

CRAB IMPERIAL
Alaska King crab baked in a highly-flavored casserole with minced green pepper. 6 servings, 1 hour. Page 121

SCALLOP KABOBS
Sea scallops marinated in an oil, lemon and butter dressing with mushrooms, green pepper, and bacon slices, skewered, then broiled and served with hot cooked rice. 4 servings, 1¼ hours. Page 124

CRAB CAKES
Sherry-flavored crab meat with eggs and crackers, served here with tartar sauce. 4 servings, 30 mins. Page 121

Shrimp/Mixed shellfish

LEEK-WRAPPED SHRIMP WITH CHEESE FILLING *Blanched leek leaves enclose large shrimp filled with fontina cheese. 4 servings, 1½ hours. Page 125*

BEER-BATTER-FRIED SHRIMP *Butterflied beer-batter-coated large shrimp deep-fried until crisp, garnished with lemon and parsley. 6 servings, 1 hour. Page 124*

ANGELS ON HORSEBACK *Broiled bacon-wrapped shrimp served with cooked long-grain rice and peas. 3 servings, 40 mins. Page 125*

SHRIMP JAMBALAYA *Pork sausage meat, tomatoes, and hot-pepper sauce mixed with rice and shrimp. 6 servings, 1¼ hours. Page 125*

SKILLET SEAFOOD NEWBURG *Shrimp and lobster in a creamy sherry sauce served with cooked rice, garnished with parsley. 6 servings, 20 mins. Page 126*

SAN FRANCISCO SEAFOOD CASSEROLE *Shellfish and white fish chunks mixed with clam juice, tomatoes, and white wine. 6 servings, 1 hour. Page 126*

PARTY PAELLA *Mussels, littleneck clams, Italian sausages, shrimp, and chicken pieces cooked with rice. 12 servings, 3½ hours. Page 127*

CHILLED SEAFOOD RISOTTO *(left) Squid, shrimp, flounder, and artichoke hearts cooked with flavorful rice, then chilled. 8 servings, 3 hours. Page 127.* **MUSSELS AND CLAMS FRA DIAVOLO** *Cherrystone clams and mussels cooked with white wine, garlic, oregano, crushed red pepper, and parsley. 4 servings, 1¼ hours. Page 126*

Bass/Bluefish/Catfish/Cod/Halibut

OVEN-STEAMED SEA BASS
Gingerroot, soy sauce, and sherry add an Oriental flavor to sea bass served with vegetables. 6 servings, 1¼ hours. Page 134

STUFFED BAKED SEA BASS
Onion, celery, Cheddar cheese, chopped parsley, nutmeg, and white wine mixed with herb-seasoned stuffing to fill a whole fish sprinkled with lime juice, and served garnished with lemon and parsley. 10 servings, 3 hours. Page 134

FRIED CATFISH
A favorite dish from the South, the cornmeal coating gives these fried fish their distinctive color. 6 servings, 2 hours. Page 135

SAUTÉED ROE
Cod or shad roe pan-fried in butter and served on a bed of shredded lettuce. 4 servings, 10 mins. Page 136

BAKED COD WITH GRAPEFRUIT
(back) 6 servings, 40 mins. **BROILED COD STEAKS MONTAUK** *Cooked with a mayonnaise mixture. 4 servings, 20 mins. Page 136*

FRIED FISH AND HUSH PUPPIES
Cornmeal-covered cod fillets and batter fritters deep fried. Served here with vegetables. 8 servings, 45 mins. Page 136

HAWAIIAN HALIBUT STEAKS
Broiled fish with lightly curried rice and pineapple tidbits, garnished with lime. 4 servings, 30 mins. Page 139

OVEN-BAKED BLUEFISH
Bread crumbs, mushrooms, green onions, and diced tomato make the light stuffing. 6 servings, 1 hour. Page 134

**SCAMPI-STYLE
FISH** *Stir-fried red
peppers and Chinese pea
pods with chunks of white fish.
4 servings, 40 mins. Page 137*

**BROILED HALIBUT STEAKS WITH
LEMON-DILL SAUCE** *Served here with
fresh asparagus and tomato slices.
4 servings, 25 mins. Page 139*

**CALIFORNIA-STYLE MARINATED
HALIBUT** *Lime juice, crushed red pepper,
and green chilies add extra zest. 4 servings,
2½ hours. Page 139*

SPINACH-STUFFED FLOUNDER
*Lemon juice and wine flavor the stuffing.
Served here with parsley rice. 6 servings,
45 mins. Page 138*

CRISP FISH CAKES
*Bread crumbs, mozzarella cheese, and celery
mixed with cod, then coated with cornmeal,
and fried. 6 servings, 40 mins. Page 137*

SWORDFISH WITH HERB BUTTER
*Broiled swordfish steaks with shallots, fresh tarragon, basil, thyme leaves, and parsley. Served
here with tomato slices and onions, garnished with lemon and parsley sprigs. 4 servings,
30 mins. Page 143*

Swordfish/Sole/Trout/Tuna/Barbecued fish

STIR-FRIED SWORDFISH
Broccoli, mushrooms, green onions, and red pepper are quickly cooked with swordfish. 4 servings, 30 mins. Page 143

CREAMY SOLE FILLETS
Poached sole fillets with a cream and tomato-based sauce. Served here with rice. 6 servings, 1¾ hours. Page 142

BAKED SOLE WITH LEMON SAUCE
Thawed frozen sole fillets with a rich sauce. Served here with mixed vegetables. 8 servings, 30 mins. Page 142

SAUTÉED FISH FILLETS WITH WALNUT COATING *Pan-fried sole, flounder or catfish with a bread-crumb and walnut coating. 4 servings, 45 mins. Page 142*

FRESH TUNA BAKE
Tuna steaks baked with a garlic-flavored tomato sauce. Served here with green beans. 4 servings, 50 mins. Page 144

TUNA-NOODLE CASSEROLE
Canned tuna baked with a cream-cheese sauce, celery, onions, and egg noodles. 6 servings, 45 mins. Page 144

GRILLED BASS FILLETS WITH MUSHROOM STUFFING *Foil-wrapped fillets baked with lemon juice and savory leaves. 6 servings, 1 hour. Page 224*

FISH FILLETS IN CORN HUSKS
Grilled flounder fillets with pimento and mozzarella and feta cheeses. 4 servings, 1 hour. Page 223

PAN-FRIED TROUT WITH VEGETABLE STUFFING *Including radishes, celery, zucchini, green pepper, and carrot. 4 servings, 1½ hours. Page 143*

Red Snapper/Salmon/Flounder/Barbecued fish

SHRIMP-FILLED FILLETS
Baked flounder with a shrimp and bread crumb stuffing, served with Hollandaise Sauce. 4 servings, 1 hour. Page 138

RED SNAPPER WITH LIME BUTTER
A broiled whole fish with a lime flavored butter and toasted almonds, garnished with lime. 4 servings, 40 mins. Page 140

RED SNAPPER CREOLE
A fish filled with a spicy bread-crumb stuffing, served with Shrimp-Olive Sauce. 10 servings, 2 hours. Page 140

SALMON MOUSSE
A creamy canned salmon mousse with mayonnaise lightly set with gelatin. 10 servings, 4 hours. Page 141

SALMON CROQUETTES WITH DILL SAUCE *Skillet-cooked patties with a mustard-and-dill-mayonnaise-based sauce served on spinach. 4 servings, 30 mins. Page 141*

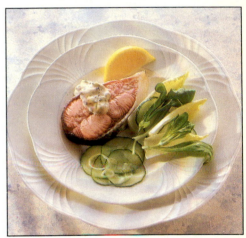

CHILLED SALMON STEAK WITH MARINATED CUCUMBER *Poached salmon steaks served with a Green Mayonnaise Dressing. 6 servings, 4 hours. Page 141*

FLOUNDER WITH GREEN-CHILI SAUCE *Skillet-cooked bread-crumb coated fillets with a zesty sauce of tomatoes, lemon, and parsley. 4 servings, 45 mins. Page 138*

GRILLED TROUT WITH SUMMER-VEGETABLE STUFFING *Zucchini, tomatoes, mushrooms, and radishes make up the stuffing. 4 servings, 1 hour. Page 224.* **GRILLED FISH STEAKS WITH CHILI BUTTER** *Swordfish or halibut steaks with a piquant sauce of chili butter. 4 servings, 45 mins. Page 223*

Whole chicken/Cut-up chicken

STUFFED CAPON WITH CRANBERRY-POACHED PEARS *Wild and long-grain rices are combined with carrots, onion, celery, and a chicken-flavor bouillon cube for the stuffing. The garnish is pears poached with spiced cranberry-juice cocktail. Served here with Giblet Gravy for Stuffed Capon and green beans. 8 servings, 4 hours. Page 147*

CHICKEN NAPA VALLEY
Chicken breasts and sausages with mushrooms in a white wine sauce. Served here with asparagus. 8 servings, 1¼ hours. Page 152

FARMHOUSE CHICKEN
A complete meal of chicken, bacon, rice, green pepper, butternut squash, and Brussels sprouts. 5 servings, 1 hour. Page 149

PARTY STUFFED CHICKEN
A pork stuffing with dry sherry fills this boned chicken. Serve with Pickled Peaches and Apricots. 6 servings, 3 hours. Page 148

COUNTRY CAPTAIN
A curried sauce of tomatoes, peppers, onion, and celery served over chicken with rice, topped with almonds. 4 servings, 1 hour. Page 152

PAPRIKA BROILED CHICKEN
Chicken pieces coated with paprika, butter, and lemon juice before broiling. Served here with a salad. 4 servings, 50 mins. Page 149

Cut-up chicken

SOUTHERN-FRIED CHICKEN
Skillet-fried chicken with a half-and-half gravy; served here with mashed potatoes and vegetables. 8 servings, 2 hours. Page 149

CHILLED ORANGE CHICKEN
Made in advance, rosemary-flavored chicken breasts are glazed with marmalade and served on lettuce. 16 servings, 6 hours. Page 156

LOUISIANA CHICKEN CASSEROLE *(left) Hot-pepper sauce flavors the casserole. 8 servings, 1½ hours.* Page 154. **JAMBALAYA CHICKEN** *(right) With Spanish sausages, rice, and pimentos. 8 servings, 2 hours.* Page 153. **CHICKEN AND OYSTER GUMBO** *With hot cooked rice. 6 servings, 1½ hours.* Page 150

CHICKEN CACCIATORE *(above left) Skillet-cooked with tomatoes, red wine, and green peppers. 4 servings, 1 hour.* **CHICKEN FRICASSEE WITH DUMPLINGS** *Chicken soup and milk make the sauce. 4 servings, 1 hour.* Page 150

DEEP-DISH CHICKEN PIE *(right) 8 servings, 2½ hours.* Page 154

Cut-up chicken/Chicken breasts/Chicken legs and thighs

CHICKEN YUCATAN *Chicken pieces coated with puréed green peppers, garlic, almonds, and oregano, then skillet-cooked. 4 servings, 1¼ hours.* **CHICKEN TOSTADAS** *Chopped chicken with green chilies, garlic, and a sour-cream mixture served with lettuce on a flour tortilla. Served here with Avocado Butter and Salsa Cruda. 4 servings, 2 hours. Page 151*

BEER-BATTER CHICKEN ROLLS *Chicken breasts coated in a beer batter and fried until crisp. Served here with carrots and beans. 8 servings, 2 hours. Page 156*

CHICKEN BURRITOS *Flour tortillas filled with chicken, chili powder, chilies, refried beans, and taco sauce. 6 servings, 1¼ hours. Page 157*

BRUNSWICK STEW *A hearty dish of chicken, beef, canned tomatoes, frozen lima beans, and frozen whole-kernel corn. 10 servings, 3 hours. Page 154*

CHICKEN BREASTS IN A PECAN CRUST *Maple-flavor syrup and chopped pecans make the crisp coating for these pan-fried chicken breasts. 4 servings, 40 mins. Page 156*

STUFFED CHICKEN QUARTERS WITH CHERRY TOMATOES *Zucchini, bread crumbs, and Swiss cheese fill honey-glazed chicken. 4 servings, 1½ hours. Page 153*

BAKED CRISPY CHICKEN THIGHS *(left) Mustard, honey, and ginger flavor the dried bread-crumb coating. Served here with French fries. 4 servings, 1 hour.* **SHRIMP-STUFFED CHICKEN LEGS** *Ginger and sherry flavor the stuffing; served with zucchini. 6 servings, 1¼ hours.* **DEVILED CHICKEN LEGS** *Served here with broccoli. 6 servings, 1 hour. Page 155*

Chicken cutlets/Cut-up chicken/Turkey

CHICKEN CROQUETTES *(left) Cooked chicken blended with a parsley-and-sage mixture, then molded, coated in bread crumbs and fried. Served here with a julienne of peppers and lettuce. 4 servings, early in day.* **CHICKEN À LA KING** *Patty shells filled with cooked chicken, mushrooms, pimentos, and sherry. 8 servings, 40 mins. Page 158*

COUNTRY TURKEY HASH
Baked in a skillet, golden potato slices top a mixture of turkey, turnips, and Muenster cheese. 6 servings, 1 hour. Page 163

CHICKEN HAVANA
Banana, golden raisins, ham, chilies, and tomatoes are added to chicken for an exotic Caribbean taste. 6 servings, 1 hour. Page 152

OLD-FASHIONED CREAMED TURKEY WITH BISCUITS *Cooked turkey with cream of mushroom soup, olives, mushrooms, and peppers. 6 servings, 30 mins. Page 163*

ROAST TURKEY WITH PECAN STUFFING *A traditional Thanksgiving Day feast. A plump, tender turkey is stuffed with crunchy Pecan Stuffing and served with Giblet Gravy and Cocktail Corn Garnish. Here the meal is completed with Cranberry Sauce and Lemon-Buttered Vegetables. 18 servings, 6½ hours. Page 160*

Chicken cutlets/livers/Cornish hens/Game/Turkey

CHICKEN CUTLETS WITH SUN-DRIED TOMATOES AND MOZZARELLA *(left) Sun-dried tomatoes cooked with wine top a cutlet with melted cheese. 4 servings, 30 mins.* **CHICKEN CUTLETS AND ARTICHOKES** *Red pepper strips and artichoke bottoms make a sophisticated dish; served with a mayonnaise sauce. 4 servings, 35 mins. Page 158*

CHICKEN-LIVER AND MUSHROOM RAGOUT *Frozen Italian beans and small whole carrots with Marsala wine complete this skillet dish. 4 servings, 45 mins. Page 168*

PEASANT-STYLE CORNISH HENS *With carrots and sausages. 2 hours, 4 servings. Page 159*

ROCK CORNISH HENS WITH WILD-RICE STUFFING *With a honey, lemon, and vermouth glaze. Served here with snow peas and tomatoes. 8 servings, 2½ hours. Page 159*

CHICKEN LIVERS WITH BACON, ONIONS, AND APPLE *Apple jelly adds sweetness to this dish with livers, apple, bacon, and onions. 4 servings, 45 mins. Page 168*

PHEASANT IN CREAM *(left) 6 servings, 2 hours. Page 168.* **CURRIED TURKEY WITH APPLES AND PEANUTS** *(above left) 8 servings, 45 mins. Page 163.* **TURKEY MARYLAND** *(center) Here with French fries. 6 servings, 2½ hours.* **TURKEY CUTLETS MARSALA** *(right) Served here with pasta. 4 servings, 40 mins. Page 162.*

Duckling/Goose/Game

ROAST DUCKLING *Sautéed apple wedges with apple jelly are served with the duckling with Bacon-Rice Stuffing and Giblet Gravy. Here, broiled link sausages are added to the apples, and buttered fresh peas complete the meal. 4 servings, 4 hours. Page 164*

BREAST OF DUCKLING WITH GREEN PEPPERCORNS *A white wine, green onion, and green peppercorn sauce is served over skillet-cooked duckling breasts. Preserved kumquats for garnish and asparagus complete this elegant dish. 2 servings, 40 mins. Page 165*

CALIFORNIA DUCK ROAST
A currant jelly glaze is brushed on duckling quarters, served with seedless red grapes and pears. 8 servings, 2½ hours. Page 165

ROAST GOOSE WITH CHESTNUT STUFFING, SAUSAGE, AND APPLES
Ginger, apple jelly, and sherry flavor apple rings. 8 servings, 4½ hours. Page 167

ROAST STUFFED GOOSE WITH CANDIED ORANGES
Corn-syrup poached oranges accompany the goose with Rye-Bread Stuffing and Creamy Mushroom Gravy. The succulent, slowly-roasted goose is served here with boiled cabbage wedges. 10 servings, 4½ hours. Page 166

Game/Barbecued poultry

ROAST WILD DUCK WITH SPICED APPLE RINGS
Two wild ducks are roasted with rosemary, apples, and onions in the cavities for extra flavor, then served with Spiced Apple Rings. The apple rings can be made ahead and served at room temperature or warm. Served here with broccoli. 4 servings, 2½ hours. Page 167

QUAIL WITH MUSHROOMS
Served on toast points, casseroled quail with onion, mushrooms, and broth. Served here with broccoli. 2 servings, 45 mins. Page 167

SUGAR-SMOKED CHICKEN
Grilled in a foil pan, the sugar burns to create "smoke." Served here with tomatoes and zucchini. 4 servings, 3 days. Page 221

OLD-WEST BARBECUED CHICKEN *(top) 8 servings, 1¼ hours. Page 221.* **CORNISH HENS WITH SWEET-AND-SOUR SAUCE** *(middle) Served with basting sauce. 4 servings, 1½ hours.* **BACON-WRAPPED CHICKEN-MUSHROOM KABOBS** *4 servings, 1¼ hours.* **SAVORY GRILLED DUCKLING** *4 servings, 2¼ hours. Page 222*

BARBECUED APRICOT CHICKEN
Chicken pieces are glazed with apricot nectar, brown sugar, catchup, and horseradish while grilling. 4 servings, 1¼ hours. Page 221

Roasts/Steaks

FAVORITE RIB-EYE ROAST
Slowly roasted beef brushed with mustard, soy sauce, and ginger, coated with minced parsley and garnished with fresh thyme. Complete the meal with Sautéed Herbed Mushrooms and Lemon-Buttered Asparagus. 16 servings, 1¾ hours. Page 177

STEAK DIANE
Rib-eye steaks flambéed with brandy and served with minced shallots, chives, and sherry. 4 servings, 20 mins. Page 175

CHICKEN-FRIED STEAK WITH CREAM GRAVY *Pounded top round steaks pan-fried, then served with pan gravy and vegetables. 4 servings, 30 mins. Page 173*

CELEBRATION FILLET MIGNON
Loin tenderloin steaks pan-fried and served on tomato slices with a mustard and caper sauce. 4 servings, 45 mins. Page 173

STANDING RIB ROAST
A succulent beef rib roast small end with individual Yorkshire Puddings and Horseradish Sauce, garnished with watercress and tomato roses. Served here with roasted potatoes and peas. 18 servings, 2 to 4 hours. Page 176

Pot roasts/Steaks

YANKEE POT ROAST
A complete meal with boneless chuck cross rib roast, potatoes, carrots, small white onions, and parsley. 12 servings, 4 hours. Page 178

LONDON BROIL
Tender flank steak flavored with onion, then broiled and thinly sliced. 6 servings, 20 mins. Page 175

SPICY BEEF BRISKET
A brisket simmered until tender with onions, garlic, and cloves, then glazed with chili sauce. 16 servings, 4 hours. Page 178

BEEFSTEAK WITH RED-WINE SAUCE *(left) Chuck arm steak is slowly cooked with red wine, meat-extract paste, mushrooms, salt pork, and a carrot. 8 servings, 2½ hours. Page 175.*
PARTY STEAK TERIYAKI *Marinated beef top round steaks are broiled, then chilled to serve with Creamy Stuffed Eggs. 10 servings, day ahead. Page 174.*

CRANBERRY POT ROAST WITH ACORN SQUASH *Canned whole-berry cranberry sauce adds flavor. Served with roasted squash and broccoli. 12 servings, 3 hours. Page 179*

CORNED BEEF WITH CABBAGE AND CARROTS *A brisket simmered with onion, celery, and carrot, then glazed. 24 servings, 4 hours. Page 178*

SHERRIED CUBED STEAKS
Sherry and minced green onions flavor the sauce for these skillet-cooked steaks. 4 servings, 30 mins. Page 174

NEW ENGLAND BOILED DINNER
Rutabaga, red potatoes, small white onions, carrots, and cabbage boiled with a brisket. 16 servings, 4 hours. Page 179

CORNED BEEF HASH
Cooked corned beef and potatoes mixed with parsley, onion, flour, and milk, then cooked in a skillet. 6 servings, 1 hour. Page 179

BEEF AND OYSTER PIE
A flaky pastry crust tops this deep-dish pie with shucked oysters. 10 servings, 2 hours. Page 181

MICHIGAN-STYLE PASTIES
Cubed top round steak with carrots, turnips, onion, and thyme leaves wrapped in pastry. 4 servings, 2 hours. Page 182

HEARTY MEATBALLS
Ground beef, pork and/or veal meatballs simmered with onion, carrot, celery, tomatoes, and wine. 6 servings, 1 hour. Page 183

BEEF ENCHILADAS
Corn tortillas filled with chili-flavored beef and Cheddar cheese, cooked in enchilada sauce. 6 servings, 2 hours. Page 181

STEAKS WITH MUSTARD BUTTER
Pan-cooked top loin steaks made extra special by topping with butter and prepared mustard. 2 servings, 15 mins. Page 173

BAKED SWISS STEAK
Green peppers, onions, and Brussels sprouts baked with top round steaks and stewed tomatoes. 8 servings, 2¾ hours. Page 174

STUFFED BEEF ROLL
Top round steak filled with salami, cheese, eggs, and peas in a tomato sauce with wine. 10 servings, 2 hours. Page 176

BLUE-CHEESE BURGERS
All-time favorites. 4 servings, 20 mins. Page 185

MEAT-LOAF ROLL WITH SPINACH STUFFING (*left*) 8 servings, 1¾ hours.
OLD-FASHIONED MEAT LOAF (*center*) *A traditional meat loaf with tomato sauce. 8 servings, 2 hours.* **MEAT AND POTATO LOAF** *Mashed potatoes are the surprise filling. 6 servings, 2 hours.* Page 184

CHILI CON CARNE (*front*) *Chili powder adds the "heat" to this dish. 10 servings, 1½ hours.* Page 182. **MEXICAN-STYLE MEATBALLS** (*top left*) *Mild, chopped green chilies and diced pimentos add a Mexican taste. 8 servings, 1 hour.* Page 183. **TEXAS-STYLE CHILI** *Slowly cooked cubed chuck blade steak. 12 servings, 2 hours.* Page 182

PORK CHOPS WITH CREAMY GRAVY
Loin blade chops skillet cooked, then served with a sauce made from pan drippings and milk. 4 servings, 30 mins. Page 189

SALISBURY STEAKS WITH ONIONS AND PEPPERS *Sherry, catchup, and soy sauce, blended to go with ground beef patties. 4 servings, 35 mins.* Page 185

Stews/Pork: Stews, Chops and Steaks, Tenderloin

STUFFED CABBAGE ROLLS
Blanched cabbage leaves wrapped around a cottage cheese, red kidney bean, and ground beef filling. 8 servings, 2 hours. Page 183

PRESSURE COOKED BEEF STEW (left) *With minced vegetables, herbs, and pimento-stuffed olives. 8 servings, 5 hours.* **BEEF IN BEER** (center) *8 servings, 2¾ hours.* **OLD-COUNTRY SHORT-RIB DINNER** *Canned white hominy, broccoli, and carrots cooked with beef ribs. 8 servings, 2½ hours.* Page 180

CORN-PONE CASSEROLE
A spicy chili mixture with tomatoes, ground beef, and red kidney beans baked with a corn-bread topping. 6 servings, 1¼ hours. Page 185

PORK AND CHICKEN STEW
Sweet potatoes, tomatoes, almonds, and chili powder combined in a family dish. 6 servings, 1½ hours. Page 193

APPLE-GLAZED PORK TENDERLOIN
8 servings, 1½ hours.
Page 191

PORK STEAKS CREOLE STYLE (left) *6 servings, 1½ hours.* Page 190. **GOLDEN GLAZED PORK CHOPS** *4 servings, 1¼ hours.* Page 189. **PORK LOIN CHOPS WITH PRUNE STUFFING** *6 servings, 2 hours.* Page 190. **CHOP SUEY** (right) *Bite-size pieces of pork with vegetables. 4 servings, 45 mins.* Page 192

Stews/Chops and steaks/Roasts/Whole ham

PORK AND APPLE GRILL
Pork butt and apples broiled with apple jelly and steak sauce, served here with succotash and a salad. 6 servings, 1¼ hours. Page 193

PORK-AND-SAUERKRAUT SUPPER
Pork chops baked with onion, apple juice, sauerkraut, potatoes, and apples. 6 servings, 2¾ hours. Page 191

COUNTRY-STYLE PORK SHOULDER ROAST *Roasted with peaches and acorn squash and served with gravy. 10 servings, 3¼ hours. Page 188*

BAKED STUFFED PORK CHOPS
Rib chops with rye-bread stuffing, served here with beans, gravy, and spiced peaches. 8 servings, 2 hours. Page 191

PORK LOIN ROAST WITH GRAVY (*left*) *Garlic salt and paprika flavor this center rib roast, served with a milk gravy. 12 servings, 3½ hours. Page 189.* **PORK CROWN ROAST WITH CRAN-APPLE STUFFING** *A crown roast filled with bread cubes, cranberries, and chopped apples, moistened with apple juice. 16 servings, 4½ hours. Page 188*

COUNTRY HAM WITH FOUR SAUCES
Smithfield ham with Buttered Raisin, Honey-Mustard, Cranberry-Wine, and Praline Sauces. 35 servings, day ahead. Page 195

Hocks/Ribs/Canned ham/Ham slices/Stews/Ham hocks

PORK HOCKS AND POTATOES
An economical dish with red potatoes and a sour-cream sauce. Here, greens complete the meal. 4 servings, 3½ hours. Page 192

OVEN-BARBECUED SPARERIBS *(left) Baked with a grapefruit, light brown sugar, and curry powder basting sauce. 10 servings, 1¾ hours.* **COUNTRY RIBS WITH RED CHILI SAUCE** *(center) Pork brushed with a purée of ancho, serrano, and green chilies. 4 servings, 1½ hours.* **PINEAPPLE-GLAZED SPARERIBS** *4 servings, 1¾ hours. Page 194*

PEACH GLAZED CANADIAN BACON *(left) 4 servings, 20 mins.* **CURRANT-GLAZED HAM STEAK** *(center back) A sauce of red currant jelly, port wine, and mustard, 4 servings, 20 mins. Page 203.* **PLUM GLAZED BAKED HAM** *(right) With plums and orange juice. 8 servings, 1½ hours.* **GLAZED SLICED HAM** *15 servings, 2¼ hours. Page 202*

VERMONT PORK AND BEANS
Pea (navy) beans, brown sugar, and an onion slowly simmered with pork. 16 accompaniment servings, 4½ hours. Page 193

LUAU KABABS
Ham, pineapple, and kumquats. 6 servings, 35 mins. Page 202

HAM AND GRITS WITH RED-EYE GRAVY *(front) A traditional southern dish with hominy grits. 6 servings, 20 mins. Page 195.* **HAM HOCKS AND COLLARD GREENS** *Slowly simmered smoked ham hocks. 4 servings, 3½ hours. Page 203*

Roasts/Chops/Shish kabobs

ROAST LEG OF LAMB (back) Parsley-, rosemary-, and garlic-flavored lamb roasted to perfection. 10 servings, 2½ hours. **STUFFED SHOULDER OF LAMB** Finely minced anchovies, seasoned pepper, and lemon juice cooked with fresh bread crumbs for a flavorful stuffing. 8 servings, 2½ hours. Page 204

BREADED LAMB SHOULDER CHOPS
Pan-fried blade chops with a dill and dried bread-crumb coating, served here with mixed vegetables. 4 servings, 30 mins. Page 205

LAMB NOISETTES
Tenderloin chops wrapped in bacon, then broiled and served with Currant-Orange Sauce. 4 servings, 1 hour. Page 206

SPRING LAMB WITH GREEN VEGETABLES Belgian endive, artichoke hearts, and peas skillet cooked with blade or arm chops. 4 servings, 1¼ hours. Page 205

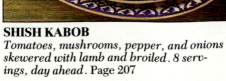

SHISH KABOB
Tomatoes, mushrooms, pepper, and onions skewered with lamb and broiled. 8 servings, day ahead. Page 207

RACK OF LAMB WITH PARSLEY CRUST
A crisp parsley and rosemary crust with bread crumbs and mayonnaise tops a tender rib roast. 8 servings, 2 hours. Page 205

Lamb/Stews, shank/Veal: Chops, Roasts, Stew/Tongue

BAKED LAMB SHANKS AND BEANS (*left*) *All-in-one dinner with green beans, lima beans, tomatoes, and wine. 4 servings, 3 hours.*
MULLIGAN STEW *A traditional meat-and-potato stew with lamb, celery, carrots, rutabaga, and cabbage. 8 servings, 2 hours. Page 207*

VEAL CHOPS WITH AVOCADO (*left*) *4 servings, 1½ hours.*
GOLDEN VEAL CHOPS (*center*) *Brushed with a seasoned bread-crumb and mayonnaise sauce. 6 servings, 45 mins.* **VEAL CHOPS WITH MUSHROOMS** *4 servings, 40 mins. Page 209*

FRESH TONGUE WITH SWEET-AND-SOUR TOMATO SAUCE *Sliced tongue with tomato sauce flavored with brown sugar and raisins. 10 servings, 3¼ hours. Page 214*

VEAL-AND-CHESTNUT RAGOUT
Chestnuts add extra crunch to this tender stew, served here with hot cooked rice. 8 servings, 1½ hours. Page 211

MUSHROOM-STUFFED BREAST OF VEAL (*front*) *A pot-roasted veal breast with mushrooms, green onions, herbs, frozen peas, and bread crumbs. 8 servings, 3½ hours.* **SPICY VEAL ROUND ROAST** *Curry powder, pickling spice, and apple juice add flavor to this pot roasted leg round roast. 8 servings, 3½ hours. Page 208.*

49

Cutlets/Venison/Calf's liver/Larger cuts/Sausages

CALIFORNIA VEAL CUTLETS (left) Topped with tomato slices, avocados, and cheese. 4 servings, 40 mins. **HAM AND CHEESE-STUFFED VEAL CUTLETS** (center) Swiss cheese and ham slices fill cutlets, fried with Sauterne. 6 servings, 1 hour. **VEAL PARMIGIANA** Fresh Tomato Sauce with Parmesan-cheese-coated cutlets. 8 servings, 45 mins. Page 210

VENISON STEW
Thick venison chunks simmered in red wine with mushrooms, onions, potatoes, carrots, and beans. 6 servings, 2 hours. Page 214

PAN-FRIED LIVER, BACON, AND ONIONS A meal with tender calf's liver slices, crisp bacon, and thin onion slices. 4 servings, 20 mins. Page 211

APPLE-GLAZED FRANKS AND CABBAGE (front) 4 servings, 1 hour. **ITALIAN SAUSAGES AND PEPPERS** 6 servings, 50 mins. Page 212

VENISON STEAKS WITH WINE SAUCE
Quince jelly, wine, nutmeg, and herbs are stirred into the pan juices to make the sauce. 4 servings, 25 mins. Page 214

PLUM-GLAZED VEAL BREAST
Fresh plums and chutney are blended together to glaze a veal breast during grilling. 4 servings, early in day. Page 218

POLISH SAUSAGE WITH RED CABBAGE (left) Cooked in a skillet with red cabbage, diced apple, and wine vinegar. 4 servings, 50 mins. Page 213. **KIELBASA WITH SAUERKRAUT** (center) 4 servings, 30 mins. Page 212. **KNACKWURST SAUERBRATEN** Crushed gingersnaps thicken the red currant jelly and Madeira sauce. 6 servings, 45 mins. Page 213

STEAK WITH ANCHOVY BUTTER (left) Grilled steak with savory topping.
8 servings, 1½ hours. **SIRLOIN STEAKS WITH FRESH-PEPPER RELISH**
Peppers and cornichons mixed with cider vinegar to serve with grilled
steaks. 4 servings, 45 mins. Page 217

APPLE-GLAZED BEEF BRISKET (left) The grilled brisket is
served here with green beans. 12 servings, early in day. Page 217.
MAPLE-GLAZED PORK TENDERLOINS Bacon wrapped
tenderloins with syrup. 6 servings, early in day. Page 218

LEMON-MARINATED GRILLED LAMB
A butterflied leg shank half is marinated
overnight with lemon juice and herbs, then
grilled. 8 servings, day ahead. Page 218

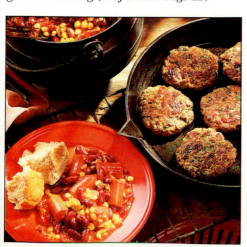

CAMP-STOVE STEW (left) With frankfurters, kidney beans, and whole-kernel corn.
6 servings, 30 mins. **BREAKFAST SAUS-
AGE PATTIES** 8 servings, 1 hour. Page 213.

BARBECUED MEATS (from back left): **BARBECUED PORK CHOPS WITH TANGY
PEAR SAUCE** 4 servings. Page 220. **TEX-MEX SPARERIBS** 4 servings. **SPARERIBS
WITH PEACH SAUCE** 6 servings. **TEXAS COUNTRY RIBS** 12 servings, Page 219.
BEEF AND VEGETABLE KABOBS WITH PEANUT SAUCE 6 servings. Page 220.

HARVARD BEETS
(left) Sliced beets with minced onion. 6 side-dish servings. 20 mins. **BROCCOLI WITH BUTTER-ALMOND SAUCE**
6 side-dish servings, 20 mins. Page 234

ASPARAGUS AND CHERRY TOMATOES *(left) Flavored with garlic. 4 side-dish servings. 15 mins.* **CALIFORNIA BRAISED ASPARAGUS AND CELERY** *Toasted pine nuts (pignolia) add extra texture and flavor. 4 side-dish servings, 30 mins. Page 230*

PRAIRIE BEAN TACOS
Spicy kidney beans in flour tacos with a sauce, served on crisp shredded lettuce. 4 main-dish servings, 30 mins. Page 233

RANCH-STYLE BEANS *(back left) Pinto beans with onions, chilies, and Monterey Jack cheese. 6 side-dish servings, 3 hours. Page 233.* **BOSTON BAKED BEANS** *(back right) Pea (navy) beans with molasses and salt pork. 12 side-dish servings, early in day.* **RED BEANS AND RICE** *With chopped ham. 8 main-dish servings, 4 hours. Page 232*

ISLAND PORK AND BEANS
Crushed pineapple and dry mustard blended with ground pork and red kidney beans. 8 main-dish servings, 3½ hours. Page 233

Eggplant/Artichokes/Dried beans/Beans

EGGPLANT PARMIGIANA
Eggplant slices fried, then baked with tomato sauce and topped with cheese. 6 side-dish servings, 1½ hours. Page 237

ARTICHOKES WITH MUSTARD SAUCE *(left) Served warm or chilled with a Dijon mustard-flavored sauce and topped with red salmon caviar. 4 side-dish servings, 45 mins.*
STUFFED ARTICHOKES MONTEREY *Onion and red and green peppers mixed with bread crumbs and Monterey Jack cheese in the stuffing. 4 main-dish servings, 1½ hours. Page 229*

HOPPIN' JOHN
Dry black-eyed beans (peas) with rice, garlic, red pepper, and unsliced bacon. 6 main-dish servings, 3 hours. Page 232

WHOLE GREEN AND WAX BEANS WITH BLUE-CHEESE SAUCE *A creamy sauce with parsley flavors this combination. 8 side-dish servings, 30 mins. Page 231*

GREEN BEAN AND ONION CASSEROLE *(top) Bacon, French-fried onions, and pimentos with beans and sour cream. 10 side-dish servings, 35 mins.* **BUTTERED-CRUMB LIMA BEANS** *(left) 4 side-dish servings, 15 mins.* **SUCCOTASH** *Whole-kernel corn and baby lima beans with green pepper, bacon, potatoes, and onions. 10 side-dish servings, 1 hour. Page 231*

Tomatoes/Peppers/Carrots/Sweet peppers/Zucchini

PAN FRIED CHERRY TOMATOES (left) With butter and parsley. 4 side-dish servings, 5 mins. **STEWED FRESH TOMATOES** (center) Garlic salt and green onions add flavor. 6 side-dish servings, 40 mins. **BACON-WRAPPED BROILED TOMATOES** For broiling or grilling, Parmesan cheese and basil add an Italian touch. 6 side-dish servings, 20 mins. Page 247

BATTER-FRIED STUFFED CHILIES A garlic and tomato sauce is served with these deep-fried green chilies filled with cheese. 8 main-dish servings, 1¼ hours. Page 240

HEARTY STUFFED PEPPERS Ground beef, frozen hash-brown potato nuggets, and kidney beans make the filling. 6 main-dish servings, 50 mins. Page 241

FRUITED CARROTS (back left) Cooked with pineapple chunks, pineapple and orange juices, and cinnamon. 10 side-dish servings, 20 mins. Page 235. **CARROTS AND GRAPES** (center) Cooked in orange juice. 8 side-dish servings, 45 mins. **GLAZED CARROTS** Coated with butter, sugar, and nutmeg. 4 side-dish servings, 25 mins. Page 234

BAKED CANDIED SWEET POTATOES (back) 10 servings, 1½ hours. **ZUCCHINI WITH RICE FILLING** 6 side-dish servings, 40 mins. Page 246

CAULIFLOWER PARMESAN *(left) Butter and Parmesan cheese sprinkled over a cooked cauliflower. 6 side-dish servings, 20 mins.* **BAKED CAULIFLOWER IN CHEESE SAUCE** *Flowerets are baked with Swiss cheese sauce. 6 side-dish servings, 1 hour. Page 235*

CHILLED LEMONY MUSHROOMS *(left) Crisp wedges of lettuce with chilled mushroom slices marinated in soy sauce and sage. 8 side-dish servings, 2 hours.* **STIR-FRIED MUSHROOMS** *Quickly-cooked mushrooms with soy sauce. 6 side-dish servings, 15 mins. Page 238*

SWEET CORN WITH HERB BUTTER *(left) 12 side-dish servings, 40 mins.* **CORN FRITTERS** *(back center) Sprinkled with confectioners' sugar. 6 side-dish servings, 30 mins.* **SKILLET CORN** *(front) 6 side-dish servings, 30 mins.* **CUSTARD CORN PUDDING** *6 side-dish servings, 1½ hours. Page 236*

RATATOUILLE IN ROASTED PEPPERS
Chilled onion, zucchini, eggplant, and mushrooms fill roasted pepper halves. 16 side-dish servings, 3 hours. Page 241

DUCHESS POTATOES *(left) 10 side-dish servings, 45 mins. Page 244.* **CARNIVAL MASHED POTATOES** *8 side-dish servings, 45 mins. Page 243*

GLAZED ONIONS *(left back) Boiled onions with sugar and butter. 6 side-dish servings, 30 mins. Page 239.* **FRENCH-FRIED ONION RINGS** *(right back) 6 side-dish servings, 40 mins. Page 238.* **CHEDDARED ONIONS** *(left front) Topped with paprika. 8 side-dish servings, 30 mins. Page 239.* **BAKED ONIONS** *10 side-dish servings, 1¾ hours. Page 238*

55

Potatoes/Peas/Squash

NEW POTATOES WITH LEMON AND CHIVES *(back)* 6 side-dish servings, 40 mins. **PARTY POTATOES WITH LEEKS** 12 side-dish servings, 1 hour. Page 243

STIR-FRIED SUGAR SNAP PEAS *(back)* 4 side-dish servings, 15 mins. **MINTED PEAS** Frozen peas cooked with mint and butter. 6 side-dish servings, 20 mins. Page 239

DELMONICO POTATOES *(top left)* Diced potatoes in a creamy sauce with cheese. 12 side-dish servings, early in day. Page 244. **HOME-FRIED POTATOES** *(top right)* 4 side-dish servings, 45 mins. Page 242. **ROASTED POTATO FANS** *(front left)* 6 side-dish servings, 1¼ hours. Page 244. **HASH BROWN POTATOES** 6 side-dish servings, 15 mins. Page 242

TWICE-BAKED POTATOES Baked potatoes are mashed, returned to the shells with a topping, then baked again. 6 side-dish servings, 1½ hours. Page 242

STUFFED ACORN SQUASH *(left)* 4 main-dish servings, 1 hour. **SPAGHETTI SQUASH WITH SPICY MEAT SAUCE** *(top center)* 4 main-dish servings, 1 hour. **MAPLE BUTTERNUT SQUASH** *(top left)* 10 side-dish servings, 15 mins. **SKILLET-BAKED ACORN SQUASH** 2 side-dish servings, 30 mins. Page 245

PEAS WITH GREEN ONIONS
Freshly shelled peas are simmered with thyme leaves, chicken broth, butter, and green onion slices. 4 side-dish servings, 30 mins. Page 239

VEGETABLES AND DILL
Artichoke hearts, tomatoes, zucchini, and squash quickly cooked with dill and lemon juice. 6 side-dish servings, 45 mins. Page 254

LEMON-BUTTERED VEGETABLES *(top left) 12 side-dish servings, 2 hours. Page 254.*
VEGETABLE BOUQUET *(top right) 4 side-dish servings, 25 mins. Page 255.* **SKILLET BRAISED ENDIVE AND RADICCHIO** *(center) 6 side-dish servings, 25 mins. Page 256.*
BROILED LEEKS, SWEET PEPPERS AND MUSHROOMS *6 side-dish servings. Page 255*

VEGETABLE KABOBS *(left) Potatoes, straight-neck squash, zucchini, and mushrooms are marinated with salad oil, vinegar, and basil, then skewered and grilled. 6 servings, early in day. Page 225.* **GRILLED CURRIED FRUIT** *Canned pear halves, peaches, and pineapple slices are grilled in foil with sugar, butter, and curry powder. 6 servings, 45 mins. Page 226*

ROASTED VEGETABLE MÉLANGE
Squash, zucchini, red and yellow peppers, onion, and mushrooms are roasted with olive oil. 8 side-dish servings, 50 mins. Page 254

Seafood/Pasta and rice/Chicken

TORTELLINI PESTO PLATTER
A summer dish of chilled pasta with basil, olive oil, salt, and garlic served with salami. 6 main-dish servings, 1½ hours. Page 282

FISH AND SEAFOOD SALADS: CRAB LOUIS (left) *Crab in a spicy sauce. 4 main-dish servings, 1 hour.* **POTATO-TUNA** (top) *A healthy and delicious combination of eggs, tuna, and vegetables. 8 main-dish servings, 40 mins.* **SHRIMP** *With celery, walnuts, and olives and Classic French Dressing. 4 main-dish servings, 1 hour. Page 279*

PICNIC PASTA SALAD FOR A CROWD
Chilled pasta with ham, cheese, olives, and vegetables, garnished with tomato wedges. 12 main-dish servings. 1 hour. Page 282

PARTY CHICKEN-AND-PASTA SALAD (left)
6 main-dish servings, 2 hours. Page 281.
CURRIED CHICKEN TOMATO CUPS
4 main-dish servings. 1 hour. Page 280

TROPICAL CHICKEN-POTATO SALAD WITH AVOCADO AND PAPAYA *Tender chicken and potatoes with green peppers in a mayonnaise and milk sauce. 4 main-dish servings, 2 hours. Page 280*

MOLDED SALADS: CUCUMBER (left) With sour cream and mayonnaise, served here with extra cucumber slices. 10 servings, early in day. **JEWELED BEET** Grated beets molded with pineapple and carrot flowers. 16 servings, early in day. Page 277

LOBSTER SALAD
Lobster meat, hard-cooked eggs, and celery mixed with mayonnaise, returned to the lobster shell, and served here with chicory leaves and lemon slices. 2 main-course servings, 1½ hours. Page 279

SALMAGUNDI
A "hodge-podge" of hard-cooked eggs, chicken, small onions, grapes, and ham, with anchovies. 6 main-dish servings, 45 mins. Page 278

DELUXE LAYERED CHEF'S SALAD
A bed of shredded spinach, with layers of Swiss cheese, lettuce, tomato, green pepper, and ham. 8 servings, 1 hour. Page 278

CONFETTI RICE MOLD
Wild rice and long-grain rice molded with peas, mushrooms, and pimento-stuffed olives. 10 servings, 5 hours. Page 282

FRUIT SALADS: FRUIT LUNCHEON (left) A light dish of cottage cheese and fruits served with Creamy Ginger-Cheese Dressing. 6 main-dish servings, 1 hour. **WALDORF** Classic combination of apples, celery, and walnuts. 4 servings, 20 mins. Page 283

AVOCADO AND GRAPEFRUIT WITH HONEY AND YOGURT (left) A delightful first course salad with pink grapefruit. 6 servings, 30 mins. **FRUIT IN MELON BASKETS** Cantaloupe, plums, nectarines, cherries, and fresh mint. 10 servings, 3 hours. Page 283

Potato/Bean and grain/Vegetable

CHICKEN AND BACON SALAD
Garbanzo beans, green onions, avocados, and Belgian endive topped with crisp bacon. 6 main-dish servings, 1 hour. Page 280.

POTATO SALADS: CREAMY POTATO AND VEGETABLE (*left*) *Garnished with fresh basil. 12 servings, 1½ hours.* **OLD-FASHIONED POTATO** (*top*) *With celery, radishes, parsley, and eggs. 6 servings, early in day.* **TANGY HOT POTATO** *Warm salad with crispy bacon and red wine vinegar dressing. 10 servings, 1 hour. Page 273*

BEAN SALADS: THREE-BEAN AND CHEESE (*left*) *8 servings, 2½ hours.* **GREEN AND WAX BEANS WITH MUSTARD SAUCE** (*top left*) *8 servings, early in day.* **TEXAS CAVIAR** (*top right*) *10 servings, 4½ hours.* **BEAN AND PEPPER SALAD** *10 servings, early in day. Page 274*

BARLEY-WALNUT SALAD (*back*) *8 servings, early in day. Page 275.* **SLICED TOMATOES WITH LEMON DRESSING** *4 servings, 20 mins. Page 276*

MARINATED GARDEN VEGETABLES
Cauliflower, broccoli, green beans, carrots, yellow squash, mushrooms, red peppers, and olives. 12 servings, 4 hours. Page 276

Green/Vegetable/Fruit/Coleslaws

SPINACH, MUSHROOM, AND BACON SALAD *A classic combination tossed with an oil and vinegar dressing, garnished with hard-cooked eggs. 6 servings, 45 mins.* Page 271

CUCUMBERS IN SOUR CREAM *(top) 6 servings, 20 mins.* **ORANGES AND TOMATOES VINAIGRETTE** *4 servings, 30 mins.* Page 276

GREEN SALADS: CAESAR *(left) Romaine in olive oil and lemon, tossed with anchovies, Parmesan cheese, and croutons. 6 servings, 1 hour.* **CALIFORNIA** *(top) Iceberg and Boston lettuce, with avocados and walnuts. 8 servings, 30 mins.* **CLASSIC TOSSED GREEN SALAD** *8 servings, 20 mins.* Page 271

GOLDEN SLAW *(left) Cabbage, red apple, and Swiss cheese. 12 servings, early in day.* **SUMMER SQUASH AND PEPPER SLAW** *(top) A crisp and crunchy dish. 10 servings, 2½ hours.* **DELUXE COLESLAW** *Cabbage, green pepper, celery, and carrot in a mayonnaise dressing. 8 servings, 1½ hours.* Page 272

FESTIVE CORN SALAD *6 servings, 1½ hours.* Page 275

CANNELLONI (left) *Homemade pasta dough filled with spinach, chicken, and ham, then baked with Parmesan Cheese Sauce. 4 main-dish servings, 3 hours.* **CREAMY CAPPELLETTI** *"Little hats" stuffed with chicken and prosciutto, then served with warmed cream, butter, and Parmesan cheese. 5 main-dish servings, 3 hours. Page 262*

ZITI WITH HEARTY HOME-STYLE MEAT SAUCE (left) *Pasta tubes in a sauce with chuck steak. 6 main-dish servings, 2¼ hours. Page 261.* **SPAGHETTI AND MEATBALLS** *6 main-dish servings, 2¼ hours. Page 259*

BAKED MACARONI AND CHEESE
Elbow macaroni with Cheddar cheese sauce baked until golden and bubbly. 4 main-dish servings, 45 mins. Page 259

LINGUINE WITH SPICY EGGPLANT SAUCE (top left) *4 main-dish servings, 1 hour.* **LINGUINE WITH RED MUSSEL SAUCE** (top right) *6 main-dish servings, 40 mins.* **ANGEL'S HAIR PASTA WITH FETA** (front left) *6 side-dish servings, 20 mins. Page 260.* **FETTUCINE ALFREDO** *With cream, Parmesan cheese and basil. 4 main-dish servings, 3½ hours. Page 261*

MONTEREY CHEESE LASAGNE (top) *10 main-dish servings, 2 hours. Page 264.* **CHEESE-FILLED MANICOTTI** *7 main-dish servings, 1¼ hours. Page 263.*

LASAGNE (*left*) *A many-layered pasta dish with ground beef, ricotta cheese, and tomatoes . 8 main-dish servings, 2½ hours .* **VEGETABLE LASAGNE** *With cabbage and straight-neck squash, tomato sauce, and cheese . 10 main-dish servings, 2½ hours . Page 264*

RICE SIDE-DISHES: WILD RICE WITH PEAS AND MUSHROOMS (*top left*) *16 servings, 1¼ hours . Page 268 .* **GOLDEN RICE** (*top right*) *6 servings, 30 mins .* **HERBED ORANGE RICE** (*center*) *4 servings, 30 mins . Page 266*

JUMBO RAVIOLI WITH SWISS CHARD
Homemade pasta dough filled with a finely chopped Swiss chard and ricotta mixture . 3 main-dish servings, 2¼ hours . Page 263

RICE AND FRUIT RING
A colorful mixture of dried fruit, celery, and long-grain rice, baked in a ring mold . 6 side-dish servings, 1 hour . Page 265

RICE SUPPER MOLD
Colorful one-dish meal with Italian sausage links and vegetables, served with zucchini . 6 main-dish servings, 1½ hours . Page 266

SUMMER-GARDEN RICE
Long-grain rice with summer vegetables in a rich Monterey Jack cheese sauce . 4 main-dish servings, 45 mins . Page 268

BACON FRIED BROWN RICE (*top left*) *4 side-dish servings, 1¼ hours . Page 266 .* **TEX-MEX STYLE RICE** (*top right*) *6 side-dish servings, 50 mins .* **PORK FRIED RICE** (*front right*) *One-dish meal Chinese style . 4 main-dish servings, 2½ hours .* **ITALIAN-STYLE RICE** *With black olives and red peppers . 4 main-dish servings, 30 mins . Page 267*

Fruits/Puddings/Mousses and Soufflés

BANANAS AND APPLES IN CARAMEL SAUCE *(left) 6 servings, 30 mins.* Page 292.
COCONUT-PINEAPPLE TAPIOCA *(center) Coconut and crushed pineapple added to quick-cooking tapioca. 6 servings, 35 mins.* Page 295. **GRILLED PINEAPPLE WEDGES** *The addition of rum makes pineapple extra special. 4 servings, 15 mins.* Page 292

CRANBERRY-PEAR COBBLER
Whole-wheat flour makes a nutty-flavored topping for this spicy dessert. 10 servings, 1½ hours. Page 289

MAPLE BREAD PUDDING
Bread cubes baked in an egg custard with maple syrup and half-and-half, then served with hot syrup. 8 servings, 2 hours. Page 298

CHESTNUT CREAM MOUSSE
Finely ground chestnuts add texture to this creamy mousse served with chestnut garnish. 12 servings, 5 hours. Page 299

PERSIMMON-DATE PUDDING
Ginger, cinnamon, and cloves add flavor to this baked dessert served with Foamy Hard Sauce. 12 servings, 2½ hours. Page 298

CHOCOLATE PUDDING *(left) Unsweetened chocolate with milk, butter, egg, vanilla and chopped pecans, served with whipped cream. 6 servings, 2½ hours.* Page 297. **BAKED INDIAN PUDDING** *Slowly baked cornmeal and molasses dessert. 8 servings, 4½ hours.* Page 298

SPRINGTIME RHUBARB REFRESHER *(left) Slowly simmered rhubarb pieces with sugar, strawberry jelly and cinnamon. 4 servings, 20 mins.* Page 291. **STRAWBERRY RHUBARB GRUNT** *Buttermilk baking mix dumplings with stewed fruit. 8 servings, 30 mins.* Page 289.

RANGE-TOP RICE PUDDING WITH FRESH FRUIT *Vanilla, cinnamon, and allspice flavor this creamy pudding with a selection of fresh fruit. 8 servings, 1 hour. Page 295*

APPLE PANDOWDY (*back left*) *Thinly sliced apples with a biscuit topping. 9 servings, 1½ hours.* **APPLE BROWN BETTY** (*back right*) *Bread cubes and apples layered with spices, served with half-and-half. 6 servings, 2 hours.* **NEW ENGLAND BAKED APPLES** (*front left*). *6 servings, 1¼ hours. Page 287.* **SNOW APPLES** *6 servings, 3½ hours. Page 288*

CRANBERRY-WINE MOLD *Dry red wine added to this cranberry-juice-cocktail mold makes it extra special. 10 servings, early in day. Page 293*

BAKED COFFEE CUSTARDS (*back*) *8 servings, 4½ hours.* **VELVETY CUSTARD WITH BANANA SAUCE** *With rum and red-currant jelly. 4 servings, 2 hours. Page 296*

GRAPE CLUSTERS IN SHIMMERING LEMON-CHEESE GEL (*back*) *10 servings, early in day. Page 294.* **MOLDED STRAWBERRIES 'N' CREAM** *A light strawberry mousse with whipped cream. 12 servings, early in day. Page 300.* **RED-WHITE-AND-BLUEBERRY MOLD** *Cream cheese base with fruit in strawberry gelatin. 10 servings, early in day. Page 293*

COOL LEMON SOUFFLÉS (top), 8 servings. Page 300. **RAINBOW ICE CREAM TORTE** 16 servings. Page 305. **EGGNOG CHARLOTTE RUSSE** 12 servings. Page 295. **BAKED ALASKA** 16 servings.

PINEAPPLE-ORANGE BAVARIAN (front) 10 servings. Page 294. **VANILLA-FUDGE-SWIRL ICE CREAM** 32 servings. Page 304. **MARBLED CHOCOLATE MOUSSE** 12 servings. Page 299

PEACHES IN STRAWBERRY AND CUSTARD SAUCE Whole peaches poached, then served with Strawberry Purée and Custard Sauce. 8 servings, 3 hours. Page 290

CRÈME BRÛLÉE WITH TROPICAL FRUITS Broiled brown sugar makes a crisp topping over chilled custard. 6 servings, early in day. Page 297

TWO-MELON GRANITA Cantaloupe and honeydew purées frozen with sugar syrups into these icy mixtures. 12 servings, early in day. Page 306

LEMON-LIME MILK SHERBET Half-and-half and milk mixed with fresh fruit juices for this summer dessert, lightly set with gelatin. 8 servings, early in day. Page 306

SPICED PEARS WITH CHOCOLATE SAUCE Pears poached in apple juice with cinnamon and cloves, served on ice cream with a sauce. 4 servings, 5 hours. Page 291

SUMMER FRUITS IN APPLE-WINE GELATIN Strawberries, grapes, blueberries, and a nectarine set in apple juice and white wine. 10 servings, 4½ hours. Page 293

Fruit/Tarts

DOWN-HOME PEACH PIE
Sweet flaky pastry with peach and tapioca filling, decorated with fluted edge and pastry leaves. 10 servings, 3 hours. Page 313

STRAWBERRY-RHUBARB PIE
Flaky pastry base filled with summer fruits, decorated with fluted edge and pastry strips. 6 servings, 3 hours. Page 314

APPLE PIES: APPLE-CUSTARD *(left) Elegantly arranged slices on a sweet-custard base. 6 servings, early in day. Page 311.* **SUGAR-FROSTED** *(top) Golden Delicious apples in flaky pastry, topped with pastry leaves and cheese. 8 servings, 2 hours. Page 309.* **OPEN-FACE** *Spiced apples drizzled with maple syrup. 6 servings, 2 hours. Page 311*

OLD-FASHIONED PEAR-APPLE PIE *(left) A favorite American fruit combination covered with a crust of flaky oil pastry. 10 servings, 3 hours.* **DEEP-DISH APPLE PIE** *Apples cooked until soft with butter, sugar, nutmeg, cinnamon, and lemon juice, decorated with a pastry lattice top. 10 servings, 2 hours. Page 312.*

RASPBERRY TART ROYALE
Sweet and crunchy tart shell with a creamy custard filling and a spectacular raspberry topping. 10 servings, 3½ hours. Page 317

Tarts/Rich Pies

CREAM PIES WITH CRUMB CRUSTS:
BANANA *(top)* 10 servings, 4½ hours.
CHOCOLATE With whipped-cream topping.
10 servings, 5½ hours. Page 320.

NUT PIES: GEORGIA-PECAN TART WITH CREAM-CHEESE PASTRY *(left) A cream-cheese pastry base with a popular nut topping. 10 servings, 3 hours.* **CHOCOLATE-PEANUT-BUTTER PIE** *(top) A sweet and nutty combination. 12 servings. 3 hours.* Page 324. **SWEET-POTATO PIE WITH WALNUT-CRUNCH TOPPING** *10 servings, 3 hours.* Page 318

LATTICE-TOPPED RAISIN PIE *(top left)*
Dark, seedless raisins flavored with orange,
decorated with woven lattice top.
8 servings, 3 hours. **MINCE PIE**
10 servings, day ahead.
Page 315

SHOOFLY PIE
Unbaked pie crust with traditional molasses
and brown sugar filling flavored with spices.
10 servings, 3 hours. Page 324

BLACK SATIN PIE
Chocolate and orange-flavor liqueur filling
with whipped cream lattice and crystalized
violets. 10 servings, 5 hours. Page 319

CHILLED PIES WITH CRUMB CRUSTS: ORANGE-CHIFFON (left) Orange filling with whipped cream and orange slices. 8 servings, early in day. Page 323. **BLACK-BOTTOM** Rum-flavored chocolate custard with whipped cream. 10 servings, early in day. Page 321

KEY-LIME (left) Graham-cracker crumb crust with sweetened condensed-milk filling flavored with lime. 8 servings, 3 hours. **GRASSHOPPER:** Creme-de-menthe and coffee filling with chocolate curls. 10 servings, 5 hours. Page 323

LEMON MERINGUE PIE
The classic American lemon custard pie with fluted edge and swirled meringue topping. 10 servings, 4 hours. Page 322

SOUR-CREAM PUMPKIN PIE (left) 10 servings, early in day. Page 318. **SLIPPED COCONUT-CUSTARD PIE** 10 servings, early in day. Page 319

BLUEBERRY PIE WITH COBBLER CRUST (top left) Deep dish pie with luscious berries and old-fashioned crust. 10 servings, 2 hours. Page 314. **CHERRY-STREUSEL PIE** (top right) 10 servings, 2 hours. Page 315. **THREE-BERRY PASTRY** Puréed strawberry base with a feast of fresh fruit. 10 servings, 3¼ hours. Page 316

69

White/Yellow/Fruit, Spice, Nut/Chocolate

CLOCKWISE FROM FRONT LEFT: BOSTON CREAM PIE *10 servings. 2½ hours. Page 328.* **STRAWBERRY SHORTCAKE** *10 servings, 45 mins. Page 341.* **GINGERBREAD RING WITH MAPLE CREAM** *Baked in a Bundt pan, spicy gingerbread with maple-syrup-flavored cream. 16 servings, 3 hours. Page 342.* **ANGEL-FOOD CAKE** *12 servings, early in day. Page 327.* **APRICOT JELLY ROLL** *A thin cake rolled around apricot preserves, then covered with whipped cream. 14 servings, 2 hours. Page 328*

SEVEN-LAYER CHOCOLATE CHIFFON CAKE *Chocolate-Cream Filling between the layers of semisweet chocolate cake with chocolate curls. 16 servings, 3 hours. Page 330*

LANE CAKE *White cake layers with a shredded coconut, pecan, cherry, raisin, and bourbon filling. 16 servings, early in day. Page 327*

CHOCOLATE SOUR-CREAM TORTE *A cocoa-flavored layer cake with luscious Chocolate Sour-Cream Frosting. 16 servings, 3 hours. Page 331*

Coffeecakes/Special Occasion/Fruit, Spice, Nut

MOTHER'S DAY CAKE
A surprisingly easy-to-make hat-shaped yellow cake, baked in a pizza pan and mixing bowl, with fresh flowers and ribbon for decoration. 16 servings, 3 hours. Page 339

4TH OF JULY CAKE
A festive yellow sheet cake with whipped cream filling and frosting. Piped decorations with fresh blueberries, strawberries, and a strawberry jelly glaze. 32 servings, 3 hours. Page 338

CHUNKY APPLE CAKE (top left) Diced apples in a cake with a walnut and coconut topping. 16 servings, 4 hours. Page 343.
CHOCOLATE FRUITCAKE (top right) A rich mixture of pecans, red candied cherries, golden raisins, raisins, and candied citron. 32 servings, up to 1 month. **OLD-FASHIONED SPICE CAKE** With sour cream. 16 servings, 4 hours. Page 342

POUND CAKE WITH COCONUT-ALMOND TOPPING *Almond-extract-flavored cake with a crunchy topping. 18 servings, 2 hours. Page 329*

PECAN-CRUMB COFFEECAKES (front) 18 servings, 1½ hours. **SOUR-CREAM COFFEECAKE** 14 servings, 2¼ hours. Page 329

Cheesecakes/Yellow/Chocolate/Fruit, Nut/Brownies

CRANBERRY SWIRL CHEESECAKE (*front left*) *With a vanilla-wafer crust. 16 servings, early in day. Page 340.* **LIGHT AND CREAMY CHEESECAKE** (*back left*) *Cottage cheese and cream cheese blended with sour cream and eggs. 16 servings, early in day.*

MANHATTAN-STYLE CHEESECAKE (*front right*) *A baked cheesecake with cream cheese. 16 servings, early in day. Page 341.* **SEMISWEET CHOCOLATE CHEESECAKE** (*back right*) *With a walnut crumb crust. 16 servings, early in day. Page 340*

BUTTERSCOTCH BROWNIES (*back*) *16 brownies, 1½ hours.* **BLONDIES** (*center left*) *15 brownies, 2½ hours.* **MARBLE BROWNIES** (*center right*) *16 brownies, 3 hours.* **CHOCOLATE-MINT BROWNIES** (*plate*) *25 brownies, 1½ hours.* **CHOCOLATE CHUNK BROWNIES** (*back rack*) *12 brownies, 2 hours. Page 345.* **PEANUT-BUTTER CUPCAKES** (*center rack*) *24 cupcakes, 2 hours. Page 343*

PINEAPPLE UPSIDE-DOWN CAKE
A brown sugar glaze with pineapple chunks and maraschino cherries for decoration. 12 servings, early in day. Page 328

CARROT CAKE WITH CREAM-CHEESE FROSTING (*front*) *with raisins. 12 servings, 3 hours. Page 343.* **DEVIL'S FOOD CAKE** *10 servings, early in day. Page 331*

Nut and Grain Cookies/Sugar Cookies/Spice Cookies

ALMOND LACE ROLLS
Ground almonds, cooked with sugar and butter, then rolled around wooden spoon handle. 30 cookies, early in day. Page 350

STRAWBERRY JAM DANDIES
Rich sugar cookies with a lemon icing, strawberry jam filling, and confectioners' sugar. 20 cookies, 3 hours. Page 348

MOLASSES SPIRALS *(back) 36 cookies, 2 hours. Page 347.* **OATMEAL COOKIES** *(center right on rack) 36 cookies, 2 hours. Page 351.* **MORAVIAN GINGER COOKIES** *(front left) 32 cookies, 4 hours. Page 347.* **DUTCH BUTTER COOKIES** *(front center back) 72 cookies, 3½ hours. Page 348.* **SNICKERDOODLES** *36 cookies, 4 hours. Page 347.*

CRUNCHY SNACK BARS *(left) With oats, pecans, and chocolate pieces. 48 bars, 3 hours.* **APRICOT MERINGUE STRIPS** *(front left) 16 cookies, 2 hours.* **PECAN CRUNCH** *With chopped pecans and semisweet chocolate pieces. 72 bars, 2 hours. Page 349*

SUGAR COOKIES *(front) Cut with cookie cutters and decorated with nonpareils. 72 cookies, 6 hours.* **SPRITZ** *A rich buttery dough flavored with orange juice. 98 cookies, 2 hours. Page 348*

Xmas/Chocolate/Nut and Grain Cookies/Candies

GINGERBREAD MEN *Crisp cookies with molasses and spices. 24 cookies, 3 hours.* Page 353. **JOLLY SANTAS** *Butter cookies with currants and frosting decorations. 42 cookies, 5 hours.* **CHRISTMAS TREE COOKIES** *With almond extract. 72 cookies, 3½ hours.*

FROSTED SNOWMEN *Quick-cooking oats and walnuts mixed with honey, then shaped, baked, and frosted. 36 cookies, 2½ hours.* Page 352. **COOKIE CHALETS** *A spicy cookie with molasses, sliced almonds, and cinnamon red-hot decorations. 24 cookies, 3 hours.* Page 353

CHOCOLATE CHIP COOKIES
An all-time favorite with semisweet chocolate pieces and chopped walnuts. 48 cookies, 2½ hours. Page 346

FILBERT COOKIE RAFTS *(back)*
32 cookies, 1½ hours. **COCONUT MACAROONS** *(center) 30 cookies, 2 hours.* **MACADAMIA MELTAWAYS** Page 351

CHOCOLATE THUMBPRINTS *(back)*
Baked cookies filled with chocolate. 36 cookies, 2 hours. **CHOCOLATE CRACKLE-TOPS** *48 cookies, early in day.* Page 346

CANDY APPLES *(back) Red delicious apples evenly coated with a light corn syrup mixture. 8 apples, early in day.* **PEANUT BRITTLE** *(center) America's well-loved candy. 1 pound, 1 hour.* **CHOCOLATE FUDGE** *32 pieces, 2½ hours.* Page 354

POPPY-SEED PINWHEELS *(back) Flavored with orange peel, cinnamon, and honey. 60 cookies, early in day* Page 351. **PEANUT BUTTER CANDY TOPS** *84 cookies, 2 hours.* **PEANUT-CHOCO NUGGETS** *50 cookies, 3 hours.* Page 350.

Grain Breads/Sweet Yeast Breads

PUMPERNICKEL-RYE BREAD *(back left) Dark and moist. 3 loaves, 6½ hours. Page 358.* **SOURDOUGH BREAD** *(back center) 2 loaves, 4 days. Page 359.* **CRUSTY WHOLE-WHEAT OATMEAL BREAD** *(back right) 1 loaf, 3½ hours. Page 357.*

QUICK-AND-EASY ANADAMA BREAD *(front left) Made from cornmeal and molasses. 1 loaf, 2½ hours. Page 358.* **WHITE BREAD** *(front center) 2 loaves, 4 hours. Page 357.* **SALLY LUNN** *Sweet white bread with sugar, milk, eggs, and butter. 1 loaf, 3½ hours. Page 358*

RAISIN-ALMOND-BRAID
Sweet yeast dough with dark seedless raisins braided and coiled, and sprinkled with sliced almonds. 1 loaf, 4½ hours. Page 359

LIMPA BREAD
Rye flour, milk, molasses, and anise seed are combined in this traditional Scandinavian bread. 2 loaves, 4½ hours. Page 360

CARDAMOM CHRISTMAS WREATH
Scented loaf decorated with dough leaves and berries, and ready to wrap with a ribbon. 1 loaf, 4½ hours. Page 360

BISCUITS:
BUTTERMILK
(back left) 18 biscuits,
35 mins. **SOUR CREAM**
(back left) 20 biscuits, 45 mins.
KENTUCKY HAM *(front left) 12 biscuits, 35 mins.*
VERMONT *(back right) 8 biscuits, 20 mins. Page 363.*
BEATEN *(front right) 15 biscuits, 1½ hours. Page 364*

CORN BREADS: CHILI-CHEESE *(left) A Tex-Mex loaf using chilies, cheese, and chorizo for extra zest. 14 side-dish servings, 1¼ hours. Page 367.* **BACON** *With cream-style golden corn, milk, and egg. 12 servings, 1 hour. Page 366*

PARKER HOUSE ROLLS
Rolls with a crease across the center, named for the famous Boston hotel. 3 dozen rolls, 3½ hours. Page 361

CHEESE QUICK BREAD
Cheddar cheese, mustard, milk, and eggs are combined in this delicious savory loaf. 1 loaf, day ahead. Page 365

BOSTON BROWN BREAD
From colonial days, a loaf with wheat, rye, and cornmeal steamed in coffee cans. 2 loaves, 2½ hours. Page 364

BANANA BREAD *(back left) A cake-like loaf using ripe bananas. 1 loaf, day ahead. Page 366.* **CRANBERRY-RAISIN BREAD** *(front left) A fruity and tasty quick bread. 2 loaves, 4 hours. Page 365.* **DATE-NUT BREAD** *(center) Delicious plain or served with a spread.*

1 loaf, 2 hours. Page 364. **PUMPKIN BREAD** *(back right) Made with canned fruit. 2 loaves, 2½ hours. Page 365.* **PEANUT-BUTTER BREAD** *(front right) With tangy orange peel, makes a delicious snack. 1 loaf, day ahead. Page 365.*

Biscuits/Corn Bread/Doughnuts/Muffins

GIANT POPOVERS
A purely American invention – a batter without leavening baked in custard cups. 8 popovers, 1½ hours. Page 364

SPOON BREAD (top) *Cornmeal mixture with a delicious, soft texture. 8 side-dish servings, 1½ hours.* Page 366. **GOLDEN CORN STICKS** *14 sticks, 35 mins.* Page 367

NEW ORLEANS BEIGNETS
A light yeast pastry deep-fried, sprinkled with sugar and served with tangy Raspberry Sauce. 12 servings, 1 hour. Page 369

LEFT PLATE: STICKY BUNS (back) *15 buns, 4 hours.* **PECAN-CINNAMON BUNS** *12 buns, 4½ hours.* Page 362. **NUTMEG SUGAR DOUGHNUTS** (right) *24 doughnuts, 2½ hours.* Page 369. **APPLE-CINNAMON FUNNEL CAKES** *7 cakes, 30 minutes.* page 369

MUFFINS: APPLE-MOLASSES (back left) *6 muffins, 40 minutes.* **ZUCCHINI-OATMEAL** (center left) *12 muffins, 45 minutes.* **MAPLE BRAN** (front left) *9 muffins, 1 hour.* **BLUEBERRY** *6 muffins, 40 minutes.* Page 368

Pancakes and Waffles/Crêpes/Pizza

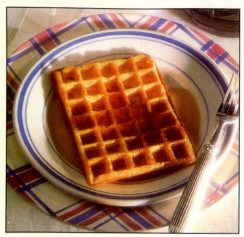

BUTTERMILK-PECAN WAFFLES
A delightful way to entertain at breakfast, lunch or dinner. 5 servings, 30 mins. Page 371

RICE FRITTERS *(left) Deep-fried and sprinkled with confectioners' sugar. 30 fritters, 1½ hours.* **COUNTRY BRUNCH PANCAKES** *(center) Shown here with Fig-Maple Syrup and crispy bacon. 6 servings, 45 mins.* **SILVER DOLLAR PANCAKES** *Served here with butter and marmalade. 6 servings, 45 mins. Page 370*

STRAWBERRY BLINTZES
Crêpes with cottage and cream cheese filling, fried and served with a Strawberry Sauce. 12 blintzes, early in day. Page 371

AVOCADO-TOMATO PIZZA *(back) With sharp Cheddar cheese, red kidney beans, and chopped parsley. 8 servings, 1 hour. Page 374* **EXTRA-CHEESE PIZZA WITH BASIL**
Mozzarella cheese gives a distinctive flavor and roasted sweet red peppers add color to this tasty pizza. 6 servings, 40 mins. Page 374

DEEP-DISH CHICAGO PIZZA
Italian-sausage links, spaghetti sauce, mozzarella cheese, and grated Parmesan. 8 servings, 1 hour. Page 374

TOP: GRAPE JELLY *Four 8-ounce glasses, early in day.* Page 380. **CRAN-APPLE JELLY** *Eight 8-ounce glasses, 4 hours.* Page 380. **RED-PEPPER FREEZER JELLY** *Six 8-ounce containers, day ahead.* Page 380. **CHUNKY APPLESAUCE** *3 cups, 2 hours.* Page 379. **CENTER: SPICED CRAB APPLES** *8 to 10 pints, day ahead.* Page 379. **SPICY WATERMELON PICKLES** *5 pints, day ahead.* Page 378. **SUNCHOKE PICKLES** *4 cups, 4 hours.* Page 377

BOTTOM: PICKLED PEACHES AND APRICOTS *6 pints, day ahead.* Page 379. **BREAD-AND-BUTTER PICKLES** *6 pints, 5 hours.* Page 377. **PICKLED BEETS** *6 servings, early in day.* Page 378. **DILL PICKLES** *A favorite American accompaniment. 20 pickles, 5 to 8 days ahead.* Page 377. **PICKLED VEGETABLE MEDLEY** *6 pints, day ahead.* Page 378. **SPICED PRUNES** *10 servings, day ahead.* Page 378

APRICOT BUTTER *(top) Slowly cooked dried apricot halves. 1½ cups, 45 mins. Page 379.* **BLUEBERRY JAM** *Succulent berries. 4½ pints, early in day. Page 381*

PEACH PRESERVES *(left) Peaches cooked to a chunky purée in a lemon-juice-and-sugar syrup are a treat no matter the season. 8 ½-pint jars, early in day.* **STRAWBERRY JAM** *Fresh strawberries boiled with sugar and lemon juice, then set with fruit pectin makes a delicious spread for toast. 8 ½-pints, early in day. Page 381*

BACK: PICCALILLI *6 pints, early in day.* **GREEN-TOMATO CHOW CHOW** *6 pints, day ahead.* **CRANBERRY-APPLE RELISH** *6 cups, early in day.* **PEPPER-PEAR RELISH** *5 pints, day ahead.* **TANGY CORN RELISH** *5 pints, day ahead.*

FRONT: AMERICAN HEIRLOOM CHUTNEY *4 cups, day ahead.* **SWEET-AND-SOUR RELISH** *5½ cups, early in day.* **CRANBERRY SAUCE** *5 cups, 10 mins.* **CUCUMBER-MINT RELISH** *10 servings, day ahead. Pages 383–384*

THE RECIPES

APPETIZERS

*"You never get a second chance
to make a first impression."*
WILL ROGERS

Over the years entertaining in America has become more and more relaxed. Informal gatherings of family and friends have ensured the popularity of quick-to-prepare and easy-to-eat nibbles and snacks; no-fuss impromptu parties are as successful today as were the long, formal dinners of yesteryear. Eating habits, too, have relaxed. Americans love finger-food (perhaps this casual approach to eating reflects the pioneer spirit within us).

We have also developed a preference for certain foods as appetizers. We often eat cheese, raw vegetables, seafood, and poultry as snacks and party foods. Unlike the European tradition of serving cheese and crackers after the main course, cheese and cheese combinations (cheese straws, spreads, and dips, for instance) are commonly offered as a cocktail tidbit or first course in American homes. Decorating a soft cheese (below) is very quick and simple, and makes a spectacular impression.

Vegetables, cooked or raw, are always welcome appetizers. Neither fattening nor filling, they make tantalizing bites that can stand alone as hors d'oeuvres or introduce a meal. Cooked hot vegetables, such as stuffed mushrooms and fried zucchini, make tasty party canapés. A small serving of steamed asparagus with a light sauce or buttered leeks makes an elegant beginning to a meal.

There is no need to confine chicken to the main course platter. Chicken pieces, especially chicken wings, have become one of the best-loved appetizers. Chicken wings are easy to prepare and easy to eat; they can be served hot or cold, as an hors d'oeuvre, first course, or as part of a buffet; they can be prepared in advance; they can be baked, grilled, or fried, and served with a variety of different sauces.

Seafood, so abundant along our North American coasts, has many uses as an appetizer. Simply dipping shrimp, crab, clams, or lobster into delectable sauces or butters tempts the appetite without spoiling it for the meal to follow. Only slightly more intricate preparations, such as marinated mussels, can make a sophisticated but light beginning to a formal dinner.

No matter what the menu, appetizers should look as stimulating as they taste. Be as creative as possible; a simple pâté or spread looks very attractive when presented on Grandmother's heirloom china. Be practical as well: remember finger bowls, small plates, forks, and plenty of napkins.

HOW TO DECORATE A WHOLE CHEESE

A whole Brie or any soft cheese makes a spectacular party presentation. Deceptively simple, it can be prepared in advance and kept refrigerated.

Surround platter with a selection of crackers or raw vegetables.

Place cheese on a large serving dish. With a sharp knife, remove top crust.

With a knife, mark cheese into 6 or 8 sections depending on size of cheese.

Press chopped nuts, herbs or spices into triangles, varying the colors and textures.

Hot appetizers

OVEN-FRIED CHICKEN WINGS

● Color index
page 18
● Begin
1 hr ahead
● 12 pieces
● 147 cals
each

6 tablespoons butter or
margarine
⅔ cup dried bread
crumbs
⅔ cup whole-wheat or
all-purpose flour

1½ teaspoons salt
¾ teaspoon rosemary,
crushed
⅛ teaspoon pepper
½ cup buttermilk
12 chicken wings

1. In 15½″ by 10½″ roasting pan in 425°F. oven, melt butter. Remove pan from oven.
2. On waxed paper, mix next 5 ingredients. Pour buttermilk into small bowl. Dip one wing at a time in buttermilk, then in crumb mixture.
3. Place chicken wings in melted butter in roasting pan, turning to coat evenly. Bake 35 minutes or until chicken wings are fork-tender.

BAKED CHICKEN WING APPETIZERS

● Color index
page 18
● Begin
1 hr ahead
● 36 pieces
● 90 cals each

18 chicken wings (about
3 pounds)
1½ cups dried bread
crumbs
¼ cup sesame seeds
1¼ teaspoons salt
¾ teaspoon ground
ginger
¾ teaspoon paprika

⅛ teaspoon ground red
pepper or 2 drops hot-
pepper sauce
1 8-ounce container plain
yogurt (1 cup)
2 tablespoons honey
6 tablespoons butter or
margarine

1. Preheat oven to 425°F. With knife, cut chicken wings at joints. Set aside.
2. On waxed paper, mix dried bread crumbs, sesame seeds, salt, ginger, paprika, and ground red pepper. In pie plate, mix yogurt and honey.
3. Dip chicken wings in yogurt mixture, then roll in crumb mixture. Place chicken wings on rack in large roasting pan (about 15″ by 10½″).
4. In small saucepan over low heat, melt butter; drizzle half over wings. Bake 15 minutes.
5. Turn chicken wings and drizzle with remaining melted butter. Bake 15 minutes longer or until chicken wings are browned and tender.

SAUCY CHICKEN WINGS

● Color index
page 18
● Begin
1 hr ahead
● 12 pieces
● 92 cals each

2 tablespoons salad oil
2 pounds chicken wings
(about 12)
3 tablespoons catchup
2 tablespoons soy sauce
2 teaspoons sugar

¼ teaspoon ground
ginger
¼ teaspoon crushed red
pepper
Water
1 tablespoon cornstarch

1. In 12-inch skillet over medium-high heat, in hot salad oil, cook chicken wings until browned on all sides. Add catchup, soy sauce, sugar, ginger, crushed red pepper, and ¾ cup water; over high heat, heat to boiling. Reduce heat to low; cover; simmer 30 minutes, stirring occasionally, until chicken wings are tender.
2. In cup, stir cornstarch with 2 tablespoons water. Gradually stir cornstarch mixture into simmering liquid in skillet; cook, stirring constantly, until mixture thickens slightly and boils.

BUFFALO-STYLE CHICKEN WINGS

This appetizer, invented in Buffalo, New York, 20 years ago, is one of our most popular finger-foods. Serve these zesty wings with celery sticks, and blue-cheese sauce.

● Color index
page 18
● Begin
40 mins
ahead
● 18 pieces
● 197 cals
each

1 8-ounce container sour
cream (1 cup)
1 4-ounce package blue
cheese, crumbled
¼ cup chopped parsley
¼ cup mayonnaise
1 tablespoon milk
1 tablespoon lemon juice
Salt

6 tablespoons butter or
margarine
2 tablespoons hot-pepper
sauce
3 pounds chicken wings
(about 18)
1 medium bunch celery
cut into sticks

1 Preheat broiler if manufacturer directs. Meanwhile, in medium-sized bowl, mix first 6 ingredients and ¼ teaspoon salt. Cover and refrigerate.

2 In small saucepan over low heat, heat butter or margarine and hot-pepper sauce, stirring occasionally, until butter or margarine melts.

3 In broiling pan, arrange chicken wings; lightly sprinkle with salt; brush with some of the hot-pepper mixture. Broil wings for 10 minutes.

4 Turn wings; brush with remaining hot-pepper mixture; broil 10 to 15 minutes longer, until wings are golden and tender.

5 To serve, arrange chicken wings and celery sticks on platter. Pass blue-cheese sauce.

Hot appetizers

HAM AND CHEESE CUPS

Based on the original French quiche, these mini cups of ham and cheese have become a favorite American appetizer.

- Color index page 19
- Begin 1½ hrs ahead or early in day
- 36 cups
- 90 cals per cup

Flaky Pastry (p.310)
1 tablespoon butter or margarine, melted
6 ounces cooked ham
3 eggs

1 cup half-and-half
¼ teaspoon salt
⅛ teaspoon pepper
¼ pound Swiss cheese, shredded (1 cup)

 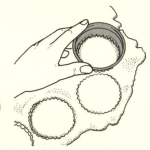

1 With a paper towel grease, then flour thirty-six 1¾-inch muffin-pan cups. Prepare Flaky Pastry, steps 1 to 3.

2 On lightly floured surface with floured rolling pin, roll dough about ⅛ inch thick. Using 3-inch round fluted cookie cutter, cut dough into 36 circles.

3 Line muffin-pan cups with pastry circles; brush pastry lightly with melted butter or margarine; cover and refrigerate.

4 On a cutting board, dice the ham into very small pieces. Cover and refrigerate if not using immediately.

 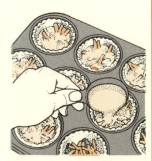

5 *About 35 minutes before serving:* Preheat oven to 400°F. In small bowl, beat eggs, half-and-half, salt, and pepper until well blended. Into each pastry cup, sprinkle some of the ham and cheese.

6 Spoon about 1 tablespoon of the egg mixture into each pastry cup. Bake 20 to 25 minutes. Remove the cups from muffin pan and serve immediately.

BRIE AND SMOKED SALMON TORTILLA TRIANGLES

- Color index page 19
- Begin 25 mins ahead
- 16 triangles
- 59 cals each

2 7- to 8-inch flour tortillas, each cut into eighths (16 triangles)
6 ounces Brie cheese
¼ pound thinly sliced smoked salmon

½ small cucumber, halved lengthwise and thinly sliced
½ teaspoon capers, drained
Dill sprigs for garnish

1. Preheat oven to 350°F. Place tortilla triangles on cookie sheet; bake 8 minutes or until crisp and lightly browned on both sides, turning often.
2. Meanwhile, cut off rind from cheese; cut cheese into thin slices.
3. When tortilla triangles are ready, arrange Brie on each triangle, cutting to fit. Bake until cheese melts. Remove from oven; arrange some salmon, 2 cucumber half-slices, and a few capers over cheese. If you like, garnish with dill sprigs.

COCKTAIL MEATBALLS

- Color index page 17
- Begin 45 mins ahead
- About 40 meatballs
- 25 cals each

1 pound ground beef
1 egg
2 teaspoons grated onion
1 teaspoon salt
¼ teaspoon pepper
Dried bread crumbs

About 4 sweet gherkin pickles, cut into ¼-inch pieces
⅓ cup minced parsley
¼ cup minced celery leaves

1. In medium bowl, mix ground beef, egg, onion, salt, pepper, and ½ cup bread crumbs.
2. Shape mixture into balls about 1 inch in diameter with a piece of pickle in the center of each.
3. Preheat broiler if manufacturer directs. On sheet of waxed paper, mix parsley, celery leaves, and 2 tablespoons bread crumbs. Roll meatballs in parsley mixture to coat evenly.
4. Place on rack in broiling pan. Broil meatballs 8 to 10 minutes until browned on all sides, turning occasionally. Serve with cocktail picks.

SAUSAGE-MUENSTER MELTS

- Color index page 19
- Begin 1 hr ahead
- 48 pieces
- 50 cals each

12 slices thin white bread (1 16-ounce loaf), crusts removed
½ pound hot Italian sausage links

3 tablespoons water
1 8-ounce package sliced Muenster cheese
Parsley sprigs for garnish

1. Lightly toast bread. Cut each slice diagonally into quarters to get 48 triangles in all.
2. In 10-inch skillet over medium heat, heat sausages and water to boiling. Cover; cook 5 minutes. Uncover; cook, turning sausages frequently, until browned, about 20 minutes. Remove to paper towels to drain.
3. Thinly slice sausages diagonally to get 48 slices. Place one slice on each bread piece. Cut cheese slices into triangles to fit on bread pieces; press parsley leaf onto each piece of cheese.
4. Preheat broiler if manufacturer directs. About 7 to 9 inches from heat, broil melts 5 minutes or until cheese melts. Garnish with parsley.

PIG-IN-A-BLANKET

An all-time favorite with adults and children alike, these sausage filled pastry hors d'oeuvres are perfect party pick-ups. Serve with cocktail sticks, and, if you like, provide a small bowl of mustard for dipping.

- *Color index page 19*
- *Begin 2½ hrs ahead*
- *32 pieces*
- *89 cals each*

8 country-style pork sausage links, each about 4 inches long
Water

½ cup butter
2 cups all-purpose flour
½ teaspoon salt
2 eggs

1 In covered 10-inch skillet over medium heat, simmer sausages and ½ cup water 5 minutes; uncover; cook until browned, turning often; refrigerate until cold.

2 In medium bowl with pastry blender, cut butter into flour and salt until mixture resembles coarse crumbs.

3 In 1-cup measure, beat eggs; add water to make ⅔ cup. Sprinkle 6 tablespoons egg mixture into flour mixture, mixing with fork until moist; shape into ball. Pre-heat oven to 425°F.

4 On a lightly floured surface, with a floured rolling pin roll the dough into a 20" by 10" rectangle. (Sprinkle extra flour on surface if dough sticks.) Cut into eight 5-inch squares.

5 Brush each square with some egg mixture; place a sausage along one edge; roll up; seal ends. Brush top of each with egg mixture.

6 Place seam side down on greased cookie sheet. Bake 20 minutes or until golden. Cool until easy to handle. Cut each roll into 4 slices.

QUESADOS

These tasty Mexican sandwiches are made by filling tortillas with cheese, sour cream, and guacamole.

- *Color index page 18*
- *Begin 30 mins ahead*
- *32 pieces*
- *50 cals each*

8 6-inch flour tortillas
1 ripe medium avocado, peeled and cut into chunks
½ small onion
1 tablespoon lemon juice
½ teaspoon salt
½ teaspoon garlic powder

2 ounces Monterey Jack cheese, shredded (½ cup)
¼ cup sour cream
4 ounces Cheddar cheese, shredded (1 cup)
Hot or mild taco sauce (optional)

1 Steam the tortillas as label directs. Or, in a 12-inch skillet in ½ inch water, place 3 inverted 6-ounce custard cups or small heat-safe bowls. Arrange the tortillas on a large heat-safe plate; set the plate on top of custard cups. Over high heat, heat water to boiling. Reduce the heat to low; cover the skillet with foil and "steam" the tortillas about 10 minutes or until they become soft and hot. Keep warm.

2 In food processor with knife blade attached or in blender at medium speed, blend next 5 ingredients until smooth.

3 In large bowl, mix avocado mixture, Monterey Jack cheese, sour cream, and ½ cup Cheddar cheese.

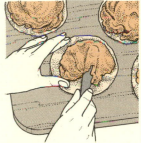

4 Spread avocado mixture evenly on one side of four steamed tortillas; top with remaining tortillas, pressing gently to seal.

5 Preheat broiler if manufacturer directs. Cut each tortilla "sandwich" into eight wedges. Place on large cookie sheet; sprinkle with remaining Cheddar.

6 Broil 3 to 5 minutes until cheese is just melted. Arrange Quesados on warm platter; serve immediately. If you like, spoon taco sauce over.

Hot appetizers

CHEDDAR-CHEESE FONDUE

- Color index page 18
- Begin 30 mins ahead
- 4 cups fondue
- 28 cals per tablespoon

2 cups half-and-half
1 tablespoon Worcestershire
2 teaspoons dry mustard
1 garlic clove, halved
1½ pounds mild or sharp Cheddar cheese, shredded (6 cups)
3 tablespoons all-purpose flour

Chunks of crusty French bread or cooked, shelled, and deveined shrimp or cooked ham chunks
Spicy Red Pepper Sauce (p.385) (optional)

1. In fondue pot or saucepan over low heat, heat half-and-half, Worcestershire, mustard, and garlic, stirring, until hot but not boiling. Discard garlic.
2. Meanwhile, in medium bowl, toss cheese with flour. Into hot mixture with fork or wire whisk, gradually stir in cheese. Cook over low heat, stirring constantly, until cheese is melted and mixture is smooth and bubbling.
3. Let each person spear chunks of French bread, shrimp, or ham chunks on long-handled fondue fork and dip in fondue. If you like, serve with Spicy Red Pepper Sauce.

STUFFED MUSHROOMS

- Color index page 19
- Begin 1 hr ahead
- 16 mushrooms
- 30 cals each

1 pound large mushrooms (about 16)
½ cup part-skim ricotta cheese
½ cup fresh white bread crumbs (about 1 slice)
1 tablespoon minced parsley
½ teaspoon salt
½ teaspoon oregano leaves
⅛ teaspoon pepper
1 egg
1 tablespoon grated Parmesan cheese

1. Preheat oven to 350°F. Trim tough ends of mushroom stems; remove and mince remaining stems; reserve mushroom caps.
2. In medium bowl, combine minced stems, ricotta cheese, and remaining ingredients, except Parmesan cheese. Spoon mixture into caps.
3. In 12″ by 8″ baking dish, arrange stuffed mushrooms, stuffing side up. Sprinkle mushrooms with Parmesan cheese. Bake in oven 20 minutes or until golden. Serve hot or chilled.

Stuffing mushroom caps: Carefully spoon stuffing mixture into the mushroom caps, molding into an attractive shape.

Baking stuffed mushrooms: Arrange stuffed mushrooms on a baking dish; sprinkle the stuffing with Parmesan cheese.

FRIED ARTICHOKE HEARTS AND ZUCCHINI

- Color index page 19
- Begin 40 mins ahead
- 4 servings
- 201 cals per serving

1 8-ounce can tomato sauce
1 tablespoon chopped fresh basil or 1 teaspoon dried basil
1 teaspoon minced green onion
1 14-ounce can artichoke hearts, drained and rinsed
2 medium zucchini (6 ounces each)
½ 12-ounce can beer
½ cup all-purpose flour
½ teaspoon salt
¼ teaspoon hot-pepper sauce
Salad oil

1. Prepare Tomato-Basil Dip: In small bowl, combine tomato sauce, basil, and green onion; set aside.
2. Pat artichoke hearts dry with paper towels. (If hearts are very large, cut in half or quarters.) Set aside. Cut zucchini lengthwise in half; cut each half lengthwise to make 4 spears. Cut each spear crosswise in half.
3. Pour beer into medium-sized bowl; with wire whisk, stir the flour, salt, and hot-pepper sauce into the beer until batter is light and frothy.
4. In deep-fat fryer set at 370°F., or in a 2-quart saucepan over medium-high heat, heat 2 inches salad oil to 370°F. on deep-fat thermometer. With a fork, dip artichokes and zucchini, one at a time, into batter; drop into oil and fry until golden, 1 to 2 minutes on each side.
5. Drain pieces on paper towels; arrange on serving dish or in basket and serve with dip.

Cutting the zucchini: Cut each zucchini in half lengthwise; then cut each again lengthwise. Cut across each spear.

Coating the pieces: With a fork, dip each piece into the beer batter to coat evenly.

"OVEN-FRIED" ARTICHOKE HEARTS AND ZUCCHINI: Prepare dip and vegetables as above but omit beer batter. Preheat oven to 400°F. Grease a large cookie sheet with *salad oil*. In a small bowl, combine *1 egg* and *2 tablespoons water*. On waxed paper, combine *⅔ cup dried bread crumbs, 1 teaspoon parsley flakes, ½ teaspoon salt*, and *½ teaspoon oregano leaves*. Dip each artichoke heart and zucchini half-spear into egg mixture, then coat with crumb mixture. Place on prepared cookie sheet. Bake 8 minutes or until golden brown; with tongs, turn pieces; bake 7 minutes longer or until lightly browned. Drain pieces on paper towels; arrange on a serving platter. Serve with dip. Makes 4 servings. 126 cals per serving.

Cold appetizers

SHRIMP COCKTAIL WITH TANGY DIP

4 cups water	Tangy Dip (below)
1 teaspoon salt	6 lettuce leaves
1 pound shelled and deveined medium shrimp	Lemon twists for garnish (p.100)

1. In 3-quart saucepan over high heat, heat water and salt to boiling; add shrimp and cook over low heat until shrimp turn pink, about 3 minutes; drain. Cover and refrigerate.
2. Prepare Tangy Dip. Cover with plastic wrap and refrigerate until needed.
3. To serve, line plates with lettuce leaves; arrange shrimp on lettuce; spoon on Tangy Dip. Garnish with lemon twists.

- Color index page 17
- Begin early in day
- 6 servings
- 111 cals per serving

TANGY DIP: In small bowl, combine ⅓ cup chili sauce, ⅓ cup catchup, 2 teaspoons horseradish, and 1½ teaspoons lemon juice. Mix well. Cover and refrigerate until needed. Makes ¾ cup. 25 cals per tablespoon.

CRAB CLAWS WITH SPICY RED PEPPER DIP

1 tablespoon salad oil	¾ teaspoon salt
2 large red peppers, chopped	⅛ teaspoon ground red pepper
1 small onion, chopped	2 12-ounce packages frozen Alaska Snow crab cocktail claws, thawed
½ cup packed fresh basil leaves or ½ teaspoon dried basil	
1 tablespoon lemon juice	
1 tablespoon capers	

1. Prepare Spicy Red Pepper Dip: In covered 3-quart saucepan over medium heat, heat oil. Add red peppers and onion, cook until tender, about 10 to 12 minutes.
2. In blender, with center of cover removed, blend pepper mixture with next 5 ingredients. Pour into small bowl; chill.
3. Serve with crab claws on bed of ice.

- Color index page 19
- Begin 1¼ hrs ahead
- 20 pieces
- 30 cals each

Instead of Spicy Red Pepper Dip, prepare:
MUSTARD DILL MAYONNAISE: In blender at low speed, blend 1 egg, 2 tablespoons Dijon mustard, 2 tablespoons lemon juice, ⅛ teaspoon salt, and ⅛ teaspoon pepper. Remove center of blender cover or uncover blender. With blender at low speed, slowly pour in ½ cup olive or salad oil in steady stream until thick and fluffy. Stir in 1 tablespoon chopped fresh dill or 1 teaspoon dill weed. Makes about 1 cup. 69 cals per tablespoon.

MARINATED MUSSELS ON THE HALF SHELL

Mussels, abundant in New England, are often inexpensive and plentiful; this elegant dish can be prepared ahead.

3 dozen large mussels	3 tablespoons mixed pickling spice, tied in cheesecloth bag	Fresh dill
1 cup water		2 tablespoons slivered roasted sweet red peppers
¼ cup cooking or dry sherry	2 tablespoons white vinegar	1 tablespoon capers, minced
¼ teaspoon peppercorns	2 teaspoons sugar	
¾ cup salad oil	2 teaspoons salt	
½ cup lemon juice		

- Color index page 19
- Begin early in day or day ahead
- 36 mussels
- 25 cals each

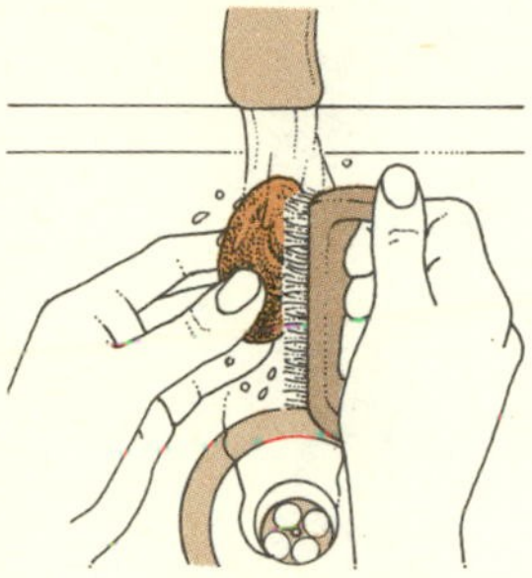

1 With stiff brush, scrub mussels with running cold water to remove any sand; remove beards.

2 In 8-quart Dutch oven or saucepot over high heat, heat water, sherry, and peppercorns to boiling.

3 Add mussels; heat to boiling. Reduce heat to low; cover; simmer until shells open, about 3 to 5 minutes, stirring occasionally.

4 With slotted spoon, remove mussels to bowl; cool slightly until easy to handle; set cooking broth aside.

5 Meanwhile, prepare marinade: In large bowl, mix salad oil, lemon juice, pickling spice, vinegar, sugar, salt, and 2 dill sprigs.

6 Remove mussels from shells; reserve 36 shells for serving later. Rinse mussels in cooking broth to remove any sand; drain well.

7 Add mussels to marinade and toss to coat well. Cover; refrigerate at least 6 hours or overnight, stirring occasionally.

8 To serve, line large platter with dill sprigs. Arrange reserved mussel shells on dill on platter.

9 With slotted spoon, remove mussels from marinade; place one mussel in each shell. Top each with some slivered red pepper and minced capers.

Cold appetizers

FRESH FRUIT IN ORANGE CUPS

- *Color index page 17*
- *Begin day ahead*
- *8 servings*
- *165 cals per serving*

Florida oranges, sweet and juicy at their best, provide their own presentation cups for this special fruit cocktail. The beautiful colors and tangy taste of the fruit make this dish a tantalizing first course.

8 large oranges	*4 kiwifruits*
1 cup sugar	*1 pint strawberries*
1/2 cup water	*1/4 cup brandy*
1/4 teaspoon salt	

1 With sharp knife, cut off one-third of each orange from stem end. Then cut thin slice off opposite end of each orange so oranges can stand upright.

2 With spoon, remove fruit from top and bottom pieces of oranges, whole if possible. Place half the fruit in bowl; cover; refrigerate. Use remainder for juice.

3 With kitchen shears, trim rim of each bottom orange shell into sawtooth pattern; cover and refrigerate orange cups.

4 From top shells, remove thin pieces of peel with vegetable peeler; cut enough peel into 1-inch-long strips to make 1 tablespoon.

5 In 1-quart saucepan over high heat, heat sugar, water, and salt to boiling. Add strips of peel; reduce heat to low; simmer 5 minutes to blend flavors. Cover and refrigerate.

6 Prepare fruit: Section peeled oranges and return sections to bowl. Peel kiwifruits; cut crosswise into slices; cut each slice in half; add to bowl. Wash and hull strawberries; cut each strawberry in half. Add to fruit in bowl. Stir brandy into chilled syrup. Pour syrup over fruit in bowl. Cover and refrigerate the syrup until well chilled, stirring mixture occasionally. To serve, spoon fruit mixture with some syrup into orange cups. Serve each orange cup on a small plate.

DEVILED EGGS

- *Color index page 17*
- *Begin 40 mins ahead*
- *12 egg-halves*
- *74 cals each*

6 hard-cooked eggs	*1/4 teaspoon pepper*
1/4 cup mayonnaise	*1 teaspoon dry mustard*
1/4 teaspoon salt	*Capers for garnish*

1. Shell eggs; with a sharp knife, cut eggs in half lengthwise.
2. Gently remove yolks; place in small bowl. With fork, finely mash yolks.
3. Add mayonnaise, salt, pepper, and mustard and mix until smooth.
4. Carefully spoon mixture into centers of egg whites; or, if you like, pipe mixture into centers. Top with capers.

Stir one of these into above egg-yolk mixture:
BACON: Add *2 1/2 tablespoons crumbled, fried bacon.*
MEXICAN STYLE: Leave out dry mustard; add *1/3 cup drained, chopped tomatoes* and *1 teaspoon chili powder.*
CAPERS: Leave out dry mustard; add *2 teaspoons minced capers.*
CUCUMBER-DILL: Leave out dry mustard; add *1/4 cup minced cucumber, 1 teaspoon dillweed,* and *1 teaspoon cider vinegar.*
TUNA: Add *3 tablespoons flaked tuna* and *2 teaspoons lemon juice.*
CURRY-CHUTNEY: Add *1/8 teaspoon curry powder* and *1 tablespoon chutney.*
SARDINE: Add *1 large sardine, chopped.*
CARROT-RAISIN: Add *2 tablespoons grated carrot, 1 tablespoon chopped raisins, 1/4 teaspoon ginger,* and *1/4 teaspoon sugar.*

LAST-MINUTE CHOICES

Often a quick appetizer must be assembled from ingredients on hand. Try combining seasonal fruits and vegetables with store-bought items to create something special.

Pineapple rings filled with soft cheese, such as cream cheese or Brie, and decorated with slices of lime and mint leaves

Half a grapefruit topped with a tablespoon of brown sugar or honey and grilled until bubbly

Slices of chilled melon and ham or salami garnished with blueberries and parsley

Avocado half stuffed with tuna salad served with a lemon wedge and coriander leaves

GUACAMOLE

1 medium tomato	1 4-ounce can chopped
2 medium avocados	mild green chilies,
2 tablespoons lemon or	drained
lime juice	Fresh coriander leaves
1¼ teaspoons salt	(optional)
½ small onion, minced	Tortilla chips or fresh
1 small garlic clove,	vegetables
minced	

1. Dip tomato in boiling water for 30 to 60 seconds, depending on ripeness. Dip into cold water, drain, then peel off skin. Dice tomato.
2. Cut each avocado in half lengthwise to the seed and twist the halves apart. Remove seeds and peel.
3. In bowl, with a fork, mash avocado with lemon juice. Stir in salt, diced tomato, onion, garlic, and chopped green chilies.
4. Spoon guacamole into a medium bowl. If you like, garnish with coriander leaves. Serve with tortilla chips or fresh vegetables. (For vegetable suggestions, see Arranging Festive Crudités, page 94.)

- Color index page 18
- Begin 1 hr ahead
- 2 cups dip
- 31 cals per tablespoon

GUACAMOLE-FILLED TOMATOES: Prepare as above for steps 1 and 2. Refrigerate. Prepare tomato shells: With small sharp knife cut off tops of *6 medium tomatoes* about one-third of the way down in a zigag pattern. With a spoon, remove flesh and seeds, leaving a "cup." Just before serving, spoon guacamole into cups. Place each cup on a small plate; garnish with coriander leaves, if you like. 70 cals each.

FIRST COURSE AVOCADO SALAD

2 small tomatoes,	1 teaspoon grated onion
chopped	1 teaspoon salt
2 tablespoons canned	¼ teaspoon ground
chopped green chilies,	cardamom
drained	1 medium avocado
2 tablespoons catchup	8 very thin salami slices
¼ teaspoon hot-pepper	Lime wedges for
sauce	garnish

1. In 2-quart saucepan over high heat, heat first 7 ingredients to boiling. Reduce heat to low; simmer, uncovered, 20 minutes, until mixture is slightly thickened. Spoon mixture into small bowl; cover and refrigerate until cool.
2. To serve, cut avocado lengthwise in half; remove seed and peel. Slice avocado halves lengthwise into 12 slices. On each of four salad plates, arrange 3 avocado slices and 2 salami slices; spoon dressing over avocado; garnish with lime wedges.

- Color index page 18
- Begin 1 hr ahead or day ahead
- 4 servings
- 165 cals per serving

COUNTRY PÂTÉ LOAF

As simple as a meat loaf, yet elegant enough to present at a dinner party, serve pâté with a variety of fancy crackers or toast points.

3 large leeks	½ teaspoon marjoram
Water	leaves
2 tablespoons salad oil	6 large pitted ripe olives,
2 green onions, chopped	coarsely chopped
1 small onion, chopped	1 envelope unflavored
1 garlic clove, crushed	gelatin
⅓ cup chopped parsley	¼ cup Madeira wine
½ teaspoon thyme leaves	¾ pound ground pork

- Color index page 17
- Begin day ahead
- 16 servings
- 125 cals per serving (without crackers)

½ pound chicken livers, ground
2 ounces ground pork fat
1 teaspoon salt
¼ teaspoon pepper
½ pound cooked smoked tongue or ham
Assorted unsalted crackers

1 Cut off the roots and trim the leaf ends of the leeks. Separate the leeks into leaves; rinse leeks well with running cold water to remove all sand. In a 10-inch skillet over high heat, heat 1 inch water to boiling, add leeks; heat to boiling. Reduce heat to low; cover skillet and simmer about five minutes or until the leeks are tender; drain, and rinse under running cold water. Arrange leeks on waxed paper and pat dry with paper towels.

2 Over medium heat, in hot oil, cook next 3 ingredients until tender, stirring. Add herbs and olives; simmer 3 minutes. Remove from heat.

3 In 1-quart saucepan, sprinkle gelatin evenly over wine. Let stand 1 minute. Cook over low heat, stirring, until gelatin is dissolved.

4 In large bowl, beat pork, chicken livers, pork fat, salt, pepper, and wine mixture until well mixed. Cut tongue into ¼-inch-wide strips.

5 Line 9″ by 5″ loaf pan with leeks, allowing leaves to hang over sides. Spread ⅓ of pork mixture in bottom of pan; top with half of onion mixture.

6 Place half of tongue strips lengthwise over top. Repeat, ending with pork mixture. Press down firmly. Fold overhanging leeks over top.

7 Bake in 350°F. oven 1 to 1¼ hours until mixture shrinks from sides of pan and juices run clear. (To check color of juices, press pâté with back of spoon.)

8 Cool on wire rack. Drain off excess fat. Cover in pan with foil-wrapped cardboard; place several cans on top to weight down pâté. Refrigerate overnight.

9 To serve, remove cans and cardboard. Unmold pâté onto cutting board or plate. Scrape off any coagulated cooking juices and excess fat. Slice pâté; serve with crackers.

Cold appetizers

HERBED GOAT CHEESE WITH SUN-DRIED TOMATOES

- Color index page 18
- Begin 30 mins ahead
- 12 servings
- 190 cals per serving

1/3 cup olive oil
1/3 cup loosely packed small basil leaves or 3/4 teaspoon dried basil
1/8 teaspoon coarsely ground black pepper
2 ounces sun-dried tomatoes, thinly sliced
1 small green onion, thinly sliced
3/4 pound goat cheese (Bucheron or Montrachet), sliced
Thinly sliced French bread or unsalted crackers (optional)

1. In small deep platter or baking dish, mix oil, basil, pepper, tomatoes, and onion. Place cheese slices in mixture, overlapping slightly; spoon mixture over slices. If not serving right away, cover; refrigerate up to 2 days.
2. If you like, serve with French bread or unsalted crackers.

HOW TO SERVE CHEESE SPREADS

The consistency of cheese spreads makes them easy to present in many forms. Try a new way with an old favorite. These spreads can be made ahead and refrigerated.

Shape spread into a ball, keeping bottom flat. Place on a small plate and press chopped parsley or other herbs into the surface.

Place cheese spread on waxed paper. Rolling wax paper, form into a log. Smooth ends with a knife and press chopped nuts into surface or scrape with a fork to give the effect of tree bark.

To create a special effect, shape cheese spread into tiny balls between palms of hands and roll balls in chopped dill or other green herbs. Arrange them in the shape of a grape cluster on a platter lined with grape leaves.

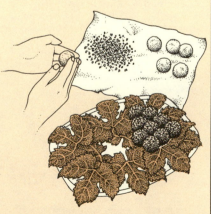

For easy handling, pack cheese spreads into small crocks or jars; smooth top with back of spoon; cover tightly with plastic wrap. Tied with a ribbon, this makes an attractive gift at holiday time.

CHEDDAR CHEESE SPREAD

- Color index page 17
- Begin 25 mins ahead or early in day
- 2 1/4 cups
- 46 cals per tablespoon

1/2 cup butter or margarine, softened
1/2 pound sharp Cheddar cheese, shredded (2 cups)
3 to 4 tablespoons milk
1 fresh mild green chili, seeded and chopped
2 green onions, finely chopped
1 small garlic clove, minced
1/4 teaspoon hot-pepper sauce

In a medium-sized bowl, with mixer at medium speed, beat butter until fluffy. Add the cheese and milk, a tablespoon at a time, until spreadable and well blended. Add the remaining ingredients and mix well.

LIPTAUER CHEESE

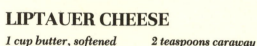

- Color index page 17
- Begin 15 mins ahead or early in day
- 3 cups
- 82 cals per tablespoon

1 cup butter, softened
2 8-ounce packages cream cheese, softened
1/2 cup sour cream
1 tablespoon sweet Hungarian paprika
1 tablespoon finely chopped onion
2 teaspoons caraway seeds
1 teaspoon dry mustard
Freshly ground pepper to taste
Chopped chives for garnish

In bowl with mixer at medium speed, or in food processor with knife blade attached, beat butter and cream cheese until smooth. Add remaining ingredients except chives; beat until well mixed. Pack into small bowl; sprinkle with chives.

BLUE CHEESE SPREAD

- Color index page 17
- Begin 20 mins ahead or early in day
- 1 3/4 cups
- 88 cals per tablespoon

1 8-ounce package cream cheese, softened
1/4 pound Roquefort or blue cheese, softened
2 tablespoons milk
1 tablespoon prepared mustard
1 teaspoon pepper

In blender at medium speed or in food processor with knife blade attached, blend all ingredients until smooth. If not serving right away, cover and refrigerate; use within one week. Before serving, let cheese mixture stand at room temperature.

HOT PEPPER PECANS

- Color index page 17
- Begin early in day
- 2 cups
- 209 cals per 1/4 cup

2 cups pecan halves
1 1/2 tablespoons butter or margarine, melted
2 teaspoons soy sauce
1/4 teaspoon salt
Dash hot-pepper sauce

Preheat oven to 300°F. In 8- or 9-inch cakepan, combine pecans and melted butter. Toast in oven 30 minutes, stirring occasionally. Add soy sauce, salt, and hot-pepper sauce; toss until coated. Spread on waxed paper to cool.

CASHEWS WITH CHILI: Prepare as above but use *2 cups salt cashews, 1 1/2 tablespoons butter or margarine*, melted, *1 tablespoon chili powder* and omit salt, soy sauce, and hot pepper sauce. Makes 2 cups. 223 cals per 1/4 cup.

VERMONT CHEDDAR STICKS

Cheese sticks can be made in many ways using various pastries and cheeses. Basically simple to prepare, it's a good idea to make a large batch to store in the freezer. For an unusual gift, wrap with a pretty ribbon.

- Color index page 17
- Begin early in day or up to 1 week ahead
- 6 dozen sticks
- 40 cals per stick

2 cups all-purpose flour
½ teaspoon salt
Ground red pepper
1 cup butter or margarine

8 ounces Cheddar cheese, shredded
½ cup iced water

1 In a large bowl with fork, combine flour, salt, and ¼ teaspoon ground red pepper. With pastry blender or two knives used scissor-fashion, cut in butter or margarine until mixture resembles coarse crumbs. With fork, stir in cheese and water just until mixture forms soft dough and leaves side of bowl. On lightly floured surface with floured hands, pat into 6″ by 6″ square.

2 Wrap dough with plastic wrap and chill in freezer for 30 minutes for easier handling.

3 Roll dough into 18″ by 8″ rectangle. Starting from one 8-inch end, fold ⅓ of dough over middle third; fold other end over middle ⅓ to make 8″ by 6″ rectangle. Repeat rolling and folding. Wrap; freeze 30 minutes again.

4 Roll and fold as above again. Then, roll into 18″ by 12″ rectangle. Sprinkle with ground red pepper; cut lengthwise in half; cut each half crosswise into 36 6″ by ½″ strips.

5 Place Cheddar sticks ½ inch apart, on ungreased large cookie sheets, pressing ends to cookie sheet to prevent ends curling up. Preheat oven to 375°F.

6 Bake 15 minutes or until golden. Remove sticks from cookie sheets; cool on wire racks. Store in tightly covered container; use up within 1 week.

CHEESE-STUFFED BREAD

Hollowed-out breads make practical containers for all sorts of fillings. Ours is stuffed with a colorful cheese-and-vegetable mixture.

- Color index page 17
- Begin 5 hrs ahead or day ahead
- 60 slices
- 45 cals per slice.

4 tablespoons butter or margarine
½ medium head green cabbage (about 1 pound), diced
½ pound mushrooms, chopped
1 large onion, diced
1 teaspoon salt
1 loaf Italian bread, about 15 inches long

1 8-ounce package cream cheese, softened
1 2-ounce jar diced pimentos, drained
⅛ teaspoon ground red pepper

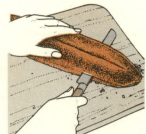

1 Prepare cheese-and-vegetable filling: In 12-inch skillet over medium heat, in hot butter, cook next 4 ingredients until vegetables are tender, about 20 minutes; stir occasionally; remove from the heat.

2 Meanwhile, cut Italian bread crosswise in half. Hollow out each bread half, leaving a ¼-inch-thick shell.

3 In large bowl with mixer at low speed, beat cream cheese until smooth; stir in pimentos, red pepper, and cabbage mixture until well mixed.

4 Pack mixture into shells. Press shells together. Wrap tightly with plastic wrap and refrigerate until mixture is firm, at least 4 hours.

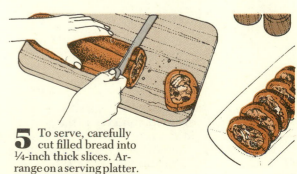

5 To serve, carefully cut filled bread into ¼-inch thick slices. Arrange on a serving platter.

Cold appetizers

DIPS

Probably the most common party appetizer in America, the dip is very easy to make from ingredients on hand. Simple dips are often made with mayonnaise, sour cream, or cheese as a base, with any combination of herbs and spices added.

CHILI-CHEESE DIP

- Color index page 17
- Begin ½ hr ahead
- 1½ cups
- 44 cals per tablespoon

2 tablespoons salad oil	¼ cup beer
1 small onion, diced	¼ teaspoon salt
½ 8-ounce package American cheese, cut in chunks	⅛ teaspoon hot-pepper sauce
½ 4-ounce can chopped green chilies, drained	1 small tomato, chopped

1. In 2-quart saucepan over medium heat, in 2 tablespoons hot salad oil, cook onion until tender, stirring occasionally.
2. Add remaining ingredients except chopped tomato; cook until cheese is melted and mixture is smooth, stirring frequently; stir in tomato.
3. Spoon cheese mixture into small bowl. Serve immediately as dip for tortilla chips and our Tex-Mex Basket (right).

HOT TUNA DIP

- Color index page 17
- Begin ½ hr ahead
- 2 cups dip
- 73 cals per tablespoon

2 cups heavy cream	1 6½-ounce can tuna, drained and mashed
2 tablespoons butter	
1 garlic clove, minced	1 teaspoon thyme leaves
1 2-ounce can anchovy fillets, drained and mashed	1 teaspoon oregano
	⅛ teaspoon red pepper

1. In 2-quart saucepan over medium-high heat, heat cream to boiling; reduce to about 1⅓ cups, stirring occasionally. Remove from heat.
2. In 1-quart saucepan, over medium heat, in hot butter, cook garlic 1 minute. Stir in next 5 ingredients. Cook, stirring until smooth. Remove from heat.
3. Gradually whisk in reduced cream until mixture is smooth. Pour into candle warmer dish and serve with a selection of prepared vegetables from the Italian Antipasto Platter and bread sticks.

ORIENTAL ONION DIP

- Color index page 17
- Begin 20 mins ahead
- 1¼ cups
- 27 cals per tablespoon

1 cup sour cream	2 tablespoons chopped fresh coriander leaves
1 envelope beef-flavor bouillon	1 tablespoon grated peeled gingerroot
¼ cup thinly sliced green onions	1 teaspoon soy sauce

1. In small bowl with spoon, mix all ingredients. Cover and refrigerate the dip if not serving it right away.
2. Spoon into serving bowl and use as dip with the Oriental Vegetable Tray.

ARRANGING FESTIVE CRUDITÉS

Create a special feeling by choosing vegetables and fruits that go together well. They should always be thoroughly cleaned, nicely cut, and beautifully arranged.

A Tex-Mex Basket can be achieved by choosing:

carrot strips
green onions
peppers; sweet and hot: red, green, and yellow
avocado chunks
cherry tomatoes
jícama strips
cucumber slices
celery stalks

For an Italian Antipasto Platter, arrange on a bed of escarole:

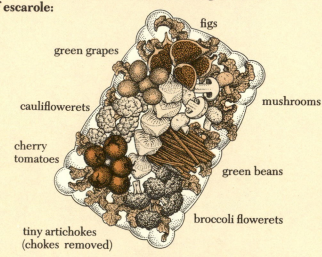

green grapes
cauliflowerets
cherry tomatoes
tiny artichokes (chokes removed)
figs
mushrooms
green beans
broccoli flowerets

For an Oriental Vegetable Tray arrange the following on a lacquered or wooden tray:

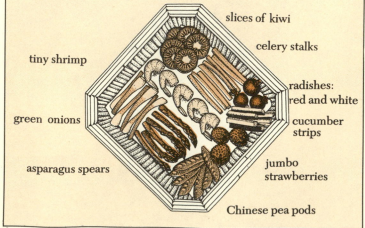

tiny shrimp
green onions
asparagus spears
slices of kiwi
celery stalks
radishes: red and white
cucumber strips
jumbo strawberries
Chinese pea pods

SOUPS

"To make a good soup, the pot must only simmer or 'smile'."

Creole proverb

The soup pot has been a welcoming mealtime feature since the country's earliest days. Into a pot full of simmering water, over a hearth or open fire, our thrifty forebears threw in whatever happened to be available – wild herbs, seeds or berries, home-grown vegetables, or leftover meat or carcasses from the game they hunted. As more and more settlers from all over the world flowed into America, they added ingredients that they had used at home, and the soup kettle literally turned into a melting pot.

French Canadian fishermen moved south into New England and added their shellfish catches to home-grown vegetables to create New England Clam Chowder. Louisiana Gumbo derives from a mixture of French, Spanish and Indian styles of cooking. This thick soup, or stew, may contain any combination of seafood, meat or poultry, vegetables and spices. It is usually thickened with okra, a vegetable brought to America by African slaves, or with filé, a powder made from dried sassafras leaves.

Americans, born and bred, have created new soups by adapting old recipes and made certain soups very popular by their continued use. However, perhaps the most obvious reason that soup has become a staple of the American diet is its versatility. Almost any soup can be offered as a first course or a main course by altering the size of the portion. For example, Cream of Fresh Tomato Soup, often served as an appetizer, makes a complete meal when teamed with a cheese quiche.

Planning an entire meal around a basic soup can be both challenging and creative. Be original by offering unusual small dishes with the soup – perhaps a crisp salad of oriental vegetables, a spicy rice and raisin pilaf, a meat or fish paté, or a vegetable dip. Warm rolls, savory muffins, and special breads like cheese or herb served in a basket make tasty dry accompaniments; crackers can be eaten in or with a soup. Soup served in a pretty tureen makes an impressive addition to the dining table.

Soups can be eaten anywhere at any time. In fact, farmers used to come in after their early morning work to a breakfast of hot soup. A small cup of soup is ideal for a mid-morning or afternoon snack; some people prefer soup as a hot bedtime drink. And for after-school snacks, a mug of your child's favorite soup is a tasty, and nutritious welcome home.

PARTY PRESENTATIONS

With very little additional time or effort, you can make soup look extra-special for serving at a party or buffet table.

Pumpkin Tureen: With a sharp knife, cut off the top of the pumpkin about one-third of the way down in a zigzag pattern. Remove top.

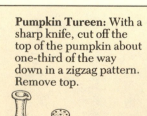

With metal spoon, scoop out the inside, leaving about 1 inch of flesh in the shell. If you like, season inside with a little oil and salt. This makes a spectacular server for pumpkin or other squash soups.

Chilled Soups: A bed of crushed ice made in a blender or food processor keeps soups cold and provides a sparkling background.

Fish Chowders: Create a seaside mood by surrounding fish soups and chowders with shells on a bed of kale or seaweed.

Vegetable soups

ONION SOUP GRATINÉ

- Color index page 20
- Begin 40 mins ahead
- 7½ cups
- 424 cals per cup

1 long loaf French bread
4 tablespoons butter or margarine
3 large onions, sliced (about 4 cups)
1 teaspoon sugar
1 tablespoon all-purpose flour

2½ cups water
½ cup dry red wine
2 10½-ounce cans condensed beef broth
6 ounces Swiss cheese, shredded (1½ cups)

1. Cut four 1-inch-thick slices bread; serve remaining bread with soup. Toast slices in 325°F. oven until lightly browned, about 10 minutes.
2. Meanwhile, in 4-quart saucepan over medium-high heat, in hot butter or margarine, cook onions and sugar 10 minutes. Stir in flour until blended. Add water, wine, and undiluted beef broth; heat to boiling. Reduce heat to low; cover; simmer 10 minutes.
3. Spoon soup into four 16-ounce oven-safe soup bowls; place 1 slice toasted bread in each bowl. Top each slice with ¼ of the shredded cheese.
4. Place bowls in jelly-roll pan for easier handling. Increase heat to 425°F. Bake 10 minutes or until cheese is melted and soup is hot.

Preparing cheese-topped toast: Top slices of French bread toast with shredded cheese.

Heating the toast and soup: Place bowls in pan and bake until cheese bubbles and soup is hot.

CORN CHOWDER

- Color index page 20
- Begin 45 mins ahead
- 9 cups
- 338 cals per cup

6 tablespoons butter or margarine
2 small potatoes (½ pound), peeled and diced
2 celery stalks, minced
1 small green pepper, minced
1 small onion, minced
1½ teaspoons salt

2 tablespoon all-purpose flour
2 tablespoons paprika
1½ cups water
2 chicken-flavor bouillon cubes or envelopes
1 16- to 20-ounce package frozen whole-kernel corn
2 pints half-and-half

1. In 4-quart saucepan over medium heat, in hot butter, cook next 5 ingredients until vegetables are tender, about 10 minutes, stirring frequently.
2. Stir in the flour and paprika until blended; cook 1 minute.
3. Stir in water and bouillon; over medium heat, cook, stirring constantly, until mixture is smooth and thickened, about 5 minutes.
4. Stir in corn kernels and half-and-half. Cook, stirring frequently, until corn is tender and mixture is heated through, about 10 minutes.

VELVETY PUMPKIN BISQUE

A squash popular with the Indians, pumpkin soon became a favorite among the colonists, who made pumpkin beer as well as soup.

- Color index page 20
- Begin 30 mins ahead
- 5 cups
- 222 cals per cup

2 tablespoons butter or margarine
1 tablespoon minced green onion
1 16-ounce can pumpkin
1 cup water
2 tablespoons brown sugar
½ teaspoon salt
⅛ teaspoon white pepper

⅛ teaspoon ground cinnamon
2 chicken-flavor bouillon cubes or envelopes
2 cups half-and-half
1 lemon, thinly sliced, for garnish
Minced parsley for garnish

1 In 2-quart saucepan over medium heat, in hot butter, cook onion until tender, stirring occasionally.

2 Stir in next 7 ingredients until blended and mixture begins to boil; cook 5 minutes to blend flavors.

3 Add half-and-half; heat through, stirring constantly.

4 To serve, ladle soup into bowls and garnish each serving.

SOUP ACCOMPANIMENTS

Crunchy textures provide a good foil for soups. Bread and crackers are traditional; try serving something different.

Corn chips

Buttered bread strips

Bread sticks

Small rolls

Garlic bread

Vegetable soups

CREAM OF FRESH TOMATO SOUP

- Color index page 20
- Begin 45 mins ahead
- 5 cups
- 302 cals per cup

Though Thomas Jefferson grew tomatoes in his own garden, few of his fellow Americans had ever seen one. Today they are grown in every state and tomato soup is a favorite.

7 medium ripe tomatoes (about 2½ pounds)
1 medium onion, coarsely chopped
1 medium celery stalk, coarsely chopped
¼ teaspoon basil
1 bay leaf
3 whole cloves
Water

4 tablespoons butter or margarine
¼ cup all-purpose flour
1½ teaspoons salt
1 cup heavy or whipping cream
3 to 4 teaspoons sugar
Fresh basil for garnish

1 With a small sharp knife, remove stem ends from tomatoes; cut into bite-sized chunks.

2 In a 3-quart non-aluminum saucepan over medium heat, heat the tomatoes, chopped onion, chopped celery, basil, bay leaf, and cloves to boiling. Reduce heat to low; cover and simmer until the vegetables are very tender, about 20 minutes. Stir the mixture occasionally to prevent any sticking. Add a little extra water if the mixture reduces too quickly.

3 Into medium bowl, press mixture through food mill or sieve; discard seeds, skin, bay leaf, and cloves.

4 Measure tomato purée. If necessary, add enough water to make 4 cups purée.

5 In same saucepan over low heat, melt butter or margarine. Stir in flour and salt until blended.

6 Stir in tomato purée; cook, stirring until thickened. Add cream and sugar; heat. Garnish with fresh basil leaf.

CREAMY CALIFORNIA ARTICHOKE SOUP

- Color index page 20
- Begin 2 hrs ahead
- 8 cups
- 222 cals per cup

6 large artichokes
Water
1 tablespoon lemon juice
2 tablespoons butter or margarine
1 large onion, chopped
2 potatoes, diced
¼ teaspoon pepper

4 cups chicken broth or 4 cups water plus 2 chicken-flavor bouillon cubes
1 cup heavy or whipping cream
Chopped parsley for garnish

1. Cut off stems and top inch of artichokes. Trim thorny tips off leaves. In 8-quart saucepot over high heat, heat 1 inch water to boiling. Add artichokes and lemon juice; return to boiling. Reduce heat to low; cover and cook 45 minutes or until an artichoke leaf can be pulled out easily.
2. Meanwhile, in 4-quart saucepan over medium heat, in hot butter or margarine, cook onion and potatoes 3 minutes, stirring occasionally. Add pepper and chicken broth; heat to boiling. Reduce heat to low; cover and simmer 15 minutes or until potatoes are tender.
3. Drain cooked artichokes; rinse with cold water; cool until easy to handle. Remove leaves from artichokes, exposing the chokes. Discard chokes. Cut up artichoke hearts. With metal teaspoon, scrape off edible part of each leaf. Add artichoke pieces to potato mixture.
4. In blender over medium speed, blend half of potato mixture until smooth; pour into bowl. Repeat with remaining half. Return all soup to saucepan; add cream; heat through. Ladle into bowls; garnish with chopped parsley.

CREAM OF MUSHROOM SOUP

- Color index page 20
- Begin 45 mins ahead
- 7 cups
- 256 cals per cup

1 pound mushrooms
½ cup butter or margarine
1 teaspoon lemon juice
1 small onion sliced
⅓ cup all-purpose flour
3½ cups water

3 chicken-flavor bouillon cubes or envelopes
1 teaspoon salt
¼ teaspoon pepper
1 cup heavy or whipping cream

1. Trim tough stem ends of mushrooms; remove stems; set aside. Slice mushroom caps thinly.
2. In 4-quart saucepan over medium-high heat, in hot butter or margarine, cook sliced mushrooms and lemon juice until mushrooms are just tender, stirring.
3. Reduce heat to medium-low; with slotted spoon, remove mushrooms to bowl. In saucepan in remaining butter, cook onion and mushroom stems; cook until onion is tender.
4. Stir in flour until blended; cook 1 minute, stirring the mixture constantly.
5. Gradually stir in water and bouillon; cook, stirring constantly, until mixture is thickened.
6. Into blender container, ladle half of mixture; cover and, at high speed, blend until smooth. Repeat with other half. Return mixture to saucepan; stir in salt, pepper, cream, and mushroom slices; reheat just until soup is boiling.

CHILLED CUCUMBER SOUP

- Color index page 20
- Begin 4 hrs ahead
- 5¼ cups
- 181 cals per cup

¼ cup butter or margarine
4 cups peeled chopped cucumbers
1 cup chopped green onions
¼ cup all-purpose flour
4 cups chicken broth
Salt and pepper
½ cup half-and-half
Cucumber slices for garnish

1. In 12-inch skillet over medium-high heat, in butter, cook cucumbers and onions. Blend flour well into the pan juices.
2. Gradually add broth, stirring; cook until mixture thickens and begins to boil. Add salt and pepper to taste.
3. Cover; simmer over low heat 10 minutes, stirring occasionally. Refrigerate until chilled.
4. In covered blender container at medium speed, blend some of mixture until smooth.
5. Strain blended mixture through sieve into bowl; discard seeds. Repeat with rest of mixture.
6. Stir in half-and-half. Pour into chilled individual bowls; garnish with cucumber slices.

Straining the mixture: Pour the blended mixture through a sieve and discard the seeds.

Serving the soup: Add the half-and-half and, if you like, serve the soup in chilled bowls on a bed of ice.

CHILLED WATERCRESS SOUP

- Color index page 20
- Begin 2½ hrs ahead or early in day
- 5⅔ cups
- 213 cals per cup

3 tablespoons butter or margarine
1 small onion, thinly sliced
1 medium celery stalk, thinly sliced
2 cups water
1 teaspoon salt
⅛ teaspoon white pepper
1 medium potato, thinly sliced
1 chicken-flavor bouillon cube or envelope
1 large bunch watercress
2 cups half-and-half

1. In 3-quart saucepan over medium heat, in hot butter or margarine, cook onion and celery until tender, stirring occasionally.
2. Add water, salt, pepper, potato, and bouillon; over high heat, heat to boiling. Reduce heat to low; cover and simmer 10 minutes.
3. Meanwhile, set aside 10 small watercress sprigs for garnish. Discard stems from remaining watercress; add leaves to saucepan; cook 5 minutes longer or until potato is very tender.
4. In blender at medium speed, blend watercress mixture until smooth. Pour mixture into large bowl; stir in half-and-half. Cover and refrigerate at least 1½ hours or until chilled. Garnish each serving with a watercress sprig.

VICHYSSOISE

In 1910 a French chef at New York's Ritz Carlton Hotel created this delicious chilled version of a traditional leek and potato soup.

- Color index page 20
- Begin 50 mins ahead
- 7 cups
- 283 cals per cup

3 medium leeks (about 1¼ pounds)
3 tablespoons butter or margarine
3 medium potatoes, peeled and sliced
3 cups water plus 2 chicken-flavor bouillon cubes or envelopes
1 cup heavy or whipping cream
1 cup milk
1 teaspoon salt
¼ teaspoon white pepper
2 tablespoons minced chives for garnish

 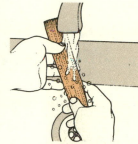

1 Cut off roots and tough leaves from leeks and discard.

2 Cut leeks lengthwise in half; rinse under running cold water to remove sand.

3 Cut crosswise into ¼-inch slices the white part of the leeks and enough of the green tops to make 2 cups.

4 In 2-quart saucepan over medium heat, in hot butter, cook leeks 5 minutes. Add potatoes and chicken stock, heat to boiling. Reduce heat to low; cover and simmer 30 minutes. Spoon half of mixture into blender; cover (with center part of blender cover removed); blend at low speed until smooth. Pour into 3-quart saucepan. Repeat with remaining mixture.

5 Stir cream, milk, salt, and pepper into leek mixture; over low heat, cook soup just until heated through.

6 Pour soup into large bowl. Cover and refrigerate until chilled. Garnish with minced chives. It is also delicious hot; serve it right after cooking or reheat to serve later.

Vegetable soups

GAZPACHO

- Color index page 21
- Begin 2½ hrs ahead
- 7 cups
- 92 cals per cup

3 cups tomato juice
3 tablespoons olive oil
3 large tomatoes, peeled, seeded, and cut up
1 cucumber, peeled, seeded, and cut up
1 small onion, cut up
1 small green pepper, cut up
1 small garlic clove
1 teaspoon sugar
¾ teaspoon salt
½ teaspoon hot-pepper sauce
½ cup cucumber, diced and seeded, for garnish
½ cup chopped onion for garnish
½ cup diced green pepper for garnish
Croutons for garnish (p.103)

In covered blender container at high speed, blend first 10 ingredients, one-third at a time, until fairly smooth. Pour into large bowl; cover and chill. Serve in soup bowls and pass chopped vegetables and croutons for garnish.

SOUP GARNISHES

Lemon/Lime Twist: Cut a slice of lemon or lime from center to edge; twist into spiral shape.

Scallion Pompom: Make several lengthwise slits to about 1 in from the root end. Soak in bowl of ice water to curl.

Carrot Curl: Peel long strips of carrot. Soak in ice water to curl.

Julienne Leeks: Cut leeks lengthwise into very thin slivers and sprinkle on individual servings.

Mushroom Pinwheel: Holding a sharp paring knife against mushroom cap, twist knife edge clockwise from center to edge of mushroom.

Fresh Herbs: Chop fresh herbs or use whole sprigs for a dainty garnish.

Hearty soups

BLACK BEAN SOUP

- Color index page 21
- Begin 3½ hrs ahead
- 10½ cups
- 202 cals per cup

Used for centuries in Central and South America and known as "Creole caviar," the black bean is a popular ingredient in many southern dishes. Here, the long cooking of ham and vegetables creates a dish more like a thick purée than a soup.

1 16-ounce package dry black beans
Water
1 ham bone with about 2 cups meat left on
2 large celery stalks, diced
1 large onion, diced
1 large carrot, diced
1 medium garlic clove, cut in half
1 bay leaf
½ teaspoon pepper
⅛ teaspoon ground cloves
Salt
Dry sherry
2 hard-cooked eggs, chopped

1 Prepare beans: Rinse beans in running cold water and discard any stones or shriveled beans. In 5-quart Dutch oven over high heat, heat beans and 8 cups water to boiling; cook 3 minutes. Remove Dutch oven from heat; cover and let stand 1 hour. Drain and rinse beans and return to Dutch oven.

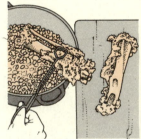

2 Add 8 cups water, ham bone, and next 7 ingredients; heat to boiling. Reduce to low; cover, simmer 2 hours or until beans are tender, stirring occasionally.

3 Discard the garlic clove halves and the bay leaf. Remove ham bone from soup to cutting board.

4 Cut meat from bone into bite-sized pieces; set aside. Discard bone. With slotted spoon, mash beans slightly.

5 Return ham pieces to soup; add salt to taste. Over medium heat, heat through. To serve, spoon soup into large bowls. Each person can add sherry to taste and garnish with chopped hard-cooked egg.

LENTIL AND FRANKFURTER SOUP

- Color index page 22
- Begin 2 hrs ahead
- 14 cups
- 227 cals per cup

1 tablespoon salad oil
1 16-ounce package frankfurters, cut into ½-inch slices
2 medium celery stalks, diced
1 medium red or green pepper, diced
1 large carrot, diced
1 large onion, diced
1 medium garlic clove, minced
1 16-ounce package dry lentils
11 cups water
1 teaspoon salt
¼ teaspoon pepper
2 chicken-flavor bouillon cubes or envelopes

1. In 5-quart Dutch oven over medium-high heat, in hot salad oil, cook frankfurters until lightly browned on all sides, stirring frequently. With slotted spoon, remove frankfurters to bowl; cover and refrigerate.
2. In drippings remaining in Dutch oven, over medium heat, cook next 5 ingredients until tender, about 10 minutes, stirring occasionally.
3. Meanwhile, rinse lentils in running cold water and discard any stones or shriveled lentils.
4. Add lentils, water, salt, pepper, and bouillon to vegetable mixture in Dutch oven; over high heat, heat to boiling. Reduce heat to low; cover and simmer 1 hour or until lentils are very tender and soup has thickened slightly.
5. Return frankfurters to Dutch oven; over medium-high heat, cook frankfurters until heated through, stirring occasionally.

MINESTRONE

- Color index page 21
- Begin 1¾ hrs ahead
- 12 cups
- 110 cals per cup

2 tablespoons olive or salad oil
1 large carrot, diced
1 large celery stalk, thinly sliced
1 medium onion, diced
1 small garlic clove, cut in half
¼ pound green beans, cut into 1-inch pieces
6 cups water
1½ teaspoons salt
½ teaspoon oregano leaves
¼ small head cabbage, shredded (3 cups)
1 medium zucchini, diced
1 8- to 8¼-ounce can tomatoes
2 beef-flavor bouillon cubes or envelopes
¼ cup elbow macaroni
½ 10-ounce bag spinach, coarsely shredded
1 15- to 19-ounce can white kidney beans (cannellini), drained
1 8- to 10½-ounce can red kidney beans, drained
Grated Parmesan or Romano cheese (optional)

1. In 4-quart saucepan over medium-high heat in hot olive oil, cook carrot, celery, onion, garlic, and green beans until lightly browned, about 15 minutes, stirring occasionally. Discard garlic.
2. Add water, salt, oregano, cabbage, zucchini, tomatoes with their liquid, and bouillon; over high heat, heat to boiling, stirring to break up tomatoes. Reduce heat to low; cover and simmer 25 minutes or until vegetables are tender.
3. Stir in macaroni, spinach, and beans; cook 10 minutes longer or until macaroni is very tender and soup is slightly thickened. If you like, pass cheese to sprinkle over each serving.

CHUNKY LAMB AND BEAN SOUP

Our version of a traditional shepherd's stew uses lamb shanks and two types of beans to create a hearty, main-course soup.

- Color index page 21
- Begin 3½ hrs ahead
- 14 cups
- 444 cals per cup

1 16-ounce package dry pea (navy) beans
Water
2 tablespoons olive or salad oil
4 lamb shanks (about 1 pound each)
2 large carrots, sliced
1 large onion, diced
1 garlic clove, minced
¼ cup cooking or dry white wine
2 teaspoons salt
½ teaspoon marjoram leaves
¼ teaspoon pepper
2 beef-flavor bouillon cubes or envelopes
1 10-ounce package frozen Italian green beans

1 Rinse beans under running cold water and discard any stones or shriveled beans. In 8-quart Dutch oven over high heat, heat the beans and 8 cups water to boiling; cook about 3 minutes. Remove saucepan from heat; cover and let it stand for about 1 hour. Drain and rinse beans; set aside. In same Dutch oven over medium-high heat, heat oil.

2 Cook lamb shanks until browned on all sides. Remove to plate.

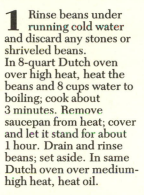

3 In drippings over medium heat, cook carrots, onion, and garlic until tender, stirring often. Return beans and lamb to Dutch oven.

4 Stir in next 5 ingredients and 10 cups water; over high heat, heat to boiling. Reduce to low; cover, simmer 1½ hours; skim fat.

5 Add frozen green beans; over high heat, heat to boiling. Reduce to low; cover; simmer 15 minutes.

6 Remove lamb shanks. Cut meat from bones into bite-sized pieces. Return cut-up lamb to soup; heat and serve.

Hearty soups

BARLEY, BEEF, AND VEGETABLE

Barley, brought to America by early settlers, helps to make a traditional winter soup.

- Color index page 21
- Begin 2½ hrs ahead
- 16 cups
- 179 cals per cup

3 tablespoons salad oil
3 beef shank cross cuts, each cut 1 inch thick (about 2 pounds)
5 large carrots, cut into 2" × ½" pieces
5 medium celery stalks, cut into 2" × ½" pieces
2 large onions, diced
¾ pound mushrooms, each cut in half

11 cups water
¾ cup medium barley
2 teaspoons salt
1 teaspoon oregano leaves
½ teaspoon pepper
2 beef-flavor bouillon cubes or envelopes
1 bunch broccoli, cut into 2" × 1" pieces

1 In 8-quart Dutch oven, in hot oil, brown beef. Remove.

2 In drippings over medium heat, cook vegetables until lightly browned, stirring often.

3 Return beef to Dutch oven; add water and next 5 ingredients; over high heat, heat to boiling, stirring to loosen brown bits from bottom.

4 Reduce heat to low; cover, simmer 1½ hours or until beef and barley are tender, stirring occasionally. Skim the fat from liquid in Dutch oven. Add broccoli. Over high heat, heat to boiling. Reduce heat to low; cover and simmer 10 to 15 minutes or until broccoli is tender, but do not overcook broccoli. Transfer the soup to a large soup tureen or serve directly from the Dutch oven into heated soup bowls.

CREAM OF PEANUT SOUP

- Color index page 21
- Begin 30 mins ahead
- 8 cups
- 441 cals per cup

5 tablespoons butter or margarine
1 small onion, minced
¼ cup minced celery
1 cup creamy peanut butter

½ cup all-purpose flour
2 13¾- to 14½-ounce cans chicken broth
3 cups milk
¼ cup salted peanuts, chopped

In 4-quart saucepan over medium-high heat, in hot butter, cook onion and celery until tender, about 5 minutes. Stir in peanut butter and flour until blended. Gradually stir in broth and milk; cook, stirring, until soup thickens and just boils. To serve, sprinkle with chopped peanuts.

BEET AND VEGETABLE SOUP

- Color index page 21
- Begin 1½ hrs ahead
- 14 cups
- 67 cals per cup

¼ cup salad oil
3 medium carrots, shredded
1 large potato, diced
1 medium onion, diced
½ small head green cabbage, shredded
8 cups water
1 14½- to 16-ounce can tomatoes

1 pound beets, shredded
3 beef-flavor bouillon cubes or envelopes
2 teaspoons sugar
1½ teaspoons salt
¼ teaspoon pepper
Sour cream for garnish (optional)

1. In 5-quart Dutch oven or saucepot over medium heat, in hot salad oil, cook carrots, potato, onion, and cabbage until lightly browned, stirring occasionally.
2. Add water, tomatoes with their liquid, beets, bouillon, sugar, salt, and pepper; over high heat, heat to boiling. Reduce heat to low; cover and simmer 35 to 40 minutes until vegetables are very tender, stirring occasionally.
3. In blender, blend about 4 cups vegetable mixture until smooth. Pour smooth mixture into the Dutch oven and stir until well blended.
4. Serve soup hot, or cover and refrigerate to serve chilled later. If you like, garnish each serving with some sour cream.

PHILADELPHIA PEPPER POT

- Color index page 21
- Begin 4½ hrs ahead
- 12 cups
- 274 cals per cup

1½ pounds precooked fresh honeycomb tripe
½ pound salt pork, diced
2 medium onions, sliced
1 medium green pepper, diced
1 large celery stalk, diced
1 medium carrot, diced
2 garlic cloves, minced
10 cups water
2¾ teaspoons salt
½ teaspoon cracked pepper

¾ teaspoon thyme leaves
½ teaspoon crushed red pepper
3 pounds veal knuckles
2 medium potatoes, peeled and diced
2 tablespoons all-purpose flour
2 tablespoons butter or margarine, softened
1 cup heavy or whipping cream

1. Rinse tripe under running cold water; drain; cut into ½-inch cubes; set aside.
2. In 8-quart Dutch oven or saucepot over medium heat, cook salt pork 10 minutes or until lightly browned, stirring frequently. Stir in onions, green pepper, celery, carrot, and garlic cloves; cook 20 minutes until vegetables are tender, stirring often.
3. Stir in water, salt, cracked pepper, thyme, crushed red pepper, veal knuckles, and tripe; over high heat, heat to boiling. Reduce heat to low; cover and simmer 3 hours.
4. Skim off fat. Remove veal to cutting board; cut meat from bone into bite-sized chunks. Return veal to soup; discard bones. Stir in potatoes; cook, covered, 30 minutes longer or until potatoes and tripe are tender.
5. In cup, mix flour and butter until smooth; slowly stir into hot soup; cook over medium heat until thickened. Into soup, stir in heavy cream; heat through.

HEARTY SPLIT PEA SOUP

This soup is traditionally made with a left-over ham bone simmered for hours; our quicker-cooking version derives its meaty flavor from ground pork meatballs.

1 16-ounce package dry split peas
3 medium carrots, cut into ¼-inch-thick slices
3 medium celery stalks, diced
2 medium onions, diced
Water
1 tablespoon salad oil
1 pound ground pork
1 cup fresh bread crumbs (2 slices white bread)
½ teaspoon rubbed sage
Salt

3 medium potatoes (1 pound), peeled and cut into bite-sized chunks
¼ teaspoon pepper

- *Color index page 23*
- *Begin 2 hrs ahead*
- *13 cups*
- *259 cals per cup*

1 Rinse peas in running cold water; discard any stones. In 5-quart Dutch oven over high heat, heat peas, carrots, half of celery, half of onion, and 8 cups water to boiling.

2 Reduce heat to low; cover, simmer 1 hour, stirring occasionally. Meanwhile, in 12-inch skillet over medium heat, in hot oil, cook remaining celery and onion until tender.

3 With slotted spoon, remove vegetables to large bowl. Add ground pork, bread crumbs, sage, 2 tablespoons water, and 1 teaspoon salt to bowl; mix well.

4 With fingers, shape ground pork mixture into 1-inch meatballs. Over medium heat, heat drippings in skillet.

5 Add meatballs; cook until browned on all sides. Remove and drain on paper towels.

6 To split-pea mixture in Dutch oven, add potatoes, pepper, and 2½ teaspoons salt; heat to boiling.

7 Reduce heat to low; cover and simmer 30 minutes. Add meatballs; heat through and serve.

HOW TO PREPARE CROUTONS

Unusual-shaped croutons make an interesting pattern in the soup bowl. Fry shapes in a mixture of butter and oil until crisp and golden, stirring constantly.

Triangle: Cut slice of bread diagonally into quarters. Cut each quarter in half.

Heart-Shaped: Cut slice of bread diagonally into quarters. With base of triangle at top, round off top 2 corners. Cut a "V" from top center.

Scalloped: Using a small curly-edged cookie cutter, cut rounds out of sliced bread.

Cubes: Cut slice of bread into small, even-sized squares.

Chicken and turkey soups

PENNSYLVANIA DUTCH CHICKEN AND CORN SOUP

German settlers, known as "Pennsylvania Dutch," were thrifty cooks who made good use of corn, a staple crop.

- Color index page 22
- Begin 2 hrs ahead
- 12 cups
- 226 cals per cup

1 3½-pound broiler-fryer
1 large onion, diced
8 cups water
1 tablespoon salt
¼ teaspoon pepper
1 10-ounce package frozen broccoli

1 10-ounce package frozen whole kernel corn
1 cup all-purpose flour
1 tablespoon milk
1 egg

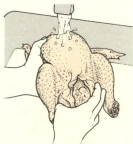

1 Rinse chicken, its giblets, and neck with running cold water. Place chicken, breast-side down, in 5-quart Dutch oven or saucepot.

2 Add giblets, neck and next 4 ingredients. Over high heat, heat to boiling. Reduce heat to low; cover; simmer 35 minutes.

3 Remove chicken, giblets and neck to large bowl; refrigerate 30 minutes. Discard skin and bones; cut meat into bite-sized pieces.

4 Skim off fat from broth in Dutch oven; over high heat, heat broth to boiling. Add chicken, broccoli, and frozen corn; heat to boiling.

5 In small bowl mix flour, milk, and egg to make a crumbly dough. Reduce heat under soup to medium until soup just simmers.

6 Sprinkle small pieces of dough into simmering soup. Cook uncovered, about 5 minutes or until vegetables are tender.

CHICKEN-ESCAROLE SOUP

1 3-pound broiler-fryer
8 cups water
2 tablespoons salad oil
1 large onion, diced
1 large carrot, diced
1 large celery stalk, diced
3 tablespoons all-purpose flour
1½ teaspoons salt

½ teaspoon thyme leaves
¼ teaspoon pepper
1 chicken-flavor bouillon cube or envelope
½ cup pastina (small star-shaped macaroni)
1 small head escarole (½ pound), coarsely sliced

- Color index page 22
- Begin 1½ hrs ahead
- 12 cups
- 162 cals per cup

1. Rinse chicken, giblets, and neck. Place chicken breast-side down, in 5- to 6-quart Dutch oven or saucepot. Add giblets, neck, and water; over high heat, heat to boiling. Reduce heat to low; cover and simmer 35 minutes.
2. Remove chicken, giblets, and neck to bowl; refrigerate 30 minutes. Discard skin and bones from chicken; cut meat into bite-sized pieces.
3. While chicken is cooling, in 2-quart saucepan over medium heat, in hot salad oil, cook onion, carrot, and celery until vegetables are tender, stirring occasionally. Stir in flour until blended; cook 1 minute. Gradually stir 1 cup chicken broth from Dutch oven into vegetables; cook, stirring constantly, until mixture is slightly thickened.
4. To remaining broth in Dutch oven, add next 6 ingredients and vegetable mixture; over high heat, heat to boiling. Reduce heat to low; cover and simmer 5 to 10 minutes until pastina and escarole are tender.
5. Skim off fat from liquid in Dutch oven. Add cut-up chicken and giblets; heat through.

MULLIGATAWNY

- Color index page 22
- Begin 1½ hrs ahead
- 8 cups
- 318 cals per cup

3 slices bacon
1 2½-pound broiler-fryer, cut up
1 tablespoon curry powder
4 cups chicken broth
2 carrots, sliced
2 celery stalks, chopped
1 apple, chopped

6 peppercorns, crushed
2 whole cloves
1 bay leaf
⅓ cup water
3 tablespoons all-purpose flour
1 cup half-and-half
1½ cups hot cooked rice

1. In 5-quart Dutch oven or saucepot over medium heat, cook bacon until crisp and browned. Remove to paper towels to drain.
2. In bacon fat remaining in Dutch oven, brown chicken pieces. Add curry powder; cook 1 minute. Add chicken broth, next 6 ingredients, and cooked bacon; over high heat, heat to boiling. Reduce heat to low; cover and simmer 30 minutes or until chicken is fork-tender.
3. Discard cloves and bay leaf. Remove chicken to cutting board; remove meat from bones; cut into bite-sized pieces. Return to soup.
4. In cup, with spoon, mix water and flour; gradually stir flour mixture into simmering soup, stirring constantly until soup thickens slightly. Stir in half-and-half; heat through.
5. To serve, ladle soup into warm bowls. Spoon a mound of hot rice into each of the bowls.

EGGS AND CHEESE

"Cheese: Milk's leap towards immortality."
CLIFTON FADIMAN

Eggs were eaten in America long before the first European settlers brought chickens here. North American Indians ate the eggs of wild birds like turkey, goose, quail, and pigeon. Even turtle and crocodile eggs were eaten in the Gulf region. Although a good number of colonists kept their own chickens, there wasn't a sufficient supply to provide eggs for many meals. Hen's eggs were something of a delicacy, and therefore very expensive, even into the nineteenth century.

Today eggs are cheap and available everywhere – and the average American consumes about 270 a year. Most of us are accustomed to preparing eggs in the simplest ways: scrambled, poached, fried, baked, or boiled. But the versatile egg can be used in making more elegant dishes: the poached egg, for instance, becomes something special when prepared as Eggs Benedict.

When we think of eggs, we usually think of breakfast but perhaps our fast-paced lives have pushed the big relaxed breakfast to a weekend-only brunch. An all-American institution, brunch can include a variety of dishes, from simple scrambled eggs to a buffet of egg, cheese, and meat dishes.

Cheese has been produced in this country since the American Revolution, when heavy taxes on imported cheeses forced colonists to make their own. Farmers in New York and Vermont made Cheddars; Adam Blumer of Wisconsin created a Swiss cheese; David Jacks of California invented a cheese similar to those made by Spanish friars and called it Monterey Jack; German immigrants in New York produced Limburger.

Both eggs and cheese can be eaten on their own as part of a meal or snack, and dishes which contain them can be served at any meal. A breakfast omelet, with a delicious filling and sauce, such as our Shrimp Creole Omelet, can make a satisfying supper dish. A vegetable quiche or savory cheese soufflé makes a tempting appetizer; add a green salad and crusty bread for lunch, brunch, or supper.

THE ALL-AMERICAN BREAKFAST

Breakfast in America was always hearty fare, often reflecting regional produce and ethnic specialties. Plan a breakfast party around one of these regional menus.

New England Country Inn:
A hearty warming meal of Corned Beef Hash and eggs or Blueberry Pancakes dripping with maple syrup. Follow this with slices of Cranberry-Nut Bread and mugs of steaming hot chocolate.

New York Deli-Style:
A sophisticated choice starting with fresh orange juice and plump bagels stuffed with lox and cream cheese. Finish with Danish pastries and coffee.

Southern Hospitality:
A modern version of Southern fare with a New Orleans flavor. Hot French Toast or Banana Bread with Strawberry Jam and French-Creole Café au Lait.

Texas Ranch-Style:
A down-home start to the day with steak and spicy Ranch-Style Eggs. Serve with Corn and Blueberry Muffins and lots of strong coffee.

Egg dishes

EGGS BENEDICT

Originally created for Mr. and Mrs. Benedict, "regulars" at New York's Delmonico's; we add peppers and onion.

- Color index page 24
- Begin 50 min ahead
- 4 servings
- 465 cals per serving

4 slices bacon
1 medium red pepper, thinly sliced
1 medium green pepper, thinly sliced
1 medium onion, thinly sliced

2 English muffins, each split in half
Water
4 eggs
Hollandaise Sauce (p. 385)

1 In 10-inch skillet over medium-low heat, cook bacon until browned; remove and drain. While warm, roll each bacon slice to form a "rose;" secure with toothpick. Keep warm.

2 Remove all but 2 tablespoons drippings from skillet. In drippings, over medium-high heat, cook peppers and onion until tender, stirring occasionally, about 15 minutes.

3 Meanwhile, toast English muffin halves; arrange on four small plates. Top muffin halves with pepper mixture; keep warm in 200°F. oven.

4 In greased 10-inch skillet, heat 1 inch water to boiling. Reduce to low. One at a time, break eggs into saucer; slip into simmering water. Cook 2 to 4 minutes.

5 Carefully remove eggs from water. Drain on towels; arrange on pepper-topped muffins; keep warm.

6 Spoon Hollandaise Sauce over eggs. Remove toothpicks from bacon roses. Garnish each serving with a bacon rose.

ZESTY MEXICAN EGGS AND BEANS

- Color index page 24
- Begin 30 mins ahead
- 4 servings
- 257 cals per serving

1 tablespoon salad oil
1 medium onion, diced
1 14½- to 16-ounce can tomatoes
1 15¼- to 19-ounce can red kidney beans, drained
1½ teaspoons chili powder
¾ teaspoon salt
4 eggs
½ cup finely shredded lettuce
Corn chips (optional)

1. In 10-inch skillet over medium heat, in hot salad oil, cook onion until tender, stirring often.
2. Stir in tomatoes with their liquid, kidney beans, chili powder and salt; over high heat, heat to boiling. Reduce heat to low; simmer 10 minutes or until slightly thickened, stirring mixture occasionally.
3. With spoon, make 4 deep indentations in tomato mixture. One at a time, break eggs into saucer and slip into indentations in simmering tomato mixture.
4. Cover skillet and cook about 10 minutes or until eggs are of desired firmness. Arrange shredded lettuce on mixture in skillet. If you like, serve at table with corn chips.

COUNTRY EGG BAKE

- Color index page 24
- Begin 1½ hrs ahead
- 6 servings
- 460 cals per serving

Salad oil
1 medium onion, diced
1 medium green pepper, diced
1 medium red pepper, diced
1 garlic clove, crushed
1 large eggplant (about 1½ pounds), cut in ½-inch cubes
1 medium zucchini, cut into ¼-inch-thick slices
1 8- to 8¼-ounce can tomatoes
½ cup water
1½ teaspoons sugar
1¼ teaspoons salt
¼ teaspoon thyme leaves
1 15½- to 19-ounce can garbanzo beans, drained
3 ounces Cheddar cheese, shredded (¾ cup)
6 eggs

1. In 12-inch skillet over medium heat, in 2 tablespoons hot oil, cook onion, peppers, and garlic until tender, stirring occasionally. With slotted spoon, remove pepper mixture to small bowl; set aside.
2. In same skillet over medium heat, in ¼ cup more hot salad oil, cook eggplant and zucchini until tender, stirring ocasionally, about 15 minutes.
3. Return pepper mixture to skillet; add tomatoes with their liquid and next 4 ingredients; over high heat, heat to boiling. Reduce heat to low; simmer 15 minutes, stirring occasionally. Stir in garbanzo beans; heat through.
4. Preheat oven to 425°F. Spoon vegetable mixture into 2½-quart shallow baking dish. With spoon make 6 deep indentations in vegetable mixture. Sprinkle 2 tablespoons Cheddar cheese into each indentation.
5. One at a time, break eggs into saucer and slip into indentations on top of cheese. Bake 12 minutes or until eggs are just set or of desired firmness.

Egg dishes

EGG-AND-SPINACH CASSEROLE

Spinach always goes well with eggs and cheese. This casserole makes the perfect light supper; serve with toasted bread.

- Color index page 26
- Begin 1 hr ahead
- 4 servings
- 429 cals per serving

2 10-ounce packages frozen chopped spinach, thawed and drained	1 cup milk
	1 4-ounce package shredded Cheddar cheese (1 cup)
Salt	6 eggs
3 tablespoons butter or margarine	Dash pepper
3 tablespoons all-purpose flour	Toast (optional)

1 Preheat oven to 325°F. In 8" by 8" baking dish, toss spinach with ½ teaspoon salt and spread in an even layer; with spoon, make 6 indentations in spinach.

2 In small saucepan over low heat, in melted butter, stir in flour until smooth; gradually stir in milk and cook, stirring constantly, until sauce is thickened.

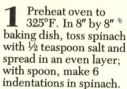

3 Stir in cheese and heat just until cheese is melted. Remove from heat so the cheese does not become stringy.

4 Break one egg into each indentation; sprinkle eggs with pepper and ¼ teaspoon salt. Pour sauce over eggs.

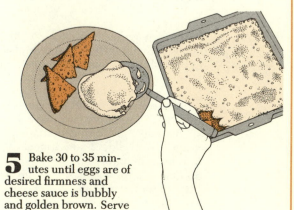

5 Bake 30 to 35 minutes until eggs are of desired firmness and cheese sauce is bubbly and golden brown. Serve with toast.

CORNED BEEF HASH AND EGGS

- Color index page 24
- Begin 45 mins ahead
- 4 servings
- 468 cals per serving

4 tablespoons butter or margarine	¾ cup milk
3 medium potatoes (1 pound), peeled and diced	1¼ cups diced cooked corned beef
	½ teaspoon salt
1 small green pepper, diced	⅛ teaspoon pepper
	4 eggs
1 small onion, minced	Chopped parsley for garnish

1. In nonstick skillet, melt butter over medium heat; add potatoes, green pepper, and onion. Cook until potatoes are brown, stirring often.
2. Add milk, corned beef, salt, and pepper; heat through.
3. With spoon, make 4 deep indentations in corned-beef mixture. One at a time break eggs into saucer and slip into indentations. Reduce heat to low; cover skillet and cook about 10 minutes. Garnish with chopped parsley.

WESTERN SCRAMBLED EGGS

- Color index page 24
- Begin 30 mins ahead
- 6 servings
- 275 cals per serving

12 eggs	1 teaspoon grated onion
⅔ cup water	½ teaspoon salt
1 medium green pepper, diced	¼ teaspoon cracked pepper
½ 4-ounce package sliced ham, diced	4 tablespoons butter or margarine

1. In large bowl with wire whisk or fork, mix eggs, water, green pepper, ham, onion, salt, and pepper.
2. In 12-inch skillet over medium heat, melt butter; add egg mixture; reduce heat to medium-low. Cook until just set, stirring occasionally.

TOMATO-SAUSAGE SCRAMBLE

- Color index page 25
- Begin 30 mins ahead
- 8 servings
- 617 cals per serving

1 8-ounce package brown-and-serve sausages, cut into ½-inch chunks	1 cup half-and-half
	8 eggs
	1 teaspoon salt
3 tablespoons butter or margarine	Dash pepper
3 tablespoons all-purpose flour	1 small tomato, cut into chunks
1 cup milk	¼ cup shredded Cheddar cheese
	Parsley for garnish

1. Cook sausage as label directs; drain any excess fat and keep sausage warm. In oven-safe medium skillet over low heat, in hot butter, stir flour until smooth; gradually stir in milk and cook, stirring constantly, until thickened.
2. In medium bowl, with fork or wire whisk, beat half-and-half, eggs, salt, and pepper until blended; stir into sauce. Cook, stirring constantly, until eggs are slightly set.
3. Meanwhile, preheat broiler if manufacturer directs. Sprinkle sausage, tomato chunks, and cheese over eggs; broil to melt cheese. Garnish with parsley.

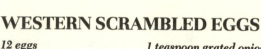

PARTY CREAMY EGGS

- Color index page 25
- Begin 1½ hrs ahead
- 8 servings
- 745 cals per serving

3 8-ounce packages thick-sliced bacon
Seasoned Avocados (below)
Sautéed Herbed Mushrooms (p. 177)
14 eggs
¼ teaspoon pepper
6 tablespoons butter or margarine
2 3-ounce packages cream cheese, diced
3 3-ounce packages sliced smoked salmon

1. Cook bacon: Preheat broiler if manufacturer directs. Arrange bacon slices, overlapping slightly, on rack in broiling pan. About 5 inches from source of heat, broil bacon at 300°F. 10 to 15 minutes or until golden. With tongs or fork, turn bacon, separating slices. Broil about 10 minutes longer or until bacon is browned and crisp. Remove to paper towels to drain; keep warm.
2. Meanwhile, prepare Seasoned Avocados; cover and refrigerate, stirring occasionally.
3. Prepare sautéed mushrooms; keep warm.
4. Prepare cream-cheese scrambled eggs: In large bowl with fork, beat eggs and pepper until just blended. In 12-inch skillet over medium-high heat, melt butter or margarine. Add egg mixture. As egg mixture begins to set, with spatula, stir slightly so uncooked egg flows to bottom. When eggs are partially cooked, add diced cream cheese. Continue cooking until egg mixture is set but still moist. Remove from heat.
5. To serve, spoon mixture into warm bowl; place on large platter. Arrange Seasoned Avocados, sautéed mushrooms, bacon strips, and smoked salmon around eggs on platter.

SEASONED AVOCADOS: In medium bowl, mix *1 tablespoon sugar*, *3 tablespoons white wine vinegar*, *2 tablespoons salad oil*, *1 tablespoon chopped parsley*, and *¾ teaspoon salt*. Peel and remove seed from *2 large avocados*. Cut avocados lengthwise in half, then crosswise into ¼-inch-thick slices. Add avocados and *1 2-ounce jar sliced pimentos*, drained, to dressing in bowl; toss to coat well with dressing. 2 cups. 40 cals per tablespoon.

PRESENTING EGGS FOR A BRUNCH

Try surrounding our Party Creamy Eggs with a selection of fruit and side dishes for a simple yet elegant brunch for friends or family.

On a large platter, arrange vegetables, bacon strips, and smoked salmon neatly around the bowl of creamy eggs.

Alternatively, serve the eggs with a plate of thinly-sliced ham, cheese, and salami, and sliced strawberries and nectarines or any other seasonal fruit.

RANCH-STYLE EGGS

- Color index page 24
- Begin 45 mins ahead
- 4 servings
- 637 cals per serving

Fried eggs, Southwestern style, are hot and spicy and something different for a hearty breakfast or light supper.

Salad oil
8 6-inch packaged corn tortillas
1 medium onion, diced
1 small garlic clove, minced
2 medium tomatoes, cut into ½-inch pieces
1 teaspoon salt
1 4-ounce can chopped green chilies, drained
3 tablespoons butter or margarine
8 eggs
¼ cup sour cream
1 medium avocado, peeled and cut crosswise into thin slices

1 In 10-inch skillet over medium heat, in 3 tablespoons hot salad oil, fry 1 tortilla at a time, a few seconds on each side.

2 Remove tortillas to paper towels to drain. Keep warm. Pour off excess oil and wipe skillet clean.

3 In 3-quart saucepan over medium heat, in 2 tablespoons hot salad oil, cook onion and garlic until tender.

4 Stir in tomatoes, salt, and chopped green chilies; heat to boiling. Reduce heat to low; cover; simmer 5 minutes, stirring often; keep warm.

5 In 10-inch skillet over medium heat, melt butter. Break each egg into saucer, then slip into skillet. Cook 2 at a time. Reduce heat to low; cook until set.

6 On each plate, arrange 2 eggs on 2 tortillas. Spoon ¼ tomato sauce over; top with 1 tablespoon sour cream. Garnish with peeled and sliced avocado.

Egg dishes

SHRIMP CREOLE OMELET

An omelet with a New Orleans flavor filled with chopped shrimp and topped with tangy tomato sauce.

Creole Sauce (below, right)
3 eggs
1 tablespoon cold water
¼ teaspoon salt
⅛ teaspoon pepper

1 tablespoon butter or margarine
¼ cup chopped cooked shrimp
1 whole shrimp for garnish
Parsley for garnish

● *Color index page 25*
● *Begin 30 mins ahead*
● *1 main-dish serving*
● *571 cals per serving*

1 Prepare Creole Sauce; keep warm. Break the eggs into a small bowl, then add the water, salt, and pepper.

2 With a wire whisk or fork, beat eggs vigorously just until the yolks and whites are mixed.

3 In a 7-inch omelet pan or skillet, over medium heat, melt butter. Tilt skillet so the butter coats the whole surface of the pan.

4 Pour in the eggs and let them set around edge. Shake the pan occasionally to keep the omelet moving freely over the bottom of the pan.

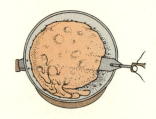

5 With a metal spatula lift omelet as it sets, tilting skillet so that any uncooked egg mixture can run under omelet.

6 Continue shaking pan for a few more seconds until you can feel the omelet sliding freely over the pan surface.

7 When omelet is set but still moist on the surface, increase the heat slightly to brown the bottom. Remove pan from heat.

8 Sprinkle the chopped shrimp evenly over half of the omelet. Tilting pan away from you, lift the edge of the omelet with a spatula and gently fold in half over the shrimp.

9 Carefully slide omelet on to a warm plate; pour Creole Sauce over the omelet. If you like, garnish with the whole shrimp and parsley.

SKILLET PEPPERS AND EGGS

Salad oil
2 medium red or green peppers, cut into ¼-inch-wide strips
1 medium onion, sliced
¼ teaspoon basil
⅛ teaspoon pepper
Salt
4 eggs
¼ cup water

1. In 4-quart saucepan over medium heat, in 1 tablespoon hot salad oil, cook peppers, onion, basil, pepper, and ½ teaspoon salt until vegetables are tender, stirring occasionally, about 10 minutes.
2. Meanwhile, in medium bowl, with fork or wire whisk, beat eggs, water, and ½ teaspoon salt until blended. In 10-inch skillet over medium heat, heat 2 tablespoons salad oil until hot. Pour egg mixture into hot oil, tilting skillet to coat bottom of skillet evenly with egg mixture.
3. Cook 3 to 5 minutes until egg is set, occasionally tilting skillet and lifting edge of cooked egg to let uncooked portion run into skillet.
4. With pancake turner, turn "egg pancake" to brown other side. To serve, top egg with pepper mixture.

● *Color index page 25*
● *Begin 30 mins ahead*
● *2 servings*
● *425 cals per serving*

HAM-AND-ONION FRITTATA

¼ cup salad oil
3 large potatoes, thinly sliced (about 4 cups)
1 small bunch green onions
12 eggs
⅓ cup water
¾ teaspoon salt
1 6-ounce package sliced cooked ham, diced

1. In 12-inch skillet over medium-high heat, in hot salad oil, cook potato slices 10 minutes or until lightly browned, occasionally turning with pancake turner.
2. With sharp knife, trim root ends and tough green tips from green onions; cut into 1-inch pieces; add to potatoes; cook 2 minutes.
3. Reduce heat to low. Cover; cook until vegetables are tender, turning occasionally.
4. Meanwhile, in medium-sized bowl, beat eggs, water, and salt until well blended. Pour egg mixture into skillet. Sprinkle with ham; cover and cook 20 minutes until egg mixture is set. Let stand 10 minutes. To serve, cut into 8 wedges.

● *Color index page 25*
● *Begin 50 mins ahead*
● *8 servings*
● *276 cals per serving*

CREOLE SAUCE: In small skillet over medium-high heat, heat *1 tablespoon salad oil*. Add *6 tablespoons each chopped green pepper* and *chopped celery*, and *2 tablespoons chopped onion*; cook until tender, about 5 minutes, stirring occasionally. Add *2 medium tomatoes*, peeled and chopped, *¼ teaspoon oregano leaves* and *¼ teaspoon salt*. Mix well; simmer, covered, for 10 minutes, stirring often. Makes enough for 2 3-egg omelets. 174 cals per tablespoon.

ROLLED MUSHROOM OMELET

1 16-ounce package sliced bacon
Thick White Sauce (below)
12 eggs, separated
1 pound mushrooms, finely chopped
¼ pound Swiss cheese, shredded (1 cup)
Parsley (optional)

- Color index page 26
- Begin 1 hr ahead
- 8 servings
- 411 cals per serving

1. In 12-inch skillet over medium-low heat, cook bacon, several slices at a time, until browned. Remove bacon to paper towels to drain; keep warm. Pour off all but ¼ cup bacon fat from skillet; set skillet aside.
2. Meanwhile, line 15½" by 10½" jelly-roll pan with waxed paper; grease waxed paper.
3. Prepare Thick White Sauce; set aside. In small bowl, beat egg yolks slightly. Into yolks, stir small amount of hot white sauce; slowly pour yolk mixture back into sauce, stirring rapidly to prevent lumping. Cook over medium heat until mixture thickens, stirring constantly (do not boil or mixture will curdle). Remove saucepan from heat; cool mixture slightly, about 15 minutes.
4. Preheat oven to 400°F. In large bowl, with mixer at high speed, beat egg whites until stiff peaks form. With rubber spatula, gently fold yolk mixture into beaten whites until blended. Spread mixture evenly in jelly-roll pan; bake 25 minutes or until omelet is puffy and golden brown.
5. Meanwhile, in bacon fat remaining in skillet, over medium-high heat, cook mushrooms until tender, about 10 minutes, stirring often. Remove from heat.
6. When omelet is done, invert onto clean cloth towel; peel off waxed paper; sprinkle mushrooms and cheese over omelet to within ¼ inch of edges. Starting at narrow end, roll omelet, jelly-roll fashion, lifting towel while rolling.
7. To serve, place rolled omelet, seam side down, on warm platter; arrange bacon slices around omelet. If you like, garnish with parsley.

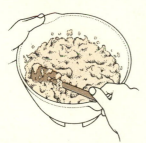 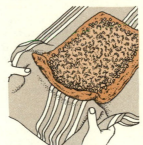

Folding in the eggs: With rubber spatula, fold yolk mixture into beaten egg whites until blended.

Rolling the omelet: Gently lift towel and roll omelet jelly-roll fashion.

THICK WHITE SAUCE: In heavy, 1-quart saucepan over low heat, melt *2 tablespoons butter* or *margarine*. Add *2 tablespoons all-purpose flour*, *½ teaspoon salt*, *⅛ teaspoon pepper*, and *⅛ teaspoon paprika*, to melted butter. Gradually stir in *1 cup milk* or *half-and-half*. Cook, stirring constantly, until the sauce is thickened and smooth. Makes about 1 cup. 29 cals per tablespoon.

PICKLED EGGS

1 16-ounce can sliced beets
12 hard-cooked eggs, shelled
¾ cup cider vinegar
½ cup sugar
2 tablespoons salt
½ teaspoon cracked pepper
⅛ teaspoon ground allspice
6 whole cloves

- Color index page 17
- Begin day ahead or up to 3 days ahead
- 12 eggs
- 90 cals per egg

1. Into 1-quart saucepan, drain liquid from beets. Place beets and eggs in 1½-quart jar or large bowl. Into beet juice, stir vinegar and remaining ingredients. Over high heat, heat to boiling. Pour hot beet-juice mixture over eggs and beets. Cover and refrigerate at least 12 hours to allow spicy flavor to penetrate eggs.
2. To serve, drain eggs and beets. For snack, light lunch, or supper, eat them plain. For appetizer, slice eggs crosswise; place each egg slice on a small cracker and top with a dollop of mustard or mayonnaise, then a piece of sliced beet. Or, use thin slices to dress up salads.

MARBLED EGGS

12 hard-cooked eggs, unshelled
6 tea bags
4 cups water
½ cup salt
½ cup soy sauce

- Color index page 17
- Begin early in day or day ahead
- 12 eggs
- 80 cals per egg

1. With back of spoon, lightly tap each egg to crack entire shell (do not remove shell; tea mixture will make attractive pattern under cracks when shells are removed); set aside.
2. In 4-quart saucepan over high heat, heat tea bags, water, salt, and soy sauce to boiling. Remove saucepan from heat; add cracked eggs. Cover and refrigerate at least 6 hours.
3. To serve, discard tea bags. Drain eggs and remove shells. For snack, light lunch, or supper, eat them plain. For appetizer, slice eggs crosswise; place each egg slice on a small cracker and top with a dollop of mustard or mayonnaise.

SPICED EGGS

2 cups water
1½ cups white vinegar
1 tablespoon sugar
1 tablespoon mixed pickling spice
1 teaspoon salt
¼ teaspoon crushed red pepper
12 hard-cooked eggs, shelled

- Color index page 17
- Begin early in day or up to 3 days ahead
- 12 eggs
- 80 cals per egg

1. In 2-quart saucepan over high heat, heat first 6 ingredients to boiling, stirring to dissolve sugar. Reduce heat to low; simmer 10 minutes.
2. With knife make several lengthwise slashes in whites of eggs. Place eggs in 1½-quart jar or large bowl. Pour hot mixture over eggs. Cover and refrigerate at least 12 hours to allow spicy flavor to penetrate eggs.
3. To serve, drain eggs. For snack, light lunch, or supper, eat them plain. For appetizer, slice eggs crosswise; place each egg slice on a small cracker and top with a dollop of mustard or mayonnaise.

Cheese dishes

ASPARAGUS QUICHE

One of America's most popular luncheon, buffet, and supper dishes, the ordinary cheese quiche can be transformed from an everyday dish into something special by adding a favorite vegetable.

- Color index page 26
- Begin 1½ hrs ahead
- 6 servings
- 261 cals per serving

1 9-inch Unbaked Piecrust (p. 310)
½ pound asparagus
Water
2 green onions, sliced

1 tablespoon all-purpose flour
½ pound Swiss cheese, shredded (2 cups)
3 eggs

1 cup half-and-half
½ teaspoon salt
¼ teaspoon basil
⅛ teaspoon pepper

1 Preheat oven to 425°F. Prepare Unbaked Piecrust, using a 9-inch quiche pan and trimming pastry edge. With fork, lightly prick pastry.

2 Bake 7 minutes or until crust is set but not browned; remove from oven. Turn oven control to 350°F.

3 Prepare asparagus: Hold base of stalk firmly and bend stalk; break off end where it is too tough to eat. Discard ends.

4 In 10-inch skillet over high heat, heat ½ inch water to boiling. Add asparagus spears. Cover; reduce to low; cook 3 minutes.

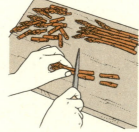

5 Drain and cool asparagus. Set aside 3 spears for garnish; cut remaining spears into 1-inch pieces.

6 In medium bowl, toss the asparagus pieces, green onions, and flour. Sprinkle cheese and asparagus mixture in piecrust.

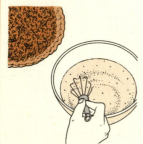

7 In same bowl with wire whisk, beat eggs, half-and-half, salt, basil, and pepper; pour over cheese and asparagus mixture.

8 Bake 25 minutes. Cut reserved spears lengthwise in half. Remove quiche from oven; arrange half-spears, cut sides down, on quiche.

9 Bake 5 to 10 minutes longer until knife inserted in center of filling comes out clean. Let stand 10 minutes before serving.

NO-CRUST ARTICHOKE QUICHE

2 6-ounce jars marinated artichoke hearts
¼ pound mushrooms, sliced
½ pound Muenster cheese, shredded (2 cups)

1¼ cups milk
½ teaspoon salt
⅛ teaspoon pepper
6 eggs

1. Preheat oven to 350°F. Drain artichokes, reserving marinade. Dice artichokes; set aside.
2. In 10-inch skillet over medium heat, heat 2 tablespoons reserved marinade; add mushrooms and cook, stirring occasionally, until tender, about 5 minutes. On bottom of 10-inch quiche dish or 9″ by 9″ baking dish, evenly distribute artichoke hearts, mushrooms, and cheese; set dish aside.
3. In large bowl, beat milk, salt, pepper, eggs, and 2 tablespoons reserved marinade. Pour egg mixture over ingredients in quiche dish. Bake 30 minutes or until knife inserted in center comes out clean.

- Color index page 26
- Begin 40 mins ahead
- 6 servings
- 320 cals per serving

BROCCOLI QUICHE WITH WHOLE-WHEAT CRUST

1¼ cups whole-wheat flour
6 tablespoons butter or margarine, melted
2 tablespoons water
½ cup cottage cheese
2 ounces Swiss cheese, shredded (½ cup)
½ cup milk

1 tablespoon salad oil
¼ teaspoon salt
¼ teaspoon basil
⅛ teaspoon pepper
4 eggs
1 10-ounce package frozen chopped broccoli, thawed and drained well

1. In small bowl, with fork, mix whole-wheat flour, melted butter and water until blended (mixture will be crumbly). With hand, press flour mixture into bottom and up side of 9-inch pie plate, making a fluted edge (p. 313). Refrigerate.
2. Preheat oven to 400°F. Into large bowl, press cottage cheese through fine strainer. Stir in Swiss cheese, milk, salad oil, salt, basil, pepper, and eggs. Add broccoli to cheese mixture; mix well.
3. Pour broccoli mixture into piecrust. Bake pie 25 to 30 minutes until knife inserted in center comes out clean.

- Color index page 24
- Begin 40 mins ahead
- 6 servings
- 320 cals per serving

SPINACH QUICHE: Prepare as above but substitute *1 10-ounce package frozen chopped spinach*, thawed and squeezed dry, for the broccoli. 421 cals per serving.

CALIFORNIA QUICHE: Prepare as above but use *¼ pound Monterey Jack cheese*, shredded, instead of Swiss cheese, and add *¼ cup canned, diced green chilies*. 458 cals per serving.

GOLDEN BUCK

- Color index page 24
- Begin 40 mins ahead
- 4 servings
- 605 cals per serving

4 tablespoons butter or margarine
¼ cup all-purpose flour
¼ teaspoon salt
⅛ teaspoon ground red pepper
1¼ cups milk
½ cup beer
6 ounces Cheddar cheese, shredded (1½ cups)

1 loaf Italian bread
2 medium tomatoes, each cut into 4 slices
Water
4 eggs
Parsley for garnish

1. In 2-quart saucepan over medium heat, melt butter; stir in next 3 ingredients; cook 1 minute.
2. Gradually stir in milk and beer; cook, stirring constantly, until mixture thickens. Stir in cheese until melted; keep sauce warm.
3. Cut eight 1-inch-thick slices from bread; toast. For each serving, arrange two toasted slices on oven-safe plate. Top each serving with 2 tomato slices; keep warm in 200°F. oven.
4. Poach eggs: In 10-inch skillet over high heat, heat 1 inch water to boiling. Reduce heat to low. One at a time, break eggs into saucer; slip into simmering water. Cook 2 to 4 minutes.
5. With slotted spoon, remove eggs from water. Drain over paper towels. Arrange on tomatoes. Spoon sauce over eggs; garnish with parsley.

Draining the eggs: With a slotted spoon, remove each egg and drain.

Arranging the eggs: Slip each egg onto the tomato slices; spoon sauce over.

WELSH RABBIT

- Color index page 25
- Begin 20 mins ahead
- 6 servings
- 375 cals per serving

4 tablespoons butter or margarine
½ cup all-purpose flour
½ teaspoon salt
⅛ teaspoon ground red pepper
⅛ teaspoon dry mustard
2 cups milk
1 teaspoon Worcestershire

½ pound sharp Cheddar cheese, shredded (2 cups)
6 toasted white or rye-bread slices
1 red pepper, seeded and thinly sliced

1. In 2-quart saucepan over low heat or in double boiler over simmering water, melt butter. Stir in next 4 ingredients; cook 1 minute.
2. Stir in milk and Worcestershire, and cook, stirring constantly, until mixture thickens. Stir in cheese; cook, stirring, just until cheese melts and mixture is smooth. Serve hot cheese mixture over warm toast. Garnish with red pepper.

CHEESY TORTILLA BAKE

This tasty tortilla pie with spicy flavorings is a Tex-Mex specialty. The sour cream provides a cool contrast.

- Color index page 24
- Begin 1 hr ahead
- 8 servings
- 360 cals per serving

12 6-inch corn tortillas
Salad oil
1 small onion, chopped
1 garlic clove, minced
½ cup water
½ teaspoon ground cumin
½ teaspoon salt
2 medium tomatoes, chopped

1 4-ounce can chopped green chilies, drained
1 chicken-flavor bouillon cube or envelope
12 eggs, beaten
½ pound sharp Cheddar cheese, shredded (2 cups)
Sour cream (optional)

1 Slice tortillas into ½-inch-wide strips. In 12-inch skillet over medium heat, in ¼ inch hot salad oil, fry several tortilla strips at a time 1 minute until golden.

2 Remove strips to paper towels; drain. Pour off all but 2 tablespoons oil from skillet, add onion and garlic; cook over medium heat stirring occasionally.

3 Stir in water, ground cumin, salt, tomatoes, green chilies, and bouillon; over high heat, heat to boiling. Remove skillet from heat. Quickly stir in eggs.

4 Preheat oven to 350°F. In 12″ by 8″ baking dish, arrange half of tortilla strips; top with half of shredded cheese. Pour egg mixture over cheese in baking dish.

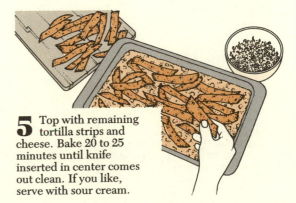

5 Top with remaining tortilla strips and cheese. Bake 20 to 25 minutes until knife inserted in center comes out clean. If you like, serve with sour cream.

Soufflés

HERB AND CHEESE SOUFFLÉ

This herb-filled soufflé, with its "top hat," makes a stylish party opener, or a light supper when served with a crisp salad and French bread.

- Color index page 26
- Begin 1¼ hrs ahead
- 6 servings
- 365 cals per serving

¼ cup butter or margarine
¼ cup all-purpose flour
1 teaspoon salt
Dash cayenne pepper
1½ cups milk
2 4-ounce packages shredded Cheddar cheese (2 cups)
6 eggs, separated

2 tablespoons chopped fresh parsley
½ teaspoon fresh thyme leaves

1 Preheat oven to 325°F. In medium saucepan over medium heat, into hot butter, stir flour, salt, and pepper until smooth.

2 Stir in milk; cook, stirring, until thick. Add cheese; stir until melted. Remove from heat. In bowl, beat yolks; stir in small amount hot sauce.

3 Slowly pour egg mixture into sauce, stirring rapidly to prevent lumping. Stir in parsley and thyme. Set aside.

4 In large bowl, with mixer at high speed, beat egg whites just until stiff peaks form when beaters are raised.

5 With rubber spatula, very gently fold cheese mixture into egg whites; pour into 2-quart soufflé dish.

6 With spoon, make 1-inch-deep circle in top of mixture, 1 inch from side of dish. Bake 1 hour. Serve at once.

WILD RICE AND CHICKEN SOUFFLÉ

- Color index page 26
- Begin 1½ hrs ahead
- 8 servings
- 270 cals per serving

⅓ cup wild rice
2 tablespoons butter or margarine
3 tablespoons all-purpose flour
¼ teaspoon salt
⅛ teaspoon pepper
¾ cup milk
½ pound Cheddar cheese, shredded (2 cups)

4 eggs, separated
1 5- to 6¾-ounce can chunk chicken, drained and flaked
1 cup bite-sized pieces cooked chicken

1. Prepare wild rice as label directs; set aside.
2. Prepare cheese sauce: In 2-quart saucepan over low heat, melt butter or margarine. Stir in flour, salt, and pepper until blended; cook 1 minute. Gradually stir in milk; cook, stirring constantly, until mixture thickens slightly. Stir in cheese; cook, stirring, just until cheese melts. Remove saucepan from heat.
3. In small bowl, beat egg yolks slightly; stir in a small amount of hot cheese sauce. Gradually pour egg-yolk mixture into cheese sauce in saucepan, stirring rapidly to prevent lumping. Remove from heat; cool slightly.
4. Preheat oven to 325°F. In large bowl, with mixer at high speed, beat egg whites until stiff peaks form. With rubber spatula, gently fold cheese mixture, one-third at a time, into egg whites just until blended. Gently fold wild rice and chicken pieces into cheese-egg mixture.
5. Pour mixture into ungreased 1½-quart soufflé dish. If desired, with back of spoon, make 1-inch-deep indentation all around in soufflé mixture about 1 inch from edge of dish. Bake 1 hour or until knife inserted into center comes out clean. Serve immediately.

HOW TO SERVE A SOUFFLÉ

Soufflés always make an eye-catching presentation. There is a trick to serving them without deflating them.

When soufflé is done, remove from the oven and serve immediately. Using two dinner forks, one in each hand, quickly break the crust into a pie-shaped wedge.

Then with a large spoon, gently cut down to the bottom of dish, scooping out the entire wedge onto warm plates. If you prefer a softer set, reduce cooking time slightly.

FISH AND SHELLFISH

"Jambalaya and crawfish pie and fillet gumbo . . . Son of a gun, we'll have big fun on the bayou."

© HANK WILLIAMS

America is endowed with miles of coastline, lakes, and rivers filled with hundreds of varieties of fish and shellfish. The size and abundance of the marine life in the Atlantic waters greatly impressed the early Viking explorers long before Christopher Columbus landed on our shores. American records of the plentiful supply of fish found along the eastern seaboard date back to the 1500s. It was said that fish were so abundant in Plymouth Bay that Pilgrims could "walk across the water" on their backs.

However, it wasn't until settlers learned to catch them efficiently that fish became an integral part of their diet. Enormous salmon were so available that settlers tired of it and restricted it to only one meal a week. Steamed salmon was always included at early 4th of July celebrations. By 1850, salmon was being canned and shipped all over the country.

The waters between Newfoundland and the Chesapeake Bay were so filled with cod that the Cape was named for it and the fish became the Massachusetts state emblem. The New England fishing industry developed around the "Cape Cod Turkey" and contributed greatly to trade with England. Although many other varieties of fish have since been depleted or become less popular, cod remains widely used and is available fresh or frozen across the country. Scrod, a young cod, best when prepared in the simplest way, has become a specialty of New England.

Oysters were available in such plentiful supply that they formed a staple part of the American Indian's diet. Southern colonists were fortunate in settling around some of the best oyster beds in the world; early records of oysters up to a foot in length may be hard to imagine! Americans were wild about oysters and cultivation on a large scale led to oyster wars and demands for shipping to the West. Many specialties became popular, especially in New Orleans where the oyster was most appreciated, and where such delights as Oysters on Half-Shell and Oysters Rockefeller originated.

Clams of the Atlantic and Pacific waters were also important in the Indian diet and culture. Clams were eaten simply on their own, and also provided the base for delicious chowders; even the shells were used as money. But the clam itself became the focus for a social gathering – the clambake – a fish feast which excited the European settlers and became a traditional American event.

SPECIAL TABLEWARE FOR FISH AND SHELLFISH

More than any other ingredient, fish and shellfish may require special tools or equipment for easy serving and eating. Although everyday utensils can be used, if you serve fish often, you may want to include some of these implements in your kitchen.

Lobster Pick
A long pick removes the small bits of meat from the body section and legs of shellfish.

Fish Cutlery
Oval-shaped blades are traditional.

Butter Warmers
Porcelain ramekins filled with melted butter kept warm over a candle flame set into a stand. Dip lobster and other seafood into the warm butter before eating.

Fish Server
A carved and etched server with its wide blade makes carving and serving a whole fish easy work.

Salt and Pepper Shells
Empty shells make attractive individual salt and pepper servers.

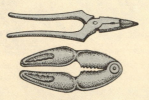

Lobster Crackers
Make easy work of cracking hard lobster and crab claws.

Clams

FAMILY CLAMBAKE

- Color index page 27
- Begin 1½ hrs ahead
- 6 servings
- 1,040 cals per serving

Pilgrims made the clambake, a meal cooked on the beach after a catch, into a popular New England social gathering. This modern version requires a very large kettle instead of the traditional outside pit.

3 dozen littleneck clams
1 3-pound bluefish, dressed
2 quarts water
6 1-pound lobsters
1 2½-pound broiler-fryer, cut up

6 ears corn, husks and silk removed
Butter or margarine
Parsley sprigs for garnish
Yogurt-Watercress Sauce (page 385)

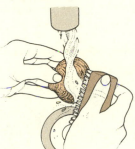

1 With stiff brush, scrub clams with running cold water until free of sand.

2 Remove head and tail from fish. Cut crosswise in half; wrap with double thickness cheesecloth.

3 In large kettle over high heat, heat water to boiling. Add clams, fish and next 3 ingredients, in order. Over high heat, heat to boiling.

4 Reduce heat to medium; cover and cook 25 to 30 minutes, until fish flakes easily, lifting lid often to let steam escape.

5 Melt 1 cup butter and pour into 6 small ramekins. Unwrap fish and cut into pieces. Arrange on platter with the remaining clambake.

6 Strain broth into mugs if you like. Garnish clambake with parsley sprigs. Serve with melted butter or Yogurt-Watercress Sauce.

STEAMED SOFT-SHELL CLAMS

- Color index page 27
- Begin 1 hr ahead
- 3 servings
- 600 cals per serving

6 dozen steamer (soft-shell) clams
1 cup water

¾ cup melted butter or margarine
Parsley for garnish

1. With stiff brush, scrub clams with running cold water to remove any sand. In steamer, or a saucepot with rack on the bottom, over high heat, heat 1 inch of water to boiling. Place clams on the rack.
2. Cover steamer with tight-fitting lid; reduce heat to low and steam clams just until they open, approximately 5 to 10 minutes.
3. Serve clams in soup bowls with 3 small individual dishes of melted butter. Pour broth from clams into mugs. Chop parsley and sprinkle over broth.
4. To eat, with fingers, pull clams from shells by neck; dip first in broth to remove any sand, then into butter. When sand settles to bottom, the broth may be drunk, if desired.

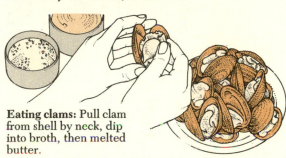

Eating clams: Pull clam from shell by neck, dip into broth, then melted butter.

CLAM FRITTERS

- Color index page 18
- Begin 45 mins ahead
- 4 servings or 2 dozen
- 216 cals per serving

1 cup all-purpose flour
1½ teaspoons baking powder
1 teaspoon sugar
¼ teaspoon salt
2 eggs

2 dozen cherrystone clams, shucked, with their liquid
1 teaspoon grated onion
Salad oil
Tartar Sauce (page 385)

1. In medium-sized bowl, combine flour with baking powder, sugar, and salt. Drain clams, reserving ½ cup liquid; coarsely chop clams.
2. In another medium-sized bowl, combine clams, eggs, onion, and reserved clam liquid; beat just until mixed. Stir clam mixture into flour mixture until blended.
3. In 12-inch skillet over medium heat, in 1 tablespoon hot salad oil, drop some clam mixture by tablespoonfuls; cook several fritters at a time until golden on both sides, turning fritters once. Place on warm platter and keep warm while cooking remaining fritters; add more oil to skillet as needed. Serve with Tartar Sauce.
COCKTAIL FRITTERS: Prepare as above, but drop rounded teaspoonfuls clam mixture, instead of tablespoonfuls, into hot salad oil. Serve on cocktail picks with Tartar Sauce or Spicy-Red Pepper Sauce (p.385). Makes about 28 (2-inch) appetizers. 31 calories each.

Crabs

- *Color index page 28*
- *Begin ½ hr ahead*
- *4 servings*
- *181 cals per crab*

PAN-FRIED SOFT-SHELL CRABS

During its growth process, the blue crab sheds its outer shell and becomes a seasonal delicacy.

8 soft-shell crabs (about 1 pound)
Salt and pepper
¼ cup butter or margarine
1 tablespoon chopped parsley
1 teaspoon lemon juice
⅛ teaspoon Worcestershire
Toast points, lemon wedges, and parsley sprigs for garnish

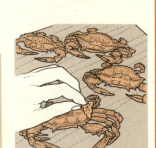

1 To clean soft-shell crabs: Cut across crab ¼ inch behind eyes; discard. With fingers, remove the flat pointed appendage (apron) on the underside.

2 Fold back, but do not remove, top shell from one of the points. Pull off spongy gills; discard. Fold top shell back. Repeat on other side. Rinse crab in cold water.

3 Sprinkle crabs with salt and pepper. In 12-inch skillet, melt butter or margarine.

4 Over medium heat, fry crabs about 3 minutes on each side or until golden. Remove crabs from skillet to a platter and keep warm.

5 Into the butter left in the skillet, stir chopped parsley, lemon juice, and Worcestershire. Pour over crabs.

6 Serve crabs with toast points; garnish with lemon and parsley sprigs. Entire crab (shell and all) is eaten.

- *Color index page 19*
- *Begin early in day*
- *6 servings*
- *122 cals per serving*

FRESH COOKED CRAB

Crab meat is one of the most delicate of all seafoods. Squeeze a lemon or lime over it; or serve with our Creamy Cocktail Sauce.

Creamy Cocktail Sauce (p. 385)
6 live crabs in season
Water
Lettuce leaves, shredded
Lemon slices for garnish
Parsley sprigs for garnish

1 Prepare Creamy Cocktail Sauce. With stiff brush, scrub crabs under running cold water to remove sand between shell and legs. In large saucepot over high heat, heat 3 inches water to boiling. Drop in crabs. Reheat to boiling; reduce the heat to medium.

2 Cover; cook 5 to 10 minutes, or until shells turn red. Remove and drain.

3 When cool, break off claws and legs; crack and remove meat. Pull off "apron" on underside.

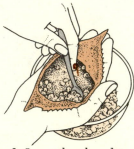

4 Insert thumb under shell. Pull off, removing top shell from body; scrape soft substance into small bowl.

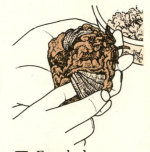

5 From body, remove and discard "dead man's fingers" and soft substance in middle of body.

6 Cut body in half; cut off thin shell around edges and remove meat between sections with nut pick or skewer.

7 Arrange lettuce on plates, place crab meat in center. Garnish with lemon slices and parsley. Serve with cocktail sauce.

CRAB IMPERIAL

- Color index page 28
- Begin 1 hr ahead
- 6 servings
- 185 cals per serving

3 tablespoons butter	1½ cups milk
2 tablespoons minced green pepper	2 tablespoons dry sherry
¼ cup all-purpose flour	2 egg yolks
¾ teaspoon dry mustard	2 6-ounce packages frozen Alaska King crab meat, thawed and well drained
¾ teaspoon salt	
¾ teaspoon Worcestershire	
⅛ teaspoon paprika	Lemon Twists (p.100) and parsley sprigs for garnish
⅛ teaspoon pepper	

1. In 2-quart saucepan over medium heat, melt butter; add green pepper; cook until tender. Stir in next 6 ingredients until well blended; cook 1 minute. Gradually stir in milk and sherry, stirring constantly, until sauce thickens and boils. Remove saucepan from heat.
2. Preheat oven to 350°F. In cup, beat egg yolks slightly; stir in ¼ cup hot sauce until blended. Slowly pour egg mixture back into saucepan stirring rapidly to prevent lumping. Fold in crab.
3. Pour into greased 1½-quart casserole. Bake 25 to 30 minutes and garnish.

CRAB CAKES

- Color index page 28
- Begin 30 mins ahead
- 4 servings
- 280 cals per serving

2 eggs	½ cup coarsely crumbled saltine crackers
1 tablespoon dry sherry	4 tablespoons butter or margarine
1 teaspoon grated onion	
¼ teaspoon salt	
⅛ teaspoon pepper	Lemon wedges and parsley sprigs for garnish
1 16-ounce container lump crab meat, picked over	

1. In medium-sized bowl, beat eggs, sherry, onion, salt, and pepper until blended; stir in crab and crumbled crackers just until mixed.
2. In 12-inch skillet over medium heat, in hot butter, spoon crab mixture into 4 mounds; with pancake turner, gently press mixture into 3½-inch round cakes. Cook until lightly browned on both sides, about 10 minutes. Garnish with lemon and parsley.

DEVILED CRAB

- Color index page 27
- Begin 45 mins ahead
- 4 servings
- 275 cals per serving

1 16-ounce container lump crab meat, picked over	1 tablespoon lemon juice
3 tablespoons butter, melted	1 teaspoon Worcestershire
	¼ teaspoon hot-pepper sauce
2 tablespoons chopped parsley	2 eggs, beaten
	½ cup dried bread crumbs
1 tablespoon prepared mustard	Lemon slices and parsley sprigs for garnish

Preheat oven to 350°F. In large bowl, with fork, mix crab and next 6 ingredients; stir in eggs and crumbs. Divide mixture among four greased 6-ounce ceramic scallop shells or ramekins; put on jelly-roll pan for easier handling. Bake 15 minutes or until golden; garnish.

Crayfish

CRAYFISH ÉTOUFFÉE

This traditional New Orleans dish, a Cajun specialty, makes good use of Louisiana's "mud bugs" or "creek crabs."

- Color index page 27
- Begin 1¼ hours ahead
- 4 servings
- 495 cals per serving

3 pounds crayfish	½ teaspoon ground red pepper
Water	
¼ cup salad oil	½ teaspoon basil
⅓ cup all-purpose flour	½ teaspoon thyme leaves
¼ cup chopped onion	2 cups hot cooked rice
¼ cup chopped celery	
¼ cup chopped green pepper	
1 teaspoon salt	

1 Rinse crayfish with running cold water. In 8-quart saucepan over high heat, heat 4 quarts water to boiling. Add crayfish; reheat to boiling.

2 Reduce heat to medium; cook 5 minutes. Drain and cool crayfish 10 minutes or until easy to handle. Remove tail meat from crayfish; set aside.

3 In 3-quart saucepan over medium-high heat, heat oil until hot. Stir in flour; cook, stirring frequently, until dark brown, about 5 minutes.

4 Reduce heat to medium; stir in next 7 ingredients; cook 1 minute. Gradually stir in ¾ cup water; cook, stirring constantly.

5 When sauce thickens and boils, reduce heat to low; cover; simmer until vegetables are tender. Add crayfish meat.

6 Heat crayfish mixture through. Spoon rice onto deep platter; arrange crayfish mixture around rice.

Lobsters

LOBSTER À L'AMERICAINE

This classic dish, contrasting sweet and tangy flavors, was probably first prepared by a French chef for dedicated American clients.

- Color index page 28
- Begin 1½ hrs ahead
- 4 servings
- 474 cals per serving

2 1½ pound lobsters
⅓ cup olive or salad oil
3 tablespoons butter or margarine
1 small onion, minced
1 garlic clove, minced
6 medium tomatoes, peeled and chopped

1 cup dry white wine
¼ cup brandy
3 tablespoons tomato paste
1½ teaspoons salt
1 teaspoon thyme leaves
Parsley sprigs for garnish

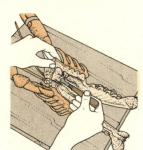

1 Prepare lobsters: Place lobster on its back. Insert point of knife through to back shell, where tail and body meet, to sever vein.

2 With knife, cut lobster in half lengthwise through shell. Devein tail. Leave greenish-gray liver and roe, if present.

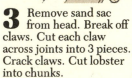

3 Remove sand sac from head. Break off claws. Cut each claw across joints into 3 pieces. Crack claws. Cut lobster into chunks.

4 In 8-quart Dutch oven over high heat, in hot oil, cook lobster pieces until shells turn red, about 5 minutes. Remove pieces; set aside.

5 Melt butter in Dutch oven. Add onion and garlic, cook until tender, stirring occasionally. Add the next 6 ingredients, heat to boiling.

6 Reduce heat; cover; simmer 20 minutes, stirring occasionally. Add lobster pieces, cover, heat through. Garnish with parsley sprigs.

LOBSTER THERMIDOR

- Color index page 28
- Begin early in day
- 4 servings
- 556 cals per serving

Water
4 1½ pound lobsters
6 tablespoons butter
3 tablespoons all-purpose flour
1 teaspoon salt
⅛ teaspoon ground nutmeg
⅛ teaspoon paprika

1½ cups half-and-half
3 tablespoons medium sherry
2 ounces Cheddar cheese, shredded (½ cup)
Lemon wedges and parsley sprigs for garnish

1. To cook lobster: in large saucepot over high heat, heat 3 inches water (or enough to cover lobsters) to boiling. Plunge lobsters head-first into boiling water. Cover; reheat to boiling. Reduce heat to medium; continue cooking 12 to 15 minutes, covered, until shell is red, lifting lid occasionally to prevent boiling over. When lobster is done, remove with tongs to large-paper-towel lined plate to drain.

2. Let lobster cool slightly. Break off claws and legs but leave lobster whole for presentation. With lobster or nut cracker, crack the large claws, remove meat to bowl. Do not twist off head from tail; with kitchen shears, cut thin underside shell from tail; gently pull meat from shell; devein tail. Reserve any red roe (coral) or green meat (tomalley) in bowl. Cut tail meat into chunks; place in bowl.

3. Lift out bony portion from head shell; add any more roe or green meat to bowl. Discard sac and spongy gray gills from top of head. Break bony portion apart; pick out any meat. Rinse and drain whole lobster shells; set aside.

4. Place meat, roe, and liver in large bowl. Cover bowl and wrap shells; refrigerate both. Recipe can be prepared ahead up to this point.

5. *About 25 minutes before serving:* In 3-quart saucepan over medium heat, in butter, blend flour, salt, nutmeg, and paprika. Stir in half-and-half and sherry; cook just until heated, stirring occasionally.

6. Preheat broiler if manufacturer directs. Place lobster shells on rack in broiling pan; carefully fill them with lobster mixture; sprinkle with cheese. Broil until mixture is hot and cheese begins to melt. Place lobsters on platter, garnish with lemon wedges and parsley sprigs.

Cracking claws: After lobster has cooled, twist claws off body; crack large claws with nut cracker; remove meat.

Picking out meat: Break bony part of lobster into a few pieces to expose the meat; pick out meat with fork or nut pick.

Oysters

OYSTERS ROCKEFELLER

Jules Alciatore of the famous New Orleans restaurant, Antoine's, created this dish in 1899. It was named after John D. Rockefeller, the wealthy industrialist.

- Color index page 18
- Begin 30 mins ahead
- 6 servings
- 144 cals per serving

18 large or 24 small oysters on the half-shell
3 tablespoons butter or margarine
½ 10-ounce package frozen chopped spinach, slightly thawed
1 tablespoon instant minced onion
1 tablespoon chopped parsley

1 bay leaf, finely crumbled
½ teaspoon salt
⅛ teaspoon cayenne pepper, hot pepper sauce, or anisette
¼ cup dried bread crumbs
Rock salt (optional)
2 bacon slices, diced
Grated Parmesan cheese (optional)

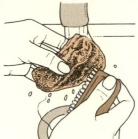

1 Scrub oysters under cold running water. Insert oyster knife between shells near hinge.

2 Run the oyster knife between the shells until you reach the opposite end.

3 With twisting motions of the knife, pry shells apart. Remove top shell.

4 Cut meat loose from shell; retain as much liquid as possible.

5 Preheat oven to 425°F. In 1-quart covered saucepan over medium heat, in melted butter, cook spinach, onion, parsley, bay leaf, salt, and cayenne stirring occasionally, until spinach is heated through. Toss in bread crumbs; set aside. If you like, place enough rock salt in bottom of large shallow baking pan to keep oysters in shell from tipping over. Place oysters in baking pan.

6 Spoon on spinach mixture. Sprinkle with bacon and cheese. Bake 10 minutes or until bacon is crisp.

OYSTERS ON HALF-SHELL

- Color index page 19
- Begin 15 mins ahead
- 16 oysters
- 140 cals per serving

1 tablespoon green peppercorns, drained
½ cup mayonnaise
3 tablespoons white wine vinegar
¼ teaspoon paprika
Crushed ice
16 oysters on the half-shell

1. In small bowl with spoon, slightly crush peppercorns. Stir in mayonnaise, vinegar, and paprika until mixed.
2. Line one or two large chilled platters with crushed ice; arrange oysters on ice. Spoon some sauce on each oyster.

SCALLOPED OYSTERS

- Color index page 18
- Begin 40 mins ahead
- 4 servings
- 192 cals per serving

⅓ cup butter or margarine
1½ cups finely crushed saltines
1 pint shucked oysters
¼ cup half-and-half
¾ teaspoon salt
⅛ teaspoon pepper
½ teaspoon Worcestershire
2 tablespoons chopped parsley

1. Preheat oven to 400°F. In 1-quart saucepan over low heat, into hot butter, stir saltines until well mixed. In 10" by 6" baking dish, arrange half of saltine mixture; top with undrained oysters.
2. In small bowl, mix half-and-half, salt, pepper, and Worcestershire and pour over oysters. Sprinkle top with parsley, then with remaining saltine mixture. Bake 20 to 25 minutes until lightly browned and bubbly.

HANGTOWN FRY

- Color index page 27
- Begin 35 mins ahead
- 4 servings
- 370 cals per serving

½ pint shucked select oysters
6 eggs
¼ cup all-purpose flour
⅔ cup dried bread crumbs
3 slices bacon
1 tablespoon butter or margarine
2 tablespoons water
½ teaspoon salt
Dash pepper

1. Drain oysters; pat dry with paper towels. In small bowl, beat 1 egg. In another small bowl, place flour. On sheet of waxed paper, sprinkle half of bread crumbs. Roll each oyster in flour to coat well. Then dip into egg and place in single layer on bread crumbs. Sprinkle oysters with remaining bread crumbs; coat well; set aside.
2. In 10-inch skillet over medium-low heat, fry bacon until crisp; remove bacon; drain on paper towels. In drippings in skillet, melt butter or margarine; add oysters in a single layer, and cook, turning once, about 5 minutes or until oysters are golden.
3. Meanwhile, into medium-sized bowl, crumble bacon; add remaining 5 eggs, water, salt, and pepper; beat with fork. When oysters are golden, reduce heat to low. Pour egg mixture over oysters; cook until mixture is set around edges. With metal spatula, gently lift edges as they set, tilting skillet to allow uncooked egg mixture to run underneath. Cook until mixture is set but still moist on surface.

Scallops

SCALLOP KABOBS

12 small mushrooms
½ large green pepper
2 tablespoons melted
   butter or margarine
2 tablespoons lemon juice
1 tablespoon salad oil
¼ teaspoon salt

Dash pepper
1 pound fresh or thawed
   frozen sea scallops
   (about 12)
4 bacon slices
2½ cups hot cooked rice

- Color index page 28
- Begin 1¼ hrs ahead
- 4 servings
- 410 cals per serving

1. Trim stems from mushrooms. Cut pepper into eight squares. In pie plate, combine next 5 ingredients. Add scallops, mushrooms, and green-pepper, tossing to coat; cover and refrigerate 30 minutes, tossing occasionally.
2. Preheat broiler if manufacturer directs. In 10-inch skillet over medium heat, fry bacon until light golden but still limp; drain on paper towels.
3. Run skewer through end of bacon slice; lace bacon between a fourth of scallops, mushrooms, and green pepper. Repeat with 3 more skewers. Place skewers on rack in broiling pan and broil 10 minutes, turning frequently.
4. Arrange hot rice on warm platter. When skewered food is done, arrange the skewers on top of the rice. If you like, remove food from skewers, keeping the shape, for easier handling.

Preparing skewers: Lace bacon between scallops, mushrooms, and green pepper.

PAN-FRIED SCALLOPS

1 pound fresh or thawed
   frozen sea scallops
⅓ cup dried bread
   crumbs
⅛ teaspoon salt
Dash pepper
Dash paprika

Butter or margarine
Toast points (optional)
2 tablespoons lemon or
   lime juice
1 tablespoon chopped
   parsley
Lime wedges for garnish

- Color index page 28
- Begin 15 mins ahead
- 3 servings
- 270 cals per serving

1. Cut large scallops in half. On waxed paper, combine bread crumbs with salt, pepper, and paprika; roll scallops in mixture until coated.
2. In 10-inch skillet over medium-high heat, in 3 tablespoons hot butter or margarine, fry scallops, turning occasionally, about 6 to 10 minutes until golden on all sides.
3. Place toast points on warm platter. With slotted spoon, arrange scallops on top; keep scallops and toast warm.
4. Into drippings remaining in skillet, stir 1 tablespoon butter or margarine, lemon juice, and parsley; heat to melt. Pour butter mixture over scallops. Garnish with lime wedges.

Shrimp

BEER-BATTER-FRIED SHRIMP

Adding beer to a simple batter makes a light, crispy coating for delicate shrimp. For a real family pleaser, serve the butterflied shrimp in a cloth-lined basket as the main course for an informal supper.

- Color index page 29
- Begin 1 hr ahead
- 6 servings
- 165 cals per serving

½ cup all-purpose flour
1 teaspoon salt
½ cup beer
1½ pounds large
   shrimp

Salad oil
Lemon wedges and
   parsley sprigs for
   garnish

1 In small bowl, mix the flour and salt. Gradually mix in beer until just blended. Do not over-mix. Set the batter aside.

2 Shell shrimp, leaving tail segment. Split shrimp along the back, cutting just enough to expose black vein.

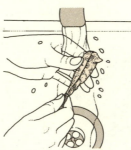

3 Spread each shrimp wide open, then rinse under running cold water to remove vein. Blot shrimp dry with paper towels.

4 In 2-quart saucepan over medium heat, heat 2 inches salad oil to 375°F. on deep-fat thermometer (or in deep-fat fryer at 375°F.).

5 Dip each shrimp into batter; drop into hot oil. Fry until lightly browned, turning once, about 1 minute. Drain shrimp on paper towels.

6 Arrange shrimp in a napkin-lined basket or bowl. Garnish with lemon wedges and parsley sprigs.

SHRIMP JAMBALAYA

1 pound large shrimp
2 tablespoons butter or
　margarine
½ pound pork-sausage
　meat
1 large onion, diced
1 large green pepper,
　diced
1 garlic clove, minced
1½ cups regular long-
　grain rice

1 14½- to 16-ounce can
　tomatoes
Water
1 chicken-flavor bouillon
　cube or envelope
¼ teaspoon salt
¼ teaspoon thyme leaves
Dash hot-pepper sauce
1 small bay leaf

- Color index
　page 29
- Begin
　1¼ hrs
　ahead
- 6 servings
- 460 cals
　per serving

1. Shell and devein shrimp; rinse with running cold water and pat dry with paper towels.
2. In 10-inch skillet over medium-high heat, in hot butter, cook shrimp 3 minutes; remove to bowl. In same skillet over medium heat, cook sausage until well browned, stirring occasionally, to break up. Stir in next 3 ingredients; cook, stirring occasionally, until tender. Add rice; cook until rice grains are opaque, stirring frequently.
3. Drain tomatoes, reserving liquid. Add enough water to tomato liquid to make 2½ cups. To rice mixture in skillet, add tomatoes with their liquid, bouillon, salt, thyme, hot-pepper sauce, and bay leaf. Over high heat, heat to boiling. Reduce heat to low; cover and cook, stirring occasionally, until rice is tender and liquid is absorbed, about 25 minutes. Discard bay leaf.
4. Stir shrimp into rice mixture; cover and cook until heated through.

ANGELS ON HORSEBACK

1 8-ounce package thick-
　sliced bacon
1 medium onion, diced
¾ cup regular long-grain
　rice
1½ cups water
1 8- to 8¼-ounce can
　tomatoes

1 chicken-flavor bouillon
　cube or envelope
½ teaspoon salt
1 cup frozen peas
¾ pound medium
　shrimp, shelled and
　deveined

- Color index
　page 29
- Begin
　40 mins
　ahead
- 3 servings
- 600 cals
　per serving

1. Cut each bacon slice crosswise in half. In 10-inch skillet over medium heat, cook bacon a few minutes on each side to render drippings. Remove bacon to paper towels to drain.
2. In drippings in skillet over medium heat, cook onion until tender, stirring occasionally. Add rice; cook until golden, stirring constantly. Add water, tomatoes with their liquid, bouillon, and salt; over high heat, heat to boiling. Reduce heat to low; cover and simmer 15 minutes. Add peas; cover and simmer 5 minutes longer or until rice and peas are tender and all liquid is absorbed.
3. Meanwhile, preheat broiler if manufacturer directs. Wrap each bacon piece around a shrimp, securing with toothpick. Place on rack in broiling pan. Broil about 8 minutes or until shrimp are tender and bacon is lightly browned, turning shrimp occasionally.
4. To serve, discard toothpicks from shrimp. Arrange rice and shrimp on large platter.

LEEK-WRAPPED SHRIMP WITH CHEESE FILLING

3 large leeks (1½ pounds)
Water
1 pound large shrimp
2 ounces fontina cheese,
　shredded (½ cup)
½ cup butter or
　margarine
¼ cup catchup

4 teaspoons lemon juice
½ teaspoon salt
⅛ teaspoon hot-pepper
　sauce
Coriander leaves and
　Lemon Twists (p. 100)
　for garnish

- Color index
　page 29
- Begin
　1½ hrs
　ahead
- 4 servings
- 390 cals
　per serving

1. Trim off roots and leaf ends of leeks. Cut each leek lengthwise in half; separate into leaves. Rinse leeks well with running cold water to remove all sand.
2. In 12-inch skillet over high heat, heat 1 inch water to boiling; add leeks; heat to boiling. Reduce heat to low; cover and simmer 5 minutes or until leeks are tender; drain. Arrange leeks on waxed paper.
3. Remove shells from shrimp, leaving tail parts of shell on. Cut each shrimp three-fourths of the way through along center back; spread each shrimp open. Rinse shrimp with running cold water to remove vein. Gently pat shrimp dry with paper towels.
4. Spoon some cheese along center back of each shrimp. Bring cut edges of each shrimp up toward cheese; firmly press shrimp to cheese.
5. Wrap each shrimp except tail with 2 or 3 strips of leek to cover completely; fasten with tooth-picks. (Use any leftover leek in soup or salad another day.)
6. Preheat broiler if manufacturer directs. In 1-quart saucepan over low heat, heat butter or margarine, catchup, lemon juice, salt, and hot-pepper sauce until butter melts, stirring mixture occasionally.
7. Arrange leek-wrapped shrimp in broiling pan; pour butter mixture over shrimp, turning shrimp to coat evenly. Broil shrimp 5 to 8 minutes until shrimp are tender, basting shrimp with butter mixture occasionally.
8. To serve, discard toothpicks. Arrange shrimp with coriander leaves on warm plates; pour pan drippings over shrimp. Garnish each serving with lemon twists.

Adding cheese: Spoon cheese along shrimp's back. Bring up edges of shrimp and press firmly to cheese.

Wrapping shrimp: Wind 2 or 3 strips of leek around shrimp to cover completely except for the tail.

Mixed shellfish

SAN FRANCISCO SEAFOOD CASEROLE

The California coast is rich in seafood, and it is especially popular in San Francisco's waterfront restaurants.

- Color index page 29
- Begin 1 hr ahead
- 6 servings
- 153 cals per serving

1 pound mussels or 18 littleneck clams
½ pound medium shrimp
1 pound cod or flounder fillets or 1 16-ounce package frozen cod or flounder fillets, thawed
2 tablespoons salad oil
1 medium onion, diced
1 large garlic clove, minced

1 28-ounce can tomatoes
1 8-ounce bottle clam juice
1 6-ounce can tomato paste
¾ cup cooking or dry white wine
¾ teaspoon salt
½ teaspoon basil
¼ teaspoon pepper

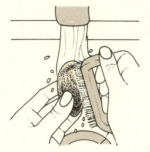

1 With stiff brush, scrub mussels under running cold water; remove beards.

2 Shell and devein shrimp; cut fish into 2-inch chunks; set aside.

3 Preheat oven to 350°F. In 3-quart saucepan over medium heat, in hot salad oil, cook onion and garlic until tender.

4 Stir in tomatoes with their liquid, clam juice, tomato paste, wine, salt, basil, and pepper; heat to boiling.

5 Pour tomato mixture into 3-quart casserole; add fish chunks, mussels, and shrimp.

6 Cover; bake 20 to 25 minutes until fish flakes, mussels open, and shrimp are tender.

MUSSELS AND CLAMS FRA DIAVOLO

- Color index page 29
- Begin 1¼ hrs ahead
- 4 servings
- 345 cals per serving

3 dozen cherrystone or littleneck clams
3 dozen large mussels
1 cup water
3 tablespoons butter or margarine
1 tablespoon olive oil
1 small onion, minced

1 garlic clove, minced
½ teaspoon oregano leaves
¼ to ½ teaspoon crushed red pepper
¼ teaspoon salt
⅓ cup chopped parsley
¼ cup dry white wine

1. With stiff brush, scrub clams and mussels under running cold water to remove any sand; remove beards from mussels.
2. In 8-quart Dutch oven or saucepot over high heat, heat water to boiling; add clams; heat to boiling. Reduce heat to medium-low; cover and cook until shells just open, about 6 to 8 minutes, stirring occasionally. With slotted spoon, remove clams to large bowl. To broth remaining in Dutch oven, add mussels; over high heat, heat to boiling. Reduce heat to medium-low; cover and cook until shells open, stirring occasionally.
3. Meanwhile, in small saucepan over medium heat, in hot butter and oil, cook next 5 ingredients until onion is tender, stirring often. Add parsley and wine; cook 2 minutes. (Although "fra diavolo" is usually a "deviled" or spicy tomato sauce, this is a lighter version.)
4. Discard top shell from each clam and mussel; rinse clams and mussels on half shell in cooking broth to remove any sand. Place clams and mussels on plate. Let broth stand a while until sand settles at bottom of Dutch oven. Carefully pour clear broth into a bowl; discard any sand.
5. Return clear broth to Dutch oven; add wine mixture in saucepan and reserved clams and mussels; over medium-high heat, heat through.

SKILLET SEAFOOD NEWBURG

- Color index page 29
- Begin 20 mins ahead
- 6 servings
- 720 cals per serving.

6 tablespoons butter or margarine
3 tablespoons all-purpose flour
1 teaspoon salt
⅛ teaspoon nutmeg
3 egg yolks
2 cups half-and-half
1 cup milk
1 pound cooked, shelled, and deveined shrimp

1 12-ounce package frozen cooked lobster meat, thawed (about 2 cups)
3 tablespoons medium sherry (optional)
3 cups hot cooked rice
Parsley sprigs for garnish

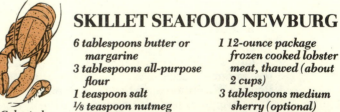

1. In 12-inch skillet over medum-high heat, into hot butter or margarine, stir flour, salt, and nutmeg until blended.
2. In medium bowl, with fork, beat egg yolks slightly and stir in half-and-half and milk; stir into flour mixture and cook, stirring constantly, until mixture is thickened.
3. Add shrimp, lobster meat, and sherry; cook until heated. Serve with hot cooked rice and garnish with parsley sprigs.

CHILLED SEAFOOD RISOTTO

1 pound fresh or frozen (thawed) squid
½ pound small shrimp, shelled and deveined
Olive oil or salad oil
1 garlic clove, minced
2 tablespoons dry sherry
¼ teaspoon pepper
Salt
1 16-ounce package frozen flounder, sole, or cod fillets, thawed
Water
1 9-ounce package frozen artichoke hearts
2 tablespoons lemon juice
2 8-ounce bottles clam juice
½ teaspoon crushed saffron threads
4 tablespoons butter or margarine
1 medium onion, diced
2 cups Italian arborio rice (short-grain pearl rice) or 2 cups regular long-grain rice
½ cup grated Parmesan cheese
½ 7-ounce jar roasted sweet red peppers, drained and cut into strips
½ cup pitted ripe olives, each cut in half

1. Pull off tentacles from squid; cut off and discard portion containing sac. Remove thin transparent cartilage and loose pieces from inside body. Gently scrape and pull off thin, dark outer skin. Rinse tentacles and body in running cold water. Slice body crosswise into ¾-inch rings. Cut large tentacles into several pieces.

2. Rinse shrimp with running cold water and pat dry with paper towels. In 10-inch skillet over medium heat, in 3 tablespoons hot oil, cook squid, shrimp, garlic, sherry, pepper, and ¾ teaspoon salt, stirring often, until squid and shrimp are tender. Spoon mixture into medium bowl.

3. Cut fish into bite-sized chunks. In same skillet over high heat, heat ½ teaspoon salt and 1 inch water to boiling; add fish. Reduce heat to low; cover and simmer 10 minutes or until fish flakes easily when tested with a fork. With slotted spoon, remove fish to bowl with squid mixture; cover and refrigerate.

4. While fish is cooking, prepare frozen artichoke hearts as label directs; drain. Return artichoke hearts to saucepan; stir in lemon juice. Add artichoke-heart mixture to bowl with squid.

5. In 3-quart saucepan over high heat, heat clam juice, saffron, 5 cups water, and 1 teaspoon salt to boiling. Reduce heat to medium-low to simmer.

6. In 5-quart Dutch oven or saucepot over medium heat, in hot butter, cook onion until tender, stirring occasionally. Add rice; cook until rice grains are opaque, stirring frequently.

7. Add 2 cups simmering clam-juice mixture to rice; cook, stirring, until liquid is absorbed. Add remaining clam-juice mixture, ½ cup at a time, stirring after each addition until liquid is absorbed. Remove Dutch oven from heat; stir in Parmesan cheese and 3 tablespoons olive oil. Add squid mixture, roasted peppers, and olives; toss to mix well. Spoon risotto onto platter. Cover and refrigerate until chilled, about 1½ hours.

- Color index page 29
- Begin 3 hrs ahead or early in day
- 8 servings
- 495 cals per serving

PARTY PAELLA

A popular recipe of Spanish origin, the colorful variety of its ingredients gives paella its festive appeal.

2 dozen mussels
2 dozen littleneck clams
Water
1 pound hot Italian-sausage links
1½ pounds large shrimp, shelled and deveined
1 2½-pound broiler-fryer, cut into 12 pieces
1 large garlic clove, minced
¾ teaspoon salt
½ teaspoon thyme leaves
Olive or salad oil
1 large onion, chopped
1 large green pepper, cut into ½-inch strips
1 14½- to 16-ounce can tomatoes

- Color index page 29
- Begin 3½ hrs ahead
- 12 servings
- 530 cals per serving

2¼ cups regular long-grain rice
½ cup dry white wine
½ teaspoon crushed saffron threads
1 chicken-flavor bouillon cube or envelope
1 9-ounce package frozen whole or cut green beans, thawed

1 With stiff brush, scrub mussels and clams with running cold water; remove beards from mussels. In 8-quart Dutch oven, to 1 inch boiling water, add mussels and clams; heat; to boiling. Reduce heat; cover, cook until shells open. Discard top shells; rinse mussels and clams in broth. Place on plate; cover; refrigerate. Let broth stand until sand settles. Spoon 2 cups clear broth into jug; discard rest.

2 In same Dutch oven over medium heat, heat sausages and ¼ cup water to boiling. Reduce heat to low.

3 Cover and simmer 5 minutes. Remove cover; cook, turning sausages often until well browned.

4 Remove sausages to paper towels to drain: Cool slightly. Cut into 1-inch slices.

5 In remaining drippings, over medium heat, cook shrimp, stirring often, about 3 minutes. Remove to bowl.

6 In medium-sized bowl, mix chicken pieces with the garlic, salt, and thyme to season.

7 In the same Dutch oven over medium-high heat, in 2 tablespoons hot oil, cook the chicken pieces until they are well browned on all sides. Remove to a large bowl; set aside. In remaining drippings in the Dutch oven, over medium heat, cook the onion and green pepper until tender, about 5 minutes, stirring often. Add tomatoes with their liquid, stirring to break up any large pieces.

8 Add the rice, dry white wine, saffron, bouillon, browned chicken pieces, and 2 cups of the reserved broth. Over high heat, heat to boiling. Reduce the heat to low; cover and simmer, stirring occasionally, until the rice is tender and all the liquid is absorbed, about 30 minutes. Preheat oven to 350°F. Stir Italian sausage, shrimp, and green beans into the cooked rice mixture.

9 Tuck mussels and clams on half shells into rice. Cover the paella, heat through about 30 minutes.

Valentine's Day Party

O n Valentine's Day, a day for love, we send romantic cards and gifts, special thoughts, heart-shaped boxes of chocolates, and red roses to sweethearts, friends, families, and teachers. What better way to celebrate than with a dessert party centered around our special heart-shaped Valentine's Devil's Food Cake, a whipped-cream-covered chocolate cake decorated with our Chocolate Lace Hearts?

Hearts are the theme for this party, so using a 3½-inch heart-shaped cookie cutter and a 1-inch round cutter to cut out cookie centers, we make our Strawberry Jam Dandies heart-shaped, too. For another special effect, make the Eggnog Charlotte Russe with Champagne cookies, tint the mixture and whipped cream pink, and garnish with Sugar-Frosted Cranberries (p. 294). Decorate with pink roses, pink ribbons, and sugared almonds, and for a very special evening, serve a sparkling pink Champagne.

MENU

12 people

*

Valentine's Devil's Food Cake
left
Strawberry Jam Dandies
page 344
Eggnog Charlotte Russe
page 295
Spiced Pears with Chocolate Sauce
(double recipe, omit ice cream)
page 291
Almond Lace Rolls
page 346

*

Pink Champagne

VALENTINE'S DEVIL'S FOOD CAKE

It's easy to turn our Devil's Food Cake (p. 337) into a spectacular heart-shaped centerpiece for Valentine's Day. It isn't necessary to buy a heart-shaped pan; follow these directions using ordinary pans.

1 Preheat oven to 350°F. Grease and flour an 8-inch round cake pan and an 8-inch square cake pan. Prepare Devil's Food Cake (p. 337) steps 1 to 3, using the round and square pans. (Do not prepare Quick Fudge Frosting.) Prepare Chocolate Lace Hearts (p. 336); chill.

2 When cakes are cool, whip 4 cups heavy or whipping cream with 2 teaspoons vanilla extract, until stiff peaks form. Cut each cake horizontally into 2 layers. Spread cut surfaces of bottom half of each cake with one-third of the cream. Replace top halves, cut side down.

3 To construct a heart-shaped cake, using round and square cakes, place the square cake on a large cake plate or aluminum-foil-covered cardboard at an angle, so one corner points upward like a diamond. Cut the round cake in half; place one half on each of the upper sides of the square cake to form heart shape.

4 With metal spatula, frost sides and top of cake with another one-third of the whipped cream. Place remaining whipped cream in a decorating bag fitted with medium star tube and pipe around edge; garnish the heart-shaped cake by placing the Chocolate Lace Hearts around the edges of the cake.

Planning Ahead

2 days ahead:	Make Devil's Food Cake layers; wrap well and chill. Bake Almond Lace Rolls and jam dandy cookies, but do not assemble. Store in air-tight containers.
Day ahead:	Prepare Eggnog Charlotte Russe; leave in pan and refrigerate. Poach pears; chill. Prepare Chocolate Lace Hearts; cover with plastic wrap and refrigerate.
Early in day:	Fill and frost Devil's Food Cake; refrigerate. Chill Champagne. Finish Strawberry Jam Dandies and dust with confectioners' sugar.
About 2 hours before serving:	Unmold Eggnog Charlotte Russe; decorate with whipped cream, cranberries, and pink ribbon; chill. Make chocolate sauce for pears. Garnish cake. Finish decorations.

ASSEMBLING THE CAKE

If you do not have a large plate or suitable tray, cover a thick piece of cardboard with several sheets of heavy-duty aluminum foil.

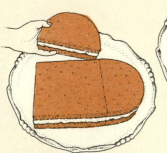

Assembling the cake: Place halves of the round cake on upper sides of square cake.

Decorating the cake: Carefully arrange the Chocolate Lace Hearts around the whipped-cream covered cake.

Easter Lunch

Easter is a joyous holiday celebrated in many ways, from the fashion parade down New York's Fifth Avenue to the delightful Easter Monday egg roll on the White House lawn, a tradition begun in 1878 by President Hayes. Children still color Easter eggs, but today's methods are easier than those of the Pennsylvania Dutch, who saved red onion skins all year to make their dyes. For an Easter lunch with a Southern theme, adapt our Glazed Sliced Ham recipe by using a whole ham.

To prepare the ham, do not pre-slice it, but score the surface of the ham forming a diamond-shaped pattern. Insert whole cloves into each diamond before glazing as directed, and garnish with chicory and Pickled Peaches and Apricots. Serve the ham with other regional specialties such as our Cream of Peanut Soup, Baked Candied Sweet Potatoes,

relishes, and a luscious Lane Cake. Set the dishes among lilies, a tiny glass basket of fragrant narcissus and baby's breath, and dyed or painted hard-cooked eggs to complete the Easter effect.

Planning Ahead

Up to 1 week ahead:	Prepare the relishes; make cake layers and freeze, if desired.
Day ahead:	Bake biscuits and corn sticks. Make soup but do not add garnish; refrigerate. Bake cake or remove from freezer.
2½ hours ahead:	Prepare ham and place in oven. Fill and frost cake. Cook and slice the potatoes.
45 minutes ahead:	Put potatoes in oven and cook vegetables.
10 mins ahead:	Warm biscuits and corn sticks. Reheat soup, garnishing with chopped peanuts.

MENU

10 people

*

Cream of Peanut Soup
page 102

*

Glazed Sliced Ham
with Pickled Peaches and Apricots
pages 202 and 379
Spicy Watermelon Pickles
Tangy Corn Relish
pages 378 and 385
Baked Candied Sweet Potatoes
page 246
Vegetable Bouquet
(double recipe) page 255
Buttermilk Biscuits/Golden Corn Sticks
pages 363 and 367

*

Lane Cake
page 333

Mother's Day Lunch

In 1908, Anna Jarvis of Philadelphia celebrated the first official Mother's Day. Now the second Sunday in May is set aside to honor all mothers. For a simple but elegant menu, serve a spectacular lamb roast with fresh new-season vegetables.

To present the lamb roasts as a "guard of honor," simply roast the two racks of lamb with their ribs interlocking, echoing the effect of swords forming a military honor guard. For a decorative look, cover every other rib with a paper frill, and arrange the vegetables around the roast before carving. The colorful Fresh Fruit in Orange Cups and extra special Mother's Day Cake can be done ahead. Decorate the table with a candy dish filled with miniature roses and wrap Mom's presents in special boxes tied with ribbons.

DECORATING THE MOTHER'S DAY CAKE

1 Prepare Mother's Day Cake, steps 1 to 6. Prepare Butter-Cream Frosting (p.348). Tint one-quarter of the frosting green, half the remaining frosting pink, and the remaining half yellow. With pink frosting, pipe roses (p.351) and set aside.

2 With green frosting, pipe dots on crown of hat. Use yellow frosting to pipe a ribbon around crown of hat: With petal tube at 45°, place wide end of opening at surface of cake, narrow end slightly up. Squeeze and move tip around crown. To make ripples, move tube up and down in short strokes.

3 With remaining yellow frosting, make a bow: Work with bag pointing toward you. Hold petal tube at 45° with wide end of opening on surface and narrow end straight up. Squeezing evenly, make loop to left. Stop pressing as you cross starting point. Squeeze again to make loop to right, stopping at starting point. From center, make 2 streamers. Decoratively arrange roses on brim.

MENU

8 people

———— ✳ ————

Fresh Fruit in Orange Cups
page 90

———— ✳ ————

Rack of Lamb with Parsley Crust
page 205
Wild Rice with Peas and Mushrooms
(½ quantity) page 268
Asparagus and Cherry Tomatoes
(double recipe) page 230
Classic Tossed Green Salad
page 271
Limpa Bread
page 360
Cucumber-Mint Relish
page 384

———— ✳ ————

Mother's Day Cake
page 351

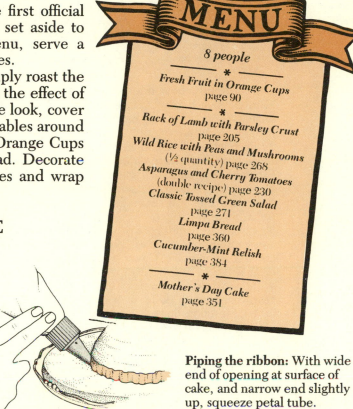

Piping the ribbon: With wide end of opening at surface of cake, and narrow end slightly up, squeeze petal tube.

Forming a bow: Make loop to left; stop pressing at starting point. Repeat with loop to right. Pipe two streamers.

PREPARING A GUARD OF HONOR

Prepare Rack of Lamb with Parsley Crust, but in step 3, arrange roasts in pan resting on their back bones.

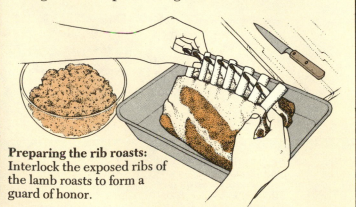

Preparing the rib roasts: Interlock the exposed ribs of the lamb roasts to form a guard of honor.

Planning Ahead

Up to 3 days ahead:	Prepare Cucumber-Mint Relish; refrigerate. Bake bread; refrigerate one loaf and if you like, freeze the other.
Day ahead:	Prepare fresh fruits for orange cups but do not assemble. Prepare salad ingredients and dressing and refrigerate separately. Bake, frost, and decorate Mother's Day Cake; cover loosely and refrigerate.
1½ hours ahead:	Begin roasting lamb; remove bread and cake from refrigerator. Assemble the orange cups. Begin cooking the rice.
15 minutes ahead:	Cook the vegetables; remove roast from the oven and allow meat to rest. Decorate with paper frills before carving.

Bass

- Color index page 30
- Begin 1¼ hrs ahead
- 6 servings
- 225 cals per serving

OVEN-STEAMED SEA BASS

4 green onions
½ small head lettuce
¼ cup water
1 3½-pound sea bass, dressed
Salt
¾ teaspoon minced, peeled gingerroot or ¼ teaspoon ground ginger
3 tablespoons soy sauce
1 tablespoon cooking or dry sherry
½ teaspoon sugar
Salad oil
2 medium carrots
¼ pound Chinese pea pods
Parsley sprigs for garnish

1. Cut green onions into 2-inch-long thin strips. Thinly slice lettuce. Place green onions and lettuce in open roasting pan large enough to hold fish; stir in water.
2. Preheat oven to 350°F. Cut 3 or 4 crosswise slashes, ½ inch deep, on each side of fish. Rinse fish with running cold water; drain well. With hands, rub ½ teaspoon salt over outside and in body cavity of fish. Arrange fish on lettuce and onion mixture.
3. In cup, mix ginger, soy sauce, sherry, sugar, and 1 tablespoon salad oil; pour mixture over fish and lettuce mixture. Cover pan with foil. Bake 40 minutes or until fish flakes easily.
4. Meanwhile, cut carrots into matchstick-thin strips. In 10-inch skillet over medium-high heat, in 1 tablespoon hot oil, cook carrots, pea pods, and ⅛ teaspoon salt until tender-crisp.
5. To serve, arrange fish and vegetables on warm platter; pour pan drippings over fish and vegetables. Garnish with parsley sprigs.

- Color index page 30
- Begin 3 hrs ahead
- 10 servings
- 452 cals per serving

STUFFED BAKED SEA BASS

1 6-pound sea bass or other whole fish, dressed
1 tablespoon lime juice
Butter or margarine
1 medium onion, minced
½ cup minced celery
1¾ cups herb-seasoned stuffing
4-ounces Cheddar cheese, shredded (1 cup)
½ cup milk
¼ cup chopped parsley
1 teaspoon salt
½ teaspoon nutmeg
½ cup dry white wine
Lemon wedges and parsley for garnish

1. Brush inside of fish with lime juice; refrigerate 1 hour.
2. Meanwhile, prepare stuffing: In 1-quart saucepan over medium heat, melt ¼ cup butter or margarine; add onion and celery and cook until tender, about 5 minutes. In large bowl, toss onion mixture, stuffing, cheese, milk, parsley, salt, and nutmeg.
3. Preheat oven to 350°F. In small saucepan, melt ½ cup butter or margarine; add wine.
4. Line a large roasting pan with foil; grease foil. Fill inside of fish with stuffing; fasten opening with toothpicks. Place fish in pan. Bake fish about 1 hour and 20 minutes, basting every 15 minutes with butter mixture.
5. Lift foil with fish onto warm, large platter; remove foil, then remove toothpicks. Pour pan liquid into gravy boat for sauce. Garnish.

Bluefish

- Color index page 30
- Begin 1 hr ahead
- 6 servings
- 750 cals per serving

OVEN-BAKED BLUEFISH

Bluefish, an oily fish with firm flesh, holds together well when cooked, making it a good choice for grilling or baking.

1 3½-pound whole bluefish, dressed
Butter or margarine
½ pound mushrooms, sliced
3 green onions, minced
3 cups soft bread crumbs (6 slices white bread)
1 medium tomato, diced
Salt
Thyme leaves
Pepper
1 tablespoon lemon juice
Lettuce, tomato, and lemon wedges for garnish

1 With fish peeler or scaler, remove any scales from fish. Cut 3 or 4 crosswise slashes, ½ inch deep, on both sides of fish.

2 In 10-inch skillet over medium heat, melt 6 tablespoons butter. Add mushrooms and onions; cook until tender; stir occasionally.

3 Remove skillet from heat; stir in bread crumbs, tomato, ½ teaspoon salt, ½ teaspoon thyme, and ¼ teaspoon pepper.

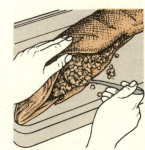

4 In 13" by 9" baking dish in 350°F. oven, melt 2 tablespoons butter; remove from oven. Place fish in dish; spoon stuffing into cavity; secure with toothpicks.

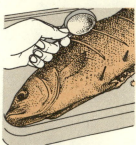

5 Sprinkle fish with lemon juice, ½ teaspoon salt, ¼ teaspoon thyme, and ⅛ teaspoon pepper.

6 Bake 35 minutes, basting occasionally. Place on warm platter; discard toothpicks; pour juices over and garnish.

Catfish

FRIED CATFISH

A Southern favorite, catfish gets its name from its distinctive whiskers. It is delicious coated with cornmeal and fried.

6 small catfish, dressed,
   with heads and tails left
   on (each about
   10 ounces)
¾ cup cornmeal
2 tablespoons all-purpose
   flour
½ teaspoon salt
¾ teaspoon pepper
¼ cup milk
Salad oil
Lemon slices and parsley
   sprigs for garnish

- Color index page 30
- Begin 2 hrs ahead
- 6 servings
- 205 cals per serving

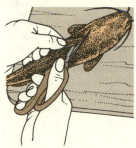

1 To skin catfish, using knife or scissors, cut off the sharp fins. Make a cut through the skin around the catfish's head.

2 Peel skin away from flesh around head; using paper towel to grasp skin, pull skin firmly toward tail to remove it in one piece. Cut off head.

3 In a plastic bag, combine cornmeal, flour, salt, and pepper. Into pie plate, pour milk. Dip catfish, one at a time, in milk to coat them well; drop into plastic bag.

4 Shake to coat evenly with cornmeal mixture. Place coated catfish on wire rack over waxed paper to dry, 30 minutes.

5 In 10-inch skillet over medium heat, heat ½ inch oil to 370°F. on deep-fat thermometer. Fry 3 catfish at a time until golden, about 8 to 10 minutes, turning once.

6 When cooked, remove catfish to drain on paper towels; keep warm while frying remaining fish.

7 Arrange fish on a large serving platter; garnish with lemon slices and parsley sprigs.

LEMON GARNISHES

Lemon is a traditional garnish for fish. Its acidity balances the oiliness of certain fish such as bluefish, salmon, and tuna; it also brings out the flavor of more delicate white fish.

Lemon/Lime Bundles: Cut each of 2 small lemons crosswise in half. Cut 4 pieces of cheesecloth, each large enough to wrap around one half.

Place one lemon half cut side down, in center of each piece of cheesecloth. Gather up edges of cloth; place one or two parsley sprigs on one side of gathered edges; tie parsley and cloth together with white kitchen string.

Julienne of Lemon Peel: With a vegetable peeler, remove the peel of a lemon in lengthwise strips trying not to take the white pith. Lay several strips on top of each other and with a very sharp knife, cut into thin julienne strips.

Lemon Loops: Slice a lemon in half lengthwise and lay it cut side down. Cut each half into slices about ¼ inch thick.

With a small sharp knife, cut the peel away from the lemon leaving about ¾ inch skin, and curl the peel under to form a loop.

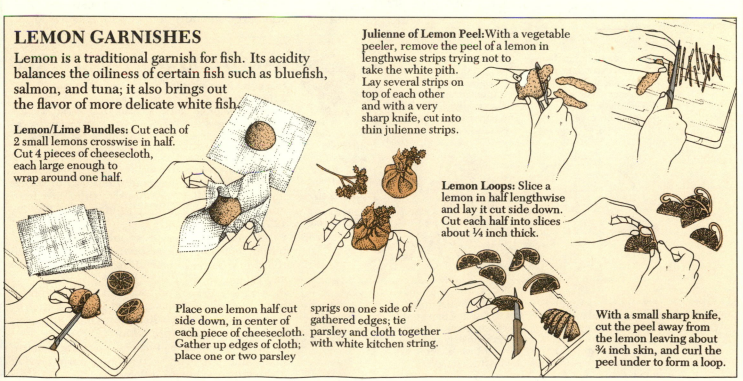

Cod

FRIED FISH AND HUSH PUPPIES

Hungry dogs begging around the table were "hushed up" with fried morsels of batter during outdoor fish frys in the Old South.

- Color index page 30
- Begin 45 mins ahead
- 8 servings
- 251 cals per serving

2 16-ounce packages frozen cod fillets, thawed
1½ cups yellow cornmeal
1 teaspoon salt
Salad oil for deep frying
½ cup all-purpose flour

2 teaspoons double-acting baking powder
¾ cup milk
1 egg
2 tablespoons minced onion

 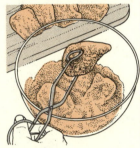

1 With sharp knife, cut each fillet crosswise into fourths. In medium bowl with fork, mix cornmeal and salt.

2 With tongs, press fish fillet pieces into cornmeal mixture, coating evenly on each side.

3 Meanwhile, in 4-quart saucepan over medium heat, heat about 1½ inches salad oil to 375°F. on deep-fat thermometer.

4 Gently drop fish into hot oil, a few pieces at a time. Cook 5 to 7 minutes, or until fish flakes easily. Drain fish on paper towels; keep warm.

5 Into remaining cornmeal mixture stir in next 5 ingredients until well mixed. Drop cornmeal mixture by measuring tablespoonfuls into hot oil.

6 Fry hush puppies, a few at a time, until golden, about 2 minutes. Drain hush puppies on paper towels. Serve fish with hush puppies.

BROILED COD STEAKS MONTAUK

- Color index page 30
- Begin 20 mins ahead
- 4 servings
- 218 cals per serving

½ cup mayonnaise
½ teaspoon prepared mustard
¼ teaspoon seasoned salt
⅛ teaspoon seasoned pepper

Salad oil
4 small cod steaks, each cut ½ inch thick
1 small orange for garnish
1 small lemon for garnish

1. Preheat broiler if manufacturer directs. Meanwhile, in small bowl, mix first 4 ingredients; set aside.
2. Lightly brush the rack in broiling pan with salad oil, to prevent fish from sticking. Place cod steaks on rack. About 7 to 9 inches from source of heat, broil cod steaks 7 minutes. Remove broiling pan from broiler; do not turn fish.
3. Spread one-fourth of mayonnaise mixture on each cod steak. Return pan to broiler; broil about 3 to 5 minutes longer or until cod flakes easily and topping is lightly browned and bubbly.
4. Thinly slice orange and lemon; cut each slice crosswise in half. Arrange cod steaks on warmed plates and garnish with orange and lemon slices.

SAUTÉED ROE

- Color index page 30
- Begin 10 mins ahead
- 4 servings
- 233 cals per serving

¼ cup butter or margarine
2 cod or shad roe (about 1 pound)

½ teaspoon salt
Dash pepper
Shredded lettuce
Lemon wedges

1. In covered 10-inch skillet over medium heat, in hot butter or margarine, cook roe, turning once, 8 minutes or until roe loses its pink color and is tender when tested with a fork.
2. Sprinkle roe with salt and pepper; Slice; arrange on shredded lettuce with lemon wedges.

BAKED COD WITH GRAPEFRUIT

- Color index page 30
- Begin 40 mins ahead
- 6 servings
- 205 cals per serving

1 large pink grapefruit
2 16-ounce packages frozen cod or haddock fillets, thawed
¾ teaspoon salt
Dash pepper

¼ cup butter or margarine
1 cup fresh bread crumbs
¼ teaspoon thyme leaves
Dill sprigs for garnish

1. Preheat oven to 350°F. Into small bowl, section grapefruit; let stand 5 minutes to collect juice. Brush fillets generously with juice from grapefruit; sprinkle with salt and pepper. Place in 12″ by 8″ baking pan.
2. In small saucepan over medium heat, melt butter or margarine; reserve 1 tablespoon; into remaining butter or margarine, stir bread crumbs and thyme; sprinkle over fish.
3. Arrange grapefruit sections over crumbs; brush grapefruit with reserved melted butter or margarine. Bake 25 to 30 minutes until fish flakes easily when tested with a fork.
4. With a pancake turner, carefully remove fillets and grapefruit sections to a warm serving dish and garnish with dill sprigs.

SCAMPI-STYLE FISH

This zesty dish uses frozen fish instead of shrimp. The red peppers and Chinese pea pods add a colorful and crunchy note.

- Color index page 31
- Begin 40 mins ahead
- 4 servings
- 210 cals per serving

Salad oil
1 medium red pepper, cut into thin strips
1 garlic clove, crushed
1 16-ounce package frozen cod, flounder, or sole fillets, thawed
½ cup water
2 tablespoons cooking or dry sherry
½ teaspoon chicken-flavor instant bouillon
Salt
½ pound Chinese pea pods
1 tablespoon chopped chives

1 In 12-inch skillet over medium-high heat, in 2 tablespoons hot salad oil, cook red pepper and garlic until pepper is tender-crisp, stirring frequently. Remove to small bowl.

2 Meanwhile, cut fish lengthwise in half, then crosswise into 16 chunks. In same skillet over high heat, heat fish chunks, water, sherry, bouillon, and ½ teaspoon salt to boiling.

3 Reduce heat to low; cover and simmer 15 minutes or until fish flakes easily when tested with a fork, stirring occasionally.

4 About 5 minutes before fish is done, in 3-quart saucepan over medium-high heat, in 1 tablespoon hot salad oil, cook pea pods and ¼ teaspoon salt until tender-crisp, stirring.

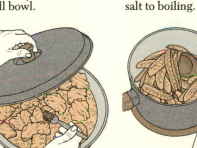

5 Return peppers and pea pods to skillet with fish; spoon mixture onto warm plates; sprinkle with chives.

CRISP FISH CAKES

Fish cakes are often made from leftovers but they become special when coated with cornmeal and served with a spicy sauce.

- Color index page 31
- Begin 40 mins ahead
- 6 servings
- 491 cals per serving

1 large celery stalk
Butter or margarine
1 16-ounce package frozen cod, flounder, or turbot, thawed
1½ cups fresh bread crumbs (about 3 slices bread)
2 ounces mozzarella cheese, shredded (½ cup)
1 tablespoon chopped parsley
1 tablespoon grated onion
1 teaspoon lemon juice
½ teaspoon salt
1 egg
¼ cup cornmeal
Parsley sprigs for garnish

1 Finely chop celery. In 12-inch skillet over medium heat, in 1 tablespoon hot butter or margarine, cook celery until tender, stirring occasionally.

2 Meanwhile, with knife, finely chop fish fillets. In large bowl, mix fish, celery, bread crumbs, mozzarella cheese, chopped parsley, grated onion, lemon juice, salt, and egg.

3 With your hands, carefully shape fish mixture into four 4-inch round cakes. Coat fish cakes with cornmeal.

4 In same skillet over medium heat, in 2 tablespoons hot butter, cook fish cakes until brown on both sides, about 10 minutes.

5 If you like, top fish cakes with Spicy Red-Pepper Sauce (p. 385). Garnish with parsley sprigs.

CODFISH BALLS: To prepare Codfish Balls to serve as an appetizer, shape mixture into balls one inch in diameter and fry as in step 4 or deep-fry as in Beer-Batter-Fried Shrimp (p. 124).

Flounder

SHRIMP-FILLED FILLETS

A lightly seasoned shellfish filling and creamy Hollandaise Sauce turn simple fish fillets into something special.

- Color index page 33
- Begin 1 hr ahead
- 4 servings
- 570 cals per serving (without sauce)

¾ cup butter or margarine
1 garlic clove, crushed
1 small onion, minced
¼ cup minced green pepper
1 pound shelled and deveined shrimp, cooked
Salt

¼ cup dried bread crumbs
1 tablespoon chopped parsley
4 flounder or sole fillets (about 1½ pounds)
Hollandaise Sauce (p. 385).
Dill sprigs for garnish

1 Preheat oven to 350°F. In 12-inch skillet heat 2 tablespoons butter; add garlic, onion, and green pepper and cook until tender.

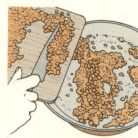

2 Reserve 4 shrimp for garnish. Dice rest of shrimp; add with ¼ teaspoon salt, crumbs, and parsley to skillet; mix well; remove from heat.

3 If large, halve fillets. On each boned side, spread 2 tablespoons shrimp down middle.

4 From narrow end, roll each fillet jelly-roll fashion; tuck any extra mixture into rolls.

5 In 9" × 9" baking pan, melt 2 tablespoons butter in oven. Arrange fillets in pan, seam side down; brush with butter. Bake 25 minutes.

6 Arrange fillets on warm platter and pour some Hollandaise Sauce over them; garnish each with a shrimp and some dill.

FLOUNDER WITH GREEN-CHILI SAUCE

- Color index page 33
- Begin 45 mins ahead
- 4 servings
- 295 cals per serving

1 lemon
2 small tomatoes
¼ cup loosely packed parsley
2 tablespoons chopped onion
1 tablespoon chopped jalapeño chili
1 4-ounce can chopped green chilies, drained

1 small garlic clove
Salad oil
½ cup dried bread crumbs
¼ teaspoon salt
1 egg
1 16-ounce package frozen flounder or sole fillets, thawed
Parsley sprigs for garnish

1. Cut lemon lengthwise in half. From one half, squeeze 1 teaspoon juice; cut remaining half into four wedges; set aside.

2. Cut 1 tomato into bite-sized chunks; thinly slice the other and set aside. In blender at low speed blend tomato chunks, next 5 ingredients, lemon juice, and 1 tablespoon salad oil.

3. Spoon green-chili mixture into 1-quart saucepan; over medium heat, heat to boiling. Reduce heat to low; cover and simmer 10 minutes to blend flavors, stirring occasionally. Keep warm.

4. On waxed paper, mix bread crumbs and salt. In pie plate with fork, beat egg slightly. Separate thawed flounder into fillets; if fillets are large, cut into serving pieces. Dip flounder fillets into beaten egg, then into bread crumbs to coat.

5. In 12-inch skillet over medium heat, in 3 tablespoons hot salad oil, cook half of the flounder fillets at a time until golden on both sides and fish flakes easily, about 5 minutes, removing fillets to warm platter as they brown.

6. To serve, garnish with tomato slices, lemon wedges, and parsley sprigs; spoon green-chili sauce over fish.

SPINACH-STUFFED FLOUNDER

- Color index page 31
- Begin 45 mins ahead
- 6 servings
- 270 cals per serving

Butter or margarine
1 10-ounce bag spinach
1 medium green onion, chopped
⅛ teaspoon pepper
1 slice white bread, cut into small pieces
Paprika

Salt
1 tablespoon cooking or dry white wine
1 teaspoon lemon juice
2 flounder or sole fillets (about ½ pound each)
Lemon slices for garnish

1. In 10-inch skillet over medium heat, in 1 tablespoon hot butter or margarine, cook spinach and onion until tender, stirring occasionally. Remove skillet from heat; stir in pepper, bread, ¼ teaspoon paprika, and ¼ teaspoon salt.

2. Preheat oven to 350°F. Place 3 tablespoons butter in 13" by 9" baking pan; place in oven until butter melts. Remove baking pan from oven; stir in wine and lemon juice until blended.

3. Place one fillet in butter mixture in pan; top with spinach mixture. Place second fillet on top; sprinkle with ¼ teaspoon paprika and ¼ teaspoon salt. Bake 15 minutes or until fish flakes easily, basting occasionally with mixture in pan.

4. To serve, arrange stuffed fish fillets on warm platter. Garnish with lemon slices.

Halibut

CALIFORNIA-STYLE MARINATED HALIBUT

- Color index page 31
- Begin 2½ hrs ahead
- 4 servings
- 370 cals per serving

⅓ cup fresh lime juice
⅓ cup salad oil
1 teaspoon salt
½ teaspoon sugar
½ teaspoon oregano leaves
⅛ teaspoon crushed red pepper

2 canned whole green chilies, seeded and cut crosswise into strips
2 large or 4 small halibut steaks, each ¾ inch thick
Lime wedges and parsley sprigs for garnish

1. In large glass or stainless-steel bowl, combine lime juice, salad oil, salt, sugar, oregano leaves, crushed red pepper, and green chilies.
2. Add halibut steaks and spoon marinade over. Cover; refrigerate 2 hours, turning often.
3. About 30 minutes before serving, preheat broiler if manufacturer directs. Place steaks on rack in broiling pan, reserving marinade.
4. Broil 8 to 10 minutes, until fish flakes when tested with a fork, spooning marinade occasionally on steaks. To serve, spoon pan juices over steaks; garnish with lime and parsley.

HAWAIIAN HALIBUT STEAKS

- Color index page 30
- Begin 30 mins ahead
- 4 servings
- 433 cals per serving

2 cups cooked rice
4 teapoons lemon juice
⅓ cup butter or margarine, melted
Seasoned salt
½ teaspoon curry powder

1 8½-ounce can pineapple tidbits, drained
2 1-pound halibut steaks
Lime slices for garnish

1. Preheat broiler if manufacturer directs. Grease broiling pan rack.
2. In a 10-inch skillet, combine rice with 3 teaspoons lemon juice, 2 tablespoons melted butter or margarine, seasoned salt, curry powder, and pineapple tidbits. Over medium heat, heat 10 minutes, stirring occasionally.
3. Meanwhile, sprinkle each halibut steak with ½ teaspoon lemon juice and ½ teaspoon seasoned salt. Place each steak on a rack in broiling pan and brush with half of the remaining butter.
4. Broil 5 minutes; turn and brush with remaining butter. Broil 5 minutes longer or until fish flakes easily when tested with a fork.
5. To serve, arrange each fish steak on a bed of rice mixture; garnish fish steaks with lime slices.

Broiling fish steaks: Brush steaks with melted butter before broiling.

Serving fish steaks: Arrange on a bed of rice; garnish with lime slices.

BROILED HALIBUT STEAKS WITH LEMON-DILL SAUCE

Halibut is a cold-seawater fish that dwells mostly in Northern waters. The flavor is subtle and needs accenting.

- Color index page 31
- Begin 25 mins ahead
- 4 servings
- 480 cals per serving

1 medium lemon
4 small halibut or salmon steaks, each cut ¾ inch thick (about 1½ pounds)
Salt
Pepper
Salad oil

2 egg yolks
2 tablespoons cooking or dry sherry
½ cup butter or margarine
⅛ teaspoon dill weed
Dill sprigs for garnish

1 Preheat broiler if manufacturer directs. Cut 4 thin slices from lemon for garnish. From lemon, squeeze 1 tablespoon juice.

2 Sprinkle halibut steaks lightly with salt and pepper. Lightly brush rack in broiling pan with salad oil.

3 Place halibut steaks on rack; broil about 6 minutes, turning steaks once with pancake turner. Place steaks on platter; keep warm.

4 Meanwhile, in double boiler over hot, *not boiling*, water, with whisk, beat yolks, sherry, and lemon juice until slightly thickened.

5 Add butter, 1 tablespoon at a time. Beat until mixture is thickened. Stir in dill weed and ¼ teaspoon salt.

6 Serve halibut with lemon-dill sauce. Garnish with dill sprigs and reserved lemon slices.

Red snapper

RED SNAPPER WITH LIME BUTTER

- *Color index page 33*
- *Begin 40 mins ahead*
- *4 servings*
- *370 cals per serving*

Found in the warm waters from North Carolina to Brazil, the best snapper seems to come from Florida.

3 to 4 large limes
4 tablespoons butter or margarine at room temperature
¼ cup heavy or whipping cream
¼ teaspoon pepper

1 2½ pound whole red snapper, dressed
½ cup vermouth
½ teaspoon salt
¼ cup sliced blanched almonds, toasted
Parsley sprigs; lime slices

1 Grate peel from 1 lime; squeeze 2 tablespoons juice. In small bowl, with mixer at medium-low, beat butter.

2 Beat in cream, then lime juice, 1 tablespoonful at a time; make sure liquid is absorbed after each addition.

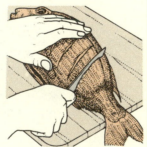

3 Increase speed to high; beat 30 seconds or until light and fluffy. Stir in pepper and lime peel. Spoon lime butter into bowl; cover; refrigerate.

4 Preheat broiler if manufacturer directs. Cut 3 or 4 crosswise slashes, ½ inch deep, on each side of red snapper. Rinse with running cold water; drain.

5 Place snapper in broiling pan. In a measuring cup, mix vermouth with salt; pour over fish. About 7 to 9 inches from source of heat, broil the fish about 6 to 8 minutes. (If you like, bake the snapper in a greased ovenproof dish, in a 450°F oven, for about 30 to 35 minutes, basting occasionally with pan juices.) Turn the fish and broil until fish flakes easily, basting with liquid occasionally. Slice remaining limes.

6 To serve, place red snapper on large platter; top with almonds and lime butter. Garnish with lime slices and parsley.

RED SNAPPER CREOLE

- *Color index page 33*
- *Begin 2 hrs ahead*
- *10 servings*
- *419 cals per serving*

⅓ cup medium sherry
1 cup fresh bread crumbs
Butter or margarine
2 cups minced onions
½ cup diced green or sweet red pepper
2 tablespoons chopped parsley
Thyme leaves

2 tablespoons chili sauce
1 5- to 6-pound red snapper, dressed, head and tail removed
Salt
Pepper
Shrimp for garnish
Shrimp-Olive Sauce (p. 385)

1. In small bowl, pour sherry over bread crumbs. In 2-quart saucepan over medium heat, in 1 tablespoon hot butter or margarine, cook minced onions until tender, about 5 minutes.

2. Add green pepper, parsley, ¼ teaspoon thyme leaves, and chili sauce; cook a few minutes. Add crumbs; cook until mixture is almost dry, about 5 minutes more.

3. Preheat oven to 350°F. Line a large baking dish with foil; grease foil. Sprinkle inside of fish lightly with salt and pepper; fill with crumb mixture; fasten opening with toothpicks.

4. In small saucepan over medium heat, melt 1 tablespoon butter or margarine; stir in 1 teaspoon salt, ¼ teaspoon pepper, and ¼ teaspoon thyme leaves. Brush fish with mixture; then place fish in baking dish. Bake 50 to 55 minutes.

5. Remove toothpicks. Garnish with shrimp and serve with Shrimp-Olive Sauce.

HOW TO SERVE A WHOLE FISH

It's useful to know how to carve a whole fish at the table. Although it is not necessary, specialized table equipment is useful to have and attractive to display.

With a sharp knife, break the skin of the fish along the backbone.

Divide the top side of the fish into serving-sized pieces, cutting just down to the bone.

Gently ease meat away from the rib bones; lift one section and place on warmed plate. Continue with remaining portions.

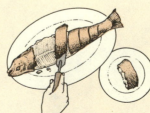
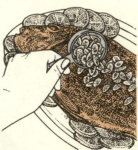

Lift off the bone by sliding a knife or fish slice to separate it from the lower section and continue portioning in the same way.

Salmon

SALMON MOUSSE

- Color index page 33
- Begin 4 hrs ahead or early in day
- 10 servings
- 230 cals per serving

¾ cup water
1 envelope unflavored gelatin
2 medium lemons
1 cup heavy or whipping cream
1 15½-ounce can salmon, drained and flaked
½ cup mayonnaise
2 tablespoons prepared white horseradish
1 tablespoon chopped fresh dill or 1 teaspoon dill weed
1 teaspoon salt
1 teaspoon paprika
⅛ teaspoon ground cardamom
2 stalks celery
Radishes for garnish
Dill sprigs for garnish

1. Into 1-quart saucepan, measure water; sprinkle gelatin evenly over water; let stand 1 minute. Cook over medium heat, stirring frequently, until gelatin is dissolved. Cover and refrigerate until mixture mounds slightly when dropped from a spoon, about 30 minutes.
2. Cut 1 lemon in half lengthwise. From 1 half, squeeze 1 tablespoon juice. Cut remaining lemons into wedges; refrigerate. Grease 9" by 5" loaf pan or 6-cup fish mold.
3. In small bowl, with mixer at medium speed, beat heavy or whipping cream until stiff peaks form. In large bowl with same beaters and with mixer at medium speed, beat salmon, next 6 ingredients, lemon juice, and gelatin mixture until blended and smooth, scraping bowl often with rubber spatula. With rubber spatula or wire whisk, fold whipped cream into salmon mixture. Spoon salmon mixture into prepared pan; cover and refrigerate until set, about 3 hours.
4. To serve, unmold mousse onto large platter. Thinly slice celery and radishes. Decorate platter with alternating slices, overlapping slightly. Garnish platter with dill sprigs.

SALMON CROQUETTES WITH DILL SAUCE

- Color index page 33
- Begin 30 mins ahead
- 4 servings
- 425 cals per serving

4 slices white bread
1 7½- to 7¾-ounce can salmon, drained and flaked
2 eggs
¼ teaspoon salt
½ teaspoon pepper
Dill weed
1 teaspoon salad oil
½ cup mayonnaise
1 teaspoon prepared mustard
1 10-ounce package frozen chopped spinach
Dill sprigs for garnish

1. Into large bowl, tear bread into small pieces; add salmon, eggs, salt, pepper, and ⅛ teaspoon dill weed; mix well. Shape salmon mixture into 8 croquettes. In 12-inch skillet over medium heat, in hot salad oil, cook patties 5 minutes or until browned on both sides, turning once.
2. Meanwhile, prepare sauce: In 1-quart saucepan over low heat, heat mayonnaise, mustard, and ⅛ teaspoon dill weed until warm. Keep sauce warm.
3. Remove croquettes from skillet; keep warm. Prepare spinach as label directs; drain. Place croquettes on spinach; garnish with dill sprigs. Serve with sauce.

CHILLED SALMON STEAK WITH MARINATED CUCUMBER

Salmon was so important to the Indians that one tribe was reported to be afraid they would starve if their supply was diminished!

- Color index page 33
- Begin 4 hrs ahead
- 6 servings
- 409 cals per serving

4 cups water
Salt
6 salmon steaks, about ½ inch thick (2 pounds)
2 large cucumbers, thinly sliced
½ cup white vinegar
2 tablespoons sugar
¼ teaspoon pepper
1 small onion, thinly sliced
Mixed salad greens and lemon wedges for garnish
Green Mayonnaise Dressing (p. 385)

1 In 12-inch skillet over high heat, heat water and 2 tablespoons salt to boiling. Add 3 steaks. Reheat to boiling.

2 Reduce heat to low; cover; simmer 5 to 8 minutes or until fish flakes. Grease 15½" by 10½" jelly-roll pan.

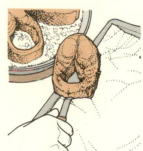

3 Remove one steak at a time and drain over paper towels. Repeat with remaining steaks; place steaks in pan; cover; refrigerate.

4 Meanwhile, in medium bowl, toss cucumbers and 1 tablespoon salt. Let stand 30 minutes; drain in colander; press out liquid.

5 Discard liquid and return cucumbers to bowl; add vinegar, sugar, pepper, onion; mix well. Cover and refrigerate.

6 On each plate arrange salmon, cucumbers, greens, and lemon. Serve with dressing.

Sole

CREAMY SOLE FILLETS

This flat fish takes its name from the Old French *sole* referring to the shape of the foot. For a special occasion fold as shown.

- Color index page 32
- Begin 1¾ hrs ahead
- 6 servings
- 260 cals per serving

6 sole fillets (about 6 ounces each)
Cooking or dry white wine
Salt
1 medium celery stalk, cut up
1 small onion, cut into quarters

1½ cups water
¼ cup packed celery leaves
⅛ teaspoon white pepper
1 cup heavy or whipping cream
1 tablespoon tomato paste
Parsley sprigs for garnish

1 Rub fillets with 2 tablespoons wine and ½ teaspoon salt; cover and refrigerate 1 hour.

2 Fold tail end of fillet over wide end and tuck under, forming pyramid shape.

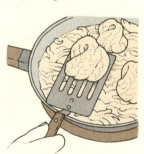

3 In 10-inch skillet over high heat, heat next 5 ingredients, 2 tablespoons wine, and ¼ teaspoon salt to boiling. Place fillets seam side down in skillet; heat to boiling.

4 Reduce heat to low; cover; simmer 6 to 8 minutes. Carefully remove fillets and drain. Arrange on warm platter; cover with foil and keep warm while preparing sauce.

5 Over high heat, heat cooking liquid in skillet until reduced to about ¼ cup. Strain and return liquid to skillet.

6 Stir in cream and tomato paste; cook, stirring constantly, until sauce boils. Pour over fish and garnish with parsley.

BAKED SOLE WITH LEMON SAUCE

- Color index page 32
- Begin 30 mins ahead
- 8 servings
- 190 cals per serving

2 16-ounce packages frozen sole, ocean perch, flounder or other fillets, thawed
1 teaspoon salt
¼ teaspoon pepper
3 tablespoons butter or margarine

2 egg yolks
1 tablespoon water
1 tablespoon all-purpose flour
¾ cup chicken broth
2 tablespoons lemon juice
Toasted almonds for garnish

1. Preheat oven to 350°F. Grease a large, shallow baking dish; arrange fillets in dish. Sprinkle with salt and pepper; dot with 2 tablespoons butter. Bake 10 minutes or until fish flakes easily.
2. Meanwhile, prepare sauce: In cup, mix egg yolks with water; set aside. In heavy 1-quart saucepan over medium heat, into 1 tablespoon hot butter or margarine, stir flour until well blended. Gradually stir in chicken broth and lemon juice and cook, stirring, until mixture is thickened; remove saucepan from heat.
3. Into egg yolks, stir small amount of hot sauce; slowly pour egg mixture into the sauce, stirring rapidly to prevent lumping. Cook, stirring, until thickened (do not boil). Spoon off any liquid from fish. Pour sauce over and garnish with almonds.

SAUTÉED FISH FILLETS WITH WALNUT COATING

- Color index page 32
- Begin 45 mins ahead
- 4 servings
- 400 cals per serving

Lime Bundles (p. 135)
⅔ cup walnuts, finely chopped
⅓ cup dried bread crumbs
1 tablespoon minced parsley

¾ teaspoon salt
1 egg
Salad oil
4 sole, flounder, or catfish fillets (about 6 ounces each)
Radishes for garnish

1. Prepare Lime Bundles; set aside.
2. On waxed paper, mix chopped walnuts, bread crumbs, minced parsley, and salt. In pie plate, beat egg slightly. Dip fillets into egg, then into walnut mixture to coat.
3. In 12-inch skillet over medium-high heat, in 2 tablespoons hot salad oil, cook two fish fillets until golden brown on both sides and fish flakes easily, about 5 minutes. Remove to warm platter; keep warm. Repeat with remaining fillets, adding more salad oil to skillet if needed.
4. Garnish platter with radishes. Serve fish fillets with Lime Bundles.

Coating the fillets: Press the mixture with your hands to be sure fillets are completely covered.

Swordfish

SWORDFISH WITH HERB BUTTER

- Color index page 31
- Begin 30 mins ahead
- 4 servings
- 395 cals per serving

2 ¾ pound swordfish steaks, each 1 inch thick
6 tablespoons butter or margarine
2 tablespoons minced shallots or green onions
1 tablespoon lemon juice
¾ teaspoon salt
½ teaspoon tarragon
½ teaspoon basil
¼ teaspoon thyme leaves
⅛ teaspoon pepper
1 tablespoon chopped parsley
Lemon wedges and parsley sprigs for garnish

1. Preheat broiler if manufacturer directs. Cut each swordfish steak crosswise in half.
2. In 1-quart saucepan over medium heat, in hot butter, cook shallots 1 minute. Remove saucepan from heat; stir in next 6 ingredients.
3. Place fish on rack in broiling pan, brush all sides with some of butter mixture. Broil 10 to 15 minutes, basting occasionally. Sprinkle with parsley. Spoon pan juices over fish and garnish.

STIR-FRIED SWORDFISH

- Color index page 32
- Begin 30 mins ahead
- 4 servings
- 355 cals per serving

1 1-pound swordfish steak, 1 inch thick
2 tablespoons dry sherry
1 tablespoon soy sauce
2 teaspoons cornstarch
½ teaspoon sugar
¼ teaspoon ground ginger
⅛ teaspoon crushed red pepper
½ pound mushrooms
½ small bunch broccoli
4 green onions
Salad oil
½ teaspoon salt
Lemon/Lime Twists (p. 100) and Scallion Pompom (p. 100) for garnish

1. Remove skin from swordfish steak; cut steak into 1-inch chunks. In medium-sized bowl, combine fish chunks and next 6 ingredients; set aside.
2. Slice mushrooms. Cut broccoli flowerets into 2" by 1" pieces; peel and cut stems into 2" by ½" strips. Cut green onions into 3-inch pieces.
3. In 5-quart Dutch oven over medium-high heat, in ¼ cup hot salad oil, cook vegetables and salt, stirring quickly and frequently until tender-crisp, about 5 minutes. Remove.
4. In same Dutch oven over medium-high heat, in 2 more tablespoons hot salad oil, cook swordfish, stirring gently, until fish is firm, about 2 minutes. Add reserved vegetables and any juices to fish; heat through and garnish.

Preparing fish: Remove skin from fish before cutting into 1-inch chunks.

Stir-frying fish: Cook until just firm; then add cooked vegetables.

Trout

PAN-FRIED TROUT WITH VEGETABLE STUFFING

- Color index page 32
- Begin 1½ hrs ahead
- 4 servings
- 545 cals per serving

Butter or margarine
6 radishes
1 medium celery stalk, thinly sliced
1 small zucchini, cut into 1" by ¼" sticks
1 small green pepper, chopped
1 small carrot, grated
Salt
1 slice white bread
4 brook trout or whiting (about ¾ pound each), dressed, with heads and tails left on if you like
1 egg
½ cup dried bread crumbs
Salad oil
½ cup water
¼ cup cooking or dry white wine
½ teaspoon chicken-flavor instant bouillon
Lemon wedges and parsley sprigs for garnish

1. In 12-inch skillet over medium heat, in 2 tablespoons hot butter or margarine, cook vegetables and ½ teaspoon salt until vegetables are tender, stirring occasionally. Place vegetables in medium bowl. Tear bread into small pieces; add to vegetables and mix well.
2. Place some vegetable stuffing in cavity of each trout. Close cavities neatly with metal skewers or toothpicks.
3. In pie plate, beat egg. On waxed paper, mix dried bread crumbs with ¾ teaspoon salt. Dip stuffed trout in egg, then into bread-crumb mixture, using hand to pat crumb mixture onto trout to coat well.
4. In 12-inch skillet over medium-high heat, in 2 tablespoons hot butter or margarine and 2 tablespoons salad oil, cook two trout about 15 minutes or until fish flakes easily when tested with a fork, carefully turning trout once with pancake turner.
5. Remove trout to warm platter; keep warm. Repeat with remaining trout, adding more butter or margarine and salad oil if necessary.
6. Into drippings remaining in skillet, stir water, wine, and bouillon; over high heat, heat wine sauce to boiling, stirring to loosen brown bits from bottom of skillet.
7. To serve, place one trout on each plate. Remove skewers or toothpicks and garnish with lemon wedges and parsley sprigs. Pour sauce from skillet over trout.

Stuffing the trout: Spoon the vegetable stuffing into the fish cavity and secure with skewer.

Coating the trout: Dip trout into beaten egg, then gently pat bread crumb mixture onto fish.

Tuna

FRESH TUNA BAKE

- Color index page 32
- Begin 50 mins ahead
- 4 servings
- 370 cals per serving

1 tuna or halibut steak, cut 1½ inches thick (about 2 pounds)
Seasoned salt
Pepper
¼ cup salad oil
4 medium tomatoes, peeled and chopped
2 tablespoons minced onion
2 garlic cloves, minced
½ teaspoon lemon juice
1 bay leaf
½ cup white wine
1 tablespoon butter or margarine
1 tablespoon all-purpose flour
Parsley sprigs for garnish

1. Preheat oven to 350°F. Sprinkle tuna with salt and pepper. In 12-inch skillet over medium heat, in hot oil, brown steak on both sides.
2. Place in 9″ by 9″ baking dish; add tomatoes and next 5 ingredients. Bake 30 minutes or until fish flakes easily when tested with a fork.
3. On warm platter, place tuna, discarding bay leaf. In 1-quart saucepan over medium heat, into hot butter, stir flour until blended. Gradually add liquid from fish; cook, stirring constantly, until thickened; pour over fish; garnish with parsley.

TUNA-NOODLE CASSEROLE

- Color index page 32
- Begin 45 mins ahead
- 6 servings
- 465 cals per serving

Butter or margarine
2 large celery stalks, thinly sliced
2 green onions, chopped
¼ cup all-purpose flour
1½ teaspoons salt
¼ teaspoon cracked pepper
3 cups milk
1 3-ounce package cream cheese, cut up
1 8-ounce package thin egg noodles
¼ cup dried bread crumbs
1 6½- ounce can tuna, drained and flaked

1. Preheat oven to 350°F. In 4-quart saucepan over medium heat, in 4 tablespoons hot butter, cook celery and green onions until tender, stirring frequently. Stir in flour, salt, and pepper until blended; cook 1 minute.
2. Gradually stir in milk; cook, stirring constantly, until mixture thickens slightly and boils. Stir in cream cheese until melted; remove from heat.
3. Meanwhile, prepare noodles as label directs; drain. In small saucepan, melt 2 tablespoons butter; stir in bread crumbs.
4. Into cheese sauce, gently stir noodles and tuna. Pour mixture into 12″ by 8″ baking dish; sprinkle with bread-crumb mixture. Bake 20 minutes or until hot and bubbly.

Baking the casserole: After pouring into dish, sprinkle with bread crumb mixture; bake until bubbly.

MOLDED TUNA PÂTÉ

This simple mold can be elegantly garnished for a special occasion or prepared quickly as a last-minute appetizer.

- Color index page 33
- Begin early in day
- 3½ cups spread
- 24 cals per tablespoon

1 3-ounce can chopped mushrooms
1 envelope unflavored gelatin
½ cup boiling water
2 6½-ounce cans tuna, drained
½ cup Green-Goddess Salad Dressing (p. 284)
½ cup pitted ripe olives
¼ cup chopped parsley
Thinly sliced radish for garnish
Lemon slices for garnish

1 Into blender, drain liquid from mushrooms; sprinkle gelatin over; let stand to soften.

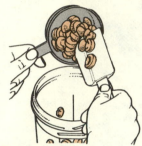

2 Add boiling water; cover and blend 10 seconds on low speed, then 20 seconds on high.

3 Add mushrooms, tuna, salad dressing, olives, and parsley; cover and blend on high speed.

4 Pour into a 1-quart greased mold; cover and refrigerate until firm.

5 To unmold, run a sharp knife between edge of mold and pâté; dip mold into hot water.

6 Place flat platter over mold; invert both together and lift off mold.

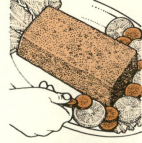

7 Garnish with overlapping slices of radish and lemon.

POULTRY

"Chicken in the bread-tray, mighty good stuff,
Mama cook him chicken an' he never get enough."

"Whoa Back, Buck" American folk song

Even before the Pilgrims arrived, native Americans enjoyed the meat of many wild birds, such as quail, goose, pheasant, and turkey, and some of these were domesticated very early. However, it is the chicken, an immigrant bird, which has become the most readily available type of poultry today.

The turkey is arguably the most American of birds. Turkey ran wild, mainly in the East, Southwest, and Mexico, long before Europeans set foot on American soil, and was part of the Indians' staple diet. There is some doubt about the story that the Indians served turkey at a feast in 1621 in Plymouth, Massachusetts, which started the tradition of Thanksgiving, but the bird was certainly presented at the Pilgrims' Thanksgiving dinner on July 30, 1623. Later, Ben Franklin became so enamored of the turkey, he proposed that it should become our national bird rather than the bald eagle. Lincoln named the last Thursday in November as the national Thanksgiving day, and although domesticated turkeys were already widely available throughout the year, many people served turkey only at Thanksgiving.

Today turkeys are sold in several forms – whole, cutlets, parts (wings, breasts, and thighs), smoked, and even pressed into turkey roll. The meat from one bird goes a long way; after a meal of roast turkey try making something different with leftovers, such as our Old-Fashioned Creamed Turkey with Biscuits or our exotic Curried Turkey with Apples and Peanuts.

Chicken was brought to America early in its history. During the seventeenth and eighteenth centuries, they were scarce, expensive, and considered a delicacy; no part of a chicken was ever wasted. By the mid-1800s, though, the breeding of poultry was well-established, and certain American breeds emerged: the Plymouth Rock, the Wyandotte, and later, the Rhode Island Red.

As chicken became more available, special dishes were created in different parts of the country. Coating parts of the chicken with flour – or dipping them into a batter – and frying them in hot fat resulted in the now famous Southern-Fried Chicken. New Englanders cut chicken into small chunks and added vegetables to fill their pot pies. Chicken-lovers in the Southwest borrowed ideas from the Mexicans and came up with Chicken Burritos and Chicken Tostadas.

Today, chickens are farmed and marketed in massive quantities – we consume an average of 33 pounds per person a year. The bird is economical and can be used in a wide variety of dishes; as a first course, a main course, part of a buffet, or in a simple sandwich.

The earliest European explorers could hardly believe the abundance of ducks in the New World. The Canvasback was probably the most commonly used duck, until the white Peking duck arrived in New York in the late 1800s, and was domesticated in Long Island, becoming known as "Long Island Duckling." Roast duckling with giblet gravy and any of a variety of stuffings can make a festive meal for any occasion. Our Breast of Duckling with Green Peppercorns makes an elegant choice for a dinner party.

Geese played a significant role in the lives of early Americans. Besides the meat they provided, their fat was used as a medicinal ointment for chest colds and their feathers supplied down for bedding and quills for pens. Geese were even good watchdogs, honking loudly at any unexpected animals, thieves, or poachers.

Goose is almost always roasted, mainly for Christmas dinner, but it certainly shouldn't be reserved for holidays alone. Along with these domesticated birds, game birds such as wild duck, pheasant, and quail often adorn American holiday tables.

Whole chicken

STUFFED CAPON WITH CRANBERRY-POACHED PEARS

This delicious bird, especially reared to improve its taste, is at its best when roasted and served with a savory stuffing.

- Color index page 34
- Begin 4 hrs ahead
- 8 servings
- 700 cals per serving

1 7-pound fresh or frozen (thawed) capon, giblets and neck reserved
Vegetable-Rice Stuffing (right)
Salad oil

Salt
Giblet Gravy (right)
Cranberry-Poached Pears (right)
About 8 Boston lettuce leaves for garnish

1 Rinse bird; drain well. Prepare the Vegetable-Rice Stuffing. Spoon some lightly into neck cavity (do not pack stuffing; it expands during cooking). Fold neck skin over the stuffing.

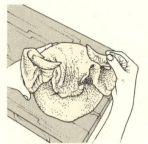

2 With capon breast side up, lift wings up toward neck, then fold under back of bird so they stay flat and keep the neck skin in place. If necessary, fasten neck skin with 1 or 2 skewers.

3 Spoon remaining stuffing lightly into body cavity. Close by folding skin lightly over opening; skewer closed. With string, tie legs and tail together.

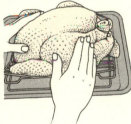

4 Place capon, breast side up, on rack in open roasting pan. Rub skin with salad oil and ½ teaspoon salt.

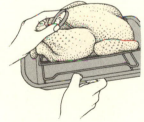

5 Insert meat thermometer into thick part between breast and thigh. Pointed end should not touch bone. Roast at 325°F, about 3 hours.

6 When golden, cover bird with tent of foil. Check for doneness during last 30 minutes. Meanwhile prepare giblets and neck for gravy, and Cranberry-Poached Pears.

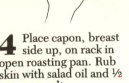

7 Remove foil during last of roasting time and, with pastry brush, brush capon generously with pan drippings for sheen. Capon is done when thermometer reaches 180° to 185°F. and thickest part of drumstick feels soft when pressed with fingers. Place capon on warm platter; let stand 20 minutes for easier carving. Meanwhile, prepare Giblet Gravy.

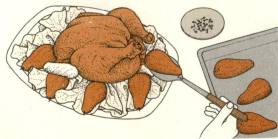

8 To serve, arrange Cranberry-Poached Pears on lettuce leaves around capon on platter.

Place a reserved whole clove in each pear half to resemble a stem. Serve with the gravy.

VEGETABLE-RICE STUFFING: Carefully rinse *½ cup wild rice* in cold running water and drain well. In 2-quart saucepan over high heat, heat *1 cup water* to boiling; stir in wild rice; heat to boiling. Reduce the heat to low; cover and simmer 45 minutes or until rice is tender and all liquid is absorbed. Meanwhile, in 3-quart saucepan over medium heat, melt *4 tablespoons butter* or *margarine*. Dice *2 medium carrots, 1 medium onion* and *1 medium celery stalk*. Add to the butter and cook until all vegetables are tender (about 7 minutes), stirring occasionally. Add *1 cup water* and *1 teaspoon chicken-flavor instant bouillon cube* or *envelope*; over high heat, heat to boiling; stir in *½ cup regular long-grain rice*; heat to boiling. Reduce heat to low; cover and simmer 20 minutes or until rice is tender and all liquid is absorbed. Stir wild rice and *1 teaspoon salt* into the rice and vegetable mixture. Use to stuff the 7-pound capon. This stuffing can also be used for a small turkey and is delicious with Rock Cornish game hen. 4 cups. 202 cals per cup.

GIBLET GRAVY FOR STUFFED CAPON: While capon is roasting, in saucepan with enough *water* to cover, heat *reserved giblets* and *neck* to boiling. Reduce heat to low; cover and simmer 1 hour or until tender. Drain, reserving broth. Pull meat from neck; discard bones. Coarsely chop neck, meat, and giblets; refrigerate. When capon is done, remove rack from roasting pan; pour pan drippings into a 2-cup measure or small bowl (set pan aside); let stand a few seconds until fat separates from meat juice. Skim 3 tablespoons fat from drippings into 1-quart saucepan; skim off and discard any remaining fat. Add reserved giblet broth to roasting pan; stir until brown bits are loosened. Add *½ teaspoon chicken-flavor instant bouillon* to meat juice in cup to make 1½ cups (add water if necessary). Into fat in saucepan over medium heat, stir *3 tablespoons all-purpose flour* until blended. Gradually stir in meat-juice mixture; cook, stirring, until mixture thickens slightly. Stir in reserved giblets and neck meat; heat through. Pour into gravy boat. 1½ cups. 74 cals per cup.

CRANBERRY-POACHED PEARS: Peel *4 large pears*. Cut each pear in half; remove core and stem. In 12-inch skillet over high heat, heat, *2 cups cranberry-juice cocktail, ½ cup sugar, ½ teaspoon whole allspice, ¼ teaspoon ground ginger, 8 whole cloves, two 3½-inch-long cinnamon sticks*, and pear halves, cut side up, to boiling. Reduce heat to low; cover and simmer 20 minutes or until pears are tender, turning pears occasionally. With slotted spoon, remove pears to 12″ by 8″ baking dish; cover and refrigerate until ready to serve. Reserve whole cloves for garnish. These pears can be done a day ahead; they will absorb more of the flavor and color of the cranberry. They also make a delicious dessert. 8 servings. 117 cals each.

Whole chicken

- Color index page 34
- Begin 3 hrs ahead
- 6 servings
- 600 cals per serving

PARTY STUFFED CHICKEN

1 3½-pound broiler-fryer
2 tablespoons butter or margarine
2 green onions, minced
¾ pound ground pork
2 slices white bread, diced
1 egg
⅓ cup milk
¾ teaspoon salt
Dry sherry
1 tablespoon salad oil
1 cup water
1 chicken-flavor bouillon cube or envelope
2 tablespoons all-purpose flour
Parsley sprigs for garnish
Pickled Peaches and Apricots (p. 379) for garnish

1. Remove giblets and neck from chicken. Reserve for use another day. Set aside chicken liver. Rinse chicken under running cold water; drain well and refrigerate.

2. Prepare stuffing: Mince chicken liver. Be sure to cut away any green spots. In 3-quart saucepan over medium heat, in hot butter or margarine, cook onions and liver until liver is firm; remove saucepan from heat.

3. Stir in the ground pork, bread, egg, milk, salt, and ¼ cup sherry; cover and refrigerate until the chicken is ready.

4. To bone the chicken: Place the chicken, breast side down, on a cutting board. With a sharp knife, or kitchen or poultry shears, cut along both sides of the backbone and discard the bone. Then, remove breastbone, wishbone, rib cage, and hip bones. If you do not have a boning knife, use a thin bladed knife.

5. Spread stuffing mixture over inside of boned chicken. Pull meat and skin over stuffing and skewer closed.

6. To reshape bird, turn chicken breast side up. Starting at neck end, with string across top of breast, bring ends of string under wings and legs; tie legs together. Fold wings under back to hold chicken steady.

7. Insert meat thermometer between breast and thigh into center of stuffing; brush bird with salad oil. Place bird, breast side up, on rack in open roasting pan.

8. Roast in 350°F. oven about 1½ hours or until meat thermometer reaches 170°F. During last 15 minutes of roasting time, brush chicken generously with pan drippings to give it an attractive sheen.

9. When chicken is done, place on warm platter and keep warm.

10. For gravy, remove rack from pan; skim all but 2 tablespoons fat from pan, leaving pan liquid and brown bits. Add water and bouillon to roasting pan; over medium heat, heat mixture to boiling, stirring to loosen brown bits. In cup, mix flour and ¼ cup sherry. Gradually stir flour mixture into hot liquid in pan; cook over medium heat, stirring until gravy thickens.

11. To serve, remove wings and set aside. Then, beginning at neck end, cut slices, ½ inch thick, through chicken and stuffing. Arrange on a platter; garnish with parsley and Pickled Peaches and Apricots. Pass the gravy separately.

PREPARING PARTY POULTRY

Any kind of poultry can be boned and stuffed to make a spectacular presentation for a party. Although it takes a little more time to prepare, it can be done in advance and refrigerated until ready to cook. When it comes time to carve the bird, it's as simple as slicing bread!

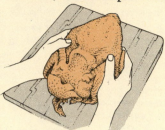

To bone poultry: Place the bird, breast side down, on a cutting board.

With a sharp knife or kitchen shears, starting at body cavity, cut along both sides of backbone to the neck; discard bone. This opens the bird.

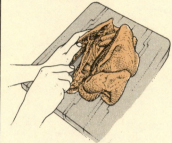

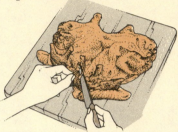

Remove breastbone by separating the flesh from the bone with the knife, always following along the breastbone as a guide.

Remove the wishbone and hip-bones. Leave the wing tips and drumsticks to keep the shape. Lay bird open on the cutting board.

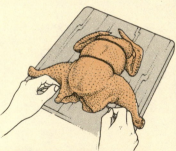

Spread the stuffing over the inside of the boned bird. Pull meat and skin over stuffing and skewer closed.

To shape: Turn breast side up. Start at neck end; with string across top of breast, tie under the wings and again under the legs.

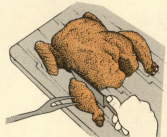

Tie legs together and fold wings under to hold bird steady.

To carve: Remove string; remove legs from body and carve thin slices. Serve hot or cold.

Cut-up chicken

SOUTHERN-FRIED CHICKEN

Finger-licking good, this Southern favorite is a real family-pleaser. Serve it hot with traditional cream gravy, or cold for a picnic.

- Color index page 35
- Begin 2 hrs ahead
- 8 servings
- 111 cals per serving

Salad oil
½ cup milk
½ teaspoon pepper
2 cups all-purpose flour
Salt
2 3- to 3½-pound broiler-fryers, cut up

1½ cups water
1 cup half-and-half
1 chicken-flavor bouillon cube or envelope

1 In 12-inch skillet over medium heat, heat ¼ inch salad oil to 350°F. on deep-fat thermometer. (Or heat oil in deep-fat fryer set at 350°F.)

2 Into pie plate, pour milk. On sheet of waxed paper, combine pepper, 1¾ cups of flour, and 2 teaspoons salt; dip chicken pieces in milk, then coat with flour mixture.

3 With tongs, carefully place ⅓ of chicken pieces, skin side up, in hot oil. Cook 10 to 12 minutes until underside of chicken is golden.

4 Turn chicken, skin side down; cook 10 to 12 minutes longer until fork-tender and skin of chicken is golden brown and crisp.

5 Remove chicken pieces, skin side up, to paper towels to drain. Keep warm. Repeat with remaining chicken.

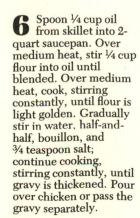

6 Spoon ¼ cup oil from skillet into 2-quart saucepan. Over medium heat, stir ¼ cup flour into oil until blended. Over medium heat, cook, stirring constantly, until flour is light golden. Gradually stir in water, half-and-half, bouillon, and ¾ teaspoon salt; continue cooking, stirring constantly, until gravy is thickened. Pour over chicken or pass the gravy separately.

PAPRIKA BROILED CHICKEN

- Color index page 34
- Begin 50 mins ahead
- 4 servings
- 345 cals per serving

1 2½-pound broiler-fryer, cut into quarters
¾ teaspoon paprika, or rosemary or dill, crushed
¾ teaspoon salt

⅛ teaspoon coarsely ground black pepper
3 tablespoons butter or margarine, cut up
1 tablespoon lemon juice

1. Preheat broiler if manufacturer directs. Sprinkle chicken quarters with paprika, rosemary or dill, salt, and pepper.
2. Place chicken quarters, skin side down, in broiling pan. Dot chicken with butter or margarine; pour lemon juice over chicken.
3. About 7 to 9 inches from source of heat (or at 450°F.), broil chicken 5 minutes, basting with melted butter in broiling pan; broil 20 minutes longer. Turn chicken and broil 15 to 20 minutes longer until fork-tender, basting with pan drippings occasionally.
4. To serve, arrange chicken quarters on platter; spoon drippings over chicken.

FARMHOUSE CHICKEN

- Color index page 34
- Begin 1 hr ahead
- 5 servings
- 610 cals per serving

4 slices bacon, diced
1 3-pound broiler-fryer, cut up
1 teaspoon salt
¼ teaspoon pepper
2 medium onions, diced
1 garlic clove, minced
½ teaspoon chili powder
2 cups water
1 chicken-flavor bouillon cube or envelope
1 cup regular long-grain rice

1 large green pepper, cut into 1-inch-wide strips
1 medium butternut squash (about 2 pounds), peeled and cut into 1-inch chunks
1 10- to 12-ounce container Brussels sprouts or 1 10-ounce package frozen broccoli

1. In 8-quart Dutch oven over medium-low heat, cook diced bacon until browned. Remove bacon to paper towels to drain. Discard all but 2 tablespoons bacon drippings.
2. Rub chicken pieces with salt and pepper. Add chicken to bacon drippings in Dutch oven; cook over medium-high heat until chicken is well browned on all sides. Remove chicken to plate.
3. In drippings in Dutch oven over medium heat, cook onions, garlic, and chili powder until onions are tender, stirring occasionally. Add water and bouillon, stirring to loosen brown bits on bottom of Dutch oven.
4. Return chicken to Dutch oven; over high heat, heat to boiling. Reduce heat to low; cover and simmer 10 minutes.
5. Skim off fat from liquid in Dutch oven. Stir rice, green pepper, squash, and Brussels sprouts into mixture in Dutch oven; over high heat, heat to boiling.
6. Reduce heat to low; cover and simmer 30 to 40 minutes or until rice and chicken are tender, stirring occasionally. Spoon chicken mixture onto warm large platter; sprinkle with bacon.

Cut-up chicken

CHICKEN FRICASSEE WITH DUMPLINGS

Once considered a humble meal because tired old chickens were used, this creamy stew is a hearty dish that satisfies everyone.

- *Color index page 35*
- *Begin 1hr ahead*
- *4 servings*
- *541 cals per serving*

1/4 cup all-purpose flour
2 teaspoons salt
1 teaspoon paprika
1/8 teaspoon pepper
1 2½- to 3-pound broiler-fryer, cut up
3 tablespoons salad oil
2 medium celery stalks, thinly sliced

2 medium carrots, thinly sliced
1 small onion, sliced
1 10¾-ounce can condensed cream of chicken soup
Milk
1 cup buttermilk-baking mix

1 On waxed paper, combine flour, salt, paprika, and pepper; coat chicken with flour mixture.

2 In 12-inch skillet over medium-high heat, in hot salad oil, cook chicken until browned. Set aside.

3 In drippings remaining in skillet, over medium heat, cook celery, carrots, and onion until tender, stirring occasionally.

4 Return chicken to skillet; stir in undiluted soup and 1½ cups milk; heat to boiling. Reduce heat to low; cover and simmer 25 minutes.

5 In small bowl with fork, stir buttermilk-baking mix and 1/3 cup milk just until blended. (Dough is soft.)

6 Drop dough by heaping tablespoons into simmering liquid. Cover; cook 10 minutes until dumplings are set.

CHICKEN CACCIATORE

- *Color index page 35*
- *Begin 1 hr ahead*
- *4 servings*
- *326 cals per serving*

1 tablespoon salad oil
1 3- to 3½-pound broiler-fryer, cut up into serving-size pieces
1 14½- to 16-ounce can tomatoes
½ cup Chianti or other dry red wine
2 teaspoons garlic salt

¾ teaspoon basil
¼ teaspoon pepper
12 small white onions, peeled
2 large green peppers, cut into ½-inch strips
1 tablespoon cornstarch
1 tablespoon water

1. In 12-inch skillet over medium-high heat, in hot salad oil, cook chicken until well browned.
2. Stir in tomatoes with their liquid, wine, garlic salt, basil, and pepper; heat to boiling. Reduce heat to low; cover and simmer 15 minutes.
3. Add onions and green peppers; cover and simmer 15 minutes longer or just until vegetables are fork-tender.
4. In cup, stir cornstarch and water until smooth. Gradually stir into chicken mixture and cook, stirring frequently, until mixture is boiling and thickened and chicken is fork-tender.

CHICKEN AND OYSTER GUMBO

- *Color index page 35*
- *Begin 1½ hrs ahead*
- *6 servings*
- *615 cals per serving*

½ cup all-purpose flour
½ teaspoon salt
¼ teaspoon pepper
1 3-pound broiler-fryer, cut up
3 tablespoons salad oil
2 medium celery stalks, diced
1 large green pepper, diced
1 large onion, diced
4 cups water

½ teaspoon hot-pepper sauce
¼ teaspoon cumin
2 chicken-flavor bouillon cubes or envelopes
1 10-ounce package frozen cut okra
1 cup regular long-grain rice
1 8-ounce container shucked oysters

1. On waxed paper, mix flour, salt, and pepper. Coat chicken pieces with flour mixture; reserve any leftover flour mixture.
2. In 5-quart Dutch oven over medium-high heat, in hot salad oil, cook chicken, a few pieces at a time, until browned on all sides. Remove chicken pieces to plate as they brown; set aside.
3. Into drippings remaining in Dutch oven, stir reserved flour mixture; cook, stirring constantly, until flour is dark brown (mixture will be thick). Add celery, green pepper, and onion; cook over medium heat until vegetables are tender, stirring occasionally. Gradually stir in water, hot-pepper sauce, cumin, and bouillon until blended.
4. Add frozen okra and chicken to Dutch oven; over high heat, heat to boiling. Reduce heat to low; cover and simmer 30 to 35 minutes. Meanwhile, prepare rice as label directs; keep warm.
5. When chicken is done, increase heat to medium-high; add oysters with their liquid; cook 5 minutes or until edges begin to curl.
6. To serve, skim off fat from liquid in Dutch oven. Spoon gumbo mixture into 6 large soup bowls. Spoon scoop of rice on top of gumbo.

CHICKEN TOSTADAS

Taking their name from the Spanish for "toasted," these crispy fried tortillas are a classic of the Southwestern table.

- Color index page 36
- Begin 2 hrs ahead
- 4 servings
- 472 cals per serving

1 2½-pound broiler-fryer
Salt
Water
Avocado Butter (right)
Salsa Cruda (right)
Salad oil

1 medium onion, finely chopped
1 garlic clove, minced
1 4-ounce can chopped green chilies, drained
½ cup sour cream

4 6-inch flour tortillas
½ small head iceberg lettuce, shredded

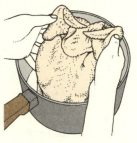

1 Rinse chicken, its giblets, and neck with runnng cold water. Place chicken, breast side down, in saucepan just large enough to hold the chicken (3- to 4-quart saucepan).

2 Add giblets, neck, 1 teaspoon salt, and 2 inches water; over high heat, heat to boiling. Reduce heat to low; cover saucepan and simmer 35 minutes or until chicken is fork-tender.

3 Remove to large bowl; refrigerate 30 minutes. Discard skin and bones from chicken; chop meat and giblets. Cover to prevent them drying out. Set aside.

4 Meanwhile, prepare Avocado Butter and Salsa Cruda; cover and refrigerate.

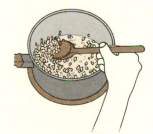

5 In 3-quart saucepan over medium heat, in 2 tablespoons hot salad oil, cook onion and garlic until tender, stirring occasionally.

6 Add chopped chicken, giblets, green chilies, sour cream, and ¾ teaspoon salt; cook over medium heat until hot; keep warm.

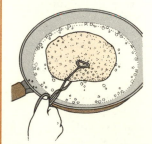

7 In 10-inch skillet over medium heat, in ¼ inch hot salad oil, fry 1 tortilla at a time, about 30 seconds on each side until lightly browned.

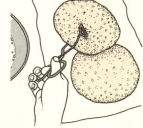

8 With tongs, remove each tortilla to paper towels to drain. Cover with cloth to keep warm until all are fried.

9 On each tortilla, arrange one fourth lettuce and one fourth chicken mixture. Serve with Avocado Butter and Salsa Cruda.

AVOCADO BUTTER: In small bowl mix 3 *tablespoons salad oil*, 2 *tablespoons cider vinegar*, 2 *teaspoons minced pickled jalapeño chili*, ½ *teaspoon sugar*, ½ *teaspoon salt*, 1 *medium avocado*, peeled and diced, and 1 *medium tomato*, diced. 1 cup. 30 cals per tablespoon.

SALSA CRUDA (Red Table Sauce): In small bowl, mix 2 *fresh* or *canned pickled minced jalapeño chilies*, 2 *medium minced tomatoes*, 1 *small grated onion*, 1 to 2 *teaspoons minced fresh coriander leaves* and ½ *teaspoon salt*. Cover; chill. 1½ cups. 5 cals per tablespoon.

CHICKEN YUCATAN

4 medium hot red or green peppers or jalapeño peppers
4 garlic cloves, unpeeled
1 small onion
⅓ cup whole blanched almonds
1½ teaspoons salt
½ teaspoon oregano leaves
¼ teaspoon cracked pepper

Water
White vinegar
1 3- to 3½-pound broiler-fryer, cut up
¼ cup peanut or salad oil
Romaine lettuce leaves for garnish
1 tablespoon all-purpose flour

1. Thread peppers and garlic cloves on long metal skewer. Rotate skewer slowly over gas flame (or electric element) on range until outside of peppers and garlic are charred. Remove peel from 1 garlic clove; set aside.
2. Mince half of onion; set aside; cut remaining half into chunks. In blender at medium speed or in food processor with knife blade attached, blend almonds until finely ground. Add peeled garlic clove, onion chunks, salt, oregano, cracked pepper, 2 tablespoons water, and 1 teaspoon vinegar; blend on medium speed until smooth.
3. Spread almond mixture over chicken pieces to coat well. In 12-inch skillet over medium-high heat, in hot peanut oil, cook chicken until browned on all sides. Remove chicken to bowl; set aside.
4. In drippings remaining in skillet over medium heat, cook minced onion until tender, stirring occasionally. Return chicken to skillet; add peppers, unpeeled garlic, ¾ cup water, and 1 teaspoon vinegar.
5. Over high heat, heat to boiling. Reduce heat to low; cover and simmer 30 minutes or until chicken is fork-tender, stirring occasionally. With slotted spoon, remove chicken, peppers, and garlic to romaine-lined platter. Skim off fat from liquid in skillet.
6. In cup, mix flour and ¼ cup water. Gradually stir flour mixture into liquid in skillet; cook over medium heat until slightly thickened, stirring constantly. Serve with chicken.

- Color index page 36
- Begin 1¼ hrs ahead
- 4 servings
- 423 cals per serving

Cut-up chicken

CHICKEN HAVANA

This sweet and spicy chicken, with its raisins, bananas, ham, and chilies, was introduced by our Caribbean neighbors.

- *Color index page 37*
- *Begin 1 hr ahead*
- *6 servings*
- *320 cals per serving*

¼ cup golden raisins
¼ cup white wine vinegar
2 tablespoons salad oil
1 2½-pound broiler-fryer, cut up
¼ pound cooked ham, diced

1 14½- to 16-ounce can tomatoes
1 4-ounce can green chilies, drained and cut into strips
1 tablespoon light brown sugar
2 firm small bananas

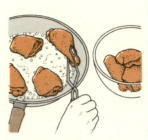

1 In small bowl, mix raisins with white wine vinegar; set aside.

2 In 12-inch skillet over medium-high heat, in hot salad oil, cook chicken pieces, a few at a time, until browned on all sides; remove pieces to bowl as they brown.

3 In drippings remaining in the skillet, over medium heat, cook the diced ham until it is lightly browned.

4 Add tomatoes with their liquid, green chilies, brown sugar, and chicken; over high heat, heat to boiling. Reduce heat to low; cover and simmer 20 minutes.

5 Add raisin mixture; cover; simmer 15 minutes more, until chicken is fork-tender. Skim off fat from liquid in skillet.

6 Slice bananas diagonally into ½-inch pieces; gently stir into chicken mixture; heat through.

COUNTRY CAPTAIN

- *Color index page 34*
- *Begin 1 hr ahead*
- *4 servings*
- *855 cals per serving*

1 3-pound broiler-fryer, cut up
⅓ cup all-purpose flour
¼ cup salad oil
2 medium onions, thinly sliced
1 garlic clove
1 medium green pepper, chopped
1 large celery stalk, chopped

1 tablespoon curry powder
1½ teaspoons salt
1 28-ounce can tomatoes
½ cup dark seedless raisins
⅓ cup slivered blanched almonds, toasted
1 tablespoon chopped parsley
Hot cooked rice (optional)

1. On waxed paper, coat chicken pieces with flour. In 12-inch skillet over medium-high heat, in hot salad oil, cook chicken, a few pieces at a time, until browned on all sides, removing pieces to bowl as they brown.

2. In drippings remaining in skillet, over medium heat, cook onions, garlic, green pepper, celery, curry powder, and salt, stirring occasionally, until vegetables are tender.

3. Stir in tomatoes with their liquid and raisins. Return chicken pieces to skillet; over high heat, heat to boiling. Reduce heat to low; cover and simmer 30 minutes or until the chicken is fork-tender.

4. To serve, arrange chicken pieces in warm deep platter. Remove garlic from sauce; spoon sauce over chicken; sprinkle with almonds and parsley. If you like, serve with hot cooked rice.

CHICKEN NAPA VALLEY

- *Color index page 34*
- *Begin 1¼ hrs ahead*
- *8 servings*
- *525 cals per serving*

¼ cup olive oil
2 garlic cloves, quartered
4 whole medium chicken breasts, boned and each cut in half
2 pounds hot Italian-sausage links
2 cups Napa Valley or other medium or dry white wine

½ pound mushrooms, sliced
½ teaspoon salt
¼ cup water
2 tablespoons cornstarch

1. In 12-inch skillet over medium heat, in hot olive oil, cook garlic until golden; with slotted spoon, remove garlic from oil; discard garlic.

2. In drippings in skillet, over medium-high heat, cook chicken and sausages, a few pieces at a time, until browned on all sides. Spoon off all but 2 tablespoons drippings. Slice sausages into ½-inch thick pieces; return to skillet with the chicken. Stir in wine, mushrooms, and salt; heat to boiling.

3. Reduce heat to low; cover skillet and simmer 30 minutes or until chicken is fork-tender, basting occasionally with liquid in skillet. Arrange chicken and sausages on warm platter.

4. In cup, blend water and cornstarch until smooth; gradually stir into hot liquid and cook over medium heat, stirring constantly, until mixture thickens and boils. Spoon some sauce over chicken. Pass remaining sauce in gravy boat.

JAMBALAYA CHICKEN

- Color index page 35
- Begin 2 hrs ahead
- 8 servings
- 416 cals per serving

1 3- to 3½-pound broiler-fryer
2 celery stalks, sliced
1 medium carrot, sliced
Salt
Water
2 tablespoons salad oil
4 chorizos (Spanish sausage) or ½ pound pork sausage links, cut into 1-inch chunks
1¼ cups regular long-grain rice
2 medium green peppers, cut into 1-inch chunks
1 medium onion, minced
1 garlic clove, crushed
1 14½- to 16-ounce can tomatoes
½ teaspoon thyme leaves
1 4-ounce jar pimentos, drained and diced
½ pound cooked ham, cut into bite-sized chunks
3 or 4 drops hot-pepper sauce

1. Rinse chicken and its giblets with running cold water. In 5-quart saucepot or Dutch oven over high heat, heat chicken, giblets, celery, carrot, 1¼ teaspoons salt, and 2 inches water to boiling. Reduce heat to low; cover and simmer 30 minutes or until chicken is fork-tender.
2. Remove chicken to large bowl; refrigerate 30 minutes or until easy to handle. Remove and discard chicken bones and skin; cut meat and giblets into bite-sized pieces; set aside.
3. Meanwhile, skim fat from broth; measure 1¾ cups broth; reserve. (Cover and refrigerate remaining broth and vegetables for favorite soup another day.)
4. In 12-inch skillet over medium heat, in hot oil, brown chorizos. With slotted spoon, remove chorizos to small bowl; set aside.
5. In same skillet over medium heat, in remaining oil, cook rice, green peppers, onion, and garlic until rice is lightly browned. Stir in reserved chicken broth, tomatoes with their liquid, thyme, and ½ teaspoon salt; heat to boiling. Reduce the heat to low. Cover skillet and simmer 15 minutes.
6. Stir in pimentos, ham, chicken, chorizos, and hot-pepper sauce; cook, covered, about 15 minutes or until rice is tender and all liquid is absorbed, stirring occasionally. Serve directly from the skillet or spoon Jambalaya into a large deep bowl.

Preparing the chicken meat: After discarding all the bones and skin from the cooked chicken, cut the meat and giblets into bite-sized pieces.

Skimming the fat: With a large spoon, carefully skim the chicken fat from the top of the broth in the Dutch oven. Then pour out 1¾ cups of broth.

STUFFED CHICKEN QUARTERS WITH CHERRY TOMATOES

Placed in a pocket made in the skin, this cheesy-vegetable filling makes a simple dish into something special.

- Color index page 36
- Begin 1½ hrs ahead
- 4 servings
- 548 cals per serving

3 tablespoons butter or margarine
2 medium zucchini (1 pound), shredded
3 slices white bread
1 egg
½ cup shredded Swiss cheese (2 ounces)
⅛ teaspoon pepper
Salt
1 2½- to 3-pound broiler-fryer, cut into quarters
Pan-Fried Cherry Tomatoes (p.247)
2 tablespoons honey

1 Prepare stuffing: In 2-quart saucepan over medium heat, melt butter; add zucchini; cook until tender, about 2 minutes, stirring.

2 Remove from heat. Into saucepan, tear bread in small pieces; stir in egg, cheese, pepper, and ½ teaspoon salt.

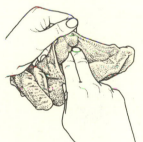

3 Preheat oven to 400°F. Carefully loosen the skin on each chicken quarter by pushing the fingers gently between skin and meat to form a pocket.

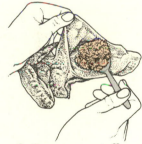

4 Spoon some stuffing into each pocket. Place chicken in 13" by 9" baking pan; bake 50 minutes or until fork-tender. Prepare Pan-Fried Cherry Tomatoes.

5 Remove chicken to warm platter; brush with honey and sprinkle lightly with salt. Serve with Pan-Fried Cherry Tomatoes.

Cut-up chicken

DEEP-DISH CHICKEN PIE

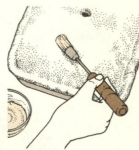

- Color index page 35
- Begin 2½ hours ahead
- 8 servings
- 399 cals (peas) 535 cals (beans) per serving

2 2½-pound broiler-fryers, cut up
½ teaspoon pepper
½ teaspoon marjoram leaves
2 bay leaves
Water
Salt
2 large carrots, sliced
1 large celery stalk, sliced
¾ pound small white onions
All-purpose flour
1¾ cups half-and-half
1 10-ounce package frozen peas or baby lima beans, thawed
½ pound small mushrooms, each cut in half
Flaky Pastry (p.310)
1 egg yolk

1. In 5-quart Dutch oven over high heat, heat first 4 ingredients, 4 cups water, and 2 teaspoons salt to boiling. Reduce heat to low; cover and simmer 35 minutes or until the chicken is fork-tender.
2. When chicken is done, reserve 1 cup broth. Cool chicken slightly; remove and discard bones and skin; cut meat into 1-inch pieces.
3. In 3-quart saucepan over high heat, heat carrots, celery, onions, and reserved broth to boiling. Reduce heat to low; cover and simmer 10 minutes or until vegetables are almost tender. Remove from heat. Remove vegetables to small bowl, leaving broth in saucepan.
4. In small bowl with fork, blend ⅓ cup flour with ¾ cup half-and-half; gradually stir into broth in saucepan until smooth; stir in remaining half-and-half. Over low heat, cook, stirring constantly, until sauce is thickened.
5. Stir in chicken, cooked vegetables, peas or lima beans, mushrooms, and 1½ teaspoons salt. Spoon chicken mixture into 13″ by 9″ baking dish. Preheat oven to 350°F. Prepare Flaky Pastry, steps 1 to 3.
6. On lightly floured surface with lightly floured rolling pin, roll dough into 14″ by 10″ rectangle. With a knife, cut out a small circle in center of pastry. (This will allow the steam to escape.) Place pastry loosely over filling.
7. Trim edge, leaving 1-inch overhang; fold overhang under; make a high stand-up edge. Crimp the edges of the pastry; use any trimmings to cut small leaves for decoration.
8. In cup, mix yolk well with 1 teaspoon water; brush pastry. Bake 1 hour or until golden brown.

Shaping the crust: Carefully fold the overhanging pastry under and shape a high stand-up edge.

Brushing the pastry: Mix yolk well with 1 teaspoon water. Brush mixture over pie top to glaze.

BRUNSWICK STEW

- Color index page 36
- Begin 3 hrs ahead
- 10 servings
- 393 cals per serving

¼ cup salad oil
3 celery stalks, sliced (1 cup)
2 medium onions, sliced
1 2½ to 3-pound broiler-fryer, cut up, or 2½ to 3-pound package frozen rabbit, thawed
2 pounds beef for stew, cut into 1-inch chunks
1 28-ounce can tomatoes
2 teaspoons salt
3 medium potatoes (1 pound), peeled and grated
½ teaspoon basil
½ teaspoon crushed red pepper
¼ teaspoon pepper
1 10-ounce package frozen lima beans
1 10-ounce package frozen whole kernel corn

1. In 8-quart Dutch oven medium heat, in hot salad oil, cook celery and onion until lightly browned. With slotted spoon, remove vegetables to small bowl; set aside.
2. In hot oil remaining in Dutch oven, cook chicken, then beef, a few pieces at a time, until well browned on all sides; set aside.
3. Return chicken, beef, and onion mixture to Dutch oven; stir in tomatoes with their liquid and next 5 ingredients; heat to boiling. Reduce heat to low; cover and simmer 35 minutes or until chicken is fork-tender, stirring occasionally. (If using rabbit simmer 1 hour.) Remove chicken to plate; set aside. Continue cooking beef mixture until meat is fork-tender, about 1 hour longer, stirring occasionally.
4. Meanwhile, cool chicken until easy to handle; discard bones and skin; cut meat into bite-sized pieces. When beef is done, return chicken to Dutch oven. Stir in frozen beans and corn and cook until hot, about 10 minutes.

LOUISIANA CHICKEN CASSEROLE

- Color index page 35
- Begin 1½ hrs ahead
- 8 servings
- 360 cals per serving

¼ cup salad oil
2 2½-pound broiler-fryers, cut up
½ cup all-purpose flour
4 medium celery stalks, thinly sliced
3 medium green peppers, cut into thin strips
2 medium onions, diced
2 chicken-flavor bouillon cubes or envelopes
3 cups water
2¼ teaspoons salt
½ teaspoon hot-pepper sauce

1. In 12-inch skillet over medium-high heat, in hot salad oil, cook chicken, a few pieces at a time, until browned on all sides. Remove chicken pieces as they brown to 4- or 5-quart casserole.
2. Into hot drippings in skillet over medium heat, stir flour; cook, stirring constantly, until flour is dark brown. Add celery, green peppers, and onions; cook until vegetables are tender, stirring frequently. Stir in bouillon, water, salt, and hot-pepper sauce; over high heat, heat mixture to boiling.
3. Preheat oven to 350°F. Pour sauce over chicken in casserole. Bake casserole, uncovered, 45 minutes or until chicken is fork-tender, occasionally basting chicken with sauce in casserole. Skim fat from sauce.

Chicken legs and thighs

SHRIMP-STUFFED CHICKEN LEGS

Prized for its juiciness and flavor, dark chicken meat, found in legs (and thighs) is especially delicious when filled with a delicate stuffing and baked.

- Color index page 36
- Begin 1¼ hrs ahead
- 6 servings
- 420 cals per serving

1 pound medium shrimp
1 green onion
1 tablespoon cooking or
   dry sherry
¼ teaspoon ground
   ginger
Salt
1 slice white bread
6 chicken legs
2 tablespoons butter or
   margarine
2 large zucchini (about
   12 ounces each)
2 tablespoons salad oil
Pepper

1 Prepare stuffing: Shell and devein shrimp; rinse and pat dry with paper towels. Mince shrimp. Mince green onion.

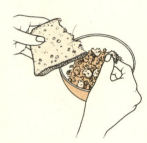

2 In small bowl, combine shrimp, green onion, sherry, ginger, and ½ teaspoon salt. Into shrimp mixture, tear bread into small pieces; mix well.

3 Preheat oven to 400°F. Carefully push fingers between the skin and meat of each chicken leg being sure not to break the skin. This will form a pocket. Place some shrimp stuffing in each pocket.

4 Rub each of the chicken legs with ¼ teaspoon salt; place each leg, stuffing side up, in an open roasting pan. Pull or dice the butter into small pieces; dot each of the chicken legs with butter pieces.

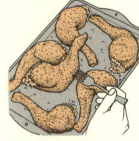

5 Bake 40 to 45 minutes until chicken is browned and fork-tender, basting chicken occasionally with pan drippings. (To prevent chicken from sticking to pan, move chicken slightly after 5 to 10 minutes of baking.)

6 About 15 minutes before the chicken is finished, slice the zucchini diagonally into ½-inch-thick pieces. Season lightly with salt and pepper to taste.

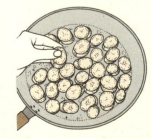

7 In 12-inch skillet over medium heat, in hot salad oil, arrange the zucchini slices in one layer if possible.

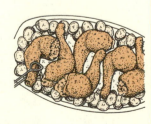

8 Cook until zucchini slices are lightly browned on both sides and tender-crisp. (Do not overcook.) To serve, arrange the shrimp-stuffed chicken legs and zucchini slices a on warm serving platter.

DEVILED CHICKEN LEGS

2 tablespoons salad oil
6 medium chicken legs
   (about 3 pounds)
1 medium onion, chopped
½ cup water
¼ cup prepared mustard
1 tablespoon prepared
   horseradish
1 tablespoon
   Worcestershire
1 teaspoon sugar or
   brown sugar
¼ teaspoon salt
1 tablespoon chopped
   parsley for garnish

1. In 5-quart Dutch oven or 12-inch skillet over medium-high heat, in hot salad oil, cook chicken legs, a few at a time, until browned on all sides, removing to plate as they brown; set aside.
2. In drippings remaining in Dutch oven over medium heat, cook onion until tender, stirring occasionally. Return browned chicken legs to Dutch oven; stir in water and remaining ingredients except parsley; over high heat, heat to boiling.
3. Reduce heat to low; cover and simmer 30 minutes or until chicken is fork-tender, stirring occasionally. Arrange chicken on warm platter. Skim off fat from liquid in Dutch oven; pour liquid over chicken; garnish with parsley.

- Color index page 36
- Begin 1 hr ahead
- 6 servings
- 350 cals per serving

BAKED CRISPY CHICKEN THIGHS

4 tablespoons butter or
   margarine
¾ cup dried bread
   crumbs
¾ teaspoon salt
⅛ teaspoon coarsely
   ground black pepper
3 tablespoons prepared
   mustard
2 tablespoons honey
1 teaspoon lemon juice
½ teaspoon ground
   ginger
1 garlic clove, crushed
8 medium chicken thighs
   (about 2 pounds)
1 16-ounce bag frozen
   crinkle-cut French-
   fried potatoes

1. Preheat oven to 425°F. In large roasting pan (about 15½" by 10½") in oven, melt butter or margarine. Remove pan from oven.
2. Meanwhile, on waxed paper, combine bread crumbs, salt, and pepper; set mixture aside. In large bowl, mix mustard, honey, lemon juice, ground ginger, and garlic. Add chicken thighs; with hand, mix until each chicken thigh is coated with mustard mixture. Then coat chicken thighs with bread-crumb mixture.
3. Arrange coated chicken thighs, skin side down, in melted butter in roasting pan. Bake 35 minutes. Turn thighs and bake 10 minutes longer or until golden brown and fork-tender.
4. While chicken is baking, prepare French-fried potatoes in skillet as label directs. Serve chicken with French-fried potatoes. Thighs can be refrigerated and served cold the next day.

- Color index page 36
- Begin 1 hr ahead
- 4 servings
- 590 cals per serving

Chicken breasts

BEER-BATTER CHICKEN ROLLS

These sophisticated chicken rolls with their lemon-butter filling and crisp beer-batter coating are an elegant alternative to the down-home batter-fried chicken.

6 tablespoons butter or margarine, softened
1 tablespoon chopped parsley
1 tablespoon lemon juice
1/8 teaspoon ground red pepper

Salt
4 whole large chicken breasts, skinned, boned, and halved
Salad oil
3/4 cup all-purpose flour
1 tablespoon sugar

1/2 teaspoon baking powder
1/2 cup beer
1 egg

- Color index page 36
- Begin 2 hrs ahead
- 8 servings
- 430 cals per serving

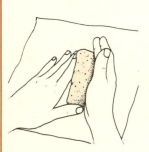

1 In small bowl, mix first 4 ingredients and 1/4 teaspoon salt. On waxed paper, pat butter mixture into a 6" by 1 1/2" piece; cover and freeze until firm, about 1 hour.

2 With meat mallet or dull edge of French knife, pound each chicken-breast half to 1/4-inch thickness; sprinkle lightly with salt.

3 Take prepared frozen butter mixture from the refrigerator and cut mixture crosswise into 8 chunks. Place one butter-mixture chunk at a narrow end of a chicken-breast half. Starting at same narrow end, roll up chicken-breast half, carefully bringing sides up over butter mixture to enclose mixture completely.

4 Secure chicken-breast rolls with toothpicks. Repeat with remaining chicken and butter mixture. Refrigerate 20 minutes.

5 In 12-inch skillet over medium heat, heat 1 inch salad oil to 350°F. on deep-fat thermometer (or heat in electric skillet at 350°F).

6 Meanwhile, in medium bowl with fork, combine flour, sugar, baking powder, and 1 teaspoon salt.

7 In small bowl with fork, beat beer, egg, and 2 teaspoons salad oil; stir into flour mixture until well mixed.

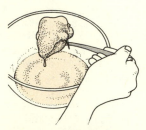

8 Dip prepared chicken into batter to coat. Cook in hot salad oil 15 minutes, turning occasionally, until golden-brown.

9 Remove cooked chicken rolls to paper towels to drain. Remove toothpicks; serve on warm platters.

CHICKEN BREASTS IN A PECAN CRUST

2 whole large chicken breasts, halved
2 tablespoons maple-flavor syrup
1 cup pecans, coarsely chopped
3 tablespoons all-purpose flour

1 teaspoon salt
2 tablespoons butter or margarine
2 tablespoons salad oil
Watercress sprigs for garnish
Lemon slices for garnish

1. On cutting board, place breast half skin side up. With tip of sharp knife, starting parallel and close to large end of rib bone, cut and scrape meat away from bone and rib cage.
2. Gently pull back meat in one piece as you cut. Discard bone and cut off white tendon.
3. Brush chicken breasts all over with maple syrup. On waxed paper, combine next 3 ingredients; coat breasts completely with mixture.
4. In 12-inch skillet over medium heat, heat butter and salad oil until butter melts; add chicken breasts.
5. Cook 12 to 15 minutes until chicken is browned on all sides and tender, turning chicken once and adding more salad oil if needed. To serve, arrange chicken on warm platter; garnish.

- Color index page 36
- Begin 40 mins ahead
- 4 servings
- 610 cals per serving

CHILLED ORANGE CHICKEN

8 whole large chicken breasts
1 1/2 teaspoons rosemary, crushed
Salt

1/2 12-ounce jar orange marmalade
1 tablespoon salad oil
16 small romaine lettuce leaves

1. With sharp knife, cut each chicken breast in half. Remove bones from each chicken-breast half but leave skin on. In large bowl, with hands, toss chicken-breast halves with rosemary and 5 teaspoons salt; cover bowl and refrigerate chicken about 4 hours to develop flavor.
2. Preheat oven to 400°F. Arrange chicken-breast halves, skin side up, in large roasting pan, overlapping chicken halves to fit, if necessary. Bake chicken about 40 minutes or until chicken is fork-tender, basting occasionally with the drippings in the pan. Remove chicken breast halves, skin side up, to a jelly-roll pan.
3. In 1-quart saucepan over low heat, heat orange marmalade, salad oil, and 1/4 teaspoon salt until marmalade is melted. Brush chicken with marmalade mixture. Cover and refrigerate at least 1 hour or until chicken is cool.
4. To serve, slice each chicken-breast half crosswise into 1/4-inch-thick slices, keeping slices together in the shape of a breast half. Place each sliced breast half on a romaine leaf on platter.

- Color index page 35
- Begin 6 hrs or day ahead
- 16 servings
- 255 cals per serving

STEAMING AND FOLDING TORTILLAS

Steaming tortillas to soften them for fillings can be done while the fillings are being prepared. If you have purchased tortillas, the directions for steaming are often on the label.

To steam:
In a skillet or roasting pan in ½ inch water, place 3 small ramekins or three oven-safe cups.

Arrange the tortillas in a stack on a large, oven-safe plate.

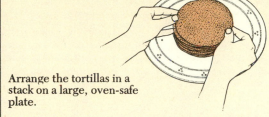

Set plate on top of ramekins or cups above water. Cover loosely with foil.

Heat the water to boiling; reduce the heat to low; cover and "steam" tortillas 10 minutes until soft and hot.

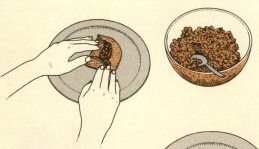

To fold:
When filled, fold left side of tortilla over the filling; turn the bottom up. This keeps the filling from falling out. Then fold the right side over to seal and form a small package.

CHICKEN BURRITOS

Spanish for "little donkey," a burrito is a flour tortilla wrapped around a hearty filling of chicken, beef, or pork, served with a taco sauce.

- *Color index page 36*
- *Begin 1¼ hrs ahead*
- *6 servings*
- *540 cals per serving*

2 whole large chicken
  breasts, halved,
  skinned, and boned
Salad oil
Salt
1 large head iceberg
  lettuce (about
  1½ pounds)
1 large onion, diced

1½ teaspoons chili
  powder
1 4-ounce can chopped
  green chilies, drained
1 8-ounce jar mild or hot
  taco sauce
6 8-inch flour tortillas
1 16-ounce can refried
  beans

3 tablespoons red wine
  vinegar
½ teaspoon sugar
¼ teaspoon oregano
  leaves
1 large tomato, cut into
  bite-sized pieces
1 large avocado, cut into
  bite-sized pieces

1 Cut breasts crosswise in ¼-inch strips. In 12-inch skillet over medium-high heat, heat 2 tablespoons oil.

2 Add chicken and ½ teaspoon salt; cook until tender, about 2 to 3 minutes, stirring frequently. Remove to bowl.

3 Coarsely chop ¼ head lettuce; reserve. Thinly slice remaining lettuce.

4 In same skillet over medium heat, in 3 tablespoons hot salad oil, cook sliced lettuce, onion, and 1 teaspoon salt until tender; stir occasionally. Stir in chili powder.

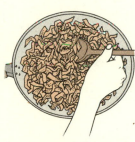

5 Cook 1 minute, stirring occasionally. Stir in cooked chicken, green chilies, and ¾ cup taco sauce; heat through. Steam tortillas (left).

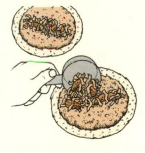

6 In 1-quart saucepan over low heat, heat refried beans. Spread about ⅓ cup beans on each tortilla; top with ½ cup chicken mixture crosswise down center.

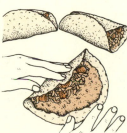

7 Fold left side of tortilla over mixture; turn bottom up; fold right side over to seal.

8 In medium bowl, mix next 3 ingredients, ¼ cup oil, and ½ teaspoon salt.

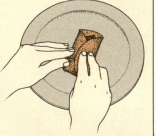

9 Add the tomato, avocado, and reserved chopped lettuce to dressing in bowl; toss the vegetables with the dressing, being sure to coat everything evenly. To serve, arrange the burritos and the vegetable-lettuce mixture on a large platter. If you like, serve the burritos with the remaining taco sauce in a bowl and let your guests serve themselves.

Chicken cutlets

CHICKEN CUTLETS AND ARTICHOKES

- Color index page 38
- Begin 35 mins ahead
- 4 servings
- 210 cals per serving

4 large chicken cutlets
1 medium red pepper
4 Artichoke Bottoms (p.229)
2 tablespoons salad oil
¼ cup mayonnaise
2 teaspoons red wine vinegar
2 teaspoons Dijon mustard
½ teaspoon chicken-flavor instant bouillon
Water

1. *About 35 minutes before serving:* With meat mallet or dull edge of French knife, pound each cutlet to ½-inch thickness; set aside. Cut red pepper into very thin strips. Prepare artichoke bottoms; keep warm.
2. In 12-inch skillet over medium-high heat, in hot salad oil, cook red-pepper strips until tender, stirring frequntly. Remove to small bowl.
3. In drippings remaining in skillet over medium-high heat, cook chicken cutlets until tender and lightly browned on both sides, about 8 minutes, removing them to plate as they brown. Keep warm while preparing sauce.
4. Spoon off fat from skillet. Over medium heat, with wire whisk, stir mayonnaise, vinegar, mustard, bouillon, and ⅔ cup water until smooth and mixture boils. Pour sauce onto platter; arrange chicken and Artichoke Bottoms over sauce. Garnish with red-pepper strips.

CHICKEN CUTLETS WITH SUN-DRIED TOMATOES AND MOZZARELLA

- Color index page 38
- Begin 30 mins ahead
- 4 servings
- 225 cals per serving

4 large chicken cutlets
2 tablespoons butter or margarine
1 shallot, thinly sliced
¼ cup cooking or dry white wine
2 tablespoons thinly sliced sun-dried tomatoes (pumate)
Water
½ 8-ounce package mozzarella cheese, sliced
1 large bunch arugula

1. With meat mallet or dull edge of chef's knife, pound each chicken-cutlet to ¼-inch thickness. Set aside.
2. In 10-inch skillet over medium-high heat, in hot butter or margarine, cook chicken cutlets just until lightly browned on both sides, about 3 to 5 minutes. Remove chicken to plate; keep warm.
3. In the remaining drippings in skillet over medium heat, cook the sliced shallot until tender, stirring occasionally. Add the wine, sliced sun-dried tomatoes, and ⅓ cup water; over high heat, heat to boiling.
4. Return the chicken cutlets to skillet. Top each cutlet with mozzarella cheese; cover and cook over medium-low heat until cheese melts, about 2 minutes.
5. To serve, arrange arugula on large platter. Top with chicken. Spoon sauce over chicken.

CHICKEN À LA KING

- Color index page 37
- Begin 40 mins ahead
- 8 servings
- 626 cals per serving

6 tablespoons butter
½ pound mushrooms, sliced
¼ cup diced green pepper
6 tablespoons all-purpose flour
3 cups half-and-half
4 cups cubed, cooked chicken or turkey
1 4-ounce jar diced pimentos, drained
2 egg yolks
2 tablespoons medium sherry
1 teaspoon salt
8 patty shells, warmed

1. In 10-inch skillet over medium heat, in hot butter, cook mushrooms and green pepper 5 minutes or until tender.
2. Stir in flour until blended. Gradually stir in half-and-half and cook, stirring, until thickened.
3. Add chicken and pimentos. Heat to boiling, stirring often. Reduce heat to low. Cover and cook 5 minutes.
4. In cup, stir yolks until mixed. Stir in a little hot sauce; slowly pour mixture back into sauce, stirring rapidly to prevent lumping. Cook, stirring, until thickened. Stir in sherry and salt; spoon into patty shells.

CHICKEN CROQUETTES

- Color index page 37
- Begin early in day or day ahead
- 4 servings
- 430 cals per serving

2½ cups ground, cooked chicken or turkey
1 cup Thick White Sauce (p. 113)
2 tablespoons chopped parsley
1 tablespoon minced onion
½ teaspoon lemon juice
⅛ teaspoon rubbed sage
Salt
1 egg
1 tablespoon water
¼ cup all-purpose flour
½ cup dried bread crumbs
Salad oil

1. In bowl, blend well first 6 ingredients. Add salt to taste. Cover; chill several hours.
2. *About 30 minutes before serving:* Shape chilled mixture into 8 cones.
3. In shallow dish with fork, beat egg with water. Place flour and bread crumbs on separate sheets of waxed paper.
4. Coat each croquette first in flour, then in egg, then in crumbs.
5. In 4-quart saucepan over medium heat, heat 1 inch oil to 370°F. Fry croquettes until golden, turning frequently. Drain on paper towels.

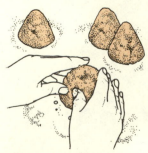

Shaping into cones: Mold chilled mixture into cone shapes with hands.

Frying the croquettes: Be sure to turn each croquette frequently so all sides are browned evenly.

Rock Cornish hens

ROCK CORNISH HENS WITH WILD-RICE STUFFING

- Color index page 38
- Begin 2½ hrs ahead
- 8 servings
- 325 cals per serving

Wild-Rice-and-Mushroom Stuffing (below)
4 1¾-pound fresh or frozen (thawed) Rock Cornish hens
¼ cup honey
2 tablespoons lemon juice
2 tablespoons dry vermouth
½ teaspoon salt
¼ teaspoon thyme leaves

1. Prepare stuffing. Meanwhile, remove giblets and necks from hens. Cut each hen in half. Rinse with running cold water; pat dry.
2. Preheat oven to 400°F. Carefully loosen skin on each hen half by pushing fingers between skin and meat to form a pocket; spoon some stuffing into each pocket. Place hen halves, breast side up, in 2 large open roasting pans.
3. In small bowl, mix next 5 ingredients. Brush hen halves with some honey mixture. Place pans on two oven racks. Bake hens about 50 minutes, basting occasionally with remaining honey mixture and drippings in pan. Switch pans between upper and lower oven racks halfway through roasting time to brown evenly.

WILD-RICE-AND-MUSHROOM STUFFING: In 3-quart saucepan over medium heat, melt 3 tablespoons butter or margarine; add 1 pound mushrooms, chopped, and cook until tender, stirring occasionally. Rinse one 8-ounce box wild rice (1½ cups); drain. To mushroom mixture, add wild rice, 3 cups water, 1 chicken-flavor bouillon cube or envelope, and 1 teaspoon salt; over high heat, heat to boiling. Reduce heat to low; cover; simmer 45 to 50 minutes until rice is tender and liquid is absorbed. 4 cups. 323 cals per cup.

Stuffing the hen: Push fingers between skin and meat to form pocket, then spoon stuffing into pocket.

SPINACH STUFFING: Thaw 1 10-ounce package frozen chopped spinach. Squeeze spinach dry with paper towels. In 4-quart saucepan over medium heat, in ½ cup hot butter or margarine, cook ¼ pound mushrooms, thinly sliced, 1 cup diced celery, and ½ cup chopped onion until tender, about 5 minutes, stirring occasionally; remove from heat. Add 3 cups fresh bread crumbs, ½ 15- to 16-ounce container ricotta cheese (1 cup), 1 egg, 1 tablespoon minced parsley, 1 teaspoon salt, ½ teaspoon poultry seasoning, ⅛ teaspoon pepper, and spinach. 3½ cups. 497 cals per cup.

PEASANT-STYLE CORNISH HENS

- Color index page 38
- Begin 2 hrs ahead
- 4 servings
- 546 cals per serving

A cross between the Plymouth Rock hen and the English Cornish game cock, the small Cornish hen offers tender white meat.

Water
Salt
10 large cabbage leaves
1 pound sweet Italian sausage links
¼ teaspoon pepper
¼ teaspoon ginger
2 1½-pound Rock Cornish hens
1 16-ounce bag carrots, thickly sliced

1 In Dutch oven over high heat, heat 1½ cups water and 1 teaspoon salt to boiling. Add cabbage; cover; cook 3 to 5 minutes. Remove; set aside. Reserve liquid.

2 In same covered Dutch oven over medium heat, cook sausages in ¼ cup water, 5 minutes; uncover and brown well; drain; reserve 2 tablespoons fat.

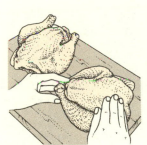

3 Meanwhile, remove giblets and neck from hens. Rub 1 teaspoon salt, pepper, and ginger into hens.

4 In same Dutch oven, in reserved hot fat, cook hens until golden on all sides. Set aside. Preheat oven to 375°F.

5 Spoon fat from Dutch oven; stir in reserved liquid. Line Dutch oven with half of cabbage leaves, overlapping slightly; place hens on top.

6 Cover with remaining leaves. Cut sausages in chunks; tuck around cabbage with carrots. Cover; bake 1 hour until hens are tender; baste often.

Turkey

ROAST TURKEY WITH PECAN STUFFING

The pride of the Thanksgiving table, a roasted, stuffed turkey, is often served with gravy, sweet potatoes, and cranberry sauce.

- *Color index page 37*
- *Begin 6½ hrs ahead*
- *18 servings*
- *710 cals per serving*

1 14-pound fresh or
   frozen (thawed) ready-
   to-stuff turkey
Pecan Stuffing (right)
Salad oil

Parsley for garnish
Cocktail Corn Garnish
   (right)
Giblet Gravy (right)

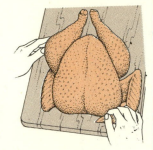

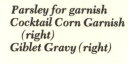

1 Remove giblets and neck from turkey; reserve for gravy. Rinse bird with running cold water; drain well.

2 Spoon some of the stuffing lightly into neck cavity. (Do not pack.) Fold neck skin over stuffing and fasten to back with 1 or 2 skewers.

3 With turkey breast side up lift wings up toward neck, then fold under back of bird so they stay in place.

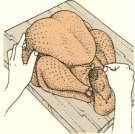
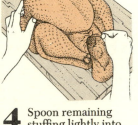
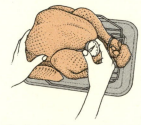

4 Spoon remaining stuffing lightly into body cavity. Close by folding skin over opening; skewer closed. With string tie legs and tail together; alternatively, push drumsticks under band of skin, or use stuffing clamp.

5 Place the turkey, with its breast side up, on a rack in a large open roasting pan. Brush the skin lightly with salad oil to keep the breasts moist and allow the skin to color evenly.

6 Insert the meat thermometer into the thickest part of the turkey between breast and thigh, being careful that the pointed end of the thermometer does not touch the bone.

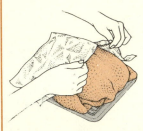

7 Roast turkey in 325°F. oven about 4¾ hours. Check for doneness during last hour of roasting. When bird turns golden, cover loosely with tent of foil.

8 Remove foil toward the end of the roasting time and with a pastry brush, brush the turkey generously with the pan drippings – this will give the turkey an attractive sheen. The turkey is done when the meat thermometer reaches 180° to 185°F. and the thickest part of the drumstick feels soft when you press it with your finger (be sure to protect your finger with paper towels). When the bird is done, place on warm platter; keep warm.

9 To serve, garnish turkey platter with sprigs of parsley and Cocktail Corn Garnish. Pass the Turkey Giblet Gravy in a large gravy boat.

PECAN STUFFING: In 8-quart Dutch oven over medium heat, in *1 cup hot butter* or *margarine*, cook *4 large celery stalks*, thinly sliced, and *2 large onions*, diced, until tender, stirring occasionally. Remove Dutch oven from heat; stir in *1 6-ounce can pecans*, toasted and chopped, *14 cups white-bread cubes* (about 22 slices), *¼ cup chopped parsley*, *1½ teaspoons poultry seasoning*, *¼ teaspoon pepper*, *3 eggs*, and *1½ teaspoons salt*. Mix well. Stuffing can be prepared a day ahead and refrigerated until ready to use. (Do not stuff turkey until it is ready to go into the oven.) 9 cups. 473 cals per cup.

COCKTAIL CORN GARNISH: Drain *1 2-ounce jar pimento* and slice pimento into strips. Drain *3 6-ounce jars pickled cocktail corn* and wrap three ears of cocktail corn with a pimento strip. Arrange corn bundle on *watercress* around turkey. Repeat with remaining corn and pimento strips. These corn bundles can be arranged on their bed of watercress, placed on a cookie sheet, set aside and refrigerated, until turkey is ready to be garnished. 33 cals per bundle.

HOW TO MAKE A CRANBERRY RELISH

Cranberry Relish is one of the easiest relishes to make and is the perfect accompaniment for all kind of poultry – not just the traditional Thanksgiving turkey.

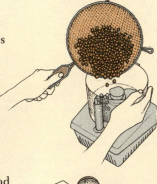

Pick over and wash a 12-ounce package of fresh cranberries.

In a food processor, process the cranberries with a washed orange, lemon, and lime, each sliced and with seeds removed, for a few seconds.

Scrape sides of bowl and process again. Mixture should be coarsely chopped. Sweeten with sugar to taste; chill.

TURKEY GIBLET GRAVY

The perfect sauce for turkey, giblet gravy is a classic example of delicious thriftiness – no usable part of the bird is discarded.

Reserved turkey giblets and neck
Water
⅓ cup all-purpose flour
Salt

- *Color index page 37*
- *Begin early in day*
- *18 servings*
- *8 cals per serving*

1 In 2-quart saucepan over high heat, heat giblets, neck, and enough water to cover to boiling. Reduce heat to low; cover and simmer 1 hour or until tender.

2 Drain, reserving broth in a bowl. Pull meat from neck; discard all the bones. Coarsely chop the neck meat and giblets; refrigerate.

3 When turkey is done, remove rack from roasting pan; pour drippings into a 4-cup measure or medium bowl (set pan aside); let stand a few seconds.

4 Skim ⅓ cup fat from drippings into 2-quart saucepan; skim off and discard remaining fat, keeping the meat juice.

5 Add reserved giblet broth to roasting pan; stir until brown bits are loosened.

6 Add to reserved meat juices. Add enough water to make 4 cups gravy.

7 Into fat in saucepan over medium heat, stir flour and 1 teaspoon salt until blended.

8 Gradually stir in meat-juice mixture; cook, stirring constantly, until mixture is thickened.

9 Stir in reserved giblets and neck meat; heat through. Pour into gravy boat.

HOW TO CARVE A TURKEY

Carving a whole turkey at the table is an important skill to master. Only a little practice is required. Remember to let the bird rest 15 to 30 minutes, depending on its size. This allows the juices to retract into the flesh and allows for easier carving as well as moist meat.

Place bird on warm platter, directly in front of you, with breast of bird at your left. With a sharp carving knife and long-tined fork, cut drumstick and thigh from body.

Separate thigh from drumstick by bending drumstick down with hand.

On a separate plate, slice dark meat from bone.

Insert fork securely into upper part of wing and make a long deep horizontal cut above wing joint through breast to rib cage.

Beginning halfway up breast, carve downward with a straight motion; when knife reaches horizontal slice made across wing, breast slices will fall free. Carve enough thin slices for serving and more as necessary.

Turkey

TURKEY MARYLAND

Though Maryland style traditionally means coated and fried, this oven-baked version offers the same taste with fewer calories.

- Color index page 38
- Begin 2½ hrs ahead
- 6 servings
- 772 cals per serving

1 5- to 6-pound fryer-roaster turkey
1 egg
⅓ cup milk
All-purpose flour
1½ cups dry bread crumbs

Salad oil
1½ teaspoons salt
¼ teaspoon pepper
1 cup water
⅔ cup half-and-half

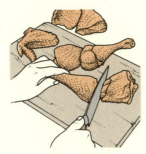

1 Preheat oven to 350°F. Cut turkey into 12 pieces. In pie plate, with fork, beat egg with milk.

2 Place ⅓ cup flour on sheet of waxed paper; place crumbs on another. Coat turkey and giblets with flour, then egg, then crumbs.

3 In 12-inch skillet over medium heat, in ¼ cup hot salad oil, cook turkey until browned.

4 Arrange turkey in 15½" by 10½" roasting pan. Sprinkle with salt and pepper; add ½ cup water.

5 Cover pan with foil and bake 1½ hours or until fork-tender; uncover for last 30 minutes. Place turkey in warm platter. For sauce, into drippings in roasting pan, stir half-and-half.

6 In cup, blend 2 tablespoons flour and ½ cup water until smooth; gradually stir into hot liquid in pan and cook over medium heat, stirring constantly, until mixture is thickened.

TURKEY CUTLETS MARSALA

Turkey cutlets make a tasty and economical alternative to veal. Cooked with Marsala wine, they're a variation of an Italian classic.

- Color index page 38
- Begin 40 mins ahead
- 4 servings
- 355 cals per serving

1 16-ounce package turkey cutlets
2 tablespoons all-purpose flour
¼ teaspoon pepper
½ teaspoon salt
1 tablespoon salad oil
1 bunch watercress

3 tablespoons butter or margarine
½ pound small mushrooms, each cut into quarters
⅛ cup dry Marsala wine
Water

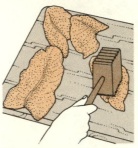

1 With meat mallet or dull edge of French knife, pound each turkey cutlet to ⅛-inch thickness.

2 In pie plate, mix flour, pepper, and ½ teaspoon salt. Coat cutlets with flour mixture.

3 In 12-inch skillet over medium heat, in hot salad oil, cook watercress until wilted. With slotted spoon, remove to bowl; keep warm. Wipe skillet clean.

4 In the same skillet over medium-high heat, in hot butter or margarine, cook mushrooms until tender. With slotted spoon, remove to bowl or oven-safe plate and keep warm.

5 In drippings remaining in skillet, cook the flour-coated turkey cutlets, a few at a time, until tender and lightly browned on both sides, removing pieces to plate as they brown, adding more butter to skillet if needed. Keep warm. To the drippings remaining in the skillet, add the Marsala wine and ⅓ cup water; over high heat, heat to boiling, stirring to loosen brown bits from bottom of skillet and blending the flavors.

6 Reduce heat to low: simmer, uncovered, until liquid thickens slightly. Return cutlets and mushrooms to skillet; heat through. Arrange watercress over cutlets

CURRIED TURKEY WITH APPLES AND PEANUTS

1¼ cups regular long-
   grain rice
3 tablespoons butter or
   margarine
1 medium onion, diced
1 green apple, peeled and
   cut into bite-sized
   chunks
1 medium celery stalk,
   diced
1 tablespoon curry
   powder
1 tablespoon all-purpose
   flour

¾ teaspoon salt
⅛ teaspoon ground red
   pepper
2½ cups milk
1 chicken-flavor bouillon
   cube or envelope
3 cups cubed (½-inch)
   cooked turkey
¾ cup peanuts
Chopped parsley for
   garnish

1. Prepare rice as label directs; keep warm. Meanwhile, in 4-quart saucepan over medium heat, in hot butter, cook onion, apple, and celery until tender, stirring occasionally.
2. Stir in next 4 ingredients until blended; cook 1 minute, stirring often.
3. Gradually stir in milk and bouillon; cook, stirring constantly, until mixture is slightly thickened and smooth.
4. Add turkey and peanuts; reduce heat to low; cover; simmer 10 minutes, stirring occasionally.
5. To serve, spoon rice onto large platter; top with turkey mixture. Garnish with parsley.

- Color index page 38
- Begin 45 mins ahead
- 8 servings
- 350 cals per serving

COUNTRY TURKEY HASH

Salad oil
4 medium turnips (about
   1 pound), shredded
1 medium onion, diced
2 cups finely chopped
   cooked turkey
½ cup shredded
   Muenster cheese
   (2 ounces)

2 tablespoons chopped
   parsley
½ teaspoon salt
2 tablespoons butter or
   margarine
4 medium potatoes (about
   1¼ pounds), thinly
   sliced.

1. In 10-inch skillet over medium heat, in 2 tablespoons hot salad oil, cook turnips and onion until tender, stirring occasionally. Remove vegetables with any liquid to medium bowl; stir in next 4 ingredients; set aside.
2. In same skillet over medium-high heat, in hot butter, and 2 tablespoons salad oil, arrange potato slices in overlapping concentric circles.
3. Cook about 10 minutes or until potatoes are tender and undersides are golden.
4. Spoon turkey mixture evenly on top of potatoes; reduce heat to low; cover and cook 15 minutes or until cheese is melted and turkey is heated through.
5. To serve, carefully invert "pie" onto platter; cut into 6 wedges.

- Color index page 37
- Begin 1 hr ahead
- 6 servings
- 325 cals per serving

OLD-FASHIONED CREAMED TURKEY WITH BISCUITS

A delicious solution for using leftover turkey meat to prepare a welcoming and warming wintertime dish is to make a stew of it and top it with flaky homemade biscuits. However, now that whole turkey and turkey pieces are available throughout the year, leftovers needn't be your only source.

2 cups all-purpose flour
2 tablespoons sugar
1 tablespoon double-
   acting baking powder
Salt
⅓ cup shortening
⅔ cup milk
1 egg
2 tablespoons butter or
   margarine
2 medium green peppers,
   cut into thin strips
½ pound mushrooms,
   sliced

1 small onion, diced
1 10¾-ounce can
   condensed cream of
   mushroom soup
1 3¼-ounce can pitted
   ripe olives, drained
   and each cut in half
1 2-ounce jar diced
   pimento, drained
3 cups bite-sized chunks
   cooked turkey
1 cup water
⅛ teaspoon pepper

- Color index page 37
- Begin 30 mins ahead
- 6 servings
- 564 cals per serving

1 Preheat oven to 450°F. Prepare biscuits: In medium bowl with fork, mix flour, sugar, baking powder, and 1 teaspoon salt. With pastry blender or 2 knives used scissor-fashion, cut in shortening to make coarse crumbs.

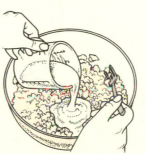

2 Add milk; with fork, quickly stir just until mixture forms soft dough and leaves side of bowl. Do not over mix, as biscuits may become heavy and tough.

3 On lightly floured surface with lightly floured hands, knead dough 10 times. Pat dough into 6½-inch circle; cut dough into 6 wedges.

4 Place wedges on cookie sheet, about 1 inch apart. In cup with fork, beat egg; brush wedges with egg. Bake 12 to 15 minutes until biscuits are golden.

5 Meanwhile, in 3-quart saucepan over medium heat, melt butter or margarine. Add green peppers, mushrooms, and onion; cook until vegetables are tender (about 7 minutes), stirring occasionally.

6 Stir in undiluted mushroom soup, olives, pimentos, turkey chunks, water, pepper, and ½ teaspoon salt; over high heat, heat to boiling. Reduce heat to low; cover and simmer 10 minutes to blend flavors.

7 To serve, spoon the creamed turkey mixture into a warm deep platter; arrange biscuit wedges on top. As the biscuits can be done ahead and the turkey kept warm, this is a good choice for a buffet dish.

Duckling

ROAST DUCKLING

Sweet, succulent roast duckling makes a delicious alternative to the traditional turkey. Prick the skin well to ensure crispiness.

- Color index page 39
- Begin 4 hrs ahead
- 4 servings
- 652 cals per serving

Bacon-Rice Stuffing (right)
1 4- to 5-pound frozen duckling, thawed
¼ teaspoon pepper

Salt
2 tablespoons butter or margarine
2 red cooking apples, cored; cut in wedges

½ cup apple jelly
Parsley sprigs for garnish
Giblet Gravy (right)

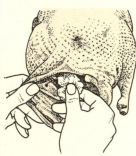

1 Prepare Bacon-Rice Stuffing. Remove giblets and neck from inside duckling. Discard fat from body cavity; rinse well. Pat dry.

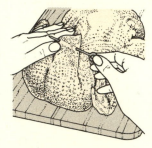

2 Spoon some stuffing lightly into neck cavity; fold neck skin over stuffing, fasten neck skin to back with skewers, if necessary.

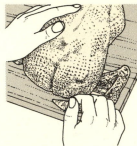

3 With duckling breast side up, lift wings up toward neck, then fold under back of duckling so they stay in place.

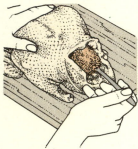

4 Spoon remaining stuffing into body cavity, fold skin over opening; skewer closed if necessary. With string, tie duckling legs together.

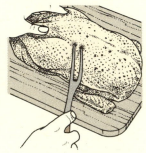

5 With two-tined fork, prick skin of duckling in several places. Rub duckling with pepper and 1 teaspoon salt. Place breast side up, on rack in open roasting pan.

6 Insert meat thermometer between breast and thigh; pointed end of thermometer should not touch bone.

7 Roast in 325°F oven 2 to 2½ hours. Meanwhile, prepare Giblet Gravy. Check doneness during last 30 minutes. Thermometer should read 185° to 190°F.; thickest part of leg will soft when pinched with fingers protected with paper towels. About 20 minutes before duckling is done, in 12-inch skillet over medium heat, melt butter. Add apples; cook until tender-crisp, turning once, about 5 to 7 minutes. Stir in apple jelly; heat through.

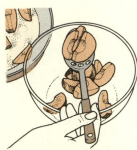

8 With slotted spoon, remove apple wedges to medium bowl; keep warm. Use butter mixture remaining in skillet to baste duckling during last 10 minutes of roasting.

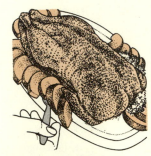

9 Place duckling on warm platter; remove skewers and strings. Arrange apple slices around bird. Garnish with parsley sprigs and serve with gravy.

BACON-RICE STUFFING: Prepare *1 cup regular long-grain rice* as label directs. Meanwhile, dice *1 8-ounce package sliced bacon*. In 2-quart saucepan over medium heat, cook bacon until browned, stirring occasionally. With slotted spoon, remove bacon to plate. Spoon off all but 3 tablespoons bacon fat from saucepan. Add *1 medium onion*, diced, to bacon fat; cook until tender, about 5 minutes. When rice is done, stir in bacon and onion and its cooking fat; set aside. 3½ cups. 423 cals per cup.

GIBLET GRAVY: In a 2-quart saucepan over high heat, heat enough *water* to cover *1 teaspoon salt*, *reserved giblets* and *neck*, and *1 medium onion*, diced. Heat to boiling. Reduce heat to low; cover and simmer 1 hour or until the giblets are tender. Drain, reserving the broth; discard the onion. Pull meat from neck; discard bones, coarsely chop the meat and giblets; refrigerate. When the duckling is done, remove the rack from the roasting pan; pour drippings into a 2-cup measure or medium bowl (set pan aside); let the drippings stand a few seconds until the fat separates from the meat juices. Skim 3 tablespoons fat from the drippings into a 2-quart saucepan; skim off and discard any remaining fat. Add the reserved broth to the roasting pan; stir until any brown bits are loosened; add to meat juices in cup to make 2 cups liquid (add water if necessary). Into fat in saucepan over medium heat, stir *3 tablespoons all-purpose flour* and *1 teaspoon salt* until blended. Gradually stir in meat-juice mixture; cook, stirring constantly, until thickened. Add giblets and neck meat; cook until heated through. Pour mixture into the gravy boat. 4 cups. 30 cals per tablespoon.

POULTRY GLAZES

In the last 10 to 20 minutes of roasting time, brush the bird with one of the glazes below. Allow about ½ cup glaze for 4- to 10-pound birds; for larger birds, double the recipe.

HONEY-BARBEQUE: In small bowl, mix *½ cup honey, 1 tablespoon soy sauce*, and *½ teaspoon ground ginger* until well blended. (Makes ½ cup.)

WINE-JELLY: In 1-quart saucepan over low heat, stir *½ cup wine jelly* with *¼ teaspoon salt* until blended. (Makes ½ cup.)

QUINCE: In 1-quart saucepan over low heat, stir *½ cup quince jelly, 1 tablespoon butter, 1 teaspoon ground cinnamon*, and *½ teaspoon ground cloves* until blended. (Makes ½ cup.)

MUSTARD: In 1-quart saucepan over low heat, stir *¼ cup Dijon mustard, ¼ cup brown sugar, 2 tablespoons salad oil, 2 tablespoons water, 1 tablespoon red-wine vinegar*, and *1 teaspoon dry mustard* until smooth. (Makes ⅔ cup.)

CALIFORNIA DUCK ROAST

2 4½- to 5-pound fresh or
  frozen (thawed)
  ducklings
Salt
Pepper
1 carrot, chopped
1 small onion, chopped
Water
⅓ cup sugar
⅓ cup cider vinegar

½ cup California blush
  wine (white zinfandel
  or white pinot noir)
¼ cup cornstarch
¼ cup currant jelly
3 small Bartlett pears,
  sliced, for garnish
½ pound seedless red
  grapes, each cut in
  half, for garnish

1. Remove giblets and necks from ducklings. Rinse ducklings, giblets, and necks with running cold water; pat dry with paper towels. Cut each duckling into quarters; trim excess fat and skin; reserve.

2. Place duckling quarters, skin side down, on rack in large open roasting pan; sprinkle lightly with salt and pepper. Roast in 350°F. oven 1 hour; turn; sprinkle with salt and pepper. Roast about 45 minutes longer or until ducklings are fork-tender and thickest part of drumstick feels soft when pinched with fingers.

3. In 3-quart saucepan over medium heat, cook duck fat and skin until crisp and browned; remove crisp pieces. Discard all but 2 tablespoons drippings.

4. In drippings remaining in saucepan, over medium heat, cook giblets and necks until browned. Add carrot and onion; cook 1 minute. Add ¼ teaspoon salt and enough water to cover; heat to boiling. Reduce heat to low; cover; simmer 1 hour. Drain, reserving 2 cups broth.

5. In 2-quart saucepan over medium-low heat, cook sugar and vinegar until liquid is golden brown and reduced to about ¼ cup. Stir in reserved broth. In cup, blend wine and cornstarch; stir into broth mixture. Over medium heat, cook sauce until thickened and smooth. Add salt to taste; keep sauce warm.

6. About 10 minutes before ducklings are done, in cup, stir currant jelly and 1 teaspoon water until smooth; brush duckling with mixture.

7. To serve, arrange duckling on warm large platter; garnish with pear slices and grape halves. Serve sauce in small bowl.

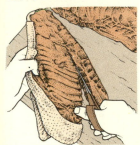

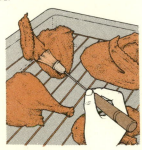

Cutting the ducklings:
With kitchen shears or a sharp knife, cut each duckling into quarters.

Basting the quarters:
About 10 minutes before ducklings are roasted, brush on jelly mixture.

- *Color index page 39*
- *Begin 2½ hrs ahead*
- *8 servings*
- *571 cals per serving*

BREAST OF DUCKLING WITH GREEN PEPPERCORNS

Much favored by contemporary chefs, pan-fried breasts served with a green peppercorn sauce make an elegant main dish.

1 4½- to 5-pound fresh or
  frozen (thawed)
  duckling
Butter or margarine
1 small green onion,
  minced

2 tablespoons cooking or
  dry white wine
2 tablespoons water
1 teaspoon green pepper-
  corns

Watercress for garnish
Preserved kumquats for
  garnish

- *Color index page 39*
- *Begin 40 mins ahead*
- *2 servings*
- *391 cals per serving*

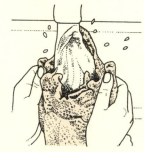

1 To remove breasts from duckling: Remove giblets and neck from duckling; set aside for use another day.

2 Rinse duckling with running cold water; pat dry with paper towels. Place duckling, breast side up, on work surface.

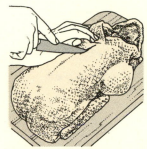

3 On one side of duckling at a time, insert tip of sharp knife between meat and breastbone. Cut and scrape meat from bone and rib cage.

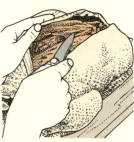

4 Gently pull meat back in one piece. Discard skin and fat from breasts. Reserve carcass and legs for use another day.

5 In 7- to 8-inch skillet over medium-high heat, in 2 tablespoons hot butter, cook breasts until underside browns, about 4 minutes.

6 Turn breasts; cook 3 minutes longer for medium-rare. Remove to warm platter; slice into thin slices; keep warm.

7 Reduce heat to medium-low. In drippings in skillet and 1 more tablespoon hot butter, cook green onion until tender.

8 Add wine, water, and green peppercorns, stirring to loosen brown bits in bottom of skillet. Drain any juice from duckling in platter into sauce in skillet.

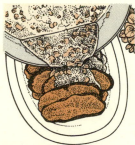

9 Remove skillet from heat; stir in 1 tablespoon butter until melted. Pour sauce over duckling breasts. Garnish platter with watercress and kumquats.

Goose

ROAST STUFFED GOOSE WITH CANDIED ORANGES

A traditional favorite of many immigrants to America, goose is usually reserved for special occasions – often as an alternative to our native turkey.

1 12-pound frozen goose, thawed, neck and giblets removed
Rye-Bread Stuffing (below)
1 teaspoon salt
¼ teaspoon pepper
8 small oranges
Water
⅓ cup light corn syrup
2 tablespoons sugar

Creamy Mushroom Gravy (below)
Parsley sprigs for garnish

- *Color index page 39*
- *Begin 4½ hrs ahead*
- *10 servings*
- *1065 cals per serving*

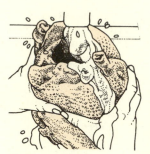 **1** Discard fat from body cavity; rinse goose with running cold water; drain well. Prepare Rye-Bread Stuffing. Spoon some into neck cavity (do not pack).

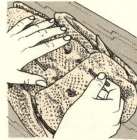 **2** Fold neck skin over stuffing; fasten skin to the back with 1 or 2 skewers. With goose breast side up, lift wings up toward neck, then fold under back of goose.

 **3** Spoon Rye-Bread Stuffing lightly into body cavity; fold skin over opening; skewer closed if necessary.

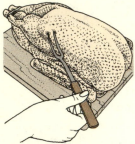 **4** With string, tie legs and tail together. With fork, prick skin of goose in several places.

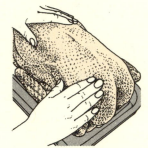 **5** Place goose, breast side up, on rack in open roasting pan. Rub with salt and pepper.

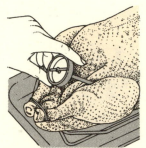 **6** Insert meat thermometer into thickest part between breast and thigh; the pointed end should not touch the bone.

 **7** Roast at 350°F. about 3 hours. Check for doneness during last 30 minutes.

 **8** About 1 hour before goose is done, prepare candied oranges: With knife, remove peel and white membrane from oranges; set aside.

9 Trim off as much of the white membrane as possible from a few pieces of orange peel; then cut orange peel into long, thin julienne strips to make about ½ cup, firmly packed. In 10-inch skillet over high heat, heat orange peel strips and the 3 cups water to boiling; cook 15 minutes. Drain, then rinse well with running cold water. With 3 cups more water, cook julienne peel 15 minutes again; drain. This removes the bitterness from the peel.

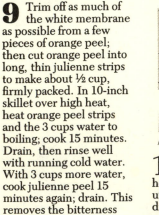

 **10** In same skillet over high heat, heat corn syrup and sugar until boiling and sugar dissolves. Add oranges and peel; coat well with syrup mixture.

 **11** Reduce the heat to medium-low and cook until the oranges are heated through, about 10 minutes; keep the orange mixture warm. Prepare Creamy Mushroom Gravy.

 **12** Goose is done when thermometer reaches 190°F, and thickest part of leg feels soft when pinched with fingers protected by paper towels. To serve, remove skewers and

strings from goose; place on warm large platter; garnish with parsley sprigs and oranges. Brush goose generously with corn-syrup mixture remaining in skillet. Serve with gravy.

RYE-BREAD STUFFING: In 5-quart Dutch oven or saucepot over medium heat, melt *½ cup butter* or *margarine*; add *2 celery stalks*, diced, and *1 medium onion*, diced. Cook until vegetables are tender, stirring frequently. Remove from heat and stir in *10 cups rye-bread cubes*, 1¼ cups milk, 2 table-spoons minced parsley, ½ teaspoon thyme leaves, ¼ teaspoon rubbed sage, and ¼ teaspoon pepper. 7 cups. 277 cals per cup.

CREAMY MUSHROOM GRAVY: In 3-quart saucepan over medium heat, melt *3 tablespoons butter*. Add *½ pound mushrooms*, thinly sliced, and *1 green onion*, sliced; cook until vegetables are tender, stirring occasionally. Stir in *2 table-spoons all-purpose flour*, ¼ teaspoon salt, and ⅛ teaspoon pepper. Stir in *2 cups milk* and *1 chicken-flavor bouillon cube*; cook, stirring, until mixture thickens. 3 cups. 307 cals per cup.

Game

ROAST GOOSE WITH CHESTNUT STUFFING, SAUSAGE, AND APPLES

- Color index page 39
- Begin 4½ hrs ahead
- 8 servings
- 870 cals per serving

Chestnut Stuffing (p. 169)
1 10-pound frozen goose, thawed
1 teaspoon salt
¼ teaspoon pepper
2 pounds pork sausage links or sweet Italian sausage links
Water
3 large red cooking apples
Butter or margarine
⅛ teaspoon ground ginger
½ cup apple jelly
1 tablespoon all-purpose flour
½ cup cooking or dry sherry
2 teaspoons chicken-flavor bouillon cube or envelope
1 teaspoon soy sauce

1. Prepare Chestnut Stuffing. Remove giblets and neck from goose. Discard fat from body cavity; rinse; drain well.
2. Spoon some stuffing into neck cavity; fold neck skin over and fasten to back with 1 or 2 skewers. With goose breast side up, lift wings up toward neck, then fold under back of goose. Spoon remaining stuffing lightly into body cavity. Close by folding skin over opening; skewer if necessary. With string, tie legs and tail together. With fork, prick skin of goose in several places. This will allow excess fat to run out.
3. Place goose, breast side up, on rack in open roasting pan. Rub goose with salt and pepper. Insert meat thermometer into thickest part between breast and thigh; pointed end should not touch bone. Roast at 350°F. about 3 hours. Check for doneness during last 30 minutes. Goose is done when thermometer reaches 190°F. and thickest part of leg feels soft when pinched with fingers protected by paper towels.
4. About 45 minutes before goose is done, prepare sausages: In 12-inch skillet over medium heat, heat sausages and ¼ cup water to boiling. Cover; simmer 5 minutes. Remove cover; continue cooking, turning frequently, until sausages are well browned. Keep warm.
5. Meanwhile, prepare apple rings: Core apples: cut into ½-inch-thick rings. In 10-inch skillet over medium heat, in 2 tablespoons hot butter or margarine, cook apple rings a few at a time, about 5 minutes, until fork-tender, turning once during cooking, adding more butter or margarine if needed. Remove rings to plate.
6. Into skillet, stir ginger and ⅓ cup apple jelly until melted; return rings to skillet, spooning apple-jelly mixture over rings to coat; heat through. With slotted spoon, remove rings to plate, leaving jelly mixture in skillet; keep the rings warm.
7. Into drippings remaining in skillet, stir flour; cook 1 minute. Add sherry, chicken-flavor bouillon, soy sauce, 1 cup water, and remaining apple jelly, stirring constantly, until slightly thickened and smooth.
8. To serve, remove skewers and strings from goose; place goose on warm large platter. Arrange sausages and apple rings around goose. Serve with sauce.

ROAST WILD DUCK WITH SPICED APPLE RINGS

- Color index page 40
- Begin 2½ hrs ahead
- 4 servings
- 669 cals per serving

2 2-pound ready-to-cook wild ducks
Salt
Pepper
1 teaspoon rosemary
2 small apples or oranges
2 small onions
Butter or margarine, melted
Spiced Apple Rings (p.290)
Watercress for garnish

1. Preheat oven to 350°F. Sprinkle cavities of ducks with salt, pepper, and rosemary; place apple and onion in each cavity, cutting them, if necessary, to fit. Brush ducks with butter.
2. Place ducks, breast side up, on rack in open roasting pan. Roast 1 to 1¼ hours until tender when pierced with two-tined fork between leg and body; juices that escape should not be pink.
3. Meanwhile, prepare Spiced Apple Rings; keep warm. If made ahead, serve at room temperature, or reheat in their syrup.
4. Remove apples and onions from ducks' cavities; discard. Place ducks on warm platter. Garnish with spiced apple rings and watercress.

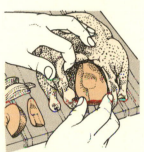 

Stuffing the ducks: Place small apples and onions in the cavities, cutting them in half, if necessary, to fit.

Arranging the platter: Place ducks in center of warm platter; arrange spiced apples and watercress around the ducks.

QUAIL WITH MUSHROOMS

- Color index page 40
- Begin 45 mins ahead
- 2 servings
- 633 cals per serving

⅓ cup butter or margarine
4 ready-to-cook quail
1 small onion, chopped
½ pound mushrooms, sliced
1 cup chicken broth
1¼ teaspoons salt
Toast points
2 tablespoons all-purpose flour
3 tablespoons Sauterne (optional)

1. Preheat oven to 350°F. In Dutch oven over medium heat, in hot butter, cook quail until browned on all sides; remove quail to platter.
2. To drippings in Dutch oven, add onion and mushrooms; cook, stirring occasionally, until onion is tender, about 5 minutes. Stir in chicken broth and salt. Add quail to mixture; cover; bake 20 minutes or until quail is tender.
3. Place quail on toast points on warm platter. In cup, blend flour and Sauterne (or 3 tablespoons water) until smooth; gradually stir into liquid in Dutch oven; cook over medium heat, stirring, until mixture is thickened. Serve with quail.

Game

PHEASANT IN CREAM

Pheasant, an increasingly popular game bird, came by way of England from China. It was first cultivated by Benjamin Franklin's son-in-law.

- Color index page 38
- Begin 2 hrs ahead
- 5 servings
- 374 cals per serving

2 1½- to 2-pound ready-to-cook pheasants, quartered
All-purpose flour
3 tablespoons butter or margarine

2 tablespoons salad oil
½ cup diced onion
1 teaspoon salt
2 teaspoons paprika
¼ teaspoon pepper
1½ cups half-and-half

1 Preheat oven to 350°F. On waxed paper, coat pheasant with about ½ cup flour.

2 In 10-inch skillet over medium heat, in hot butter and salad oil, cook pheasant until browned on all sides.

3 Remove pieces to shallow 2-quart baking pan as they are browned. Pour off all but 2 tablespoons drippings from skillet; add onion and cook until tender, about 5 minutes.

4 Stir 3 tablespoons flour, salt, paprika, and pepper into the onion in the skillet until well blended.

5 Gradually stir in half-and-half and cook, stirring constantly, until mixture is thickened; pour over pheasant.

6 Cover and bake 1 hour or until fork-tender. Remove pheasant to warm platter; stir sauce until smooth and pour over pheasant.

Chicken livers

CHICKEN LIVERS WITH BACON, ONIONS, AND APPLE

- Color index page 38
- Begin 45 mins ahead
- 4 servings
- 550 cals per serving

1 8-ounce package sliced bacon
2 medium onions, sliced
1 large red cooking apple, cut into wedges

1 pound chicken livers, each cut in half
½ cup water
1 tablespoon apple jelly
¼ teaspoon salt

1. With kitchen shears, cut each bacon slice into 1-inch pieces. In 12-inch skillet over medium heat, cook bacon pieces until browned, stirring occasionally.
2. With slotted spoon, remove bacon to paper towels to drain. In drippings remaining in skillet over medium heat, cook onions 5 minutes, stirring occasionally.
3. Add apple wedges, cook about 5 minutes longer or until onions and apple wedges are lightly browned and tender.
4. With slotted spoon, remove onions and apples to bowl. In drippings remaining in skillet over medium-high heat, cook chicken livers until lightly browned but still pink inside, stirring frequently.
5. Return the bacon, onions, and apple to the skillet; add water, apple jelly, and salt. Cook over medium heat until the mixture is hot, stirring frequently to loosen any brown bits from the bottom of the skillet.

CHICKEN-LIVER AND MUSHROOM RAGOUT

- Color index page 38
- Begin 45 mins ahead
- 4 servings
- 380 cals per serving

1 pound chicken livers
¾ pound mushrooms
1 medium onion
4 tablespoons butter or margarine
1 teaspoon salt
⅛ teaspoon pepper
½ cup water

1 tablespoon all-purpose flour
3 tablespoons dry Marsala wine
1 10-ounce package frozen Italian beans
1 16-ounce can or jar whole carrots, drained

1. Cut each chicken liver in half; remove white membrane. Cut mushrooms in halves or quarters if they are large. Slice onion.
2. In 12-inch skillet over medium heat, in hot butter or margarine, cook onion until almost tender, about 5 minutes, stirring occasionally. Increase heat to medium-high; add chicken livers, mushrooms, salt, and pepper and cook until livers are tender but still pink inside, about 5 minutes, stirring often.
3. In measuring cup, mix water, flour, and Marsala wine. Gradually stir flour mixture into mixture in skillet; cook, stirring constantly, until mixture is slightly thickened.
4. Add frozen Italian beans to mixture in skillet; over high heat, heat to boiling. Reduce heat to low; cover and simmer 10 minutes, separating beans with fork. Add the carrots and continue cooking until the beans are tender and carrots are heated through.

Stuffings

SAUSAGE-RICE STUFFING

¾ cup regular long-grain rice
½ pound sweet Italian sausage links, casings removed
1 green onion, thinly sliced
⅛ teaspoon pepper

- Begin 25 mins ahead
- 3 cups
- 306 cals per ½ cup

1. Prepare rice as label directs; meanwhile, in 10-inch skillet over medium heat, cook sausage until well browned, breaking apart with fork. Drain excess fat. Toss rice with sausage, onion, and pepper. Use to stuff one roasting chicken.

CHESTNUT STUFFING

1½ pounds chestnuts
Water
½ cup butter or margarine
2 medium celery stalks, diced
1 medium onion, diced
2 tablespoons minced parsley
1 teaspoon salt
½ teaspoon poultry seasoning
¼ teaspoon pepper
9 cups white-bread cubes (about 18 slices)
1 egg, slightly beaten

- Begin 1 hr ahead
- 7½ cups
- 360 cals per serving

1. In 4-quart saucepan over high heat, heat chestnuts and enough water to cover to boiling. Reduce heat to medium; cover; cook 10 minutes.
2. Remove saucepan from heat. With slotted spoon, remove 3 or 4 chestnuts at a time to cutting board. Cut each chestnut in half.
3. With tip of small knife, scrape out chestnut meat from its shell. (Skin will stay in shell.) Chop chestnut meat; set aside. Discard cooking water.
4. In same saucepan over medium heat, melt butter; add celery and onion; cook until vegetables are tender, about 10 minutes, stirring occasionally. Remove saucepan from heat; stir in remaining 6 ingredients, ½ cup water, and reserved chestnuts; mix well. Use to stuff small turkey or two chickens.

NUTTY BROWN-RICE STUFFING

1 12-ounce package brown rice (2 cups)
2 chicken-flavor bouillon cubes or envelopes
4 tablespoons butter or margarine
3 large celery stalks, sliced
2 large onions, diced
1 8-ounce can walnuts (2 cups), toasted and chopped
½ teaspoon rubbed sage

- Begin 30 mins ahead
- 12 cups
- 175 cals per ½ cup

1. In 3-quart saucepan, prepare brown rice as label directs, adding chicken-flavor bouillon.
2. In 12-inch skillet or 5-quart Dutch oven over medium heat, in hot butter or margarine, cook celery and onions until tender, about 7 minutes, stirring occasionally.
3. Remove skillet from heat; stir in toasted walnuts, sage, and cooked rice. Use to stuff 12- to 16-pound turkey. Or, spoon stuffing into 13" by 9" baking dish; cover and bake in 325°F. oven 1 hour or until heated through.

SAUSAGE AND CORN-BREAD STUFFING

Among the most popular of the seasoned mixtures used to stuff poultry, this is one of the many uses of corn, Benjamin Franklin's "most agreeable and wholesome grains."

1 12- to 14-ounce package corn-muffin mix
½ pound hot Italian sausage links
Water
3 medium celery stalks
½ teaspoon rosemary
¼ teaspoon salt
⅛ teaspoon thyme leaves
1 egg

- Begin 1 hr ahead
- 6 cups
- 180 cals per ½ cup

1 Preheat oven to 400°F. Grease 8" by 8" baking pan. Prepare corn-muffin mix as label directs. Spoon batter into prepared pan.

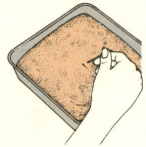

2 Bake 20 minutes or until toothpick inserted in center comes out clean. Cool corn bread in pan on wire rack slightly (will be sticky if crumbled when too hot).

3 Meanwhile, in 12-inch skillet over high heat, heat Italian sausage links and ¼ cup water to boiling. Reduce heat to low; cover and simmer 5 minutes.

4 Uncover skillet and cook over medium heat, turning sausages frequently to brown on all sides, about 15 minutes. Remove sausages to paper towels to drain.

5 Discard all but 2 tablespoons of the sausage drippings from the skillet.

6 Dice celery; in drippings in skillet over medium heat, cook until tender, stirring occasionally. Remove skillet from heat. Dice sausages and crumble corn bread; add to mixture in skillet with rosemary, salt, thyme leaves, egg, and 1 cup water; mix well. Use to stuff one 7-pound capon or small turkey.

Stuffings

APPLE-HERB STUFFING

Bread stuffing is traditionally flavored with sage; here the addition of apples makes it moist and sweet.

- Begin 30 mins ahead
- 5 cups
- 157 cals per cup

½ 14-inch-long loaf Italian bread
¼ teaspoon rubbed sage
¼ teaspoon thyme leaves
⅛ teaspoon salt
⅛ teaspoon pepper
Butter or margarine

3 medium red cooking apples
2 tablespoons minced green onions
¾ cup apple juice or white grape juice

1 Cut bread into ¾-inch cubes (about 5 cups loosely packed). In 12-inch skillet over medium heat, heat next 4 ingredients and 4 tablespoons butter until butter melts.

2 Add bread cubes; cook until lightly browned on all sides, turning bread cubes to brown evenly. Remove bread cubes to bowl. Wipe skillet clean.

3 Cut apples into ¾-inch chunks to make about 4 cups.

4 In same skillet over medium heat, melt 1 more tablespoon butter or margarine. Add apple chunks and green onions; cook until tender, stirring occasionally.

5 Return the bread cubes to the skillet; add the apple juice (or white grape juice). Heat through, stirring gently. This stuffing goes particularly well with roast duckling or goose.

MOIST BREAD STUFFING

1 cup butter or margarine
2 cups diced celery
1½ cups chopped onions
18 cups white-bread cubes (about 36 slices)
¼ cup minced parsley

2 teaspoons poultry seasoning
1¾ teaspoons salt
½ teaspoon pepper
3 eggs, slightly beaten

- Begin 30 mins ahead
- 10 cups
- 175 cals per ½ cup

1. In 5- to 8-quart Dutch oven or saucepot over medium heat, in hot butter or margarine, cook celery and onions until tender, about 8 minutes, stirring occasionally.
2. Remove Dutch oven from heat; add bread cubes and remaining ingredients; toss to mix well. Use to stuff 12- to 16-pound turkey. Or spoon stuffing into 13″ by 9″ baking dish; cover with foil and bake in preheated 325°F. oven 45 minutes or until heated through.

OYSTER STUFFING

- Begin 30 mins ahead
- 10 cups
- 190 cals per ½ cup

3 ½-pint containers shucked "standard" oysters
1 cup butter or margarine
1½ cups chopped celery
¾ cup chopped onion

12 cups white-bread cubes (about 24 slices)
1½ teaspoons salt
1 teaspoon pepper
¾ teaspoon poultry seasoning

1. Drain oysters, reserving ½ cup liquid. Coarsely chop oysters and set aside.
2. In 5- to 8-quart Dutch oven over medium heat, in hot butter or margarine, cook celery and onion until tender, stirring occasionally.
3. Remove Dutch oven from heat; add oysters, reserved oyster liquid, bread cubes, and remaining ingredients; toss to mix well. Use to stuff 12- to 16-pound turkey. Or spoon stuffing into 13″ by 9″ baking dish; cover with foil and bake in preheated 325°F. oven 45 minutes or until heated through.

HOW TO CALCULATE STUFFING QUANTITIES

Most poultry stuffings can be used for any type of bird, although some are traditionally used with certain types of poultry, such as chestnut stuffing and turkey.

Weight of bird (pounds)	Amount of stuffing (cups)
1½ – 4	1 – 3
4 – 8	3 – 6
8 – 12	6 – 9
12 – 16	9 – 12
16 – 20	12 – 15
20 – 24	15 – 18

Allow about ¾ to 1 cup stuffing per pound of bird. Spoon stuffing lightly into bird so it can expand during roasting and absorb the juices and flavor of the bird. Any extra stuffing can be baked in a greased covered casserole for about 45 minutes to an hour.

MEAT

*"Wish I had time for just
one more bowl of chili!"*

KIT CARSON'S alleged dying words

The Spanish were the first to bring cows and pigs to Florida in the 1500s, but most American cattle are descended from English breeds. There were cows in Jamestown by 1611, and commercial meat-packing began as early as 1662, when William Pynchon established a slaughterhouse in Boston.

In 1711 Philadelphians imitated their English cousins by starting a "Beef Stake Club." At that time, beefsteak was a flattened piece of meat, fried, and served with gravy — something like our Chicken-Fried Steak with Cream Gravy; it was usually eaten very rare. By the mid-1700s there were "beefsteak houses" in several American cities, a tradition that still prevails.

Texans started herding cattle, especially the Longhorn steer, in the early 1800s, and by the 1850s Chicago had become a center for meat-packing. The demand for beef grew rapidly after the Civil War, and the first cattle were shipped by railroad from Abilene, Kansas, in 1867.

With the introduction of the refrigerated railway car in 1871, beef became more available to Easterners, and by the late 1800s it was even being shipped to England. Veal, or calf's meat, also became more plentiful, especially in the South and Midwest. It didn't really become popular in the East, though, until the early 1900s, when European immigrants introduced tempting veal dishes, such as Veal Piccata and Veal Parmigiana, which later took prominent places on restaurant menus. By the twentieth century, beef was widely consumed, and a dinner of thick steak and potatoes became an American institution.

Although the early colonists had plenty of room for raising cattle, pork was eaten more often as pigs were easier to keep and feed; cows often wandered off into the woods, becoming wild. The first domesticated pigs in America were brought to Florida from Spain in 1539 by Hernando de Soto; all North American pigs are descended from that herd. Since pigs lived on scraps, colonists found them cheap and easy to keep. Salting and smoking pork were the main methods of preparing the meat, and salt pork became the most important meat in the early American diet. Virginia hams, particularly the specially cured Smithfield ham, quickly gained fame for their delicious taste.

In the South, every part of the pig was used, not only the meat, but the fat for soap-making. Ham Hocks and Collard Greens is a traditional Southern favorite, as is Ham and Grits with Red-Eye Gravy, a gravy made from ham drippings, water, and sometimes with coffee.

As with beef, demand for pork grew after the Civil War, and the meat-packing industry, centered in Chicago, boomed. As beef became more popular, however, pork's popularity decreased, perhaps because it was associated with a poor man's diet. Today pigs are bred to produce leaner meat, and pork is eaten more frequently; it is prepared as roasts, ribs, chops, in sausages and stews.

Although lamb has always been abundant in the U.S., it has never been as popular as other meats. Perhaps this is a throwback to the violent feuds between cattle ranchers and sheepherders when sheep were brought to the western steer country in the 1800s. Lamb is eaten more frequently in parts of the West and Southwest than in other areas of the country, perhaps due to the early Spanish influence.

Most American lamb is spring lamb. Some is raised in New Jersey and Pennsylvania, but a lot of the lamb we eat is imported from New Zealand. The most popular cuts are the chops, leg, rack, saddle, and shoulder.

Today, although the amount of meat consumed nationwide has declined in the past few years, America remains famous for its beef and as a country of meat eaters.

Steaks

STEAKS WITH MUSTARD BUTTER

- Color index page 43
- Begin 15 mins ahead
- 2 servings
- 690 cals per serving

Butter or margarine
2 beef top loin or rib eye steaks, each cut about ¾ inch thick
1½ teaspoons lemon juice
1½ teaspoons prepared mustard
Salt
Pepper

1. In 12-inch skillet over medium-high heat, melt 1 tablespoon butter or margarine.
2. Add steaks; cook until browned on both sides, about 8 minutes for rare or until of desired doneness.
3. Meanwhile, in cup, mix lemon juice, mustard, and 3 tablespoons softened butter or margarine. If you like, the mustard butter can be done ahead, stored in a small crock and refrigerated until ready to use.
4. When steaks are done, remove to warm plates; sprinkle with salt and pepper to taste and top with mustard butter.

LEMON-PEPPER STEAK: Prepare as in steps 1 and 2 above. In cup, mix *1 tablespoon grated lemon peel, 1 tablespoon butter,* softened, *2 teaspoons cracked black pepper, ½ teaspoon salt,* and *⅛ teaspoon garlic powder*. Finish as in step 4, omitting salt and pepper. 750 cals per serving.

CELEBRATION FILET MIGNON

- Color index page 41
- Begin 45 mins ahead
- 4 servings
- 380 cals per serving

¼ pound medium mushrooms
1 large or 2 medium tomatoes
Butter or margarine
1 large onion, cut into ¾-inch-thick slices
4 beef loin tenderloin steaks, each cut 1 inch thick
½ cup water
2 tablespoons prepared mustard
4 teaspoons capers, drained
Watercress sprigs for garnish

1. If you like, flute mushrooms (p.100). Set aside. Cut four thick center slices from tomatoes.
2. In 10-inch skillet over medium heat, in 1 teaspoon hot butter or margarine, cook tomato slices until heated through. Remove to warm large platter, keep warm.
3. Meanwhile, in 12-inch skillet over medium heat, in 2 tablespoons hot butter or margarine, cook onion until tender, stirring occasionally. Remove onion to bowl and set aside.
4. In drippings remaining in skillet, over medium-high heat, cook mushrooms and beef loin tenderloin steaks about 5 minutes for medium or until of desired doneness, turning steaks once. Remove steaks and mushrooms to platter, placing one steak on each tomato slice; keep warm.
5. Into drippings remaining in skillet, stir water, mustard, and capers; over medium heat, cook until mixture boils and thickens slightly, stirring constantly.
6. Return onions to skillet; heat through. Pour sauce over and around steaks. Garnish platter with watercress sprigs.

CHICKEN-FRIED STEAK WITH CREAM GRAVY

This beef dish, a favorite of roadside cafés in the South, Midwest, and Southwest, gets its name from its similarity to the recipe for Southern fried chicken.

- Color index page 41
- Begin 30 mins ahead
- 4 servings
- 504 cals per serving

1 pound beef top round steak, cut about ½ inch thick
All-purpose flour
3 tablespoons salad oil
½ cup water
1 cup milk
1 teaspoon salt
⅛ teaspoon pepper
3 cups hot mashed potatoes

1 On cutting board, coat top round steak with 3 tablespoons flour. With meat mallet or dull edge of French knife, pound both sides of meat well; cut into 4 pieces.

2 In 12-inch skillet over medium-high heat, in hot salad oil, cook steaks 3 to 5 minutes on each side, until well browned and of desired doneness. Remove to warm platter; keep warm.

3 In cup with fork, mix water with 2 tablespoons flour until smooth. (Use flour left over from coating steak plus more, if needed.)

4 Gradually stir flour mixture into drippings in skillet, stirring and scraping until brown bits are loosened from bottom of pan.

5 Stir in milk, salt, and pepper and cook over medium heat, stirring constantly, until gravy is thickened and boils.

6 Serve the Chicken-Fried Steak with mashed potatoes and pass the hot gravy, separately, in a gravy boat.

Steaks

PARTY STEAK TERIYAKI

Hawaiians adapted Chinese and Japanese recipes, creating Polynesian specialties like this delicious teriyaki marinated steak. Ideal for a party, it can be prepared in advance.

- Color index page 42
- Begin day ahead
- 10 servings
- 350 cals per serving

1 medium onion, sliced
1 small garlic clove, minced
½ cup soy sauce
2 tablespoons brown sugar
2 tablespoons lemon juice
1 tablespoon salad oil

1¼ teaspoons salt
½ teaspoon ground ginger
2 beef top round steaks, each cut 1 inch thick (about 1½ pounds each)
2 medium cucumbers

Creamy Stuffed Eggs
10 eggs
Water
½ cup mayonnaise
4 teaspoons lemon juice
1 tablespoon milk
½ teaspoon salt
¼ teaspoon pepper

1 In 12″ by 8″ baking dish, mix first 8 ingredients. Place steaks in marinade; turn to coat evenly. Cover; refrigerate 8 hours or overnight; turn occasionally.

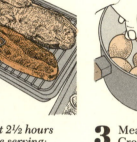

2 About 2½ hours before serving: Preheat broiler if manufacturer directs. Broil steaks 10 to 15 minutes for rare, turning once. Refrigerate.

3 Meanwhile, prepare Creamy Stuffed Eggs: In 4-quart saucepan, place eggs and enough water to cover; water should come 1 inch above tops of eggs.

4 Over high heat, heat to boiling. Remove pan from the heat; cover tightly and let eggs stand in hot water for about 15 minutes; drain.

5 Peel eggs under running cold water. Slice eggs lengthwise in half. Remove yolks and place in medium bowl; with fork, finely mash.

6 Stir in next 5 ingredients until the mixture is smooth. Pipe egg-yolk mixture into egg-white centers.

7 Mince enough cucumber to make 2 tablespoons; thinly slice remaining ones; set aside.

8 Remove steaks to cutting board and thinly slice; arrange on center of large platter.

9 Arrange cucumber slices and eggs around meat. Sprinkle with minced cucumber.

SHERRIED CUBED STEAKS

1 pound beef cubed steaks
Butter or margarine
3 tablespoons minced green onions

⅓ cup dry sherry
¼ teaspoon salt
⅛ teaspoon pepper
Radishes for garnish

1. If beef cubed steaks are large, cut each in half. In 12-inch skillet over medium-high heat, melt 2 tablespoons butter or margarine.

2. Add 2 or 3 pieces of steak at a time, cooking until browned on both sides and tender, about 4 minutes. Remove steaks to 4 dinner plates; keep steaks warm until ready to serve.

3. In drippings remaining in skillet, over medium heat, in 2 more tablespoons hot butter or margarine, cook green onions until tender, stirring occasionally.

4. Stir in sherry, salt, and pepper; cook until mixture boils, stirring to loosen brown bits from bottom of skillet. Pour sauce over steaks. Garnish with radishes.

- Color index page 42
- Begin 30 mins ahead
- 4 servings
- 365 cals per serving

BAKED SWISS STEAK

4 beef top round steaks, each ¼ inch thick (about 1½ pounds each)
⅓ cup all-purpose flour
2 tablespoons salad oil
4 medium onions, sliced
1 14½- to 16-ounce can stewed tomatoes
1 cup water
¾ teaspoon salt

½ teaspoon sugar
½ teaspoon Worcestershire
¼ teaspoon pepper
3 medium green peppers, cut into 1-inch-wide strips
1 10- to 12-ounce container Brussels sprouts

1. Cut each of the top round steaks crosswise in half. On a sheet of waxed paper, or on a plate, coat the meat evenly with flour.

2. In 8-quart Dutch oven over medium-high heat, in hot salad oil, cook meat, a few pieces at a time, until browned on both sides, removing meat to 13″ by 9″ baking dish as it browns and adding more oil if needed.

3. In drippings remaining in Dutch oven, over medium heat, cook onions until lightly browned, stirring occasionally and adding more oil if needed. Add stewed tomatoes, water, salt, sugar, Worcestershire, and pepper, stirring to loosen brown bits from bottom of Dutch oven; over high heat, heat to boiling.

4. Pour tomato mixture over meat in baking dish. Cover baking dish tightly with foil and bake in 350°F. oven 1 hour.

5. Add green peppers and Brussels sprouts to meat mixture in baking dish. Bake, covered, for 1 to 1½ hours longer, until meat and vegetables are tender. Remove to warm platter.

- Color index page 43
- Begin 2¾ hrs ahead
- 8 servings
- 345 cals per serving

BEEFSTEAK WITH RED-WINE SAUCE

- Color index page 42
- Begin 2½ hrs ahead
- 8 servings
- 385 cals per serving

2 tablespoons salad oil
1 beef chuck arm steak, 1 inch thick (about 2½ pounds)
1 pound medium mushrooms, each cut in half
¼ pound salt pork, diced
1 carrot, minced
1 garlic clove, minced

1½ cups dry red wine
1 tablespoon dark-brown sugar
1 teaspoon meat-extract paste
¼ teaspoon pepper
Chopped parsley and parsley sprigs for garnish

1. In 8-quart Dutch oven over medium-high heat, in hot salad oil, cook beef until well browned on both sides. Remove steak to plate; set aside.
2. Add mushrooms; cook over medium heat 5 minutes; with slotted spoon, remove to bowl; set mushrooms aside.
3. In same Dutch oven, cook salt pork until lightly browned. Add carrot and garlic; cook, stirring over medium-high heat until mixture is well browned.
4. Stir in the dry red wine, dark-brown sugar, and meat-extract paste. Return steak to Dutch oven; over high heat, heat to boiling. Reduce heat to low; cover and simmer 1½ hours, turning steak occasionally.
5. Stir in mushrooms and continue cooking until the steak and vegetables are tender, about 15 minutes.
6. To serve, arrange the steak on a warm platter. Skim the fat from the remaining liquid in Dutch oven. Spoon liquid and vegetables around steak; sprinkle with chopped parsley; garnish with a sprig of parsley.

LONDON BROIL

- Color index page 42
- Begin 20 mins ahead
- 6 servings
- 190 cals per serving

1 beef flank steak (about 1½ pounds)
1 tablespoon minced onion or 1 small garlic clove, minced
1 tablespoon salad oil

1 teaspoon salt
⅛ teaspoon pepper
1 tablespoon butter or margarine
2 teaspoons chopped parsley

1. Preheat broiler if manufacturer directs. With sharp knife, score both sides of flank steak for even broiling. Place steak on rack in broiling pan.
2. In small bowl, mix onion, salad oil, salt, and pepper. Rub steak on both sides with onion mixture.
3. Broil steak 5 minutes. With tongs, turn steak and continue to broil 5 more minutes for rare or until of desired doneness.
4. To serve, place steak on carving board or warm platter; spread with butter; sprinkle with parsley. With knife held in slanting position almost parallel to the cutting surface, cut thin slices across width of steak; spoon drippings over slices. (If you like, London Broil can also be grilled ahead and left to cool. Any leftover meat is delicious served cold.)

STEAK DIANE

Previously prepared at the table in restaurants only, Americans now make this flaming steak for parties or intimate dinners.

- Color index page 41
- Begin 20 mins ahead
- 4 servings
- 620 cals per serving

4 beef rib-eye steaks, each cut about ½ inch thick
Salt
Pepper
4 tablespoons butter or margarine

¼ cup brandy
2 small shallots, minced
3 tablespoons chopped chives
½ cup dry sherry

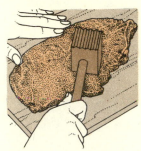

1 On cutting board, with meat mallet or the dull edge of a French knife, pound the beef rib-eye steaks until flattened to about ¼-inch thick, turning over occasionally. Sprinkle each of the steaks with salt and pepper to taste.

2 In a chafing dish at the table, or in a frying pan in the kitchen, over high heat, in 1 tablespoon hot butter or margarine, cook one beef rib-eye steak just until both sides are browned. (Do not overcook steak.)

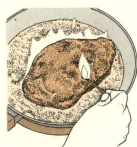

3 Pour 1 tablespoon brandy over steak and using a long match set the steak aflame. It should flare up at once.

4 When the flaming stops, stir in ¼ each of shallots and chives; cook, stirring constantly, until the shallots are tender, about 1 minute.

5 Add 2 tablespoons sherry to steak and shallots in pan; heat through. Place steak on a warm dinner plate.

6 Pour sherry mixture over steak. Keep warm. Repeat the same process with the three remaining steaks.

Steaks

Roasts

STUFFED BEEF ROLL

Italian immigrants brought this flavorful Sicilian dish to America. Originally called "Farsu Margru," or "fake lean," it starts with lean meat, but surprises with a rich filling.

1 beef top round steak cut 1 inch thick (about 1¼ pounds)
½ pound ground beef
1 egg
1 cup fresh bread crumbs (2 slices white bread)
2 tablespoons chopped parsley
1 tablespoon grated onion

Salt
1 4-ounce package sliced salami
½ 8-ounce package mozzarella cheese, cut into ¼-inch-thick strips
2 hard-cooked eggs, each cut lengthwise into 4 wedges

- Color index page 43
- Begin 2 hrs ahead
- 10 servings
- 374 cals per serving

½ cup frozen peas
2 tablespoons olive or salad oil
2 medium carrots, sliced
1 medium onion, sliced
1 14½- to 16-ounce can tomatoes
½ cup cooking or dry white wine
½ teaspoon basil

1 Butterfly the round steak: Holding knife parallel to work surface and starting from a long side of steak, cut steak horizontally almost but not all the way through.

2 Spread steak open to form 1 large piece; with meat mallet or dull edge of French knife, pound steak to about ¼-inch thickness.

3 Prepare the meat filling: In a medium bowl, mix ground beef (or you can use a combination of ground beef and veal or ground veal, if you prefer), egg, bread crumbs, parsley, grated onion, and ½ teaspoon salt. Spread this ground-beef mixture all over the flattened steak. Arrange the salami slices along the center of the steak in a lengthwise row over the ground-beef mixture, overlapping the slices if necessary.

4 Place cheese strips along one side of salami; place egg wedges along other side of salami; sprinkle with peas.

5 Starting at a long side, roll steak, jelly-roll fashion. With string, tie beef roll crosswise in several places.

6 In 8-quart Dutch oven over medium-high heat, in hot olive oil, cook beef roll until well browned on all sides.

7 Reduce heat to medium; add carrots and onion. Cook; stir often.

8 When the vegetables are lightly browned and tender, stir in the tomatoes with their liquid, cooking or dry white wine, basil, and ¾ teaspoon salt, stirring to break up the tomatoes; over a high heat, heat to boiling. Reduce heat to low; cover and simmer about 1 hour or until the meat is fork-tender, stirring frequently.

9 Arrange beef roll in deep platter; discard strings; spoon sauce over.

STANDING RIB ROAST

1 2- to 3-rib beef rib roast small end (4 to 6 pounds)
Salt
Pepper
Yorkshire Pudding (optional) (below)

Horseradish sauce (optional, p.385)
Watercress and Tomato Roses (p. 230) for garnish

1. Place roast on rib bones in open roasting pan. Sprinkle with salt and pepper. Insert meat thermometer into thickest part, making sure it is in center of roast and not resting on bone or fat.
2. Roast in 325°F. oven until internal temperature reaches 140°F. for rare (1¾ to 2½ hours); or until of desired doneness.
3. When roast is done, rest at room temperature 15 minutes for easier carving. If serving with Yorkshire Pudding, begin preparation about 5 minutes before end of roasting time.
4. Transfer roast to warm platter. Garnish with watercress and Tomato Roses. If you like, serve with Yorkshire Pudding and Horseradish sauce.

- Color index page 41
- Begin 2 to 4 hrs ahead
- 18 servings
- 513 cals per serving

YORKSHIRE PUDDING: In medium bowl with wire whisk beat *2 eggs* until foamy; beat in *1 cup milk* and *½ teaspoon salt*. Gradually beat in *1 cup all-purpose flour* until batter is smooth. When roast is done, spoon off 2 tablespoons drippings and divide into twelve 3-inch muffin cups; tilt to coat evenly; turn oven to 400°F. Heat muffin pan in oven 5 minutes; pour 2½ tablespoons batter in each greased muffin cup. Bake 30 minutes. Loosen Yorkshire Pudding; transfer to platter and serve immediately. Makes 12 individual puddings. 82 cals each.

Baking Yorkshire Pudding: Heat reserved drippings from Standing Rib Roast in muffin cups for 5 minutes before pouring batter into each cup. Bake for 30 minutes.

ROAST BEEF HASH: In large bowl, mix *2 cups finely chopped roast beef, 2 cups chopped cooked potatoes, ½ cup beef broth, ¼ cup minced onion, 2 tablespoons all-purpose flour,* and *2 teaspoons Worcestershire.* In 10-inch skillet over medium heat, in *¼ cup hot butter,* cook hash until well browned and crusty, pressing and turning occasionally with pancake turner, about 30 minutes. 4 servings. 421 cals per serving.

FAVORITE RIB-EYE ROAST

Always a favorite choice for Sunday dinner, this rib-eye roast, tender and succulent, is given a special herb coating.

- Color index page 41
- Begin 1¾ hrs ahead
- 16 servings
- 474 cals per serving

1 medium garlic clove
½ cup prepared mustard
2 tablespoons soy sauce
2 tablespoons olive or salad oil
½ teaspoon coarsely ground black pepper
¼ teaspoon ground ginger

1 4-pound beef rib-eye roast
Sautéed Herbed Mushrooms (right)
Lemon-Buttered Asparagus (right)
2 tablespoons minced parsley
Fresh thyme for garnish

1 Into small bowl with a garlic press, press garlic. Stir in mustard and next 4 ingredients. Place beef rib-eye roast on rack in open roasting pan.

2 With a pastry brush, brush half of mustard mixture over top of roast. Insert meat thermometer into center of thickest part of roast.

3 Roast in 350°F. oven until thermometer reaches 140°F. for rare (about 20 minutes per pound) or until meat is of desired doneness.

4 Meanwhile, prepare Sautéed Herbed Mushrooms and Lemon-Buttered Asparagus; keep vegetables warm until ready to serve.

5 About 10 minutes before beef rib-eye roast is done, with pastry brush, brush top of roast with remaining mustard, soy, and oil mixture.

6 To serve, press parsley on roast. Place on warm platter. Surround with mushrooms and asparagus. Garnish with fresh thyme.

SAUTÉED HERBED MUSHROOMS: In 5-quart Dutch oven over medium-high heat, melt **4 tablespoons butter**. Add **2 pounds medium mushrooms**, sliced, **½ teaspoon salt**, **¼ teaspoon thyme leaves**, and **⅛ teaspoon pepper**; cook, stirring often, until mushrooms are tender, about 10 minutes. 16 servings. 38 cals per serving.

LEMON-BUTTERED ASPARAGUS: Prepare **2½ pounds asparagus**: Hold base of each stalk firmly and bend (end will break off at spot where it becomes tough); discard ends; with sharp knife, remove scales. If you like, trim rough end of each stalk even. In 12-inch skillet over medium heat, melt **3 tablespoons butter** or **margarine**. Add asparagus, **1 tablespoon lemon juice**, and **¾ teaspoon salt**; cover; cook until asparagus is tender-crisp, about 5 minutes, turning occasionally. 16 servings. 28 cals per serving.

HOW TO CARVE ROAST BEEF

It is important to let roasted meat rest for 15–20 minutes after removing from the oven; this allows the juices to settle back into the meat, and makes for easier carving. Transfer the meat to a warm platter and cover with foil; keep in a warm place while you prepare the gravy and last-minute vegetables.

For a Rib of Beef:
After leaving the meat to rest for 15–20 minutes, place on a board or platter, bone (large) end down, ribs to your left. Insert carving fork between the top 2 ribs. With a sharp carving knife, carefully cut across meat toward the rib bone, making a ¼-inch-thick slice.

Then with the tip of the knife, cut down along the rib bone, cutting as close to the bone as possible, to release slice; transfer the slice to a warm plate. Continue cutting the meat, removing each bone as it is exposed.

For a Boneless Roast:
Place cooked, roast meat on a board or warm platter; remove any strings, wooden picks or skewers (or leave one or two in place if roast starts to fall apart). Anchor meat with fork: with sharp, carving knife, cut roast crosswise, against the grain, into slices ¼- to ½-inch thick.

Pot roasts

YANKEE POT ROAST

Harsh winter climates may have inspired New Englanders to produce this warming dish of slow-cooked meat and vegetables.

- Color index page 42
- Begin 4 hrs ahead
- 12 servings
- 722 cals per serving

2 tablespoons salad oil	Water
1 4- to 4½-pound beef chuck cross rib roast, boneless	8 medium potatoes, peeled and halved
2 teaspoons salt	8 medium carrots, cut into 3-inch pieces
1 teaspoon sugar	1 pound small white onions
½ teaspoon pepper	¼ cup all-purpose flour
½ teaspoon thyme leaves	Parsley sprigs for garnish
1 bay leaf	

 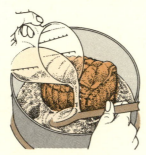

1 In 8-quart Dutch oven over medium-high heat, in hot salad oil, brown beef chuck cross rib roast until the meat is well browned on all sides.

2 Stir in salt, sugar, pepper, thyme leaves, bay leaf, and 3 cups water; heat to boiling. Reduce the heat to low; cover and simmer for for 2¼ hours.

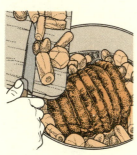 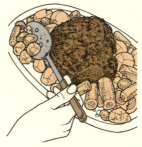

3 Add the vegetables; over high heat, heat to boiling. Reduce heat to medium-low; cover; cook 45 minutes or until the meat and vegetables are fork-tender.

4 Remove strings from the meat, if tied. Arrange vegetables and meat on warm platter; keep warm. Skim off fat from liquid in Dutch oven. Discard bay leaf.

5 In small bowl, blend flour and ½ cup water; gradually stir into liquid in Dutch oven.

6 Over medium heat, stir until thickened. Serve in gravy boat; garnish dish with parsley.

CORNED BEEF WITH CABBAGE AND CARROTS

- Color index page 42
- Begin 4 hrs ahead
- 24 servings
- 355 cals per serving

1 6-pound corned-beef brisket	Water
1 medium onion, cut in half	⅔ cup packed brown sugar
1 celery stalk, cut up	2 tablespoons prepared mustard
1 large carrot, cut up	2 tablespoons catchup
2 garlic cloves, each cut in half	Sautéed Cabbage (below)
½ teaspoon whole black peppercorns	Orange Baby Carrots (below)

1. Prepare corned beef as label directs, or in 8-quart Dutch oven or saucepot over high heat, heat first 6 ingredients with enough water to cover meat to boiling. Reduce heat to low; cover and simmer 3 hours or until meat is fork-tender.
2. Preheat oven to 350°F. Cut meat into slices. Arrange meat, overlapping slices, on ovenproof platter or in open roasting pan.
3. In bowl, mix sugar, mustard, and catchup; spread on top and between meat slices; bake 20 minutes or until glaze is browned. To serve, arrange vegetables on platter with meat.

SAUTÉED CABBAGE: Coarsely slice *2 small heads green cabbage*. In 8-quart Dutch oven over high heat, heat *¼ cup salad oil* until very hot; stir in cabbage, *1 teaspoon salt*, and *¼ teaspoon sugar*; cook, stirring often, until cabbage is tender-crisp, about 5 to 10 minutes.

ORANGE BABY CARROTS: In 2-quart saucepan over medium heat, heat *⅓ cup orange marmalade*, *1 tablespoon orange juice*, *1 teaspoon chopped parsley*, and *⅛ teaspoon salt* to boiling. Add *two 16-ounce cans whole baby carrots*, drained; heat through.

SPICY BEEF BRISKET

- Color index page 42
- Begin 4 hrs ahead
- 16 servings
- 215 cals per serving

2 small onions	2 tablespoons salad oil
1 garlic clove	½ cup chili sauce
1 4-pound beef brisket	1½ teaspoons sugar
10 whole cloves	1 teaspoon
Water	Worcestershire

1. Cut 1 onion into quarters; cut garlic clove in half. In 8-quart Dutch oven or saucepot over high heat, heat brisket, whole cloves, quartered onion, garlic, and enough water to cover meat to boiling. Reduce heat to low; cover and simmer 2½ to 3 hours, until meat is tender.
2. *About 15 minutes before meat is done, prepare glaze:* Dice remaining onion. In 2-quart saucepan over medium heat, in hot salad oil, cook diced onion until tender, stirring occasionally. Add chili sauce, sugar, Worcestershire, ¼ cup water; cover and simmer 5 minutes.
3. When meat is done, preheat oven to 325°F. Place meat in 13″ by 9″ baking pan; pour glaze over meat. Bake about 15 minutes or until glaze is bubbly and set.

NEW ENGLAND BOILED DINNER

1 4-pound corned-beef
  brisket
1 garlic clove
½ teaspoon whole black
  peppercorns
Water
1 medium rutabaga
  (about 2 pounds), cut
  into 2-inch chunks
16 small red potatoes
16 small white onions
6 medium carrots, cut
  into 2-inch pieces
1 medium head green
  cabbage (about
  2 pounds), cut into
  wedges

1. Prepare brisket as label directs, or in 8-inch Dutch oven over high heat, heat brisket, garlic, peppercorns, and enough water to cover to boiling. Reduce heat to low; cover; simmer about 3 hours or until meat is fork-tender. Remove brisket from Dutch oven; keep warm.
2. Taste brisket cooking liquid; if too salty, discard enough liquid, replacing it with fresh water, to reach desired salt level. Add rutabaga, potatoes, onions, and carrots; over high heat, heat to boiling. Reduce heat to low; cover and simmer 20 minutes. Add cabbage; cook 10 minutes more or until all vegetables are tender.
3. To serve, arrange brisket and vegetables on warm large platter.

- Color index page 42
- Begin 4 hrs ahead
- 16 servings
- 400 cals per serving

CORNED BEEF HASH

3 cups finely chopped
  cooked corned beef
3 cups finely chopped
  cooked potatoes
½ cup milk
3 tablespoons all-purpose
  flour
2 tablespoons chopped
  parsley
2 tablespoons finely
  chopped onion
¼ teaspoon salt
¼ teaspoon pepper
¼ cup butter or
  margarine
Parsley sprigs for garnish

1. In large bowl, mix first 8 ingredients.
2. In 10-inch skillet, preferably with non-stick surface, over medium heat, in 2 tablespoons hot butter, spread corned beef mixture to cover skillet evenly. Cook until underside is well browned and crisp, about 20 to 30 minutes, pressing hash firmly into a cake with pancake turner. Remove from heat.
3. Invert a large plate over the skillet; holding plate and skillet together with pot holders, invert the hash onto the plate.
4. In same skillet over medium heat, in 2 tablespoons hot butter, slide hash into skillet; cook until brown and crisp on other side.
5. To serve, invert hash onto plate again. Garnish with parsley sprig.

- Color index page 43
- Begin 1 hr ahead
- 6 servings
- 589 cals per serving

RED FLANNEL HASH: Prepare as above but reduce corned beef to **2 cups** and add **1 cup chopped cooked beets**. 442 cals per serving.

CRANBERRY POT ROAST WITH ACORN SQUASH

This all-American pot roast, with sweet and spicy cranberry gravy, is served with delicious roast acorn squash, one of the favorite winter squashes of the Indians.

2 tablespoons salad oil
1 4-pound boneless beef
  chuck arm pot roast
½ teaspoon ground
  cinnamon
¼ teaspoon ground
  ginger
¼ teaspoon pepper
Water
Salt
3 medium acorn squash
½ cup butter or
  margarine
2 tablespoons sugar
1 16-ounce can whole-
  berry cranberry sauce
2 tablespoons cornstarch

- Color index page 42
- Begin 3 hrs ahead
- 12 servings
- 470 cals per serving

1 In 8-quart Dutch oven over medium-high heat, in hot salad oil, cook roast until browned on all sides. Add cinnamon, ginger, and pepper.

2 Stir in ⅓ cup water, and 2 teaspoons salt; heat to boiling. Reduce heat to low; cover and simmer 2 hours, turning meat occasionally.

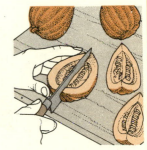

3 After cooking beef chuck arm pot roast for 1 hour, prepare acorn squash: Cut each squash into quarters; scoop out the seeds.

4 In 15½" by 10½" roasting pan, in a 350°F. oven, melt butter or margarine. Remove the pan from the oven; stir in sugar and 1½ teaspoons of salt.

5 Place squash in roasting pan; brush with the butter mixture. Cover pan with foil; bake 30 minutes; remove foil; bake 30 minutes longer or until squash is tender.

6 About 15 minutes before roast is done, add cranberry sauce to liquid in Dutch oven; when roast is fork-tender, remove to cutting board.

7 Skim fat from liquid. In cup, blend cornstarch and 2 tablespoons water until smooth.

8 Stir into liquid in Dutch oven; cook, stirring constantly, until gravy thickens and boils.

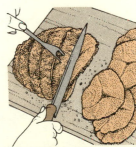

9 With sharp knife, cut meat into thin slices; serve roast with gravy and acorn squash.

Stews and pieces

BEEF IN BEER

- Color index page 45
- Begin 2¾ hrs ahead
- 8 servings
- 518 cals per serving

This traditional American stew originated on the prairies, where beef, and sometimes buffalo, were simmered in a tasty sauce.

4 slices bacon, cut into 1-inch pieces
3 large onions (1½ pounds), sliced
3 pounds beef for stew cut into 2-inch chunks
Salad oil
2 tablespoons all-purpose flour
1 12-ounce can beer

1 cup water
1 beef-flavor bouillon cube or envelope
1 small bay leaf
2 teaspoons sugar
¾ teaspoon salt
¼ teaspoon thyme leaves
⅛ teaspoon pepper
2 tablespoons red wine vinegar

1 In 12-inch skillet over medium heat, cook the bacon until browned; with slotted spoon, remove bacon to 3-quart casserole.

2 In drippings remaining in skillet, cook onions until tender and lightly browned, stirring often. With slotted spoon, remove to casserole.

3 In drippings in skillet over medium heat, cook beef pieces a few at a time, until brown (add oil if needed); remove to casserole.

4 In same skillet over medium heat, into an additional 2 tablespoons hot salad oil, stir flour; cook, stirring constantly, until dark brown.

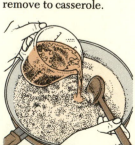

5 Gradually stir in beer and remaining ingredients except vinegar; cook until thickened. Add to casserole.

6 Bake, covered, in 350°F. oven 1¾ hours. Spoon off fat. Stir in vinegar.

OLD-COUNTRY SHORT-RIB DINNER

- Color index page 45
- Begin 2½ hrs ahead
- 8 servings
- 855 cals per serving

2 tablespoons salad oil
4 pounds beef chuck short ribs
1 28-ounce can tomatoes
1 cup water
1 tablespoon Worcestershire
2 teaspoons salt
1 teaspoon sugar
½ teaspoon pepper

1 medium onion, thinly sliced
2 16-ounce cans white hominy, rinsed and drained
2 medium carrots, cut into 2-inch pieces
1 small bunch broccoli, cut into 1½-inch pieces
¼ teaspoon basil

1. In 5-quart Dutch oven over medium-high heat, in hot salad oil, cook short ribs, a few pieces at a time, until browned on all sides, removing short ribs to large bowl as they brown. Spoon off fat remaining in Dutch oven.

2. Return short ribs to Dutch oven; add tomatoes with their liquid, water, Worcestershire, salt, sugar, pepper, and sliced onion; over high heat, heat to boiling. Reduce heat to low; cover and simmer 1¼ hours, stirring occasionally.

3. Skim fat from liquid in Dutch oven. Stir in hominy and carrots; over high heat, heat to boiling. Reduce heat to low; cover and simmer 30 minutes. Stir in broccoli and basil; over high heat, heat to boiling. Reduce heat to low; cover and simmer, 10 minutes longer, stirring occasionally, until vegetables and meat are tender. To serve, arrange ribs and vegetables on warm platter.

PRESSURE-COOKED BEEF STEW

- Color index page 45
- Begin 5 hrs ahead
- 8 servings
- 450 cals per serving

2 pounds beef for stew, cut into 1½-inch chunks
½ cup dry red wine
2 tablespoons salad oil
¼ pound lean salt pork, cut into ½-inch cubes
1 14½- to 16-ounce can tomatoes
1 large onion, minced
1 large carrot, minced
1 celery stalk, minced

1 small garlic clove, minced
1 bay leaf
1½ teaspoons salt
1 teaspoon thyme leaves
3 parsley sprigs
12 pimento-stuffed olives, each cut in half
1 4-ounce can whole mushrooms, drained
4 cups buttered, hot cooked noodles

1. In large bowl, combine meat, wine, and salad oil. Cover and refrigerate at least 4 hours.

2. About 30 minutes before serving: Drain meat, reserving marinade. In 4-quart pressure cooker over medium-high heat, cook salt pork until golden; add meat and cook until well browned. Add reserved marinade, tomatoes with their liquid, and remaining ingredients except mushrooms and noodles. Cover and bring cooker to 15 pounds pressure as manufacturer directs; cook 20 minutes.

3. Remove cooker from heat and reduce pressure quickly as manufacturer directs before uncovering stew. Add mushrooms and heat through gently. Discard parsley and bay leaf. Serve beef stew over buttered, hot cooked noodles.

BEEF ENCHILADAS

Enchilada, a Spanish-American word for "filled with chili," is a tortilla folded around a mixture of meat, cheese, chili, or other ingredients.

Salad oil
1½ pounds beef for stew
1 medium onion, chopped
2 teaspoons chili powder
¾ cup water
¾ teaspoon salt

1 4-ounce package shredded Cheddar cheese
1 7-ounce package 6-inch corn tortillas (12)
3 10-ounce cans mild enchilada sauce

- Color index page 43
- Begin 2 hrs ahead
- 6 servings
- 670 cals per serving

½ medium head iceberg lettuce, thinly sliced
1 3.2-ounce can (drained weight) pitted ripe olives, drained and thinly sliced

1 In 2-quart saucepan over medium-high heat, in 2 tablespoons hot salad oil, cook meat and onion until the meat is browned, stirring occasionally. Stir in chili powder; cook 1 minute.

2 Stir in water and salt; heat to boiling. Reduce the heat to low; cover and simmer, stirring occasionally, until the meat is very tender and begins to fall apart, about 1½ hours. Remove from heat.

3 When meat is done, shred with 2 forks. Place in bowl and stir in half of cheese. In 10-inch skillet over medium heat, in ¼ inch hot salad oil, fry 1 tortilla at a time.

4 Fry a few seconds on each side until soft and blistered. Remove tortilla to paper towels to drain. Preheat oven to 350°F. Grease 13" by 9" baking dish.

5 Assemble the enchiladas: Pour 2 cans of enchilada sauce into pie plate. Slip fried tortillas, one at a time, into enchilada sauce to soften slightly.

6 Using a slotted pancake turner, lift tortilla to a large plate. Spread 2 rounded tablespoons of the meat mixture in lengthwise strip along center of tortilla.

7 Fold left and right sides of tortilla over mixture; place, seam side down, in a baking dish. Repeat to make eleven more enchiladas.

8 Pour the remaining can of sauce over the enchiladas and sprinkle the enchiladas evenly with the remaining cheese. Bake about 30 minutes or until the enchiladas are hot and bubbly. Arrange the sliced lettuce around the enchiladas and top with the olives. If you like, serve the enchiladas with some additional lettuce or extra shredded cheese.

BEEF AND OYSTER PIE

1 beef kidney (about 1 pound)
¼ cup all-purpose flour
2 pounds beef for stew, cut into 1-inch chunks
Salad oil
1 garlic clove, cut in half
4 medium carrots, cut into 1-inch chunks
1 large onion, chopped
1 12-ounce can or bottle beer
2 tablespoons steak sauce
½ teaspoon salt
¼ teaspoon pepper
Water
1 8-ounce container shucked oysters
1 9-inch Unbaked Piecrust (p.310)
1 egg yolk

1. Rinse kidney. With knife, remove membranes and hard white parts from kidney; cut the kidney into 1-inch chunks.
2. On waxed paper, coat kidney chunks with 1 tablespoon flour; place in small bowl. Coat beef for stew with remaining flour; place coated beef on a large plate.
3. In 5-quart Dutch oven over medium-high heat, in ¼ cup hot salad oil, cook garlic until golden; discard garlic. In same Dutch oven, cook kidney until well browned. With slotted spoon, remove kidney to bowl; set aside.
4. In oil remaining in Dutch oven, cook beef for stew until well browned. With slotted spoon, remove beef for stew to plate. In drippings remaining in Dutch oven (add 2 tablespoons salad oil if necessary) over medium heat, cook carrots and onion until lightly browned, stirring frequently.
5. Return browned beef for stew to Dutch oven; stir in the beer, steak sauce, salt, pepper, and ½ cup water; over high heat, heat to boiling. Reduce heat to low; cover and simmer for 1½ hours or until the beef is fork-tender, stirring occasionally to prevent sticking.
6. When beef is tender, stir kidney and oysters with their liquid into beef mixture; spoon into 2½-quart round casserole. Prepare Unbaked Piecrust, steps 1 and 2. Meanwhile, preheat the oven to 400°F.
7. On lightly floured surface with lightly floured rolling pin, roll dough into a circle about 1½ inches larger all around than the top of the casserole with the beef mixture.
8. Place pastry loosely over meat mixture. With kitchen shears, trim pastry edge, leaving 1-inch overhang. Fold overhang under and press gently all around casserole rim to make a high stand-up edge on the pie.
9. With top of knife, cut several slits in pastry top. In cup with fork, mix egg yolk with 1 teaspoon water. Brush the slit crust with the egg-yolk mixture.
10. If you like, reroll scraps and use a cookie cutter to cut out shapes to decorate top of pie; brush cut-outs with yolk mixture. Bake pie 20 minutes or until crust is golden and mixture is heated through.

- Color index page 43
- Begin 2 hrs ahead
- 10 servings
- 485 cals per serving

Stews and pieces

MICHIGAN-STYLE PASTIES

These all-in-one lunches were originally the fare of Cornish miners who settled in Michigan in the 1800s. They are now so popular that May 24th is Michigan Pasty Day.

1 pound beef top round steak, cut about ½ inch thick
Unseasoned meat tenderizer
4 small carrots, thinly sliced

2 medium turnips, diced
1 medium onion, minced
¾ teaspoon thyme leaves
¼ teaspoon pepper
Salt
2 cups all-purpose flour

¾ cup shortening
5 to 6 tablespoons cold water
Milk
Watercress for garnish

- Color index page 43
- Begin 2 hrs ahead
- 4 servings
- 822 cals per serving

1 Prepare steak with meat tenderizer as label directs; cut into ½-inch cubes. In large bowl mix well meat, vegetables, thyme, pepper, and 1 teaspoon salt.

2 In medium bowl, stir 1 teaspoon salt into flour. With pastry blender or two knives used scissor-fashion, cut shortening into mixture to resemble coarse crumbs.

3 Sprinkle water, a tablespoon at a time, into flour mixture, mixing lightly with fork after each addition until dough just holds together. Shape dough into a ball.

4 Divide into 4 pieces. On lightly floured surface with floured rolling pin, roll one dough piece into a circle 9 inches in diameter and ⅛-inch thick; trim edge.

5 Place pastry circle on large cookie sheet; spoon ¼ meat mixture onto center, spreading it into an oval mound.

6 Gently pull pastry edges up around meat mixture, pinching firmly together to seal; trim edges to ½ inch and fold edges over. Repeat to make 4 pasties in all.

7 Reroll trimmings to about 10″ by 3″ rectangle; cut lengthwise into 12 thin strips. Form 3 strips into a braid.

8 Moisten sealed edge of a pasty with milk; place braid on edge, pressing lightly along length of the edge.

9 Repeat with remaining strips. Brush with milk. Bake in 400°F. oven 1 hour until golden. Garnish with watercress.

Ground

TEXAS-STYLE CHILI

1 3½- to 4-pound boneless beef chuck blade steak
¼ cup salad oil
2 cups chopped onions
3 medium green peppers, diced
4 garlic cloves, crushed
2 28-ounce cans tomatoes
1 12-ounce can tomato paste
2 cups water

⅓ cup chili powder
¼ cup sugar
2 tablespoons salt
2 teaspoons oregano leaves
¾ teaspoon cracked pepper
½ cup shredded Monterey Jack
Shredded cheese for garnish

1. With sharp knife, cut chuck blade steak into ½-inch cubes.
2. In 8-quart Dutch oven over medium-high heat, in hot salad oil, cook ⅓ meat at a time, until browned on all sides. With slotted spoon, remove meat to bowl; set aside.
3. Reserve ½ cup onions; cover; set aside. Add remaining onions, green peppers, and garlic to drippings in Dutch oven; over medium heat, cook 10 minutes, stirring occasionally, adding more oil if necessary.
4. Return meat to Dutch oven; add tomatoes and their liquid and remaining ingredients except cheese for garnish and reserved onion; over high heat, heat to boiling. Reduce heat to low; cover and simmer 1½ hours or until meat is fork-tender, stirring occasionally.
5. Spoon chili into large bowl; sprinkle shredded cheese over top for garnish. Pass reserved onion to sprinkle over each serving, if you like.

- Color index page 44
- Begin 2 hrs ahead
- 12 servings
- 155 cals per serving

CHILI CON CARNE

1 tablespoon salad oil
2 pounds lean ground beef
1 cup coarsely chopped onions
¼ cup diced green pepper
2 large garlic cloves, minced

2 14½- to 16-ounce cans tomatoes or 4 cups chopped, peeled, fresh tomatoes
¼ to ⅓ cup chili powder
1½ teaspoons salt
2 15¼- to 19-ounce cans red kidney or pinto beans

1. In 5-quart Dutch oven over medium-high heat, in hot salad oil, cook ground beef, chopped onions, diced green pepper, and minced garlic until onion is tender, about 10 minutes, stirring frequently.
2. Add tomatoes and their liquid, chili powder, and salt; heat to boiling. Reduce heat to low; cover and simmer 1 hour, stirring occasionally.
3. Stir in beans and their liquid; heat. Serve in soup bowls with a choice of accompaniments. (Serve any of the following in a small bowl: minced onions, chopped coriander, fresh chilies, or shredded Monterey Jack cheese.)

- Color index page 44
- Begin 1½ hrs ahead
- 10 servings
- 240 cals per serving

HEARTY MEATBALLS

1½ pounds ground beef, pork, and/or veal
¾ cup dried bread crumbs
¼ cup water
⅛ teaspoon pepper
1 egg
Salt
2 tablespoons salad oil
1 medium onion, diced
1 medium carrot, diced
1 medium celery stalk, diced
1 14½- to 16-ounce can tomatoes
¼ cup cooking or dry white wine
½ teaspoon basil
1 tablespoon minced parsley
2 teaspoons grated lemon peel

1. In large bowl, mix first 5 ingredients and 1 teaspoon salt. Shape into six meatballs.
2. In 10-inch skillet over medium-high heat, in hot salad oil, cook meatballs until browned on all sides, removing to plate as they brown. In drippings remaining in skillet over medium heat, cook onion, carrot, and celery until lightly browned and tender, stirring occasionally.
3. Return meatballs to skillet. Stir in tomatoes with their liquid, wine, basil, and ¾ teaspoon salt; stir to break up tomatoes; over high heat, heat to boiling. Reduce heat to low; cover and simmer 30 minutes; stirring occasionally.
4. Skim off fat from liquid in skillet. Spoon meatballs and sauce into warm deep platter. Sprinkle with parsley and lemon peel.

- *Color index page 43*
- *Begin 1 hr ahead*
- *6 servings*
- *324 cals per serving*

MEXICAN-STYLE MEATBALLS

Salad oil
1 medium onion, minced
1½ pounds ground beef
1 8- to 8¾-ounce can red kidney beans, drained and mashed
½ cup dried bread crumbs
¼ teaspoon pepper
1 egg
Salt
Chili powder
1 4-ounce can mild chopped green chilies, drained
1 10¾-ounce can condensed tomato soup, undiluted
1 2-ounce jar diced pimentos, drained
1 cup water
1 teaspoon sugar

1. In 12-inch skillet over medium-high heat, in 2 tablespoons hot salad oil, cook onion until tender, about 5 minutes. In large bowl, mix onion and next 6 ingredients with 1 teaspoon chili powder and 1 tablespoon green chillies. Shape mixture into 1-inch meatballs.
2. In same skillet over medium-high heat, in 3 more tablespoons hot oil, cook meatballs, a few at a time, until well browned on all sides; remove to bowl. Pour off any oil in skillet.
3. Return meatballs to skillet; add last 4 ingredients, 1 teaspoon salt, 1 teaspoon chili powder, and remaining green chillies. Over medium heat, heat to boiling. Reduce heat to low; cover; simmer 15 minutes, stirring occasionally.

- *Color index page 44*
- *Begin 1 hr ahead*
- *8 servings*
- *305 cals per serving*

STUFFED CABBAGE ROLLS

Early Dutch settlers probably brought the first cabbages to America; later, East European immigrants introduced their favorite dishes, such as stuffed cabbage.

1 small head green cabbage (about 1½ pounds)
1 pound lean ground beef
1 medium onion, chopped
1 15¼- to 19-ounce can red kidney beans, drained
1 8-ounce container creamed cottage cheese (1 cup)
½ teaspoon ground allspice
Salt
1 14½- to 16-ounce can tomatoes
1 tablespoon brown sugar
¼ cup water
2 teaspoons cornstarch

- *Color index page 45*
- *Begin 2 hrs ahead*
- *8 servings*
- *227 cals per serving*

1 Discard tough outer cabbage leaves; remove the core. Fill 5-quart saucepot ¾ full with water; heat water to boiling. Add cabbage cut side up.

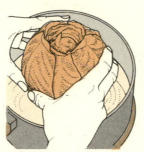

2 Using 2 large spoons, gently separate the leaves as the outer leaves soften slightly; remove 16 leaves from cabbage and let drain in colander.

3 Trim rib of each reserved leaf very thin. Drain and coarsely shred remaining cabbage; set aside.

4 In 12-inch skillet over medium-high heat, cook beef and onion until meat is browned and onion is tender, about 10 minutes.

5 Remove from heat; stir in beans, cottage cheese, allspice, and 1 teaspoon salt. On center of each leaf, place about ¼ cupful beef mixture.

6 Fold 2 sides of cabbage leaf toward center over meat, overlapping edges. From one narrow edge, roll jelly-roll fashion.

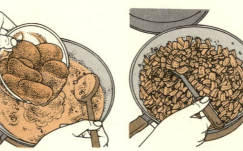

7 In same 12-inch skillet, add the tomatoes with their liquid, brown sugar, and ¾ teaspoon salt.

8 Over high heat, heat to boiling, stirring to break up tomatoes; reduce heat to low. Spread cabbage in skillet.

9 Arrange the stuffed cabbage rolls, seam side down, on cabbage in skillet. Cover and simmer 45 minutes or until the cabbage rolls are fork-tender. In cup, stir water and cornstarch until well blended; gradually stir cornstarch mixture into tomato mixture in skillet. Cook over medium heat, stirring constantly, until the mixture is slightly thickened. Arrange cabbage on warm platter; pour over sauce and serve hot.

Ground

MEAT AND POTATO LOAF

Here's an unusual way to serve two all-time favorites – ground beef and potatoes. When the round loaf is sliced, there's a mashed potato surprise in the center.

3 medium potatoes (about 1 pound), unpeeled
Water
1 tablespoon salad oil
1 medium green pepper, diced
1½ pounds ground beef

2 cups fresh bread crumbs (4 slices white bread)
½ teaspoon basil
1 egg
Salt
Water

Pepper
3 tablespoons milk
4 tablespoons butter or margarine
2 large onions, sliced
2 ounces Swiss cheese, shredded (½ cup)

- *Color index page 44*
- *Begin 2 hrs ahead*
- *6 servings*
- *466 cals per serving*

1 In 2-quart saucepan over high heat, heat potatoes and water to cover, to boiling. Reduce heat to low; cover; cook 30 minutes until tender.

2 Meanwhile, in 12-inch skillet over medium heat, in hot salad oil, cook the diced green pepper until tender, stirring occasionally.

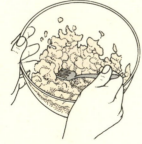

3 Remove skillet from heat; stir in ground beef, the bread crumbs, basil, egg, ¼ cup water, 1½ teaspoons salt, and ¼ teaspoon pepper.

4 In deep 1½-quart oven-safe bowl, press the ground-beef mixture to line inside of bowl, creating a 1-inch thick shell.

5 Peel cooked potatoes. In a medium bowl, mash the potatoes until smooth; stir in the milk and ½ teaspoon salt. Mix thoroughly.

6 Spoon the mashed potatoes into the center of the ground-beef mixture, pressing firmly. Bake in 350°F. oven 1 hour 15 minutes.

7 About 15 minutes before loaf is done, in a 10-inch skillet over medium-high heat, in hot butter, cook onions with ¼ teaspoon salt until tender; stir occasionally.

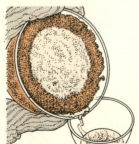

8 When loaf is done, remove bowl from oven and carefully pour off fat. To serve, invert bowl onto oven-safe platter; carefully remove bowl.

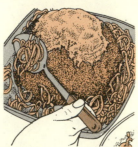

9 Sprinkle the meat and potato loaf with shredded Swiss cheese. Bake loaf for 3 minutes or until cheese is melted. Garnish platter with sautéed onions.

OLD-FASHIONED MEAT LOAF

1 cup fresh bread crumbs (2 slices white bread)
½ cup milk
2 eggs
1 small onion, minced
1 teaspoon salt
½ teaspoon thyme leaves
¼ teaspoon pepper

2 pounds ground beef
1 15-ounce can tomato sauce
¼ cup packed light brown sugar
½ teaspoon dry mustard
Thyme sprigs for garnish

1. In large bowl, with fork, mix first 7 ingredients; let stand 5 minutes. Add ground beef; mix well. In 13″ by 9″ baking pan, shape beef mixture into 9″ by 5″ loaf, pressing firmly.
2. Bake meat loaf in 350°F. oven 1 hour. Meanwhile, in 1-quart saucepan over medium heat, heat tomato sauce, brown sugar, and mustard to boiling. Reduce heat to low; keep tomato sauce mixture warm.
3. Remove meat loaf from oven; brush lightly with some tomato sauce mixture. Bake loaf 15 minutes longer or until glazed.
4. To serve, with two pancake turners, carefully place meat loaf on warm platter. Garnish with thyme sprigs. Serve with remaining tomato sauce mixture.

- *Color index page 44*
- *Begin 2 hrs ahead*
- *8 servings*
- *333 cals per serving*

MEAT-LOAF ROLL WITH SPINACH STUFFING

1 medium onion
2 pounds ground beef
2 cups fresh white or whole-wheat bread crumbs (4 slices bread)
½ cup milk

¼ teaspoon pepper
3 eggs
Salt
1 10-ounce package frozen chopped spinach, thawed

1. Mince onion; set aside 1 tablespoon for use in spinach mixture. In large bowl, mix remaining minced onion with ground beef, bread crumbs, milk, pepper, 2 eggs, and 1 teaspoon salt.
2. On sheet of waxed paper, pat meat mixture into 14″ by 8″ rectangle; set aside.
3. Squeeze spinach dry. In same large bowl, mix spinach, ½ teaspoon salt, remaining egg, and reserved minced onion. Spread spinach mixture on meat rectangle. Do not spread right to the edge as it will squeeze out.
4. Starting from the narrow end, roll meat mixture, jelly-roll fashion, lifting waxed paper and using long metal spatula to loosen meat from waxed paper. Place rolled loaf, seam side down, in shallow baking pan. Bake in 350°F. oven 1¼ hours. When loaf is done, remove from oven and let stand in baking pan 15 minutes for easier slicing. If you like, slice ahead and arrange on warm platter so the spiral pattern can be seen more easily.

- *Color index page 44*
- *Begin 1¾ hrs ahead*
- *8 servings*
- *320 cals per serving*

SALISBURY STEAKS WITH ONIONS AND PEPPERS

- Color index page 44
- Begin 35 mins ahead
- 4 servings
- 490 cals per serving

2 tablespoons butter or margarine	1 egg
4 medium onions, sliced	Salt
3 peppers, red, green, or yellow, cut into thin strips	Pepper
	1 tablespoon all-purpose flour
1 pound ground beef	1 cup water
1 cup fresh bread crumbs (2 slices bread)	2 tablespoons catchup
	1 tablespoon dry sherry
	½ teaspoon soy sauce

1. In 12-inch skillet over medium heat, in hot butter, cook onions and peppers until tender, stirring frequently. Remove onion mixture to warm platter; keep warm.
2. Meanwhile, in medium-sized bowl, with fork, mix ground beef, bread crumbs, egg, ½ teaspoon salt, and ¼ teaspoon pepper. Shape mixture into four ½-inch-thick oval patties.
3. In same skillet over medium-high heat, cook patties about 5 minutes for medium-rare or until of desired doneness, turning once. Arrange patties on serving platter with onions and peppers; keep warm.
4. Into drippings in skillet over medium heat, stir flour, ½ teaspoon salt, and ⅛ teaspoon pepper; cook 1 minute. Add water, catchup, sherry, and soy sauce; cook, stirring constantly, until mixture thickens slightly; pour the sauce over the patties.

CORN-PONE CASSEROLE

- Color index page 45
- Begin 1¼ hrs ahead
- 6 servings
- 533 cals per serving

Pone, the Indian word for baked, was a bread made from cornmeal, salt, and water, and was a colonial favorite.

1 pound ground beef	1 15¼- to 19-ounce can red kidney beans, drained
1 medium onion, diced	
4 teaspoons chili powder	
1 28-ounce can tomatoes	1 12- to 15-ounce package corn-muffin mix
1½ teaspoons sugar	
1½ teaspoons salt	
¼ teaspoon cracked pepper	

1. In 4-quart saucepan over high heat, cook beef and onion until all pan juices evaporate and meat is browned, stirring occasionally. Stir in chili powder; cook 1 minute.
2. Stir in tomatoes with their liquid, sugar, salt, and pepper; over high heat, heat to boiling. Reduce heat to low; cover; simmer 30 minutes, stirring often. Stir in beans. Spoon mixture into 12" by 8" baking dish.
3. Preheat oven to 400°F. Prepare corn-muffin mix batter as label directs. With back of spoon, spread corn-muffin batter evenly over top of meat mixture in casserole.
4. Bake casserole, uncovered, 15 to 20 minutes until golden and toothpick inserted into corn bread comes out clean. Serve casserole hot, directly from baking dish.

BLUE-CHEESE BURGERS

The hamburger probably originated in Germany where a pounded beefsteak was popular in the mid-1800s. J. Wellington Wimpy, Popeye's friend and notorious hamburger addict, would have loved this version served on a sesame-seeded hamburger bun with French fries.

- Color index page 44
- Begin 20 mins ahead
- 4 servings
- 370 cals per serving

1 pound ground beef	1 tablespoon butter or margarine, softened
¼ pound blue-cheese, crumbled	
2 tablespoons half-and-half	½ teaspoon salt
	¼ teaspoon pepper

1 Shape ground beef into four ½-inch-thick patties. Heat 10-inch skillet over high heat until hot.

2 Add patties and cook about 15 minutes for medium-rare or until of desired doneness, turning the patties once.

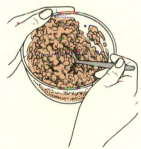 

3 Meanwhile, in small bowl, mix the blue-cheese, half-and-half, butter, salt, and pepper until smooth and well blended.

4 Top each patty with ¼ blue-cheese mixture. Cover and cook over medium-low heat until melted.

SAUTÉED-ONION TOPPING: In 10-inch skillet over medium heat, in *2 tablespoons hot salad oil*, cook *2 medium onions*, sliced, *2 teaspoons white-wine vinegar*, *½ teaspoon dry mustard*, and *½ teaspoon salt* until onions are tender, stirring often. Stir in *1 tablespoon chopped parsley*. Makes ¾ cup. 85 cals per serving.

MUSHROOM-AND-PEPPER TOPPING: In 10-inch skillet over medium-high heat, *in 1 tablespoon hot salad oil*, cook *½ pound mushrooms*, sliced, *2 small red* or *green peppers*, cut into thin strips, and *½ teaspoon salt* until tender, stirring occasionally. Toppings can be served directly over hamburgers or served in a small bowl and passed separately. Makes about 1 cup. 60 cals per serving.

Ground

The All-American Hamburger

A good hamburger, juicy and full of flavor, is an excellent dish, and is rightfully regarded as the best of fast food. The original hamburger was introduced by German immigrants at the Louisiana Purchase Exposition in St. Louis in 1904. It has never lost its appeal; since the 1920s, hamburgers have been America's most popular form of meat, making them the favorite choice for children's parties, outdoor barbecues, and house specialties in famous city restaurants and bars.

A good quality hamburger, served on a firm toasted bun or roll, topped with a savory relish, and served with a vegetable accompaniment, such as French fries or salad, makes a tasty and wholesome meal. Just season the meat and form it into 1-inch-thick patties. Heat the skillet until very hot; add the patties and cook 3 to 4 minutes on each side, turning once, or broil about 2 inches from the heat, about 8 minutes, turning once.

Hamburgers provide the opportunity for using a variety of sauces and toppings; here are suggestions, making the most of regional ingredients and seasonings.

THE BIG APPLE BAGEL BURGER

A juicy hamburger on a bagel with traditional New York delicatessen condiments makes a big city treat.

Cover the bottom half of a *split bagel* with a *Boston* or *Iceberg lettuce leaf*; this will cover the hole. Place the *grilled beef patty* on the lettuce, top with *Russian dressing*, *slices of dill pickle*, and the top half of the bagel. Serve with *potato salad* or *French fries* and *creamy coleslaw*.

THE SLOPPY JOE

Not a true hamburger, but served on a bun, this classic sandwich is based on well-seasoned hamburger meat cooked in a sauce.

Brown *one pound ground chuck* and *1 small onion*, chopped. Stir in ⅔ cup bottled barbecue sauce, ¼ cup chopped parsley, *1 tablespoon soy sauce*, 2 teaspoons sugar, ½ teaspoon salt, ½ teaspoon ginger, and ¼ teaspoon pepper. Simmer 3 minutes until flavors are blended. Spoon over toasted hamburger buns and serve with *shoe-string potatoes*. If you like, top with *shredded cheese* and broil until cheese begins to melt.

THE CALIFORNIA GOAT CHEESE BURGER

An up-to-the-minute hamburger topped with fresh sun-drenched ingredients.

Cut a 6-inch piece from a *French bread*. Split and toast on a grill. Shape *hamburger meat* into a *2″ × 5″* rectangle and barbecue. Cover toasted bread with *arugula leaves*, *grilled beef patty*, and *thin slices of goat cheese*. Sprinkle with *chopped artichoke hearts* and *sun-dried tomatoes*. If you like, broil 2 minutes, just until cheese begins to melt. Garnish with *fresh chives* and serve with *fresh tomatoes* and *cucumber* or *Sliced Tomatoes with Lemon Dressing* (p.276).

THE CHICAGO PIZZA BURGER

Combine a hamburger with the special flavor of pizza, Chicago-style. Add one or more favorite toppings.

Place a *broiled beef patty* on half a toasted *English muffin* or slice of *Italian bread*. Top with *Italian-style tomato sauce*, *shredded mozzarella cheese*, *anchovy fillets*, and *ripe olives*. Sprinkle with *oregano* and *Parmesan cheese* and broil until cheese begins to melt. If you like, use a variety of toppings such as *pepperoni*, *onions*, *green* and *red peppers*, and sprinkle with *crushed red chilies*. Serve with a *green salad* tossed in a *vinegar and olive oil dressing*.

THE FLORIDA SURF 'N' TURF BURGER

For a sunny flavor, top a burger with shrimp and avocado from the sunshine state.

THE LOUISIANA CREOLE BURGER

Top a hearty hamburger on a traditional bun with a warming combination of spicy flavors for this Southern treat.

Split and toast a *hamburger bun*. Place a *barbecued beef patty* on bottom half of bun and top with *Creole Sauce* (p.112). Sprinkle with extra *tabasco sauce* and cover with top half of bun. Serve with a salad of *okra*, *rice*, and *beans* for a flavorful and complete Creole-style light meal.

Place a *barbecued beef patty* on a slice of *toasted whole-wheat bread*. Top with *large shrimp*, *avocado slices*, and a *Creamy Cocktail Sauce* (p.385). Garnish with *a fresh parsley sprig* and serve with a salad of *peeled orange and grapefruit slices* or *Oranges and Tomatoes Vinaigrette* (p.276).

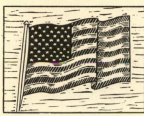

THE CLASSIC BACON CHEESEBURGER

A juicy grilled burger covered with American Cheddar and topped with crispy bacon slices makes a hearty choice.

THE TEX-MEX CHILI-BURGER

Chili, a favorite Mexican-American dish, is often used as a piquant topping for hamburgers and hot dogs.

Toast a *sesame seed hamburger bun*. Just before the hamburger is done, cover with a *slice of Cheddar cheese* and continue cooking until cheese begins to melt. Place on bottom of bun, cover with *crispy bacon slices* and top half of bun. Serve with *catchup*, *mustard*, and *relishes* and lots of *French fries* or *Hash Brown Potatoes* (p.242).

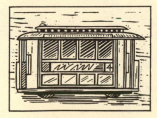

THE SAN FRANCISCO BURGER

A slice of sourdough bread, a specialty of San Francisco, provides the base for this peppery burger.

Cover a hot *tortilla* with *shredded lettuce* and a *cooked beef patty*. Spoon *chili* over burger and top with *chopped onions*, *shredded cheese*, and *sour cream*. Serve with *Salsa Cruda* (p.151) accompanied by an *avocado* and *tomato* salad sprinkled with *chopped coriander*.

Toast a *slice of sourdough bread* and cover with a *slice of tomato*. Meanwhile, press *coarsely ground* or *cracked pepper* into *hamburger patty* and fry in a hot skillet. Place over slice of tomato and top with *watercress sprigs* and *catchup*. Serve with *Home-Fried Potatoes* (p.242) or a tossed salad.

Roasts

PORK CROWN ROAST WITH CRAN-APPLE STUFFING

Entertaining in high style became important in the 1800s; large crown roasts like this one, stuffed with home-grown cranberries and apples, still make a spectacular presentation.

- Color index page 46
- Begin 4½ hrs ahead
- 16 servings
- 542 cals per serving

1 14- to 16-rib pork crown roast (about 7 pounds)
Salt
Pepper
2 cups cranberries, finely chopped

½ cup sugar
½ cup butter or margarine
2 small onions, diced
2 cups diced celery
8 cups white bread cubes (about 10 slices)

2 medium cooking apples, peeled and finely chopped
½ cup apple juice
1 egg
1 teaspoon poultry seasoning

1 Preheat oven to 325°F. Sprinkle pork with 1 teaspoon salt and ¼ teaspoon pepper.

2 Place roast, rib ends down, on a rack in open roasting pan; roast for 2 hours.

3 Meanwhile, in small bowl, mix well cranberries and sugar and set aside.

4 In Dutch oven over medium heat, in hot butter or margarine, cook onions and celery until tender, about 10 minutes.

5 Into celery mixture, stir reserved cranberries, 2 teaspoons salt, ¼ teaspoon pepper, bread cubes, and next 4 ingredients; toss well.

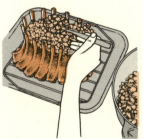

6 Remove roast from oven; invert roast so ribs are up. Fill cavity of roast with the cran-apple stuffing.

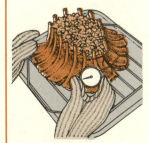

7 Carefully insert meat thermometer between two ribs into the thickest part of the meat, being careful that the pointed end of the thermometer does not touch bone.

8 Return to oven; continue roasting about 1½ hours or until thermometer reaches 170°F. (If the stuffing becomes too brown, cover it with foil.)

9 Place roast on warm platter; let stand 15 minutes for easier carving. To carve, slice between ribs. Accompany each serving with a spoonful of stuffing.

COUNTRY-STYLE PORK SHOULDER ROAST

½ teaspoon ground ginger
¼ teaspoon garlic powder
¼ teaspoon sage leaves
Salt
Cracked pepper
1 5-pound pork shoulder or leg roast
2 small acorn squash
Water
1 29-ounce can cling-peach halves, drained, and each peach cut in half

½ cup packed brown sugar
3 tablespoons butter or margarine
¾ cup milk
3 tablespoons all-purpose flour
¼ teaspoon bottled sauce for gravy

1. In small bowl, mix ginger, garlic powder, sage, 1½ teaspoons salt, and ¼ teaspoon cracked pepper; rub mixture onto pork roast. Place roast fat side up on rack in open roasting pan. Insert meat thermometer into center of pork, being careful that pointed end of thermometer does not touch bone.

2. Roast in 325°F. oven 2½ to 3 hours until meat thermometer reaches 170°F. (30 to 35 minutes per pound). Pork near bone will be slightly pink. If you prefer that no pink shows, roast until thermometer reaches 185°F.

3. About 30 minutes before pork roast is done, prepare acorn squash and peaches: Cut squash lengthwise in half; discard seeds; cut halves crosswise into ¾-inch-thick slices. In 12-inch skillet over high heat, heat ½ inch water and squash to boiling. Reduce heat to low; cover and simmer 10 minutes or until the squash is fork-tender; drain off water.

4. To squash in skillet add peaches, brown sugar, and butter. Over medium heat, cook mixture until sugar and butter melt and peaches are heated, stirring gently; keep warm.

5. When roast is done, place on warm large platter and let stand at least 15 minutes for easier carving.

6. Prepare gravy: Remove rack from roasting pan; pour pan drippings into 2-cup measure or medium bowl (set pan aside); let stand a few seconds until fat separates from meat juices. Skim off 3 tablespoons fat; pour into 2-quart saucepan; skim off and discard any remaining fat. Add milk to roasting pan; stir until brown bits are loosened from pan; add to meat juice in cup with enough water to make 2 cups.

7. Into fat in saucepan over medium heat, stir flour, ¾ teaspoon salt, and ⅛ teaspoon cracked pepper; gradually stir in meat-juice mixture and cook, stirring constantly, until gravy thickens slightly and boils. Stir in bottled sauce for gravy.

8. To serve, spoon squash and peaches with brown-sugar sauce around roast. Serve pork roast immediately with the gravy.

- Color index page 46
- Begin 3¼ hrs ahead
- 10 servings
- 610 cals per serving

Chops and steaks

PORK LOIN ROAST WITH GRAVY

Today American pork is 50% leaner than it was 25 years ago, making it easy to use for lighter but rich-tasting meals, such as this roast with an old-fashioned milk gravy.

2 teaspoons garlic salt
2 teaspoons paprika
Pepper
1 5-pound pork loin center rib roast, cut French style*

¾ cup milk
Water
3 tablespoons all-purpose flour
½ teaspoon salt

- Color index page 46
- Begin 3½ hrs ahead
- 12 servings
- 505 cals per serving

*If you like, ask butcher to expose about 1 inch of rib bone by cutting out meat between ribs and to loosen backbone from ribs.

1 On waxed paper, mix garlic salt, paprika, and ¼ teaspoon pepper; rub the mixture onto the pork roast.

2 Place roast, fat side up, in open roasting pan. Insert meat thermometer into center; do not let pointed end touch the bone.

3 Roast in 325°F. oven 2½ to 3 hours, until meat thermometer reaches 170°F. (30 to 35 minutes per pound).

4 With sharp knife, cut backbone from ribs; discard. Place the roast on warm platter; let roast stand 15 minutes for easier carving of meat.

5 To prepare gravy: Pour pan drippings into 2-cup measure or medium bowl (set pan aside); let stand a few seconds until fat separates.

6 Skim 3 tablespoons fat from drippings into 2-quart saucepan; skim off and discard any remaining fat.

7 Add milk to roasting pan; stir until brown bits are loosened from pan; add to meat juice in cup with enough water to make 2 cups.

8 Into fat in saucepan over medium heat, stir flour, salt, and ⅛ teaspoon pepper until well blended.

9 Gradually stir in meat-juice mixture and cook, stirring constantly, until the gravy thickens slightly and boils. Serve the hot pork roast with gravy.

PORK CHOPS WITH CREAMY GRAVY

4 pork loin blade chops or pork loin chops, each cut ¾ inch thick
Milk
All-purpose flour

Salt
Pepper
3 tablespoons salad oil
½ cup water

1. Trim excess fat from chops. Into pie plate, pour 2 tablespoons milk. On waxed paper, combine ¼ cup flour, ¼ teaspoon salt, and ⅛ teaspoon pepper. Dip pork chops in milk, then into flour mixture to coat well.
2. In 12-inch skillet over medium-high heat, in hot salad oil, cook pork chops until browned on both sides and fork-tender, about 15 minutes, turning occasionally. Remove chops to warm platter; keep warm.
3. In cup with fork, mix water with 2 tablespoons flour until smooth. Stir flour mixture into drippings in skillet, stirring and scraping to loosen brown bits from bottom of skillet. Gradually stir in 1 cup milk and ⅛ teaspoon pepper; cook, stirring constantly, until gravy is thickened and boils. Add salt to taste.
4. Serve pork chops with gravy. If you like, serve with mashed potatoes.

- Color index page 44
- Begin 30 mins ahead
- 4 servings
- 405 cals per serving

GOLDEN GLAZED PORK CHOPS

4 pork loin chops, each cut ¾ inch thick
1 cup pineapple juice
½ teaspoon salt

3 tablespoons apricot preserves
¼ cup pecans, toasted and chopped

1. Trim several pieces of fat from edges of pork loin chops. In 12-inch skillet over medium heat, heat pork fat and, with spoon, press and rub fat to grease bottom of skillet. Discard pieces of fat. In greased skillet over medium-high heat, cook pork chops, two at a time, until well browned on both sides, removing the pork chops from skillet as they brown.
2. Add pineapple juice and salt, stirring to loosen brown bits from bottom of skillet.
3. Return pork chops to skillet; over high heat, heat to boiling. Reduce heat to low; cover and simmer 45 minutes or until pork chops are fork-tender, stirring occasionally and turning chops once during cooking.
4. Remove chops to warm platter. Into liquid in skillet, stir apricot preserves; over high heat, heat to boiling, stirring constantly until mixture thickens slightly.
5. Pour apricot mixture over pork chops. To serve, sprinkle pork chops with the toasted and chopped pecans.

- Color index page 45
- Begin 1¼ hrs ahead
- 4 servings
- 465 cals per serving

Chops and steaks

PORK LOIN CHOPS WITH PRUNE STUFFING

Many Scandinavians settled in the Midwest, bringing favorite recipes with them, like this delicious combination of sweet prunes and succulent pork chops.

- *Color index page 45*
- *Begin 2 hrs ahead*
- *6 servings*
- *627 cals per serving*

2 tablespoons butter or margarine
1 small onion, diced
1½ cups whole-wheat bread cubes (about 3 slices)
1½ cups pitted prunes, coarsely chopped

¼ teaspoon sage leaves
Water
Salt
Pepper
6 pork loin rib chops, each cut about 1 inch thick

2 chicken-flavor bouillon cubes or envelopes
¼ cup milk
1 tablespoon all-purpose flour

1 In 12-inch skillet over medium heat, in hot butter, cook onion until tender, stirring occasionally. Remove skillet from heat. Add bread cubes, prunes, sage, ⅓ cup water, 1 teaspoon salt, and ¼ teaspoon pepper; mix well. With sharp knife, on a cutting board, trim several pieces of fat from edge of pork loin rib chops; reserve the fat to use later.

2 Cut each pork chop, from fat side, horizontally almost to the bone to form a pocket.

3 Spoon some prune mixture firmly into each pocket; close the pockets with toothpicks.

4 Lightly sprinkle pork chops on both sides with salt and pepper. In the same skillet over medium-high heat, heat the reserved fat until it is lightly browned.

5 Use spoon to press and rub fat over the bottom of skillet to grease it well; discard fat. Add 3 chops to skillet; over high heat, cook until well browned on both sides.

6 Remove chops from skillet as they brown. Repeat with remaining chops. Return chops to skillet; add bouillon and 1 cup water; over high heat, heat to boiling.

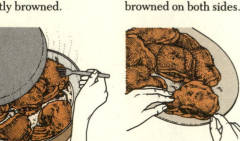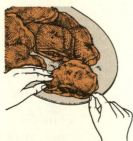

7 Reduce heat to low; cover and simmer 1½ hours or until pork chops are fork-tender, turning chops once.

8 Remove pork chops to a large platter; discard toothpicks. Keep pork chops warm.

9 Skim off any remaining fat from the liquid in the skillet. In a small cup, mix the milk and flour until well blended. Be sure there are no lumps. Gradually stir the flour mixture into the liquid in the skillet. Simmer over medium heat, stirring constantly, until the gravy is slightly thickened and the flour is cooked. Arrange chops on warm platter; pass the gravy separately.

PORK STEAKS CREOLE STYLE

2 tablespoons salad oil
2 pork shoulder arm steaks, each about ¾ inch thick (about 2 pounds)
2 tablespoons all-purpose flour
1 medium celery stalk, diced

1 small green pepper, diced
1 small onion, diced
1 14½- to 16-ounce can tomatoes
2 teaspoons sugar
1 teaspoon salt
½ teaspoon hot-pepper sauce

1. In 12-inch skillet over medium-high heat, in hot salad oil, cook pork steaks until well browned on both sides. Remove steaks to plate; set aside.
2. Into drippings in skillet, stir flour; cook, stirring constantly, until flour is dark brown (mixture will be thick). Add celery, green pepper, and onion; cook over medium heat until vegetables are tender, about 10 minutes, stirring often. Return pork steaks to skillet; add tomatoes with their liquid, sugar, salt, and hot-pepper sauce; over high heat, heat to boiling. Reduce heat to low; cover and simmer, stirring occasionally, 45 minutes to 1 hour, until the pork is fork-tender. Transfer to warm serving platter.

- *Color index page 45*
- *Begin 1½ hrs ahead*
- *6 servings*
- *454 cals per serving*

HOW TO PREPARE GRAVY

Natural juices from roasting or pan-frying meats provide the base for the most appropriate sauce for all meats – pan gravy.

1. Remove the roast or meat from the pan to a platter; keep warm. Pour off fat and meat juices into a measuring cup.

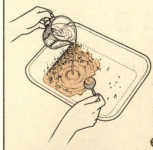

2. Pour ¼ of this fat into a saucepan; discard remaining fat, reserving juices. Pour *1 cup water* into pan, stirring to loosen brown bits. Add *meat juices* from cup.

3. Into fat in saucepan, over medium heat, gradually stir ¼ *cup flour* until smooth.

4. Slowly stir in liquid from roasting pan, add *1 cup water* and heat to boiling, stirring until thickened. Season to taste.

Tenderloin

BAKED STUFFED PORK CHOPS

- Color index page 46
- Begin 2 hrs ahead
- 8 servings
- 402 cals per serving

8 rib pork chops, each cut about 1½ inches thick
2 tablespoons butter or margarine
¼ cup minced celery
2 tablespoons minced green onions
½ small garlic clove, minced
2 cups cubed rye bread with caraway seeds (about 3 slices)
1 egg
Salt
Pepper
Canned spiced peaches for garnish
Gravy (p.190)

1. Preheat oven to 325°F. With sharp knife, next to bone, cut meat of each pork chop horizontally to form a pocket.
2. In 2-quart saucepan over medium heat, in hot butter, cook celery, green onions, and garlic until tender, about 5 minutes. Remove from heat; stir in bread, egg, and ¼ teaspoon salt until well mixed. Stuff each chop with stuffing. Sprinkle meat on both sides with salt and pepper.
3. On rack in open roasting pan, arrange pork chops in one layer. Bake 1 hour and 15 minutes or until chops are fork-tender.
4. Arrange pork chops on warm platter; keep warm; garnish with spiced peaches.
5. Prepare gravy, using chicken broth for liquid. Spoon some over chops and serve remainder in gravy boat.

PORK-AND-SAUERKRAUT SUPPER

- Color index page 46
- Begin 2¾ hrs ahead
- 6 servings
- 555 cals per serving

2 tablespoons salad oil
6 pork rib or loin chops, each ¾ inch thick
1 medium onion, diced
1¾ cups apple juice
2 16-ounce bags or cans sauerkraut, drained
3 medium potatoes (about 1 pound), cut in ¼-inch-thick slices
2 medium red cooking apples, cored and cut into ½-inch chunks
2 teaspoons brown sugar
½ teaspoon salt
⅛ teaspoon pepper

1. In 12-inch skillet over medium-high heat, in hot salad oil, cook pork chops, half at a time, until browned on both sides. Remove chops to plate.
2. In drippings remaining in skillet, over medium heat, cook onion until tender, stirring occasionally. Add ¼ cup apple juice, stirring to loosen brown bits from bottom of skillet.
3. In 13" by 9" baking dish, combine onion mixture, sauerkraut, potatoes, apples, brown sugar, and remaining apple juice. Tuck pork chops in sauerkraut mixture; sprinkle chops with salt and pepper.
4. Cover baking dish with foil and bake in 350°F. oven 2 hours, occasionally basting meat and potatoes with liquid in baking dish, until meat and potatoes are fork-tender.

APPLE-GLAZED PORK TENDERLOIN

The pork tenderloin is a popular cut, as it is very tender and there is no waste. Since it is very lean, it requires frequent basting to keep it moist; a traditional American condiment, such as the sweet apple jelly we've used here, is perfect for the job.

- Color index page 45
- Begin 1½ hrs ahead
- 8 servings
- 287 cals per serving

1 medium lemon
1 cup apple jelly
2½ teaspoons salt
¼ teaspoon pepper
2 pork tenderloins (each about 1 pound)

1 Preheat oven to 325°F. Shred enough lemon peel to make 4 teaspoons; squeeze juice from lemon to make 1 teaspoon.

2 In small saucepan over low heat, heat lemon peel and juice, apple jelly, salt, and pepper until jelly melts, stirring occasionally.

3 Place tenderloins on rack in open roasting pan, tucking ends under to make roasts of uniform thickness.

4 Carefully insert a meat thermometer, on an angle if necessary, into the center of one pork tenderloin.

5 Roast 1 hour or until meat thermometer reaches 170°F., brushing tenderloins occasionally with some of the apple glaze prepared in small saucepan.

6 With knife slanting, carve meat into thin slices. Arrange the slices around one edge of eight individual dinner plates. Serve remaining apple glaze as sauce.

Tenderloin

CHOP SUEY

- Color index page 45
- Begin 45 mins ahead
- 4 servings
- 486 cals per serving

Though this oriental-sounding dish does not exist in China, Chinese cooks served it to laborers who worked on the Pacific Railroad in the 1800s. A delicious combination of vegetables and either pork or chicken, the name may come from the Chinese word for "odds and ends."

1 pound pork-sirloin cutlets or pork tenderloin
2 tablespoons cornstarch
3 tablespoons soy sauce
1 tablespoon dry sherry
1½ teaspoons salt
¼ teaspoon ground ginger
Water
2 tablespoons salad oil
2 cups thinly shredded Chinese cabbage
1 cup thinly sliced celery

1 bunch green onions, cut into 1-inch pieces
1 16-ounce can bean sprouts, drained
1 6- or 8½-ounce can water chestnuts, drained and thinly sliced
1 5- or 6-ounce can bamboo shoots, drained and sliced
3 cups hot cooked rice

1 With sharp knife, on a cutting board, slice the pork cutlets into thin, bite-sized pieces.

2 In small bowl, combine the cornstarch, soy sauce, dry sherry, salt, ginger, and ½ cup water. Mix thoroughly and set aside until pork is browned.

3 In 12-inch skillet over medium-high heat, in hot salad oil, cook pork until browned; stir quickly and frequently, about 5 minutes.

4 Add cornstarch mixture and all ingredients except rice; cook and stir until the vegetables are tender-crisp, about 5 minutes. Serve with rice.

SHRIMP CHOP SUEY: Use *one 16-ounce package frozen, shelled,* and *deveined shrimp,* thawed, instead of pork. Prepare as above but cook shrimp in hot salad oil only 2 minutes or until pink. Finish cooking as above and serve with hot cooked rice. 378 cals per serving.

Hocks

PORK HOCKS AND POTATOES

- Color index page 47
- Begin 3½ hrs ahead
- 4 servings
- 680 cals per serving

The colonists, especially Southerners, loved pork and ate every part of the animal, including the feet and the legs, or hocks.

4 pork hocks
1 medium onion, sliced
10 cups water
2 tablespoons dry sherry
Salt
8 small red potatoes
1 8-ounce container sour cream (1 cup)

2 tablespoons prepared mustard
½ teaspoon cracked pepper
½ teaspoon thyme leaves

1 In 8-quart Dutch oven or saucepot over high heat, heat pork hocks, onion, water, dry sherry, and 2 teaspoons salt to boiling. Reduce heat to low; cover and simmer 2½ hours or until the meat is almost fork-tender.

2 Peel ½-inch-wide strip around center of each potato. Add the potatoes to Dutch oven; over high heat, heat to boiling. Reduce heat to low; cover and simmer 30 minutes longer or until the meat and potatoes are tender.

3 Meanwhile, in a 1-quart saucepan, mix sour cream, mustard, pepper, thyme, and ¼ teaspoon salt.

4 Gradually stir in ⅔ cup cooking liquid from Dutch oven; over medium heat, heat through (do not boil).

5 With slotted spoon, remove pork hocks and potatoes to a warm platter; spoon some sauce over pork hocks. Pass the remaining sauce.

Stew and pieces

VERMONT PORK AND BEANS

2 16-ounce packages dry
  pea (navy) beans
Water
½ pound pork for stew,
  cut into ½-inch chunks
1 large onion, diced

¾ cup packed dark
  brown sugar
⅓ cup dark molasses
5 teaspoons salt
1 tablespoon dry mustard

1. Rinse beans in running cold water and discard any stones or shriveled beans. In 5-quart Dutch oven over high heat, heat beans and 8 cups water to boiling; cook 3 minutes. Remove Dutch oven from heat; cover and let stand 1 hour. Drain and rinse the beans well; set aside.

2. In same Dutch oven over medium-high heat, cook pork for stew and onion until pork is browned and onion is tender, stirring often.

3. Return beans to Dutch oven; add 8 cups water; over high heat, heat to boiling. Reduce heat to low; cover and simmer 1 hour.

4. Add sugar, molasses, salt, and mustard; cover; simmer 2 hours longer or until beans are tender, stirring occasionally to prevent sticking.

5. If bean mixture becomes too thick on standing, add water, half cup at a time; cook over low heat, stirring occasionally, until of desired consistency. If you like, serve Vermont Pork and Beans in a traditional New England bean pot, as an accompaniment to corned beef, sliced ham, or frankfurters.

- Color index page 47
- Begin 4½ hrs ahead
- 16 accompaniment servings
- 161 cals per serving

PORK AND APPLE GRILL

½ cup apple
  jelly
½ cup bottled
  steak sauce
4 tablespoons butter
  or margarine

2 pounds boneless
  fresh pork butt
3 Golden Delicious or
  other cooking
  apples

1. In small saucepan over medium-low heat, heat apple jelly, steak sauce, and butter until melted, stirring frequently. Remove saucepan from the heat.

2. Trim excess fat from fresh pork butt; cut meat into 2-inch chunks.

3. Cut apples into thick wedges.

4. Preheat broiler if manufacturer directs. Place the pork chunks and the apple wedges on rack in the broiling pan.

5. About 7 to 9 inches from source of heat (or with oven control set at 450°F.), broil 35 to 40 minutes until pork and apples are tender, turning pork and apple wedges occasionally.

6. Brush with apple-butter sauce during last 15 minutes of cooking. Transfer the pork chunks and apple wedges to a large warm platter.

- Color index page 46
- Begin 1¼ hrs ahead
- 6 servings
- 390 cals per serving

PORK AND CHICKEN STEW

This unusual mix of pork, chicken, and vegetables is simmered in a Mexican-style sauce of almonds, tomatoes, and chilies.

2 tablespoons salad oil
4 medium chicken legs
  (about 2 pounds)
½ pound pork pieces, cut
  into 1-inch chunks
1 medium onion, diced
1 medium sweet green
  pepper, diced
½ cup blanched whole
  almonds

2 teaspoons chili powder
1 8- to 8¼-ounce can
  tomatoes
1¼ cups water
1¼ teaspoons salt
¼ teaspoon ground
  cinnamon

- Color index page 45
- Begin 1½ hrs ahead
- 6 servings
- 535 cals per serving

2 large sweet potatoes
  (about 2 pounds) or
  1 16- to 17-ounce can
  sweet potatoes, drained
1 large red cooking apple

1 In a 12-inch skillet over medium-high heat, in hot salad oil, cook chicken until browned. Remove to plate.

2 In drippings remaining in skillet over medium-high heat, cook pork until well browned Remove to plate.

3 In drippings remaining in skillet over medium heat, cook onion, pepper, and almonds until vegetables are tender.

4 Stir in chili powder; cook 1 minute, stirring frequently. Remove skillet from heat; stir in tomatoes with their liquid, water, salt, and cinnamon, stirring to loosen brown bits on bottom of skillet. In blender at low speed or in food processor with knife blade attached, blend tomato mixture until smooth. Return the tomato mixture to the skillet.

5 Add pork; over high heat, heat to boiling. Reduce the heat to low; cover the skillet; simmer 30 minutes, stirring occasionally.

6 Peel sweet potatoes; cut into bite-sized chunks. Add with chicken to pork mixture. (If using canned sweet potatoes, cut into chunks; reserve.)

7 Over high heat, heat to boiling; stir occasionally. Reduce heat to low; cover, simmer 25 mnutes, stir occasionally.

8 Cut apples into wedges; add to skillet and heat through. (If using canned sweet potatoes add with apples.)

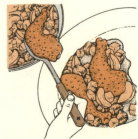

9 When stew is done, with large spoon or ladle, transfer to warm serving dish. Serve stew immediately.

Ribs

COUNTRY RIBS WITH RED CHILI SAUCE

Originally this Tex-Mex chili sauce would have been used to marinate the country ribs so they would keep in a hot climate. Today, we enjoy it for its zesty flavor.

- Color index page 47
- Begin 1½ hrs ahead
- 4 servings
- 988 cals per serving

4 pounds pork loin country-style ribs, cut into serving pieces
Water
5 dried ancho chilies, stems removed
6 serrano chilies, stems removed
1 4-ounce can chopped green chilies, drained
1 garlic clove, minced
¾ cup vinegar

2½ teaspoons salt
¼ teaspoon ground cumin
¼ teaspoon oregano leaves
1 medium avocado, peeled and cut into ½-inch pieces
1 medium bunch radishes, cut into ½-inch pieces

1 With sharp knife, cut ribs into serving-sized pieces. In 5-quart Dutch oven or saucepot, cover pork loin country-style ribs with water; over high heat, heat to boiling. Reduce heat to low; cover and simmer for 1 hour or until the ribs are fork-tender. Meanwhile, in a 1-quart saucepan, cover the ancho chilies with water; over high heat, heat chilies to boiling.

2 Reduce heat to low; cover; simmer 5 minutes until soft; drain.

3 In blender at medium speed or in food processor with knife blade attached, blend ancho chilies with the serrano chilies and next 6 ingredients until puréed.

4 Preheat broiler if manufacturer directs. Remove ribs from water; arrange on rack in broiling pan; broil 15 to 20 minutes, brushing with chili mixture occasionally and turning once.

5 To serve, arrange ribs on warm platter. Garnish with avocado and radish pieces.

PINEAPPLE-GLAZED SPARERIBS

- Color index page 47
- Begin 1¾ hrs ahead
- 4 servings
- 940 cals per serving

¾ cup soy sauce
¼ cup dry sherry
1 tablespoon minced peeled gingerroot or 1 teaspoon ground ginger
2 green onions, diced
1 garlic clove, crushed

4 pounds pork spareribs, cut into 2-rib portions
2 14- to 20-ounce cans pineapple chunks in juice
½ cup packed brown sugar

1. In large open roasting pan, mix first 5 ingredients. Place spareribs in soy-sauce mixture, turning each portion to coat well. Arrange spareribs, meat side down, in roasting pan. Bake in 325°F. oven 1 hour. With pastry brush, baste ribs occasionally with soy-sauce mixture in pan.
2. Turn ribs meat side up and bake 20 minutes. Meanwhile, into 1-cup measure, drain ¼ cup pineapple juice from pineapple chunks; stir in brown sugar.
3. Brush spareribs with brown-sugar mixture. Bake 10 minutes longer or until spareribs are fork-tender.
4. Spoon drained pineapple chunks over spareribs; bake 5 minutes or just until pineapple is heated through. Arrange spareribs on warm large platter with pineapple.

OVEN-BARBECUED SPARERIBS

- Color index page 47
- Begin 1¾ hrs ahead
- 10 servings
- 327 cals per serving

4 pounds pork spareribs, cut into 2-rib portions
⅔ cup unsweetened grapefruit juice
½ cup packed light brown sugar

2 teaspoons cornstarch
1 teaspoon salt
1 teaspoon curry powder
⅛ teaspoon ground allspice

1. Arrange pork spareribs in large open roasting pan in one layer. Roast spareribs in 325°F. oven 1½ hours or until fork-tender.
2. Meanwhile, in 1-quart saucepan over medium heat, heat grapefruit juice and remaining ingredients to boiling; cook 1 minute, stirring mixture constantly to prevent sticking.
3. During last 30 minutes of roasting time, brush ribs frequently with grapefruit mixture.

HOW TO PREPARE A FINGER BOWL

Sticky ribs often call for an easy and polite clean-up remedy at the table. Prepare individual finger bowls and place on the table in advance. Have plenty of extra napkins handy.

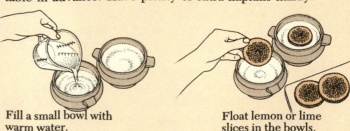

Fill a small bowl with warm water.

Float lemon or lime slices in the bowls.

Whole ham

COUNTRY HAM WITH FOUR SAUCES

America is famous for its specially cured country-style hams, a feature of Southern cuisine and some New England states. Our sweet sauces complement the ham's strong smoky flavor.

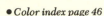

- *Color index page 46*
- *Begin day ahead*
- *35 servings*
- *170 cals per serving (without sauce)*

1 12-pound cook-before-eating Smithfield ham or country-style ham
Water

Buttered Raisin Sauce (right)
Honey-Mustard Sauce (right)

Cranberry-Wine Sauce (right)
Praline Sauce (right)
Dark corn syrup

1 *Day ahead:* Prepare ham as label directs or, place ham, skin side down, in large saucepot; add water to cover ham completely. Let the ham stand in water at room temperature at least 12 hours or overnight.

2 *6 hours before serving:* Discard water from ham. With vegetable brush, scrub and rinse ham well. In same saucepot, again cover ham with water; over high heat, heat to boiling.

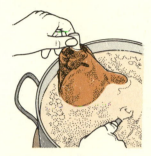

3 Reduce heat to low; cover and simmer about 4 hours (about 20 minutes per pound) or until the bone on small end of ham (shank bone) pokes out about 1 inch and feels loose.

4 *1½ hours before the ham is done:* Prepare Buttered Raisin Sauce, Honey-Mustard Sauce, Cranberry-Wine Sauce, and Praline Sauce.

5 Keep the sauces warm until needed or, if preferred, spoon each into a small sauce bowl to serve at room temperature.

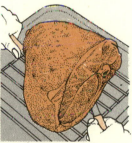

6 When done, remove ham to rack in large, open roasting pan. Discard water in saucepot. Cool ham slightly until easy to handle.

7 Preheat oven to 325°F. With sharp knife, remove skin and trim excess fat from ham, leaving about ¼ inch fat.

8 Brush ham with dark corn syrup. Bake ham 30 minutes or until lightly browned; brush often with corn syrup.

9 To serve, place ham on cutting board; cut it into paper-thin slices. Serve with any or all of the four sauces.

BUTTERED RAISIN SAUCE: In 2-quart saucepan over medium heat, heat *2 cups apple juice*, *1 cup dark seedless raisins*, and *1 cup golden raisins* to boiling. Reduce heat to low; cover and simmer 30 minutes; stir in *4 tablespoons butter or margarine* until melted. In cup, stir *1 tablespoon water* and *1 teaspoon cornstarch* until smooth; add to raisin mixture; cook, stirring constantly, until mixture thickens slightly and boils. Serve sauce warm or serve at room temperature. Makes about 2½ cups. 40 calories per tablespoon.

HONEY-MUSTARD SAUCE: In 1-quart saucepan with wire whisk or fork, mix *1 cup honey*, *½ cup prepared mustard*, *¼ cup water*, *2 tablespoons soy sauce*, and *1 teaspoon cornstarch* until smooth. Over medium heat, heat mixture to boiling, stirring frequently. Serve sauce warm or at room temperature. Makes about 2 cups. 35 calories per tablespoon.

CRANBERRY-WINE SAUCE: In 3-quart saucepan over medium heat, heat *one-half of 12-ounce package cranberries* (about 1½ cups), *⅔ cup sugar*, *½ cup orange juice*, and *⅓ cup red port wine* to boiling, stirring occasionally. Reduce heat to low; cover and simmer mixture 15 minutes, stirring occasionally. Serve sauce warm or at room temperature. Makes 1¾ cups. 25 calories per tablespoon.

PRALINE SAUCE: In 2-quart saucepan over medium-low heat, in *½ cup hot butter* or *margarine*, cook *1 cup pecans*, finely chopped, until pecans are lightly browned. Stir in *½ cup packed dark brown sugar*. In cup, stir *¾ cup water* and *2 teaspoons cornstarch* until smooth. Stir into pecan mixture; cook over medium-high heat until mixture thickens slightly and boils, stirring constantly. Serve warm. Makes about 2 cups. 60 calories per tablespoon.

HAM AND GRITS WITH RED-EYE GRAVY

Enriched white hominy grits
1 tablespoon salad oil

6 country-ham slices, each ¼-inch thick (about 1½ pounds)
2 cups water

1. Prepare enough hominy grits for 6 servings as label directs; keep warm.
2. Meanwhile, in 12-inch skillet over medium heat, in hot salad oil, cook 3 slices country ham at a time until ham is browned on both sides; remove ham to platter.
3. Add water to drippings in skillet; over medium heat, heat to boiling, stirring to loosen brown bits on bottom of skillet. Cook 5 minutes, stirring occasionally. Serve the gravy over the ham and grits.

- *Color index page 47*
- *Begin 20 mins ahead*
- *6 servings*
- *330 cals per serving*

Memorial Day Picnic

Memorial Day originated during the Civil War when Southern women chose May 30 to decorate the graves of the Union and Confederate soldiers. Now this patriotic holiday honors all American servicemen who have given their lives for their country. Usually observed as a legal holiday on the last Monday in May, this date was finally made a federal holiday in 1971. Civil and military groups commemorate this day with parades and special ceremonies. Often the weather is warm and friends and families gather in backyards and on porches for casual outdoor meals.

Our Southern-style country picnic revolves around an all-American favorite, Southern-Fried Chicken, accompanied by tasty salads like Three-Bean and Cheese, Potato, and Festive Corn. Add Kentucky Ham Biscuits and Deviled Eggs, using some of our variations. The grand finale is a rich Georgia-Pecan Tart with Cream-Cheese Pastry and whipped cream; follow with ripe, juicy peaches and glasses of tangy lemonade, for a cool finish.

BEST SPARKLING LEMONADE

Spanish friars transported lemons from Florida to California where, by the mid-19th century, they were flourishing. Today, California produces 80 percent of America's lemon crop and lemonade is one of America's favorite summer drinks; club soda adds extra sparkle to a real thirst quencher.

8 to 10 lemons   *Ice cubes*
1½ cups sugar   *Club Soda*
Water

1 Grate lemons to make 1 tablespoon finely grated peel. Squeeze lemons to make 1½ cups juice. Set juice aside.

2 In a 1-quart jar with tight-fitting lid, put lemon peel, lemon juice, and sugar; add 1½ cups very hot water.

3 With lid fitting firmly, shake jar until sugar is dissolved; refrigerate.

4 To serve, pour into a pitcher with ice cubes and top with club soda. Or pour ¼ cup syrup over ice cubes in individual glasses, and stir in ¾ cup club soda.

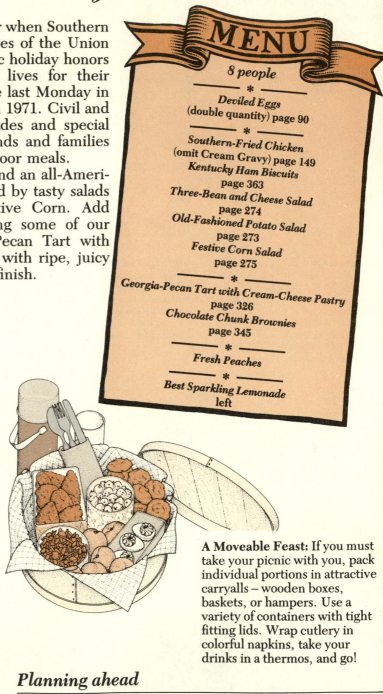

A Moveable Feast: If you must take your picnic with you, pack individual portions in attractive carryalls – wooden boxes, baskets, or hampers. Use a variety of containers with tight fitting lids. Wrap cutlery in colorful napkins, take your drinks in a thermos, and go!

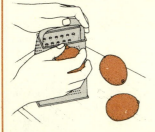

Grating the lemons: Using a grater, grate the lemon skin; do not to take any white pith.

Dissolving the sugar: Tighten the lid of the jar firmly and shake to dissolve the sugar.

Planning ahead

Day ahead: Prepare the salads; cover each and refrigerate. Prepare the pecan tart and bake the brownies; cool and cover.

Early in day: Bake Kentucky Ham Biscuits; cool; wrap. Fry chicken; drain and cool. Prepare eggs and lemonade. Pack individual portions or arrange food in bowls and on plates if serving at home.

MENU

8 people

*

Deviled Eggs
(double quantity) page 90

*

Southern-Fried Chicken
(omit Cream Gravy) page 149
Kentucky Ham Biscuits
page 363
Three-Bean and Cheese Salad
page 274
Old-Fashioned Potato Salad
page 273
Festive Corn Salad
page 275

*

Georgia-Pecan Tart with Cream-Cheese Pastry
page 326
Chocolate Chunk Brownies
page 345

*

Fresh Peaches

*

Best Sparkling Lemonade
left

Fourth of July Barbecue

July 4th, Independence Day, is America's birthday. On this day we commemorate the signing of the Declaration of Independence in 1776. The first Independence Day was observed in Philadelphia on July 8th, 1776; the Declaration was read, bells were rung, bands played, and people rejoiced. In 1941, Congress declared the 4th of July a legal holiday; we still celebrate with fairs, picnics, barbecues, parades, and often elaborate fireworks.

Planning Ahead

Day ahead:	Prepare pickles. Make fruit mold and refrigerate; do not unmold.
Early in day:	Prepare vegetables and set aside to marinate. Make coleslaw; cover and refrigerate. Make hamburger patties; refrigerate.
1½ hours ahead:	Prepare grill for barbecuing. Prepare chicken and spareribs. Place chicken first, then spareribs, on grill. Unmold fruit mold; garnish; refrigerate. Wrap potatoes in foil and cook on coals.
45 minutes ahead:	Prepare dip and serve. Warm garlic bread; cook hamburgers to order.

We honor our patriotic holiday with a Western-style barbecue and recreate a pioneer-days' atmosphere using traditional American spongeware, wooden baskets, an antique patchwork tablecloth, and a flag. For the menu, we choose all-American favorites like barbecued ribs and chicken, and the most popular of all barbecue recipes, the traditional juicy charcoal-grilled hamburger! Tangy accompaniments like our Deluxe Coleslaw, Marinated Garden Vegetables, Sweet-and-Sour Relish, and Bread-and-Butter Pickles, pay homage to America's vegetable bounty. It's a good idea to borrow an extra grill to accommodate the barbecue dishes. Make a tasty loaf of garlic bread by brushing slices of Italian bread with garlic and butter, wrapping in foil, and cooking in the coals for 15 minutes. Watermelon slices and a spectacular star-shaped Red-White-and-Blueberry Mold provide a colorful and refreshing finish.

MENU

12 people

*

Chili-Cheese Dip
(with potato chips) page 94

*

The All-American Hamburger
(your choice) pages 186, 187
Old-West Barbecued Chicken
page 221
Spareribs with Peach Sauce
page 219
Deluxe Coleslaw/Marinated Garden Vegetables
pages 272, 276
Barbecued Potato Packs
page 225
Garlic Bread
Sweet-and-Sour Relish/Bread-and-Butter Pickles
pages 384, 377

*

Red-White-and-Blueberry Mold
page 293
Watermelon Slices

*

Iced Tea

Labor Day Clambake

In 1894, President Grover Cleveland signed a bill making Labor Day a national holiday. Labor Day honors all working people, and also has become a symbol of the end of the summer and the start of the new school year. The weather is still warm, sometimes hot, and many people take advantage of a last weekend at the beach.

Celebrate with a New-England-style Family Clambake — a kind of barbecue-picnic-social gathering, held on the beach after a fresh catch. Indoor clambakes can be just as much fun; just follow our easy recipe for a delicious all-in-one meal of lobsters, clams, chicken, fish, and corn. Add some baked potatoes, some tasty biscuits and cornbread, and finish with a succulent blueberry pie and seasonal fruit. Using pewter, wood, old enamelware, and boards and baskets, will create an authentic New England seaside atmosphere.

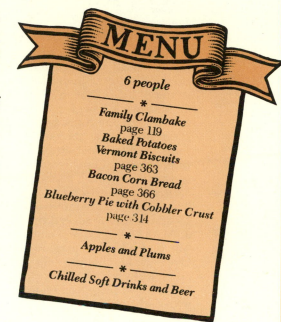

MENU

6 people

*

Family Clambake
page 119
Baked Potatoes
Vermont Biscuits
page 363
Bacon Corn Bread
page 366
Blueberry Pie with Cobbler Crust
page 314

———

*

Apples and Plums

*

Chilled Soft Drinks and Beer

Planning Ahead

Early in day:	Bake Vermont Biscuits and Bacon Corn Bread; store in tightly covered containers. Bake Blueberry Pie with Cobbler Crust. Chill drinks.
1½ hours ahead:	Prepare Family Clambake and bake some potatoes.
15 minutes before serving:	Heat Blueberry Pie with Cobbler Crust.

HOW TO EAT A LOBSTER

When the first settlers arrived in America, lobsters were so common they were sometimes washed up onto the Massachusetts beaches in piles two feet high! Nowadays, they are expensive, but the sweet meat makes an extravagant treat. Follow these simple directions to remove and eat the meat.

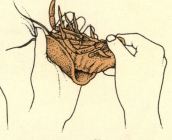

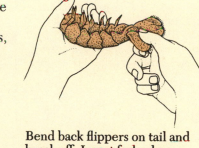

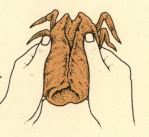

Twist off claws; crack or cut each with lobster crackers or shears, nutcracker, or pliers.

Separate tail piece from body by arching back until it cracks, then pull tail from body.

Bend back flippers on tail and break off. Insert fork where flippers were broken off and push out lobster meat.

Pull body apart sideways and crack it apart. There are tender bits of meat at the base of the small claws.

Remove tomalley (green liver) from body and any lobster coral (pinkish-red roe). Lift body out of the back shell.

Canned ham

● Color index
page 47
● Begin
1½ hrs
ahead
● 8 servings
● 436 cals
per serving

PLUM GLAZED BAKED HAM

1 3-pound canned ham
⅓ cup packed brown
sugar
1 tablespoon cornstarch
1 17-ounce can plums

¼ cup orange juice
½ teaspoon dry mustard
¼ teaspoon ground
ginger
Curly endive for garnish.

1. Remove any gelatin from ham. Place ham on rack in small open roasting pan. Score top in diamond pattern. Insert meat thermometer into center of ham. Bake in 325°F. oven 1 hour.

2. Meanwhile, in 1-quart saucepan, combine brown sugar and cornstarch. Into saucepan, drain syrup from plums. Set aside plums. Stir orange juice, mustard, and ginger into cornstarch mixture. Over medium heat, heat to boiling, stirring constantly. Remove plum glaze from heat.

3. Brush ham with glaze. Continue to bake ham 20 minutes or until internal temperature reaches 130°F., brushing several times with glaze.

4. With knife, cut each plum in half; remove pit. Add plums to plum glaze remaining in saucepan. Over low heat, keep plum glaze warm, stirring occasionally.

5. To serve, place ham on warm platter. Garnish with curly endive. Serve the ham with plums in plum glaze.

APRICOT-MAPLE GLAZED HAM: Prepare and bake ham as above in step 1. Meanwhile, in 1-quart saucepan over high heat, heat *1¼ cups water*, *½ cup dried apricots*, and *1 teaspoon minced onion* to boiling. Reduce heat to low; cover and simmer 15 minutes or until apricots are tender. Pour apricots and their liquid into blender; add *¼ cup maple* or *maple-flavor syrup*, *2 tablespoons lemon juice*, and *¼ teaspoon salt*. Blend until smooth. Use glaze to brush over ham and serve the rest with ham. 415 cals per serving.

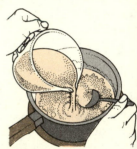

● Color index
page 47
● Begin
35 mins
ahead
● 6 servings
● 665 cals
per serving

LUAU KABOBS

¾ cup packed brown
sugar
½ cup butter or
margarine
1 teaspoon ground
cinnamon
½ teaspoon ground
ginger
¼ teaspoon ground
cloves

1 2-pound canned ham,
cut into 1½-inch cubes
1 large pineapple, cut
into 1-inch chunks
1 9- to 10-ounce jar
preserved kumquats,
drained

1. In 1-quart saucepan over low heat, heat first five ingredients, stirring often, until butter melts. Remove saucepan from heat.

2. Preheat broiler if manufacturer directs. On six 14-inch all-metal skewers, thread ham cubes alternately with pineapple chunks and kumquats.

3. Place on rack in broiling pan; broil 15 minutes or until ham is heated through. Brush often with butter mixture and turn occasionally.

Ham slices

GLAZED SLICED HAM

Ham is traditionally served in a sweet glaze or sauce. This sliced ham in a tangy orange glaze is delicious served hot or cold.

● Color index
page 47
● Begin
2¼ hrs
ahead
● 15 servings
● 300 cals
per serving

1 5-pound boneless fully
cooked smoked half
ham
¼ cup sugar
2 tablespoons cornstarch
1½ cups orange
juice

⅓ cup prepared white
horseradish
2 tablespoons cider
vinegar
1 tablespoon grated
orange peel

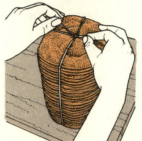

1 Cut ham into ¼-inch slices, then reassemble into original shape by tying slices together with string. (This will make for easier serving, but, if you prefer, the ham can be prepared whole.)

2 Place reassembled, tied ham slices in rack in open roasting pan. Insert meat thermometer into center of ham. Bake ham in 325°F. oven for 2 hours or until thermometer reaches 140°F.

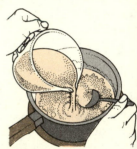

3 Meanwhile, in a heavy 1-quart saucepan, stir sugar with cornstarch; add orange juice and the remaining ingredients.

4 Cook over medium heat, stirring constantly, until the mixture thickens and boils; boil 1 minute. Remove saucepan from heat.

5 During last 30 minutes of baking time, brush ham occasionally with the orange mixture. Serve warm, or, if you like, cover and refrigerate ham to serve later.

Ham hocks

CURRANT-GLAZED HAM STEAK

- Color index page 47
- Begin 20 mins ahead
- 4 servings
- 274 cals per serving

1 fully cooked smoked ham center slice, cut ¾ inch thick (about 1 pound)
⅓ cup red currant jelly
1 tablespoon port wine
¾ teaspoon dry mustard
Salt
Parsley sprigs for garnish

1. Trim several pieces of fat from edge of ham steak. In 10-inch skillet over medium-high heat, heat fat trimmings until lightly browned; using spoon, press and rub fat over bottom of skillet to grease it well; discard fat pieces.
2. Add ham to skillet; over medium-high heat, cook ham steak until well browned on both sides. Remove ham steak to platter; keep warm.
3. In same skillet over low heat, stir currant jelly, port wine, and dry mustard until jelly is melted and sauce is hot; add salt to taste if needed; pour over ham steak.
4. To serve, garnish with parsley sprigs.

Trimming the fat: With sharp knife, trim several pieces of excess fat from the edge of the smoked ham steak.

Greasing the skillet: With a large metal spoon, press fat gently, spreading evenly over the bottom of the skillet.

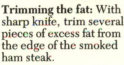

PEACH-GLAZED CANADIAN BACON

- Color index page 47
- Begin 20 mins ahead
- 4 servings
- 485 cals per serving

1 pound Canadian-style bacon slices, each about ¼ inch thick
1 16-ounce can sliced cling peaches in heavy syrup
3 tablespoons butter or margarine
½ cup packed light-brown sugar

1. Remove any casing from bacon slices. In 10-inch skillet over medium heat, cook bacon slices, a few at a time, until lightly browned on both sides, removing pieces to warm platter as they brown; keep warm.
2. Drain peaches and reserve 3 tablespoons syrup. Into drippings in skillet, over medium heat, stir butter, sugar, and reserved syrup, stirring constantly, until sugar is melted. Add peaches; heat through.
3. To serve, spoon peaches and sauce over Canadian bacon.

HAM HOCKS AND COLLARD GREENS

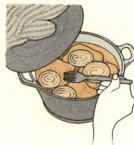

This delicious Southern dish uses a traditional combination of ham hocks and collard greens. The richness of the meat is cut by the slight sharpness of the greens. The same effect can be achieved with a ham slice and a choice of any other seasonal green.

- Color index page 47
- Begin 3½ hrs ahead
- 4 servings
- 325 cals per serving

4 smoked ham hocks
1 medium onion, sliced
Water
1½ pounds collard greens
Salt
Pepper

1 In 8-quart saucepot or Dutch oven over high heat, heat smoked ham hocks, onion, and enough water to cover meat to boiling.

2 Reduce heat to low; cover and simmer 2½ to 3 hours, until meat is fork-tender.

3 Meanwhile, wash the collard greens thoroughly; remove hard center vein; chop the leaves coarsely.

4 About 20 minutes before meat is done, add greens to liquid in Dutch oven and cook, covered, for 20 minutes. Season with salt and pepper, if you like.

5 To serve, using a slotted spoon, arrange the ham hocks and collard greens on a warm large platter. If you like, serve with warm Corn Muffins (p.367).

203

Roasts

ROAST LEG OF LAMB

The traditional seasoning for lamb – garlic and herbs – comes from the heritage of Basque shepherds, whose descendants still tend sheep in the Rocky Mountains.

- Color index page 48
- Begin 2½ hrs ahead
- 10 servings
- 415 cals per serving

1 4½-pound lamb leg shank half
⅓ cup chopped parsley
¼ cup olive or salad oil
2 teaspoons salt
2 teaspoons rosemary, crushed

½ teaspoon pepper
1 garlic clove, crushed
8 medium potatoes (about 2½ pounds) peeled and cut into 1½-inch chunks

1 With knife, cut 3 crosswise slits on top (fat side) of lamb leg, each about 4 inches long and ¼ inch deep.

2 In small bowl, combine next 6 ingredients. Lightly press some parsley mixture into slits in lamb; put remaining mixture on top.

3 Place lamb, fat side up, on small rack in 17¼" by 11½" open roasting pan.

4 Gently insert a meat thermometer into the center of the lamb, being very careful that the pointed end of the thermometer does not touch the bone. Roast lamb in 325°F. oven until thermometer reaches 165°F. for medium (allowing 40 to 45 minutes per pound) or until lamb is of desired doneness. If parsley mixture becomes too brown, cover loosely with foil.

5 *About 35 minutes before lamb is done:* Add potatoes to pan with meat, turning potatoes to coat all sides with pan drippings; turn potatoes occasionally to brown on all sides.

6 When lamb is done, place on warm large platter; let lamb stand 10 minutes for easier carving. Continue roasting the potatoes about 10 minutes longer. Spoon the potatoes around lamb.

STUFFED SHOULDER OF LAMB

- Color index page 48
- Begin 2½ hrs ahead
- 8 servings
- 406 cals per serving

¼ cup butter or margarine
1 small garlic clove, minced
2 cups fresh bread crumbs
4 teaspoons lemon juice

1 tablespoon minced anchovies
½ teaspoon seasoned pepper
1 3-pound cushion shoulder of lamb with pocket

1. Preheat oven to 325°F. In 2-quart saucepan over medium heat, in hot butter, cook garlic until browned, about 5 minutes; remove from heat.
2. Stir in bread crumbs, lemon juice, anchovies, and seasoned pepper; spoon into pocket in lamb shoulder; tie with string.
3. Place lamb, fat side up, on rack in open roasting pan. Insert meat thermometer into center of lamb, being careful not to touch the stuffing.
4. Roast about 2 hours or until meat thermometer reaches 165°F. for medium or 170° to 180°F. for well done.
5. Let meat stand 15 minutes for easier carving. Remove string and slice.

Stuffing the lamb: Spoon stuffing into the pocket and tie string around shoulder of lamb.

HOW TO CARVE A LEG OF LAMB

Carving a leg of lamb can be simple to do at the table. Before carving, be sure to let the meat rest on a warm platter; this allows the meat to set, making carving easier.

Anchor meat with a carving fork. Holding knife almost parallel to the bone, make a ¼-inch-thick slice about ⅓ of the way along the leg toward the shank end; remove slice.

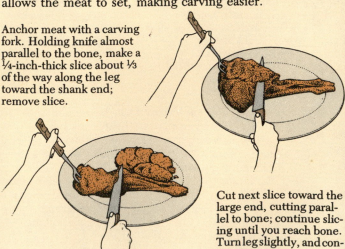

Cut next slice toward the large end, cutting parallel to bone; continue slicing until you reach bone. Turn leg slightly, and continue carving.

Chops

RACK OF LAMB WITH PARSLEY CRUST

After leg of lamb, chops are the most popular cut, but the rack of lamb is gaining popularity as it makes an impressive main course for a special occasion.

2 garlic cloves
Salt
2 7- or 8-rib lamb rib
   roasts (about 2½
   pounds each)*
1 cup fresh bread crumbs
   (about 2 slices white
   bread)

½ cup mayonnaise
¾ teaspoon rosemary,
   crushed
¼ teaspoon pepper
1 egg
¼ cup minced parsley
Parsley sprigs for garnish

- Color index page 48
- Begin 2 hrs ahead
- 8 servings
- 670 cals per serving

* Ask butcher to cut through the backbone to separate ribs for easier carving and scrape the bones to expose about 1½ inches for decoration if desired.

1 Into cup, press garlic through garlic press; stir in 1 teaspoon salt.

2 Trim excess fat from rib roasts, leaving about ⅛ inch fat. Rub garlic mixture over lamb.

3 Place the lamb roasts on their rib bones in a large open roasting pan.

4 Insert the meat thermometer into center of a roast, making sure that pointed end of thermometer does not touch bone.

5 Roast in 375°F. oven about 1¼ hours or until meat thermometer reaches 140°F. for medium-rare (about 30 minutes per pound) or until of desired doneness.

6 Meanwhile, in medium bowl, mix bread crumbs, mayonnaise, rosemary, pepper, egg, minced parsley, and ½ teaspoon salt. Cover and refrigerate.

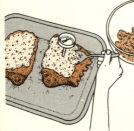

7 About 15 minutes before lamb is done, move from the oven. read parsley mixture nly over the top of a roast.

8 Return to oven and continue roasting until done. When done, remove to cutting board; let stand 10 minutes for easier carving.

9 To serve, with knife, slice roasts between each rib. Arrange ribs on a warm serving platter. Garnish with the parsley sprigs.

SPRING LAMB WITH GREEN VEGETABLES

2 tablespoons salad oil
1 small onion, diced
4 lamb shoulder blade or
   arm chops, each
   ¾ inch thick
1 teaspoon lemon juice
¾ teaspoon salt
¼ teaspoon dill weed
⅛ teaspoon pepper
Water

2 medium Belgian endive
1 9-ounce package frozen
   artichoke hearts
1 cup frozen peas
1 tablespoon all-purpose
   flour
1 tablespoon grated
   lemon peel for garnish
1 tablespoon minced
   parsley for garnish

1. In 12-inch skillet over medium-high heat, in hot salad oil, cook onion until tender; spoon onion onto plate. In oil remaining in skillet, cook 2 lamb shoulder blade chops at a time until browned on both sides, removing chops to plate with onion as they brown.
2. Return onion and lamb chops to skillet. Add lemon juice, salt, dill, pepper, and ¾ cup water; over high heat, heat to boiling, stirring to loosen brown bits from bottom of skillet. Reduce heat to low; cover and simmer 30 minutes. Skim fat from liquid in skillet.
3. Cut each endive lengthwise in half. Add endive, frozen artichoke hearts, and frozen peas to skillet with lamb; over high heat, heat to boiling, separating frozen vegetables with a fork. Reduce heat to low; cover and simmer 10 to 15 minutes longer, until tender,
4. In cup, stir flour and 2 tablespoons water until blended. Gradually stir flour mixture into simmering liquid in skillet; cook, stirring constantly, until mixture thickens slightly.
5. To serve, transfer to large warmed platter and garnish with lemon peel and minced parsley.

- Color index page 48
- Begin 1¼ hrs ahead
- 4 servings
- 443 cals per serving

BREADED LAMB SHOULDER CHOPS

2 eggs
1 tablespoon water
¾ teaspoon salt
½ teaspoon dill weed
1 cup dried bread crumbs

4 lamb shoulder blade
   chops, about ¾ inch
   thick
2 tablespoons salad oil

1. In pie plate, mix eggs, water, salt, and dill weed. On waxed paper, place bread crumbs. Dip lamb chops into egg mixture, turning to coat both sides, then dip into crumbs. Repeat until each chop is coated twice.
2. In 12-inch skillet over medium heat, in hot salad oil, cook chops until browned and of desired doneness, about 15 minutes, adding more oil if necessary.

- Color index page 48
- Begin 30 mins ahead
- 4 servings
- 470 cals per serving

hops

LAMB NOISETTES

Lamb chops, probably the most frequently consumed cut of lamb, needn't be boring: try our savory-sweet bacon-wrapped lamb with dried fruit for an elegant alternative.

- Color index page 48
- Begin 1 hr ahead
- 4 servings
- 610 cals per serving

8 pitted prunes
8 dried apricot halves
Water
3 tablespoons butter or
   margarine
2 slices white bread,
   diced

⅛ teaspoon thyme leaves
⅛ teaspoon basil
Salt
4 lamb loin chops, each
   1¼ inches thick
8 slices bacon
Pepper

Currant-Orange, Almond-
   Curry, Cran-Apple
   Wine, or Cranberry-
   Pear Wine Sauce (right)

1 In 1-quart saucepan over high heat, heat prunes, apricots, and 3 tablespoons water to boiling; remove the saucepan from heat; let stand 10 minutes; drain; set aside.

2 Meanwhile, in 2-quart saucepan over medium heat, melt butter or margarine; add bread, thyme, basil, 1 teaspoon salt, and 2 teaspoons of water; toss to mix well.

3 Remove bones from lamb chops: With knife, starting at one side of backbone, cut through meat along bone, keeping knife blade against bone.

4 Cut along both sides of bone to separate bone from meat, making sure that the meat remains in one piece. Trim any excess fat from the lamb chops.

5 Preheat broiler if the manufacturer directs. With a teaspoon, fill each chop where the bone has been removed with one-fourth of bread mixture, 2 prepared pitted prunes, and 2 prepared apricot halves.

6 Push meat tightly around filling. Wrap 2 bacon slices tightly around side of each chop; secure bacon slices with toothpicks. (This will help keep the filling in place.)

7 Place lamb chops on rack in broiling pan; sprinkle lightly with salt and pepper. Broil lamb chops 8 minutes; gently turn lamb chops; broil about 8 minutes longer for medium-rare, or until of desired doneness. While lamb chops are broiling, prepare the Currant-Orange Sauce, or other sauce as preferred. Keep sauce warm until needed.

8 To serve, place lamb chops on warm meat platter. Pass sauce in a small bowl to spoon over the lamb noisettes.

CURRANT-ORANGE SAUCE

2 teaspoons grated
   orange peel
½ cup freshly squeezed
   orange juice

¼ cup red-currant jelly
1 teaspoon honey

In 1-quart saucepan, combine the orange peel and orange juice. Stir in the red-currant jelly and honey. Cook over medium heat until mixture boils; reduce heat to low; simmer 5 minutes, stirring frequently.

- About ½ cup
- 27 cals per tablespoon

ALMOND-CURRY SAUCE

2 tablespoons butter or
   margarine
2 tablespoons slivered
   blanched almonds
1 small onion, sliced
1 clove garlic, minced
1 tablespoon curry
   powder
1 tablespoon all-purpose
   flour

1 cup water
1 beef-flavor bouillon
   cube or envelope
¼ cup dried currants

1. In 2-quart saucepan over medium heat, in hot butter or margarine, cook the slivered blanched almonds until golden brown. Add the onion, garlic, and curry powder. Cook until onion is tender, stirring occasionally.
2. Stir flour into almond mixture until well mixed. Add water, bouillon cube, and currants. Over medium heat, heat mixture to boiling, stirring constantly. Reduce heat to low; cover and simmer 15 minutes, stirring occasionally.

- 1⅔ cups
- 17 cals per tablespoon

CRAN-APPLE WINE SAUCE

1 red cooking apple
1 tablespoon butter or
   margarine
1 8-ounce can jellied
   cranberry sauce

⅓ cup red port wine
2 teaspoons cornstarch
⅛ teaspoon salt

1. Core and cut apple into ¼-inch thick wedges. In 2-quart saucepan over medium heat, in hot butter or margarine, cook apple wedges until tender-crisp, stirring occasionally. Stir in cranberry sauce; heat through.
2. In cup, mix wine, cornstarch, and salt until smooth; stir into cran-apple mixture. Over medium heat, cook until mixture boils and thickens slightly, stirring constantly.

- About 2 cups
- 19 cals per tablespoon

CRANBERRY-PEAR WINE SAUCE: Prepar as above but omit red cooking apple, and u instead, *1 large Anjou* or *Bartlett pear*, peele Makes about 2 cups. 19 cals per tablespoon.

Stew and shanks

Shish kabob

MULLIGAN STEW

2 pounds lamb for stew, cut into 2-inch chunks
1 medium onion, sliced
1 13¾- to 14½-ounce can chicken broth
1 bay leaf
2 teaspoons salt
½ teaspoon pepper
½ teaspoon thyme leaves
Water
6 medium potatoes, peeled and cut into bite-sized pieces
3 medium celery stalks, sliced
3 medium carrots, sliced
1 medium rutabaga, peeled and cut into 1-inch chunks
1 small head green cabbage (about 1 pound), cut into bite-sized pieces
2 tablespoons all-purpose flour
1 tablespoon minced parsley

1. In 8-quart Dutch oven or saucepot over medium-high heat, heat first 7 ingredients and 2½ cups water to boiling. Reduce heat to low; cover and simmer, stirring often, for 1 hour or until meat is almost tender.
2. Add vegetables; heat to boiling. Reduce heat to low; cover; simmer 30 minutes or until vegetables are tender.
3. In cup, blend flour and ¼ cup water; gradually stir into hot liquid in Dutch oven, and cook, stirring constantly, until mixture thickens slightly. Sprinkle with parsley.

- Color index page 49
- Begin 2 hrs ahead
- 8 servings
- 475 cals per serving

BAKED LAMB SHANKS AND BEANS

3 tablespoons salad oil
4 lamb shanks (about 1 pound each)
2 medium onions, sliced
1 garlic clove, sliced
2 14½- to 16-ounce cans tomatoes
½ cup water
¼ cup cooking or dry red wine
1½ teaspoons sugar
½ teaspoon salt
¼ teaspoon rosemary
1 10-ounce package frozen Fordhook lima beans
1 9-ounce package frozen whole green beans

1. In 8-quart Dutch oven over medium-high heat, in hot salad oil, cook lamb shanks until meat is well browned on all sides. Remove shanks to plate. In drippings in Dutch oven over medium heat, cook onions and garlic until tender, stirring occasionally.
2. Return shanks to Dutch oven. Add tomatoes, with their liquid, and next 5 ingredients; over high heat, heat to boiling. Cover and bake in 350°F. oven 2 hours, stirring occasionally.
3. Remove Dutch oven from oven; skim off fat from sauce in Dutch oven. Add frozen lima beans and frozen whole green beans, separating vegetables with fork as they soften. Bake 30 minutes longer or until meat and vegetables are tender, stirring occasionally.

- Color index page 49
- Begin 3 hrs ahead
- 4 servings
- 1095 cals per serving

SHISH KABOB

Early settlers cooked meat on skewers over open fires, while later immigrants from the Mediterranean added the marinade and vegetables that have made this dish famous.

1 2½-pound boneless lamb shoulder or leg roast
Olive oil
¼ cup red wine vinegar or lemon juice
2 garlic cloves, minced
1½ teaspoons salt
1 teaspoon oregano leaves
¼ teaspoon pepper
16 small white onions
1 large green pepper
3 firm medium tomatoes
½ pound large mushrooms

- Color index page 48
- Begin day ahead
- 8 servings
- 243 cals per serving

1 Day ahead: Cut strings and unroll lamb shoulder, trimming excess fat; cut lamb into 1½-inch chunks.

2 Prepare marinade: In large bowl, mix well ½ cup olive oil and next 5 ingredients.

3 Add lamb and stir to coat with marinade. Cover; refrigerate overnight; turn occasionally.

4 45 minutes before serving: Preheat broiler if manufacturer directs. In 2-quart saucepan over medium heat, in 2 inches boiling water, cook onions 10 minutes until tender-crisp.

5 Cut green pepper into 1½-inch chunks and tomatoes into quarters. Remove stems from mushrooms. Reserve in refrigerator for use in soup another day.

6 On five 12- or 14-inch all-metal skewers, skewer lamb chunks alternately with green-pepper chunks and onions; reserve marinade. Place skewers on rack in broiling pan.

7 Into the reserved marinade, stir 3 tablespoons olive oil; brush vegetables with some of marinade. Broil prepared skewers for 10 to 12 minutes.

8 Meanwhile, on more skewers, thread the mushrooms and the tomatoes. Turn lamb; place skewers with the tomatoes and mushrooms on broiling-pan rack.

9 Brush meat and vegetables with remaining marinade mixture and broil 10 to 12 minutes more until lamb is of desired doneness.

Roasts

MUSHROOM-STUFFED BREAST OF VEAL

During the Depression veal, called "mock chicken," was substituted for the more expensive bird. Today, although the reverse is often true, this is a very economical cut.

Butter or margarine
½ pound mushrooms, sliced
½ cup sliced green onions
⅛ teaspoon fines herbes
1 10-ounce package frozen peas, thawed

2 cups fresh bread crumbs (4 slices)
Salt
Pepper
1 5-pound veal breast with pocket

- *Color index page 49*
- *Begin 3½ hrs ahead*
- *8 servings*
- *565 cals per serving*

1½ cups Rhine wine or Sauterne
½ cup water
¼ cup all-purpose flour
Chopped parsley for garnish

1 Preheat oven to 325°F. In 10-inch skillet over medium heat, in 3 tablespoons hot butter, cook mushrooms and onions about 5 minutes.

2 Remove skillet from heat. Stir in fines herbes, peas, 1½ cups bread crumbs, 1 teaspoon salt, and ¼ teaspoon pepper. Mix well.

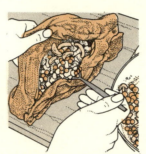

3 Sprinkle veal inside and out lightly with salt and pepper. Into the pocket, lightly stuff the mushroom mixture.

4 Carefully secure pocket opening with small skewers or toothpicks to prevent stuffing spilling out as it expands during cooking. Place in large open roasting pan.

5 Pour Rhine wine or Sauterne over stuffed veal breast in roasting pan. Cover pan tightly with aluminum foil; bake for 2½ to 3 hours, until the meat is fork-tender.

6 In small saucepan over medium heat, melt 2 tablespoons butter. Add remaining bread crumbs, stirring frequently until crumbs are golden. Keep warm.

7 Place veal on warm platter; keep warm. Pour liquid from pan into 2-quart saucepan.

8 In cup, blend water with flour; gradually stir into liquid in saucepan; cook over medium heat, stirring constantly.

9 Spoon small amount of sauce over meat; sprinkle with buttered crumbs and parsley. Pass remaining sauce.

SPICY VEAL ROUND ROAST

2 tablespoons salad oil
1 4-pound veal leg round roast, boneless
1 tablespoon pickling spice
1 medium onion, diced
1 tablespoon curry powder
1½ cups apple juice

1 teaspoon salt
Dash pepper
4 small red cooking apples, halved and cored
3 tablespoons all-purpose flour
⅓ cup water

1. In 8-quart Dutch oven over medium-high heat, in hot salad oil, cook veal roast until well browned on all sides.

2. Meanwhile, prepare bouquet garni: Cut a double-thickness of cheesecloth, 5 inches square; on it, place pickling spice; pull corners up to form small bag; tie with colorfast string.

3. Remove meat from Dutch oven. In drippings over medium heat, cook onion and curry powder, stirring occasionally, until onion is tender, about 5 minutes. Stir in apple juice, salt, and pepper; add bouquet garni. Return meat to Dutch oven; heat to boiling. Reduce heat to low; cover and simmer 2–2¼ hours or until meat is fork-tender, turning meat occasionally.

4. About 10 minutes before meat is done, add apples and continue cooking until apples are tender. Place on warm platter; keep warm.

5. Discard bouquet garni. In cup, blend flour and water until smooth; gradually stir into hot liquid in Dutch oven and cook over medium heat, stirring constantly, until mixture is thickened. Serve gravy over meat.

- *Color index page 49*
- *Begin 3½ hrs ahead*
- *8 servings*
- *312 cals per serving*

HOW TO MAKE A BOUQUET GARNI

The classic bouquet garni is a small bundle of herbs – usually parsley, thyme, and bay leaf – tied together with kitchen string.

Cut a double thickness of cheesecloth, about 5 inches square; place herbs and spices in the center.

Pull corners of cloth up to form a small bag and tie securely with color-fast kitchen string.

Chops

VEAL CHOPS WITH MUSHROOMS

● Color index page 49
● Begin 40 mins ahead
● 4 servings
● 395 cals per serving

3 tablespoons butter or margarine
1 small garlic clove, minced
¾ pound mushrooms, thickly sliced
2 tablespoons olive or salad oil
4 veal loin chops, each ½ inch thick
⅓ cup brandy
¾ cup half-and-half
1 small bunch arugula, coarsely sliced

1. In 12-inch skillet over medium-high heat, in hot butter or margarine, cook garlic until lightly browned. Add mushrooms; cook until tender. With slotted spoon, remove mushrooms and garlic to bowl.
2. In same skillet over medium-high heat, in hot olive or salad oil, cook veal chops until browned on both sides and cooked through, about 10 minutes. Remove veal chops to warm platter; keep warm.
3. Spoon off fat, if any, from skillet. Add brandy to drippings in skillet; over high heat, heat to boiling, stirring to loosen brown bits from bottom of skillet. Add half-and-half and mushroom mixture; cook until mixture thickens slightly. Remove skillet from heat; stir in arugula and salt to taste. Pour sauce over veal chops.

GOLDEN VEAL CHOPS

● Color index page 49
● Begin 45 mins ahead
● 6 servings
● 310 cals per serving

⅓ cup mayonnaise
¼ cup seasoned dried bread crumbs
¼ cup minced parsley
3 tablespoons white wine
1 tablespoon prepared mustard
1 tablespoon lemon juice
1 teaspoon salt
¾ teaspoon sugar
6 veal rib chops, each cut about ¾ inch thick

1. Preheat broiler if manufacturer directs.
2. Meanwhile, in small bowl, mix mayonnaise, bread crumbs, parsley, white wine, mustard, lemon juice, salt, and sugar.
3. Place veal chops on rack in broiling pan; broil 10 to 15 minutes until chops just lose their pink color and brown lightly, turning once and brushing with mayonnaise mixture occasionally.

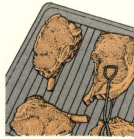

Broiling the veal chops: Place the veal chops on a rack in the broiling pan. Broil chops about 10 to 15 minutes until they are lightly browned.

Glazing the chops: Turn the veal chops once during broiling and brush them occasionally with the mayonnaise and bread crumb mixture.

VEAL CHOPS WITH AVOCADO

Avocados, grown extensively in California, Florida, and Hawaii, make a special topping for baked veal chops.

● Color index page 49
● Begin 1½ hrs ahead
● 4 servings
● 436 cals per serving

4 veal loin chops, each cut about ¾ inch thick (about 1½ pounds)
2 tablespoons butter or margarine
¼ pound mushrooms, sliced
¼ cup minced onion
2 tablespoons medium sherry
1 teaspoon salt
Dash hot pepper sauce
1 small ripe avocado
2 teaspoons cornstarch
½ cup heavy or whipping cream
Fresh dill sprigs for garnish

1 Preheat the oven to 350°F. With a sharp knife, slash the fat on the edge of the 4 veal loin chops in several places. In a 10-inch skillet with an oven-safe handle, over medium heat, in the hot butter or margarine, cook the sliced mushrooms and the minced onion until they are tender, about 5 minutes. Arrange the veal chops in the skillet on top of the cooked sliced mushrooms and onion.

2 Add sherry, salt, and the hot-pepper sauce; heat to boiling. Cover and bake 1 hour or until meat is fork-tender.

3 Cut avocado in half; remove the seed and skin. Thinly slice the avocado and carefully arrange the slices over the veal chops.

4 Bake, uncovered, 10 minutes or until avocado is heated through. With pancake turner, place veal chops on a warm platter.

5 In a cup, blend cornstarch and 1 tablespoon cream until smooth; stir in remaining cream. Gradually stir into hot liquid in skillet.

6 Cook over medium heat, stirring constantly, until thickened. Garnish with dill. Serve chops immediately with the sauce.

Cutlets

HAM AND CHEESE-STUFFED VEAL CUTLETS

We've stuffed the traditional veal cutlet with the favorite All-American combination of ham and Swiss cheese to create a special occasion dish.

- Color index page 50
- Begin 1 hr ahead
- 6 servings
- 431 cals per serving

6 large veal cutlets, each cut about ½ inch thick
6 Swiss cheese slices
6 paper-thin cooked ham slices
2 tablespoons all-purpose flour

½ teaspoon paprika
3 tablespoons butter or margarine
1 cup Sauterne
¼ cup half-and-half

1 On cutting board, with meat mallet or dull edge of French knife, pound veal cutlets well until they are about ¼-inch thick.

2 On each cutlet, place 1 cheese slice, then 1 ham slice. Fold each veal cutlet in half; fasten with toothpicks.

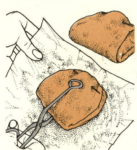 

3 On waxed paper, combine flour and paprika. Lightly coat ham and cheese-stuffed veal cutlets with flour and paprika mixture.

4 In a 12-inch skillet over medium-high heat, in hot butter, cook until lightly browned on both sides. Add Sauterne; heat to boiling.

5 Reduce heat to low; cover; simmer 10 to 15 minutes until meat is fork-tender. Remove to warm platter; remove toothpicks; keep warm.

6 Simmer the pan liquid, uncovered, over medium heat until reduced to ½ cup. Stir in half-and-half; heat; serve over the veal cutlets.

VEAL PARMIGIANA

- Color index page 50
- Begin 45 mins ahead
- 8 servings
- 230 cals per serving

1 egg
Water
⅓ cup all-purpose flour
¼ cup grated Parmesan cheese
8 veal cutlets, each cut about ½ inch thick (about 2 pounds)

About ⅓ cup salad oil
1 teaspoon salt
⅛ teaspoon pepper
2 cups Spaghetti Sauce (p.259)
Chopped parsley for garnish
Spaghetti (optional)

1. In a pie plate, with a fork, beat the egg with 1 tablespoon water. On waxed paper, mix the flour with ¼ cup Parmesan cheese.
2. Dip the veal cutlets, one at a time, into the egg mixture, then in the flour mixture, coating each cutlet on both sides.
3. In 10-inch skillet over medium-high heat, in 2 tablespoons hot salad oil, cook cutlets, a few at a time, until browned on both sides, adding more oil as needed.
4. Return all meat to skillet; sprinkle with salt and pepper.
5. Pour the Spaghetti Sauce over the meat; sprinkle with ½ cup grated Parmesan cheese; heat to boiling. Reduce heat to medium-low; cover and cook for 15 minutes more.
6. To serve, transfer Veal Parmigiana to a warmed platter. Sprinkle with the chopped parsley. If you like, serve with spaghetti.

CALIFORNIA VEAL CUTLETS

- Color index page 50
- Begin 40 mins ahead
- 4 servings
- 530 cals per serving

Lemony Vinaigrette (below)
4 veal cutlets (about 1 pound)
2 tablespoons butter or margarine
Salt

1 small tomato, sliced
1 small avocado, sliced
4 ounces Monterey Jack cheese with jalapeño peppers, shredded (1 cup)
Red leaf lettuce

1. Prepare Lemony Vinaigrette; keep warm.
2. On cutting board, with meat mallet or dull edge of French knife, pound each veal cutlet to about ⅛-inch thickness.
3. In 12-inch skillet over medium-high heat, in hot butter or margarine, cook veal cutlets, in two batches if necessary, until browned on both sides, about 3 to 4 minutes, removing cutlets to plate as they brown.
4. Arrange cooked veal cutlets in skillet in one layer; sprinkle lightly with salt if you like. Top cutlets with tomato slices, avocado slices, then shredded cheese. Reduce heat to low; cover skillet and heat until cheese melts.
5. To serve, arrange the red leaf lettuce on a warm platter. Then arrange the cutlets on the lettuce leaves with edges slightly overlapping. Pour Lemony Vinaigrette over all, or serve separately in a gravy boat.

LEMONY VINAIGRETTE: In small saucepan over medium heat, heat *3 tablespoons lemon juice, 3 tablespoons olive or salad oil, 1 tablespoon water, 1½ teaspoons sugar,* and *⅛ teaspoon salt.* ½ cup. 30 cals per tablespoon.

Stew

- Color index page 49
- Begin 1½ hrs ahead
- 8 servings
- 350 cals per serving (without rice)

VEAL-AND-CHESTNUT RAGOUT

When the first settlers arrived, America was covered with tall chestnut trees, but a blight destroyed most of them at the beginning of this century. Today, most of the chestnuts we use are imported from Europe. They provide a nutty taste and texture for this satisfying and warming winter veal stew.

2 tablespoons salad oil
2 pounds veal for stew, cut into 1½-inch chunks
1 large onion, diced
1 medium rutabaga (about 1¾ pounds), cut into bite-sized pieces
1½ teaspoons salt
½ teaspoon sugar
¼ teaspoon pepper
1 chicken flavor bouillon cube or envelope
Water
1 pound chestnuts
2 tablespoons all-purpose flour
2 tablespoons minced parsley for garnish
Hot cooked rice (optional)

1. In 5-quart Dutch oven over medium-high heat, in hot salad oil, cook veal and onion until veal is browned on all sides and onion is tender. Stir in rutabaga, salt, sugar, pepper, bouillon, and 3 cups water; over high heat, heat to boiling. Reduce heat to low; cover and simmer for 40 minutes, stirring stew occasionally, until the veal is almost tender.
2. Meanwhile, in 2-quart saucepan over high heat, heat chestnuts and enough water to cover to boiling. Reduce heat to medium; cover and cook 15 minutes. Remove saucepan from heat. With slotted spoon, immediately remove 4 chestnuts from water. With kitchen shears, carefully cut each chestnut on flat side through shell. With fingers, peel off shell and skin, keeping chestnuts whole if possible. Repeat with remaining chestnuts. (Chestnuts will be difficult to peel if allowed to cool.)
3. Gently stir chestnuts into veal mixture; continue cooking until veal, rutabaga, and chestnuts are tender, about 15 minutes.
4. When veal mixture is ready, skim fat from liquid in Dutch oven. In cup, stir flour and ¼ cup water until blended. Gradually stir flour mixture into veal mixture in Dutch oven; cook over medium heat, stirring, until mixture thickens slightly. Spoon veal mixture into warm bowl; garnish with parsley. Serve with rice if you like.

Cutting the chestnuts: With kitchen shears, cut each chestnut on its flat side completely through the shell.

Peeling the chestnuts: With fingers, gently peel off the shell and the skin; try to keep the chestnuts whole.

Calf's liver

- Color index page 50
- Begin 20 mins ahead
- 4 servings
- 445 cals per serving

PAN-FRIED LIVER, BACON, AND ONIONS

Highly nutritious calf's liver tastes delicious when cooked with its traditional companions, bacon and onion. A squeeze of lemon gives additional zest.

1 8-ounce package sliced bacon
2 medium onions, sliced
1 pound calf's liver, sliced about ¼ inch thick
2 tablespoons all-purpose flour
¼ teaspoon salt
4 lemon wedges (optional)
Chopped parsley for garnish

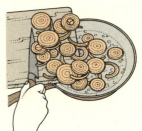

1 In 10-inch skillet over medium heat, fry bacon until crisp but not brittle; drain on paper towels; keep bacon warm between 2 plates.

2 Pour off and reserve all but 2 tablespoons drippings; add onions and cook until tender. Remove; set aside and keep warm.

3 Meanwhile, trim any membrane from the edges of liver slices. On waxed paper, coat liver with the flour.

4 Add 2 more tablespoons drippings to skillet. Over medium heat, cook liver about 4 minutes, turning once, until the liver is crisp and browned on the outside, and a delicate pink on the inside (medium done). Add more drippings if necessary. (Be careful not to over-cook or liver will be tough.) Sprinkle with salt and squeeze a little lemon juice over liver slices. Add the onions and heat through.

5 Place liver, onions, and bacon on warm platter; garnish with parsley.

LIVER AND ONIONS: Omit bacon. Use 2 tablespoons bacon drippings, butter or margarine to cook 2 medium onions, sliced; place on warm platter. In 2 more tablespoons drippings, cook liver as before. 4 servings. 437 cals per serving.

Sausages

APPLE-GLAZED FRANKS AND CABBAGE

- Color index page 50
- Begin 1 hr ahead
- 4 servings
- 595 cals per serving

The frankfurter in a bun appeared in St. Louis in the 1800s and became *the* American ballpark favorite. Teamed with apples and cabbage, they remain true to their German heritage.

1 medium head green cabbage (about 2 pounds)
Salad oil
½ teaspoon salt
1 16-ounce package frankfurters, cut into 2-inch pieces

2 red medium cooking apples, cut into ½-inch wedges
¼ cup apple jelly

1 Discard any tough green outer leaves from the cabbage. With knife, coarsely slice the cabbage to make about 10 cups, discarding any tough ribs.

2 In 12-inch skillet over medium heat, in 2 tablespoons hot salad oil, cook cabbage and salt until cabbage is tender, stirring occasionally.

3 Spoon the cabbage into a bowl. Then, in the same skillet over a medium-high heat, in 1 tablespoon hot salad oil, cook the frankfurter pieces until they are browned on all sides; spoon into bowl with the cabbage. In drippings remaining in skillet over medium-low heat, cook the apple wedges about 5 minutes until they are just tender.

4 Using a pancake turner, carefully turn the apple wedges once during cooking.

5 When the apples are lightly browned and tender, stir in apple jelly, being careful not to break up the apple; heat through.

6 Put the cooked frankfurter pieces and the cabbage in skillet with apple wedges and jelly; over medium heat, heat through.

ITALIAN SAUSAGES AND PEPPERS

- Color index page 50
- Begin 50 mins ahead
- 6 servings
- 275 cals per serving

1½ pounds hot or sweet Italian-sausage links
¼ cup water
2 large sweet peppers, cut into strips

2 large onions, sliced
½ teaspoon salt
½ teaspoon oregano leaves

1. In 12-inch skillet over medium heat, heat Italian-sausage links with water to boiling. Cover and cook 5 minutes. Remove cover; continue cooking, turning sausages frequently, until water evaporates and sausage links are well browned, about 20 minutes. Remove sausages to paper towels to drain.
2. Pour off all but about 3 tablespoons fat from skillet; add green peppers, onions, salt, and oregano leaves; over medium heat, cook, stirring frequently, until vegetables are tender.
3. Add cooked sausage links to vegetables; heat through and arrange on warm platter.

Browning the sausages: Add water to the sausage links pan. Cook, covered, turning frequently until water evaporates.

Adding sausage links: Carefully add the cooked sausages to the vegetable mixture to heat through.

KIELBASA WITH SAUERKRAUT

- Color index page 50
- Begin 30 mins ahead
- 4 servings
- 481 cals per serving

1 1-pound kielbasa (smoked Polish sausage), cut into 2-inch pieces
2 tablespoons salad oil
1 small onion, diced
1 small green pepper, diced
1 16-ounce can or package sauerkraut, drained

¾ cup water
2 tablespoons brown sugar
¼ teaspoon salt
1 large red cooking apple, cut into thin wedges
Parsley sprigs for garnish

1. In 10-inch skillet over medium-high heat, cook kielbasa until lightly browned; set aside.
2. In same skillet over medium heat, in hot salad oil, cook onion and green pepper until tender, stirring occasionally.
3. Add sauerkraut, water, brown sugar, salt, and kielbasa; heat to boiling. Reduce the heat to low; cover and simmer for about 15 minutes, stirring occasionally.
4. Add apple wedges to sauerkraut mixture; simmer 5 minutes or until heated through.
5. Serve on a warm platter; garnish with parsley.

POLISH SAUSAGE WITH RED CABBAGE

- Color index page 50
- Begin 50 mins ahead
- 4 servings
- 420 cals per serving

1 small red cabbage, coarsely shredded
1 small apple, peeled and diced
1 tablespoon lemon juice
Salt
Water
1 tablespoon butter or margarine
1 small onion, chopped
1 tablespoon wine vinegar
1 pound Polish sausage, cut into chunks

1. In covered 4-quart saucepan over medium heat, simmer cabbage with apple, lemon juice, 2 teaspoons salt, and ½ cup water for 15 minutes, stirring occasionally.
2. Meanwhile, in 10-inch skillet over medium heat, in hot butter, cook onion until tender.
3. Stir in cabbage mixture, 1 teaspoon salt, vinegar, and Polish sausage chunks. Reduce heat to low; cover and simmer 30 minutes or until sausage chunks are cooked through.

KNACKWURST SAUERBRATEN

- Color index page 50
- Begin 45 mins ahead
- 6 servings
- 515 cals per serving

3 medium potatoes (1 pound), each cut in half
Salt
Water
2 12-ounce packages knackwurst
2 tablespoons butter or margarine
4 medium celery stalks, cut into 2-inch pieces
3 large carrots, cut into 2-inch pieces
1 medium onion, sliced
½ teaspoon beef-flavor bouillon cube or envelope
½ teaspoon thyme leaves
¼ teaspoon cracked pepper
⅛ teaspoon ground cloves
5 gingersnaps, crushed
¼ cup red wine vinegar
3 tablespoons red currant jelly
2 tablespoons Madeira wine

1. Cook potatoes: In 2-quart saucepan over high heat, heat potatoes, ½ teaspoon salt, and enough water to cover to boiling. Reduce heat to medium-low; cover and cook 20 minutes or until potatoes are fork-tender. Drain; keep warm.
2. Meanwhile, cut each of the knackwurst lengthwise in half. In 12-inch skillet over medium heat, in hot butter, cook the knackwurst, half at a time, until they are lightly browned, about 5 to 7 minutes, removing knackwurst to a bowl as they brown.
3. To drippings in skillet, add celery, carrots, onions, bouillon, thyme, cracked pepper, ground cloves, 1¾ cups water, and ½ teaspoon salt; over high heat, heat to boiling.
4. Reduce the heat to medium-low; cover and cook for about 15 minutes or until the vegetables are tender.
5. Add crushed gingersnaps, red wine vinegar, red currant jelly, and the Madeira wine; cook until mixture is slightly thickened and boils, stirring constantly.
6. Return the knackwurst to the skillet; heat through. Arrange the potatoes on top of the knackwurst mixture in skillet; heat through.

BREAKFAST SAUSAGE PATTIES

- Color index page 51
- Begin 1 hr ahead
- 8 servings
- 326 cals per serving

A hearty breakfast featuring sausages was a necessary start to the day for people engaged in physical labor. Our sausage patties are easy to make and provide a warm and nourishing morning meal.

2 pounds pork shoulder blade roast boneless, cut into 1-inch cubes
¼ cup chopped parsley
2½ teaspoons salt
1 teaspoon rubbed sage
½ teaspoon pepper

1 With food grinder, using coarse cutting disk, grind cubed pork into large bowl.

2 Add the chopped parsley, salt, rubbed sage, and pepper; mix well. Shape the meat mixture into patties.

3 In 12-inch skillet over medium-low heat, cook the patties about 25 minutes or until they are browned and well done.

4 Carefully turn the patties occasionally with pancake turner to ensure they cook and brown evenly. Serve patties immediately.

CAMP-STOVE STEW

- Color index page 51
- Begin 30 mins ahead
- 6 servings
- 419 cals per serving

3 tablespoons butter or margarine
1 medium onion, coarsely chopped
1 16-ounce package frankfurters, quartered lengthwise
1 tablespoon all-purpose flour
1½ teaspoons chili powder
1 teaspoon salt
2 15¼- to 19-ounce cans red kidney beans
1 14½- to 16-ounce can tomatoes
1 12-ounce can whole-kernel corn, drained

1. In large saucepot or Dutch oven over medium heat, in hot butter, cook onion with frankfurters until lightly browned; with spoon, stir in flour, chili powder, and salt.
2. Add beans and tomatoes with their liquid and corn. Cover and simmer 15 minutes.

Tongue

- Color index page 49
- Begin 3¼ hrs ahead
- 10 servings
- 432 cals per serving

FRESH TONGUE WITH SWEET-AND-SOUR TOMATO SAUCE

Tongue was one of the many dishes brought to America by East European immigrants. Use plump California raisins for the sauce.

1 3½-pound fresh beef tongue
½ teaspoon peppercorns
3 whole cloves
1 bay leaf
Salt
Water
1 28-ounce can plum tomatoes

1 6-ounce can tomato paste
⅓ cup lemon juice
¼ cup dark seedless raisins
¼ cup packed light brown sugar
Parsley sprigs for garnish

1 In 5-quart Dutch oven over high heat, heat the first 4 ingredients, 2 teaspoons salt, and enough water to cover to boiling. Reduce the heat to low; cover and simmer 2¾ hours or until the tongue is fork-tender. Meanwhile, prepare the tomato sauce: In 12-inch skillet over medium heat, heat tomatoes with their liquid, tomato paste, lemon juice, raisins, sugar, and 1 teaspoon salt to boiling.

2 Stir the mixture frequently to break up the tomatoes and to prevent the raisins and sugar from sticking.

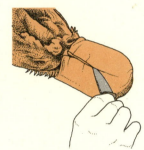

3 Reduce heat to low; cover and simmer sauce 15 minutes to blend flavors; stir occasionally.

4 When tongue is tender, drain and rinse with cold water. Slit skin on underside from thick end to tip; loosen skin all around thick end.

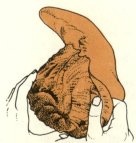

5 Grasp skin at thick end and pull it off. With sharp knife, trim all bones and gristle from thick end of tongue.

6 Cut tongue crosswise into thin slices. Arrange slices in skillet; cover; cook until heated through. Garnish.

Venison

- Color index page 50
- Begin 25 mins ahead
- 4 servings
- 355 cals per serving

VENISON STEAKS WITH WINE SAUCE

Pilgrims learned to substitute foods that were abundant in the New World for those that had been familiar at home. Venison often replaced beef in the diet of early New Englanders.

4 venison T-bone or loin steaks, cut about ½-inch thick (about 1½ pounds)
3 tablespoons butter or margarine
Salt and pepper
½ cup dry red wine

1 tablespoon chopped parsley
1 tablespoon chopped chives
1 tablespoon quince or currant jelly
⅛ teaspoon nutmeg

1. Trim off any excess fat from steaks. In 10-inch skillet over medium heat, in hot butter, fry steaks 3 or 4 minutes on each side until medium or well done; sprinkle lightly with salt and pepper; place on warm platter.

2. In drippings, heat remaining ingredients; spoon over steaks.

VENISON STEW

- Color index page 50
- Begin 2 hrs ahead
- 6 servings
- 409 cals per serving

2 tablespoons salad oil
1½ pounds venison for stew, cut into 1¼-inch chunks
2 tablespoons butter or margarine
½ pound small mushrooms
6 small white onions
2 cloves garlic, chopped
1 teaspoon salt
½ teaspoon thyme leaves

¼ teaspoon pepper
1½ cups dry red wine
Water
1 pound small red potatoes
½ 16-ounce bag carrots
½ pound green beans
3 tablespoons all-purpose flour
2 tablespoons chopped parsley

1. In 5-quart Dutch oven over high heat, in hot salad oil, cook venison, half at a time, until well browned. With slotted spoon, remove venison to bowl as pieces brown.

2. To drippings in Dutch oven, add butter or margarine. Over medium heat, in hot butter or margarine, cook mushrooms, onions, and garlic until lightly browned, stirring frequently.

3. Return venison and its juices to Dutch oven. Add salt, thyme, pepper, wine, and ¾ cup water. Over high heat, heat to boiling. Reduce heat to low; cover and simmer 1 hour.

4. Meanwhile, cut each potato in half. Cut carrots into 1-inch pieces. Stir potatoes and carrots into venison mixture; cover and cook 20 minutes. Trim ends from green beans; cut each in half. Stir beans into venison mixture. Cook 10 minutes longer or until venison and vegetables are fork-tender.

5. In cup, blend flour and ¼ cup water until smooth. Into venison mixture, stir flour mixture. Over medium-high heat, cook until sauce boils and thickens, stirring carefully. Sprinkle with chopped parsley.

BARBECUE

*"Bacon's in the pan and coffee's in the pot,
come on round and get it while it's hot."*

Cowboy song

Outdoor cooking is certainly in our heritage: the present passion for barbecuing has been described as a "national mania" pursued on any warm weekend. The earliest Spanish explorers used the word *barbacoa* (frame of sticks) to describe the way the Indians of Haiti grilled meat outdoors. Ponce de León and other explorers of the South Atlantic coast noticed that the Indians used primitive wooden racks over open fires to smoke their fish, game, and fowl. Settlers took this cooking method with them to ranches in Texas, New Mexico, Arizona, and California; but it was the Spaniards who provided the zesty sauces, using hot peppers, and garlic for flavoring.

By the late 1700s the barbecue was already associated with a large social gathering. It became popular in Texas, where a community barbecue brought together farmers, ranchers, rangers, and neighbors. Wood was piled into ditches made just for the purpose and was left to burn all night before being used for cooking the next day. In 1850, a big Kansas barbecue boasted 6 cows, 20 hogs, 50 sheep, pigs, and lambs, and 100 hams!

The barbecue became a social event. Parties, holiday celebrations, and political meetings were often centered around the outdoor feast. In the mid-1800s politicians used the barbecue as a way to get votes; people were often swayed by the food and drink provided for them at the barbecue rather than by the platforms of the candidates. Years later, Eleanor Roosevelt created a great stir when she served hot dogs to England's King George VI on the White House lawn.

Although outdoor cooking was made popular by British colonials in the East, and Spaniards in the South and West, the barbecue has become a legend in Texas. A true Texas barbecue involves very slow cooking over a wood fire in an open pit. The meat is cooked for about an hour per pound without turning, until it is very well done. Although many different meats are used, the main choice for barbecuing in Texas is beef, and brisket, from the breast of the animal, is considered the best cut of all.

Adding a smoking wood, such as hickory, mesquite, oak, or alder, to a charcoal, gas, or electric grill has become a popular way of giving the barbecued food extra flavor. Herbs (rosemary, thyme, basil, or marjoram, for example) or fruit rinds (orange or lemon) sprinkled around the edges of the coal or wood toward the end of the cooking time add a beautiful aroma.

GLOSSARY OF BARBECUE EQUIPMENT

Barbecuing is an all-American pastime and most people manage with ordinary kitchen equipment, but certain utensils do make it easier and safer.

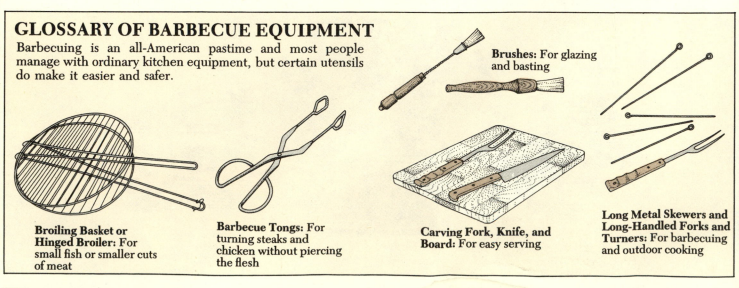

Brushes: For glazing and basting

Broiling Basket or Hinged Broiler: For small fish or smaller cuts of meat

Barbecue Tongs: For turning steaks and chicken without piercing the flesh

Carving Fork, Knife, and Board: For easy serving

Long Metal Skewers and Long-Handled Forks and Turners: For barbecuing and outdoor cooking

Meat/Steaks

SIRLOIN STEAKS WITH FRESH-PEPPER RELISH

- Color index page 51
- 4 servings
- Begin 45 mins ahead
- 422 cals per serving

1 large red pepper, diced	1/8 teaspoon celery seeds
1 large green pepper, diced	1/2 teaspoon salt
1 large yellow pepper, diced	Water
2 tablespoons cider vinegar	1/3 cup gherkins
2 teaspoons sugar	4 boneless top sirloin steaks, cut about 3/4-inch thick
	2 tablespoons salad oil

1. Prepare outdoor grill for barbecuing.
2. Meanwhile, prepare fresh-pepper relish: In 2-quart saucepan over high heat, heat peppers, vinegar, sugar, celery seeds, salt, and 2 tablespoons water to boiling; boil 1 minute. Remove saucepan from heat.
3. If gherkins are large, cut each lengthwise in half. Add gherkins to pepper mixture. Keep pepper relish warm on the side of the grill. (If you like, you can prepare the relish early in the day and refrigerate until ready to use.)
4. Trim any excess fat from steaks. Brush steaks with the salad oil. Place steaks on grill over high heat; grill 5 to 7 minutes for rare or until of desired doneness, turning occasionally. Serve with the fresh-pepper relish.

Preparing pepper relish: Heat peppers, vinegar, sugar, celery seeds, salt, and water to boiling.

Preparing the steaks for grilling: With a sharp knife, remove any excess fat. Brush with oil.

STEAK WITH ANCHOVY BUTTER

- Color index page 51
- Begin 1 1/2 hrs ahead
- 8 servings
- 290 cals per serving

1/2 2-ounce can anchovy fillets, drained	2 teaspoons lemon juice
4 tablespoons butter or margarine, softened	1/2 teaspoon sugar
2 tablespoons minced parsley	1 beef top round steak, cut 1 1/2 inches thick, about 2 pounds
1 tablespoon prepared mustard	

1. Prepare outdoor grill for barbecuing.
2. In small bowl with fork, mash anchovies with next 5 ingredients until well mixed; set aside.
3. Place top round steak on grill over medium heat; grill 25 minutes for rare or until of desired doneness, turning occasionally. Remove steak to cutting board. With metal spatula, spread top of steak with anchovy butter; Serve immediately.

Meat/Brisket

APPLE-GLAZED BEEF BRISKET

- Color index page 51
- Begin early in day or day ahead
- 12 servings
- 423 cals per serving

1 4- to 4 1/2-pound beef brisket	3 tablespoons minced green onions
1 small onion, cut into quarters	3 tablespoons prepared mustard
1 garlic clove, cut in half	1 1/2 teaspoons salt
10 whole cloves	3/4 teaspoon curry powder
Water	1/2 teaspoon cracked pepper
1 10-ounce jar apple jelly	
1/3 cup cooking or dry white wine	

1. In 8-quart Dutch oven or saucepot over high heat, heat beef brisket, onion, garlic, cloves, and enough water to cover meat to boiling.
2. Reduce heat to low; cover and simmer 2 1/2 to 3 hours until meat is fork-tender. Remove meat to platter; cover and refrigerate.
3. About 1 hour before serving: Prepare outdoor grill for barbecuing. Meanwhile, in small metal-handled saucepan, mix apple jelly, white wine, green onions, mustard, salt, curry powder, and cracked pepper.
4. Heat mixture on grill until jelly is melted, stirring occasionally.
5. Place cooked brisket on grill over medium heat; cook 30 minutes or until heated through, brushing with jelly mixture and turning occasionally. Serve remaining jelly mixture with meat.

HOW TO PRESENT A PLANKED STEAK

The most important step in preparing a planked steak is choosing the proper plank. Unfinished hardwood, such as oak, maple, or hickory, is best. Season the plank or planks by brushing with oil and heating in a 300°F. oven for an hour.

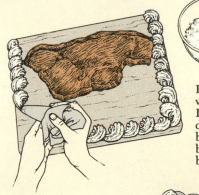

Place barbecued steak on well-seasoned plank. Pipe Duchess Potatoes (p.244) onto plank to form a border. If you like, lightly broil potatoes until browned.

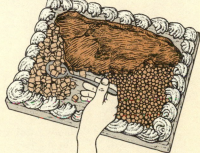

Arrange accompanying vegetables, such as carrots, peas, Brussels sprouts, or lima beans, around the steak, inside the potato border.

Meat/Larger cuts

LEMON-MARINATED GRILLED LAMB

Chops are the traditional cut for barbecued lamb, but a succulent leg, butterflied and marinated in a mixture of herbs, spices, and lemon juice, makes the outdoor meal an extra special occasion.

- Color index page 51
- Begin a day ahead or early in day
- 8 servings
- 409 cals per serving

1 4-pound lamb leg shank half
3 tablespoons salad oil
2 medium onions, thinly sliced

1 garlic clove, minced
1 tablespoon salt
2 teaspoons sugar
1½ teaspoons thyme leaves

1 teaspoon rosemary
½ teaspoon pepper
¾ cup lemon juice

1 Place lamb with fat side down on cutting board. With sharp knife, cut through meat parallel to bone, exposing main leg bone.

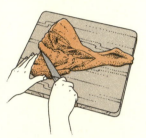

2 Keeping the knife blade against the bone, begin scraping the meat from around the bone until reaching the knee joint.

3 Turn the leg slightly and still holding the knife blade against the bone, continue cutting away the meat around the knee joint.

4 Continue to cut meat from knee down to the second leg bone. Remove the bone.

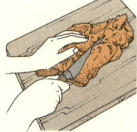

5 The boned lamb has an uneven thickness, so cut the thicker muscles almost in half.

6 Open like a butterfly to make lamb flatter for more even thickness (shape will still be irregular). Trim excess fat.

7 Prepare marinade: In 2-quart saucepan over medium-high heat, in hot salad oil, cook the onions and next 6 ingredients until onions are tender, stirring mixture occasionally.

8 Spoon onion mixture into 13" by 9" baking dish; stir in lemon juice. Add butterflied leg of lamb, turning to coat with the marinade. Cover and refrigerate it overnight, turning occasionally.

9 Prepare outdoor grill. Place lamb on grill over medium heat. Grill 25 minutes for rare or until of desired doneness; brush occasionally with marinade; turn often.

MAPLE-GLAZED PORK TENDERLOINS

1 teaspoon salt
¼ teaspoon pepper
2 pork tenderloins, whole, trimmed, (about ¾ pound each)

6 bacon slices
½ cup maple-flavor syrup

1. *Early in day:* With hands, rub salt and pepper into pork tenderloins. Place tenderloins in medium bowl; cover and refrigerate tenderloins at least 4 hours.
2. *About 1 hour before serving:* Prepare outdoor grill for barbecuing.
3. Place two tenderloins with thick ends pointing away from each other and thin ends overlapping slightly to make a long piece of meat of even thickness. Wrap bacon slices around tenderloins; secure with small metal skewers.
4. Into small metal-handled saucepan, measure maple-flavor syrup.
5. Place pork tenderloins on grill over medium heat; cook 25 to 30 minutes until pork is lightly browned and fork-tender, brushing frequently with maple-flavor syrup and turning meat occasionally. (Internal temperature of meat should be 170°F. on meat thermometer.) Transfer to warmed platter. Remove metal skewers from tenderloins; slice and serve.

- Color index page 51
- Begin early in day
- 6 servings
- 435 cals per serving

PLUM-GLAZED VEAL BREAST

1 4-pound veal breast
Water
1 17-ounce bottle chutney

4 large plums, peeled and cut up
½ teaspoon salt

1. *Early in day:* In 8-quart saucepot or Dutch oven, cover veal breast with water; over high heat, heat to boiling. Reduce heat to low; cover and simmer 1½ hours or until meat is fork-tender. Remove veal breast to platter; cover and refrigerate until ready to grill.
2. *About 1 hour before serving:* Prepare outdoor grill for barbecuing.
3. Meanwhile, in blender at medium speed or in food processor with knife blade attached, blend chutney, plums, and salt until smooth. Remove plum mixture to small saucepan and keep warm on the side of the grill.
4. Place cooked veal breast on grill over medium heat; cook 30 minutes or until heated through, turning veal breast occasionally and brushing with plum mixture during the last 10 minutes of cooking time.
5. Place glazed veal breast on a cutting board. Slice into ¼-inch-thick slices. If you like, accompany with a tossed green salad.

- Color index page 50
- Begin early in day
- 4 servings
- 820 cals per serving

Meat/Ribs

TEX-MEX BARBECUED SPARERIBS

4 pounds pork spareribs, cut into 2-rib portions
Water
4 canned pickled serrano chilies, stems removed and chopped (about 1 tablespoon)
2 tablespoons drained, chopped, canned green chilies
½ cup chili sauce
½ cup cider vinegar
2 tablespoons brown sugar
1 tablespoon salad oil
1 teaspoon salt
⅛ teaspoon ground cumin
⅛ teaspoon oregano leaves

1. In 6-quart saucepot or Dutch oven, cover ribs with water; over high heat, heat to boiling.
2. Reduce heat to low; cover; simmer 1 hour or until ribs are fork-tender. Remove to platter.
3. *About 1 hour before serving:* Prepare outdoor grill. Prepare barbecue sauce: In blender at medium speed or in food processor with knife blade attached, blend serrano chilies with remaining ingredients until smooth; set aside.
4. Place cooked spareribs on grill over medium heat; cook 20 minutes, brushing occasionally with barbecue sauce and turning once.

- *Color index page 51*
- *Begin 1½ hrs ahead*
- *4 servings*
- *775 cals per serving*

SPARERIBS WITH PEACH SAUCE

½ cup soy sauce
¼ cup cooking or dry sherry
¼ cup water
6 pounds pork spareribs, cut into 2-rib portions
1 28-ounce can cling peach halves, drained
⅓ cup chili sauce
2 tablespoons honey
2 teaspoons minced, peeled gingerroot or ½ teaspoon ground ginger
¾ teaspoon salt
¼ teaspoon garlic powder

1. In large open roasting pan, mix soy sauce, sherry, and water. Place spareribs in soy-sauce mixture in one layer, turning ribs to coat well. Bake in 350°F. oven 1 hour. Baste occasionally with soy-sauce mixture in pan.
2. Meanwhile, in covered blender at medium speed or in food processor with knife blade attached, blend peaches with remaining ingredients until smooth. Spoon mixture into small bowl; set aside.
3. *About 1 hour before serving:* Prepare outdoor grill for barbecuing. Remove roasting pan from oven; spoon ½ cup soy-sauce mixture from pan into peach mixture. Place ribs on grill over medium heat; grill 20 minutes.
4. Brush ribs with some peach sauce. Grill 20 minutes longer or until ribs are fork-tender, brushing frequently with sauce.

- *Color index page 51*
- *Begin 1¾ hrs ahead*
- *6 servings*
- *630 cals per serving*

TEXAS COUNTRY RIBS

Pork ribs are traditional barbecue fare. They're grilled here in the typical zesty garlic and pepper sauce handed down to us by the first Spanish settlers. This sauce can be made ahead and can be used with beef ribs and steaks too.

8 pounds pork loin country-style ribs
Water
¼ cup salad oil
1 garlic clove, sliced
1 medium onion, minced
1 14-ounce bottle catchup
¼ cup dark molasses
2 tablespoons cider vinegar
2 teaspoons Worcestershire
1 teaspoon dry mustard
1 teaspoon hot-pepper sauce
½ teaspoon salt
Pickled hot red and green cherry peppers for garnish

- *Color index page 51*
- *Begin early in day or day ahead*
- *12 servings*
- *600 cals per serving*

1 In 12-quart saucepot or Dutch oven, cover ribs with water; over high heat, heat to boiling.

2 Reduce heat to low; cover and simmer 1 hour or until ribs are fork-tender. Remove to large platter; cover with foil and refrigerate.

3 Meanwhile, prepare barbecue sauce: In 3-quart saucepan over medium heat, in hot oil, cook garlic until lightly browned; discard garlic.

4 In oil remaining in saucepan, cook onion uncovered, until tender. With wooden spoon, stir frequently.

5 Stir in catchup, molasses, vinegar, Worcestershire, mustard, hot pepper sauce, and salt. Over high heat, heat mixture to boiling.

6 Reduce heat to medium; cook 5 minutes, stirring occasionally. Remove from heat. Cover and refrigerate barbecue sauce.

7 *About 1 hour before serving:* Prepare outdoor grill. Place cooked ribs on grill over medium heat.

8 Cook 20 minutes or until hot, turning ribs often and brushing with sauce occasionally to coat thoroughly.

9 To serve, arrange ribs on platter. Garnish with pickled hot red and green cherry peppers. Serve hot.

Meat/Kabobs and chops

BEEF AND VEGETABLE KABOBS WITH PEANUT SAUCE

Americans have been cooking food on skewers for more than 300 years. These kabobs have a unique flavor with a zesty sauce made from America's favorite spread, peanut butter.

- *Color index page 51*
- *Begin 3 hrs ahead*
- *6 servings*
- *445 cals per serving*

1 1½-pound beef top
  round steak
¼ cup soy sauce
2 tablespoons salad oil
½ teaspoon caraway
  seeds, crushed
½ teaspoon ground
  coriander
1 garlic clove, sliced

Lemon juice
Ground red pepper
¾ cup water
½ cup chunky peanut
  butter
3 medium yellow straight-
  neck squash (about
  8 ounces each), cut
  into 1½-inch chunks

½ pound medium
  mushrooms
1 large green pepper, cut
  into 1-inch pieces
3 tablespoons butter or
  margarine, melted

1 With a sharp knife, slanting – almost parallel to cutting surface, slice the beef top round steak crosswise into ⅛-inch-thick slices.

2 In medium bowl, mix meat slices, next 5 ingredients, 2 tablespoons lemon juice, and ¼ teaspoon ground red pepper. Toss to coat well.

3 Cover and refrigerate the meat in soy-sauce mixture for at least 2 hours, stirring occasionally, allowing the meat slices to absorb the flavors. *About 1 hour before serving:* Prepare outdoor grill. Meanwhile prepare peanut sauce: In a metal-handled 2-quart saucepan, mix water, peanut butter, 1 tablespoon lemon juice, and ⅛ teaspoon ground red pepper; set aside while preparing kabobs.

4 On 3 long skewers, alternately thread squash chunks, mushrooms, and the green-pepper pieces.

5 On 6 more skewers, thread meat pieces accordion-style, reserving soy-sauce marinade.

6 Place the vegetable kabobs on grill over medium heat.

7 Cook about 15 minutes or until vegetables are tender-crisp, basting frequently with melted butter.

8 Cook meat about 10 minutes or until fork-tender, basting often with reserved marinade. Turn kabobs occasionally.

9 Meanwhile, place saucepan with sauce on grill; heat through, stirring occasionally. Serve with meat.

BARBECUED PORK CHOPS WITH TANGY PEAR SAUCE

1 16-ounce can sliced
  pears in heavy syrup
¼ cup prepared mustard
3 tablespoons catchup
2 tablespoons prepared
  white horseradish

1 tablespoon salad oil
1 teaspoon salt
4 pork loin blade or
  sirloin chops, each cut
  ¾-inch thick

1. Prepare outdoor grill for barbecuing.
2. Meanwhile, drain pears, reserving ½ cup syrup. In blender at medium speed or in food processor with knife blade attached, blend pears with reserved syrup until puréed. Pour puréed pears into medium bowl, stir in mustard, catchup, horseradish, salad oil, and salt until blended; set sauce aside.
3. Place pork loin blade chops on grill over medium heat; cook 30 to 35 minutes until pork is fork-tender and just loses its pink colour, brushing with sauce frequently and turning pork chops occasionally.

- *Color index page 51*
- *Begin 1 hr ahead*
- *4 servings*
- *370 cals per serving*

TIPS ON PREPARING KABOBS

Kabobs are a favorite for barbecuing. To ensure success follow these tips:

If the foods you are using require different cooking times, grill them on separate skewers, as in our Beef and Vegetable Kabobs (left).

Leave a small space between each piece of food on the skewer so that the pieces of food can cook evenly.

Wrap the entire skewer (except the handle) in aluminum foil.

Leave the skin on fish pieces to hold the fish together.

Poultry

OLD-WEST BARBECUED CHICKEN

- Color index page 40
- Begin 1¼ hrs ahead
- 8 servings
- 432 cals per serving

1 12-ounce bottle chili sauce
2 tablespoons wine vinegar
2 tablespoons Worcestershire
4 teaspoons sugar
1 teaspoon salt

1 teaspoon chili powder
¼ teaspoon hot-pepper sauce
2 2½- to 3-pound broiler-fryers, each cut into quarters
Coriander leaves for garnish (optional)

1. Prepare outdoor grill for barbecuing. Meanwhile, prepare barbecue sauce: In medium bowl, combine first 7 ingredients; set aside.
2. Place chicken on grill over medium heat; cook until golden on both sides, about 10 minutes. Then, to avoid charring, stand chicken pieces upright, leaning one against the other. Rearrange pieces from time to time and cook until chicken is fork-tender, about 30 minutes.
3. Lay chicken pieces flat; brush with sauce; cook 5 minutes longer. Arrange on warm platter; if you like, garnish with coriander leaves.

BARBECUED APRICOT CHICKEN

- Color index page 40
- Begin 1¼ hrs ahead
- 4 servings
- 650 cals per serving

1 5½-ounce can apricot nectar
2 tablespoons brown sugar
1 tablespoon orange peel
1 tablespoon catchup
2 teaspoons cornstarch
1 teaspoon prepared horseradish

Salt
1 3-pound broiler-fryer, cut into quarters
1 16-ounce can peeled whole apricots, drained
Basil leaves for garnish (optional)

1. Prepare outdoor grill for barbecuing. Meanwhile, prepare apricot glaze: In small saucepan with spoon, mix first 6 ingredients and ½ teaspoon salt. Over medium heat, heat to boiling; boil 1 minute. Reduce heat to low; simmer 5 minutes to blend flavors. Remove from heat.
2. Rub chicken lightly with salt. Place on grill over medium heat; cook until golden on both sides, about 10 minutes; then, to avoid charring, stand pieces upright, leaning one against the other; rearrange from time to time; and cook until fork-tender, about 25 minutes more.
3. During last 5 to 10 minutes of cooking, brush often with glaze. Arrange chicken on warm large platter. Garnish with apricots and basil.
4. To broil in oven: About 1 hour before serving, preheat broiler if manufacturer directs. Rub chicken pieces lightly with salt. Brush bottom of broiling pan with salad oil. Place chicken quarters, skin side down, in broiling pan. About 7 to 9 inches from source of heat (or at 450°F.), broil 20 minutes or until golden. Meanwhile, prepare apricot glaze as above.
5. Brush chicken generously with some apricot glaze; broil 2 to 3 minutes. Turn chicken skin side up; broil 10 minutes. Brush with remaining glaze; broil 10 to 15 minutes longer or until chicken is fork-tender. Garnish as above.

SUGAR-SMOKED CHICKEN

- Color index page 40
- Begin 3 days ahead
- 4 servings
- 381 cals per serving

In this revival of an old-fashioned technique, chicken is bathed in smoke created by burning sugar. Chilling mellows the strong flavor.

1 3½-pound broiler-fryer
2 tablespoons salt
Water

¾ cup packed dark brown sugar

1. Remove giblets and neck. Rinse chicken with running cold water; drain well (do not pat dry).
2. With hands, rub salt over outside and in body cavity of bird; place in large bowl; cover with plastic wrap; refrigerate 24 hours.
3. With knife and kitchen shears, cut chicken lengthwise in half. In 4-quart saucepan or Dutch oven, in 1 inch water, place 2 inverted 6-ounce custard cups.
4. Place chicken halves, skin side up, on 5- or 6-inch oven-safe plate; set plate on top of custard cups. Over high heat, heat water to boiling. Reduce heat to medium-low; cover and steam chicken 40 minutes.
5. Remove chicken and plate from saucepan. Drain any liquid in plate. Cover and refrigerate chicken overnight.
6. About 4 hours before serving: Prepare outdoor covered grill for barbecuing.

7 Using heavy-duty foil, make a small pan by folding edges up to form ½-inch stand-up rim. Evenly sprinkle brown sugar in foil pan.

8 Place pan directly on hot coals. Place the chicken, skin side up, on grill directly over pan. Cover grill; close cover vents. Smoke chicken 20 minutes or until golden brown. The sugar will burn, creating "smoke" to smoke chicken.

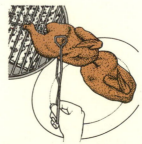
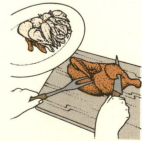

9 Remove the smoked chicken to platter. Immediately discard the foil pan.

10 Cover chicken and refrigerate 3 hours to mellow flavor. Slice chicken into thin slices. Serve cold.

Poultry

BACON-WRAPPED CHICKEN-MUSHROOM KABOBS

- Color index page 40
- Begin 1¼ hrs ahead
- 4 servings
- 370 cals per serving

2 whole large chicken breasts
10 large mushrooms (about 1 pound)
¼ cup soy sauce
¼ cup cider vinegar
2 tablespoons honey
2 tablespoons salad oil

2 small green onions, minced
1 8- or 8¼-ounce can sliced pineapple, drained
1 8-ounce package sliced bacon

1. Skin and bone chicken breasts. Cut each chicken breast in half; then cut each breast half into 5 chunks.
2. Cut each mushroom in half. In large bowl, mix mushroom halves, chicken pieces, soy sauce, cider vinegar, honey, salad oil, and green onions.
3. Prepare outdoor grill for barbecuing. Meanwhile, cut each pineapple slice into 3 pieces. Cut each bacon slice crosswise in half. Wrap each bacon piece around a piece of chicken and a mushroom half. On 4 long skewers, thread bacon-wrapped chicken and pineapple pieces, being sure to leave space between each so bacon will cook completely. Reserve soy-sauce mixture for basting.
4. Place skewers on grill over medium heat. Cook about 15 to 20 minutes until chicken is fork-tender and bacon is crisp, brushing chicken kabobs frequently with soy-sauce mixture and turning skewers occasionally. If you like, serve these kabobs over rice or with a green salad with a sharp vinaigrette dressing.

CORNISH HENS WITH SWEET-AND-SOUR SAUCE

- Color index page 40
- Begin 1½ hrs ahead
- 4 servings
- 370 cals per serving

2 1½- to 2-pound fresh or frozen (thawed) Rock Cornish hens*
Salad oil
⅓ cup red wine vinegar
⅓ cup packed light brown sugar

¼ cup orange juice
3 tablespoons soy sauce
½ teaspoon salt
½ teaspoon anise seeds, crushed

1. Prepare outdoor grill for barbecuing. Meanwhile, remove giblets and necks from inside hens; refrigerate to use in soup another day.
2. Rinse hens with running cold water; pat dry with paper towels. With poultry or kitchen shears, cut each hen in half; rub hens well with salad oil.
3. In small bowl, mix red wine vinegar, brown sugar, orange juice, soy sauce, salt, anise, and 1 tablespoon salad oil.
4. With tongs, place hens on grill. Cook over medium heat 30 to 35 minutes until hens are fork-tender, basting frequently with sauce mixture and turning hens often. Accompany these hens with our Confetti Rice Mold (p.282) or a pasta salad, which can be made ahead.

*Frozen Rock Cornish hens will thaw in original wrapping overnight in refrigerator.

SAVORY GRILLED DUCKLING

Long Island duckling is usually roasted. Here, we barbecue duckling quarters in foil to retain the juices, and add a zesty sauce.

- Color index page 40
- Begin 2¼ hrs ahead
- 4 servings
- 795 cals per serving

1 8-ounce can tomato sauce
3 medium green onions, chopped
3 tablespoons brown sugar
1 tablespoon red wine vinegar

1 tablespoon prepared mustard
2 teaspoons Worcestershire
1¼ teaspoons salt
1 5-pound fresh or frozen (thawed) duckling

1 Prepare the outdoor grill for barbecuing. Meanwhile, prepare the sauce: In a 1-quart saucepan over medium-high heat, heat tomato sauce, onions, sugar, red wine vinegar, mustard, Worcestershire, and salt to boiling. Reduce heat to low; simmer, uncovered, 15 minutes or until sauce is slightly thickened; set the sauce aside. Remove the giblets and the neck from the duckling and refrigerate them to use another day.

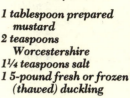

2 Rinse duckling with running cold water and drain well. Pat with paper towels. Cut duckling into quarters; trim excess fat and skin.

3 Wrap each piece of duckling in double thickness of heavy-duty foil; be sure seam of foil is folded several times to seal in the juices.

4 Place packets on grill over medium heat, about 4 inches above the heat. Roast 1 hour, turning packets with tongs every 10 to 15 minutes.

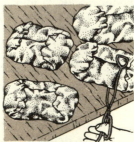

5 Be sure not to puncture foil (if the juices leak out, flame may get too high and char duckling). After cooking 1 hour, remove packets to work surface.

6 Carefully open the foil packets and spoon sauce over duckling. Close foil and roast 20 minutes longer or until duckling is fork-tender. Serve at once.

Fish

GRILLED FISH STEAKS WITH CHILI BUTTER

4 tablespoons butter or margarine, softened
1 teaspoon chili powder
½ teaspoon salt
¼ teaspoon pepper
1 teaspoon chopped coriander

2 swordfish or halibut steaks, each cut about ¾-inch thick (about ¾ pound each)
Lime for garnish

1. Prepare outdoor grill for barbecuing.
2. Meanwhile, prepare chili butter: In a small saucepan, beat the softened butter or margarine. Add the chili powder, salt, pepper, and chopped coriander and mix until well blended. Set aside.
3. Place fish on grill over medium heat; cook about 5 minutes or until fish flakes easily when tested with a fork. Meanwhile, place saucepan with butter mixture on grill; heat until butter or margarine is melted, stirring occasionally.
4. To serve, arrange fish on platter. Pour chili butter over fish; garnish with lime slices.

- Color index page 33
- Begin 45 mins ahead
- 4 servings
- 305 cals with swordfish
- 270 cals with halibut

BARBECUE MARINADES

SOY-SESAME MARINADE: In medium bowl, combine ½ cup minced onion, ½ cup soy sauce, 2 tablespoons light brown sugar, 2 tablespoons sesame seeds, 2 tablespoons salad oil, 2 teaspoons salt, 2 teaspoons lemon juice, ½ teaspoon pepper, and ½ teaspoon ground ginger. This oriental-style marinade is particularly well-suited to shrimp, scallops, and fresh tuna, but may also be used with chicken, turkey, duckling, beef, and lamb. Makes about 1 cup. 35 cals per tablespoon.

GINGER MARINADE: In medium bowl, combine one 7-ounce bottle lemon-lime soft drink (about 1 cup), ¼ cup soy sauce, 2 tablespoons sugar, 1 tablespoon garlic salt, and 1 tablespoon ground ginger. Use to marinate whole fish, such as bluefish, shrimp, chicken, and chicken pieces. May also be used with any meat before barbecuing. Makes about 1¼ cups. 11 cals per tablespoon.

MEXICALI MARINADE: Begin 30 mins ahead. In small saucepan over medium heat, in ⅓ cup hot olive oil, cook 2 crushed garlic cloves 2 to 3 minutes. Stir in ⅓ cup cider vinegar, ⅓ cup apple juice, 1 teaspoon chili powder, 1 teaspoon sugar, 1 teaspoon salt, and ¼ teaspoon pepper. Heat through, stirring until smooth; cool. Chicken and fish quickly absorb the flavors. Use with chicken breasts, thighs, and wings; and fish steaks or fillets. Suitable also for marinating beef, lamb, pork, or veal and for basting during cooking. Makes 1 cup. 43 cals per tablespoon.

FISH FILLETS IN CORN HUSKS

Fish and corn have shared an affinity since the Indians showed the first settlers how to catch fish, grow corn, and cook both.

4 large ears corn with husks
Water
String
2 medium lemons
4 flounder fillets (about 1 pound) or 1 16-ounce package frozen flounder fillets, thawed

Salt
Pepper
3 tablespoons drained chopped pimento
6 ounces mozzarella cheese, coarsely shredded (1½ cups)

- Color index page 32
- Begin 1 hr ahead
- 4 servings
- 310 cals per serving

2 ounces feta cheese, finely crumbled (½ cup)
4 tablespoons butter or margarine, diced

1 Carefully pull husks back from each ear of corn; remove corn and silk, leaving husks on stem. Reserve corn or serve with fish.

2 Place husks with enough water to cover in large saucepan. Cut four 12-inch-long pieces of string; place in pan with husks; set aside.

3 Prepare outdoor grill for barbecuing. Cut one lemon into wedges. From remaining lemon, squeeze 1 tablespoon of juice; set aside.

4 If using frozen fish, separate thawed fish into fillets. Sprinkle fish lightly with salt and pepper. In bowl, mix pimento and lemon juice.

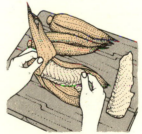

5 Remove corn husks and string from the water. Shake any excess water from husks. Into each, place a fish fillet; fold to fit if necessary.

6 Top each fillet with one-fourth mozzarella cheese, feta cheese, diced butter or margarine, and pimento mixture.

7 Bring husks together, enclosing filling totally; tie open end of each tightly with string; cut off loose ends of string and discard.

8 Place fish in corn husks on grill over medium heat; cook 20 minutes or until fish flakes easily, turning husks occasionally.

9 Separate husks slightly with fork to test fish for doneness. Serve fish in corn husks. Garnish with reserved lemon wedges.

Fish

GRILLED TROUT WITH SUMMER-VEGETABLE STUFFING

Trout was so abundant that it became an everyday food for early settlers, who probably copied the Indian method of cooking it on a wooden rack placed over a fire.

- Color index page 33
- Begin 1 hr ahead
- 4 servings
- 661 cals per serving

4 brook trout, bluefish, or other locally caught fish (about ¾ pound each)
¾ cup butter or margarine
3 tablespoons lemon juice
1 cup white-bread cubes (2 slices)
1 small zucchini (6 ounces), thinly sliced
1 small tomato, diced
¼ pound mushrooms, thinly sliced
6 radishes, thinly sliced
1 teaspoon savory
¾ teaspoon salt
⅛ teaspoon cracked pepper

1 Prepare outdoor grill for barbecuing. Meanwhile, with peeler or fish scaler, remove scales from fish. With sharp knife, gut the fish.

2 Then cut 3 slashes on each side of fish. Rinse fish with running cold water; pat dry inside and outside with paper towels.

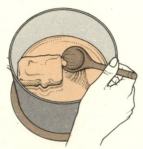

3 In a small metal-handled saucepan over low heat, heat the butter and lemon juice until the butter is melted. Remove from heat.

4 Into medium bowl, measure ⅓ cup butter mixture. Add bread crumbs and the remaining ingredients; toss gently to mix well.

5 Spoon ¼ of stuffing into each fish; pack mixture firmly; secure the openings with small metal skewers.

6 Wrap fish in heavy-duty foil (or place in large, flat, wire barbecue basket).

7 Cook on grill over medium heat about 5 minutes each side or until fish flakes and stuffing is heated through.

8 Brush each fish occasionally with some butter mixture. Serve fish with remaining butter mixture.

GRILLED BASS FILLETS WITH MUSHROOM STUFFING

1 3½-pound whole striped bass or sea bass
Butter or margarine
¾ pound mushrooms, sliced
¼ cup minced green onions
2½ cups soft white bread crumbs (about 5 slices)
¼ cup water
Savory leaves
Salt
Pepper
1 tablespoon lemon juice
Lemon wedges for garnish

1. Prepare outdoor grill for barbecuing.
2. Scale striped bass and rinse under running cold water. Cut flesh from bones to make 2 large fillets with skin left on.
3. In 10-inch skillet over medium high heat, melt 6 tablespoons butter or margarine; add mushrooms and green onions and cook until tender, stirring occasionally. Remove skillet from heat; stir in bread crumbs, water, 1 teaspoon savory, ½ teaspoon salt, and ¼ teaspoon pepper.
4. On double thickness of heavy-duty foil place a fillet, skin side down. Spoon mushroom mixture onto fillet; top with remaining fillet, skin side up. Sprinkle fish with lemon juice, ¼ teaspoon savory, ¼ teaspoon salt, and ⅛ teaspoon pepper; dot with 2 tablespoons butter. Wrap with foil; fold seam several times to seal in juices.
5. Place packet on grill over medium heat; cook 30 minutes until fish flakes easily when tested with fork; turn once. Serve with lemon wedges.

- Color index page 32
- Begin 1 hr ahead
- 6 servings
- 291 cals per serving

HOW TO PREPARE BARBECUE FISH PACKS

The delicate texture of fish makes it tricky to barbecue successfully. Making a fish pack is a great alternative.

For about 1 lb of fish: Mix about 1 cup fresh thinly sliced vegetables.

Place ¼ of fish on foil, with ¼ of vegetables, and 1 teaspoon of oil

Fold edges of foil to tightly seal the "envelope." Repeat with remaining fish. Grill 20 minutes.

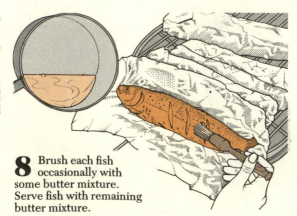

Vegetables

VEGETABLE KABOBS

For a complete meal cooked outdoors, serve these tasty kabobs as an accompaniment to barbecued meat, fish, or poultry.

- Color index page 57
- Begin early in day or 5½ hrs ahead
- 6 servings
- 145 cals per serving

8 small red potatoes
Water
2 small yellow straight-neck squash (about 6 ounces each)
2 small zucchini (about 6 ounces each)

½ pound medium mushrooms
⅔ cup white vinegar
⅓ cup salad oil
5 teaspoons sugar
2 teaspoons salt
1 teaspoon basil

1 Peel ¼-inch-wide strip around center of each potato. In 2-quart saucepan over high heat, heat with enough water to cover to boiling.

2 Reduce heat to low; cover; simmer 20 minutes or until potatoes are fork-tender. Drain potatoes well, then set aside while preparing vegetables.

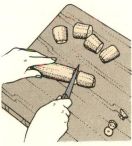

3 Meanwhile, cut each yellow squash and zucchini crosswise into 4 chunks. Trim tough stem ends from mushrooms.

4 In large bowl, mix white vinegar, salad oil, sugar, salt, and basil; add potatoes, yellow squash, zucchini, and mushrooms; toss well to coat vegetables with vinegar mixture. Cover and refrigerate at least 4 hours, tossing mixture occasionally, allowing the vegetables to absorb the flavors of the vinegar mixture. *About 1 hour before serving:* Prepare the outdoor grill for barbecuing.

5 Meanwhile, on 4 long skewers, alternately thread the potatoes, yellow squash, zucchini, and mushrooms, reserving the leftover marinade in the bowl.

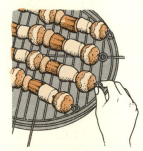

6 Place skewers on grill over medium heat; cook about 20 minutes, brushing frequently with reserved marinade and turning often, until the vegetables are tender-crisp.

HOW TO BARBECUE CORN-ON-THE-COB AND OTHER VEGETABLES

It's easy and convenient to use the hot coals of the barbecue for cooking vegetables; it avoids the need to light the stove or oven indoors. Wrapping the vegetables in heavy-duty foil saves on dish-washing as well as sealing in the juices.

Corn-on-the-cob: Remove husks and silk from corn. Place each ear of corn on a sheet of heavy-duty foil; brush with a barbecue sauce or butter.

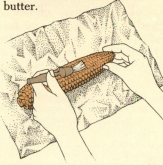

Wrap each ear tightly and grill over medium coals 30 minutes, turning frequently.

Onions in foil: For each serving, peel 3 or 4 small white onions and score each end. Dot with butter or margarine.

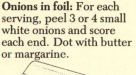

Wrap tightly in heavy-duty foil and bake in coals 30 minutes.

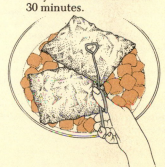

Grilled eggplant or zucchini: Place chunks of eggplant or zucchini on skewers; brush with seasoned oil or a favorite salad dressing. Grill, turning often until tender, about 10 minutes.

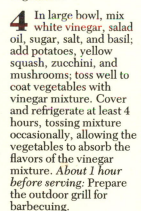

Potatoes: Cut 2 or 3 large unpeeled potatoes (scrubbed) into thick slices. Overlap slices slightly on a sheet of heavy-duty foil; dot with butter or margarine.

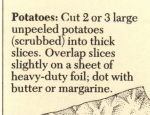

Sprinkle potatoes with chopped chives. Wrap tightly; cook on coals about 45 minutes until tender, turning once.

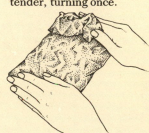

Fruit

- Color index page 57
- Begin 45 mins ahead
- 6 servings
- 215 cals per serving

GRILLED CURRIED FRUIT

1 16-ounce can pear halves, drained
1 16-ounce can cling peach halves, drained
1 8- to 8½-ounce can sliced pineapple, drained and each slice cut in half

½ cup packed brown sugar
2 tablespoons butter or margarine, cut into small pieces
4 teaspoons mild curry powder

1. Prepare outdoor grill for barbecuing.
2. Meanwhile, on double thickness of heavy-duty foil, mix all ingredients. Wrap fruit mixture in foil, being careful that seam of foil is folded several times to seal in juices.
3. Place foil packet on grill over medium heat; cook 15 to 20 minutes, turning packet occasionally with tongs, until mixture is hot. Just before serving, stir fruit to mix well. Serve with barbecued poultry, ham, steak, or lamb.

QUICK BARBECUE DESSERTS

While the coals are still glowing, there are great opportunities for quick desserts. The ingredients can be prepared ahead and assembled on the grill at the last minute.

Hot Apple and Pear Slices:
Cook thick wedges of unpeeled apples and pears in melted butter or margarine in disposable aluminum cake pan on grill. When heated through, sprinkle with sugar on all sides.

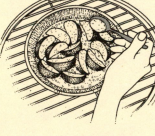

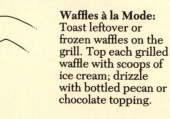

Waffles à la Mode:
Toast leftover or frozen waffles on the grill. Top each grilled waffle with scoops of ice cream; drizzle with bottled pecan or chocolate topping.

Cheese-Topped Apple Pie: Arrange wedge-shaped slices of American or Cheddar cheese on top of a purchased, baked apple pie. Cover the pie loosely with foil and heat on grill until cheese begins to melt.

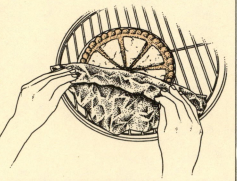

BARBECUE SAUCES

No matter what you plan to cook, steaks, hamburgers, poultry or other meat, backyard barbecues always taste better when brushed with a zesty barbecue sauce. To prevent sugar-based sauces from burning, precook the meat or chicken on the grill or in the oven. Then brush frequently with the sauce during the last 10 to 15 minutes on the grill.

FIERY CHILI BARBECUE SAUCE: In small bowl, mix *one 8-ounce can stewed tomatoes, 2 pickled jalapeño chilies,* minced (or add more chilies if you prefer), *2 tablespoons brown sugar, 2 tablespoons salad oil, 1 teaspoon salt, 1 teaspoon Worcestershire,* and *⅛ teaspoon garlic powder.* Makes about 1½ cups. 19 cals per tablespoon.

CRANBERRY-HONEY BARBECUE SAUCE: In small bowl, mix *one 8-ounce can whole berry cranberry sauce, 3 tablespoons honey, 1 tablespoon salad oil, 1 tablespoon red wine vinegar, 1½ teaspoons salt,* and *½ teaspoon ground cinnamon.* Makes about 1 cup. 55 cals per tablespoon.

PEANUT-GINGER BARBECUE SAUCE: In small bowl, mix *¾ cup packed light brown sugar, ⅓ cup red wine vinegar, 3 tablespoons soy sauce, 1 tablespoon creamy peanut butter, 1¼ teaspoons ground ginger (or 1 tablespoon minced fresh gingerroot),* and *¾ teaspoon salt.* Makes about 1 cup. 47 cals per tablespoon.

GREEN-ONION-SOY SAUCE: In small bowl, with back of spoon, mash slightly *¼ cup minced green onions.* Stir in *⅓ cup soy sauce, 2 tablespoons dry white wine, 2 tablespoons catchup, 1 tablespoon salad oil,* and *1 teaspoon Worcestershire.* Makes ¾ cup. 22 cals per tablespoon.

PEPPERY HOT SAUCE: In 2-quart saucepan over medium-high heat, in *2 tablespoons hot salad oil,* cook *1 medium onion,* chopped, *1 garlic clove,* minced, until tender, stirring occasionally. Stir in *⅔ cup catchup, 2 tablespoons cider vinegar, 2 teaspoons brown sugar, 2 teaspoons minced fresh* or *canned jalapeño peppers, ½ teaspoon salt,* and *¼ teaspoon dry mustard.* Over medium heat, heat sauce to boiling, stirring often. Reduce heat to low; simmer gently 5 minutes to blend flavors. Makes about 1 cup. 24 cals per tablespoon.

TANGY BEER SAUCE: In medium bowl, mix *⅓ cup chili sauce, ¼ cup beer, 1 tablespoon soy sauce, 1 tablespoon salad oil, ½ teaspoon sugar, ½ teaspoon salt, ½ teaspoon grated onion, ¼ teaspoon dry mustard,* and *⅛ teaspoon hot pepper sauce.* Makes about ¾ cup. 13 cals per tablespoon.

EAST INDIES SAUCE: In small bowl, mix *¼ cup lemon juice, 2 tablespoons salad oil, 1½ teaspoons turmeric, 1 teaspoon ground cardamom, 1 teaspoon ground ginger, 1 teaspoon salt, ¾ teaspoon sugar,* and *1 small garlic clove,* minced. Makes about ⅓ cup. 42 cals per tablespoon.

ROSEMARY-BUTTER SAUCE: In mortar with pestle, crush *1 teaspoon rosemary.* In small saucepan over low heat, heat rosemary, *4 tablespoons butter* or *margarine, 1 tablespoon lemon juice, ¾ teaspoon salt,* and *⅛ teaspoon pepper* until butter or margarine melts. Makes about ⅓ cup. 80 cals per tablespoon.

VEGETABLES

*"Cauliflower is nothing but a cabbage
with a college education."*

MARK TWAIN

Some native American plants, such as corn, squash, and chili peppers, have been cultivated since our earliest history; others were brought to American shores by immigrants.

Corn was part of Indian rituals, religion, and diet, and quickly became a staple crop for the colonists. During hard times, a family may have eaten fresh, dried, or ground corn three times a day. Succotash, an Indian vegetable stew of corn and dried beans, was probably served at the first Thanksgiving in 1621. Today, the dish is made with corn and lima beans and is very popular in the South. By 1779, there were records of Indians along the Susquehanna River "roasting ears" in their husks over open fires, but it wasn't until the mid-1800s that corn-on-the-cob became a common sight on American tables. By the 1880s, the corn-producing states of the midwest were called the "Corn Belt."

Indians often planted squash as a rotation crop after corn, introducing the colonists to several varieties. Zucchini became widely known in the 1920s thanks largely to Italian immigrants. Zucchini and most squashes are versatile vegetables; they can be fried, baked, stuffed, and puréed. Zucchini is now so popular, an annual festival occurs in Harrisville, N.H., complete with a peeling contest. Spaghetti squash, named for its strandlike flesh, has recently become a successful crop in California. It provides an unusual base for a dish like our Spaghetti Squash with Spicy Meat Sauce.

When Columbus arrived, the Indians were already cultivating and using chili peppers as seasoning in many dishes. Chili powder was used to give zest to food in the Caribbean and Gulf states and has become a main ingredient in Tex-Mex cooking.

Dried beans were often planted in fields with corn and were transported by Indians from Mexico to North America. There are many theories about the origin of baked beans but the mixture of pea, or navy beans, with maple syrup and salt pork or bacon certainly fortified New Englanders against the harsh winters, and Boston Baked Beans remains a wintertime favorite.

It is not known if the white potato was native to North America, but it was not very popular and believed to be poisonous. It was not until the 19th century, when it became associated with the Irish and the potato famine in 1845, that the potato became more acceptable and recipes for potato dishes began to appear. By the end of the century, potatoes were an essential part of the American diet and prepared in many ways – boiled, baked, mashed, roasted, fried, or creamed. They were sold by street vendors, roasted over coals, celebrated in famous hotels, featured in restaurants of the sophisticated Eastern cities; Delmonico potatoes was one of the most famous dishes.

Tomatoes, although cultivated in North America since the 1700s, were also thought to be poisonous. In the 1800s, they were mostly used in preserves and sauces but rarely eaten raw. By the early 1900s, however, tomatoes were being farmed on a large scale and today are the most often-planted garden vegetable. It is hard to imagine cooking without the tomato; dishes like Stewed Fresh Tomatoes, Bacon-Wrapped Grilled Tomatoes, delicate Pan-Fried Cherry Tomatoes, and fresh tomato sauces would certainly be missed.

The artichoke, popularized by Italian immigrants in California, was considered too much trouble to eat. The Italians showed the Californians better methods of growing and cooking the artichoke and today it is one of the state's major crops. Artichoke recipes are increasing because it can be used in many ways; hot or cold, as an appetizer, main-course meal accompaniment, or mixed with other vegetables.

America has become known for the variety of vegetables produced and the versatility of their preparation, especially our quick-cooking methods which retain the crunchy texture and fresh flavor of vegetables.

Artichokes

STUFFED ARTICHOKES MONTEREY

4 large artichokes
3 slices bacon
1 small onion, minced
1 medium red pepper, chopped
1 medium green pepper, chopped

1 8-ounce loaf French or Italian bread
¾ pound Monterey Jack cheese, shredded (3 cups)
Water

1. Prepare artichokes as Artichokes with Mustard Sauce (right), steps 1 to 5.
2. Meanwhile, in 12-inch skillet over medium-low heat, cook bacon until browned. Remove bacon to paper towels to drain. Crumble bacon; set aside. In bacon drippings in skillet over medium heat, cook onion and peppers until tender. Remove skillet from heat.
3. Into vegetable mixture in skillet, tear bread into small pieces. Stir in cheese and 1¼ cups water until mixed.
4. Preheat oven to 350°. Spoon bread mixture into centers and between leaves of artichokes. Place stuffed artichokes in 13" by 9" baking dish. Cover with foil; bake 25 minutes or until stuffing mixture is hot and cheese melts. Sprinkle with bacon to serve.

- Color index page 53
- Begin 1½ hrs ahead
- 4 main-dish servings
- 700 cals per serving

HOW TO PREPARE ARTICHOKE BOTTOMS

Artichoke bottoms make tasty, sophisticated containers for other vegetables or sauces. Surround roast beef with warm artichoke bottoms filled with green peas and carrots; serve cold with Classic French Dressing (p.284) as an appetizer; or use in recipes like our Chicken Cutlets and Artichokes (p.158). Prepare artichokes as for Artichokes with Mustard Sauce (right), drain and cool.

Pull off all leaves from each artichoke. (Serve leaves with a dip as an appetizer.)

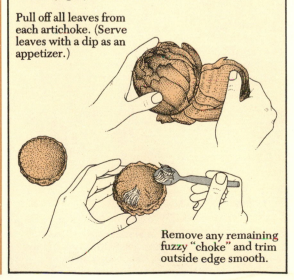

Remove any remaining fuzzy "choke" and trim outside edge smooth.

ARTICHOKES WITH MUSTARD SAUCE

Introduced by the Spanish, artichokes are a major crop in California and Castroville is known as the artichoke capital of the world.

4 medium artichokes
Water
2 tablespoons Dijon mustard
¼ teaspoon sugar

1 tablespoon white wine vinegar
1 egg yolk
Salad oil
¼ teaspoon salt

- Color index page 53
- Begin 45 mins ahead or early in day
- 4 side-dish servings
- 355 cals per serving

¼ cup milk
2 tablespoons red salmon caviar

1 Prepare artichokes: With sharp knife, cut off stem from each artichoke; then carefully cut 1 inch straight across top of each artichoke.

2 Pull off any small, loose, or discolored leaves from around bottom. With kitchen shears, carefully trim thorny tips of leaves.

3 Gently spread artichoke leaves apart and remove leaves from center to expose fuzzy and prickly portion (choke) inside each.

4 With spoon, carefully scrape out and discard the choke from the center of each of the artichokes.

5 Rinse the artichokes with running cold water. Place the artichokes in a 5-quart saucepot or Dutch oven; add 1 inch water; over high heat, heat to boiling. Reduce heat to low; cover and simmer the artichokes 30 minutes or until a leaf can be pulled off easily. Remove the artichokes from the water. Turn artichokes upside down to allow excess water to drain; keep warm if serving immediately.

6 Meanwhile, prepare sauce: In blender at low speed, blend mustard, sugar, vinegar, egg yolk, 2 tablespoons salad oil, and salt until ingredients are smooth.

7 Remove center of blender cover and very slowly pour ⅓ cup salad oil in steady stream into mixture. Continue blending until mixed. Quickly blend in milk.

8 Serve artichokes warm or refrigerate to serve chilled later. To serve, place an artichoke on each dinner plate.

9 With hands, spread leaves open on plate to resemble a flower. Spoon sauce into the center of each artichoke; lightly sprinkle some caviar over sauce.

Asparagus

ASPARAGUS AND CHERRY TOMATOES

- Color index page 52
- Begin 15 mins ahead
- 4 side-dish servings
- 55 cals per serving

Although wild asparagus probably grew in the New World, it was not widely cultivated until after the 1850s. A jumbo variety produced in California is particularly sought after. Cherry tomatoes add an extra-colorful touch.

1 pound asparagus
Water
Salt
½ pint cherry tomatoes

1 tablespoon olive or salad oil
1 garlic clove, sliced

1 Prepare asparagus: Hold base of stalk firmly and bend stalk; end will break off at the spot where it becomes too tough to eat. Discard ends; trim the scales if the stalks are gritty.

2 In 12-inch skillet over medium heat, in ½ inch boiling water, heat the asparagus and ½ teaspoon salt to boiling. Reduce heat to low; cover and simmer 5 minutes until asparagus is just tender-crisp.

3 Remove asparagus to plate. Wash and dry skillet. With sharp knife, carefully cut each cherry tomato in half.

4 In same skillet over medium heat, in hot olive or salad oil, cook the garlic slices until light golden, stirring occasionally; remove and discard garlic slices.

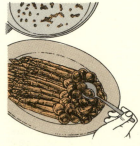

5 Add asparagus and cherry tomatoes; cook over medium heat until heated through.

6 Transfer to a heated oval serving platter or special asparagus dish and serve immediately.

CALIFORNIA BRAISED ASPARAGUS AND CELERY

- Color index page 52
- Begin 30 mins ahead
- 4 side-dish servings
- 70 cals per serving

¾ pound asparagus
3 medium celery stalks
1 tablespoon salad oil
Water

2 tablespoons pine nuts (pignolia), toasted
Salt

1. Discard the tough ends and trim scales from asparagus. With sharp knife, cut asparagus and celery diagonally into 2-inch pieces.

2. In 10-inch skillet over medium heat, in hot salad oil and 2 tablespoons water, cook asparagus and celery, covered, stirring occasionally, until tender-crisp, about 10 minutes; drain.

3. Toss vegetables with pine nuts and salt.

DECORATING WITH VEGETABLES

Vegetables with their beautiful natural shapes and fresh colors, liven up plate presentations, add zest to many dishes, and, best of all, can be eaten.

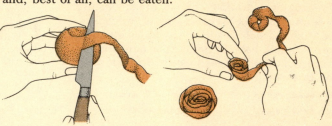

Tomato Rose: With a small sharp knife, cut thin slice from tomato top being careful not to cut completely through. Continue peeling in one continuous strip about ¾-inch wide.

Carefully remove as much flesh as possible from the strip. Begin rolling the strip from the end to the round base and set the roll on the base; flare top to resemble rose.

Cucumber Cases: With sharp-tined fork, draw lines down side of cucumber to create a striped effect. Cut into even 2-inch lengths.

Remove the inside with a small spoon or melon baller, leaving at least a ¼-inch shell. Fill with a dip or vegetable purée and top with fresh herbs or red salmon caviar.

Tomato Loops: With sharp knife cut center out of cherry tomato leaving a ¼-inch shell.

Encircle small green beans or carrot sticks with loops and use to garnish meat platters.

Beans

GREEN BEAN AND ONION CASSEROLE

- Color index page 53
- Begin 35 mins ahead
- 10 side-dish servings
- 126 cals per serving

12 bacon slices
3 9-ounce packages frozen whole green beans
½ 4-ounce jar pimentos, cut up
½ cup crumbled, canned French-fried onion rings
½ teaspoon seasoned salt
½ cup sour cream

1. In 12-inch skillet over medium heat, cook the bacon slices until well browned; remove to paper towels to drain. Crumble the bacon.
2. Cook green beans as label directs; drain well.
3. Toss the fried bacon with the cooked green beans. Add the pimentos, the crumbled onion rings, and the seasoned salt; toss well.
4. Pour the mixture into a large serving dish; spoon sour cream into the center and serve.

BUTTERED-CRUMB LIMA BEANS

- Color index page 53
- Begin 15 mins ahead
- 4 side-dish servings
- 232 cals per serving

1 10-ounce package frozen baby lima beans
2 tablespoons butter or margarine
½ cup fresh bread crumbs
1 tablespoon lemon juice (optional)
½ cup shredded Cheddar or grated Parmesan cheese (optional)

1. Cook lima beans as label directs; drain.
2. Meanwhile, in small skillet or saucepan over medium heat, melt butter. Add breadcrumbs; cook tossing lightly, until crumbs are golden. If you like, add lemon juice and cheese; toss well.
3. To serve, sprinkle the buttered crumb mixture over the drained, hot lima beans.

SUCCOTASH

- Color index page 53
- Begin 1 hr ahead
- 10 side-dish servings
- 175 cals per serving

4 slices bacon
6 medium potatoes (about 2 pounds), peeled and diced
1 medium green pepper, diced
1 small onion, minced
2 medium tomatoes, chopped
1 10-ounce package frozen baby lima beans
1 10-ounce package frozen whole-kernel corn
¾ cup water
1½ teaspoons salt
1½ teaspoon sugar
⅛ teaspoon pepper

1. In 5-quart Dutch oven or saucepot over medium-low heat, cook bacon until well browned; remove to paper towels to drain. Crumble the bacon; reserve.
2. In drippings remaining in the Dutch oven over medium heat, cook the potatoes, green pepper, and onion, stirring frequently, until the pepper and onion are tender.
3. Add the tomatoes and remaining ingredients; over high heat, heat to boiling. Reduce heat to low; cover and simmer 20 minutes, stirring occasionally, until the vegetables are tender and the mixture thickens slightly.
4. To serve, spoon vegetable mixture into a large bowl; sprinkle with reserved crumbled bacon.

WHOLE GREEN AND WAX BEANS WITH BLUE-CHEESE SAUCE

Wax beans have a sweet buttery flavor. Mix them with crisp green beans and top with a blue-cheese sauce for extra zest.

- Color index page 53
- Begin 30 mins ahead
- 8 side-dish servings
- 105 cals per serving

Water
1 pound green beans
1 pound wax beans
1 tablespoon butter or margarine
1 tablespoon all-purpose flour
½ teaspoon salt
¼ teaspoon pepper
¾ cup milk
½ cup blue cheese
Chopped parsley for garnish

1 In 12-inch skillet over medium heat, in 1-inch boiling water, heat beans to boiling; reduce heat to low; cover and simmer 10 minutes or until just tender-crisp. Drain well.

2 Meanwhile, prepare sauce: In 2-quart saucepan over medium heat, into hot butter, stir flour, salt, and pepper until well blended.

3 Gradually stir in the milk; cook, stirring constantly, until sauce is smooth and thickened. Reduce heat to low.

4 Meanwhile, in small bowl, with a fork, or back of a spoon, lightly mash the blue cheese, until it crumbles.

5 Remove the sauce from the heat; stir in the crumbled blue cheese until well blended.

6 Arrange beans on warm platter. Pour sauce over the beans and sprinkle with the parsley.

Dried beans

BOSTON BAKED BEANS

- Color index page 52
- Begin early in day or day ahead
- 12 side-dish servings
- 411 cals per serving

Puritan women of Boston made a large pot of beans for Saturday dinner and, as no cooking was allowed on the Sabbath, served them for Sunday breakfast with fish cakes and Boston Brown Bread, and again for lunch. Today Boston is still known as "Bean Town."

2 16-ounce packages dry pea (navy) beans
4 teaspoons salt
Water
¾ cup dark molasses
½ cup packed dark brown sugar

1 tablespoon dry mustard
1 teaspoon pepper
1 large onion
4 whole cloves
1 8-ounce piece salt pork

1 Rinse the beans in running cold water and discard any stones or shriveled beans. In a 5-quart Dutch oven or saucepot over high heat, heat the beans, salt and 8 cups water to boiling; boil 2 minutes. Remove from heat; cover and let stand 1 hour. Heat beans to boiling. Reduce the heat to low; cover and gently simmer the beans 1 hour.

2 Add molasses, sugar, mustard, and pepper to beans; stir well.

3 Stud the onion with cloves. With a sharp knife, carefully make several slashes in the salt pork rind.

4 Tuck the clove-studded onion and the salt pork into the bean mixture. Preheat oven to 250°F.

5 Remove Dutch oven from heat; cover and bake 7 hours, adding more water if necessary to keep the beans moist but not too wet during cooking time.

6 Remove and discard the clove-studded onion. Transfer the baked beans to a large warm serving bowl. Serve the beans immediately.

RED BEANS AND RICE

- Color index page 52
- Begin 4 hrs ahead
- 8 main-dish servings
- 408 cals per serving

1 16-ounce package red kidney beans
6½ cups water
½ teaspoon salt
¼ cup salad oil
1 medium onion, diced
1 garlic clove, minced

1 leftover ham bone, 1½ cups meat left on
1 teaspoon parsley flakes
½ teaspoon crushed red pepper
6 cups hot cooked rice

1. Rinse beans in running cold water; discard any stones or shriveled beans. In 8-quart Dutch oven, heat beans, water, and salt to boiling; boil 2 minutes. Remove from heat; tightly cover and let stand 1 hour.
2. In 1-quart saucepan over medium heat, in hot salad oil, cook onion and garlic until tender, about 10 minutes, stirring frequently.
3. Stir onion and garlic into beans with all the remaining ingredients, except the rice.
4. Over high heat, heat onion mixture to boiling. Reduce heat to low; cover; simmer 1½ hours or until beans are tender and mixture is slightly thickened, stirring often.
5. Remove ham bone to cutting board; cut meat into bite-size chunks. Return cut-up ham to beans; discard bone. Serve spooned over rice.

BLACK BEANS AND RICE: Prepare *1 16-ounce package dry black beans* as for Red Beans and Rice, step 1, but omit salt. Drain, rinse beans; set aside. In Dutch oven over medium heat, cook *½ pound salt pork*, diced, until lightly browned. Add *1 medium onion*, diced and *1 medium celery stalk*, diced, and cook until vegetables are tender, stirring occasionally. Return beans to Dutch oven; add *1¾ teaspoons salt*, *¼ teaspoon crushed red pepper* and *5½ cups water*. Continue as Red Beans and Rice, step 4. Serve immediately with the rice. Makes 4 main-dish servings. 458 cals per serving.

HOPPIN' JOHN

- Color index page 53
- Begin 3 hrs ahead
- 6 main-dish servings
- 520 cals per serving

1 16-ounce package dry black-eyed beans/peas
½ pound unsliced bacon
Water
1 large onion, chopped
1 clove garlic, chopped

1 bay leaf
1½ teaspoons salt
¼ teaspoon crushed red pepper
1 cup regular long-grain rice

1. Prepare the beans as in Red Beans and Rice, step 1 (above).
2. In 8-quart saucepot over high heat, heat bacon and 6 cups water to boiling. Reduce heat to low. Cover, simmer 1 hour.
3. Drain and rinse the beans. Add beans, onion, garlic, bay leaf, salt, and red pepper to bacon. Over high heat, heat to boiling. Reduce heat to low; cover and simmer gently 30 minutes or until beans are almost tender.
4. Stir in rice; cook 20 minutes longer or until beans and rice are tender. With slotted spoon, remove bacon to cutting board. Discard bay leaf. Dice bacon and stir into bean mixture.

RANCH-STYLE BEANS

- Color index page 52
- Begin 3 hrs ahead
- 6 side-dish servings
- 466 cals per serving

1 16-ounce package dry pinto beans
Water
2 tablespoons salad oil
2 medium onions, sliced
2 garlic cloves, minced
1 10-ounce can whole green chilies, drained and cut into bite-sized pieces

1 or 2 canned jalapeño chilies, diced
1 tablespoon salt
1 teaspoon sugar
1 teaspoon ground cumin
1 28-ounce can tomatoes
½ teaspoon oregano leaves
2 cups shredded Monterey Jack cheese (8 ounces)

1. Rinse beans in running cold water and discard any stones or shriveled beans. In 5-quart Dutch oven over high heat, heat beans and 8 cups water to boiling; cook 3 minutes.
2. Remove the Dutch oven from the heat; cover and let the beans stand 1 hour. Drain and rinse beans; set beans aside.
3. In same Dutch oven over medium heat, in hot salad oil, cook onions and garlic until tender, stirring occasionally.
4. Add beans, chilies, salt, sugar, cumin, and 3 cups water; over high heat, heat to boiling. Reduce heat to low; cover and simmer 1 hour, stirring occasionally
5. Add tomatoes with their liquid and oregano, stirring to mix well and break up tomatoes; over high heat, heat to boiling. Reduce heat to low; cover and simmer about 30 minutes longer or until the beans are tender.
6. Stir in half of the cheese and cook until the cheese is melted, stirring occasionally. Spoon the bean mixture into a large warm serving bowl; sprinkle with the remaining cheese.

ISLAND PORK AND BEANS

- Color index page 52
- Begin 3½ hrs ahead
- 8 main-dish servings
- 256 cals per serving

1 16-ounce package dry red kidney beans
Water
1 pound ground pork
1 large onion, diced
2 tablespoons brown sugar
2 tablespoons Worcestershire

2½ teaspoons salt
1 teaspoon dry mustard
½ teaspoon pepper
1 8¼-ounce can crushed pineapple
½ cup catchup

1. Rinse the beans in running cold water and discard any stones or shriveled beans. In 8-quart Dutch oven over high heat, heat beans and 8 cups water to boiling; cook 3 minutes. Remove from heat; cover; let stand 1 hour. Drain and rinse the beans.
2. In the same Dutch oven over medium-high heat, cook the ground pork and the diced onion until the pan juices evaporate and the pork is browned, stirring to prevent pork sticking.
3. Return the beans to the Dutch oven; add the sugar, Worcestershire, salt, mustard, pepper, and 4 cups water; over high heat, heat to boiling. Reduce heat to low; cover; simmer 1¼ hours.
4. Add pineapple with its liquid and catchup; over high heat, heat to boiling. Reduce heat to low; cover; simmer 15 minutes until tender.

PRAIRIE BEAN TACOS

Roll this hearty mix of beans, chilies, and onions into tortillas for a tasty supper dish. Garnish with lots of cool, shredded lettuce.

- Color index page 52
- Begin 30 mins ahead
- 4 main-dish servings
- 285 cals per serving

4 6-inch flour tortillas (about ½ 10-ounce package)
2 tablespoons salad oil
1 medium onion, diced
1 15¼- to 19-ounce can red kidney beans or 1 16-ounce can pink beans

1 4-ounce can chopped green chilies, drained
3 tablespoons catchup
¼ teaspoon salt
½ small head iceberg lettuce, shredded (1⅓ cups)
Shredded lettuce for garnish

1 Steam tortillas (p.157). In 2-quart saucepan over medium heat, in hot salad oil, cook onion until tender, stirring the mixture occasionally.

2 Into the onion in saucepan, measure 2 tablespoons bean liquid. In a colander drain the beans; discard the remaining bean liquid.

3 Add drained beans, green chilies, catchup, and salt to onion; cook the mixture over medium heat 5 minutes.

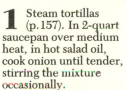

4 Mash beans slightly with the back of a spoon and stir occasionally. Line a warm tortilla with ⅓ cup lettuce.

5 Spoon one-fourth of the bean mixture on the lettuce in lengthwise strip. Carefully roll up tortilla. Repeat with remaining tortillas.

6 To serve, with knife, carefully cut filled tortillas crosswise in half. Place, seam side down, on platter and garnish.

Beets/Broccoli

Carrots

HARVARD BEETS

- Color index page 52
- Begin 20 mins ahead
- 6 side-dish servings
- 115 cals per serving

¼ cup sugar
1 tablespoon cornstarch
½ teaspoon salt
⅓ cup vinegar
1 tablespoon butter or margarine

½ teaspoon instant minced onion
2 16-ounce cans sliced beets, drained (about 3 cups)
6 lettuce leaves

1. In a small saucepan, combine the sugar, cornstarch, and salt; slowly stir in the vinegar; add the butter and onion; over medium heat, cook until thickened, stirring constantly.
2. Reduce heat to low; add the beets and cook the beets just until heated through, stirring occasionally. Transfer to a warmed platter and serve the beets hot; garnish with lettuce leaves.
BEETS IN ORANGE SAUCE: Prepare as above but use *½ cup orange juice* instead of vinegar and *1 teaspoon grated orange peel* instead of onion. Makes 6 servings. 120 cals per serving.

BROCCOLI WITH BUTTER-ALMOND SAUCE

- Color index page 52
- Begin 20 mins ahead
- 6 side-dish servings
- 146 cals per serving

2 pounds fresh broccoli
Water
4 tablespoons butter or margarine
¼ cup sliced almonds

2 tablespoons lemon juice
½ teaspoon salt
½ teaspoon grated lemon peel
⅛ teaspoon sugar

1. Remove any large leaves and cut off any woody stalk ends from broccoli. Split stalks lengthwise 2 or 3 times to speed cooking. Rinse well.
2. In large skillet over medium heat, in 1 inch boiling water, heat broccoli to boiling; cover and cook 10 minutes; drain, set aside.
3. Meanwhile, in 1-quart saucepan over medium-low heat, in hot butter, cook almonds 5 minutes, stirring often. Stir in lemon juice and remaining ingredients.
4. To serve, arrange broccoli in bowl; pour sauce over broccoli.

Preparing the broccoli: Cut off ends and split stalks to speed cooking.

Cooking the almonds: Add the almonds to the butter, cook 5 minutes.

BROCCOLI WITH SOUR-CREAM SAUCE Preheat oven to 350°F. Prepare as above but arrange broccoli in baking dish. Mix *½ cup sour cream*, *2 tablespoons prepared mustard*, and *½ teaspoon salt*; spoon over broccoli. Bake 8 minutes. Makes 6 side-dish servings. 196 cals per serving.

CARROTS AND GRAPES

An unusual combination of carrots and grapes, this dish makes a fresh-tasting accompaniment to broiled or roasted meats.

- Color index page 54
- Begin 45 mins ahead
- 8 side-dish servings
- 125 cals per serving

2 16-ounce bags carrots
½ cup orange juice
⅓ cup olive oil
½ teaspoon salt
½ teaspoon sugar

Dash ginger
1 cup seedless green grapes
2 tablespoons chopped parsley for garnish

1 With a sharp knife on cutting board, carefully cut each of the carrots into 1-inch-thick diagonal slices.

2 In medium saucepan over medium heat, heat the carrots and next 5 ingredients to boiling; cover, then simmer gently 15 minutes.

3 Meanwhile, with a small, sharp knife, cut each seedless grape in half. Add the halved grapes to carrots.

4 Cook 5 minutes more or until carrots are fork-tender. Drain; sprinkle with parsley and serve immediately.

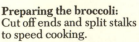

GLAZED CARROTS

- Color index page 54
- Begin 25 mins ahead
- 4 side-dish servings
- 98 cals per serving

Water
1 pound carrots, cut into 2-inch sticks
Salt
2 tablespoons butter or margarine

1 tablespoon sugar or brown sugar
¼ teaspoon ground nutmeg

1. In a medium saucepan over medium heat, in 1 inch boiling water, heat the carrots and ¼ teaspoon salt to boiling. Cover, then cook 15 minutes or until the carrots are tender-crisp; drain well. Return the carrots to the saucepan.
2. Mix in the butter or margarine, the sugar, ¼ teaspoon salt, and the nutmeg. Return the mixture to the heat and cook, stirring constantly, until the carrots are glazed. Transfer glazed carrots to a large warmed bowl and serve.

Cauliflower

FRUITED CARROTS

Early English settlers first brought carrots to the New World. Today they are mostly grown in California, Texas, and Wisconsin. Although naturally sweet, we have combined them with pineapple for extra fruitiness.

- Color index page 54
- Begin 20 mins ahead
- 10 side-dish servings
- 62 cals per serving

Water
10 medium carrots, thickly sliced
1 16-ounce can pineapple chunks

1 cup orange juice
1 tablespoon cornstarch
1 teaspoon salt
½ teaspoon cinnamon

1 In medium saucepan over medium heat, in 1 inch boiling water, heat the thick carrot slices until boiling.

2 Cover the saucepan and cook about 15 minutes or until the carrots are just tender-crisp; drain well.

3 Into a large sauce-pan, drain the liquid from the can of pineapple chunks, then add the orange juice.

4 In a small bowl, mix the cornstarch, salt, and cinnamon; stir in a few tablespoons of the pineapple-orange juice; mix well to form a smooth paste.

5 Heat the pineapple-orange liquid in saucepan, then stir in the cornstarch mixture. Simmer gently, stirring constantly, until the liquid is thickened.

6 Add the pineapple chunks and carrots; cook over low heat, stirring constantly, until the mixture is hot and bubbly. Transfer to a serving bowl; Serve immediately.

BAKED CAULIFLOWER IN CHEESE SAUCE

Cauliflower, a member of the cabbage-family, is still grown in Long Island, N.Y., where it was introduced in the 17th century.

- Color index page 55
- Begin 1 hr ahead
- 6 side-dish servings
- 313 cals per serving

Water
1 medium head cauliflower, trimmed, rinsed, and separated into flowerets
Salt
3 tablespoons butter
3 tablespoons chopped onion

2 tablespoons all-purpose flour
1¼ cups milk
½ pound Swiss cheese, shredded (2 cups)
2 eggs, beaten

1 In 4-quart saucepan over high heat, in 1 inch boiling water, heat cauliflower and ½ tea-spoon salt to boiling; cover and cook 10 minutes; drain; set aside.

2 Meanwhile, grease a 10″ by 6″ baking dish. In 2-quart saucepan over medium heat, melt butter; add onion and cook until tender, stirring the mixture often.

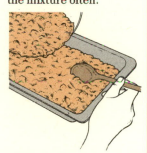

3 Stir in flour; cook 1 minute. Preheat oven to 325°F. Slowly stir in milk. Cook, stirring constantly, until mixture begins to boil; quickly remove from heat.

4 Stir in the cheese and cauliflower until cheese melts slightly; stir in eggs. Pour mixture into the baking dish; bake 30 minutes or until firm to the touch.

CAULIFLOWER PARMESAN

- Color index page 55
- Begin 20 mins ahead
- 6 side-dish servings
- 135 cals per serving

Water
1 medium head cauliflower
½ teaspoon salt

¼ cup butter or margarine, melted
Grated Parmesan cheese
Seasoned pepper

1. In large saucepan over medium heat, in 1 inch boiling water, heat cauliflower and salt to boiling. Cover and cook 10 to 15 minutes until just fork-tender; drain well.
2. Place whole cauliflower in serving dish. Pour on butter. Sprinkle with cheese, then pepper.

Corn

SWEET CORN WITH HERB BUTTER

Our corn-on-the-cobs are boiled in their own husks, keeping them sweet and juicy. Serve with a herb butter for a change.

- Color index page 55
- Begin 40 mins ahead
- 12 side-dish servings
- 240 cals per serving

12 large ears corn with husks
Water
Watercress
1½ cups butter or margarine

2½ teaspoons sugar
1 teaspoon thyme leaves
1 teaspoon salt

1 Pull the husks back from corn; remove silks, leaving the husks on. Bring the husks back together to completely enclose the corn.

2 In 8-quart saucepot over high heat, in 2 to 3 inches boiling water, heat corn in husks to boiling. Reduce heat to low; cover and gently simmer 5 minutes.

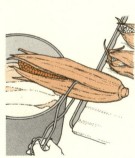

3 With tongs, carefully remove corn from water; drain corn well on paper towels.

4 Meanwhile, with sharp knife, finely chop enough watercress to measure ¼ cup.

5 In 2-quart saucepan over low heat, heat watercress, butter, sugar, thyme, and salt until butter melts. Pour this butter mixture into tall, narrow container for serving at table.

6 To serve, pull husks all the way back on each ear of corn and arrange corn on platter. Let each person wrap napkin around husks and dip ear of corn in the warm herb butter to eat.

SKILLET CORN

- Color index page 55
- Begin 30 mins ahead
- 6 side-dish servings
- 282 cals per serving

8 ears corn, husked
¼ cup butter or margarine
1 cup thinly sliced onions
½ cup green-pepper strips

1½ teaspoons salt
¼ teaspoon oregano leaves
½ cup half-and-half
2 medium tomatoes, cut up

1. On cutting board, with sharp knife, cut kernels from corn (about 4 cups).
2. In covered, large, heavy skillet over medium heat, in melted butter, cook corn, onions, pepper, salt, and oregano leaves until the corn is tender, about 6 minutes; carefully shake the skillet occasionally to prevent sticking.
3. Remove cover; add half-and-half and tomato pieces and simmer, uncovered, 1 or 2 minutes until tomatoes are hot but still firm.

CORN FRITTERS

- Color index page 55
- Begin 30 mins ahead
- 6 side-dish servings
- 185 cals per serving

Salad oil
1 16-to 17-ounce can whole-kernel corn, drained
1 cup all-purpose flour
¼ cup milk

1 teaspoon baking powder
½ teaspoon salt
2 eggs
Confectioners' sugar or maple syrup

1. In heavy saucepan over medium-high heat, heat ½ inch salad oil to 400°F. on deep-fat thermometer (or in electric skillet, heat ½ inch salad oil to 400°F.).
2. In medium-sized bowl, stir 1 tablespoon oil and next 6 ingredients just until blended.
3. Drop batter by tablespoons into hot oil; fry 3 to 5 minutes, until golden brown; turn once.
4. With slotted spoon, carefully remove fritters to paper towels to drain.
5. Sprinkle with confectioners' sugar or serve with maple syrup; or serve as an accompaniment to grilled chicken or fish.

CUSTARD CORN PUDDING

- Color index page 55
- Begin 1½ hrs ahead
- 6 side-dish servings
- 170 cals per serving

2 cups milk
2 tablespoons butter or margarine
2 eggs
1½ teaspoons salt

1 teaspoon sugar
¼ teaspoon pepper
1 12-ounce can whole-kernel corn, drained

1. Preheat oven to 325°F. In medium saucepan over low heat, heat milk and butter until tiny bubbles form around the edge and butter melts.
2. Meanwhile, in small bowl with wire whisk or fork, beat eggs, salt, sugar, and pepper.
3. Stir in the corn. Slowly add the warmed milk to the egg mixture, beating constantly with a wire whisk or spoon.
4. Pour the mixture into a 1½-quart casserole. Set the casserole in a shallow baking pan on the oven rack.
5. Fill pan with hot water to come half-way up side of casserole. Bake 1 hour or until a knife inserted in center comes out clean.

Eggplant

EGGPLANT PARMIGIANA

Thomas Jefferson first brought the eggplant to America from France in the 17th century, but it was Italian-Americans who popularized this classic preparation.

Olive oil
1 garlic clove, minced
1 large onion, chopped
2 14½- to 16-ounce cans
*   tomatoes*
2 teaspoons sugar
½ teaspoon oregano
*   leaves*
½ teaspoon basil
½ teaspoon salt
1 cup dried bread crumbs
2 eggs
Water

1 large eggplant, cut into
*   ½-inch slices*
½ cup grated Parmesan
*   cheese*
1 8-ounce package
*   mozzarella cheese, cut*
*   into ¼-inch slices*

- *Color index page 53*
- *Begin 1½ hrs ahead*
- *6 side-dish servings*
- *390 cals per serving*

1 In a medium skillet over medium heat, in 2 tablespoons hot olive oil, cook the garlic and chopped onion until tender, about 5 minutes, stirring occasionally.

2 Add the tomatoes, sugar, oregano leaves, basil, and salt. Reduce heat to low and cook, tightly covered, 30 minutes; stir occasionally.

3 Meanwhile, grease 13" by 9" baking dish. On sheet of waxed paper, place bread crumbs. In small dish, with fork, beat eggs with 2 tablespoons water.

4 Dip eggplant into egg mixture, then into the crumb mixture. Repeat so each piece is well coated twice.

5 In large skillet over medium heat, heat 2 tablespoons olive oil until very hot.

6 Cook a few eggplant slices at a time until golden brown, adding a little more oil as needed; drain on paper towels.

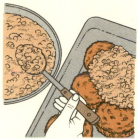

7 Preheat oven to 350°F. Arrange half of eggplant slices in baking dish; cover with half tomato mixture.

8 Sprinkle with half Parmesan and then top with half mozzarella; repeat. Bake 25 minutes or until lightly browned.

SOUTHERN COOKING

Southern cooking can generally be characterized by its combination of textures and flavors. Native products like corn and greens are intermingled with imported crops, now locally grown, such as peanuts and okra. The latter features prominently in "soul food."

Peanuts: Nut-like seeds of native South American vine; used in many ways. Its oil is especially revered in Southern cooking for frying; the nut itself is used in hundreds of dishes from Tuskegee Soup (named for the Institute) to Peanut Brittle.

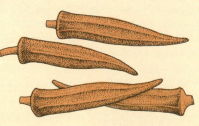

Greens: Leafy vegetables such as beet, collard, turnip, mustard, and dandelion; also kale, spinach, and Swiss chard. Mild to strong-flavored greens simmered in bouillon provide a good sharp contrast to fat-flavored meats like pork.

Okra: A finger-shaped vegetable (often called "lady fingers") used on its own or as a thickener in soups, stews, and gumbos.

Hominy and Grits: Finely ground, dried, hulled corn kernels used as a traditional Southern Breakfast food, but prepared and used in many ways. Grits are more finely ground than hominy: more grinding results in cornmeal.

Mushrooms

STIR-FRIED MUSHROOMS

Pennsylvania is the leading mushroom producer in the country. The mushroom's delicate flavor benefits from quick cooking.

- *Color index page 55*
- *Begin 15 mins ahead*
- *6 side-dish servings*
- *99 cals per serving*

2 teaspoons corn-
  starch
Water
¼ cup salad oil
1 tablespoon soy sauce

1 pound medium
  mushrooms, whole or
  sliced
¼ teaspoon sugar

1 In a small bowl, combine cornstarch with 2 teaspoons cold water, stirring until well mixed; set aside.

2 In a wok or 12-inch skillet over high heat, in very hot oil, cook next 3 ingredients; stir quickly and often (stir-fry).

3 Reduce heat to medium-high; stir-fry 5 to 6 minutes until mushrooms are tender.

4 Stir cornstarch paste into mushroom mixture; cook, stirring until thickened.

CHILLED LEMONY MUSHROOMS

1 pound medium
  mushrooms
1 medium lemon
¼ cup salad oil
2 tablespoons water

1½ teaspoons soy sauce
¼ teaspoon salt
¼ teaspoon sugar
¼ teaspoon rubbed sage
2 small heads Bibb lettuce

- *Color index page 55*
- *Begin 2 hrs ahead or early in day*
- *8 side-dish servings*
- *83 cals per serving*

1. Rinse mushrooms; trim and slice. From lemon, cut 6 very thin slices; squeeze 2 teaspoons juice from remainder; set aside.
2. In 3-quart saucepan over medium-high heat, in hot salad oil, cook mushrooms, stirring frequently, until mushrooms are coated with oil.
3. Stir in next 5 ingredients, lemon slices, and lemon juice; heat to boiling. Reduce heat to medium; cook 3 minutes longer, stirring frequently. Spoon mixture into bowl; cover with plastic wrap and refrigerate until well chilled.
4. To serve, cut each head of lettuce into 4 wedges. Arrange lettuce and mushrooms on plates.

Onions

FRENCH-FRIED ONION RINGS

Onions must be the most versatile of vegetables in the kitchen. Deep fried, they are a popular American accompaniment to hamburgers, and barbecued meats.

- *Color index page 55*
- *Begin 40 mins ahead*
- *6 side-dish servings*
- *140 cals per serving*

3 large onions
Salad oil
½ cup milk

1 cup all-purpose
  flour
½ teaspoon salt

1 On a cutting board with a sharp knife, carefully cut each of the onions crosswise into ¼-inch thick slices.

2 In 3- to 4-quart heavy saucepan over medium heat, heat 2 inches salad oil to 370°F. on deep-fat thermometer (or heat in deep-fat fryer set at 370°F.).

3 In small dish, place milk. In small bowl, stir flour and salt until mixed. Dip onion rings into milk, then into flour mixture. Repeat to coat twice

4 In hot salad oil, cook onion rings 3 to 5 minutes, until golden brown. Drain thoroughly on paper towels. Serve immediately.

BAKED ONIONS

¾ cup water
1 envelope chicken-flavor
  bouillon
10 medium onions

2 tablespoons butter or
  margarine, cut up
Salt
Paprika

- *Color index page 55*
- *Begin 1¾ hrs ahead*
- *10 side-dish servings*
- *51 cals per serving*

1. In 8″ by 8″ baking dish, combine the water and chicken-flavor bouillon. Add the onions, dot with butter, then sprinkle lightly with salt.
2. Cover the dish with foil and bake in 350°F. oven 1½ hours or until the onions are tender, occasionally basting onions with the cooking liquid in the dish.
3. To serve, carefully remove the onions from the baking dish and arrange in a warmed deep serving dish and sprinkle lightly with paprika.

Peas

CHEDDARED ONIONS

- Color index page 55
- Begin 30 mins ahead
- 8 side-dish servings
- 210 cals per serving

There were many onion varieties native to America, but the common onion, brought from Europe, is most usually grown.

Water
Salt
2 pounds small white onions
6 tablespoons butter or margarine

3 tablespoons all-purpose flour
1½ cups milk
4 ounces Cheddar cheese, shredded (1 cup)
Paprika

1 In medium saucepan over medium heat, in 1 inch boiling water with ¼ teaspoon salt, heat onions to boiling; cover and cook 10 to 15 minutes, until tender.

2 Meanwhile, in medium saucepan over medium heat, melt butter; stir in flour until smooth; stir in milk and ¼ teaspoon salt. Cook, stirring, until thickened

3 Stir in cheese; cook over very low heat, stirring constantly, until cheese is melted.

4 Drain onions and place in serving dish; pour on sauce and sprinkle with paprika

CREAMED ONIONS: Prepare Cheddared Onions as above, but omit shredded cheese. Pour sauce over onions; sprinkle with paprika. 160 cals per serving.

GLAZED ONIONS

- Color index page 55
- Begin 30 mins ahead
- 6 side-dish servings
- 166 cals per serving

Water
1½ pounds small onions
⅓ cup sugar

2 tablespoons butter or margarine
¼ teaspoon salt

1. In a medium saucepan over medium heat, in 1 inch boiling water, heat the onions to boiling; cover and cook 15 to 20 minutes until tender-crisp; drain.
2. In large skillet over low heat, stir sugar, butter, 2 teaspoons water, and salt. Add onions; cook until glazed, about 5 minutes, stirring.

PEAS WITH GREEN ONIONS

- Color index page 57
- Begin 30 mins ahead
- 4 side-dish servings
- 160 cals per serving

2 pounds fresh peas
2 tablespoons butter
2 bunches green onions, cut in 1-inch pieces
2 teaspoons all-purpose flour

½ teaspoon sugar
¼ teaspoon salt
¼ teaspoon thyme leaves
⅛ teaspoon pepper
¾ cup chicken broth

1. Shell peas (there should be about 2¾ cups). In 3-quart saucepan over medium heat, in hot butter, cook onions 2 minutes. With wooden spoon, stir in flour, sugar, salt, thyme leaves, pepper, and chicken broth.
2. Heat to boiling. Reduce heat to low; cover; simmer 5 to 7 minutes or until peas are tender.
3. Transfer to warm serving dish; serve hot.

Shelling peas: Press pods between thumb and forefinger; gently press the peas out.

Adding the liquid: With spoon, stir in peas, flour, sugar, and seasonings, then stir in broth.

MINTED PEAS

- Color index page 56
- Begin 20 mins ahead
- 6 side-dish servings
- 135 cals per serving

2 10-ounce packages frozen peas
1 tablespoon chopped onion

1 tablespoon chopped fresh mint
¼ cup butter or margarine

1. Cook the frozen peas as the label directs but add the chopped onion and chopped fresh mint; drain well.
2. Add butter and toss gently until butter is melted. Serve hot.

STIR-FRIED SUGAR SNAP PEAS

- Color index page 56
- Begin 15 mins ahead
- 4 side-dish servings
- 94 cals per serving

1 pound sugar snap peas*

1 tablespoon salad oil
¼ teaspoon salt

1. Remove stem ends and strings along both sides of pods of sugar snap peas (do not shell); rinse with cold water.
2. In 3-quart saucepan over medium heat, heat salad oil until very hot. Add Sugar Snap peas and salt; cook until tender-crisp, about 3 to 5 minutes, stirring quickly and frequently.

*Sugar snap peas are a new variety of edible pea pods. They are shorter and rounder than Chinese pea pods with fully formed peas and thick pods. The peas and pod are eaten together – either quickly cooked, as in this recipe, or raw.

Peppers

BATTER-FRIED STUFFED CHILIES

By the time Columbus arrived in the New World, the Indians had been cultivating the "chili pepper" and using it as seasoning in their food. This tasty Tex-Mex dish is a good example of the ways chilies can be used.

1 10-ounce can whole green chilies, drained
Salad oil
1 small onion, minced
1 small garlic clove, minced
1 28-ounce can tomatoes
1 teaspoon sugar
1 teaspoon oregano leaves
¼ teaspoon pepper
Salt

All-purpose flour
¾ pound Monterey Jack cheese, cut into thin strips
8 eggs, separated

- *Color index page 54*
- *Begin 1¼ hrs ahead*
- *8 main-dish servings*
- *381 cals per serving*

1 Set 8 whole green chilies aside; with a sharp knife on cutting board, chop the remaining green chilies to make the stuffing mixture.

2 Prepare tomato sauce: In 2-quart saucepan over medium heat, in 2 tablespoons hot oil, cook onion and garlic until tender, stir often.

3 Add the chopped green chilies, the tomatoes with their liquid, then the sugar, oregano, pepper, and ½ teaspoon salt, stirring to break up the tomatoes; over medium-high heat, heat the mixture to boiling. Reduce the heat to low and simmer, uncovered, 45 minutes, or until the mixture is slightly thickened. With a wooden spoon, stir the mixture occasionally to prevent it from sticking.

4 Meanwhile, place 2 tablespoons all-purpose flour on a sheet of waxed paper. With sharp knife, carefully make a lengthwise slit in side of each whole chili.

5 Stuff each of the chilies with some of the cheese; roll lightly in flour on waxed paper to coat; set chilies aside while preparing the batter mixture.

6 Prepare batter: In a large bowl with mixer at high speed, beat the egg whites and ½ teaspoon salt until stiff peaks form. In small bowl with mixer at medium speed, beat egg yolks slightly. With rubber spatula, fold egg yolks and ⅓ cup flour into beaten whites. In 5-quart Dutch oven or saucepot over medium heat, carefully heat about ½ inch oil to 375°F. on deep-fat thermometer (or heat oil in electric skillet set at 375°F.).

7 Carefully spoon ⅓ cup batter onto hot oil. With a greased spoon, spread in an oval 1 inch larger than stuffed chili. Carefully top batter with a stuffed chili.

8 Cover with another ⅓ cup batter; very carefully seal edges together with spoon. Cook 2 to 3 minutes until underside is golden. With pancake turner and spoon, carefully turn and cook until underside is golden. Remove chili from skillet. Drain well on paper towels; keep warm. Repeat with remaining stuffed chilies and batter. Serve the chilies immediately, topped with tomato sauce.

HOW TO PREPARE CHILIES

Chilies, hot and mild, are available canned, frozen, dried, and fresh. The many varieties make it a confusing plant, but more chilies are produced and consumed than any other spice in the world. Chilies are most often found in Tex-Mex dishes. Knowing how to prepare them is useful; if possible wear rubber gloves and keep hands away from face and eyes.

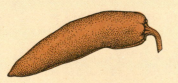

Mild New Mexico
(Chile de ristra)

Poblano
(ancho)

Mulato
(poblano pasilla)

Serrano
(hot or mountain chilies)

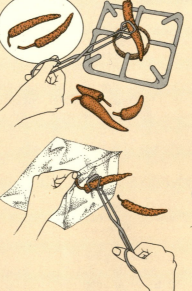

Place blistered chilies in a bag to steam and soften about 10 minutes.

Hold chili over gas flame or electric burner, turning frequently until all sides are blistered. Alternatively, if doing a large number, dip them into very hot oil (400°F.); this will blister them more quickly and evenly.

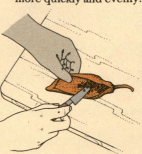

When cool, peel chilies starting at the stem end; rinse under running water. Cut out veins and seeds (the hottest part).

HEARTY STUFFED PEPPERS

During the early 1900s, peppers were used as containers to serve leftovers in a new way. Ours make a delicious supper dish.

¾ pound ground beef
1 small onion, diced
½ 32-ounce package frozen hash-brown potato nuggets (4 cups)
Salad oil
1¼ teaspoons salt
½ teaspoon oregano leaves

¼ teaspoon pepper
Chili powder
1 15¼- to 19-ounce can red kidney beans, drained
1 15-ounce can tomato sauce
3 large green peppers
¾ cup water

1 In 12-inch skillet over medium-high heat, cook ground beef, onion, and potatoes until meat is browned and onion and hash-brown potato nuggets are tender, stirring often.

2 Turn occasionally with pancake turner; add salad oil if necessary. Stir in salt, oregano, pepper, 1 teaspoon chili powder, ½ cup kidney beans and half of tomato sauce; remove from heat.

3 Cut each green pepper lengthwise in half; remove seeds.

4 Stuff green-pepper halves with meat mixture; set aside.

5 In same skillet, stir water, remaining kidney beans, tomato sauce, and ½ teaspoon chili powder. Arrange green peppers in sauce.

6 Over high heat, heat to boiling. Reduce heat to low; cover; simmer until peppers are fork-tender, about 25 minutes; stir occasionally.

- Color index page 54
- Begin 50 mins ahead
- 6 main-dish servings
- 333 cals per serving

RATATOUILLE IN ROASTED PEPPERS

Sweet red, green, and yellow peppers are often called "bell peppers" because of their shape. We fill ours with a popular French vegetable stew, ratatouille.

Salad oil
1 garlic clove, sliced
8 medium peppers, red, green and/or yellow
1 medium onion, chopped
2 medium zucchini, cut into ¼-inch-thick slices

½ pound mushrooms, cut into ¼-inch slices
Salt
1 large eggplant (about 1½ pounds), cut into ½-inch cubes

1 14½- to 16-ounce can tomatoes
1 tablespoon sugar
½ teaspoon basil
Parsley sprigs for garnish

- Color index page 55
- Begin 3 hrs ahead
- 16 side-dish servings
- 97 cals per serving

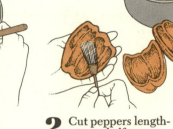

1 Preheat oven to 450°F. In 1-quart saucepan over low heat, heat 3 tablespoons oil and garlic until garlic is light brown; discard.

2 Cut peppers lengthwise in half; remove seeds and stems. Brush peppers on all sides with oil mixture. Arrange in large open roasting pan.

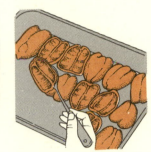

3 Roast the peppers 30 to 35 minutes until skin puckers and peppers are tender, turning them occasionally. Cover and refrigerate.

4 Meanwhile, in 8-quart Dutch oven or saucepot over medium heat, in 1 tablespoon hot salad oil, cook onion until tender, stirring occasionally. With slotted spoon, remove onion to bowl; set aside. In same Dutch oven or saucepot over medium heat, in 2 more tablespoons hot oil, cook zucchini, mushrooms, and ¼ teaspoon salt until tender, stirring occasionally. Remove and place in bowl with the cooked onion.

5 In same Dutch oven over medium heat, in ⅓ cup more hot oil, cook eggplant until tender, stirring occasionally, about 15 minutes.

6 Add onion mixture to Dutch oven, with tomatoes with their liquid, sugar, basil, and 1¾ teaspoons salt; over high heat, boil.

7 Reduce heat to medium-low. Simmer, uncovered, 20 minutes, stirring occasionally to blend flavors and thicken mixture slightly.

8 Place the mixture in large bowl; cover with plastic wrap and refrigerate at least 2 hours or until well chilled.

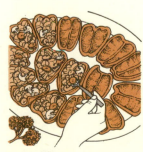

9 To serve, arrange pepper halves on large platter. Fill pepper halves with eggplant mixture. Garnish with parsley sprigs.

Potatoes

TWICE-BAKED POTATOES

The Idaho potato is considered one of the finest in the world; its light, floury texture makes it ideal for baking. This dish makes a festive addition to any table.

- *Color index page 56*
- *Begin 1½ hrs ahead*
- *6 side-dish servings*
- *239 cals per serving*

6 medium baking potatoes, washed and unpeeled
3 tablespoons butter or margarine
1 teaspoon salt
Dash white pepper

⅓ cup milk
Toppings
Minced onion, chopped chives, diced American cheese or crumbled bacon

1 Preheat oven to 450°F. Place the potatoes in the oven and bake them for 45 minutes or until fork-tender.

2 With a sharp knife, holding a potato with a clean pot holder, slice lengthwise, to remove top fourth from each of the potatoes.

3 With a spoon, carefully scoop out potatoes to form 6 shells. Scrape potato from top quarters and discard tops.

4 In large bowl with mixer at low speed, beat potatoes, butter, salt, and pepper until well combined and fluffy.

5 Slowly add the milk, beating the mixture constantly until smooth. With a spoon, pile the mashed potato mixture back into the reserved potato shells.

6 Sprinkle generously with the topping of your choice. Place the potatoes on a cookie sheet; return to the oven and bake 10 minutes or until the tops are golden.

HOME-FRIED POTATOES

Today, the average American eats about 120 pounds of potatoes per year. Home-fried is one of the most popular styles, often garnishing hamburgers and omelets.

- *Color index page 56*
- *Begin 45 mins ahead*
- *4 side-dish servings*
- *225 cals per serving*

4 medium potatoes
4 tablespoons butter or margarine

1 small onion, chopped
Salt

1 Leave potato skin on if you like; with a sharp knife, on cutting board, cut potatoes into ¼-inch-thick slices. In 12-inch skillet over medium heat, melt butter.

2 Add potato slices and sprinkle with chopped onion; cook until potatoes are golden brown on the bottom. Reduce heat to low; cover; cook 5 minutes.

3 With a pancake turner, turn the potatoes over; continue cooking over medium heat until the potatoes are light golden brown on the other side.

4 Reduce heat to low; cover and cook 5 to 10 minutes longer, until the potatoes are tender. Sprinkle with salt to taste. Transfer to a serving platter; serve immediately.

HASH BROWN POTATOES

½ cup butter or margarine
5 or 6 medium potatoes, coarsely shredded or finely diced (about 6 cups)

1 teaspoon salt
½ teaspoon paprika
¼ teaspoon pepper

- *Color index page 56*
- *Begin 15 mins ahead*
- *6 side-dish servings*
- *310 cals per serving*

1. In medium skillet (preferably with a non-stick finish) over medium heat, melt the butter or margarine; in hot butter cook the potatoes, covered, for 10 minutes.

2. Uncover and sprinkle with remaining ingredients. Continue cooking 15 minutes or until the potatoes are tender and lightly browned, occasionally turning with pancake turner. Serve immediately.

PARTY POTATOES WITH LEEKS

12 medium potatoes
Water
2 small leeks (about
  ¾ pound)
¾ cup butter or
  margarine

2 cups milk
2 teaspoons salt
¼ teaspoon pepper

- Color index page 56
- Begin 1 hr ahead
- 12 side-dish servings
- 220 cals per serving

1. In 5-quart Dutch oven or saucepot over high heat, heat potatoes and enough water to cover to boiling. Reduce heat to low; cover and cook 25 to 30 minutes, until fork-tender; drain and peel.
2. Meanwhile, cut off root end of leeks; separate leeks into leaves. Thoroughly rinse leeks with running cold water to wash away sand and grit.
3. Cut leeks crosswise into ½-inch pieces. In 10-inch skillet over medium heat, in 2 tablespoons hot butter, cook the leeks until they are very tender, stirring occasionally.
4. In 2-quart saucepan over medium-low heat, heat milk and remaining butter until butter melts and mixture is hot.
5. In large bowl, with mixer at low speed, beat half of potatoes and half of hot milk mixture until smooth, scraping bowl often with rubber spatula. Increase speed to high; beat until light and fluffy.
6. Spoon potato mixture into warm, large bowl. Keep warm. Repeat with remaining potatoes and milk mixture. With rubber spatula, stir salt, pepper, and leek mixture into potato mixture. Serve potatoes immediately.

NEW POTATOES WITH LEMON AND CHIVES

Water
2 pounds new potatoes,
  washed and unpeeled
Salt
¼ cup butter or
  margarine

Grated peel 1 lemon
2 tablespoons lemon juice
2 tablespoons chopped
  chives

- Color index page 56
- Begin 40 mins ahead
- 6 side-dish servings
- 213 cals per serving

1. In large saucepan over medium heat, in 1 inch boiling water, heat potatoes and 1 teaspoon salt to boiling; cover and cook 15 to 20 minutes, until fork-tender; drain.
2. Cool potatoes slightly, then if you like, peel.
3. Return to saucepan. Add remaining ingredients and heat. Or, omit lemon peel, juice, chives, and butter and while potatoes are still hot, add ¼ cup of the following flavored butters:

CHILI BUTTER: In small bowl, with spoon, beat *½ cup butter* or *margarine*, softened, *1 teaspoon chili powder*, and *¼ teaspoon pepper* until well blended. Refrigerate until firm. Makes ½ cup. 105 cals per tablespoon.
CHIVE BUTTER: Prepare as above, but substitute *2 teaspoons chopped chives* for chili powder. Makes ½ cup. 100 cals per tablespoon.
DILL BUTTER: Prepare as above, but substitute *1 teaspoon dill weed* for chili powder. Makes ½ cup. 100 cals per tablespoon.

CARNIVAL MASHED POTATOES

A large bowl of creamy mashed potatoes is one of America's most popular potato dishes. Swirled with a colorful vegetable mixture it creates a holiday mood any time of the year.

- Color index page 55
- Begin 45 mins ahead
- 8 side-dish servings
- 215 cals per serving

8 medium potatoes (about
  2½ pounds), peeled
  and each cut in half
Water
6 tablespoons butter or
  margarine
2 green onions, minced

1 large carrot, diced
1 12-ounce can whole-
  kernel corn with sweet
  peppers, drained
¾ cup hot milk
1 teaspoon salt
¼ teaspoon pepper

1 In 5-quart saucepot over high heat, heat the peeled potato halves and enough water to cover to boiling.

2 Reduce heat to low; cover and simmer 15 to 20 minutes or until potatoes are fork-tender. Drain potatoes.

3 Meanwhile, in 10-inch skillet over medium heat, in hot butter, cook green onions and carrot until tender, stirring occasionally.

4 Add the whole-kernel corn with sweet peppers and cook just until heated through; remove from the heat and keep warm.

5 In large bowl, with mixer at low speed, beat potatoes until fluffy. Gradually add hot milk, salt, and pepper; beat until smooth.

6 To serve, spoon mashed potato mixture into warm, large bowl. Swirl the vegetable mixture through the hot mashed potatoes.

Potatoes

DUCHESS POTATOES

Duchess Potatoes are originally French, but they are an important part of the traditional American steak presentation, the Planked Steak (p.217); the egg yolks keep them firm.

- *Color index page 55*
- *Begin 45 mins ahead*
- *10 side-dish servings*
- *155 cals per serving*

6 medium potatoes Water ½ cup butter or margarine	1 teaspoon salt 2 eggs, slightly beaten

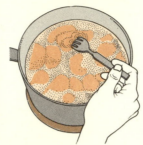

1 Rinse potatoes with running cold water; peel. Cut each potato into quarters. In 3-quart saucepan over high heat, heat the potato quarters and enough water to cover to boiling.

2 Reduce the heat to low; cover, then simmer 20 to 30 minutes, until the potatoes are fork-tender. Drain the potatoes well.

3 Preheat broiler if manufacturer directs. In large bowl, with mixer at low speed, beat potatoes, 4 table-spoons butter, and salt until fluffy.

4 Add the beaten eggs and, at medium speed, continue beating the mixture until it is smooth, about 2 minutes.

5 In a small saucepan over low heat, melt remaining butter. On a greased cookie sheet, pipe or mound mashed potato leaving 2 inches between each mound.

6 Brush potato mounds with melted butter. Broil 5 to 8 minutes, until the potatoes are golden brown. Use to garnish Planked Steak.

- *Color index page 56*
- *Begin 1¼ hrs ahead*
- *6 side-dish servings*
- *220 cals per serving*

ROASTED POTATO FANS

6 medium potatoes 6 tablespoons butter or margarine ½ teaspoon salt	¼ teaspoon basil ¼ teaspoon marjoram leaves ⅓ teaspoon pepper

1. Peel potatoes. With sharp knife, cut each potato crosswise into ¼-inch-thick slices, being careful to cut each slice only three-quarters of the way through potato.
2. In 13" by 9" baking pan in 400°F. oven, melt butter. Arrange potatoes, cut side up, in pan; brush with melted butter; sprinkle with salt, basil, marjoram, and pepper.
3. Bake 1 hour or until potatoes are golden and slices fan out, occasionally brushing potatoes with butter in pan. Serve immediately.

Cutting the potatoes: Carefully slice each potato only three-quarters of the way through.

Brushing the potatoes: Brush the potatoes occasionally with the butter in the pan.

- *Color index page 56*
- *Begin early in day*
- *12 side-dish servings*
- *385 cals per serving*

DELMONICO POTATOES

Water 9 medium potatoes, unpeeled Salt ⅓ cup butter or margarine ⅓ cup all-purpose flour 2¼ cups half-and-half or milk	Salt 1 4-ounce package shredded Cheddar cheese (1 cup) 3 tablespoons dried bread crumbs

1. In a large covered saucepan over medium heat, in 1 inch boiling water, cook unpeeled potatoes and 1 teaspoon salt for 20 to 30 minutes until potatoes are fork-tender; drain and cool.
2. *About 1 hour before serving*: Preheat oven to 375°F. Grease 12" by 8" baking dish. Peel and dice potatoes.
3. In large saucepan over medium-high heat, melt butter. With wire whisk or slotted spoon, stir in flour until well blended and smooth.
4. Gradually stir in half-and-half and cook, stirring constantly, until mixture is thick and bubbly. Stir in 1 teaspoon salt; gently stir in the diced potatoes.
5. Pour the potato mixture evenly into the baking dish; sprinkle the mixture with the shredded cheese, then the bread crumbs.
6. Bake 25 minutes or until cheese is melted and mixture is bubbly. Serve hot.

Squash

STUFFED ACORN SQUASH

2 medium acorn squash
(2 pounds)
½ cup brown rice
1 16-ounce package pork-
sausage meat
1 egg

1 3-ounce can sliced
mushrooms, drained
1 tablespoon maple syrup
or maple-flavor syrup
½ teaspoon salt

- Color index
page 56
- Begin
1 hr ahead
- 4 main-dish
servings
- 527 cals
per serving

1. Preheat oven to 350°F. Cut each acorn squash lengthwise in half; discard seeds. Place squash halves, cut side down, in 12" by 8" baking dish; bake 45 minutes. Meanwhile, prepare rice as label directs.
2. In 10-inch skillet over medium heat, cook pork-sausage meat until browned. With slotted spoon, remove meat (discard drippings) to medium bowl; toss with egg, mushrooms, syrup, and cooked brown rice.
3. Turn the squash halves cut side up, in the baking dish; sprinkle the squash with salt.
4. Spoon the meat mixture into the squash halves. Cover with foil and bake 15 minutes or until tender. Transfer to warm platter.

SKILLET-BAKED ACORN SQUASH

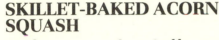

1 medium acorn squash
2 tablespoons butter or
margarine

2 tablespoons brown
sugar

- Color index
page 56
- Begin
30 mins
ahead
- 2 side-dish
servings
- 250 cals
per serving

1. Cut squash lengthwise in half; remove seeds. Cut halves crosswise into ½-inch-thick slices.
2. In 12-inch skillet over medium-low heat, melt butter or margarine. Arrange squash slices in one layer in melted butter.
3. Cover skillet and cook about 20 minutes, turning squash occasionally, until browned on both sides and tender.
4. Sprinkle squash with brown sugar; cover skillet to melt sugar.

MAPLE BUTTERNUT SQUASH

2 medium butternut
squash (about 1¾
pounds each)
Water
½ cup maple or maple-
flavor syrup

6 tablespoons butter or
margarine
Chopped parsley for
garnish

- Color index
page 56
- Begin
15 mins
ahead
- 10 side-dish
servings
- 175 cals
per serving

1. Cut each squash lengthwise in half; discard seeds. Then cut each squash half crosswise into slices about 1 inch thick; cut off peel.
2. In 4- to 5-quart saucepot over high heat, in 1 inch boiling water, heat squash to boiling. Reduce heat to low; cover and simmer 15 minutes stirring occasionally, or until squash is fork-tender. Drain.
3. In large bowl, with mixer at low speed, beat squash, maple syrup, and butter until smooth, scraping bowl often with rubber spatula. Spoon into warm bowl; sprinkle with parsley.

SPAGHETTI SQUASH WITH SPICY MEAT SAUCE

Named for its strandlike flesh, we treat this squash like the pasta and serve it with a Spicy Meat Sauce.

1 2½-pound spaghetti
squash
Water
1 beef top round steak,
cut ½ thick (about
1 pound)
2 tablespoons salad oil
1 small onion, diced

1 small garlic clove,
minced
¾ teaspoon chili powder
4 medium tomatoes
(about 1½ pounds),
diced (4 cups)
2 teaspoons sugar
¾ teaspoon salt

- Color index
page 56
- Begin
1 hr ahead
- 4 main-dish
servings
- 410 cals
per serving

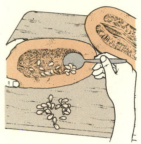 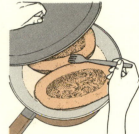

1 Cut squash lengthwise in half; discard seeds. In 12-inch skillet over high heat, in 1 inch boiling water, place the squash, cut side up; heat squash to boiling.

2 Reduce heat to low; cover and simmer 40 minutes or until squash is fork-tender. Meanwhile, with sharp knife, dice beef top round steak.

3 In 3-quart saucepan over high heat, in hot salad oil, cook the beef, onion, and garlic until the juices from the meat evaporate and the meat is browned, stirring frequently. Stir in the chili powder and cook 1 minute. Add the tomatoes, sugar and salt to saucepan. Heat the mixture to boiling. With wooden spoon, stir to loosen the brown bits on the bottom of the pan and to prevent sticking.

4 Reduce heat to low; cover and simmer 30 minutes or until meat is tender and sauce is slightly thickened; with wooden spoon, stir occasionally.

5 Drain squash. With 2 forks, lift up pulp of squash to form spaghetti-like stands.

6 Transfer to large warm platter. Spoon meat sauce over squash; serve like spaghetti.

Squash

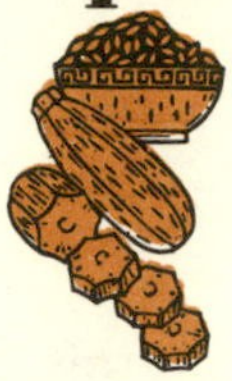

ZUCCHINI WITH RICE FILLING

Thanks to Italian immigrants, zucchini has become widely available in America. Often stir-fried, we stuff it with a tasty rice filling.

- *Color index page 54*
- *Begin 40 mins ahead*
- *6 side-dish servings*
- *201 cals per serving*

3 medium zucchini (about 8 ounces each)
1 tablespoon butter or margarine
1 small onion, diced
¾ cup regular long-grain rice
¼ teaspoon salt
Water
¾ cup frozen peas
½ cup milk
¼ pound Cheddar cheese, shredded (1 cup)

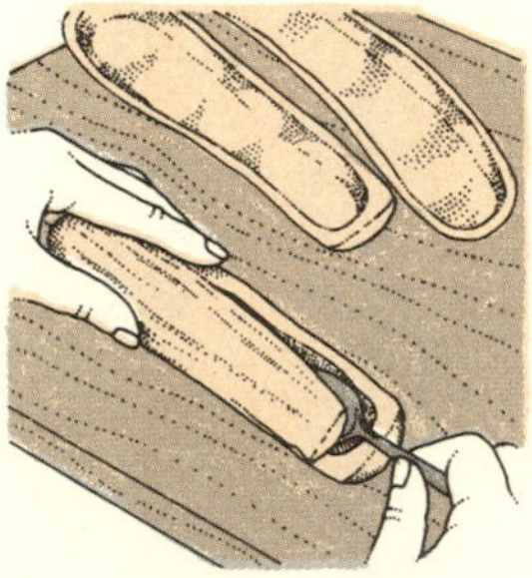

1 Cut each zucchini lengthwise in half. Scoop out and dice centers, leaving ¼-inch-thick shell; set aside.

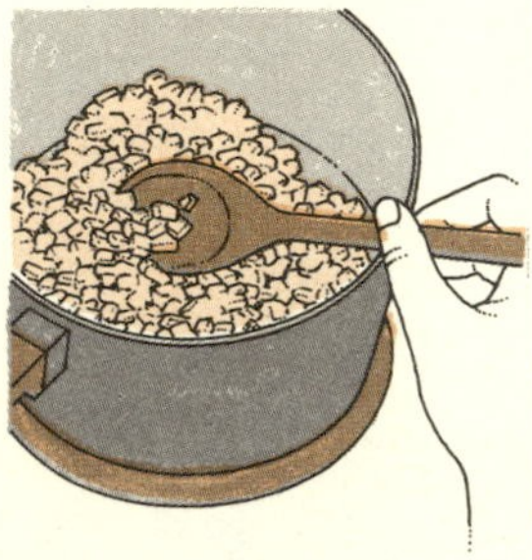

2 In 3-quart saucepan over medium heat, in hot butter, cook onion and diced zucchini until tender, stirring occasionally.

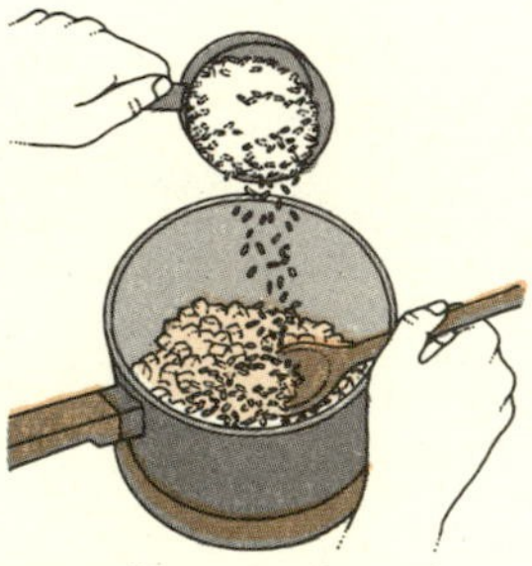

3 Add rice, salt, and 1½ cups water; heat to boiling. Reduce heat to low; cover and simmer 10 minutes.

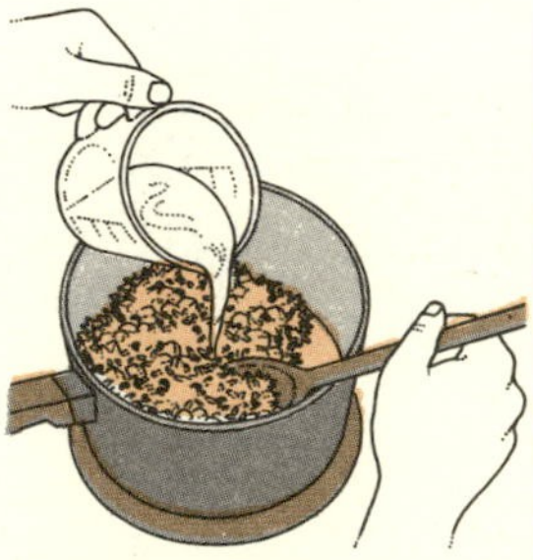

4 Add peas; cover and simmer 10 minutes or until liquid is absorbed. Stir in milk and ¾ cup cheese; remove from heat.

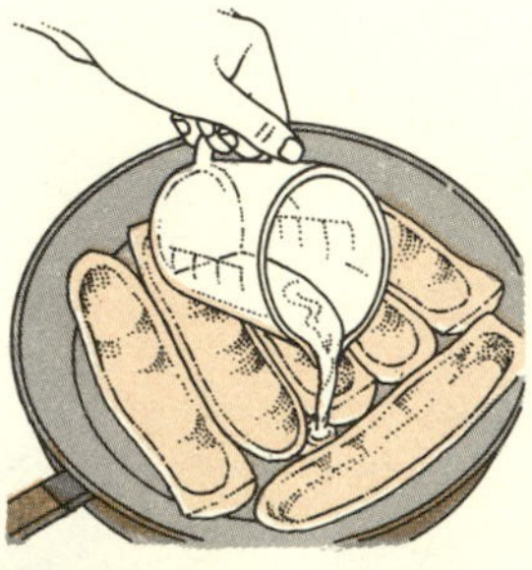

5 Meanwhile, in 12-inch skillet over high heat, heat zucchini halves and ¼ cup water to boiling. Reduce heat to low; cover and simmer 5 minutes or until tender-crisp.

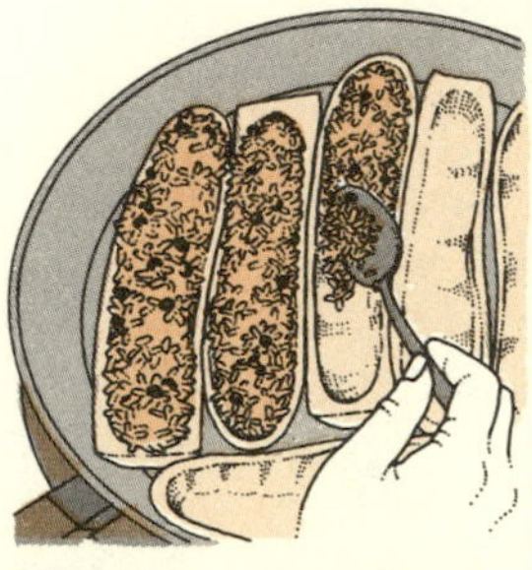

6 Fill zucchini halves with rice mixture; sprinkle with remaining cheese. Cover and cook zucchini halves over low heat until filling is completely heated through.

Sweet potatoes

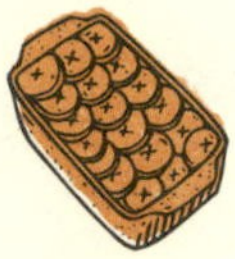

BAKED CANDIED SWEET POTATOES

Sweet potatoes, an important crop in the South, can be baked, boiled, mixed in pies and biscuits, or candied as we do here.

- *Color index page 54*
- *Begin 1½ hrs ahead*
- *10 side-dish servings*
- *214 cals per serving*

6 large sweet potatoes (about 3 pounds)
Water
Salt
½ cup packed brown sugar
4 tablespoons butter or margarine, cut into small pieces

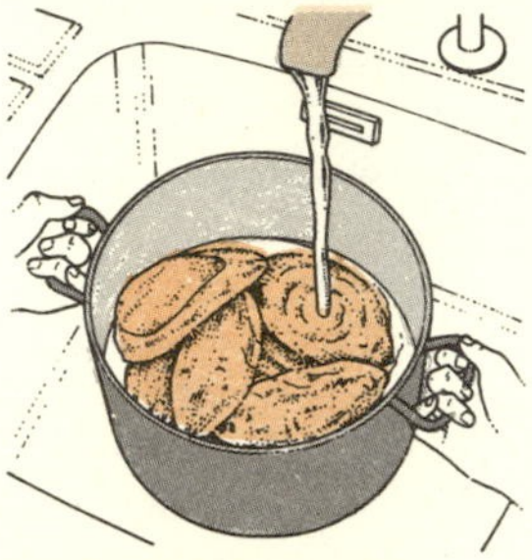

1 In 4-quart saucepan over high heat, heat unpeeled sweet potatoes and enough water to cover to boiling.

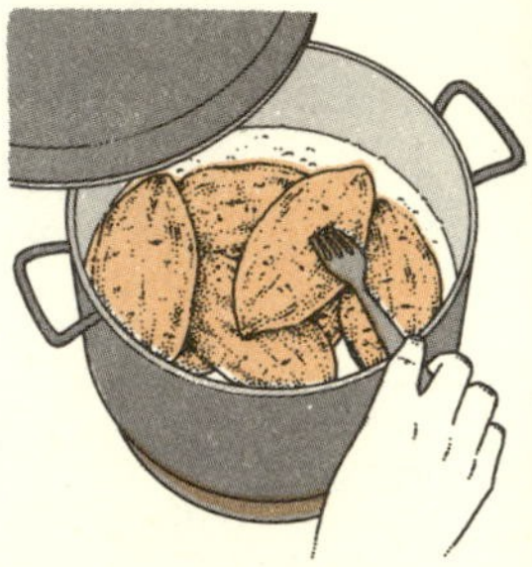

2 Reduce heat to low; cover and simmer 25 to 30 minutes until the potatoes are tender. Drain potatoes; let cool slightly until possible to handle.

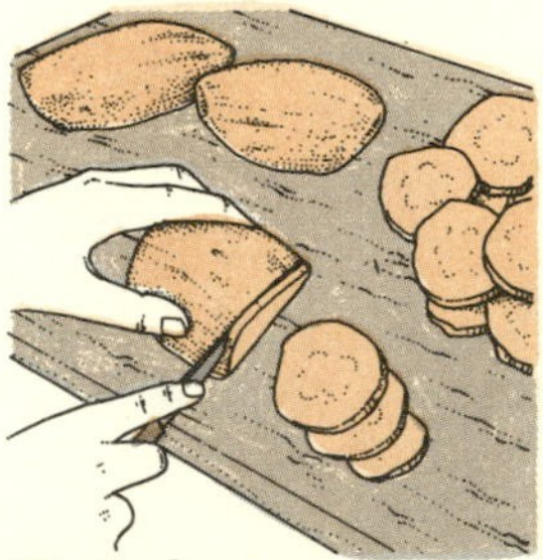

3 Preheat oven to 325°F. Grease 12″ by 8″ baking dish. Peel the potatoes; cut potatoes into ¼-inch-thick slices.

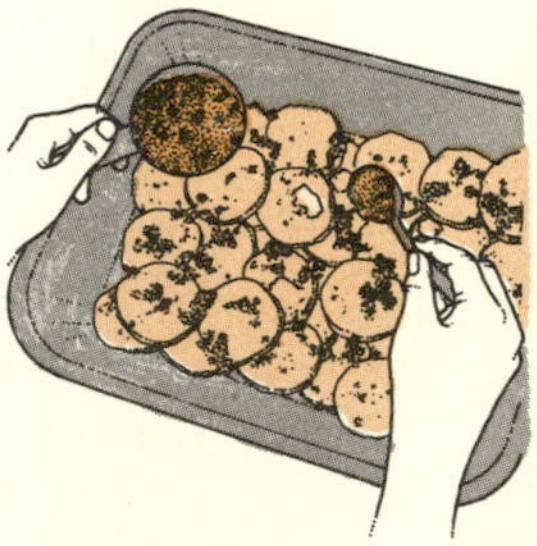

4 Arrange one-third of potato slices in baking dish; lightly sprinkle with some salt; then sprinkle with one-third of brown sugar; dot with one-third of butter.

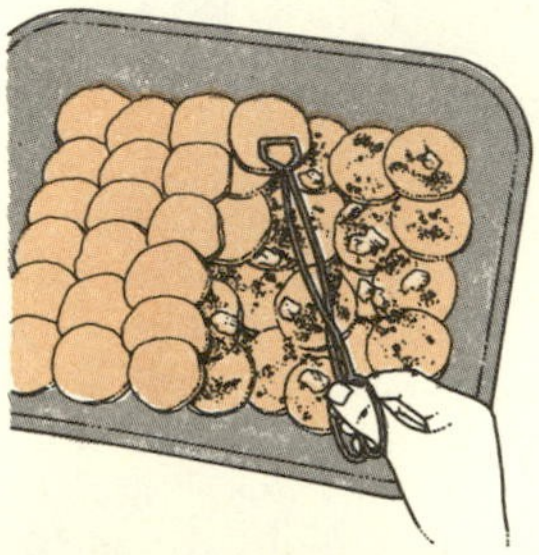

5 Repeat with the remaining potato slices, salt, brown sugar, and butter to make 3 layers in all.

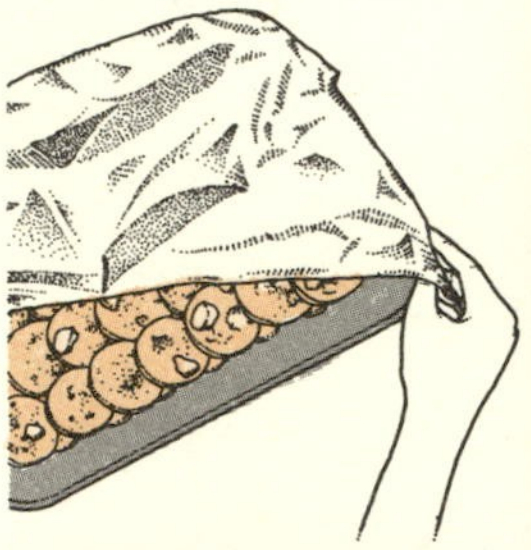

6 Cover baking dish with foil, bake 45 minutes or until potatoes are heated through and the sugar and butter are melted.

Tomatoes

STEWED FRESH TOMATOES

- Color index
  page 54
- Begin
  40 mins
  ahead
- 6 side-dish
  servings
- 68 cals
  per serving

Although the tomato is actually a fruit, in 1893 the Supreme Court classified it as a vegetable for trade purposes. If you are lucky enough to grow tomatoes, this is an easy and traditional way to use any excess.

Water
2 pounds tomatoes
2 tablespoons butter or
   margarine
4 green onions, chopped
1½ teaspoons sugar

1½ teaspoons garlic salt
¼ teaspoon seasoned
   pepper
Fresh basil or parsley for
   garnish

1 In a large saucepan, bring enough water to cover the tomatoes to the boil. Add the tomatoes and return to the boil 30 to 60 seconds depending on ripeness.

2 Drain tomatoes and dip into cold water. With sharp knife, pull away loosened skin from tomatoes. Cut out stem end. Cut the tomatoes into wedges.

3 In 10-inch skillet over medium heat, in butter, cook green onions 1 minute. Add tomatoes, sugar, salt, and pepper; cook about 10 minutes, stirring occasionally.

4 To serve, spoon the hot stewed fresh tomatoes into a warmed serving dish and garnish with the fresh basil or fresh parsley.

PAN FRIED CHERRY TOMATOES

- Color index
  page 54
- Begin
  5 mins
  ahead
- 4 side-dish
  servings
- 82 cals
  per serving

2 tablespoons butter or
   margarine
1 pint cherry tomatoes

Chopped parsley for
   garnish

1. In 3-quart saucepan over high heat, melt the butter. Add the cherry tomatoes.
2. Cook just until tomatoes are heated through and skins start to wrinkle, stirring frequently. Transfer to warm serving dish. Sprinkle with chopped parsley.

BACON-WRAPPED BROILED TOMATOES

- Color index
  page 54
- Begin
  20 mins
  ahead
- 6 side-dish
  servings
- 115 cals
  per serving

The tomato, or "love apple" as it used to be called, may have been native to parts of South America, but was not introduced to North America until the 18th century. This is a delicious garnish for barbecued meats.

12 bacon slices
6 medium tomatoes
1 teaspoon marjoram
   leaves
1 teaspoon grated
   Parmesan cheese

1 teaspoon salt
½ teaspoon basil
Dash pepper
Fresh basil leaves for
   garnish

1 Preheat broiler if manufacturer directs or prepare outdoor grill for barbecuing. In large skillet over medium heat, fry bacon just until limp.

2 Cut each tomato about ¾ way through into 6 wedges, gently spreading the wedges apart.

3 In cup, combine marjoram and next 4 ingredients; sprinkle on tomatoes.

4 Wrap 2 bacon slices around each tomato and secure the slices with toothpicks.

5 For broiling, place tomatoes in broiling pan and broil 5 to 10 minutes until the bacon is golden and the tomatoes are tender. Do not overcook.

6 For grilling, loosely wrap each tomato halfway up with foil and grill. Remove the toothpicks from the tomatoes. Arrange on warm serving platter and garnish with fresh basil.

Halloween Party Buffet

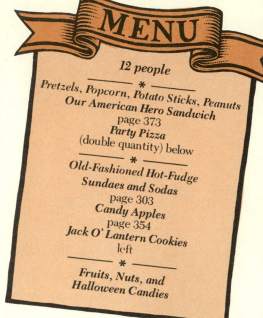

MENU

12 people

*

Pretzels, Popcorn, Potato Sticks, Peanuts
Our American Hero Sandwich
page 373
Party Pizza
(double quantity) below

*

**Old-Fashioned Hot-Fudge
Sundaes and Sodas**
page 303
Candy Apples
page 354
Jack O' Lantern Cookies
left

*

*Fruits, Nuts, and
Halloween Candies*

Halloween celebrations became popular in the 1800s, when Scottish and Irish immigrants arrived bringing their special customs with them. Nowadays, it is a festival enjoyed mostly by children who dress in costumes and masks and go "trick or treating." Neighbors give them candy, fruit, pennies, and sometimes home-baked cookies. Parties of all kinds have become popular on this evening, so we have planned one which can be enjoyed by everyone. Our American Hero Sandwich won't leave room for much else, but we serve a tasty Party Pizza just in case! As a special treat, set up your own ice-cream fountain; provide toppings and sauces for do-it-yourself sundaes and sodas! Set the scene with Candy Apples, apples and tangerines, nuts, candy, Jack O' Lantern cookies, and carved pumpkins to provide a Halloween atmosphere.

JACK O'LANTERN COOKIES

1 Prepare Cookie Chalets dough (p.353); refrigerate 1 hour or until dough is firm enough to handle. Make pattern (below). Preheat oven to 350°F.

2 On lightly floured surface with lightly floured rolling pin, gently roll out half of dough ⅛ inch thick. Using a sharp knife and pattern, cut as many cookie pumpkins as possible from half the dough. With pancake turner, place pumpkin shapes on an ungreased cookie sheet, about ½ inch apart.

3 Bake cookies 5 to 6 minutes. With pancake turner or metal spatula, remove cookies to wire rack to cool. Repeat with remaining cookie dough.

4 Meanwhile, make Ornamental Cookie Frosting (p.338). Using red and yellow food colorings, tint two-thirds frosting orange and one-third frosting yellow. Spoon some of each color into small decorating bags with small plain writing tubes.

5 When cookies are cool, using a metal spatula, frost cookies or leave plain. Pipe on Jack O' Lantern faces; let dry. Store in an airtight container.

Party Pizzas make ideal party fare. Make the toppings as varied as you like. Prepare Basic Pizza Dough (p.374, steps 1 to 3). Shape dough into ½-inch-high rim at edge of pan. Spread tomato sauce over and bake 15 minutes; remove from oven. Top alternate sections with Sautéed Herbed Mushrooms (p.374), fried mixed peppers, and pepperoni slices with mozzarella cheese; bake 10 more minutes.

Making a pattern: Draw a pumpkin shape 2½ inches high on a piece of thin cardboard; cut out pattern.

Cutting the cookies: Using the tip of a knife, cut around pattern on rolled out cookie dough.

Planning Ahead

Up to 1 week ahead:	Bake Jack O' Lantern Cookies; store in tightly covered container.
Early in day:	Make Candy Apples; set aside.
Up to 2 hours ahead:	Prepare hero sandwich (do not add any dressing); wrap in plastic wrap. Put toppings and sauces for sundae bar in individual bowls; cover and refrigerate if necessary.
1 hour ahead:	Make pizzas.
Just before serving:	Add dressing to sandwich; scoop ice cream as necessary.

Thanksgiving Day

Thanksgiving, the most popular American holiday, is a family feast celebrating the first successful harvest of the Plymouth Colony in 1621. In 1789, President George Washington proclaimed the first nationally observed Thanksgiving, but it wasn't until 1941 that Congress officially established the date as the last Thursday in November. No one knows if the first feast included turkey, now the traditional main course for the meal and the symbol of Thanksgiving itself. Our menus must seem restrained compared to the Pilgrims' first dinner which is said to have included oysters, eels, venison, goose, cornbread, leeks, watercress, plums, and berries, accompanied by a sweet wine.

This celebration centers around a plump Roast Turkey with Pecan Stuffing and Giblet Gravy garnished with pickled baby corns to symbolize that early harvest. We offer the traditional accompaniments and then some – from freshly baked rolls to apple cider. Create a colonial New England mood with baskets of nuts, seasonal and traditional fruits, dried flowers, and autumn leaves.

Planning Ahead

Up to 2 days ahead:	Bake the rolls and store in an airtight container. Make relishes and refrigerate.
Day ahead:	Prepare stuffing; refrigerate. Bake pies.
7 hours ahead:	Stuff the turkey and begin roasting; make the broth for the gravy and refrigerate; prepare corn garnish and refrigerate.
2 hours ahead:	Begin preparing Lemon-Buttered Vegetables and Party Potatoes with Leeks; keep warm.
½ hour ahead:	Remove turkey from roasting pan and keep warm; prepare the gravy.
Just before serving:	Pipe cream on pumpkin pie; heat raisin pie.

MENU

12 people

*

Oyster Soup
page 106

*

**Roast Turkey with Pecan Stuffing and
Turkey Giblet Gravy/Cocktail Corn Garnish**
pages 160-161
Cranberry Sauce/Cranberry-Apple Relish
page 383
Party Potatoes with Leeks
page 243
Lemon-Buttered Vegetables
page 254
Parker House Rolls
page 361

*

Sour-Cream Pumpkin Pie
page 318
Lattice-Topped Raisin Pie
page 315

*

Fruit and Nuts

*

Apple Cider

Christmas Eve Party

The bustle of the Christmas season usually culminates with a trim-the-tree party on Christmas Eve. It is an ideal time to invite family and friends to join in the festivities and, with some planning ahead and organization, you will have a beautifully-decorated tree and a lively party.

A selection of appetizers, and a generous plate or tray of elegant, but simple, open sandwiches provide a filling supper; choose a variety of meats and fish with pretty garnishes. Toast the tree with rich Eggnog or Glögg (Swedish mulled wine), Christmas cookies, and a slice of Chocolate Fruitcake. For gifts, pack some cookies in little wooden boxes lined with colorful tissue paper.

EGGNOG
Eggnog is a rich, thick drink made from eggs and spirits (we use bourbon) served at Christmastime in America.

12 eggs, separated	6 cups milk
1 cup sugar	Ground nutmeg
1½ cups bourbon	1 cup heavy or whipping
½ cup brandy	cream

1 In large bowl with mixer at low speed, beat egg yolks with sugar. At high speed, beat until thick and lemon-colored, about 15 minutes, frequently scraping bowl. Carefully beat in bourbon and brandy, one tablespoon at a time, to prevent curdling mixture. Cover and chill.

2 About 20 minutes before serving: In chilled 5 to 6-quart punch bowl, stir yolk mixture, milk, and 1¼ teaspoons nutmeg.

3 In large bowl with mixer at high speed, beat egg whites until soft peaks form. In small bowl, using same beaters, with mixer at medium speed, beat cream until stiff peaks form.

4 Gently fold egg whites and cream into yolk mixture until just blended; sprinkle with nutmeg.

Planning Ahead

Up to 1 month ahead:	Bake the fruitcake; wrap and refrigerate until ready to serve.
Up to 1 week ahead:	Bake and decorate cookies. Make fudge; store in containers with tight-fitting lids.
Early in day:	Make Eggnog, cover and refrigerate. Make meatballs but do not broil; cover and refrigerate. Make Ham and Cheese Cups. Make Pig-in-a-Blanket but do not bake; cover and refrigerate.
1½ hours ahead:	Prepare sandwiches; cover with plastic wrap. Bake Pig-in-a-Blanket; keep in a warm oven. Broil meatballs.

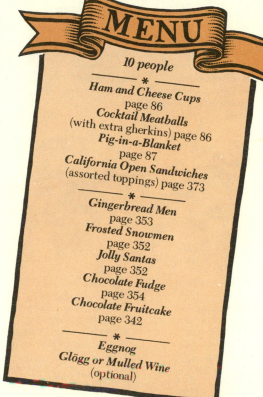

MENU

10 people

*

Ham and Cheese Cups
page 86
Cocktail Meatballs
(with extra gherkins) page 86
Pig-in-a-Blanket
page 87
California Open Sandwiches
(assorted toppings) page 373

*

Gingerbread Men
page 353
Frosted Snowmen
page 352
Jolly Santas
page 352
Chocolate Fudge
page 354
Chocolate Fruitcake
page 342

—

*

Eggnog
Glögg or Mulled Wine
(optional)

MAKING COOKIE ORNAMENTS
Before baking, make a hole in the top of each cookie, using a small plain tube. Thread with ribbon after cooling.

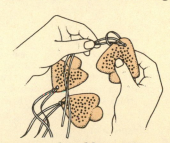

Threading the ribbon: Fold ribbon in half; gently push folded end through hole.

Knotting the ribbon: Take the loose ends through the folded loop and gently pull.

Wrapping the cookies: Fill boxes or tins with cookies, separating layers with colorful tissue paper; use as gifts.

Mixed vegetables

LEMON-BUTTERED VEGETABLES

This rich combination of vegetables includes Brussels sprouts, a small member of the cabbage family. The most popular American variety is the Improved Long Island.

Water
2 10-ounce containers
  Brussels sprouts
1 chicken-flavor bouillon
  cube or envelope
1 pound green beans
2 16-ounce bags medium
  carrots

2 large acorn squash
  (1 pound each)
2 pounds small white
  onions
½ cup butter or
  margarine

- *Color index page 57*
- *Begin 2 hrs ahead*
- *12 side-dish servings*
- *180 cals per serving*

2 tablespoons lemon juice
½ teaspoon savory
¼ teaspoon salt
¼ teaspoon cracked black
  pepper

1 In 5-quart Dutch oven over high heat, in 1 inch boiling water, heat Brussels sprouts and the chicken-flavor bouillon to boiling.

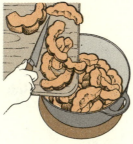

2 Reduce heat to low; cover; simmer 10 to 15 minutes until tender. With slotted spoon, remove Brussels sprouts to large pan; keep warm.

3 In broth remaining in Dutch oven over high heat, heat whole green beans to boiling. Reduce heat to low; cover; simmer 10 minutes or until tender. With slotted spoon, remove to pan with Brussels sprouts; keep warm. In broth remaining in Dutch oven over high heat, heat whole carrots to boiling. Reduce heat to low; cover; simmer 20 minutes or until tender. Remove to pan with vegetables; keep warm.

4 Cut each acorn squash lengthwise in half; remove seeds. Place halves cut side down, and cut crosswise into ½-inch-thick slices.

5 In broth remaining in Dutch oven (add more water if necessary to make 1 inch) over high heat, heat the squash slices to boiling.

6 Reduce heat to low; cover and simmer 10 minutes or until tender. With pancake turner, remove squash to pan with vegetables; keep warm.

7 Meanwhile, in 3-quart saucepan over high heat, in 1 inch boiling water, heat onions to boiling. Reduce heat to low; cover and simmer 15 to 20 minutes until onions are tender; drain. In the same saucepan over medium heat, in 2 tablespoons hot butter, cook the onions until well browned, stirring frequently. Remove onions to pan with Brussels sprouts, whole green beans, carrots, and acorn squash slices; keep warm.

8 In same saucepan over medium heat, heat remaining 6 tablespoons butter and remaining ingredients until butter melts.

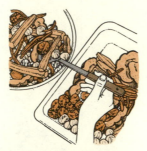

9 To serve, spoon vegetables into bowl, or arrange in piles around roasted meat or poultry. Pour butter sauce over the vegetables.

ROASTED VEGETABLE MÉLANGE

2 small yellow straight-
  neck squash (about
  6 ounces each)
2 small zucchini (about
  6 ounces each)
2 medium red peppers
2 medium yellow peppers
1 medium red onion
½ pound mushrooms

¼ cup olive or salad oil
1½ teaspoons chopped
  fresh thyme or ½
  teaspoon dried thyme
  leaves
½ teaspoon cracked
  pepper
Salt

1. Cut yellow straightneck squash, zucchini, red and yellow peppers into about 2″ by ½″ strips. Slice red onion. If mushrooms are large, cut into quarters. Place vegetables in large roasting pan.
2. Preheat oven to 400°F. To vegetables in roasting pan, add olive oil, thyme, and pepper; mix well.
3. Cook vegetables about 20 minutes or until tender-crisp, stirring occasionally. Add salt to taste.

Cutting the vegetables: With sharp knife cut squash, zucchini, and peppers into 2″ by ½″ strips.

Preparing to roast: Arrange vegetables in roasting pan; mix with olive oil, thyme and pepper.

- *Color index page 57*
- *Begin 50 mins ahead*

- *8 side-dish servings*
- *105 cals per serving*

VEGETABLES AND DILL

1 6-ounce jar marinated
  artichoke hearts
3 medium tomatoes, each
  cut into quarters
2 small zucchini (about
  6 ounces each), thinly
  sliced
2 small yellow straight-
  neck squash (about
  6 ounces each), thinly
  sliced

1 tablespoon minced fresh
  dill or 1 teaspoon dill
  weed
2 teaspoons lemon juice
½ teaspoon salt
¼ teaspoon sugar
Fresh dill weed for
  garnish

1. In 12-inch skillet over medium heat, cook all ingredients until vegetables are tender-crisp, about 5 minutes, stirring occasionally.
2. To serve, spoon into heated serving dish and garnish with fresh dill weed.

- *Color index page 57*
- *Begin 45 minutes ahead*

- *6 side-dish servings*
- *150 cals per serving*

VEGETABLE BOUQUET

1 medium carrot
2 medium turnips, peeled
Water
¼ pound green beans,
*   ends trimmed*

¼ teaspoon salt
1 tablespoon butter or
*   margarine*
Fresh mint to garnish

1. Cut carrots diagonally into ¼-inch slices; cut turnips into quarters.
2. In 3-quart saucepan over high heat, in 1-inch boiling water, heat turnips and salt to boiling. Reduce heat to medium; cover and cook 5 minutes.
3. Add carrot slices and green beans; over high heat, heat to boiling. Reduce heat to low; cover and simmer 10 minutes longer.
4. Drain vegetables; return to saucepan and stir in butter. Garnish with fresh mint.

- *Color index page 57*
- *Begin 25 minutes ahead*
- *4 side-dish servings*
- *62 cals per serving*

HOW TO MAKE VEGETABLE PURÉES

Quick and easy to make, vegetable purées offer a good way to use fresh and left-over vegetables. Hard vegetables such as carrots and parsnips should be cooked until tender (not crisp); soft vegetables should be cooked in a little butter until tender.

Cook vegetables until tender; drain well and pass through a food mill, or purée in a blender or food processor. Add a small amount of butter or cream, season, and serve as a vegetable or fill Artichoke Bottoms (p.229) with purée to garnish meats or poultry.

Stir a spoonful into scrambled eggs, or fill an omelet, or add a spoonful to a Thick White Sauce (p.113) for extra flavor.

BROILED LEEKS, SWEET PEPPERS, AND MUSHROOMS

These marinated vegetables make a delicious accompaniment to roast chicken or lamb, and can be prepared ahead. Be sure to rinse leeks well to remove sand.

6 large leeks
6 large peppers (red,
*   yellow and/or green)*
Salt
6 jumbo mushrooms
¾ cup olive or salad oil

¼ cup tarragon vinegar
1 tablespoon minced fresh
*   oregano or 1 teaspoon*
*   dried oregano leaves*

1 teaspoon sugar
1 teaspoon coarsely
*   ground black pepper*

- *Color index page 57*
- *Begin 4 hrs ahead*
  or early in day
- *6 side-dish servings*
- *180 cals per serving*

1 Cut off roots and trim leaf ends of leeks. Cut the leeks lengthwise in half to within 2 inches of the root ends.

2 Separate leaves slightly; rinse with running cold water to wash away sand and grit. Cut each pepper lengthwise in half; discard seeds.

3 Parboil vegetables: In 8-quart saucepot over high heat, in 2 inches boiling water, heat the leeks and 2 teaspoons salt to boiling.

4 Reduce heat to low; cover; simmer 5 to 10 minutes until leeks are tender. With tongs, remove leeks to large roasting pan or baking dish.

5 Add peppers to saucepot; over high heat, heat to boiling. Reduce heat to low; cover; simmer 5 to 10 minutes until tender-crisp.

6 Remove to same roasting pan. Add mushrooms, olive oil, vinegar, oregano, sugar, pepper, and 1 teaspoon salt. Mix well.

7 Cover vegetables in roasting pan and refrigerate at least 2 hours, turning vegetables occasionally to coat with the marinade.

8 *About 40 minutes before serving:* Preheat broiler if manufacturer directs; remove vegetables to rack in broiling pan.

9 About 7 to 9 inches from source of heat, broil 10 minutes or until heated through, turning and brushing with the marinade occasionally.

Mixed vegetables

SKILLET BRAISED ENDIVE AND RADICCHIO

Belgian endive and radicchio are types of chicory with a slightly bitter flavor; they are delicious braised as well as in salads.

- Color index page 57
- Begin 25 mins ahead
- 6 side-dish servings
- 105 cals per serving

4 slices bacon
3 large heads Belgian endive
2 medium heads radicchio

⅛ teaspoon pepper
Salt

1 In 12-inch skillet over medium-low heat, cook bacon until browned. Remove bacon to paper towels to drain; crumble bacon.

2 Meanwhile, remove a few outside leaves from the endive and the radicchio heads for garnish. Cut each endive lengthwise in half; cut the radicchio into wedges.

3 In hot bacon drippings remaining in skillet over medium heat, cook endive and radicchio, covered, 15 minutes or until lightly browned and tender.

4 Turn vegetables occasionally and sprinkle vegetables with pepper and salt to taste.

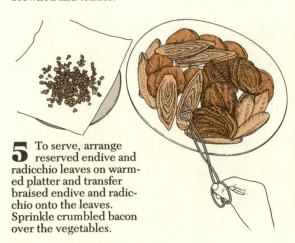

5 To serve, arrange reserved endive and radicchio leaves on warmed platter and transfer braised endive and radicchio onto the leaves. Sprinkle crumbled bacon over the vegetables.

Sauces

SAUCES FOR VEGETABLES

Vegetables can be delicious prepared on their own, but sometimes a sauce can add a new zest.

SOUR-CREAM MUSTARD SAUCE: In small saucepan over very low heat, heat *1 cup sour cream* with *1 tablespoon minced onion, 1 tablespoon prepared mustard, ¼ teaspoon salt*, and *dash pepper* just until hot. Sprinkle with *1 tablespoon chopped parsley* before serving. Makes about 1 cup. 32 cals per tablespoon.

LEMON BUTTER: In small saucepan over medium heat, melt *¼ cup butter* or *margarine*; stir in *1 tablespoon lemon juice, 1 tablespoon chopped parsley, ½ teaspoon salt*, and *dash cayenne*. (Or, in a small bowl, with spoon, stir butter or margarine until creamy. Slowly stir in the rest of the ingredients.) Serve hot on hot cooked vegetables. Makes about ⅓ cup. 90 cals per tablespoon.

FINE HERBS: Prepare as above but substitute *3 tablespoons dry white wine* for lemon juice; add *2 tablespoons chopped chives* and *1 teaspoon chopped fresh dill*. Makes about ⅓ cup. 95 cals per tablespoon.

BUTTER SAUCE FOR VEGETABLES: Into measuring cup, pour liquid from vegetables; measure and return to vegetables in pan. For each ½ cup liquid (add water to make ½ cup if necessary), in another cup, stir *1 tablespoon butter* or *margarine* and *1 tablespoon flour* to make smooth paste. Stir mixture into vegetables and liquid; over medium heat, cook, stirring gently, until sauce is thickened and smooth. Add *salt* and *pepper* to taste. Makes about ½ cup. 19 cals per tablespoon.

COLD CHIFFON SAUCE: In heavy, 1-quart saucepan over low heat, melt *2 tablespoons butter* or *margarine*. Add *2 tablespoons all-purpose flour, ½ teaspoon salt, ⅛ teaspoon pepper, ⅛ teaspoon paprika* to butter. Over low heat, stir together until smooth. Gradually stir in *1 cup milk* or *half-and-half*; cook stirring constantly, until thickened and smooth; remove from heat. Separate *1 egg* and in cup, beat egg yolk with fork; pour the beaten egg yolk into the hot sauce, stirring rapidly until blended; let stand for 10 minutes. Stir in *2 tablespoons cider vinegar* and *1 teaspoon tarragon*; cool 1 hour. In small bowl, with mixer at high speed, beat egg white and *¼ teaspoon salt* until stiff peaks form. With rubber spatula, fold beaten white into sauce. Cover sauce and refrigerate. Spoon sauce over cold cooked vegetables. Makes 1⅓ cups. 25 cals per tablespoon.

MORNAY SAUCE: In 2-quart saucepan over medium heat, melt *3 tablespoons butter* or *margarine*; with wooden spoon, stir *2 tablespoons all-purpose flour* into butter until smooth. Gradually stir in *1 cup chicken broth* and *1 cup half-and-half* and cook, stirring, until sauce is thickened; remove pan from heat. In a small bowl with wire whisk or fork, beat *1 egg yolk* slightly; then beat into egg yolk a small amount of hot sauce. Slowly pour egg mixture back into hot sauce, stirring vigorously to prevent the sauce from lumping. Add *½ cup shredded natural Swiss cheese* and *¼ cup grated Parmesan cheese* and cook over low heat, stirring constantly, just until thickened (do not boil). Serve hot on cooked vegetables. Makes about 2⅓ cups. 28 cals per tablespoon.

PASTA AND RICE

"Red beans and ricely yours"

LOUIS ARMSTRONG signed his letters this way

It was probably Thomas Jefferson who started America's love affair with pasta when he sent to Naples for a macaroni machine (he received a spaghetti machine instead). In 1802, he served his dinner guests a macaroni pie with Parmesan cheese, an early macaroni and cheese casserole. By 1848, America's first pasta factory was opened by Antoine Zerega in Brooklyn, New York. He used horse-drawn machinery and hung the pasta on the roof to dry.

Throughout the 19th century all pasta was called macaroni regardless of its shape, and was a luxury. Italian immigrants popularized pasta in America; for them, it was a link with the homeland. World War II put a stop to imports, but brought about the growth of the American pasta industry.

Durum wheat is the essential ingredient in pasta; when ground, it is called semolina and has a granular consistency which gives the pasta its firm texture. Mark Carleton planted its seed in North Dakota in 1898; 95 per cent of it is now grown there.

By the 1950s, pasta dishes such as our Lasagna and Cannelloni were standard party fare. Mario Lanza used to make his own spaghetti at his dinner parties and claimed it was the one thing that made him sing!

Traditionally, long pasta is served with tomato or seafood sauces, such as our Spaghetti with Meatballs and Linguine with Red Mussel Sauce; short pasta goes best with meaty or creamy sauces, such as our Ziti with Hearty Meat Sauce and Creamy Cappelletti. Pasta is nourishing, non-fattening, inexpensive, easy to prepare, and is now an all-American tradition.

There are many stories accounting for the introduction of rice to America; it was sown as early as 1647 and South Carolina soon became the leading producer of long-grain rice. During the Revolution the British captured Charleston and shipped the entire rice crop home, leaving no seed behind. Again it was Thomas Jefferson who managed to bring some Italian rice seed back to the Carolinas. For generations rice was a staple part of the American diet. In the South, dishes such as Red Beans and Rice, Hoppin' John and Tex-Mex Style Rice were produced; the Chinese popularized rice dishes such as Pork Fried Rice. Rice combines easily with fruit and nuts as in our Rice and Fruit Ring and can make a simple yet elegant dish.

Wild rice, a tall grass with a nutty flavor, grows mostly in Minnesota where it is still harvested in canoes by Indians using traditional methods.

Although not native to America, both pasta and rice have become associated with many of our best-loved specialties.

SPAGHETTI HELPERS

Spaghetti is one of America's most popular pastas; certain hints and gadgets make cooking it a lot easier. Always add pasta to boiling water gradually so water does not stop boiling.

Spaghetti Measure: Helps estimate the amount of spaghetti per person if the hole corresponding to the servings required is used.

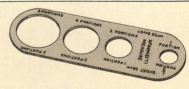

Spaghetti Fork: A wooden fork with pegs to separate the pasta.

Large Deep Pasta Pot: Capable of holding at least 8 cups of water for every 8 ounces of pasta.

Oil: A small amount of oil added to the water prevents pasta from sticking.

Colander: A large colander makes the draining safer and easier.

Pasta

BAKED MACARONI AND CHEESE

- Color index page 62
- Begin 45 mins ahead
- 4 main-dish servings
- 652 cals per serving

1 8-ounce package elbow macaroni
4 tablespoons butter or margarine
¾ cup fresh bread crumbs
1 small onion, minced
1 tablespoon all-purpose flour
1 teaspoon salt
¼ teaspoon dry mustard
Dash pepper
1½ cups milk
2 4-ounce packages shredded Cheddar cheese (2 cups)

1. Cook macaroni as label directs; drain. Preheat oven to 350°F. Grease 2-quart casserole. In small saucepan over medium heat, melt 2 tablespoons butter; add bread crumbs; toss to coat; set aside.
2. Meanwhile, in medium saucepan over medium heat, melt remaining 2 tablespoons butter; add onion and cook until tender, about 5 minutes. Stir in flour, salt, mustard, and pepper until blended. Slowly stir in milk; cook until smooth and slightly thickened, stirring constantly. Remove from heat; stir in cheese until melted.
3. Place drained macaroni in casserole. Pour cheese mixture over macaroni. Sprinkle reserved crumb mixture over top.
4. Bake 20 minutes or until bubbly and bread crumbs are golden.

Tossing bread crumbs: Add the bread crumbs to 2 tablespoons melted butter and toss to coat well.

Assembling the casserole: Place drained macaroni in dish; add cheese mixture; sprinkle with crumbs.

SPAGHETTI SAUCE

- Color index page 62
- Begin 1 hr ahead
- 4 cups
- 364 cals per cup

2 tablespoons salad oil
1 medium onion, diced
1 medium garlic clove, minced
2 15-ounce cans tomato sauce
1 12-ounce can tomato paste
2 teaspoons brown sugar
2 tablespoons chopped parsley
1 teaspoon oregano leaves
1 teaspoon salt
⅛ teaspoon cracked pepper
1 bay leaf

1. In 3-quart saucepan over medium heat, in hot salad oil, cook onion and garlic until tender, stirring frequently, about 10 minutes.
2. Add tomato sauce and remaining ingredients; over high heat, heat to boiling.
3. Reduce heat to medium-low; partially cover and cook 30 minutes. Discard bay leaf.

SPAGHETTI AND MEATBALLS

Spaghetti, topped with tender meatballs and a zesty tomato sauce, has become an all-American favorite family meal.

- Color index page 62
- Begin 2¼ hrs ahead
- 6 main-dish servings
- 797 cals per serving

Spaghetti Sauce (left)
1½ pounds lean ground beef
1 cup fresh bread crumbs
1 egg
½ teaspoon oregano leaves
⅛ teaspoon pepper
Salt
Salad oil
4 quarts water
1 16-ounce package spaghetti
Grated Parmesan cheese

1 Prepare Spaghetti Sauce. Prepare meatballs: In large bowl, combine ground beef, bread crumbs, egg, oregano, pepper, and 2 teaspoons salt.

2 With hands, shape mixture into 1-inch balls. In 12-inch skillet over medium-high heat, in 2 tablespoons oil, cook meatballs until browned.

3 Spoon off drippings from the skillet. Add Spaghetti Sauce; heat to boiling. Reduce heat to low; cover; simmer for 10 minutes.

4 Meanwhile, in 8-quart saucepot, heat to boiling water and 2 teaspoons salt. Add spaghetti; cook until spaghetti is tender but firm (al dente).

5 Drain spaghetti in colander. Toss with 1 tablespoon oil to prevent spaghetti sticking.

6 Arrange on warm plate. Serve the meatballs and sauce over spaghetti. Pass grated Parmesan cheese.

Pasta

LINGUINE WITH RED MUSSEL SAUCE

In season, sweet plump mussels can be found all along the east coast from Maine to South Carolina. As with other seafood, they make a tasty sauce for linguine.

- Color index page 62
- Begin 40 mins ahead
- 6 main-dish servings
- 425 cals per serving

2 dozen large mussels
Water
2 tablespoons salad oil
1 medium onion, chopped
1 garlic clove, crushed
1 14½- to 16-ounce can tomatoes

1 6-ounce can tomato paste
3 tablespoons chopped parsley
2 tablespoons dry white wine

1½ teaspoons salt
1 teaspoon sugar
¼ teaspoon crushed red pepper
1 16-ounce package linguine

1 With stiff brush, scrub mussels with running cold water; remove beards. In 5-quart saucepot or Dutch oven over high heat, heat mussels and 1 inch water to boiling.

2 Reduce heat to medium-low; cover and cook until mussel shells open, about 5 minutes (discard any that do not open).

3 Discard shells from mussels; rinse the mussels in cooking broth to remove any sand.

4 Chop mussels; set aside. Let broth stand until sand settles to bottom of saucepot. Reserve ¾ cup clear broth; set aside.

5 Meanwhile, in 4-quart saucepan over medium heat, in hot salad oil, cook onion and garlic until tender.

6 Add reserved mussel broth, tomatoes with their liquid, and next 6 ingredients, stirring to break up tomatoes.

7 Over high heat, heat to boiling. Reduce heat to low; cover and simmer 15 minutes, stirring occasionally.

8 While sauce is simmering, prepare linguine as label directs; drain completely.

9 To serve, stir mussels into tomato sauce; heat through. Serve mussel sauce over the linguine.

LINGUINE WITH SPICY EGGPLANT SAUCE

1 pound hot or sweet Italian sausage links
¼ cup olive or salad oil
1 medium eggplant (about 1½ pounds), diced

2 tablespoons water
½ 16-ounce package linguine
½ cup minced parsley

1. Remove sausage meat from casings. In 4-quart saucepan over medium-high heat, in hot olive oil, cook the sausage meat until browned, stirring frequently to break up the sausage meat. With a slotted spoon, remove the sausage meat to a bowl. Set aside.
2. In the drippings remaining in the saucepan over medium heat, cook the diced eggplant and water until the eggplant is very tender, 10 to 15 minutes, stirring frequently.
3. Meanwhile, in a saucepot, prepare linguine as label directs. Drain; return to saucepot; keep the linguine warm.
4. When the eggplant is done, add it to the linguine in the saucepot with the minced parsley and the sausage meat; toss to mix well. Transfer to large warmed bowl and serve.

- Color index page 62
- Begin 1 hr ahead
- 4 main-dish servings
- 655 cals per serving

LINGUINE WITH WHITE CLAM SAUCE

Drain juice from *3 8-ounce cans of minced clams*, reserving juice. In 2-quart saucepan over medium heat, in *¼ cup hot olive* or *salad oil*, cook *1 clove garlic*, minced, until tender. Stir in reserved clam juice and *¾ cup chopped parsley*, *2 tablespoons white wine* (optional), *1 teaspoon basil*, and *½ teaspoon salt*. Cook sauce 10 minutes, stirring occasionally. Meanwhile, in saucepot, prepare *1 16-ounce package linguine* as step 3 above. When sauce is ready, stir in clams; cook sauce just until clams are heated through. Add to linguine in saucepot; toss to mix well. Makes 4 main-dish servings. 350 cals per serving.

ANGEL'S HAIR PASTA WITH FETA

½ 16-ounce package angel's hair pasta or cappellini
3 tablespoons olive or salad oil
1 medium tomato, diced

1 8-ounce package feta cheese, crumbled
1 3.2-ounce can (drained weight) pitted ripe olives, drained and each cut into quarters

1. In saucepot, prepare pasta as label directs. Drain; return to saucepot.
2. Add olive oil and tomato to pasta in saucepot; cook over medium heat until hot, gently tossing pasta with 2 forks. Add feta and olives; heat through. Transfer to large warmed bowl.

- Color index page 62
- Begin 20 mins ahead
- 6 side-dish servings
- 330 cals per serving

ZITI WITH HEARTY HOME-STYLE MEAT SAUCE

3 tablespoons olive or salad oil
2 tablespoons butter or margarine
2 tablespoons chopped parsley
1 medium onion, diced
1 large carrot, coarsely shredded (1 cup)
1 pound beef chuck shoulder steak, boneless, finely chopped

⅔ cup milk
1 28-ounce can tomatoes
1½ teaspoons salt
¾ teaspoon sugar
½ teaspoon cracked pepper
1 16-ounce package ziti macaroni

1. In heavy 4-quart saucepan over medium heat in hot oil and butter, cook parsley, onion, and carrot until tender; stir occasionally.
2. Add chopped chuck shoulder steak and cook just until meat loses its pink color.
3. Increase heat to medium-high. Add milk and continue cooking until it evaporates; stir often.
4. Stir in tomatoes with their liquid and next 3 ingredients; over high heat, heat to boiling. Reduce heat to low; simmer, uncovered, 1½ hours or until meat is very tender, stirring occasionally. Skim off fat from sauce, if necessary.
5. Meanwhile, prepare ziti as label directs. Drain. Serve meat sauce over ziti.

- Color index page 62
- Begin 2¼ hrs ahead
- 6 main-dish servings
- 595 cals per serving

FETTUCCINE ALFREDO

Homemade Pasta Dough (right)
6 quarts water
1 tablespoon salad oil
Salt
1 cup heavy or whipping cream
Grated Parmesan cheese

6 tablespoons butter or margarine
¼ teaspoon cracked pepper
Fresh basil leaves for garnish.

1. About 2½ hours before serving: Prepare Homemade Pasta Dough, steps 1 to 6 for fettuccine noodles.
2. About 25 minutes before serving: Cook fettuccine noodles. In 8-quart saucepot over high heat, heat water, oil, and 1 teaspoon salt to boiling. Add noodles; with long fork, gently stir to separate noodles; heat to boiling. Reduce heat to medium; cook 3 minutes or until tender but firm (al dente). Drain.
3. Return noodles to saucepot; over low heat, gently toss noodles with heavy or whipping cream, ½ cup Parmesan cheese, butter, ½ teaspoon salt, and cracked pepper until butter melts and mixture is heated through.
4. Serve immediately. Pass more Parmesan cheese, if you like. Garnish with fresh basil.

- Color index page 62
- Begin 3½ hrs ahead
- 4 main-dish servings
- 866 cals per serving

HOMEMADE PASTA DOUGH

Italian influence made pasta an everyday American dish, but noodles are also part of our Dutch, German, and Middle European heritage. This dough is easy to make.

2¼ to 2½ cups all-purpose flour
⅓ cup water (if using pasta machine, follow manufacturer's directions)

2 eggs
1 egg yolk
1 tablespoon olive or salad oil
1 teaspoon salt
6 quarts water

- Color index page 62
- Begin 2½ hrs ahead
- 1 pound pasta dough
- 1593 cals

1 teaspoon salt
1 tablespoon salad oil

1 In large bowl, combine 1 cup flour and remaining ingredients. With mixer at low speed, beat 2 minutes, occasionally scraping the side of the bowl.

2 With wooden spoon, stir in enough additional flour to make a soft dough.

3 Turn dough onto lightly floured surface, knead until smooth and elastic, about 10 minutes. Cover dough and let rest 30 minutes.

4 Cut dough in half. On floured surface with floured rolling pin, roll half of dough into 20" by 14" rectangle; fold in half crosswise and fold in half again to form 5" by 14" rectangle.

5 For fettuccine, cut into ¼-inch strips or for wide noodles, cut ½-inch strips. Open the dough strips and place them in a single layer on clean cloth towels.

6 Repeat with remaining dough. Let the strips dry at least 1 hour before cooking them.

7 About 25 minutes before serving: In 8-quart saucepot over high heat, heat to boiling water, salt and oil.

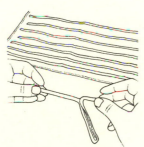

8 Break noodles in smaller lengths, if desired, and add to saucepot; stir to separate noodles, heat to boiling.

9 Reduce heat to medium; cook 3 minutes until tender but firm; drain. Serve with any Sauce for Pasta (p.265).

Pasta

CREAMY CAPPELLETTI

Cappelletti, "little caps" traditionally stuffed with chicken, scoop up the creamy sauce in this classical dish. The whole family can help form the pasta, but children, with their slim fingers, are ideal for shaping the "hats."

Salad oil
2 whole small chicken breasts, skinned, boned, and diced (about 3 cups)
¼ pound sliced prosciutto, mortadella, or cooked ham, cut up.

Salt
1 egg
⅛ teaspoon pepper
⅛ teaspoon ground nutmeg
Homemade Pasta Dough (p.261)
Water

- Color index page 62
- Begin 3 hrs ahead
- 5 main-dish servings
- 840 cals per serving

1 cup heavy or whipping cream
1 cup grated Parmesan cheese
½ cup butter or margarine, softened

1 In 10-inch skillet over medium-high heat, in 1 tablespoon hot salad oil, cook the diced chicken breast, stirring frequently, about 5 minutes or until tender. Remove the skillet from heat. In blender at medium speed, or in food processor with knife blade attached, finely grind the cooked chicken and prosciutto ham. Scrape side of blender or bowl occasionally.

2 Taste and add salt if needed. Add egg, pepper, and nutmeg; grind until paste forms; cover and refrigerate.

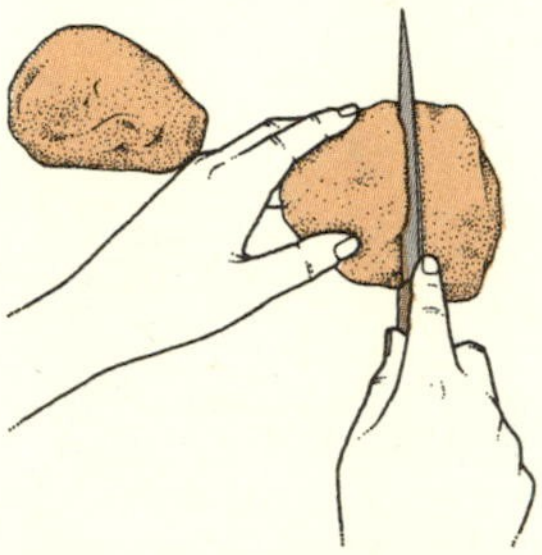

3 Prepare Homemade Pasta Dough, steps 1 to 3. Cut into 3 pieces. Cover 2 pieces with plastic wrap; set aside.

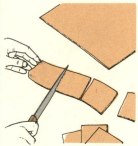

4 On floured surface with floured rolling pin, roll first piece of dough into a 26" by 8" rectangle. Cut into 2-inch squares.

5 Place scant ½ teaspoon chicken filling in center of each square; brush edges with water. Fold each in half to make a triangle; press to seal.

6 To shape, place folded edges of dough at right angle to finger; bend around finger until 2 ends meet; press ends to seal.

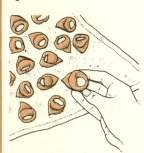

7 Place cappelletti in single layer on floured clean cloth towel. Repeat with remaining dough and filling.

8 For easier handling, let cappelletti dry 30 minutes before cooking. To cook, about 30 minutes before serving, in 8-quart saucepot over high heat, heat 5 quarts water and 2 teaspoons salt if desired to boiling. Add cappelletti; with spoon, stir gently to separate pieces. Heat to boiling. Reduce heat to medium; cook until cappelletti are tender but firm (al dente), about 5 minutes; drain the cappelletti.

9 Return to saucepot; over medium-low heat, toss with cream, Parmesan cheese, butter, and salt to taste.

CANNELLONI

Homemade Pasta Dough (p.261)
2 tablespoons butter or margarine
1 tablespoon chopped green onion
1 10-ounce package frozen spinach, thawed and squeezed dry
1 cup finely chopped cooked chicken
½ cup finely chopped cooked ham

Grated Parmesan cheese
1 tablespoon dry sherry
¼ teaspoon ground ginger
1 egg, beaten
Salt
5 quarts water
1 tablespoon salad oil
Parmesan-Cheese Sauce (below)
Chopped parsley

1. Prepare Homemade Pasta Dough, steps 1 to 3. Cut dough into 3 pieces; on well-floured surface with floured rolling pin, roll 1 piece of dough into 16" by 8" rectangle. Cut the rectangle into 8 4-inch squares.

2. Place squares on floured, clean, cloth towel. Repeat with remaining dough, making 24 squares in all. Cover with plastic wrap; set pasta squares aside to rest at least 1 hour. Meanwhile prepare the cannelloni filling.

3. Prepare filling: In a 2-quart saucepan over medium heat, in hot butter, cook green onion until tender. Stir in the spinach, cooked chicken, cooked ham, ½ cup Parmesan cheese, dry sherry, ground ginger, beaten egg, and ¼ teaspoon salt; heat through.

4. Remove from heat and set mixture aside. Grease 13" by 9" baking pan or broiler-safe baking dish; set aside.

5. In 8-quart saucepot, heat water, salad oil, and 1 teaspoon salt to boiling. Add a few squares of pasta at a time and cook 5 minutes. With slotted spoon, remove the pasta squares to colander to drain.

6. While the squares are still warm, assemble cannelloni: With spoon, spread rounded tablespoon of filling across center of each square. Roll squares jelly-roll fashion; place, seam side down, in pan.

7. Preheat oven to 350°F. Prepare Parmesan-Cheese Sauce. Pour sauce over cannelloni; sprinkle with chopped parsley. Bake cannelloni 20 minutes.

8. Turn oven control to broil. Remove baking pan to broiler and broil 5 minutes or until sauce is browned and bubbly. Serve cannelloni very hot and, if you like, pass additional grated Parmesan cheese separately.

PARMESAN-CHEESE SAUCE: In 2-quart saucepan over medium heat, melt *4 tablespoons butter* or *margarine*. Stir in *¼ cup all-purpose flour* until blended; cook 1 minute. Gradually stir in *3 cups milk* and *2 chicken-flavor bouillon cubes* or *envelopes*. Cook, stirring constantly, until sauce thickens. Stir in *½ cup grated Parmesan cheese* until cheese melts.

- Color index page 62
- Begin 3 hrs ahead
- 4 main-dish servings
- 1003 cals per serving

JUMBO RAVIOLI WITH SWISS CHARD

- Color index page 63
- Begin 2¼ hrs ahead
- 3 main-dish servings
- 835 cals per serving

Homemade Pasta Dough (p.261)	¼ teaspoon pepper
Butter or margarine	2 eggs
1 small onion, minced	Grated Parmesan cheese
1 pound Swiss chard	Lemon juice to taste
Water	2 teaspoons dried bread
⅔ cup ricotta cheese	crumbs

1. Prepare Homemade Pasta Dough steps 1 to 3. Refrigerate dough for 30 minutes.
2. Meanwhile, prepare filling: In 4-quart saucepan over medium heat, in 1 tablespoon hot butter, cook onion until tender. Spoon into medium bowl.
3. In same saucepan over high heat, heat Swiss chard and 1 inch water to boiling. Reduce heat to low; cover and simmer 10 minutes. Drain; let cool until easy to handle. Finely chop; squeeze dry. Place Swiss chard in bowl with onion; stir in ricotta cheese, pepper, eggs, and ¼ cup grated Parmesan cheese.
4. Divide dough into 4 equal pieces; place 1 piece dough on lightly floured surface (keep remaining dough in plastic wrap). With floured rolling pin, roll dough into 15″ by 6″ rectangle.
5. With ravioli cutter or knife, cut rectangle crosswise into five 6″ by 3″ strips. For each ravioli, place 1 tablespoon Swiss-chard filling near a short end of a dough strip.
6. Moisten edges of dough with water; fold opposite end of strip over to enclose filling. With fork dipped in flour, press edges together to seal. Repeat with remaining dough and filling.
7. In 8-quart saucepot or Dutch oven over high heat, in 3 inches boiling water, cook the ravioli 2 minutes; drain completely; place the ravioli in a large bowl.
8. Meanwhile, in 1-quart saucepan over low heat, heat 4 tablespoons butter and lemon juice until butter melts. Pour sauce over ravioli.
9. Sprinkle bread crumbs and 2 tablespoons grated Parmesan cheese over ravioli. If you like, pass additional grated Parmesan cheese.

CHEESE FILLING: In small bowl, combine *1¼ cups ricotta cheese* with *¼ cup minced parsley*, *2 teaspoons grated onion*, *½ teaspoon salt*, and *1 egg*. Mix well.

MEAT FILLING: In 10-inch skillet over medium-high heat, cook *½ pound ground beef*, *⅓ cup minced onion*, *1 garlic clove*, minced, until meat is browned; remove from heat; spoon off juices. Stir in *1 egg*, *¼ cup minced parsley*, *2 tablespoons grated Parmesan cheese*, and *½ teaspoon salt*. Stir ingredients until well mixed.

SPINACH FILLING: In small bowl, combine *one 10-ounce package frozen chopped spinach*, thawed and well drained, *⅓ cup grated Parmesan cheese*, *2 egg yolks*, *1 tablespoon butter*, softened, *¼ teaspoon salt*, *⅛ teaspoon pepper*, *⅛ teaspoon ground nutmeg*. Stir ingredients until well mixed.

CHEESE-FILLED MANICOTTI

Jumbo manicotti, stuffed with fresh ricotta and melting mozzarella, and baked with a zesty sauce make a satisfying meatless meal.

- Color index page 62
- Begin 1¼ hrs ahead
- 7 main-dish servings
- 633 cals per serving

2 15- to 16-ounce containers ricotta cheese (4 cups)	Salt
	Pepper
1 8-ounce package mozzarella cheese, shredded	1 8-ounce package manicotti shells
2 eggs	4 tablespoons butter or margarine
Grated Romano cheese	2 tablespoons all-purpose flour
Chopped parsley	2 cups milk

1 In large bowl, mix ricotta cheese, mozzarella cheese, eggs, ¼ cup grated Romano cheese, 2 tablespoons chopped parsley, ½ teaspoon salt, and ½ teaspoon pepper; set aside.

2 Cook manicotti as label directs. Drain immediately under running warm tap water to stop cooking (do not use cold water; it will cause shells to break); drain again.

3 Meanwhile, prepare sauce: In 1-quart saucepan over medium heat, melt the butter; stir in the flour, ¼ teaspoon salt, and ¼ teaspoon pepper; stir until well blended. Gradually stir in the milk; cook over medium heat until slightly thickened, stirring constantly. Stir in 3 tablespoons of grated Romano cheese. Spoon half of sauce into 13″ by 9″ baking dish; spread evenly over bottom.

4 Preheat oven to 375°F. Using pastry bag without tip, or with spoon, fill manicotti shells with cheese mixture.

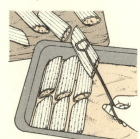

5 Arrange filled shells in baking dish over sauce in one layer. Spoon remaining sauce over manicotti.

6 Bake 25 minutes or until mixture is hot and bubbly. If you like, garnish with some chopped parsley.

Pasta

VEGETABLE LASAGNA

Shortly after World War II, layered lasagna became a popular party dish. Use fresh vegetables for this tasty version of the dish.

1 head green cabbage (about 2½ pounds)
2 yellow straight-neck squash (about 6 ounces each)
⅓ cup salad oil
1 15-ounce can tomato sauce
1 6-ounce can tomato paste
½ cup water

1½ teaspoons sugar
1½ teaspoons minced fresh basil or ½ teaspoon dried basil
¾ teaspoon salt
¼ teaspoon pepper
2 medium tomatoes, chopped
1 15- to 16-ounce container ricotta cheese

1 pound Monterey Jack cheese, shredded (4 cups)
2 eggs
⅔ 16-ounce package lasagna noodles (about 14 noodles)

- *Color index page 63*
- *Begin 2½ hrs ahead*
- *10 main-dish servings*
- *505 cals per serving*

1 Remove core from green cabbage; separate cabbage leaves; cut and discard tough ribs from leaves. Thinly slice cabbage leaves and yellow squash. In 12-inch skillet over medium heat, in hot salad oil, cook the cabbage 10 minutes or until it is tender-crisp. Add the squash and cook 10 minutes longer or until the squash slices and cabbage slices are tender; remove the skillet from the heat.

2 In 2-quart saucepan, heat tomato sauce and next 7 ingredients to boiling. Reduce heat to medium; cook 15 minutes.

3 In medium bowl, mix cheese and eggs; set aside. Prepare lasagna noodles as label directs; drain.

4 Preheat oven to 350°F. Into 13" by 9" baking dish, evenly spoon 1⅓ cups tomato-sauce mixture.

5 Arrange half of lasagna noodles over sauce, overlapping to fit. Spoon over half of cheese mixture.

6 Top with all but ½ cup cabbage mixture (reserve remaining cabbage mixture to spoon on top of lasagna later).

7 Spoon half of remaining sauce over cabbage mixture; top with remaining noodles and cheese, then sauce.

8 Bake lasagna 45 minutes or until heated through; remove from oven.

9 Let lasagna stand 10 minutes for easier serving. Reheat reserved cabbage mixture; spoon on top of lasagna.

LASAGNA

1 pound ground beef
1 small onion, diced
1 28-ounce can tomatoes
1 12-ounce can tomato paste
1 tablespoon sugar
1½ teaspoons salt
½ teaspoon oregano leaves
1½ teaspoons thyme leaves
½ teaspoon crushed red pepper

¼ teaspoon garlic salt
1 bay leaf
⅔ 16-ounce package lasagna noodles (about 14 noodles)
2 eggs
1 15- to 16-ounce container ricotta cheese
1 16-ounce package mozzarella cheese, diced

1. In 5-quart Dutch oven over high heat, cook ground beef and onion until pan juices evaporate and beef is browned. Add next 9 ingredients.

2. Heat mixture to boiling, stirring to break up tomatoes. Reduce heat to low; cover; simmer 30 minutes, stirring mixture occasionally.

3. Discard bay leaf. Tilt pan and spoon off any fat which accumulates on top of sauce. Cook lasagna noodles as label directs; drain well in colander.

4. In 13" by 9" baking dish, arrange half of noodles overlapping. Preheat oven to 375°F.

5. In a small bowl with spoon, combine eggs and ricotta cheese; spoon one half over noodles.

6. Top with one half sauce and one half mozzarella. Repeat layers. Bake in oven 45 minutes. Remove from oven; let rest 10 minutes.

- *Color index page 63*
- *Begin 2½ hrs ahead*
- *8 main-dish servings*
- *601 cals per serving*

MONTEREY CHEESE LASAGNA

Marinara Sauce (p. 265)
⅔ 16-ounce package lasagna noodles
3 tablespoons butter
1 pound medium shrimp, shelled and deveined
¼ cup all-purpose flour

¼ teaspoon salt
1¼ cups milk
½ cup dry white wine
½ pound Monterey Jack cheese, diced
Chopped parsley for garnish

1. Prepare Marinara Sauce. Prepare lasagna noodles as label directs; drain. In 10-inch skillet over medium-high heat, in hot butter, cook shrimp just until pink. Remove to bowl.

2. In drippings in skillet, over medium heat, stir in flour and salt; cook 1 minute. Gradually stir in milk and wine. Cook until thickened, stirring. Remove from heat; stir in cheese until melted. Reserve 10 shrimp; chop remaining shrimp.

3. Preheat oven to 375°F. In 13" by 9" baking dish, spread ¾ cup Marinara Sauce. Arrange 4 noodles lengthwise over sauce; spread a third of cheese sauce; sprinkle with half of chopped shrimp; drizzle with a third of remaining Marinara Sauce. Repeat layering twice, except for shrimp. Cover with foil. Bake 25 minutes. Uncover; add reserved shrimp; bake 5 minutes. Let rest 10 minutes; sprinkle with parsley.

- *Color index page 62*
- *Begin 2 hrs ahead*
- *10 servings*
- *329 cals per serving*

SAUCES FOR PASTA

Piping hot pasta, tossed with a tasty sauce, is always a welcoming dish. Serve additional sauce and pass a small dish of grated cheese.

MEAT SAUCE: In 5-quart Dutch oven over medium heat, in 2 *tablespoons hot olive oil*, cook *1 pound ground beef* with *1 medium onion*, chopped, and *1 garlic clove*, minced, until meat is well browned; spoon off excess fat. Stir in *1 16-ounce can tomatoes* with their liquid and *1 12-ounce can tomato paste*. Add *4 teaspoons sugar*, *2 teaspoons oregano leaves*, *1¾ teaspoons salt*, *⅛ teaspoon cayenne pepper*, and *1 bay leaf*, crumbled. Reduce heat to low; partially cover and simmer the meat-tomato mixture 35 minutes or until very thick, stirring occasionally. Makes 4 cups. 348 cals per cup.

MARINARA SAUCE: In 2-quart saucepan over medium heat, in *2 tablespoons olive* or *salad oil*, cook *2 garlic cloves*, minced, and *1 small onion*, chopped, until tender, 5 minutes. Stir in *1 16-ounce can tomatoes* with their liquid. Add *1 6-ounce can tomato paste*, *1 tablespoon sugar*, *2 teaspoons basil*, and *1½ teaspoons salt*. Reduce heat to low; cover; cook 20 minutes or until sauce is thickened, stirring occasionally. Makes 3 cups. 171 cals per cup.

PESTO: In blender container, place *⅓ cup olive* or *salad oil* with *¼ cup grated Parmesan cheese*, *¼ cup chopped parsley*, *1 small garlic clove*, quartered, *2 tablespoons dried basil* or *½ cup fresh basil*, *1 teaspoon salt*, and *¼ teaspoon ground nutmeg*. Cover and blend at medium speed until well mixed. Makes ½ cup. 92 cals per tablespoon.

SPINACH SAUCE: In 2-quart saucepan over medium heat, in *¼ cup hot butter*, cook *1 10-ounce package frozen chopped spinach* and *1 teaspoon salt* 10 minutes. Reduce heat to low; add *1 cup ricotta cheese*, *½ cup grated Parmesan cheese*, *¼ cup milk*, and *⅛ teaspoon ground nutmeg*. Mix the sauce well; cook the sauce until it is just heated through (do not allow sauce to boil). Makes 2½ cups. 444 cals per cup.

WALNUT SAUCE: In 9-inch skillet over medium heat in *¼ cup hot butter* or *margarine*, lightly brown *1 cup walnuts*, coarsely chopped, about 5 minutes, stirring occasionally. Stir in *½ cup milk*, *2 tablespoons minced parsley*, and *1 teaspoon salt*. Heat sauce through. Makes 1⅓ cups. 1005 cals per cup.

FOUR-CHEESE SAUCE: In 3-quart saucepan over medium heat, in *¼ cup hot butter* or *margarine*, stir in *1 tablespoon all-purpose flour* until blended; cook 30 seconds. Gradually stir in *1½ cups half-and-half*; cook, stirring, until mixture boils and slightly thickens. Stir in *1 cup shredded mozzarella cheese*, *1 cup shredded fontina cheese*, *½ cup grated provolone cheese*, *¼ cup grated Parmesan cheese*, *¼ teaspoon salt*, and *¼ teaspoon cracked pepper* until smooth and cheeses are melted. Makes 4 cups. 857 cals per cup.

ANCHOVY SAUCE: in 1-quart saucepan over medium-high heat, in *¼ cup hot olive oil*, brown *1 small garlic clove*, halved. Remove from heat; discard garlic. Stir in *1 2-ounce can anchovy fillets*, drained and chopped, *2 tablespoons minced parsley*, *2 tablespoons grated Parmesan cheese*, and *1 teaspoon lemon juice*, until well mixed. Makes ½ cup, 66 cals per tablespoon.

Rice

- Color index page 63
- Begin 1 hr ahead
- 6 side-dish servings
- 340 cals per serving

RICE AND FRUIT RING

The combination of rice and fruit is often found in Middle Eastern cooking. This rice ring makes a festive addition to any meal.

1 11-ounce package mixed dried fruit
2 tablespoons butter or margarine
1 large celery stalk, diced

1½ cups regular long-grain rice
3 cups water
1½ teaspoons salt

1 Set aside 6 apricot halves and 2 prunes from mixed dried fruit for garnish.

2 Cut each of the remaining prunes in half; remove pits and dice prunes. Dice remaining dried fruit.

3 In 3-quart saucepan over medium heat, in hot butter, cook celery until tender, stirring occasionally. Add diced fruit, rice, water, and salt; over high heat, heat mixture to boiling.

4 Reduce heat to low; stir ingredients to mix well. Cover and simmer rice and fruit mixture 20 minutes or until rice is tender and all liquid is absorbed.

5 Preheat oven to 350°F. Grease 6-cup ring mold. Spoon rice mixture into mold, packing mixture lightly. Cover with foil and bake 20 minutes.

6 To serve, invert rice ring onto warm platter. Arrange 6 reserved apricot halves and 2 reserved prunes in center of rice ring.

Rice

RICE SUPPER MOLD

It was Thomas Jefferson who brought rice into the Carolinas; it became a major crop for 200 years. Italian sausage and vegetables make this a colorful one-dish meal.

*1 chicken-flavor bouillon
    cube or envelope*
Water
Butter or margarine
Salt
Pepper
*1½ cups regular long-
    grain rice*
*1 pound sweet Italian-
    sausage links*

*½ pound mushrooms,
    thinly sliced*
1 small onion, diced
1 cup milk
*1 10-ounce package
    frozen peas, thawed*
*1 4-ounce package
    shredded Cheddar
    cheese (1 cup)*

*2 4- or 1 7-ounce jar
    diced pimentos,
    drained*
*3 small zucchini, sliced
    (about 6 ounces each)*

- *Color index page 63*
- *Begin 1½ hrs ahead*
- *6 main-dish servings*
- *685 cals per serving*

1 In 4-quart saucepan over high heat, heat bouillon, 3 cups water, 1 tablespoon butter, 1 teaspoon salt, and ¼ teaspoon pepper to boiling; stir in rice. Reduce heat to low; cover; simmer 20 minutes or until rice is tender and all liquid absorbed. Meanwhile, in 10-inch skillet over medium heat, heat sausages and ¼ cup water to boiling. Reduce heat to low; cover; simmer 5 minutes. Remove cover.

2 Continue cooking, turning sausages often, until water evaporates and sausages brown, about 20 minutes.

3 Remove sausages to paper towels to drain. Cut sausages into ¼-inch-thick slices.

4 In drippings remaining in skillet over medium heat, cook mushrooms and onion, stirring occasionally.

5 Gently stir mushroom mixture, sausages, milk, peas, cheese, and pimentos into rice. Preheat oven to 350°F.

6 Grease 2½-quart heat-safe bowl. Spoon rice mixture into bowl, packing firmly. Cover bowl with foil.

7 Bake 30 minutes. Remove from oven; and let stand 5 minutes. In same skillet over medium heat, melt 3 tablespoons butter.

8 Add zucchini, ½ teaspoon salt, and ¼ teaspoon pepper; cook over medium-high heat, stirring often, until zucchini is tender-crisp.

9 To serve, with metal spatula, gently loosen rice from bowl; invert onto warm large platter. Spoon zucchini around rice.

BACON FRIED BROWN RICE

¾ cup brown rice
2 cups water
*1 8-ounce package sliced
    bacon, diced*
Salad oil

4 eggs
1 tablespoon soy sauce
*2 tablespoons chopped
    green onions*

1. In 3-quart saucepan over high heat, heat brown rice and water to boiling. Reduce heat to low; with fork, stir rice. Cover and cook about 45 minutes or until the rice is tender and all the liquid has been absorbed. Fluff the rice with a fork to separate the grains.

2. Meanwhile, in 12-inch skillet over medium-low heat, cook diced bacon until crisp and browned. With slotted spoon, remove bacon to paper towels to drain. Discard bacon fat; wipe skillet clean.

3. When the rice is done, in the same skillet over high heat, heat 2 tablespoons salad oil until very hot. In medium bowl, with fork, beat the eggs slightly.

4. Pour the egg mixture into hot oil; cook, stirring quickly and constantly with a spoon, until the eggs are the size of peas and leave the side of the skillet.

5. Reduce heat to low; gently stir in the cooked rice, bacon, soy sauce, and 1 tablespoon salad oil; heat through completely. Transfer rice mixture to warm bowls; sprinkle with green onions.

- *Color index page 63*
- *Begin 1¼ hrs ahead*
- *4 side-dish servings*
- *415 cals per serving*

PLAIN BOILED BROWN RICE: Prepare as step 1, above, but use *2½ cups water, 1 cup brown rice*, and *1 tablespoon salt.* Makes 4 cups or 5 to 6 accompaniment servings. 135 cals per serving.

HERBED ORANGE RICE

*4 tablespoons butter or
    margarine*
*⅔ cup chopped celery
    with leaves*
*2 tablespoons minced
    onion*
1½ cups water
*1 tablespoon grated
    orange peel*

1 cup orange juice
1 teaspoon salt
⅛ teaspoon thyme leaves
*1 cup regular long-grain
    rice or ¾ cup part-
    boiled rice*
*Orange sections for
    garnish (optional)*

1. In 2-quart saucepan over medium heat, in hot butter, cook celery and onion until tender, about 5 minutes.

2. Add water, grated orange peel, orange juice, salt, and thyme leaves. Heat to boiling; stir in the rice. Reduce the heat to low; cover and simmer mixture 15 to 20 minutes, or until rice is tender and all the liquid has been absorbed. Fluff the rice with a fork to separate the grains. Transfer rice to a warm bowl, garnish, and serve.

- *Color index page 63*
- *Begin 30 mins ahead*
- *4 side-dish servings*
- *315 cals per serving*

PORK FRIED RICE

1½ cups regular long-
grain rice (or 4½ cups
cold, cooked rice)
1 pound pork loin sirloin
cutlets
1 tablespoon cooking or
dry sherry
1 tablespoon soy sauce

1 teaspoon cornstarch
Salt
2 eggs
1 10-ounce package
frozen chopped
spinach, thawed and
squeezed dry
Salad oil

- Color index
  page 63
- Begin
  2½ hours
  ahead
- 4 main-dish
  servings
- 928 cals
  per serving

1. Prepare the rice as the label directs; transfer the rice to a bowl and refrigerate until the rice is completely chilled.
2. *About 30 minutes before serving:* With a sharp knife, cut the pork loin sirloin cutlets into matchstick-thin strips. In a small bowl, mix the pork strips, sherry, soy sauce, cornstarch, and 1¼ teaspoons salt; set aside. In a medium bowl with a fork, beat the eggs and ½ teaspoon salt; set aside. Mince the thawed and dried spinach; remove to bowl and set aside.
3. In a 12-inch skillet over high heat, in 2 tablespoons hot salad oil, cook the pork mixture until the pork loses its pink color, about 3 to 4 minutes; stir the pork mixture quickly and frequently. Spoon the pork mixture into a small bowl; keep warm.
4. In the same skillet over high heat, in 2 more tablespoons hot salad oil, cook the eggs, stirring quickly and constantly until the eggs are the size of peas and leave the side of the pan. Reduce heat to low. Push the eggs completely to one side of the skillet.
5. In the same skillet, gently stir the rice and 3 tablespoons salad oil until the rice is well coated with oil. Add the pork mixture and spinach; gently stir the mixture to mix well the ingredients in the skillet; heat through. Transfer the fried rice to a warm platter and serve.

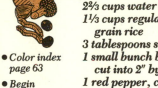

ITALIAN-STYLE RICE

2⅔ cups water
1⅓ cups regular long-
grain rice
3 tablespoons salad oil
1 small bunch broccoli,
cut into 2" by 1" pieces
1 red pepper, cut into
strips
1 small garlic clove,
minced

¾ teaspoon salt
1 cup milk
¾ cup grated Parmesan
cheese
¼ cup pitted ripe olives,
each cut in half
2 ounces salami, chopped

- Color index
  page 63
- Begin
  30 mins
  ahead
- 4 main-dish
  servings
- 505 cals
  per serving

1. In 3-quart saucepan over high heat, heat water and rice to boiling, stirring occasionally. Reduce heat to low; cover and simmer 20 minutes or until rice is tender and all liquid is absorbed.
2. Meanwhile, in 10-inch skillet over medium heat, in hot salad oil, cook broccoli, red pepper, garlic, and salt until tender, stirring frequently.
3. When rice is done, stir in milk and cheese; cook over low heat until cheese melts, stirring frequently. Stir in broccoli mixture, olives, and salami; heat through.

TEX-MEX STYLE RICE

In this Tex-Mex side dish, Carolina rice, cooked in chicken stock, is given more zest with salt pork, peas, and olives.

- Color index
  page 63
- Begin
  50 mins
  ahead
- 6 side-dish
  servings
- 280 cals
  per serving

¼ pound salt pork, diced
1 medium onion, chopped
¾ cup regular long-grain
rice
1 medium tomato, diced
1 chicken-flavor bouillon
cube or envelope

1⅓ cups water
¾ teaspoon salt
⅛ teaspoon pepper
1 cup frozen peas
¼ cup pitted ripe olives,
sliced

1 In 3-quart saucepan over medium heat, cook salt pork until golden, pressing frequently with back of spoon to render all liquid fat.

2 With slotted spoon, remove browned salt pork to paper towels to drain excess fat.

3 In pork fat over medium heat, cook onion until tender, stirring occasionally. Stir in rice; cook until golden, stirring often.

4 Add tomato, bouillon, water, salt, and pepper; over high heat, heat mixture to boiling. Reduce heat to low; cover; simmer 15 minutes.

5 Add frozen peas and browned salt pork; cover; simmer 5 minutes longer or until rice and peas are tender and all liquid absorbed.

6 Remove saucepan from heat; stir in sliced olives. Transfer rice to large warm platter and serve.

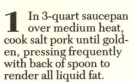

Rice

WILD RICE WITH PEAS AND MUSHROOMS

5 tablespoons butter or margarine
1 pound mushrooms, sliced
1 medium onion, diced
3½ cups water
½ teaspoon salt
⅛ teaspoon pepper

2 beef-flavor bouillon cubes or envelopes
1½ cups wild rice
1 cup brown rice
1 10-ounce package frozen peas

1. Preheat oven to 350°F. In 2-quart saucepan over medium heat in hot butter, cook mushrooms and onion, stirring occasionally, until onion is tender. Stir in water, salt, pepper, and bouillon; heat to boiling.
2. Meanwhile, rinse wild rice with water; drain. In 4-quart casserole, combine wild rice, brown rice, and mushroom mixture. Cover casserole and bake 45 minutes.
3. Stir in frozen peas; cover and bake 5 minutes longer or until peas are cooked, rice is tender, and all liquid is absorbed.

- Color index page 63
- Begin 1¼ hrs ahead
- 16 side-dish servings
- 145 cals per serving

GOLDEN RICE

1 cup regular long-grain rice or ¾ cup parboiled rice
2 cups water

3 tablespoons butter or margarine
1 teaspoon salt

1. In medium saucepan over medium heat, cook rice, stirring constantly, until rice is golden. Stir in water, butter, and salt.
2. Over high heat, heat to boiling; reduce heat to low, cover and simmer 15 minutes for long-grain rice and 25 minutes for parboiled rice, or until water is absorbed and rice is tender.

- Color index page 63
- Begin 30 mins ahead
- 6 side-dish servings
- 172 cals per serving

RICE PLUS: Prepare 4 servings of regular long-grain rice as label directs; toss with one of the following additions until well mixed:

ALMONDS: ¼ cup chopped or slivered almonds, toasted. 245 cals per serving.

CURRIED APPLE: Cut 1 apple, cored and unpeeled, into chunks. In small skillet over medium heat, in 3 tablespoons hot butter or margarine, cook apple and ¼ teaspoon curry powder 5 minutes or until apple is tender. 300 cals per serving.

BACON: 6 slices bacon, cooked and crumbled. 255 cals per serving.

OLIVES: ¼ cup pimento-stuffed green olives or pitted ripe olives, sliced. 220 cals per serving.

ONION: In small skillet over medium heat, in 2 tablespoons hot butter or margarine, cook 1 small onion, diced, 5 minutes. 260 cals per serving.

SUMMER-GARDEN RICE

This richly flavored rice topped with a combination of summer vegetables in a light cheese sauce makes a hearty one-dish meal.

2 tablespoons butter or margarine
1 small onion, sliced
1 garlic clove, minced
1 chicken-flavor bouillon cube or envelope
Water
Salt
Cracked pepper
1 cup regular long-grain rice

3 tablespoons salad oil
½ small bunch broccoli, cut into 2" by 1" pieces
2 large carrots, thinly sliced diagonally
2 medium yellow straightneck squash (about 8 ounces each), cut into matchstick-thin strips
1 cup half-and-half

- Color index page 63
- Begin 45 mins ahead
- 4 main-dish servings
- 695 cals per serving

1 tablespoon all-purpose flour
½ pound Monterey Jack cheese, shredded (2 cups)
2 medium tomatoes, diced

1 In 3-quart saucepan over medium heat, melt butter. Add onion and garlic; cook until tender, stirring occasionally.

2 Stir in bouillon, 2 cups water, ½ teaspoon salt, and ⅛ teaspoon cracked pepper; over high heat, heat to boiling.

3 Stir in rice; reduce heat to low; cover and simmer 20 minutes or until rice is tender and all liquid is absorbed.

4 Meanwhile, in 12-inch skillet over medium-high heat, in hot salad oil, stir broccoli and carrots until well coated with oil; add ¼ cup water; cover and cook 3 minutes. Add yellow straightneck squash, ½ teaspoon salt, and ⅛ teaspoon cracked pepper; cook the vegetables, uncovered, stirring frequently, until vegetables are tender-crisp. Reduce the heat to medium and simmer gently.

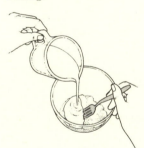

5 In small bowl, blend half-and-half and flour; gradually stir into vegetable mixture in the skillet.

6 Cook vegetable mixture, stirring constantly, until mixture thickens slightly.

7 Add 1½ cups shredded cheese to mixture; stir until cheese melts.

8 When rice is done, gently stir in tomatoes and remaining ½ cup shredded cheese, stirring until cheese melts.

9 To serve, spoon rice mixture onto warm platter; spoon vegetable mixture onto rice.

SALADS

"All my soul is in delight when mommy fixes kraut just right."

Pennsylvania Dutch saying

Salad greens, with or without added ingredients, were not in common use until the late 1800s. The earliest form of salad, coleslaw, was brought to our country by the Dutch during the colonial period; salads were made from cabbage because it stayed crisp and fresh long after many other garden greens were killed by frost. After the Civil War, a salad usually consisted of seafood or poultry and vegetables, with a few lettuce leaves around the platter. Only wealthy Americans who frequented new restaurants in the big cities could try European-style salads. In 1893 the famous "Oscar" of New York's old Waldorf Hotel created the Waldorf Salad, which was an immediate sensation.

In the late 1800s the molded salad appeared; it was an American invention made with gelatin and sugar or sweet fruits. Today the molded salad is still popular, and unusual-shaped molds, garnished and decorated with cut-up fruits or vegetables, make attractive additions to a buffet-table or special-occasion dinner.

At the turn of the century, fancier salads, made with fruit, cheese, and nuts, became fashionable. They were served with sweet dressings and often decorated with bright red maraschino cherries.

In the 1920s salads became very popular, especially in southern California, where delicious fresh vegetables and fruits were readily available. Caesar salad, created by Caesar Cardini, an Italian immigrant who owned restaurants just across the Mexican border, became a favorite of Hollywood movie stars. Italian immigrants also made tomatoes an important ingredient in salads.

Potato salad hasn't been around as long as lettuce salads, but it is now an American favorite, whether served hot at the table or cold for a barbecue or picnic. Hot potato salad was a favorite of German immigrants.

The salad bar, an innovation of the health-conscious 70s, became a major feature in restaurants throughout the country. Americans took to the salad bar with enthusiasm, helping themselves to the selection of greens, vegetables, condiments, and dressings. Cold pasta salads and rice salads also became a popular addition to the salad bar counter. Today a salad is often the main course, both in restaurants and at home.

Greens such as romaine, Bibb lettuce, iceberg lettuce, and leaf lettuce form the base for most salads, but some of the more unusual greens and herbs, such as Chinese cabbage, Belgian endive, fresh basil, and tarragon are becoming increasingly popular.

SALAD COMBINATIONS

Endless salad combinations are possible by varying greens and adding herbs, fruits, nuts, and vegetables.

Boston and red-tipped leaf lettuces with grapefruit or orange sections and our Honey-Caraway Dressing (p. 284).

Belgian endive and chicory or escarole with sliced beets, chopped parsley, and our Green-Goddess Dressing (p. 284).

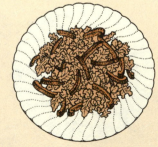

Shredded Chinese cabbage, julienned red peppers, chopped coriander leaves, toasted sesame seeds with soy-flavored French dressing or our Creamy Ginger-Cheese Dressing (p. 284).

Watercress or arugula, thinly sliced pears, and walnut halves, with a French dressing made with walnut oil and red wine vinegar, or our Creamy Blue-Cheese Dressing (p. 284).

Green salads

CAESAR SALAD

- Color index page 61
- Begin 1 hr ahead
- 6 servings
- 200 cals per serving

1/4 cup olive or salad oil
Juice of 1 lemon
1 garlic clove, halved
1/4 teaspoon salt
Dash coarsely ground pepper
1 medium head romaine
1 cup croutons
1/4 cup grated Parmesan cheese
4 anchovy fillets, chopped
1 egg

1. In large salad bowl, combine olive oil, lemon juice, garlic, salt, and pepper.
2. Cover bowl; let stand 1 hour. Discard garlic.
3. *About 10 minutes before serving:* Into dressing, tear romaine into bite-sized pieces. Add croutons, cheese, and anchovies; toss well. Add raw egg and toss again. Serve at once.

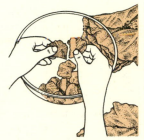

Preparing the dressing: Combine olive oil, lemon juice, garlic, salt, and pepper and mix well.

Adding the lettuce: Tear lettuce into bite-sized pieces; add croutons, cheese, and anchovies.

CLASSIC TOSSED GREEN SALAD

- Color index page 61
- Begin 20 mins ahead
- 8 servings
- 94 cals per serving

1/2 head Boston lettuce
1/4 head chicory
1/2 head romaine
1/4 cup sliced radishes
1/2 cup Classic French Dressing (p.284)

1. Into large salad bowl, tear Boston lettuce, chicory, and romaine into bite-sized pieces.
2. Add radishes and salad dressing; toss gently to coat lettuce well.

CALIFORNIA SALAD

- Color index page 61
- Begin 30 mins ahead
- 8 servings
- 204 cals per serving

1/4 cup salad oil
1 tablespoon sugar
2 tablespoons white wine vinegar
2 teaspoons minced parsley
1/2 teaspoon garlic salt
1/2 teaspoon seasoned salt
1/4 teaspoon oregano leaves
1/8 teaspoon seasoned pepper
1/2 large head iceberg lettuce
1/2 large head Boston lettuce
2 large avocados, peeled and sliced
1/2 cup walnuts

1. In large salad bowl, mix well oil, sugar, white wine vinegar, parsley, garlic salt, seasoned salt, oregano and pepper.
2. Into dressing, tear iceberg and Boston lettuce into bite-sized pieces.
3. Add the sliced avocados; gently toss to coat avocados and lettuce with dressing. Garnish with walnuts before serving.

SPINACH, MUSHROOM, AND BACON SALAD

- Color index page 61
- Begin 45 mins ahead
- 6 servings
- 210 cals per serving

Most of the spinach grown in the United States comes from California, and is available all year round to use in one of America's favorite salads. If you like, try this classic combination using other salad greens, such as romaine, arugula, watercress, or the colorful red leaf lettuces and radicchio.

Dressing
1/3 cup salad oil
3 tablespoons cider vinegar
1 tablespoon sugar
1/2 teaspoon dry mustard
1/4 teaspoon salt
1/8 teaspoon pepper
4 slices bacon
1 10-ounce bag spinach or 3/4 pound spinach
1/4 pound mushrooms, sliced
2 hard-cooked eggs, chopped, for garnish

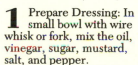

1 Prepare Dressing: In small bowl with wire whisk or fork, mix the oil, vinegar, sugar, mustard, salt, and pepper.

2 In a 10-inch skillet over medium heat, cook the bacon slices until they are crisp, turning with wooden spoon.

3 Remove the cooked bacon to paper towels to drain. Crumble and set aside.

4 Into a large salad bowl, tear the spinach into bite-sized pieces; add mushrooms.

5 Pour dressing over salad and toss gently. Sprinkle with bacon and chopped eggs. Serve salad immediately.

Coleslaws

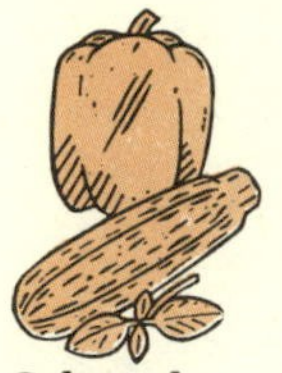

SUMMER SQUASH AND PEPPER SLAW

- Color index page 61
- Begin 2½ hrs or day ahead
- 10 servings
- 172 cals per serving

Squash comes from the Narraganset Indian word meaning "eaten raw" and that's exactly what you do with the yellow straight-neck squash in this sweet but zesty squash-and-red-pepper mixture.

5 medium yellow straight-neck squash (10 ounces each)	2¼ teaspoons salt
	2 teaspoons sugar
	¼ teaspoon basil
5 medium red peppers	¼ teaspoon marjoram leaves
1 medium onion	
⅔ cup salad oil	¼ teaspoon crushed red pepper
⅓ cup cider vinegar	

1 Cut yellow straightneck squash and red peppers into matchstick-thin strips; thinly slice onion. Place vegetables in large oven-safe bowl; set aside.

2 In 1-quart saucepan over high heat, heat salad oil and remaining ingredients to boiling. Pour hot mixture over the vegetables in bowl, tossing to mix well.

3 Cover and refrigerate about 2 hours to blend flavors.

4 Stir occasionally to coat vegetables evenly with dressing.

GOLDEN SLAW

- Color index page 61
- Begin early in day.
- 12 servings
- 179 cals per serving.

1 medium head cabbage, finely shredded (8 cups)	⅔ cup mayonnaise
	¼ cup prepared mustard
	2 teaspoons salt
2 cups diced, unpeeled red apple	1½ teaspoons pepper
2 cups shredded natural Swiss cheese	

1. In large salad bowl, toss cabbage, apple, and cheese; cover and refrigerate.
2. In small bowl or jar, mix mayonnaise, mustard, salt, and pepper; refrigerate.
3. Just before serving, toss cabbage mixture with mayonnaise mixture.

DELUXE COLESLAW

- Color index page 61
- Begin 1½ hrs ahead or early in day.
- 8 servings
- 123 cals per serving.

½ cup mayonnaise or cooked salad dressing	⅛ teaspoon pepper
	1 medium head cabbage
1 tablespoon milk	1 small green pepper
1 tablespoon vinegar or lemon juice	1 large celery stalk
	1 large carrot
½ teaspoon sugar	2 tablespoons minced onion
¼ teaspoon salt	
⅛ teaspoon paprika	

1. Prepare dressing: Into cup, measure first 7 ingredients; with fork or wire whisk, stir until well blended. Set aside.
2. With sharp knife, shred cabbage and thinly slice green pepper.
3. With a sharp knife, cut the celery stalk into ¼-inch-wide pieces. Then using a grater, finely shred the carrot.
4. In large bowl, gently toss prepared cabbage, green pepper, celery, carrot, onion, and dressing. Cover and refrigerate.

CABBAGES FOR SLAWS

Cabbage, one of the oldest cultivated vegetables, is one of the least costly and most nutritious. For variety in coleslaws, add shredded carrots, zucchini, sweet peppers, or other vegetables. Add chopped nuts or raisins for additional texture, or a variety of spices, such as caraway, sesame, cardamom, cumin, or thyme.

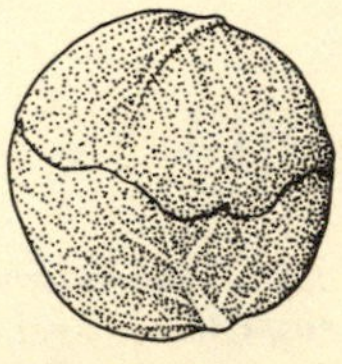

Green cabbage is good for storing and for grating; the number one coleslaw cabbage

Red cabbage is associated with vinegar; may be eaten raw or cooked

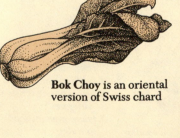

Savoy cabbage has curly leaves and a delicate flavor and texture

Bok Choy is an oriental version of Swiss chard

Chinese cabbage is similar in shape to romaine lettuce. It is interchangeable with green cabbage

Round head cabbage is available year-round; eaten raw or cooked

Potato salads

OLD-FASHIONED POTATO SALAD

1 cup mayonnaise
1 tablespoon cider
    vinegar
1½ teaspoons salt
2 teaspoons prepared
    mustard
½ teaspoon celery seed
Dash pepper
4 hard-cooked eggs,
    chopped
4 cups diced cooked
    potatoes
1½ cups sliced celery
½ cup sliced green onions
¼ cup sliced radishes
2 tablespoons chopped
    parsley
Lettuce leaves

1. Prepare the dressing: In a large bowl, stir mayonnaise with cider vinegar, salt, mustard, celery seed, and pepper until well mixed.
2. Add the eggs, potatoes, celery, green onions, radishes, and chopped parsley. Mix gently; do not break up the potatoes. Cover the potato salad and refrigerate if not using immediately.
3. To serve, arrange lettuce leaves around the edge of a large platter. Mound the potato salad in the center of the platter.

- Color index page 60
- Begin early in day
- 6 servings
- 408 cals per serving

CREAMY POTATO AND VEGETABLE SALAD

12 medium potatoes
    (about 4 pounds)
Water
1 9-ounce package frozen
    cut green beans
1 7-ounce jar roasted
    sweet red peppers,
    drained
1 3½-ounce can (drained
    weight) pitted ripe
    olives, drained
1 cup mayonnaise
⅓ cup milk
2 tablespoons lemon juice
1½ teaspoons salt
1 teaspoon sugar
½ teaspoon basil
¼ teaspoon coarsely
    ground black pepper
Fresh basil leaves for
    garnish

1. In 8-quart Dutch oven or saucepot over high heat, heat potatoes and enough water to cover to boiling. Reduce heat to low; cover and simmer 30 minutes or until potatoes are fork-tender; drain. Cool potatoes until easy to handle; peel potatoes; cut into ¾-inch chunks.
2. Meanwhile, prepare green beans as label directs; drain. Cut roasted sweet peppers into ½-inch-wide strips. Reserve 2 tablespoons red-pepper strips for garnish. Cut each olive in half.
3. In large bowl, mix mayonnaise, milk, lemon juice, salt, sugar, and basil. Add potatoes, green beans, olives, and remaining red-pepper strips. Gently toss to coat with dressing. If not serving right away, cover and refrigerate.
4. To serve, garnish salad with reserved red-pepper strips. Sprinkle with coarsely ground pepper; garnish with basil leaves.

- Color index page 60
- Begin 1½ hrs ahead or
    early in day
- 12 servings
- 260 cals per serving

TANGY HOT POTATO SALAD

Potatoes did not really feature in American cooking until the mid-nineteenth century. A hot potato salad, introduced by German immigrants, increased the potato's popularity.

8 large potatoes (about
    4 pounds)
Water
4 slices bacon, diced
2 large celery stalks,
    thinly sliced
1 medium onion, sliced
⅓ cup salad or olive oil
¼ cup red wine
    vinegar
2 tablespoons chopped
    parsley
1½ teaspoons salt
1¼ teaspoons sugar
2 teaspoons prepared
    mustard

- Color index page 60
- Begin 1 hr ahead
- 10 servings
- 195 cals per serving

1 In 5-quart saucepot over high heat, heat unpeeled potatoes and enough water to cover to boiling. Reduce heat to medium-low; cover; cook for 30 minutes.

2 When potatoes are fork-tender, drain. With sharp knife, cut potatoes into bite-sized pieces (do not peel); return the potatoes to saucepot.

3 Meanwhile, in a 2-quart saucepan over medium-low heat, cook the diced bacon until it is browned, turning with wooden spoon.

4 Remove bacon to paper towels to drain, leaving drippings in saucepan.

5 In the drippings remaining in the saucepan over medium heat, cook celery and onion until tender, stirring occasionally.

6 With slotted spoon remove the vegetables to the saucepot with the potatoes.

7 In same 2-quart saucepan, mix oil, vinegar, parsley, salt, sugar, and mustard; heat over medium heat to boiling. Reduce heat to low. Stir occasionally.

8 Simmer dressing 5 minutes to blend flavors. Pour hot dressing over potato and vegetable mixture in the saucepot.

9 Add bacon to potato and vegetable mixture; gently toss potatoes and dressing to mix well. Spoon potato salad onto warm large platter.

Bean and grain salads

TEXAS CAVIAR

- Color index page 60
- Begin 4½ hrs ahead
- 10 servings
- 205 cals per serving

Arriving here in 1734, black-eyed beans or peas were a staple of the colonial diet; they still feature in Southern and Western dishes.

1 16-ounce package dry black-eyed beans (peas)
Water
½ cup cider vinegar
⅓ cup olive or salad oil
1 tablespoon salt
2 teaspoons sugar
¼ teaspoon ground red pepper

1 small garlic clove, minced
½ cup chopped parsley
3 green onions, minced
2 celery stalks, thinly sliced
1 hard-cooked egg, chopped, for garnish
Watercress sprigs for garnish

1 Rinse the beans in running cold water; discard any stones. In 4-quart saucepan over high heat, heat the beans and 6 cups water to boiling; boil for 2 minutes.

2 Remove saucepan from heat; cover and let stand 1 hour. Drain beans; return to saucepan; add 6 cups water; over high heat, heat to boiling.

3 Reduce heat to low; cover and simmer 45 minutes or until beans are tender; drain.

4 In a medium bowl with a fork, beat the next 6 ingredients until well mixed.

5 Add beans, parsley, green onions, and celery; toss gently to coat with dressing. Cover the bowl and refrigerate at least 2 hours.

6 While salad is in refrigerator, uncover and stir occasionally. To serve, garnish with the chopped egg and the watercress sprigs.

THREE-BEAN AND CHEESE SALAD

- Color index page 60
- Begin 2½ hrs ahead
- 8 servings
- 320 cals per serving

Water
1 pound green beans, cut into 1-inch pieces
Salt
1 15½- to 19-ounce can garbanzo beans
1 15¼- to 19-ounce can red kidney beans

½ pound Swiss cheese, cut into ½-inch cubes
¼ cup salad oil
3 tablespoons chili sauce
2 tablespoons cider vinegar
1 teaspoon sugar

1. In 2-quart saucepan over high heat, in 1 inch boiling water, heat green beans and ½ teaspoon salt to boiling. Reduce heat to low; cover; simmer 5 to 10 minutes until tender; drain.
2. Place in large bowl. Drain garbanzo and kidney beans; place in bowl with remaining ingredients, and ½ teaspoon salt; toss to mix well.
3. Cover the salad and refrigerate at least 2 hours to blend flavors, stirring occasionally. Serve chilled with sliced, cold meats or hamburgers.

GREEN AND WAX BEANS WITH MUSTARD SAUCE

- Color index page 60
- Begin early in day
- 8 servings
- 220 cals per serving

1½ pounds green beans
1½ pounds wax beans
Water
1 8-ounce package cream cheese, softened

⅓ cup prepared mustard
⅓ cup mayonnaise
½ cup milk

1. Cut ends from green and wax beans. In 5-quart Dutch oven or saucepot over high heat, heat 1 inch water to boiling.
2. Add beans to Dutch oven; heat to boiling. Reduce heat to low; cover; simmer 8 to 10 minutes until tender-crisp, stirring occasionally; drain; cover and refrigerate.
3. In a small bowl, with mixer at medium speed, beat remaining ingredients until smooth. Cover; refrigerate. Serve sauce over the beans.

BEAN AND PEPPER SALAD

- Color index page 60
- Begin early in day or day ahead
- 10 servings
- 110 cals per serving

2 pounds green beans
2 large yellow peppers
Water
Salad oil
2 tablespoons white wine vinegar
2 tablespoons lemon juice
1 tablespoon sugar

1 tablespoon minced fresh basil or 1 teaspoon dried basil
½ teaspoon salt
¼ teaspoon pepper
1 cup Mediterranean or small ripe olives

1. Slice green beans diagonally into 2-inch pieces. Cut yellow peppers into thin strips.
2. In 5-quart Dutch oven over high heat, in 1 inch boiling water, heat green beans to boiling. Reduce heat to low; cover; simmer 10 minutes or until tender-crisp. Drain; place in large bowl.
3. In same Dutch oven over medium-high heat, in 2 tablespoons hot salad oil, cook peppers, stirring often until tender-crisp. Add to beans.
4. To vegetables in bowl, add next 7 ingredients and 3 tablespoons salad oil; toss to coat. Cover; refrigerate at least 1 hour to blend flavors, stirring occasionally.

FESTIVE CORN SALAD

The Indians referred to their plentiful maize, or corn, as the "giver of life." Early settlers called it "Indian corn," and found it invaluable in getting them through the first harsh years in the New World.

- Color index page 61
- Begin 1½ hrs ahead or early in day
- 6 servings
- 125 cals per serving

6 medium ears corn
Water
Salt
2 tablespoons salad oil
2 medium red peppers, cut into ¼-inch strips

3 tablespoons cider vinegar
¾ teaspoon sugar
½ teaspoon dry mustard

1 Pull back and remove the husks and silk from each ear of corn. Remove any remaining silk and discard.

2 Cut kernels from corn to make 4 cups. In 3-quart saucepan over high heat, in ½ inch boiling water, heat corn kernels and ½ teaspoon salt to boiling.

3 Reduce heat to low; cover and simmer the corn about 5 minutes or until the corn is tender; drain well.

4 Meanwhile, in a 2-quart saucepan over medium-high heat, in hot salad oil, cook the red peppers just until tender-crisp, stirring the peppers occasionally.

5 Remove saucepan from heat; add corn, vinegar, sugar, mustard, and 1¼ teaspoons salt; toss to mix well.

6 Cover with plastic wrap or aluminum foil and then refrigerate the salad for at least 1 hour to blend the flavors.

BARLEY-WALNUT SALAD

America is the world's second-largest producer of barley. Team it with delicious walnuts for a tasty, healthy salad.

- Color index page 60
- Begin early in day or day ahead
- 8 servings
- 300 cals per serving

Water
⅔ cup barley
1 medium carrot
1 medium green pepper
1 medium celery stalk, thinly sliced
1 green onion
¼ cup salad oil

1 8-ounce can walnuts (2 cups)
¼ cup minced parsley
1 tablespoon sugar
5 tablespoons cider vinegar
½ teaspoon salt

1 In 3-quart saucepan, heat 2 quarts water to boiling. Add barley; heat to boiling.

2 Reduce heat to low; cover; simmer 40 minutes or until tender. Drain; rinse; drain again.

3 Meanwhile, coarsely shred carrot. Cut green pepper lengthwise into quarters; then cut each quarter crosswise into thin strips. Thinly slice celery.

4 Place vegetables and barley in large bowl. Cut onion into 2-inch pieces. In 1-quart saucepan over medium heat, in hot oil, cook green onion until lightly browned.

5 Discard green onion. Add oil to barley mixture, tossing to coat. In same saucepan over low heat, cook walnuts until lightly toasted, stirring them frequently.

6 Stir walnuts into barley mixture with parsley, sugar, vinegar, and salt. Cover bowl with plastic wrap or aluminum foil and refrigerate at least 2 hours to blend flavors.

Vegetable salads

MARINATED GARDEN VEGETABLES

Marinated salads make a change from raw fresh vegetables and they keep longer too. This salad can be done a day ahead; the longer they are chilled the better they taste.

1¾ cups olive or salad oil
½ cup cider vinegar
½ cup red wine vinegar
4½ teaspoons sugar
2¼ teaspoons salt
½ teaspoon crushed red
   pepper
½ teaspoon oregano
   leaves

1 medium head
   cauliflower
1 medium bunch broccoli
1 pound green beans
4 medium carrots
2 medium yellow
   straightneck squash

- Color index page 60
- Begin 4 hrs ahead
- 12 servings
- 72 cals per serving

½ pound mushrooms
4 medium red peppers
Water
1 6-ounce can (drained
   weight) pitted ripe
   olives, drained

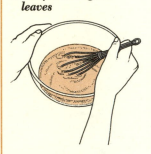

1 Prepare dressing: In medium-sized bowl, with wire whisk or fork, mix oil, vinegar, sugar, salt, pepper, and oregano; set dressing aside.

2 Separate cauliflower into flowerets; cut broccoli into 2" by 1" pieces; cut green beans into 1-inch pieces.

3 Cut the carrots, yellow straight-neck squash, and mushrooms into ¼-inch-thick slices; cut the red peppers into 1-inch pieces.

4 In 8-quart Dutch oven over high heat, in 1 inch boiling water, heat cauliflower, broccoli, green beans, and carrots to boiling.

5 Reduce heat to low; cover and simmer 5 minutes or until vegetables are tender-crisp; drain. Spoon vegetables into large bowl.

6 In same Dutch oven over high heat, in 1 inch boiling water, heat squash, mushrooms, and red peppers to boiling.

7 Reduce heat to low; cover and simmer 1 minute; drain. Spoon vegetables into bowl with cauliflower mixture.

8 Cut each olive in half; add olives and dressing to vegetables. With rubber spatula, gently stir to coat well.

9 Cover and refrigerate at least 3 hours, stirring the mixture occasionally, to blend the flavors.

SLICED TOMATOES WITH LEMON DRESSING

2 medium tomatoes
Lettuce leaves
1 medium lemon
⅓ cup olive or salad oil
1 teaspoon minced
   parsley

½ teaspoon salt
½ teaspoon sugar
⅛ teaspoon pepper

1. Slice tomatoes; arrange carefully on lettuce-leaf-lined platter.
2. From lemon, grate ½ teaspoon peel and squeeze 1 tablespoon juice.
3. In small bowl, with wire whisk or fork, mix lemon peel, juice, olive oil, and remaining ingredients. Spoon dressing over tomatoes.

- Color index page 60
- Begin 20 mins ahead
- 4 servings
- 175 cals per serving

ORANGES AND TOMATOES VINAIGRETTE

2 large oranges
2 medium tomatoes
¼ cup pitted ripe olives
⅓ cup olive or salad oil
3 tablespoons tarragon
   vinegar

2 teaspoons sugar
¼ teaspoon salt
Boston lettuce leaves

1. Peel and section oranges; place in large bowl. Cut tomatoes into thin wedges; slice olives; add to oranges in bowl.
2. In small bowl, with wire whisk or fork, mix next 4 ingredients until well blended.
3. Pour dressing over fruit; gently toss to coat. Serve mixture on lettuce leaves.

- Color index page 61
- Begin 30 mins ahead
- 4 servings
- 230 cals per serving

CUCUMBERS IN SOUR CREAM

1 cup sour cream
3 tablespoons minced
   chives or onion
2 tablespoons lemon juice

1½ teaspoons salt
Dash pepper
3 large cucumbers

1. In large bowl, combine sour cream, minced chives, lemon juice, salt, and pepper.
2. Peel and thinly slice cucumbers; add and mix well. Serve immediately.
3. Or, cover with plastic wrap and refrigerate to serve later.

- Color index page 61
- Begin 20 minutes ahead or early in day
- 6 servings
- 79 cals per serving

CUCUMBERS IN DILLED YOGURT: In large bowl, combine *1 8-ounce container plain yogurt, 1 teaspoon lemon juice, ½ teaspoon chopped fresh dill, ½ teaspoon salt,* and *dash pepper.* Prepare cucumbers as above; add and mix well. Makes 4 cups. 45 cals per serving.

Molded salads

MOLDED CUCUMBER SALAD

1 3-ounce package lemon-flavor gelatin	1/4 cup mayonnaise
1 teaspoon salt	1 large cucumber, finely shredded and well drained
2/3 cup boiling water	
3 tablespoons cider vinegar	Mint-Lime Dressing (p.284)
1 teaspoon grated onion	Lime Twists and mint leaves for garnish
2 cups sour cream	

1. In medium bowl, stir gelatin and salt; add boiling water and stir until gelatin is dissolved. Stir in vinegar and onion.
2. Refrigerate until mixture mounds slightly when dropped from a spoon, about 40 minutes.
3. With wire whisk or hand beater, beat in sour cream, mayonnaise, and cucumber until well mixed. Pour into 6-cup mold. Chill until set.
4. Unmold onto platter; garnish with Lime Twists (p.100) and mint; serve with dressing.

- Color index page 59
- Begin early in day or day ahead
- 10 servings
- 239 cals per serving

HOW TO MOLD AND PRESENT A GELATIN SALAD

Gelatin salads should be prepared well ahead of time, preferably the night before, to allow the gelatin to set. Unmold the gelatin directly onto a slightly wet serving platter and then garnish.

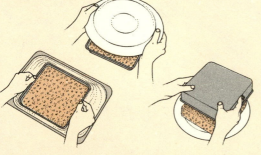

Before filling the gelatin mold, rinse it out with cold water and shake it out, leaving a few moisture droplets—this will make unmolding easier.

Run a small knife or metal spatula between the finished gelatin and mold to loosen the edges.

Dip mold into warm water just to the rim for about 10 seconds; do not melt gelatin. Wipe bottom dry.

Place platter upside down over mold and shake gently; invert mold and shake it downwards onto platter; carefully remove mold.

JEWELED BEET SALAD

The English were the first to introduce beets to our country and the Dutch imported them soon after. Today, most American-grown beets are either canned or pickled, but fresh beets are sweet, beautifully red, and make a festive-looking mold for a special occasion.

- Color index page 59
- Begin early in day or day ahead
- 16 servings
- 40 cals per serving

3 medium beets (3/4 pound)	1/4 teaspoon salt	1 8 1/4-ounce can crushed pineapple
Water	3 envelopes unflavored gelatin	1/3 cup red wine vinegar
1/4 cup sugar	1 medium carrot	Carrot curls for garnish

1 In 3-quart saucepan over high heat, heat the unpeeled beets and enough water to cover to boiling. Reduce the heat to low; cover and simmer for 25 to 30 minutes until the beets are tender; drain. Cool the beets slightly until they are easy to handle, then peel them. Meanwhile, in 2-quart saucepan, mix the sugar, salt, and 3 cups water. Evenly sprinkle the unflavored gelatin over the mixture.

2 Cook over medium heat until gelatin is completely dissolved, stirring frequently. Set gelatin aside at room temperature.

3 From carrot, cut 16 thin slices. With a small flower-shaped canapé cutter, cut carrot slices so they resemble flower shapes.

4 From beets, cut 16 thin slices. Shred remaining beets. Into 8" by 8" baking dish, pour 1/4-inch layer of gelatin mixture; chill in refrigerator about 20 minutes or until gelatin is set.

5 Arrange carrot flowers on top of gelatin in dish so that when salad is cut later, carrots will be in the center of each of the sixteen servings.

6 Place a beet slice on each carrot flower. Spoon a thin layer of gelatin over beet slices; refrigerate 30 minutes or until gelatin is set.

7 Into the remaining gelatin mixture, stir crushed pineapple with its juice, vinegar, and shredded beets.

8 Spoon beet mixture over gelatin in pan. Chill in refrigerator until salad is set, about 3 hours

9 To serve, unmold gelatin salad carefully onto chilled serving platter (left). Garnish salad with carrot curls (p.100).

Chef's salads

SALMAGUNDI

Based on a popular American colonial dish, this Southern-style chef's salad is made with ham and chicken. Done ahead, it makes an easy summer lunch or supper.

- *Color index page 59*
- *Begin 45 mins ahead*
- *6 main-dish servings*
- *325 cals per serving*

3 hard-cooked eggs
2 whole large chicken breasts
Salad oil
Salt
1/3 cup white wine vinegar
2 tablespoons chopped parsley

1 tablespoon sugar
1 teaspoon prepared mustard
1 small head radicchio
1 16-ounce jar or can boiled small whole onions, drained

1/2 pound red or green seedless grapes
1 4-ounce package sliced cooked ham, cut into 1/4-inch-wide strips
1 2-ounce can anchovy fillets, drained

1 Peel and slice eggs. Meanwhile, on a cutting board, cut each chicken breast in half. Working with one half at a time, place skin side up.

2 With tip of sharp knife, starting parallel and close to large end of rib bone, cut and scrape meat away from bone and rib cage.

3 Gently pull back meat in one piece as you cut. Discard bones and skin and cut off the white tendon.

4 With knife slanting, almost parallel to surface, slice across each half into 1/8-inch-thick slices. Cut each slice into matchstick thin strips.

5 In 10-inch skillet over medium-high heat in 2 tablespoons hot oil, cook chicken strips and 1/2 teaspoon salt, stirring quickly and often.

6 Continue cooking over medium-high heat until the chicken is tender, about 2 to 3 minutes. Set the chicken aside.

7 In small bowl, mix together vinegar, parsley, sugar, mustard, 1/4 cup salad oil, and 3/4 teaspoon salt.

8 Line large platter with radicchio. Arrange cooked chicken, sliced eggs, onions, grapes, and ham in the center of the platter.

9 Arrange the anchovy fillets on the salad in a lattice pattern. Serve salad with dressing at room temperature or chill to serve later on.

DELUXE LAYERED CHEF'S SALAD

4 eggs
1/2 10-ounce bag spinach
1/2 small head iceberg lettuce
1/2 pound Swiss cheese
1/2 pound cooked ham
2 medium tomatoes
1 large green pepper
1/2 cup mayonnaise

1/4 cup salad oil
2 tablespoons milk
2 tablespoons red wine vinegar
3/4 teaspoon sugar
1/2 teaspoon salt
1/4 teaspoon basil
Packaged seasoned croutons for garnish

1. In 2-quart saucepan, place eggs and enough water to come 1 inch above tops of eggs; over high heat, heat to boiling. Remove saucepan from heat; cover and let eggs stand in hot water 15 minutes; drain.
2. Carefully peel eggs under running cold water. Thinly slice eggs crosswise; set aside.
3. Meanwhile, coarsely shred spinach and lettuce. Cut Swiss cheese and ham into 1/2-inch cubes. Cut tomatoes into wedges; dice green pepper.
4. Place shredded spinach in bottom of 2 1/2-quart glass bowl; top with cheese cubes, then with layers of lettuce, tomato, pepper, and ham.
5. In small bowl with fork or wire whisk, mix mayonnaise and next 6 ingredients until blended. Pour dressing over salad in bowl. Arrange egg slices on top. Garnish salad with croutons.

- *Color index page 59*
- *Begin 1 hr ahead*
- *8 servings*
- *460 cals per serving*

PRESENTING A CHEF'S SALAD

Chef's Salad is a prime example of a one-dish main meal. In the classic presentation, the vegetables are combined in a bowl and strips of meat, chicken, and cheese are arranged in spoke fashion on top. The dressing is then poured over the strips.

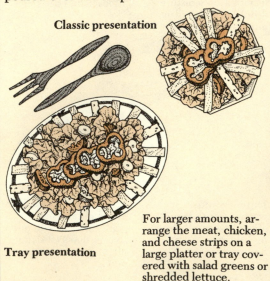

Classic presentation

Tray presentation

For larger amounts, arrange the meat, chicken, and cheese strips on a large platter or tray covered with salad greens or shredded lettuce.

Seafood salads

SHRIMP SALAD

- Color index page 58
- Begin 1 hr ahead
- 4 main-dish servings
- 290 cals per serving

2 cups cooked, shelled and deveined shrimp, chilled
1½ cups sliced celery
½ cup chopped walnuts (optional)
¼ cup sliced stuffed olives
¼ cup Classic French Dressing, (p.284)
¼ cup mayonnaise
1 teaspoon minced onion
Lettuce leaves

1. Cut shrimp in half lengthwise.
2. Place shrimp in large bowl. Add next 6 ingredients; mix. Cover; refrigerate. On 4 dishes, arrange lettuce. Top with shrimp salad.

CRAB LOUIS

- Color index page 58
- Begin 1 hr ahead
- 4 main-dish servings
- 400 cals per serving

1 cup mayonnaise
3 tablespoons catchup
2 tablespoons chopped green onion
1 tablespoon Worcestershire
1 tablespoon red wine vinegar
2 teaspoons lemon juice
½ teaspoon salt
⅛ teaspoon white pepper
1 pound cooked fresh crab or 3 6-ounce packages frozen Alaska King crab, thawed and drained
Lettuce leaves
3 hard-cooked eggs, sliced
1 cucumber, sliced
1 tomato, sliced

1. In medium bowl, combine mayonnaise, catchup, onion, Worcestershire, wine vinegar, lemon juice, salt, and pepper; refrigerate 30 minutes.
2. In center of each of 4 plates, heap crab; encircle with lettuce, egg, cucumber, and tomato slices; pass the dressing separately.

LOBSTER SALAD

- Color index page 59
- Begin 1½ hrs ahead
- 2 main-dish servings
- 390 cals per serving

2 1¼-pound lobsters, cooked
2 hard-cooked eggs
1 celery stalk
3 tablespoons mayonnaise
1 tablespoon milk
Chopped parsley for garnish
Lettuce leaves
1 lemon, sliced

1. Working with one lobster at a time, twist lobster from head to tail. With kitchen shears, cut thin underside shell from tail; discard. Gently pull out tail meat from shell; reserve shell; devein tail meat.
2. Break off claws. With lobster cracker, crack claws; remove meat.
3. With hands, pull bony portion from head shell and break into pieces; with lobster pick or fork, pick out meat. Discard sac and spongy grayish gills; save red roe (coral) or green-gray liver (tomalley) for salad. Reserve head shell.
4. Cut lobster meat into bite-sized pieces; chop eggs; slice celery; place in bowl. Stir in mayonnaise and milk.
5. Put head and tail shells together, overlapping them slightly. Holding shells at a slight angle, fill with lobster salad. Garnish with parsley. Arrange lettuce on platter. Place salad-filled shells on lettuce. Garnish with lemon slices.

POTATO-TUNA SALAD

A variation on the traditional potato salad, this healthy dish combines eggs, tuna, and vegetables to make a satisfying main course.

- Color index page 58
- Begin 40 mins ahead
- 8 main-dish servings
- 340 cals per serving

1 pound small red potatoes
Water
4 eggs
1 9-ounce package frozen French-style green beans
½ cup salad oil
⅓ cup red wine vinegar
2 tablespoons prepared mustard
2 teaspoons sugar
1 teaspoon salt
½ teaspoon basil
1 12½- to 13-ounce can tuna, drained
1 8-ounce can pitted ripe olives, drained and each cut in half
1 medium tomato, cut into bite-sized chunks
1 tablespoon capers, drained
3 cups thinly sliced red cabbage or 2 16-ounce cans julienne beets, drained

1 In 3-quart saucepan over high heat, heat unpeeled potatoes and enough water to cover to boiling. Reduce heat to medium-low; cover and cook 15 minutes or until potatoes are fork-tender; drain. Cut potatoes into bite-sized pieces (do not peel). Meanwhile, in a small saucepan, hard-cook the eggs. In another small saucepan, cook the green beans as label directs; drain well.

2 Peel eggs. Separate yolks from whites; coarsely chop the whites and set aside.

3 In large bowl, mash the hard-cooked egg yolks; stir in the salad oil, red wine vinegar, prepared mustard, sugar, salt, and the basil.

4 Add the cooked potatoes, green beans, hard-cooked egg whites, tuna, olives, tomato, and capers, tossing to coat with dressing.

5 To serve, arrange sliced red cabbage on large platter; top with potato-salad mixture.

Chicken salads

TROPICAL CHICKEN-POTATO SALAD WITH AVOCADO AND PAPAYA

Christopher Columbus found papayas in the West Indies. Today, many of the best papayas come from Hawaii. Combine them with avocados for a tropical chicken salad.

- *Color index page 58*
- *Begin 2 hrs ahead or early in day*
- *4 main-dish servings*
- *713 cals per serving*

1 3- to 3½-pound
  broiler-fryer
Salt
Water
2 medium potatoes

1 small green pepper,
  chopped
¾ cup mayonnaise
½ cup milk
¼ teaspoon white pepper

2 large papayas or 1 small
  cantaloupe
1 large avocado
Lettuce leaves

1 Cook chicken: Rinse chicken, its giblets, and neck with running cold water.

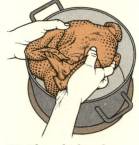

2 Place chicken, breast side down, in 5-quart saucepot or Dutch oven; add giblets, neck, 1 teaspoon salt, and 2 inches water; over high heat, heat to boiling.

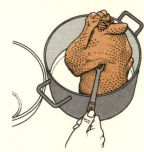

3 Reduce heat to low; cover and simmer 35 minutes or until chicken is fork-tender. Remove chicken to a large bowl; refrigerate 30 minutes or until easy to handle.

4 Discard all the skin and bones from the chicken; cut the meat and giblets into bite-sized pieces. Set aside.

5 In 2-quart saucepan over high heat, heat unpeeled potatoes and enough water to cover to boiling. Reduce heat to medium-low.

6 Cover; cook 20 to 30 minutes until fork-tender; drain. Cool the potatoes until easy to handle. Peel and cut into bite-sized pieces.

7 In large bowl, gently toss chicken, potatoes, next 4 ingredients and 1½ teaspoons salt until they are all well mixed.

8 Peel and remove the seeds from the papayas or cantaloupe and avocado; cut the fruit into thin slices.

9 Arrange fruit slices on half of large platter. Line other half of platter with lettuce leaves; top fruit and lettuce with chicken salad.

CURRIED CHICKEN TOMATO CUPS

2 whole large chicken
  breasts, halved,
  skinned and boned
Salad oil
1 medium onion, diced
1 teaspoon curry powder
1 teaspoon salt

½ cup mayonnaise
1 tablespoon lemon juice
1 large celery stalk, sliced
4 medium tomatoes
4 large lettuce leaves
2 tablespoons golden
  raisins

1. With knife held in slanting position, almost parallel to the cutting surface, slice across width of each breast half into ¼-inch-thick slices. In 12-inch skillet over high heat, in 2 tablespoons hot salad oil, cook onion until tender. Stir in chicken, curry powder, and salt; cook about 5 minutes, stirring frequently, until chicken is tender. Remove to large bowl.

2. To chicken, add mayonnaise, lemon juice and sliced celery, stirring to mix well.

3. To serve, cut each tomato into 6 to 8 wedges, being careful not to cut all the way through. Spread wedges apart slightly. Place each tomato on a lettuce-lined plate. Top each tomato with some chicken mixture. Garnish with raisins.

- *Color index page 58*
- *Begin 1 hr ahead or early in day*
- *4 main-dish servings*
- *385 cals per serving*

CHICKEN AND BACON SALAD

½ 8-ounce package sliced
  bacon
2 whole large chicken
  breasts, skinned and
  boned
2 green onions, sliced
1 15½- to 19-ounce can
  garbanzo beans,
  drained

2 tablespoons red wine
  vinegar
1 tablespoon sugar
½ teaspoon dry mustard
¼ cup water
3 small avocados
1 medium head Belgian
  endive

1. In 12-inch skillet over medium-low heat, cook bacon until browned. Remove bacon to paper towels to drain. Crumble bacon; set aside.

2. Cut each chicken breast in half. With knife held in slanting position, almost parallel to the cutting surface, slice each chicken breast half crosswise into ⅛-inch-thick slices.

3. In bacon fat in skillet over medium-low heat, cook green onions until tender. Stir in chicken; over medium-high heat, cook until chicken is tender and just loses its pink color, about 2 to 3 minutes, stirring quickly and constantly. Remove to a large bowl.

4. Into drippings in skillet, stir next 5 ingredients; over high heat, heat to boiling. Remove from heat; stir in chicken; add salt to taste.

5. Peel and cut each avocado in half. Arrange salad and avocados on large platter. Sprinkle with bacon; garnish with endive leaves.

- *Color index page 60*
- *Begin 1 hr ahead*
- *6 main-dish servings*
- *440 cals per serving*

PARTY CHICKEN-AND-PASTA SALAD

Americans often serve chicken and macaroni salads on their own. Put them together, add fresh vegetables, and you get an inventive main-course party dish.

1 3-pound broiler-fryer
1 small onion, cut into quarters
Water
½ 16-ounce package rotelle, corkscrew, or shell macaroni
Salad oil
2 large carrots, thinly sliced diagonally
Salt
½ pound mushrooms, each cut into quarters

½ small bunch broccoli, cut into 2" by 1" pieces
½ small head cauliflower separated into flowerets
1 bunch green onions, cut into 1-inch pieces
2 tablespoons soy sauce

- Color index page 58
- Begin 2 hrs ahead
- 6 main-dish servings
- 525 cals per serving

1 Rinse chicken, its giblets and neck with running cold water. Place the chicken, breast side down, in a saucepan or saucepot just large enough to hold the chicken (4- to 5-quart size). Add giblets, neck, onion, and 2 inches water; over high heat, heat to boiling. Reduce heat to low; cover the saucepan and simmer 35 minutes or until chicken is fork-tender. Remove chicken, giblets, and neck to large bowl; refrigerate for 30 minutes.

2 Discard skin and bones from chicken; cut meat and giblets into bite-sized pieces. Meanwhile, prepare macaroni as label directs; drain the macaroni.

3 In 8-quart Dutch oven or saucepot over medium heat, in 1 tablespoon hot salad oil, cook carrots and ¼ teaspoon salt, stirring the carrots frequently.

4 Cook carrots until tender-crisp, about 3 to 5 minutes. Remove to large bowl. In same Dutch oven, heat 2 more tablespoons salad oil.

5 In hot oil, cook mushrooms and ¼ teaspoon salt, stirring occasionally, until the mushrooms are tender, about 5 minutes.

6 Remove mushrooms to bowl with carrots. In 2 more tablespoons hot salad oil, stir the next 3 ingredients until they are coated with oil.

7 Add ¼ cup water and ½ teaspoon salt; cover; cook 5 to 10 minutes, stirring occasionally, until vegetables are tender-crisp.

8 With slotted spoon, remove broccoli, cauliflower, and onions to bowl with mushrooms and carrots. Discard any liquid in Dutch oven. Return all vegetables to the Dutch oven. Add chicken pieces, macaroni, soy sauce, 3 tablespoons salad oil, and ½ teaspoon salt; toss gently to mix. Spoon the mixture onto large platter. Serve salad at room temperature, or cover and refrigerate to serve chilled later.

SALAD SHELLS

Fruits and vegetables make pretty and practical containers for serving salad. Cut a thin slice from the underside of round fruits and vegetables so they stand upright.

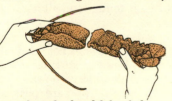

Fresh seafood and fish salads look attractive in a lobster or crab shell.

After removing meat, put lobster shell together, overlapping body and tail; fill with salad.

Small patty pan squashes make pretty receptacles for dips and salad dressings.

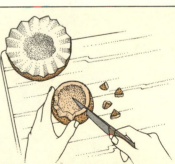

Oranges, grapefruits, and melons can be cut with a zig-zag edge or into a basket shape.

Coleslaws make a spectacular presentation served in a large hollowed-out leafy cabbage.

Carve out the cabbage center with a sharp spoon and reserve for coleslaw or soup.

Scooped-out tomatoes and peppers look pretty filled with salad. Place top over salad.

A pineapple half, scooped out and filled with fruit makes a beautiful centerpiece.

Pasta and rice salads

PICNIC PASTA SALAD FOR A CROWD

Pasta is always a favorite for outdoor eating. Easy to make in advance, this Italian-style salad is a real crowd-pleaser.

- Color index page 58
- Begin 1 hr ahead or early in day
- 12 main-dish servings
- 480 cals per serving

1 16-ounce package penne or ziti macaroni
1 pound cooked ham
1 pound Jarlsberg or Swiss cheese
3 small zucchini (about 6 ounces each)
2 medium red peppers
2 medium green peppers
1 5.6-ounce can colossal pitted ripe olives, drained

1 8-ounce bottle red wine vinegar and oil salad dressing or other favorite dressing
1 cup chopped parsley
½ cup mayonnaise
2 medium tomatoes

1 Prepare macaroni as label directs; drain. Meanwhile, cut the ham and cheese into ¾-inch chunks. Cut zucchini into ¼-inch-thick slices.

2 Cut peppers into bite-sized pieces. Cut each olive in half. In a large bowl, mix salad dressing, chopped parsley, and mayonnaise.

3 Add the macaroni, ham, cheese, peppers, zucchini, and olives; toss to coat well with dressing.

4 Serve salad at room temperature. Or, cover and refrigerate to serve chilled later.

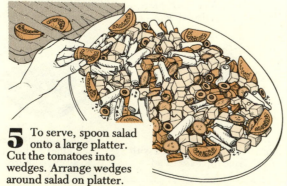

5 To serve, spoon salad onto a large platter. Cut the tomatoes into wedges. Arrange wedges around salad on platter.

TORTELLINI PESTO PLATTER

12 ounces fresh or frozen cheese or meat tortellini or ½ 16-ounce package shell macaroni
2 cups loosely packed basil leaves
¼ cup olive oil
¼ teaspoon salt
1 small garlic clove
½ cup grated Parmesan cheese

½ pound Fontina cheese, cut into bite-sized chunks
½ 7-ounce jar roasted sweet red peppers, drained and cut into strips
¼ pound thinly sliced salami

- Color index page 58
- Begin 1½ hrs ahead or early in day
- 6 main-dish servings
- 545 cals per serving

1. Prepare tortellini as label directs; drain. Return tortellini to saucepot.
2. Meanwhile, in blender at medium speed or in food processor with knife blade attached, blend basil, olive oil, salt, and garlic until smooth.
3. To tortellini in saucepot, add basil mixture, Parmesan, Fontina, and roasted peppers; toss gently with rubber spatula to coat mixture well with dressing. Refrigerate tortellini mixture until chilled, at least 1 hour.
4. Spoon tortellini mixture onto chilled platter; arrange salami slices around pasta.

CONFETTI RICE MOLD

1 cup wild rice
Water
Chicken-flavor bouillon cube or envelope
Salad oil
½ pound mushrooms, sliced
1 10-ounce package frozen peas

¾ cup regular long-grain rice
⅓ cup pimento-stuffed olives, sliced
3 tablespoons red wine vinegar
¾ teaspoon salt
Tomato slices for garnish

- Color index page 59
- Begin 5 hrs ahead or day ahead
- 10 servings
- 190 cals per serving

1. Rinse wild rice; drain. In 2-quart saucepan over high heat, heat 2 cups water to boiling. Stir in wild rice and half the bouillon; heat to boiling. Reduce heat to low; cover and simmer 45 to 50 minutes until wild rice is tender and all liquid is absorbed.
2. Meanwhile, in 3-quart saucepan over medium-high heat, in 2 tablespoons hot salad oil, cook mushrooms until tender, stirring often. With slotted spoon, remove to large bowl.
3. In same 3-quart saucepan, prepare peas as label directs but omit salt; drain. Spoon into bowl with mushrooms.
4. In same saucepan over high heat, heat 1½ cups water to boiling. Stir in long-grain rice and remaining bouillon; heat to boiling. Reduce heat to low; cover and simmer 20 minutes or until rice is tender and all liquid is absorbed.
5. Brush 2½-quart bowl with salad oil. Press 2 tablespoons sliced olives to bottom and sides; add rest of olives to vegetable mixture.
6. Toss wild rice, long-grain rice, vinegar, salt, and 2 tablespoons salad oil with vegetable mixture; pack into greased bowl. Cover and refrigerate at least 4 hours. To serve, carefully invert rice mold onto platter and garnish with tomatoes.

Fruit salads

AVOCADO AND GRAPEFRUIT WITH HONEY AND YOGURT

2 medium avocados
Lemon juice
2 medium pink grapefruit
Boston lettuce leaves
Fresh mint leaves for
garnish

½ 8-ounce container
plain yogurt (½ cup)
2 tablespoons honey
¼ teaspoon dry mustard

1. Cut avocados in half lengthwise; discard seeds and skin. Cut each avocado half into lengthwise slices. Dip slices in lemon juice to prevent avocado from darkening.
2. Remove peel and white membranes from grapefruit. Cut grapefruit into sections. Line a large platter with lettuce leaves; arrange avocado and grapefruit on lettuce. If you like, garnish with mint leaves.
3. Prepare dressing: In small bowl, mix yogurt, honey, mustard, and ½ teaspoon lemon juice. Pass yogurt dressing to serve with fruit.

- Color index page 59
- Begin 30 mins ahead
- 6 servings
- 190 cals per serving

WALDORF SALAD

3 medium Red Delicious
apples
2 celery stalks
½ cup walnuts
½ cup mayonnaise

2 tablespoons lemon juice
½ cup dark seedless
raisins
4 large Boston lettuce
leaves

1. Dice the unpeeled apples and place in a medium bowl. Thinly slice the celery and add to the apples. Coarsely chop the walnuts and add to the apples and celery; toss to combine.
2. In medium bowl, stir mayonnaise with lemon juice until smooth. Add the apples, celery, and walnut mixture. Add raisins; toss gently to mix well. Serve mixture on lettuce leaves or in Salad Shell (p.281).

- Color index page 59
- Begin 20 mins ahead
- 4 servings
- 400 cals per serving

FRUIT LUNCHEON SALAD

1 head Boston lettuce
1½ 16-ounce containers
cottage cheese (3 cups)
1 small pineapple, cut
into chunks
1 cantaloupe, cut into
balls

1 pint strawberries
2 oranges, sectioned
Creamy Ginger-Cheese
Dressing (p. 284)

1. Line large salad bowl with lettuce; spoon cottage cheese into center of lettuce; arrange pineapple, melon, strawberries, and oranges around cottage cheese; chill.
2. Serve with Creamy Ginger-Cheese Dressing.

- Color index page 59
- Begin 1 hour ahead
- 6 main-dish servings
- 413 cals per serving

FRUIT IN MELON BASKETS

America abounds with wild and cultivated fruits. A refreshing summer salad is a healthy way to satisfy your family's sweet tooth, and our melon baskets make pretty containers.

2 large honeydew melons
1 medium cantaloupe
3 plums
2 nectarines

½ pound sweet cherries
⅓ cup sugar
1 teaspoon almond
extract

Light corn syrup
2 large bunches mint
leaves

- Color index page 59
- Begin 3 hrs ahead or early in day
- 10 servings
- 168 cals per serving

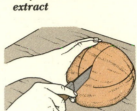

1 Into each honeydew make a horizontal cut from each end 2 inches from top (do not cut through); leave 1-inch strip in center.

2 Then make two vertical cuts, from the top of the melon down to the horizontal cuts, just deep enough to carve out a handle.

3 Carefully remove the melon wedges from both sides of the "handle" (wrap well and refrigerate to serve another day).

4 Discard seeds from honeydew melons. Scoop out and cut pulp from melon baskets into bite-sized pieces, or use melon baller to scoop into small balls; place in large bowl.

5 Cut scalloped edge around rim of melon baskets; slice thin piece of rind from bottom of each so that the baskets stand level. Wrap the melon baskets with plastic wrap; refrigerate.

6 Cut cantaloupe into bite-sized pieces; cut the unpeeled plums and nectarines into wedges. If you like, remove stems and pits from cherries.

7 Place all fruit in bowl with honeydew. Add sugar and almond extract; toss to mix well. Cover and refrigerate at least 2 hours to blend flavors, stirring occasionally.

8 To serve, brush handles of baskets lightly with corn syrup. Attach some mint leaves to handles to make an attractive arrangement.

9 Spoon fruit mixture into melon baskets. Carefully arrange the remaining mint leaves on a large platter; place the melon baskets on top of the mint leaves on platter.

Salad dressings

BLENDER MAYONNAISE

Famous American salad dressings, such as Green Goddess, Thousand Island, Russian, and Creamy Blue-Cheese all use a good mayonnaise base.

- Begin 10 mins ahead
- 1¼ cups
- 29 cals per tablespoon

Olive or salad oil
1 egg
2 tablespoons cider vinegar
1 teaspoon sugar
1 teaspoon dry mustard
¾ teaspoon salt
⅛ teaspoon white pepper

1. In covered blender container at low speed, blend ¼ cup oil and remaining ingredients for 1 or 2 seconds until thoroughly mixed.
2. Remove center of cover and, at low speed, very slowly pour ¾ cup oil in steady stream into mixture; continue blending until well mixed.

Mixing the ingredients: In covered blender, blend ¼ cup of olive or salad oil with the other ingredients for a couple of seconds until well mixed.

Pouring the oil: After removing the center of blender cover, with blender at low speed, pour ¾ cup oil very slowly into mixture.

GREEN GODDESS DRESSING: In small bowl, stir together ¾ cup mayonnaise, 2 anchovy fillets, minced, 1 tablespoon chopped parsley, 1 tablespoon chopped chives, 1 tablespoon chopped green onion, 1 tablespoon tarragon vinegar, and ¾ teaspoon tarragon until well mixed. Cover with plastic wrap and refrigerate. Makes 1 cup. 90 cals per tablespoon.

THOUSAND ISLAND DRESSING: In small bowl, stir 1 cup mayonnaise, 2 tablespoons chili sauce, 2 tablespoons minced green pepper, 1 tablespoon chopped parsley, and 1 teaspoon grated onion until well mixed. Makes 1⅓ cups. 73 cals per tablespoon.

RUSSIAN DRESSING: In small bowl, stir 1 cup mayonnaise, 3 tablespoons chili sauce, and 1 teaspoon minced onion or chopped chives until ingredients are well mixed. Makes 1 cup. 102 cals per tablespoon.

CREAMY BLUE-CHEESE DRESSING: In small bowl, with fork, mash 4 ounces Danish or other blue cheese, crumbled (about ½ cup), with 3 tablespoons half-and-half until smooth and creamy. Add ½ cup mayonnaise, 6 tablespoons olive or salad oil, ¼ cup white wine vinegar, 1 teaspoon prepared mustard, ⅛ teaspoon salt, and ⅛ teaspoon pepper. With hand beater or wire whisk, beat until well mixed. Makes about 1 cup. 134 cals per tablespoon.

CLASSIC FRENCH DRESSING

¾ cup olive or salad oil
¼ cup cider or wine vinegar
¾ teaspoon salt
⅛ teaspoon pepper

- Begin 10 mins or day ahead
- 1 cup
- 90 cals per tablespoon

Into a small bowl or a covered jar, measure all ingredients; stir with fork or cover and shake until thoroughly mixed. Cover and chill. Stir or shake the dressing just before serving.

MIXED HERB: Prepare as for Classic French Dressing but add 2 teaspoons chopped fresh parsley and ½ teaspoon tarragon or basil.

POPPY-SEED DRESSING

1 cup salad oil
½ cup sugar
⅓ cup cider vinegar
1 tablespoon poppy seeds
1 tablespoon grated onion
1 teaspoon salt
1 teaspoon dry mustard

- Begin 10 mins ahead or early in day
- 1½ cups
- 97 cals per tablespoon

In a covered blender container at medium speed, blend the salad oil, sugar, vinegar, poppy seeds, grated onion, salt, and mustard until thoroughly mixed; the dressing will be thick. Store in a tightly covered jar in refrigerator. Stir well before using. Serve dressing on tossed green salad, fruit salad, or cottage cheese.

MINT-LIME DRESSING

¼ cup lime juice
1 cup mint leaves
⅓ cup sugar
2 3-ounce packages cream cheese, softened

- Begin 10 mins ahead or early in day
- 1⅓ cups
- 46 cals per tablespoon

In covered blender container at medium speed, blend lime juice and mint until mint is finely chopped. Add sugar and cream cheese; blend at medium speed just until smooth. (Do not overblend or dressing will be thin.)

CREAMY GINGER-CHEESE DRESSING

1 8-ounce package cream cheese, softened
¼ cup milk
2 tablespoons sugar
3 tablespoons lemon juice
¾ teaspoon ground ginger

- Begin 10 mins ahead or early in day
- 1⅓ cups
- 52 cals per tablespoon

In small bowl, with mixer at medium speed, beat cream cheese, milk, sugar, lemon juice, and ground ginger until smooth.

HONEY-CARAWAY DRESSING

¾ cup mayonnaise
2 tablespoons honey
1 tablespoon lemon juice
1 tablespoon caraway seeds

- Begin 10 mins ahead or early in day
- 1 cup
- 98 cals per tablespoon

In small bowl, with wire whisk or fork, stir mayonnaise, honey, lemon juice, and caraway seeds until blended; cover and refrigerate. Stir before using.

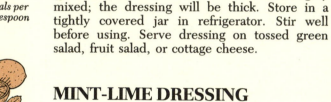

DESSERTS

"Give me the luxuries of life and I will willingly do without the necessities."

FRANK LLOYD WRIGHT

"What's for dessert?" is probably the most frequently asked question at the dinner table. Despite the trend in recent years towards low-calorie diets and healthier eating habits, most Americans find it hard to resist the sweet last course. We have become a nation famous for our love of desserts – fruit dishes, puddings, and especially ice cream.

Settlers, and later immigrants, from every part of the world brought their recipes for sweet dishes to America, but many desserts, springing from native fruits and other foods, are inherently American.

Apples have been used in thousands of desserts since our earliest history. Besides apple pie, the most American of apple dishes may well be Apple Pandowdy, which, according to the song, "makes your eyes light up and your stomach say 'howdy'." This is a simple dish with a sliced apple filling topped with a crust that may be broken up by being stirred into the filling. The down-home and slightly dowdy appearance of the dessert accounts for its name. Baked in kitchens since the early 1800s, Apple Pandowdy seems to be a totally American invention.

The origin of the name Apple Brown Betty is unknown, but the dish was mentioned in print as early as 1864. It has layers of apple slices and buttered crumbs and was popular with East Coast traders, who brought it south along the coast in their ships; the recipe spread westward from there.

Perhaps the first big promotion of the baked apple originated in the dining cars of the Northern Pacific Railroad, whose kitchens boasted two North-western products in their baked potatoes and baked apples. Today baked apples are often flavored and stuffed, or covered with a syrup.

Fruit cobblers, a traditional deep-dish "pie" with a thick crunchy topping, were made with a wide variety of fruits, while wild berries gave rise to a colonial dessert called a grunt: fruit covered with a dough and steamed in a kettle of boiling water. Our version of the grunt uses strawberries and rhubarb topped with biscuit dumplings.

Europeans used the word "pudding" as a general term for both hot and cold pies and other desserts; when they settled in the New World the lack of familiar ingredients forced them to make puddings from whatever was available – usually coarse cereals and sweeteners, such as whole meal, maple syrup, and molasses. Cornmeal mush, or hasty pudding, was made in the late 1600s from cornmeal, milk, and molasses. Some of the early desserts – Indian pudding, custard, and creams – still exist.

Homemade desserts like tapioca pudding and rice pudding may be considered old-fashioned, but nonetheless make deliciously rich and creamy courses. The persimmon, or "date plum," was very popular with the Indians and then with the earliest settlers, and persimmon pudding is a Thanksgiving dessert in the Southeast and Midwest.

However famous our fruits and puddings have become, America's first choice for desserts and snacks must be ice cream: in ice-cream pies and cakes; in sundaes; on waffles, pancakes, and fruit pies; sandwiched between cookies; or simply placed in wafer cones.

Philadelphians were probably the first Americans to make ice cream popular on a grand scale; the city became famous for its own style of rich ice cream, which was made without eggs. The term "Philadelphia ice cream" has been used since the early 1800s, and by the end of the century there were fifty ice cream factories in Philadelphia.

In 1846 a woman named Nancy Johnson made ice cream available to the average family by inventing a small ice cream freezer which could be cranked by hand; making ice cream at home in a hand-churned freezer became a summertime event.

Ice cream was soon mass-manufactured and became cheaper to buy in the markets. By the late 1800s, Americans were consuming ice cream at home, in ice cream parlors, and at ice cream stands. Ice cream rightly remains one of America's favorite desserts.

Fruit

APPLE BROWN BETTY

2 cups lightly packed
  fresh bread cubes
1/3 cup butter or
  margarine, melted
1/2 cup sugar
1/2 teaspoon ground
  nutmeg
1/2 teaspoon ground
  cinnamon
6 cooking apples, peeled,
  cored, and sliced
1/4 cup water
1 tablespoon lemon juice
Half-and-half for topping

1. Preheat oven to 375°F. Grease 2-quart casserole. In small bowl, toss bread cubes with butter. In another small bowl, stir sugar, nutmeg, and cinnamon. Add more sugar if the apples are especially tart.
2. Place one-third of bread cubes in even layer in casserole; cover with half of apples; sprinkle with half the sugar mixture. Repeat layering once. (Bread cubes will be left over.)
3. In cup, mix 1/4 cup water with lemon juice; pour over mixture. Sprinkle the remaining bread cubes over the mixture.
4. Cover and bake 30 minutes; uncover and bake 30 minutes longer or until the apples are tender. Serve the Apple Brown Betty warm and top with half-and-half.

BANANA COCONUT BETTY: About 1 hour before serving: Prepare as above but use 1½-quart casserole and substitute 4 bananas, thinly sliced, for apples; use 1/3 cup sugar and increase lemon juice to 2 tablespoons. Add 1 tablespoon grated lemon peel to sugar mixture. In step 3 toss the remaining bread cubes with 1/2 cup shredded coconut, then sprinkle over mixture. Cover the mixture and bake 30 minutes; uncover and bake the Banana Coconut Betty 5 minutes longer or until coconut is golden. Makes 6 servings. 244 calories per serving.

NEW ENGLAND BAKED APPLES

6 large baking apples
3 tablespoons butter or
  margarine, softened
1/4 cup dried currants or
  chopped dark seedless
  raisins
2 tablespoons finely
  chopped walnuts
1 teaspoon ground
  cinnamon
1 cup maple syrup or
  maple-flavor syrup

1. Preheat oven to 350°F. Prepare apples: Wash well; starting from stem end, core apples being careful not to go through to the bottom and making opening about 1 inch in diameter. Peel apples 1/3 of the way down.
2. Arrange apples in 13" by 9" shallow baking dish, peeled end up. In cup, combine butter, dried currants, walnuts, and cinnamon. Place some butter mixture in the hollow center of each of the apples. Pour the maple syrup over and around the filled apples.
3. Bake apples 50 minutes or until fork-tender, basting with syrup in baking dish occasionally. Serve apples hot, or cover and refrigerate apples to serve cold later.

APPLE PANDOWDY

Also called "Apple Jonathan" in the Northeast, this simple dish was probably named for its somewhat homey, dowdy-looking crust.

5 large cooking apples
  (about 3 pounds)
1/3 cup sugar
1 teaspoon ground
  cinnamon
Salt
3 tablespoons butter or
  margarine
1/3 cup light molasses
1/4 cup water
1 cup all-purpose flour
2 teaspoons double-acting
  baking powder
3 tablespoons shortening
3/4 cup milk
Heavy or whipping cream
  (optional)

1 Peel, core, and thinly slice apples to make 8 cups. In large bowl with rubber spatula, lightly toss apples, sugar, cinnamon, and 1/4 teaspoon apple salt; spoon apple mixture into 8" by 8" by 2" baking dish. In small saucepan over low heat, melt butter; remove saucepan from heat. Stir in the molasses and the water to make a sauce for the apples.

2 Pour over apple mixture in baking dish; set aside.

3 Preheat oven to 375°F. Prepare biscuit crust: In medium bowl with fork, mix flour, baking powder, and 3/4 teaspoon salt.

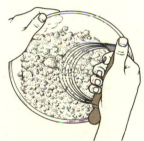

4 With pastry blender or two knives used scissor-fashion, cut in shortening until mixture resembles coarse crumbs. With fork, stir in milk just until flour is moist.

5 With spoon, drop dough by heaping tablespoons into 9 mounds on apple mixture. Bake 45 minutes or until crust is golden and apples are tender.

6 To serve, with spoon, break up crust and stir into apple mixture; serve warm in dessert bowls. If you like, pour some cream over each serving.

Fruit

SNOW APPLES

A very popular dessert at the beginning of this century, our snow apples are made with one of America's top varieties, McIntosh.

1 large lemon
6 medium McIntosh
* apples*
1 envelope unflavored
* gelatin*
¼ cup water
2 egg whites, at room
* temperature*
⅓ cup sugar
½ teaspoon vanilla
* extract*
¼ teaspoon salt
Lemon leaves for garnish

• *Color index page 65*

• *Begin 3½ hours ahead or early in day*

• *6 servings*

• *137 cals per serving*

1 Grate peel of lemon; set peel aside. Cut lemon; squeeze juice into 2-quart saucepan. Cut stem end from apples, ½ inch from top. Dip cut surfaces in some lemon juice to prevent darkening.

2 With spoon or melon baller, scoop out fruit from cut apples and tops into saucepan, discarding the core and leaving ⅛-inch-thick apple shells.

3 Discard tops. Brush inside of shells with some lemon juice. Wrap shells with plastic wrap; refrigerate while preparing the filling.

4 Heat apple pieces and remaining lemon juice in saucepan over high heat to boiling. Reduce heat to low; cover; simmer 8 to 10 minutes until apples are tender, stirring often.

5 Meanwhile, in cup, sprinkle the gelatin over water; let stand at least 1 minute to soften. Stir the gelatin mixture into the cooked apples until gelatin is dissolved.

6 In covered blender container at medium speed, blend mixture until smooth; chill until it mounds when dropped from spoon but is not set, about 2 hours.

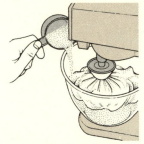

7 In small bowl with mixer at high speed, beat egg whites until soft peaks form. Beating at high speed, gradually sprinkle in sugar; beat until sugar is dissolved.

8 When sugar is dissolved and egg whites stand in stiff, glossy peaks, with wire whisk, gently fold apple mixture, vanilla, salt, and half of the grated lemon peel into the beaten egg whites. Spoon this mixture into the apple shells, making it mound slightly; sprinkle the top of the apples with the remaining lemon peel. (Spoon any leftover mixture into dessert dishes.) Refrigerate Snow Apples and any leftover mixture until set.

9 To serve, line chilled dessert platter with lemon leaves; place Snow Apples on top. Serve each with a spoon. Or, if you like, serve with a knife and fork to eat the shell.

BEST WAYS TO USE APPLE VARIETIES

All apples can be eaten fresh or cooked, but some lose their shape when baked, while others may be too tart for out-of-hand eating. Use this chart to guide your choice.

	Eating	Baking	Cooking	Sauce	Salad	Pie
Cortland	X	X	X	X	X	X
Golden Delicious	X	X	X	X	X	X
Granny Smith	X	X	X	X	X	X
Gravenstein	X	X	X	X	X	X
Jonathan	X	X	X	X	X	X
McIntosh	X		X	X	X	X
Newtown Pippin		X	X	X		X
Northern Spy	X	X	X	X	X	X
Red Delicious	X					
Rome Beauty		X	X	X		X
Winesap	X	X	X	X	X	X

McIntosh

Red Delicious

Rome Beauty

Golden Delicious

Newtown Pippin

Jonathan

CRANBERRY-PEAR COBBLER

An old New-England dessert sometimes known as "crow's nest pudding," the cobbler can be made with almost any fruit. We combine sweet pears with cranberries for a winning combination.

- *Color index page 64*
- *Begin 1½ hrs ahead or early in day*
- *10 servings*
- *235 cals per serving*

1 12-ounce package cranberries
¾ cup sugar
1½ cups water
3 tablespoons cornstarch
½ teaspoon ground cinnamon
¼ teaspoon salt
⅛ teaspoon ground cloves
5 medium Bartlett or other cooking pears

Cobbler Topping
1 cup whole-wheat flour
½ cup all-purpose flour
⅓ cup sugar
1 tablespoon baking powder
½ teaspoon salt
½ cup butter or margarine
½ cup whipping cream

Heavy cream (optional)

1 In 3-quart saucepan, combine first seven ingredients. Over high heat, heat mixture to boiling, stirring constantly. Spoon mixture into 13" by 9" baking dish.

2 Peel pears. Cut each lengthwise in half; remove cores and slice pears. Arrange pear slices on top of the cranberry mixture, overlapping the slices to fit.

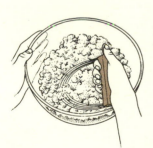

3 Preheat oven to 400°F. Prepare Cobbler Topping: In bowl, mix the flours, sugar, baking powder, and salt. With pastry blender, cut in butter until mixture resembles coarse crumbs.

4 Add whipping cream to dry ingredients in bowl; stir gently with fork until the dough leaves the side of the bowl. Crumble the Cobbler Topping over the pear layer.

5. Bake for 25 to 30 minutes until the topping is golden and fruit mixture is hot and bubbly. Serve cobbler warm.

6. If you like, pour heavy cream over each serving. Or cool cobbler completely to serve later. To reheat, just before serving, place cobbler in 400°F. oven 10 minutes to heat through.

STRAWBERRY RHUBARB GRUNT

The colonial dessert known as a grunt was made with berries and a steamed dough. Here we use strawberries and rhubarb.

- *Color index page 64*
- *Begin 30 mins ahead*
- *8 servings*
- *236 cals per serving.*

1 pint strawberries, hulled and each cut in half
1 pound rhubarb, cut into 1-inch pieces
½ cup sugar
3 tablespoons water
½ teaspoon ground cinnamon
½ teaspoon lemon juice

1 cup buttermilk baking mix
⅓ cup milk
1 cup heavy or whipping cream

1 In 10-inch skillet over medium heat, heat strawberry halves, rhubarb, sugar, water, cinnamon, and lemon juice to boiling.

2 Reduce heat to low; cover and simmer 5 to 10 minutes until the rhubarb is tender, stirring occasionally.

3 Meanwhile, in small bowl with fork, mix buttermilk baking mix and milk just until baking mix is moistened.

4 Drop dough by heaping tablespoons on top of simmering strawberry mixture, forming eight dumplings.

5 Cover and cook the strawberry mixture about 8 to 10 minutes until dumplings are set.

6 To serve, spoon strawberry mixture and dumplings into individual dessert bowls. Pass cream separately.

Fruit

- Color index page 66
- Begin 3 hrs ahead or early in day
- 8 servings
- 245 cals per serving.

PEACHES IN STRAWBERRY AND CUSTARD SAUCE

The Spanish brought peaches to the New World in the 1500s; by 1661 William Penn noted that no Indian plantation was without them. Today they are our second largest crop.

6 cups water
1¼ cups sugar
1 tablespoon vanilla extract

8 medium peaches, peeled
Custard Sauce (right)
Strawberry Purée (right)
Mint leaves for garnish

1 In 5-quart Dutch oven or saucepot over high heat, heat water, sugar, and vanilla extract until mixture boils and sugar is completely dissolved, stirring occasionally.

2 Add peaches; heat to boiling. Reduce heat to low; cover and simmer 5 to 10 minutes until the peaches are tender, occasionally basting the peaches with syrup in the Dutch oven.

3 With slotted spoon, remove peaches to 12" by 8" baking dish; cover and refrigerate until peaches are chilled, about 2 hours.

4 Meanwhile, prepare Custard Sauce and Strawberry Purée. Cover both and refrigerate at least 1 hour or until completely chilled.

5 To serve, into center of chilled deep platter, spoon Strawberry Purée. Spoon Custard Sauce around purée.

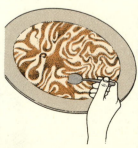

6 With spoon, swirl sauces together to create a marbleized effect. Arrange peaches in sauce. If you like, garnish peaches with mint leaves.

CUSTARD SAUCE: In 2-quart saucepan, mix *2 cups milk, 3 tablespoons sugar, 1 tablespoon cornstarch, ¼ teaspoon salt,* and *2 egg yolks.* Cook over medium heat, stirring constantly, until mixture boils; boil 1 minute. Remove from heat; add *½ teaspoon almond extract.* Makes 2½ cups. 19 cals per tablespoon.

STRAWBERRY PURÉE: In blender at high speed, blend *1 pint strawberries* and *2 tablespoons sugar* until smooth. Makes 1⅓ cups. 9 cals per tablespoon.

RASPBERRY SAUCE: In blender at high speed blend *1 pint raspberries* and *½ teaspoon sugar* until smooth, adding water if needed to thin to desired consistency. If you like, press sauce through fine sieve to remove seeds. Makes 1½ cups. 7 cals per tablespoon.

BITTERSWEET CHOCOLATE DESSERT SAUCE: In heavy 1-quart saucepan over medium heat, heat *⅓ cup sugar* with *⅓ cup water, 2 squares unsweetened chocolate, 2 squares semisweet chocolate, 2 tablespoons butter* or *margarine,* and *⅛ teaspoon salt* to boiling, stirring frequently. (Mixture will look separated.) Reduce heat to medium-low; simmer, uncovered, until sauce is smooth and thickened, about 3 minutes, stirring mixture constantly. Remove saucepan from heat; stir in *¾ teaspoon vanilla extract.* Serve sauce warm over poached pears, sautéed bananas, ice cream, or pound cake. Or, refrigerate sauce to serve later; reheat in heavy 1-quart saucepan over low heat, stirring mixture constantly. Keeps up to 1 week in the refrigerator. Makes about 1 cup sauce. 65 calories per tablespoon.

HOW TO MAKE SPICED APPLE RINGS

Apples, abundant all year round, make an unusual garnish for roast poultry, game, and salads when poached in a spicy syrup. For extra color, add a few red-hot cinnamon candies.

Peel the apples and core; sprinkle with lemon juice. Slice into ¼-inch rounds. If you like, cut the edges with a scalloped-edge cookie cutter for a more decorative look.

In a 12-inch skillet, poach the apple rounds as Spiced Pears with Chocolate Sauce, step 2 (p.291), but cooking only 15 minutes. Chill or serve warm.

HOW TO PRESENT FRESH FRUIT

When cut in unusual ways, fresh fruits can be used on their own to create a spectacular effect or as a garnish for other desserts. For best results, use a sharp knife with a thin blade.

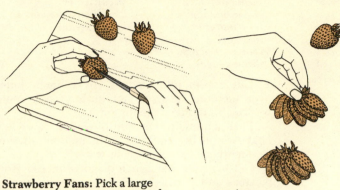

Strawberry Fans: Pick a large strawberry with a nice stem and cut into it lengthwise making as many thin slices as possible. Fan out by pressing the strawberry lightly at an angle.

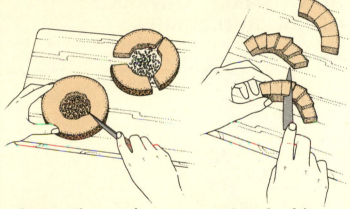

Melon Steps: Slice a cantaloupe or other melon into 1-inch-thick rounds and cut each round into three pieces.

Remove the seeds and skin, producing a basic fan shape. Make 4 or 5 radiating cuts on the surface of the melon about ¼-inch deep. Cut down to remove the wedge leaving the "steps."

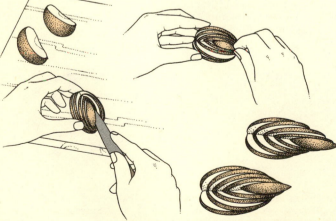

Apple Chevrons: Cut apple into 6 wedges; then cut each wedge into 4 layered V-shaped slices.

Reassemble the wedges, spreading them out slightly. Sprinkle cut surfaces with lemon juice to prevent darkening.

- *Color index page 66*
- *Begin 5 hrs or day ahead*
- *4 servings*
- *559 cals per serving*

SPICED PEARS WITH CHOCOLATE SAUCE

American pears came from European varieties, and the Bartlett is the most popular. They're delicious raw or cooked this way.

4 small pears	6 3-inch-long cinnamon
3 cups apple juice	sticks
¼ cup packed light	6 whole cloves
brown sugar	Bittersweet Chocolate
1 tablespoon grated	Dessert Sauce (p.290)
lemon peel	½ pint vanilla ice cream

1 Peel the pears. With an apple corer, remove the cores from the bottom of the pears, but do not remove the stems. This will make pears easier to serve.

2 In 2-quart saucepan over medium heat, heat pears and next 5 ingredients to boiling. Reduce heat to low; cover; simmer 30 minutes; turn occasionally.

3 Spoon pears and liquid into bowl; cover; refrigerate until well chilled, about 4 hours; turn occasionally.

4 About 10 minutes before serving, prepare chocolate sauce. Place 4 dessert dishes in refrigerator to chill. Remove the chilled pears from their liquid; reserve the liquid for use another day. In each of the chilled dessert dishes, place ¼ cup ice cream; arrange a pear on top of the ice cream. Drizzle the chocolate sauce in an attractive pattern over the fruit and ice cream in each bowl. Serve at once.

- *Color index page 64*
- *Begin 20 mins ahead*
- *4 servings*
- *115 cals per serving*

SPRINGTIME RHUBARB REFRESHER

1 pound rhubarb, cut	¼ cup strawberry jelly
into 1-inch pieces	¼ teaspoon ground
(about 2½ cups)	cinnamon
¼ cup sugar	⅛ teaspoon salt

1. In 2-quart saucepan over medium heat, heat all ingredients to boiling.
2. Reduce heat to low; cover and simmer 10 minutes or until rhubarb is tender, stirring the mixture occasionally.
3. Spoon the rhubarb mixture into four dessert dishes. Serve the rhubarb warm or refrigerate to serve cold later.

Fruit

GRILLED PINEAPPLE WEDGES

The pineapple is a native American fruit – Columbus found the "pine of the Indians" on Guadeloupe in 1493. Washington tried it in Barbados in 1751 and liked it better than any other tropical fruit. Today it is Hawaii's largest crop.

- Color index page 64
- Begin 15 mins ahead
- 4 servings
- 220 cals per serving

1 small pineapple 4 tablespoons butter or margarine, melted	⅓ cup packed brown sugar ¼ cup rum (optional)

1 Preheat broiler if manufacturer directs. Cut pineapple lengthwise into quarters from bottom through crown; leave on crown.

2 Cut out cores. Loosen fruit from peel by cutting close to peel; cut fruit crosswise into slices.

3 Place pineapple wedges in broiling pan; cover leafy crown with foil to prevent it from burning.

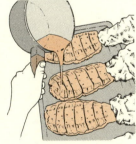

4 Pour melted butter over pineapple; sprinkle with brown sugar. Broil 4 to 5 minutes just until pineapple is heated through.

5 To serve, place pineapple on warm platter; remove foil. Pour any juice from broiling pan over pineapple.

6 If you like, heat rum in small saucepan over medium heat until hot but not boiling. Light the rum with a match; pour the flaming rum over the pineapple wedges.

BANANAS AND APPLES IN CARAMEL SAUCE

- Color index page 64
- Begin 30 mins ahead
- 6 servings
- 335 cals per serving

2 medium Golden Delicious apples ½ cup butter or margarine ½ cup packed light brown sugar	⅓ cup water 3 medium bananas ½ cup pecans

1. Cut apples into wedges. In 12-inch skillet over medium heat, in hot butter, cook apple wedges 5 minutes, stirring often.

2. Push apples to one side of skillet. Over low heat, stir in brown sugar until melted, stirring frequently. Gradually stir in water.

3. Cut bananas into 2-inch diagonal pieces. Add bananas and pecans to mixture in skillet; over medium heat, cook 3 minutes or until bananas are heated through, gently turning fruit occasionally. Serve warm.

HOW TO MAKE WHIPS AND OTHER FRUIT PURÉES

Prune whip, a popular American dessert based on a fruit purée, adorned many turn-of-the-century tables. Other dried, fresh, or canned fruits can also be puréed quickly and easily and used in whips or with other desserts.

In a food processor or blender, purée 1½ cups pitted cooked prunes with ¼ cup confectioners' sugar and ½ teaspoon grated orange or lemon peel.

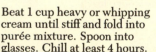

Beat 1 cup heavy or whipping cream until stiff and fold into purée mixture. Spoon into glasses. Chill at least 4 hours.

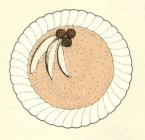

Purée fresh strawberries, raspberries, or cut-up mango; add a squeeze of lemon juice and sweetener to taste. Spoon onto a large plate as a background for presenting sliced fruits, and garnish with fresh berries.

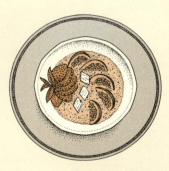

Ladle into a soup plate or bowl and use as a base for "fruit soup"; add cut-up fruits; garnish with mint leaves.

Molded desserts

SUMMER FRUITS IN APPLE-WINE GELATIN

¼ cup sugar
5 cups apple juice
4 envelopes unflavored gelatin
2½ cups dry white wine
1 pint strawberries
¼ pound seedless green grapes
1 large nectarine
½ cup blueberries
¼ cup loosely packed mint leaves, coarsely chopped

1. Into 3-quart saucepan, measure sugar and 2 cups apple juice; evenly sprinkle unflavored gelatin over the mixture.
2. Cook over medium heat until the gelatin and sugar are completely dissolved, stirring frequently to prevent gelatin from lumping.
3. Remove saucepan from heat; stir in dry white wine and remaining 3 cups apple juice. Refrigerate until mixture mounds slightly when dropped from a spoon, about 1 hour; stir occasionally
4. Meanwhile, wash and hull strawberries; cut each strawberry in half. Cut each grape in half. Thinly slice nectarine.
5. Stir strawberries, grapes, nectarine, blueberries, and mint leaves into gelatin mixture.
6. Pour mixture into 10 individual dessert glasses, or 1 10-cup glass bowl. Cover; refrigerate until set, about 3 hours.

- *Color index page 66*
- *Begin 4½ hrs ahead or early in day*
- *10 servings*
- *170 cals per serving*

CRANBERRY-WINE MOLD

4 packages unflavored gelatin
1 cup water
3 cups cranberry-juice cocktail or red grape juice
1½ cups dry red wine
½ cup packed light brown sugar
Red and green grapes for garnish

1. In 1-quart saucepan, evenly sprinkle unflavored gelatin over water; let stand 1 minute to soften. Place saucepan over medium heat and cook gelatin until it is completely dissolved, stirring frequently.
2. Pour the gelatin mixture into a large bowl with the cranberry juice, red wine, and brown sugar. Stir the mixture well until the sugar is completely dissolved.
3. Pour the cranberry-juice and gelatin mixture into a 6-cup mold. Cover and refrigerate until the mold is well set, about 4 hours. About 30 minutes before serving, place a dessert platter in the refrigerator to chill.
4. To serve, using a knife dipped in hot water unmold the Cranberry-Wine Mold onto the chilled platter. Garnish with grapes.

- *Color index page 65*
- *Begin early in day or day ahead*
- *10 servings*
- *131 cals per serving*

RED-WHITE-AND-BLUEBERRY MOLD

Wild berries were so abundant in the New World, the Indians held feasts to celebrate the strawberry harvest. This beautiful mold is perfect for a Fourth of July party.

1 pint strawberries
1 3-ounce package strawberry-flavor gelatin
Water
1 pint blueberries
½ cup sugar

1 envelope unflavored gelatin
½ cup milk
2 eggs, separated
2 8-ounce packages cream cheese, softened

- *Color index page 65*
- *Begin early in day or day ahead*
- *10 servings*
- *305 cals per serving*

1 teaspoon almond extract
¼ teaspoon salt
Mint leaves for garnish

1 Slice enough strawberries to measure ¾ cup; reserve the remaining strawberries for garnish.

2 In medium bowl, stir strawberry gelatin with ¾ cup boiling water until gelatin is completely dissolved. Stir in ¾ cup cold water.

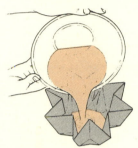

3 Pour ⅛-inch layer strawberry gelatin into 6-cup mold; refrigerate until almost set, about 10 minutes.

4 Arrange a few strawberry slices and some blueberries on gelatin layer to make a pretty design; refrigerate until set.

5 Refrigerate remaining strawberry-flavor gelatin until it mounds when dropped from a spoon.

6 Fold in ¼ cup blueberries and the remaining sliced strawberries (reserve the remaining blueberries for garnish); spoon over the gelatin layer in the mold. Refrigerate. Meanwhile, in a 2-quart saucepan, mix the sugar and the unflavored gelatin. In a cup with a fork beat milk and egg yolks until blended; stir milk and egg mixture into gelatin mixture.

7 Cook over medium-low heat, stirring constantly, until gelatin is dissolved and mixture coats the back of a spoon (do not boil). Remove saucepan from heat.

8 In small bowl with mixer at high speed, beat egg whites until stiff. In large bowl with mixer at low speed, beat cream cheese, almond extract, and salt until smooth. Gradually beat in gelatin mixture until blended. With rubber spatula or wire whisk, fold beaten egg whites into cream-cheese mixture. Pour cream-cheese mixture over strawberry layer in mold. Cover and refrigerate until set, about 4 hours.

9 To serve, unmold salad onto platter. Garnish the mold with mint leaves and the reserved whole strawberries and blueberries.

Molded desserts

GRAPE CLUSTERS IN SHIMMERING LEMON-CHEESE GEL

Early settlers made wine from the wild grapes they found all over the country; jellies, preserves, and juices soon followed. This mold makes a pretty summer dish.

- Color index page 65
- Begin early in day
- 10 servings
- 160 cals per serving.

Fresh mint leaves
2 3-ounce packages lemon-flavor gelatin
Boiling water
1 16-ounce container cottage cheese

1 tablespoon sugar
1 teaspoon grated lemon peel
½ teaspoon vanilla extract

½ pound seedless green grapes
½ pound seedless red grapes

1 Chop enough mint leaves to make 2 teaspoons. In small bowl, stir 1 package lemon-flavor gelatin with ½ cup boiling water until dissolved.

2 In blender at high speed, blend gelatin mixture with next 4 ingredients, and chopped mint until smooth; pour into 8" by 3" springform pan. Chill until almost set.

3 In medium bowl, stir remaining package lemon-flavor gelatin with 2 cups boiling water until gelatin is completely dissolved. Refrigerate until cool but not set, about 1 hour. Meanwhile, cut each grape from ¼ pound green grapes and ¼ pound red grapes in half. With kitchen shears, cut remaining green and red grapes into small bunches; wrap in plastic wrap and refrigerate for garnish.

4 Arrange grape halves in two clusters on cheese layer in springform pan. Place a few mint leaves at stem end of grape clusters to resemble grape leaves.

5 Carefully pour enough lemon-flavor gelatin mixture over the grape design to just cover the grapes so the grapes do not float.

6 Cover and refrigerate the gelatin mold until almost set, about 20 minutes. Leave remaining gelatin mixture at room temperature while the mold is chilling so it does not set. Pour the remaining lemon-gelatin mixture over grapes. (There may not be enough lemon gelatin-mixture to completely cover the grapes; some may extend out of mixture.) Cover and refrigerate until set, about 3 hours.

7 Using a metal spatula, first dipped into a cup of hot water, gently loosen the edge of the dessert from the pan.

8 Carefully remove the side of the springform pan. Transfer the dessert to a large serving dish.

9 Arrange reserved whole mint leaves and grape bunches around the finished dessert.

PINEAPPLE-ORANGE BAVARIAN

1 8½-ounce can crushed pineapple in heavy syrup
1 3-ounce package orange-flavor gelatin

¾ cup boiling water
1 cup heavy or whipping cream
1 tablespoon sugar

1. Drain pineapple, reserving ½ cup syrup. In medium bowl, stir orange-flavor gelatin and boiling water until gelatin is dissolved; stir in reserved syrup. Refrigerate gelatin mixture about 45 minutes or until mixture mounds slightly when dropped from a spoon.

2. In small bowl with mixer at medium speed, beat heavy or whipping cream and sugar until soft peaks form. With rubber spatula or wire whisk, fold whipped cream and pineapple into gelatin mixture.

3. Pour mixture into ten 4-ounce molds or one 5-cup mold; cover and refrigerate 3 hours or until the mixture is set.

4. To serve, unmold Bavarian onto chilled dessert dishes or platter.

- Color index page 66
- Begin early in day
- 10 servings
- 160 cals per serving

SUGAR-FROSTED FRUITS

Sugar-frosted fruits make a festive centerpiece when arranged in a glass bowl, or used as a special garnish for any dessert.

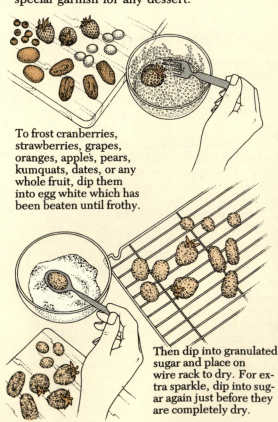

To frost cranberries, strawberries, grapes, oranges, apples, pears, kumquats, dates, or any whole fruit, dip them into egg white which has been beaten until frothy.

Then dip into granulated sugar and place on wire rack to dry. For extra sparkle, dip into sugar again just before they are completely dry.

Puddings

EGGNOG CHARLOTTE RUSSE

Perhaps named for the French hat style "Charlotte" which it resembled, this was a popular party dessert in the late 1800s.

- Color index page 66
- Begin early in day or day ahead
- 12 servings
- 248 cals per serving

2 envelopes unflavored gelatin
Sugar
½ teaspoon salt
½ teaspoon ground nutmeg
4 eggs, separated
2 cups milk
¼ cup brandy (or 2 tablespoons brandy-flavor extract)

1 3-ounce package ladyfingers, split
1½ cups heavy or whipping cream
1 square semisweet chocolate, grated, for garnish

1 In double boiler, stir gelatin with ½ cup sugar, salt, and nutmeg. In small bowl, with wire whisk or fork, beat egg yolks with 1 cup milk until well mixed; stir into gelatin mixture. Cook over hot, not boiling, water, stirring constantly with spoon or rubber spatula, until mixture thickens and coats spoon, about 30 minutes. Stir in remaining 1 cup milk and brandy.

2 Cover with waxed paper; refrigerate until mixture mounds slightly when dropped from spoon, about 1 hour. Remove paper.

4 In large bowl, with mixer at high speed, beat egg whites until soft peaks form; beating at high speed, gradually sprinkle in ¼ cup sugar; beat until the sugar is completely dissolved. (Whites should stand in stiff, glossy peaks.) Do not scrape the sides of the bowl during the beating process. With a rubber spatula or large spoon, fold in chilled mixture.

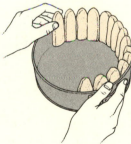

3 Meanwhile, line side of 8-inch springform pan with ladyfingers.

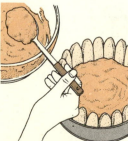

5 In small bowl, with mixer at medium speed, beat 1 cup heavy cream until soft peaks form; with rubber spatula, fold into dessert mixture. Spoon into lined pan; refrigerate until set.

6 To serve, carefully remove side of springform pan. In small bowl, with mixer at medium speed, beat remaining ½ cup cream to soft peaks; use to garnish top; sprinkle with chocolate.

RANGE-TOP RICE PUDDING WITH FRESH FRUIT

- Color index page 65
- Begin 1 hr ahead or early in day
- 8 servings
- 213 cals per serving

4½ cups milk
⅔ cup regular long-grain rice
2 tablespoons sugar
¼ teaspoon salt
2 eggs
1 teaspoon vanilla extract
¼ teaspoon ground cinnamon

¼ teaspoon ground allspice
½ pint strawberries
2 small bananas
Lemon juice
1 large kiwifruit
½ cup red grapes
Maple or maple-flavor syrup

1. In 10-inch skillet over high heat, heat milk, rice, sugar, and salt just to boiling. Reduce heat to low; cover and simmer 20 minutes, stirring occasionally.

2. In small bowl with fork, beat eggs slightly; stir in small amount of hot rice mixture. Slowly pour egg mixture back into rice mixture, stirring rapidly to prevent lumping.

3. Cook over low heat until rice mixture is slightly thickened, about 1 minute, stirring. (Do not boil, or it will curdle.)

4. Remove from heat; stir in vanilla extract, cinnamon, and allspice. Serve rice pudding warm or refrigerate to serve cold later.

5. Just before serving, hull strawberries; cut into thick slices. Slice bananas; sprinkle with lemon juice to prevent browning. Peel and thinly slice kiwifruit. Cut each grape lengthwise in half; remove seeds.

6. Arrange the fruit in a pretty design on top of the pudding. Pass the maple syrup separately to pour over each serving.

COCONUT-PINEAPPLE TAPIOCA

- Color index page 64
- Begin 35 mins ahead
- 6 servings
- 215 cals per serving

2 cups milk
¾ cup cream of coconut
3 tablespoons quick-cooking tapioca
1 egg
⅛ teaspoon salt

½ teaspoon vanilla extract
¼ cup flaked coconut
1 8-ounce can crushed pineapple, drained

1. In 3-quart saucepan, mix milk, cream of coconut, tapioca, egg, and ⅛ teaspoon salt; let stand 5 minutes to soften the tapioca. Over medium heat, heat to boiling, stirring constantly. Remove the saucepan from heat; stir in the vanilla extract. Let the tapioca mixture stand 20 minutes to set.

2. Meanwhile, toast coconut: In a small skillet over medium-high heat, heat flaked coconut until lightly toasted, about 4 minutes, stirring the coconut flakes frequently.

3. To serve, reserve 2 tablespoons crushed pineapple for garnish. With rubber spatula, gently fold remaining pineapple into tapioca mixture. Pour into bowl. Sprinkle top with toasted coconut and reserved pineapple. Serve the tapioca warm or cover and refrigerate the tapioca until ready to serve.

Puddings

BAKED COFFEE CUSTARDS

We are known as a nation of coffee-drinkers, and coffee-flavored desserts, like this luscious custard, are always winners.

- Color index page 65
- Begin 4½ hrs ahead or early in day
- 8 servings
- 270 cals per serving

1 teaspoon instant-coffee granules
Sugar
6 eggs
2¼ cups milk

½ cup coffee-flavor liqueur
¼ teaspoon salt
18 chocolate "coffee beans" for garnish

1 Preheat oven to 350°F. Grease eight 6-ounce custard cups. In small saucepan over medium heat, stir coffee and ¾ cup sugar until smooth, stirring constantly. Immediately pour into custard cups.

2 In large bowl with wire whisk or fork, beat eggs and ¾ cup sugar until blended. Beat in milk, coffee-flavor liqueur, and salt until mixed; pour mixture into custard cups.

3 Place custard cups in large open roasting pan; fill pan with hot water to come halfway up side of custard cups.

4 Bake 1 hour or until knife inserted in center of custard comes out clean.

5 Remove custard cups from the pan of water. Place cups on cookie sheet; cover; refrigerate until well chilled, at least 3 hours.

6 To serve, with knife, carefully loosen custard from cups; invert each onto a dessert plate; allow syrup to drip from cup onto custard. Garnish each with 3 chocolate "coffee beans."

VELVETY CUSTARD WITH BANANA SAUCE

- Color index page 65
- Begin 2 hrs ahead or early in day
- 4 servings
- 204 cals per serving

2 cups skim milk
2 eggs
¼ cup sugar

½ teaspoon rum extract
¼ cup red currant jelly
1 medium banana

1. In 2-quart saucepan with wire whisk, combine skim milk, eggs, and sugar. Cook over low heat until mixture thickens and coats spoon well (do not boil or mixture will curdle) about 20 minutes, stirring constantly.
2. Stir in rum extract. Spoon custard into four 8-ounce goblets or dessert dishes.
3. Cover and refrigerate mixture until well chilled, about 1 hour.
4. To serve, in 1-quart saucepan over low heat, melt currant jelly. Remove saucepan from heat. Dice banana; gently stir banana into melted jelly. Spoon ¼ of banana mixture onto each serving of chilled custard.

HOW TO MAKE FIG FLOWERS

Small fig flowers can be a dessert on their own, or they can be served as an accompaniment to a cheese plate or other dessert when filled with a flavored whipped cream, instant pudding, or dessert topping.

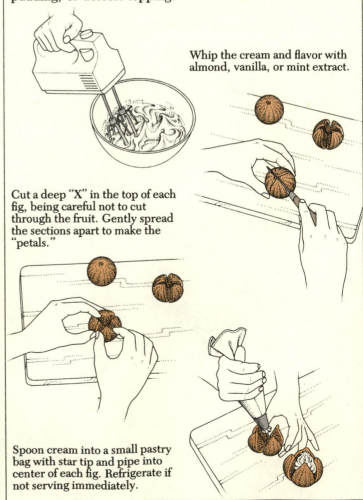

Whip the cream and flavor with almond, vanilla, or mint extract.

Cut a deep "X" in the top of each fig, being careful not to cut through the fruit. Gently spread the sections apart to make the "petals."

Spoon cream into a small pastry bag with star tip and pipe into center of each fig. Refrigerate if not serving immediately.

CRÈME BRÛLÉE WITH TROPICAL FRUITS

- Color index page 66
- Begin early in day
- 6 servings
- 380 cals per serving without fruit

2 cups heavy or whipping cream
4 egg yolks
¼ cup sugar
½ teaspoon vanilla extract
3 tablespoons brown sugar

Fruits: cut-up papayas, mangoes, kiwifruit, star fruit, tamarillo, or other favorite fruits such as peaches, pineapple, berries

1. In 1-quart saucepan over medium heat, heat cream until tiny bubbles form around the edge (do not boil).
2. In heavy 2-quart saucepan, with wire whisk, beat egg yolks with sugar until blended; slowly stir in hot cream.
3. Cook over medium-low heat, stirring constantly, until the mixture thickens and coats the back of a spoon well, about 15 minutes. (Be careful not to boil the mixture or it will curdle.)
4. Stir in vanilla extract. Pour custard into six 3- to 4-ounce heat-safe ramekins. Refrigerate until custard is well chilled, at least 1 hour.
5. About 1 hour before serving: Preheat broiler if manufacturer directs. Place brown sugar in small sieve; with a spoon, press the sugar through the sieve over the top of the chilled custard. Broil 2 to 3 minutes until the sugar just melts. Refrigerate until ready to serve. The melted sugar will form a crisp crust over the custard. If the crust is done too early in the day, the sugar will become soft and lose its crisp texture.
6. To serve, place a ramekin of Crème Brûlée on a plate and garnish it with a selection of the fruits. Or, if you like, arrange a selection of fruits in a large dessert bowl and pass it to accompany the individual Crème Brûlées.

GINGERED CRÈME BRÛLÉE: Prepare as above but heat cream with *1 teaspoon ground ginger*. Stir *¼ cup minced crystalized ginger* into cooked mixture with vanilla. Pour into ramekins; refrigerate. Add brown sugar; broil as above; chill. Serve with selection of tropical fruits listed above or other favorite fruits. 6 servings. 390 cals per serving without fruit.

Melting the sugar topping: Preheat broiler if manufacturer directs and broil sugar-topped custard 2 to 3 minutes until sugar just melts; refrigerate.

Coating the custard with sugar: About 1 hour before serving, place brown sugar in a sieve; press the sugar through the sieve onto the top of the chilled custard.

CHOCOLATE PUDDING

American chocolate was first produced in Massachusetts in 1765; dishes like chocolate pudding have since become famous.

- Color index page 64
- Begin 2½ hrs ahead or early in day
- 6 servings
- 440 cals per serving

⅔ cup sugar
¼ cup all-purpose flour
¼ teaspoon salt
Ground cinnamon
2 cups milk
4 tablespoons butter or margarine
3 squares unsweetened chocolate, chopped

1 egg
1 teaspoon vanilla extract
½ 3- to 4-ounce can pecans (½ cup), chopped
½ cup heavy or whipping cream

1 In heavy 3-quart saucepan, mix sugar, flour, salt, and ¼ teaspoon cinnamon; add milk, butter, and chocolate. Cook over medium heat until chocolate melts and mixture thickens slightly and boils; stir often. In a small bowl, beat egg with fork or wire whisk; stir small amount of the hot chocolate mixture into the beaten egg.

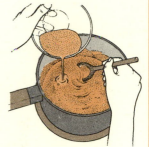

2 Slowly pour egg mixture back into chocolate mixture, stirring rapidly to prevent mixture from lumping.

3 Cook over low heat, stirring constantly, until pudding is thickened, about 2 minutes. (Do not boil, or mixture will curdle.) Remove saucepan from heat; stir in vanilla extract and chopped pecans.

4 Carefully spoon the pudding into 6 custard cups or small dessert dishes. Cover the custard cups or dessert dishes with aluminum foil. Refrigerate until well chilled, at least 2 hours.

5 In small bowl with mixer at medium speed, beat the heavy or whipping cream until soft peaks form.

6 To serve, spoon a dollop of whipped cream on each serving; lightly sprinkle cream with cinnamon.

Puddings

BAKED INDIAN PUDDING

The Indians used cornmeal in many ways – one was in a pudding, cooked with milk and molasses for about 3½ to 4 hours.

- Color index page 64
- Begin 4½ hrs ahead
- 8 servings
- 282 cals per serving

6 cups milk
½ cup yellow cornmeal
1½ teaspoons all-purpose flour
½ teaspoon ground cinnamon
¼ teaspoon ground ginger

¼ teaspoon ground cloves
2 tablespoons butter or margarine
¾ cup molasses
1 egg, beaten
1 cup heavy or whipping cream (optional)

1 Preheat oven to 300°F. In heavy 3-quart saucepan over medium heat, heat 4 cups milk until very hot; do not boil.

2 Meanwhile, in a small bowl, combine cornmeal, flour, cinnamon, ginger, and cloves.

3 Slowly stir cornmeal mixture into hot milk. Cook, stirring constantly, until mixture is very thick, about 15 minutes.

4 Remove pan from heat. With wire whisk or spoon, stir in butter or margarine until melted. Beat in molasses and egg until well mixed.

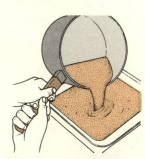

5 Beat in remaining 2 cups milk. Pour mixture into greased 2-quart casserole. Bake 3 hours or until knife inserted in center comes out clean.

6 Remove pudding from oven. Cool on wire rack 1 hour. Serve pudding warm. If you like, pour some cream over each serving.

MAPLE BREAD PUDDING

1 tablespoon butter or margarine
3 cups fresh bread cubes (about 6 to 8 slices)
1¼ cups maple syrup or maple-blended syrup
4 eggs

1 cup half-and-half
½ cup milk
2 tablespoons sugar
1½ teaspoons vanilla extract
1¼ teaspoons salt

- Color index page 64
- Begin 2 hrs ahead
- 8 servings
- 273 cals per serving

1. Grease 1½-quart casserole. In 2-quart saucepan over medium-low heat, melt butter. Stir in bread cubes; gently toss to coat well. Pour into casserole; pour ½ cup maple syrup over bread cubes in casserole.

2. In medium bowl with fork, beat eggs with next 5 ingredients; pour this mixture over the bread-cube mixture.

3. Set casserole in 9″ by 9″ baking pan; place pan on oven rack. Pour hot water in pan to come halfway up side of casserole. Bake in 350°F. oven 1 hour and 15 minutes or until knife inserted in center comes out clean.

4. To serve, in small saucepan heat remaining maple syrup until hot. Invert pudding onto warm plate. Serve pudding warm with hot syrup.

PERSIMMON-DATE PUDDING

2 cups all-purpose flour
2 cups sugar
4 teaspoons baking soda
1 tablespoon double-acting baking powder
½ teaspoon ground cinnamon
¼ teaspoon ground ginger
¼ teaspoon ground cloves
2 cups coarsely chopped walnuts
1 cup dark seedless raisins

1 cup chopped dates
1 teaspoon grated orange peel
2 cups persimmon pulp (about 1½ quarts home-grown or 4 large Japanese persimmons)
1 cup milk
3 tablespoons butter or margarine, melted
2 teaspoons vanilla extract
Foamy Hard Sauce (below)

- Color index page 64
- Begin 2½ hrs ahead
- 12 servings
- 540 cals per serving

1. Preheat oven to 325°F. Into large bowl, sift and mix first 7 ingredients; stir in nuts, raisins, dates, and orange peel; set aside.

2. Prepare persimmon pulp: Wash persimmons and remove caps. Peel and slice Oriental varieties and mash; press native persimmons through a food mill to remove seeds and skin.

3. With large spoon, stir persimmon pulp, milk, butter, and vanilla extract into the flour mixture until it is well mixed.

4. Spoon evenly into a greased and floured 13″ by 9″ baking dish. Bake 50 to 60 minutes until toothpick inserted in center comes out clean. Serve warm with Foamy Hard Sauce (below).

To store, cover pudding with foil and refrigerate up to 2 weeks. To reheat, preheat oven to 325°F. Heat covered pudding about 40 minutes or until heated through.

FOAMY HARD SAUCE: To Brandy Hard Sauce (p.315), softened, fold in *1 stiffly beaten egg white* and *½ cup heavy cream*, whipped. Refrigerate. Makes 1½ cups. 70 cals per tablespoon.

Mousses and soufflés

CHESTNUT CREAM MOUSSE

- Color index page 64
- Begin 5 hrs or day ahead
- 12 servings
- 171 cals per serving

1½ pounds chestnuts
Water
2½ cups milk
Sugar
2 envelopes unflavored gelatin
½ teaspoon salt
4 egg whites, at room temperature
2 cups heavy or whipping cream
¼ cup light corn syrup
1 teaspoon cocoa

1. In 3-quart saucepan over high heat, heat chestnuts and enough water to cover to boiling. Reduce heat to medium; cover and cook 15 minutes. Remove saucepan from heat. Immediately, with slotted spoon, remove 3 chestnuts from water. With sharp knife or kitchen shears, carefully cut each chestnut on flat side through shell; with fingers, peel off shell and skin, keeping chestnuts whole. (Chestnuts will be hard to peel when cool.) Repeat with 3 more chestnuts. Reserve the whole peeled chestnuts to garnish the mousse.

2. Quickly remove remaining chestnuts, 3 or 4 at a time, from hot water to cutting board; cut each in half. With tip of small knife, scrape out chestnut meat from its shell into medium bowl. In food mill or in meat grinder, using fine cutting disk, finely grind chestnuts. (Do not use a blender or food processor or chestnuts will be too gummy.)

3. In 1-quart saucepan, mix 1½ cups milk with ⅓ cup sugar; sprinkle gelatin evenly over mixture; over medium-low heat, cook, stirring constantly, until gelatin is completely dissolved. In a medium bowl, mix the gelatin mixture with the chestnuts, salt, and remaining 1 cup milk. Cover and refrigerate mixture until mixture mounds when dropped from a spoon, about 45 minutes.

4. Meanwhile, prepare collar for 1½-quart soufflé dish: Fold a 20-inch strip of waxed paper or foil into 20" by 6" strip; wrap around outside of dish so collar stands 2 inches above rim. Secure the collar with tape.

5. In small bowl with mixer at high speed, beat egg whites until soft peaks form. Beating at high speed, gradually sprinkle in ¼ cup sugar, beating until sugar is dissolved.

6. In large bowl with mixer at medium speed, beat heavy or whipping cream until stiff peaks form. With rubber spatula or wire whisk, fold chestnut mixture and egg whites into whipped cream until blended. Spoon mixture into soufflé dish; cover and refrigerate the mousse until it is set, about 2½ hours.

7. Meanwhile, prepare garnish: In 1-quart saucepan over high heat, heat corn syrup to boiling. Reduce heat to medium; cook 2 minutes. Remove saucepan from heat. With fork, dip reserved whole chestnuts, one at a time, in corn syrup. Place coated chestnuts on wire rack to cool and allow coating to harden.

8. To serve, remove collar from soufflé dish. Sprinkle top of mousse with cocoa; garnish with whole chestnuts.

MARBLED CHOCOLATE MOUSSE

Originally a French dessert, light and airy chocolate mousse has become very popular in American homes and restaurants.

- Color index page 66
- Begin early in day or day ahead
- 12 servings
- 247 cals per serving

3 eggs, separated, at room temperature
2 cups milk
¾ cup sugar
2 envelopes unflavored gelatin
1½ teaspoons vanilla extract
¼ cup cocoa
2 cups heavy or whipping cream

1 Prepare collar for 1-quart soufflé dish: From roll of waxed paper, tear off a 20-inch strip; fold lengthwise in half. Wrap around outside of dish so collar stands 2 inches above rim. Secure with cellophane tape. In 2-quart saucepan with wire whisk, beat egg yolks, milk, and sugar; sprinkle gelatin evenly over mixture. Over medium-low heat, cook, stirring constantly, until gelatin dissolves and mixture coats a spoon, about 10 minutes. Stir in the vanilla extract.

2 Pour half of yolk mixture into medium bowl; stir in cocoa until smooth. Cover and refrigerate both mixtures until they mound slightly when dropped from a spoon, about 30 minutes.

3 In small bowl with mixer at high speed, beat egg whites until stiff peaks form. In large bowl with mixer at medium speed, beat heavy cream until soft peaks form.

4 With rubber spatula, fold half of beaten egg whites and half of beaten cream into chocolate mixture; fold remaining whites and cream into vanilla mixture.

5 Alternately spoon chocolate and vanilla mixtures into soufflé dish. With knife, cut through mixtures for marble effect.

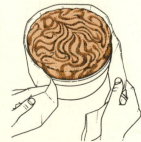

6 Cover and refrigerate the mousse until set, about 3 hours. Carefully remove the collar before serving.

Mousses and soufflés

MOLDED STRAWBERRIES 'N' CREAM

Strawberry festivals, a tradition started in the 1850s, are still held all over the country. Try this rich mold for a special day.

2 pints strawberries
2¼ cups milk
¼ teaspoon salt
4 eggs, separated
Sugar
2 envelopes unflavored gelatin

½ teaspoon almond extract
2 cups heavy or whipping cream
Mint leaves for garnish

- *Color index page 65*
- *Begin early in day or day ahead*
- *12 servings*
- *255 cals per serving*

1 Reserve 12 whole strawberries for garnish. Hull remaining strawberries. In blender at medium speed or in food processor with knife blade attached, blend hulled strawberries until puréed. In heavy 3-quart saucepan, with fork or wire whisk, beat milk, salt, egg yolks, and ¼ cup sugar until mixed. Sprinkle gelatin over milk mixture; let stand 1 minute to soften gelatin slightly.

2 Cook over medium-low heat, stirring constantly, until gelatin dissolves and mixture coats back of spoon, about 30 minutes (do not boil).

3 Pour the gelatin mixture into a large bowl; stir in the strawberry purée and almond extract.

4 Cover and refrigerate until mixture mounds slightly when dropped from a spoon, about 40 minutes, stirring occasionally.

5 In small bowl, with mixer at high speed, beat egg whites to soft peaks. Sprinkle in ⅓ cup sugar; beat until sugar dissolves and whites stand in stiff peaks.

6 Spoon beaten egg whites over gelatin mixture. Using same bowl and beaters, with mixer at medium speed, beat 1¼ cups cream to soft peaks.

7 With wire whisk or rubber spatula, fold beaten egg whites and whipped cream into strawberry gelatin mixture. Pour mixture into 1½-quart bowl. Cover with plastic wrap and refrigerate until mixture is set, about 4 hours. *About 30 minutes before serving:* In small bowl, with mixer at medium speed, beat remaining ¾ cup cream until soft peaks form.

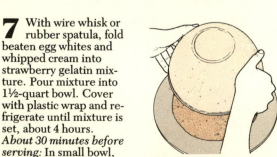

8 Spoon 1 cup whipped cream into decorating bag with large star tube. Unmold dessert onto chilled plate.

9 Decorate sides and top of mold with whipped cream. Place 6 whole berries around bottom and 6 on top. Garnish with mint leaves.

COOL LEMON SOUFFLÉS

2 teaspoons all-purpose flour
Sugar
¾ cup milk
2 eggs, separated, at room temperature

4 medium lemons
¼ teaspoon salt
1 cup heavy or whipping cream

1. In heavy 1-quart saucepan, mix flour and ½ cup sugar; stir in milk. Over medium heat, cook, stirring, until mixture thickens and boils; boil 1 minute. Remove from heat.

2. In small bowl, beat egg yolks slightly; stir in small amount of hot-milk mixture. Slowly pour egg-yolk mixture back into milk mixture, stirring rapidly. Cook over low heat, stirring constantly, until mixture thickens and coats the back of a spoon well, about 5 minutes (do not boil). Remove from heat. Cover surface of custard with plastic wrap and refrigerate until well chilled, at least 1 hour.

3. Meanwhile, prepare collars for eight 2-ounce ramekins or soufflé dishes: From roll of 12-inch-wide foil, tear off eight 4-inch strips; fold each in half into 12″ by 2″ strips. Wrap foil around outside of each ramekin so collar stands about 1½ inches above rim; secure with cellophane tape.

4. From 3 lemons, grate 1 tablespoon peel and squeeze ⅔ cup juice.

5. When custard is cool, in small bowl, with mixer at high speed, beat egg whites and salt until soft peaks form. Gradually beat in ⅓ cup sugar, 1 tablespoon at a time, until sugar dissolves and whites stand in stiff peaks.

6. In large bowl, with same beaters and mixer at medium speed, beat heavy or whipping cream until soft peaks form. With rubber spatula or wire whisk, fold custard, lemon peel, and lemon juice into whipped cream. Then, fold beaten egg whites into whipped-cream mixture. Spoon soufflé mixture into ramekins; freeze about 4 hours or overnight.

7. To serve, remove collars. Let soufflés stand at room temperature about 10 minutes to soften slightly. Cut remaining lemon into desired shapes; use to garnish tops of soufflés.

Preparing collars: Fold strips of foil into 12″ by 2″ lengths.

Wrapping ramekins: Wrap around ramekin; tape or tie with string.

- *Color index page 66*
- *Begin early in day or day ahead*

- *8 servings*
- *225 cals per serving*

Ice-cream desserts

BAKED ALASKA

Thomas Jefferson served a baked ice cream dessert in 1802; it may have been the earliest version of Baked Alaska.

2 pints chocolate ice
   cream, softened
2 pints raspberry
   sherbet, softened
1 11¾-ounce package
   white or yellow cup-
   cake mix
6 egg whites, at room
   temperature
½ teaspoon cream of
   tartar

⅔ cup sugar
½ cup raspberry jam
1 square unsweetened
   chocolate, grated

● Color index page 66

● Begin early in day
   or up to 1 week ahead

● 16 servings

● 296 cals per serving

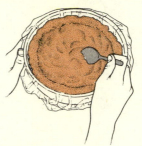

1 Chill 2-quart bowl, measuring about 8 inches across the top. Line chilled bowl with plastic wrap, leaving overhang.

2 With back of spoon, spread chocolate ice cream evenly in bowl to form a 1-inch-thick shell. Cover the bowl.

3 Chill in freezer about 40 minutes or until firm. Fill center of shell with raspberry sherbet; cover; freeze at least 3 hours until firm.

4 Meanwhile, preheat oven to 350°F. Prepare cupcake mix as label directs but pour the batter into a greased 9-inch-round cake pan.

5 Bake 20 to 25 minutes until cake springs back when lightly touched with finger. Cool cake; remove from pan. If not using same day, wrap cake and freeze.

6 About 20 minutes before serving: In large bowl with mixer at high speed, beat egg whites and cream of tartar until soft peaks form. Beating at high speed, gradually beat in sugar, about 2 tablespoons at a time, until sugar is completely dissolved. Whites should stand in stiff glossy peaks. Preheat oven to 500°F. Place cake on chilled heat-safe platter or cookie sheet. Platter is chilled to prevent ice cream melting when placed in hot oven.

7 In small bowl mix raspberry jam and grated chocolate; spread on cake. Invert ice cream onto cake; peel off plastic wrap. Spread meringue over ice cream and cake.

8 Bake 3 to 4 minutes until meringue is lightly browned. Serve immediately. Keep any leftover Baked Alaska frozen, wrapped in foil or plastic wrap.

HOW TO MAKE ICE-CREAM SANDWICHES

Ice-cream sandwiches have always been a popular snack. Try inventing your own sandwich using cakes, crackers, or cookies. Extra toppings make it less portable, but more fun.

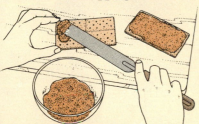

For a Portable Sandwich: For one serving, spread each of 2 graham crackers thinly with strawberry preserves.

For a Party Sandwich: Split 1 9-inch chocolate cake layer, unfrosted, in half horizontally.

From 1 pint ice cream "brick" cut a 1-inch-thick slice of ice cream; trim to fit cracker.

Place one half, cut side up, on plate; spread with 1 pint vanilla or strawberry ice cream, softened.

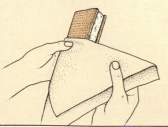

Place on spread side of one cracker; top with other cracker, spread side down. Serve immediately in paper napkin.

Top with remaining cake half, cut side down; freeze. To serve, soften 15 minutes; slice into wedges; top with Fudge Sauce (p.304).

Ice creams

Ice cream – The All-American Dessert

The history of ice cream in America dates back to Revolutionary times. George Washington was an early ice-cream lover and is said to have owned an ice-cream machine. Thomas Jefferson loved the dessert and is credited with bringing the custard-based version back from his trips to France and Italy where it was already very popular among the European nobility. However, it was Dolly Madison who really made ice cream popular when she served it at the White House.

With the Exposition of 1876, Philadelphia gained a country-wide reputation for its ice cream. Americans, and especially Philadelphians, had become ice cream crazy and the first ice-cream parlors emerged. "Philadelphia ice cream" is a term which still symbolizes a rich, quality ice cream made with cream, sugar, and flavorings, especially vanilla. Today, America makes and consumes more ice cream than any other country in the world and half of it is vanilla!

CHERRIES JUBILEE

The United States is the world's leading producer of cherries. The Bing cherry makes the best Cherries Jubilee, an elegant dessert of the 1880s.

At the table, in a medium skillet or chafing dish over medium heat, melt *one 10-ounce jar red currant jelly*, stirring gently. Add *two 17-ounce cans pitted dark sweet cherries*, well drained, and heat to simmering. Pour in *½ cup brandy*; heat 1 minute; then light with a match. Spoon flaming cherries over *6 scoops of vanilla ice cream* in 6 individual dessert dishes. **BRANDIED-CHERRY SAUCE** (made with fresh cherries): In 2-quart saucepan combine *1 pound sweet cherries*, pitted, *½ cup brandy*, *½ cup sugar*, and *2 teaspoons cornstarch*. Over medium heat, cook, stirring constantly, until thickened and boiled; remove from heat; stir in *¼ teaspoon almond extract*; use as above.

GEORGIA PEACH MELBA

Named for the famous opera singer, Nellie Melba, this combination of peaches topped with raspberry sauce makes a simple yet elegant dessert.

Place *1 poached peach half* (p.290), or *a well-drained canned peach half*, in bottom of dessert bowl; top with *1 scoop vanilla ice cream*, spoon over *2 tablespoons Melba Sauce* (p.306).

BROOKLYN BANANA SPLIT

Originally, bananas were brought to the U.S. from Cuba about 1804. They make a delicious base for this well known ice-cream extravaganza.

Peel and split *1 ripe banana* lengthwise; place halves, cut side up, on dessert plate. Top with *1 scoop each vanilla, chocolate*, and *strawberry ice creams*. Pour *2 tablespoons Hot Butterscotch Sauce* (p.306) over vanilla ice cream, *2 tablespoons hot Fudge Sauce* (p.304) over chocolate ice cream, and *2 tablespoons Brandied Strawberry Sauce* (p.306) over strawberry ice cream. Top with *whipped cream, nuts*, and a *maraschino cherry* or a *fresh strawberry*.

PHILADELPHIA ICE-CREAM SODA

The first ice-cream soda was served in Philadelphia in 1874. It's still one of America's most popular soda-fountain specials.

For a "Black and White" soda, so called because of the chocolate syrup base and vanilla ice cream, in a tall glass, mix *¼ cup milk* with *3 tablespoons chocolate syrup*. Add *1 cup soda water*, or flavored soft drink, and *2 scoops vanilla ice cream*. Top with *whipped cream* and add a straw. Experiment with other flavors.

OLD-FASHIONED HOT-FUDGE SUNDAE

Sundaes, an American classic, were originally served only on Sunday as they contained no soda water, a mix associated with alcohol.

ALASKAN ICE-CREAM SNOWBALL

On a hot summer's day, a "snowball" is a welcome relief. Try this traditional dessert with a variety of flavors and coatings.

LIBERTY ICE-CREAM CONES

Ice-cream cones first became popular at the 1904 St. Louis World Fair. Sugar cones, wafer cones, and a variety of toppings are fun at parties.

For each ice-cream snowball, roll *a scoop of vanilla ice cream* in a coating of *shredded coconut*, *chopped nuts*, or *cake crumbs* and arrange on a tray; refreeze. Place three balls on a plate; top with *Raspberry Sauce* (p.290). If you like, use any favorite ice cream. Serve with any of our *Dessert* (p.290) or *Ice-Cream Sauces* (p.306).

Place *2 scoops Chocolate Fudge Swirl Ice Cream* (p.304), or another favorite flavor, in lacy-edged ice cream sundae glasses or any dessert bowl; pour over *2 tablespoons Fudge Sauce* (p.304) or other Sauce for Ice Cream (p. 306); top with *whipped cream* and *Shaved Chocolate* or *Chocolate Curls* (p.330).

JOHNNY APPLESEED À LA MODE

Traditionally, a scoop of vanilla ice cream made apple pie "à la mode." Keep the combination to top a warm nutty waffle.

Fill a *sugar wafer cone* with a scoop or two of any flavor *ice cream*. Dip into a favorite topping such as *melted chocolate*, *shredded chocolate* or *coconut*, *chopped toasted almonds*, *chocolate sprinklers*, *crushed peppermint* or *other crushed candies*. Offer small bowls of toppings for each child to dip; provide lots of napkins and watch them enjoy themselves.

SAN FRANCISCO STRAWBERRY PARFAIT

California strawberries look especially pretty in this parfait; layers of ice cream and a dessert sauce or fruit. Use any pretty chilled glass.

In a glass, alternate layers of *strawberry-ripple ice cream* with *Brandied Strawberry Sauce* (p.306). Top with *whipped cream* and *strawberries*. For a raspberry parfait, use *raspberry-ripple ice cream* with *Raspberry Sauce* (p.290). Top with some *whipped cream* and *raspberries*.

Lightly toast or warm in the oven a *Buttermilk Pecan Waffle* (p.371); place on a warmed dessert plate. Top with a scoop of *vanilla ice cream* and pour over *¼ cup warm Chunky Applesauce* (p.379). Garnish with *chopped pecans*.

DOLLY MADISON ICE-CREAM CRÊPES

Using crêpes is a sophisticated way to serve ice cream. Try them with one of our Sauces for Ice Cream (p.306) or a fruit purée.

Scoop softened *strawberry ice cream* on center of a *Crêpe* (p.371). Fold 2 sides over and place crêpe seam side down on large dessert or dinner plate. Spoon some warm *Brandied Strawberry Sauce* (p.306) or *Bitter-Sweet Chocolate Dessert Sauce* (p.290) over the crêpe and sprinkle with *toasted almonds*. If you like garnish with a fresh *strawberry*.

Ice-cream desserts

CHOCOLATE FUDGESWIRL ICE CREAM

Ice cream was sold in colonial days, and a record states that George Washington spent $200 on it in one summer! We think our vanilla ice cream marbled with fudge would have pleased him.

- Color index page 66
- Begin early in day or up to 1 month ahead
- 32 servings or 4 quarts
- 265 cals per serving

2 cups sugar
⅓ cup all-purpose flour
1½ teaspoons salt
6 cups milk
6 eggs
3 cups heavy or whipping cream
3 tablespoons vanilla extract
2 cups water
About 10 to 20 pounds cracked ice
About 3 cups rock salt or 2 cups table salt for ice cream freezer
Fudge Sauce (right)

1 In heavy 4-quart saucepan, mix sugar, flour, and salt; stir in milk. Cook over medium heat until custard mixture thickens slightly and boils; stir the mixture frequently.

2 In medium bowl, beat eggs slightly; stir in small amount of hot mixture. Slowly pour egg mixture back into custard mixture, stirring rapidly to prevent the mixture from lumping.

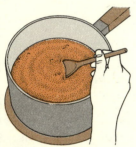

3 Cook over low heat, stirring constantly, until custard mixture thickens, about 5 minutes. (Do not boil, or mixture will curdle.) Remove from heat.

4 Pour custard into medium bowl; cover surface with plastic wrap; refrigerate until completely cooled, about 3 hours, stirring occasionally.

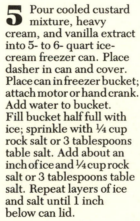

5 Pour cooled custard mixture, heavy cream, and vanilla extract into 5- to 6- quart ice-cream freezer can. Place dasher in can and cover. Place can in freezer bucket; attach motor or hand crank. Add water to bucket. Fill bucket half full with ice; sprinkle with ¼ cup rock salt or 3 tablespoons table salt. Add about an inch of ice and ¼ cup rock salt or 3 tablespoons table salt. Repeat layers of ice and salt until 1 inch below can lid.

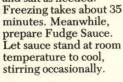

6 Freeze as manufacturer directs, adding more ice and salt as needed. Freezing takes about 35 minutes. Meanwhile, prepare Fudge Sauce. Let sauce stand at room temperature to cool, stirring occasionally.

7 After freezing, ice cream will be soft. Remove motor or crank; wipe lid clean. Remove dasher. Spoon vanilla ice cream into 15½" by 10½" roasting pan or 6-quart bowl.

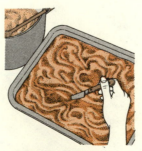

8 With knife or metal spatula, quickly swirl Fudge Sauce into ice cream to create a marbled effect. Cover surface with plastic wrap, then cover pan with foil. Place roasting pan in freezer for 2 to 3 hours to harden.

HOW TO RIPPLE ICE CREAM

Commercial ice creams are convenient to have on hand; rippled with other flavors they create a quick and pretty dessert. First, remove ice cream from freezer and place in refrigerator for about 40 minutes to soften slightly.

Berry Swirl: Place 1 pint vanilla ice cream in 8" by 8" baking pan. With fork, swirl 1 cup crushed strawberries or raspberries through ice cream. Refreeze until firm.

Maple Nut: Place 1 pint butter-pecan ice cream in 8" by 8" baking pan. Swirl maple or maple-flavored syrup through ice cream. Refreeze until firm.

Holiday Loaf: Spread 1 pint softened rum-raisin ice cream, in a 9" by 5" by 3" loaf tin. Swirl ½ cup prepared mincemeat through ice cream and refreeze until it is firm.

To serve, run knife dipped in hot water around edge of container to loosen; unmold and slice onto dessert plates. If you like, serve with whipped cream.

FUDGE SAUCE: In 2-quart saucepan over medium-high heat, heat *1 cup sugar, 1 cup heavy or whipping cream, 2 tablespoons butter, 1 tablespoon light corn syrup,* and *4 squares unsweetened chocolate* to boiling, stirring constantly. Reduce heat to medium; cook 5 minutes, stir often. Remove from heat; add *1 teaspoon vanilla extract.* Makes 1⅓ cups. 96 cals per tablespoon.

RAINBOW ICE CREAM TORTE

Layers of America's best-loved ice cream flavors in a gingery crust make a colorful dessert when sliced into wedges.

2 pints chocolate ice cream
⅓ cup gingersnap crumbs (about 20 gingersnaps)
¼ cup butter or margarine, softened
2 pints chocolate-chip-mint ice cream
2 17-ounce cans pitted dark sweet cherries, well drained

2 pints strawberry ice cream
2 pints vanilla ice cream
½ 4-ounce can walnuts (½ cup), chopped

- *Color index page 66*
- *Begin early in day or up to 1 week ahead*
- *16 servings*
- *378 cals per serving*

1 Remove chocolate ice cream from the freezer and place in the refrigerator about 40 minutes to soften slightly.

2 Meanwhile, in 10" by 3" springform pan, combine gingersnap crumbs and butter. With fingers, firmly press onto bottom of pan; freeze 10 minutes until firm.

3 Evenly spread chocolate ice cream on top of crumb crust. Place pan in freezer about 4 minutes to harden ice cream slightly.

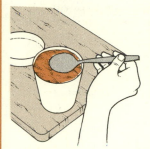

4 While waiting for chocolate ice cream to harden, place chocolate-chip-mint ice cream in the refrigerator. Leave to soften slightly.

5 Remove pan from freezer. Spread chocolate-chip-mint ice cream on chocolate ice cream; top with cherries. Return ice creams to the freezer to harden.

6 Repeat with strawberry and vanilla ice creams; sprinkle with walnuts. Cover and freeze ice cream until firm, about 3 hours.

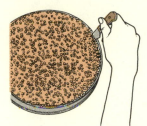

7 To serve, carefully run knife or metal spatula, dipped in hot water, around the edge of the springform pan to loosen the ice cream torte.

8 Gently remove side of springform pan. Let Rainbow Ice Cream Torte stand at room temperature about 15 minutes for easier slicing.

HOW TO MAKE AN ICE-CREAM PIE

Ice-cream pies make a convenient all-in-one dessert or party presentation. They can even be decorated ahead of time and frozen. Remember to remove pie from the freezer 10–15 minutes before serving. Try this Peanut-Butter Ice-Cream Pie for a children's birthday party.

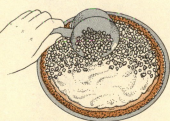

Sprinkle with ⅔ cup unsalted peanuts, chopped, and cover with another 1 pint vanilla ice cream, softened.

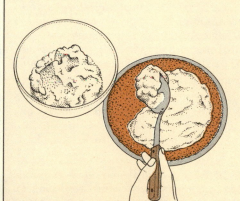

Prepare Peanut-Butter Cookie Crumb Crust (p.321). When cool, spread with 1 pint vanilla ice cream, softened.

In small bowl, blend ½ cup light corn syrup with ⅓ cup creamy peanut butter and spread over ice cream in pie crust.

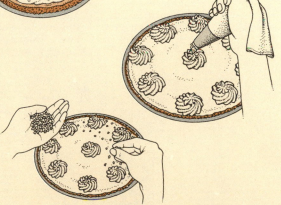

Cover and freeze until firm, about 4 hours. If you like, decorate with whipped cream and more chopped nuts.

Fruit ices/sauces

LEMON-LIME MILK SHERBET

Lemon-lime is an all-time favorite fruit combination, especially for fruit ices. Milk gives this deep flavor an extra rich texture.

- Color index page 66
- Begin early in day
- 8 servings
- 258 cals per serving

2 cups milk
1 envelope unflavored gelatin
2 cups half-and-half
1⅓ cups sugar
2 tablespoons grated lemon peel

1 tablespoon grated lime peel
½ cup lemon juice
¼ cup lime juice
Thin lemon or lime slices for garnish

1 In 2-quart saucepan over 1 cup milk, evenly sprinkle gelatin. Cook over medium-low heat, stirring until gelatin is dissolved. Remove the pan from heat.

2 Stir in the remaining milk and the half-and-half. Add the sugar, grated lemon peel, grated lime peel, lemon juice, and lime juice. (Mixture may look curdled.)

3 Pour the mixture into a 13" by 9" baking pan. Cover the top of the baking pan and freeze the mixture until partially frozen, about 3 hours, stirring occasionally.

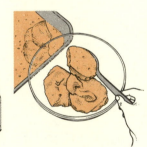

4 Spoon the mixture into a chilled large bowl. With the mixer at medium speed, beat the mixture until smooth but still frozen; return mixture to baking pan. Cover; freeze until firm.

5 To serve, let the sherbet stand at room temperature 10 minutes for easier scooping. Scoop into dessert glasses. Garnish with fruit slices.

TWO-MELON GRANITA

2 cups water
1 cup sugar
¼ cup lemon juice
1 ripe small cantaloupe (about 2 pounds)

1 ripe small honeydew melon (about 2 pounds)
Mint leaves for garnish

- Color index page 66
- Begin early in day or up to 1 week ahead
- 12 servings or 4 cups
- 95 cals per serving

1. In small saucepan over high heat, heat water and sugar to boiling. Reduce heat to medium; cook 5 minutes. Remove saucepan from heat; stir in lemon juice.

2. Cut cantaloupe into chunks. In blender at medium speed or in food processor with knife blade attached, blend cantaloupe until smooth; pour mixture into 8" by 8" baking pan. Repeat with honeydew melon; pour into another 8" by 8" baking pan.

3. Pour half of sugar mixture into each baking pan; stir until well mixed. Cover pans with foil or plastic wrap and freeze melon mixtures until firm, about 5 hours, stirring occasionally so mixtures freeze evenly.

4. To serve, let the granitas stand at room temperature about 5 minutes to soften slightly. With spoon, scrape across the surface of granitas in pans to create a pebbly texture. Spoon some cantaloupe granita and some honeydew granita into each of 12 chilled dessert bowls. Garnish with the fresh mint leaves. Or if you like, serve in hollowed-out melon shells (p.281).

SAUCES FOR ICE CREAM

Sauces make an ordinary scoop of ice cream into a special dessert. Pour them over other frozen desserts, custards, or fresh fruit; top with chopped nuts for extra crunch.

HOT BUTTERSCOTCH SAUCE: In small saucepan over medium heat, heat *1 cup packed light brown sugar, ¼ cup half-and-half, 2 tablespoons butter* or *margarine,* and *2 tablespoons light corn syrup* to boiling, stirring occasionally. Makes 1 cup. 79 cals per tablespoon.

CHOCOLATE-MARSHMALLOW SAUCE: In medium saucepan over low heat, cook *2 cups miniature marshmallows, ⅓ cup heavy* or *whipping cream, ⅓ cup honey, 1½ squares unsweetened chocolate,* and *⅛ teaspoon salt,* stirring constantly, until marshmallows and chocolate are melted. Serve hot. Makes 1½ cups. 47 cals per tablespoon.

MELBA SAUCE: In medium saucepan over low heat, melt *¼ cup red currant jelly;* stir constantly; *add 1½ 10-ounce packages frozen raspberries;* heat. In cup, mix *2 tablespoons cornstarch* with *1 tablespoon water* until smooth; stir into berries. Over medium heat, cook until thick; stir often. Makes 2 cups. 12 cals per tablespoon.

BRANDIED-STRAWBERRY SAUCE: Drain *3 10-ounce packages frozen sliced strawberries,* thawed, reserving ½ *cup juice.* In 2-quart saucepan over low heat, melt ½ cup redcurrant jelly, stirring. In bowl, mix juice and *1 tablespoon cornstarch* until smooth. Gradually stir into jelly; over medium heat, cook until thickened; stir often. Stir in berries and ½ *cup brandy.* Makes 4 cups. 12 cals per tablespoon.

PIES

*"Apple pie without cheese is like a kiss
without a squeeze."*

19th century American saying

Pies have been standard fare in America since the first English settlers brought their tradition of pie-making to the New World. They made many types of pastry pies filled with meats, fish, poultry, and, of course, wild fruit, which grew in abundance. Early American pies often consisted of wild berries or other fresh fruit. Dried fruit was often used, especially in winter. The pies were sometimes covered with a layer of custard for extra richness.

Since home-baked pies were so common, many recipes never appeared in early cookbooks; they were handed down by word of mouth or recorded in household diaries. Apple pie rarely appeared in any cookbook as each housewife had her own special pie recipe and it was assumed everyone knew how to make one. America has become the world's foremost apple-producing country and apple pie has come to symbolise the nation's culture, hence the statement "as American as apple pie." There are hundreds of apple pie recipes from every part of the country, some mixed with other fruits, such as raisins, pears, or cranberries, and some with nuts.

Berries and cherries, wild-growing or cultivated, have always been a prime choice for pies and tarts. Like apple pie, few written recipes for berry pies existed in our early history as it was assumed everyone knew how to make them. Favorites have traditionally been blueberry, strawberry, raspberry, and cherry, which has become a symbol of George Washington's birthday due to the story of the young boy chopping down the cherry tree.

Citrus fruits, mostly grown in California and Florida, are also important in our pie heritage. Lemon custard pie was Calvin Coolidge's favorite; today lemon meringue pie is probably on the menu of most American diners and coffee shops. Key lime pie, first made in the Florida Keys in the 1850s, when sweetened condensed milk became available, is a true American invention. As there were not many cows on the Keys, and fresh milk was scarce, condensed milk was used in this tangy pie made with lime juice. Today, true Key limes are difficult to obtain, as most are grown privately, so Tahiti limes, grown in Florida and California, are used most often.

A garden vegetable (though thought of as a fruit), rhubarb was considered a tonic and was used so commonly in pies that it became known as the "pie plant." It is used either as a main pie ingredient, often topped with custard, or combined with strawberries, as in our Strawberry-Rhubarb Pie.

American-grown nuts, such as pecans, walnuts, and peanuts, give a delicious flavor and crunchy texture to pies and piecrusts, and provide the base for pecan pies, walnut pies, and peanut-butter pies. These nut pie recipes vary from state to state. Shoofly pie, a Pennsylvania Dutch specialty, was originally made with molasses, which must have attracted flies, thus giving the pie its amusing name.

Among the many squashes in the New World, pumpkins were so abundant it was natural for the English colonists to invent the now-famous pumpkin pie. Some records report this favorite pie was served at the Pilgrim's second Thanksgiving in 1623; it certainly has become a traditional Thanksgiving dessert. Northerners almost always used pumpkin in this one-crust pie, but Southerners often preferred sweet potatoes; our Sweet-Potato Pie with Walnut-Crunch Topping gives an old favorite some extra texture.

It wasn't until the late 1800s that the cream pies we know today, such as banana and chocolate, began to appear. They remain a favorite dessert pie along with chiffon pies which appeared in the 1930s when a restaurant in Iowa served the first one recorded.

The pie is still one of the most welcome desserts on the American table; the countless varieties of fillings, crusts, and toppings make it a popular year-round choice.

Fruit pies

SUGAR-FROSTED APPLE PIE

America is the world's foremost apple producer. Our decorated flaky pastry filled with juicy apples, then topped with cheese, is truly an all-American dessert.

- *Color index page 67*
- *Begin 2 hrs ahead or early in day*
- *10 servings*
- *379 cals per serving*

8 medium Golden
    Delicious apples
2 teaspoons lemon juice
2 tablespoons all-purpose
    flour
¼ teaspoon salt
Sugar
Ground cinnamon
Flaky Pastry (p.310)
1 tablespoon butter or
    margarine, cut into
    small pieces
Milk
5 slices American cheese

1 Peel, core, and thinly slice apples, (makes 8 cups). Sprinkle with lemon juice; this helps prevent the apples from darkening.

2 In a large bowl with a rubber spatula, lightly toss the apples, flour, salt, ½ cup sugar, and ¾ teaspoon cinnamon; set aside.

3 Prepare the Flaky Pastry, steps 1 to 6. Spoon the apple and spice mixture into the pastry-lined pie plate.

4 Dot with butter, set aside. Preheat oven to 425°F. Roll out smaller ball; slash, then center top over apple filling.

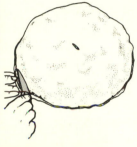

5 Trim pastry edge, leaving 1-inch overhang. Fold overhang under, then bring up over pie-plate rim; pinch to form stand-up edge; form Fluted Edge (p.313).

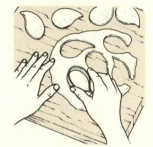

6 Reroll pastry trimmings. With floured leaf-shaped cookie cutter or knife, cut 5 leaves, rerolling dough if necessary. Arrange the leaves on pie top.

7 Lightly brush top of pie with milk. In a small bowl, mix 1 tablespoon sugar with ⅛ teaspoon cinnamon. Sprinkle evenly over pie.

8 Place pie on cookie sheet. Bake pie 45 minutes or until crust is golden and apples are tender. Remove pie to wire rack, cool slightly.

9 Cut each cheese slice into a leaf. Gently tuck cheese leaves under pastry leaves on pie top. Serve warm, or cool pie to serve later.

HOW TO DECORATE WITH PASTRY

It is easy work to make a pie look very special simply by cutting trimmings of pastry into various shapes and decorating the top.

A covered pie can be decorated with shapes of any kind.

Using a sharp knife, cookie cutter, or pastry wheel, cut rolled out pastry trimmings into various shapes:

Lattice Strips

Diamonds

Holly Leaves and Berries

Hearts

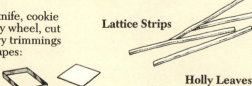

Leaves

Grape Leaves and Cluster of Grapes

An open-face pie can be partly covered by joining a pattern of diamonds or leaves over the top to form a kind of top crust.

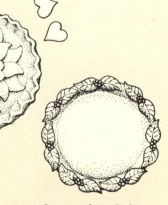

Open-face pies benefit from a decorative edge made by overlapping leaves and berries on the rim, or a larger design placed in the center.

Fruit pies

FLAKY PASTRY

This flaky pastry makes enough dough for a two-crust pie. It is light and tender, yet firm enough to hold a substantial fruit filling. Using cold water, chilling the dough, and rolling out the pastry as quickly as possible should guarantee excellent results.

- *Begin early in day*
- *1 8- or 9-inch two-crust pie*
- *2350 cals*

2 cups all-purpose flour
1 teaspoon salt

¾ cup shortening
Water

1 About ½ hour before making pastry, chill flour in medium bowl in refrigerator. With fork, stir salt into flour.

2 With pastry blender or two knives used scissor fashion, cut the shortening into the flour until the mixture resembles coarse crumbs.

3 Sprinkle 5 to 6 tablespoons water, a tablespoon at a time, into flour mixing lightly with a fork until pastry just holds together.

4 With hands, shape pastry into 2 balls, one slightly larger, and flatten slightly. Wrap in waxed paper and refrigerate for half an hour before rolling.

5 For bottom crust, on lightly floured surface, with lightly floured rolling pin, roll larger ball into a circle ⅛-inch thick and about 2 inches larger all around than pie plate.

6 Roll pastry circle gently onto rolling pin; transfer to the pie plate and unroll it, carefully easing the pastry into the bottom and side of the pie plate.

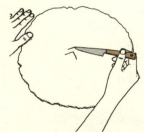

7 For top crust, roll smaller ball as for bottom crust. With sharp knife, cut a few short slashes or a design in center of circle; this will allow the steam to escape during baking.

8 Center the top crust over the filling. With kitchen scissors or sharp knife, carefully trim the pastry edges, leaving a 1-inch overhang. Fold the overhang under.

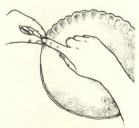

9 Carefully bring overhang up over the pie-plate rim; pinch to form a stand-up edge, then make a Decorative Pie Edge (p.313). Bake as directed in recipe.

UNBAKED PIECRUST

1 cup all-purpose flour
½ teaspoon salt

¼ cup plus 2 tablespoons shortening
Water

1. In medium bowl, with fork, stir flour and salt. With pastry blender or two knives used scissor fashion, cut shortening into flour until mixture resembles coarse crumbs.

2. Sprinkle 2 to 3 tablespoons cold water, a tablespoon at a time, into flour mixture, mixing lightly with a fork after each addition until pastry is just moist enough to hold together. Shape pastry into a ball and flatten slightly. Wrap in waxed paper and refrigerate for half an hour.

3. On lightly floured surface, with lightly floured rolling pin, roll pastry into circle ⅛-inch thick and about 2 inches larger all around than an 8- or 9-inch pie plate.

4. Roll pastry circle gently onto rolling pin; transfer to pie plate and unroll, easing into bottom and side of plate. With kitchen scissors or sharp knife, trim pastry edges, leaving a 1-inch overhang. Fold overhang under, then bring up over pie-plate rim; pinch to form a stand-up edge, then make a Decorative Pie Edge (p.313). Bake as directed in recipe.

BAKED PIECRUST: Preheat oven to 425°F. Prepare as for Unbaked Piecrust. With four-tined fork, prick bottom and side of crust in many places to prevent puffing during baking. Bake 15 minutes or until golden. Cool on a wire rack.

- *Begin 2 hrs ahead or early in day*
- *1 8- or 9-inch piecrust*
- *1895 cals*

HOW TO ROLL OUT PASTRY

Chilling the pastry makes the rolling a lot easier. If possible, use a stockinette-covered rolling pin on a lightly floured surface; otherwise flour rolling pin by hand.

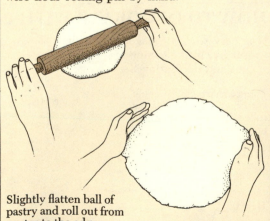

Slightly flatten ball of pastry and roll out from center to the edges, turning pastry to keep it circular. Add more flour if pastry begins to stick to counter top.

Push the sides in by hand if necessary and lift rolling pin slightly as you near the edges to avoid making them too thin.

OPEN-FACE APPLE PIE

- Color index page 67
- Begin 2 hrs ahead
- 6 servings
- 491 cals per serving

1 9-inch Unbaked Piecrust (p.310)
6 cups thinly sliced, peeled, and cored cooking apples
⅔ cup sugar
2 tablespoons all-purpose flour
1 teaspoon grated lemon peel

2 teaspoons lemon juice
½ teaspoon cinnamon
¼ teaspoon nutmeg
⅛ teaspoon salt
1 tablespoon butter or margarine
Maple syrup (optional)

1. Prepare Unbaked Piecrust with Turret Edge (p.313). Preheat oven to 425°F.
2. In large bowl, toss apples with next 7 ingredients; arrange in piecrust. Dot the filling with butter or margarine.
3. Cover top of pie with sheet of foil; place another sheet of foil on oven shelf below pie to catch any drips.
4. Bake 45 minutes; remove foil from top of pie. Bake 10 to 15 minutes more until the apples are tender.
5. If you like, drizzle maple syrup over top of hot pie. Serve warm or cold.

HOW TO MAKE APPLE DUMPLINGS

This is an old-fashioned dessert, easy to make with Flaky Pastry (p.310) and apples. Peel apples; remove ¾ of core, leaving stem end intact and stem attached.

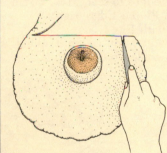

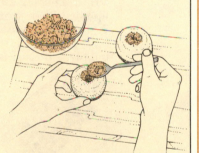

Roll pastry out ⅛-inch thick. Cut a square large enough to wrap an apple.

Fill core of apple with a mixture of ground cinnamon, sugar, and small cubes of butter, and place in center of pastry. If you like add a few raisins to the filling.

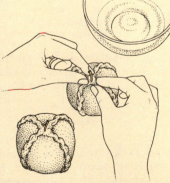

Trim excess pastry from edges; moisten with water and pinch edges together to seal seams. Decorate with pastry leaves.

Brush dumpling with beaten egg and bake about 25 to 30 minutes, until pastry is brown and the fruit tender.

APPLE-CUSTARD PIE

This version of the ordinary apple pie is rich and creamy, yet light, and makes an elegant dessert for a special dinner party. Arrange the thin apple slices neatly in overlapping circles to make a pretty circular pattern.

- Color index page 67
- Begin early in day or day ahead
- 8 servings
- 270 cals per serving

2 lbs cooking apples
1 9-inch Unbaked Piecrust (p.310)
Sugar
3 tablespoons all-purpose flour

½ teaspoon salt
¼ teaspoon cinnamon
2 eggs
¾ cup half-and-half or milk
Dash ground nutmeg

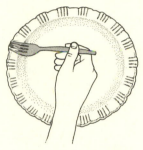

1 Peel and core apples; cut into thin slices. This will make about 6 cups. Prepare Unbaked Piecrust with Fork-Scalloped Edge (p.313).

2 Preheat oven to 375°F. In large bowl, toss apple slices with ½ cup sugar, flour, salt, and cinnamon until apples are well coated.

3 Carefully arrange prepared apple slices in overlapping circles in the unbaked piecrust, working from the outer edge of the pie plate toward the center.

4 In small bowl with wire whisk or fork, beat eggs with ¼ cup sugar, half-and-half, and the ground nutmeg; pour mixture over apple slices in piecrust.

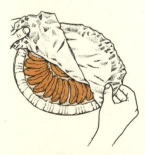

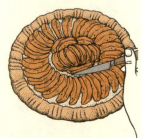

5 Cover loosely with foil. Bake pie 45 minutes; remove foil and bake 30 minutes more.

6 Pie is done when knife inserted in custard comes out clean. Cool, then refrigerate.

Fruit pies

OLD-FASHIONED PEAR-APPLE PIE

In America, apples and pears have always been a favorite fruit combination. They are especially delicious when baked until soft under an old-fashioned covered crust.

- Color index page 67
- Begin 3 hrs ahead or early in day
- 10 servings
- 395 cals per serving

4 medium Granny Smith apples, peeled, cored, and thinly sliced (about 4 cups)
4 large pears, peeled, cored, and thinly sliced (about 4 cups)
½ cup packed light brown sugar

¼ cup sugar
¼ cup all-purpose flour
¾–1 teaspoon ground cinnamon
¼ teaspoon ground nutmeg
Salt

Flaky Oil Pastry (for 9½" by 1½" deep pie plate)
2⅓ cups all-purpose flour
1 teaspoon salt
½ cup plus 1 tablespoon salad oil
3–4 tablespoons cold water

1 In large bowl, with rubber spatula, gently toss first 7 ingredients and ¼ teaspoon salt until well mixed; set aside. Prepare Flaky Oil Pastry: In medium bowl, stir flour and salt. Stir in salad oil until mixture resembles coarse crumbs. Add cold water, a tablespoon at a time, into mixture, mixing lightly with fork after each addition until the pastry is moist and cleans the side of bowl. Shape the pastry into a ball.

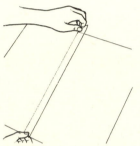

2 Moisten counter top. Place two 15-inch-long strips of waxed paper on top, overlapping to make a 15-inch square.

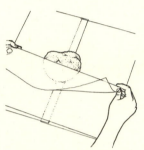

3 For bottom crust, place two-thirds of pastry in center of square; cover with another square of waxed paper.

4 With rolling pin, carefully roll pastry into a 15-inch round. Line pie plate with the pastry; trim edge, leaving ½-inch overhang.

5 Spoon fruit mixture into pastry-lined pie plate; dot filling with the butter or margarine. Preheat oven to 425°F.

6 For top crust, roll remaining pastry between two 12-inch squares of waxed paper into a 12-inch round; place over filling.

7 Make Fork Edge: Fold the overhang under; press it down lightly. Trim the pastry even with the rim.

8 With floured, four-tined fork, press pastry to rim, leaving a 1-inch gap between the fork marks.

9 With sharp knife, cut a few slashes in top crust to allow steam to escape during baking. Bake pie 50 minutes, or until crust is golden and fruit is tender. If pastry browns too quickly, cover the pie loosely with foil to prevent over-browning. Remove pie from oven and cool on a wire rack 1 hour; serve warm. If you like, cool completely to serve later.

DEEP-DISH APPLE PIE

Flaky Pastry (p.310)
6 medium cooking apples, peeled, cored, and sliced
2 tablespoons butter
¾ cup sugar
¼ cup all-purpose flour

1 teaspoon ground cinnamon
1 teaspoon lemon juice
½ teaspoon ground nutmeg
¼ teaspoon salt
Egg Glaze (below)

1. Prepare Flaky Pastry, steps 1 to 4. Preheat oven to 425°F.
2. Roll larger ball of pastry into a rectangle large enough to line a 10″ by 6″ baking dish. Line baking dish with the pastry; trim pastry, leaving a 1-inch overhang.
3. Arrange apple slices in baking dish; dot with butter. In small bowl, combine next 6 ingredients and sprinkle over apples.
4. Add trimmings to remaining pastry and roll into a rectangle 12 inches long. With a pastry wheel or sharp knife, cut 4 ½-inch strips, 12 inches long. Reroll remaining pastry and cut 6 ½-inch strips 8 inches long.
5. Moisten edge of bottom crust with water. Place the 4 12-inch long strips evenly across the length of the filling, twisting strips. Place the 6 8-inch long strips at right angles to the first layer, gently twisting the strips.
6. Trim strips even with overhang, pressing ends of overhang to seal. Turn overhang up over the strips, pinching the edges to seal. Make a stand-up edge, then form Fluted Edge (right).
7. Brush top crust with Egg Glaze.
8. Bake pie 45 to 50 minutes until filling is bubbly and crust is golden brown.

Forming pastry top: Twist long pastry strips lengthwise over fruit.

Fluting the edge: Keeping index finger inside edge, pinch pastry.

EGG GLAZE: For a golden glaze, before baking brush top crust with beaten whole egg or egg yolk. For added sparkle, sprinkle with sugar.

- Color index page 67
- Begin 2 hrs ahead or early in day
- 10 servings
- 376 cals per serving

DEEP-DISH PLUM PIE: Preheat oven and prepare crust as directed above, but use *2 pounds of plums*, halved; dot with *2 tablespoons butter* or *margarine*. In small bowl, combine *1¼ cups sugar, 3 tablespoons all-purpose flour* and *¼ teaspoon almond extract*; sprinkle over plums. Top with pastry as directed above; bake as above. Makes 10 servings. 384 cals per serving.

DECORATIVE PIE EDGES

Any pie can look extra special by making a decorative edge. It can be as simple as a Fluted Edge or as fancy as a Braided Edge. Use our easy directions to create a special look.

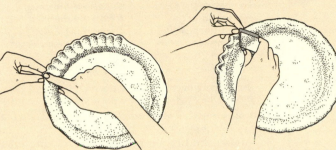

Fluted Edge: Place one index finger on the inside edge of pastry and, with index finger and thumb of the other hand, pinch pastry to make a flute. Repeat around the edge, leaving a 1/4-inch space between each flute.

A Fluted Edge can be varied either by angling the fingers to the edge of the rim as you pinch the pastry to make the flute, or by using the back of a knife or a diamond-shaped cutter to make a deeper indentation in the pastry.

Turret Edge: Form a stand-up edge. With kitchen scissors or knife, cut through pastry to rim at 1/2-inch intervals. Press alternate strips of pastry flat around edge to give turret effect.

Pinched Edge: Form a stand-up edge. Pinch edge between thumb and index finger. Place thumb in groove left by index finger and repeat all around the pie edge.

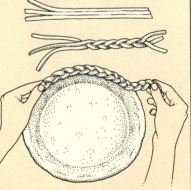

Fork-Scalloped Edge: Form a stand-up edge. Place thumb against outside edge of the pie edge and press it toward pie while pressing down next to it with 4-tined fork. Continue around edge leaving alternate fork marks and a ruffle effect.

Braided Edge: Cut strips of remaining rolled out pastry 1/4-inch wide. Braid together and press to lightly moistened piecrust edge.

- Color index page 67
- Begin 3 hrs ahead or early in day
- 10 servings
- 400 cals per serving

DOWN-HOME PEACH PIE

Peach pie is a favorite in Georgia, where peaches are a major crop. Decorate the top of this sugar pastry crust with pretty leaves for a fancier effect.

Sweet Flaky Pastry
2 1/3 cups all-purpose flour
1 teaspoon salt
2 teaspoons sugar
3/4 cup butter or margarine
Water

Peach Filling
14 large peaches (5 pounds)

1/4 cup quick-cooking tapioca
2 tablespoons lemon juice
1 teaspoon ground cinnamon
1/8 teaspoon ground ginger
1 cup sugar
Butter
1 egg yolk, beaten

1 Prepare Sweet Flaky Pastry as Flaky Pastry (p.310), steps 1 to 4, using the above ingredients and adding sugar to flour mixture before cutting in the butter. Roll bottom crust 2 1/2 inches larger than a 9 1/2" by 1 1/2" deep pie plate. Line pie plate; trim edge leaving 1-inch overhang. Peel and slice peaches. In bowl, gently toss peaches with next 5 ingredients. Let stand 30 minutes, stirring often.

2 Spoon peach mixture into pie plate. Cut 1 tablespoon butter into small pieces; sprinkle over peach mixture.

3 Preheat oven to 425°F. Roll top crust as Flaky Pastry (p.310) steps 7 to 9. Make Fluted Edge at an angle (left).

4 Reroll pastry trimmings; cut out a few leaves and arrange on top of pie. Brush pastry with beaten egg yolk.

5 Place pie on cookie sheet to catch drips during baking. Bake 50 minutes, until crust is golden and fruit is tender.

6 If pie crust begins to brown too much, cover loosely with foil. Remove pie to wire rack. Serve pie warm or cool.

Fruit pies

STRAWBERRY-RHUBARB PIE

Rhubarb, also called the "pie plant," has long been a Pennsylvania Dutch favorite, especially when baked with strawberries.

- Color index page 67
- Begin 3 hrs ahead
- 6 servings
- 573 cals per serving

Flaky Pastry (p.310)
2 pints strawberries, each cut in half
1 pound rhubarb (without tops), cut into ½-inch pieces, or 1 16-ounce package frozen rhubarb
¾ cup sugar

⅓ cup all-purpose flour
2 tablespoons quick-cooking tapioca
½ teaspoon vanilla extract
½ teaspoon salt
1 tablespoon butter or margarine

1 Prepare Flaky Pastry, steps 1 to 4. In a large bowl, with rubber spatula, toss next 7 ingredients to mix.

2 Let stand 30 minutes, stirring often. Roll crust as Flaky Pastry, steps 5 to 6; line a 9½" by 1½" deep pie plate.

3 Spoon fruit mixture into piecrust. Cut butter into small pieces; sprinkle over fruit. Preheat oven to 425°F; Roll out remaining pastry.

4 With a pastry wheel, cut long strips, ½-inch wide. Place on pie in 6 "V" shapes. Use more strips to make smaller "V" shapes inside larger ones.

5 Moisten edge of bottom pastry; press strip ends to edge. Finish as in Flaky Pastry, steps 8 and 9, (p.310) with a Fluted Edge (p.313).

6 Bake pie 50 minutes or until fruit begins to bubble and crust is golden. Cool pie on wire rack 1 hour; serve warm or cool completely.

BLUEBERRY PIE WITH COBBLER CRUST

- Color index page 69
- Begin 2 hrs ahead or early in day
- 10 servings
- 222 cals per serving

Flaky Pastry (p.310)
⅔–¾ cup sugar
¼ cup all-purpose flour
½ teaspoon cinnamon
⅛ teaspoon grated lemon peel

¼ teaspoon nutmeg
6 cups blueberries
2 teaspoons lemon juice
1 tablespoon butter or margarine

1. Prepare Flaky Pastry, steps 1 to 6, and line a 9½" by 1½" deep pie plate. In large bowl, combine next 7 ingredients; let stand half an hour. Preheat oven to 425°F.
2. Spoon the blueberry filling evenly into crust; dot with butter or margarine.
3. For Cobbler Crust: Roll out remaining pastry 2 inches larger all around than a 9½" by 1½" deep pie plate. Place over filling. Trim edges, leaving a 1-inch overhang. Pinch to form stand-up edge, then make Fluted Edge (p.313). Cut a 4-inch "X" in center of crust. Fold back points from center to make a square opening. Bake 50 minutes or until golden. Serve warm.

Forming Cobbler Crust: Cover pie with top crust; trim; flute edge. Using a sharp knife, cut a 4-inch "X" in center.

Folding the pastry: Fold back the 4 points of the "X" to make a square opening; this allows the filling to show.

BLACKBERRY PIE: Prepare filling as above but use *5 cups blackberries* instead of blueberries and omit lemon juice. Top with *Cobbler Crust* as above. Makes 10 servings. 219 cals per serving.

HOW TO PREPARE STRAWBERRIES

California strawberries are available almost all year round and it's easy to take advantage of their abundance. Prepare berries by rinsing quickly under running cold water. Discard any crushed or bruised ones; drain and dry.

Remove stems from the top; this is called hulling. If very large, cut strawberries in half.

Perfect berries can be rolled in sugar while still wet to make an attractive garnish.

CHERRY-STREUSEL PIE

Streusel Topping (below)
1 cup sugar
¼ cup cornstarch
½ teaspoon salt
5 cups pitted fresh tart cherries
1 9-inch Unbaked Piecrust (p.310)

1. Prepare Streusel Topping; set aside. In a large bowl, combine the sugar, cornstarch, salt, and cherries; toss well; let stand while preparing the pastry for Unbaked Piecrust.
2. Prepare Unbaked Piecrust, steps 1 to 4. Using the blunt edge of a knife instead of fingers, make a Fluted Edge (p.313). (The knife makes a deeper indentation in the pastry.)
3. Spoon cherry filling evenly into crust. Pinch Streusel Topping into small pieces and arrange in lattice-top design over cherry mixture.
4. Bake 50 to 60 minutes until crust is golden. Loosely cover pie with aluminum foil if topping and edge brown too quickly. Serve warm or cold.

- Color index page 69
- Begin 2 hrs ahead or early in day
- 10 servings
- 237 cals per serving

STREUSEL TOPPING: In small saucepan over medium heat, melt *4 tablespoons butter* or *margarine*; remove from heat. Stir in *⅓ cup all-purpose flour* and *2 tablespoons sugar* to form a soft dough.

MINCE PIE

1 18-ounce jar prepared mincemeat (2 cups)
1½ cups coarsely broken walnuts
2 large apples, cored and diced
½ cup packed brown sugar
¼ cup brandy or rum (optional)
1 tablespoon lemon juice
Flaky Pastry (p.310)
Brandy Hard Sauce (below)

1. In medium bowl, stir first 6 ingredients until well mixed; cover and refrigerate overnight to allow flavors to blend.
2. Prepare Flaky Pastry, steps 1 to 6. Preheat oven to 425°F. Fill crust with undrained mincemeat mixture.
3. Roll out the top crust as in Flaky Pastry, steps 7 to 9. Flatten stand-up edge. Decorate rim with Pastry Holly Leaves and Berries (p.309).
4. Bake 30 to 40 minutes until crust is golden. Serve warm with Brandy Hard Sauce.

- Color index page 68
- Begin day ahead
- 10 servings
- 494 cals per serving

BRANDY HARD SAUCE: In small bowl with mixer at medium speed, beat *¼ cup butter* or *margarine*, softened, until light and fluffy. Gradually beat in *¾ cup confectioners' sugar*, *1 tablespoon brandy*, and *¼ teaspoon vanilla extract* until creamy. Refrigerate. Makes ½ cup. 106 cals per tablespoon.

LATTICE-TOPPED RAISIN PIE

California is the largest raisin-producing region in the world; combining the fruit with oranges, another favorite crop, produces a scrumptious pie.

- Color index page 68
- Begin 3 hrs ahead or day ahead
- 8 servings
- 355 cals per serving

1 15-ounce package dark seedless raisins
Water
2 tablespoons cornstarch
1 small orange
2 tablespoons butter or margarine
¾ teaspoon salt
Flaky Pastry (p.310)

1 In 2-quart saucepan over high heat, heat raisins and 2 cups water to boiling. Reduce heat to low; cover and simmer 5 minutes, stirring mixture occasionally.

2 In cup with fork, mix cornstarch and ½ cup water; gradually stir into raisin mixture. Cook over medium heat until it thickens and boils; stir constantly; cook 1 minute. Remove from heat.

3 Grate 1 teaspoon peel and squeeze 2 tablespoons juice from orange. Add orange peel, orange juice, butter, and salt to the raisin mixture, then set aside.

4 Prepare Flaky Pastry steps 1 to 6. Spoon raisin mixture into pastry-lined pie plate. Preheat oven to 425°F.

5 For Woven Lattice Top: Roll remaining pastry into 12-inch circle; carefully cut pastry into ¾-inch-wide strips.

6 Place some strips about 1¼-inches apart across pie filling; do not seal ends.

7 Fold every other strip back halfway from center. Place the center cross-strip on pie and replace folded part of the pastry strips.

8 Fold back alternate strips and place second cross-strip in place. Repeat to "weave" lattice. Trim the strips; moisten and seal ends, folding all ends under.

9 Bake pie 30 to 35 minutes until crust is golden and raisin mixture begins to bubble. Cool pie on wire rack. If you like, serve with Brandy Hard Sauce (left).

Fruit tarts

TART SHELL

- Begin 2 hrs ahead or early in day
- 1 10-inch tart shell
- 1595 cals

A small amount of sugar added to a basic pastry dough creates a slightly sweet and crunchy crust for fruit tarts and tartlets.

1¼ cups all-purpose flour
6 tablespoons cold butter or margarine, cut into ¼-inch pieces
1 tablespoon sugar

2 tablespoons shortening
¼ teaspoon salt
3 to 4 tablespoons ice water
1 egg white

1 Preheat oven to 425°F. Into medium bowl, measure flour, cold butter or margarine, sugar, shortening, and salt. With fingertips, blend mixture until it resembles coarse crumbs.

2 Add ice water, a tablespoon at a time, mixing lightly after each addition until pastry is just moist enough to hold together. Shape into ball; cover in waxed paper; refrigerate before rolling.

3 On a lightly floured surface, with floured rolling pin, roll pastry into a round 1 inch larger than 10-inch tart pan with removable bottom.

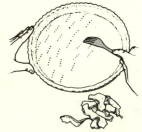

4 Line tart pan with the pastry, gently pressing pastry onto the bottom and up side of pan; trim edge. With a fork, gently prick pastry in many places.

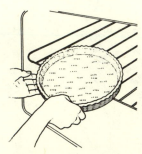

5 Bake 12 to 15 minutes until pastry is golden brown. If the pastry puffs up, gently press it to the bottom of the pan with a spoon.

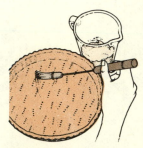

6 In cup, with a fork, beat egg white until frothy and quickly brush hot tart shell. Cool tart shell in pan on wire rack. Remove side from pan; place tart on platter.

THREE-BERRY PASTRY

- Color index page 69
- Begin 3¼ hrs ahead or early in day
- 10 servings
- 285 cals per serving

Tart Shell (left)
1½ pints strawberries, hulled
½ cup water
¼ cup sugar
1 envelope unflavored gelatin

½ cup heavy or whipping cream
1 pint blueberries or blackberries
1 pint raspberries
¼ cup red currant jelly
1 teaspoon lemon juice

1. Prepare Tart Shell; cool but do not remove the side from pan.
2. In blender at medium speed or in food processor with knife blade attached, blend 1 pint strawberries until smooth to make about 1½ cups of fresh strawberry purée.
3. In 2-quart saucepan, stir water and sugar; evenly sprinkle gelatin over mixture; let stand 1 minute to soften gelatin slightly. Cook over medium-low heat until sugar and gelatin are completely dissolved, stirring occasionally. Remove saucepan from heat; stir in strawberry purée. Refrigerate about 20 to 25 minutes until mixture mounds slightly when dropped from a spoon, stirring occasionally.
4. In small bowl with mixer at medium speed, beat heavy or whipping cream until soft peaks form. With rubber spatula or wire whisk, fold strawberry mixture into whipped cream. Evenly spread mixture into cooled tart shell. Refrigerate 1 hour or until mixture is set.
5. *About ½ hour before serving:* Slice remaining strawberries; arrange with other fruit on top of tart. (If fruit is put on too early, it will become watery.)
6. In small saucepan over low heat, heat currant jelly and lemon juice until jelly is melted. Brush fruit with jelly mixture; refrigerate dessert about 15 minutes longer to set glaze.
7. Carefully remove side from pan and place dessert on serving plate.

ARRANGING FRUIT TARTS

The natural shapes of fruits make a spectacular tart without much fuss. Cutting them and arranging them in a Tart Shell (left) produces a great effect.

Berries: Use berries sliced or whole, alone or combined with others. Arrange them in strips or circles alternating their colors, then glaze (p.317).

Peaches and Pears: Poached fruits can be used halved, cut side down, or thinly sliced and "pushed out" to produce a fan effect. Canned fruit can be substituted for a quick tart; be sure to drain well, then glaze (p.317).

Exotic Fruits: Lightly poached figs, whole or quartered, can be stood up in a tart shell. Overlapping slices of kiwi, papaya, or mango, glazed, make beautiful tarts and tartlets. If you like, garnish with pomegranate seeds.

Grapes and Cherries: Seedless grapes, black grapes with seeds removed, or pitted sour cherries, cut in half, arranged cut side down, in concentric circles on the tartlets, are easy to assemble.

HOW TO MAKE SUMMER TARTS AND TARTLETS

For the shells, below, prepare Unbaked Piecrust (p.310), steps 1 to 2; roll out the pastry ⅛-inch thick.

Making a heart-shaped shell: Line a heart-shaped tart ring. Trim excess leaving a 1-inch overhang. Fold overhang to the inside forming a stand-up edge.

Make Fluted Edge (p.313). With four-tined fork, prick bottom and side of pastry to prevent puffing during baking. Bake as for Baked Piecrust (p.310).

When cool, cover bottom of pastry with whipped cream and fill with strawberries, raspberries, red currants, or blueberries and brush with a red currant jelly glaze (below).

With thumbs press pastry into pans; trim off any excess.

Forming tartlet shells: Place tartlet pans on top of pastry; using a sharp knife, cut pastry slightly larger than each.

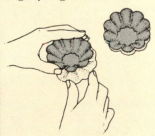

Place another tartlet pan the same size on top and press gently; this will keep the pastry from puffing up.

Bake for slightly shorter time than large tart and remove top pan. Cool on rack and fill with fresh fruits, then glaze (below).

Glazes: Glazes give a lovely sheen and prevent fruit from drying out; melt a little red currant jelly (for red fruit) or strained apricot preserves (for yellow fruit) with a little water. Boil until it coats a spoon and brush over tart.

- Color index page 67
- Begin 3½ hrs ahead or early in day
- 10 servings
- 315 cals per serving

RASPBERRY TART ROYALE

Raspberries were among the first wild fruits picked by New England settlers. They make a spectacular effect in this tart.

Tart Shell (p.316)
¼ cup sugar
3 tablespoons all-purpose flour
1 envelope unflavored gelatin
¼ teaspoon salt

2 eggs
1 egg yolk
1½ cups milk
½ cup heavy or whipping cream
3½ pints raspberries

1 Prepare Tart Shell. Prepare custard filling: In heavy 2-quart saucepan, stir the sugar, flour, gelatin, and salt.

2 With fork, beat eggs and egg yolk with milk; stir into sugar mixture; let stand 1 minute to soften gelatin slightly.

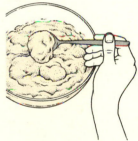

3 Cook over medium-low heat, stirring until gelatin is dissolved and mixture thickens and coats the back of a spoon, about 20 minutes. (Do not boil.)

4 Remove from heat. Pour into large bowl; cover; refrigerate until mixture mounds slightly when dropped from a spoon, about 1 hour, stirring occasionally.

5 In small bowl, with mixer at medium speed, beat cream until stiff peaks form. With rubber spatula or wire whisk, fold whipped cream into custard.

6 Spoon custard filling into cooled tart shell. Pile the raspberries on top of the custard. Refrigerate tart for 1 hour or until the custard is completely set.

Rich pies

SWEET-POTATO PIE WITH WALNUT-CRUNCH TOPPING

George Washington Carver thought of more than a hundred uses for the sweet potato; this pie is a famous Southern specialty.

- *Color index page 68*
- *Begin 3 hrs ahead or early in day*
- *10 servings*
- *375 cals per serving*

1 9-inch Unbaked Piecrust (p.310)
2 16-ounce cans sweet potatoes, drained
½ cup packed brown sugar
½ cup milk
2 eggs
2 tablespoons butter or margarine

2 tablespoons lemon juice
¾ teaspoon salt
¼ teaspoon ground cinnamon
Walnut Crunch Topping
2 tablespoons butter or margarine
1 cup walnuts, chopped
½ cup packed brown sugar

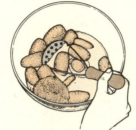

1 Preheat oven to 400°F. Prepare Unbaked Piecrust. Using a diamond-shaped pastry cutter, form a pointed Fluted Edge (p.313).

2 In large bowl with potato masher, mix sweet potatoes with the remaining pie ingredients until smooth; spoon sweet-potato mixture into piecrust.

3 Bake 45 minutes or until knife inserted into the center comes out clean. Remove pie to wire rack to cool.

4 Prepare Walnut-Crunch Topping: In pan over low heat, melt butter. Remove from the heat; stir in walnuts and brown sugar.

5 Preheat broiler if manufacturer directs; spoon Walnut-Crunch Topping evenly over pie. About 5 to 7 inches from source of heat, broil pie about 2 minutes. Cool on rack.

SOUR-CREAM PUMPKIN PIE

- *Color index page 69*
- *Begin early in day or day ahead*
- *10 servings*
- *213 cals per serving*

1 9-inch Unbaked Pie-crust (p.310)
3 eggs, separated
1 16-ounce can pumpkin (2 cups)
1 cup sugar
1 cup sour cream
1 teaspoon cinnamon
½ teaspoon ground ginger

¼ teaspoon ground nutmeg
¼ teaspoon ground cloves
¼ teaspoon salt
Whipping or heavy cream, whipped

1. Prepare Unbaked Piecrust with Spoon Scalloped Edge (below), and refrigerate. Preheat oven to 450°F.
2. In small bowl, with mixer at high speed, beat egg whites just until soft peaks form.
3. In large bowl, with same beaters and with mixer at low speed, beat pumpkin with egg yolks and the remaining ingredients, except whipped cream, until well blended.
4. With wire whisk or rubber spatula, gently fold whites into pumpkin mixture.
5. Place pie plate on oven rack; pour pumpkin mixture into piecrust. Bake 10 minutes; turn oven control to 350°F and bake pie one hour and 5 minutes more or until filling is set. Refrigerate.
6. To serve, pipe with whipped cream or serve whipped cream separately if you like.

PECAN-CRUNCH PUMPKIN PIE: Prepare pie as above, steps 1 to 5. When pie is cool, preheat broiler if manufacturer directs. Prepare Pecan Crunch Topping: In small bowl, mix *1 cup pecan halves*, chopped, *¾ cup packed brown sugar*, and *4 tablespoons butter* or *margarine*, melted. Spoon topping evenly over pie. About 5 to 7 inches from source of heat, broil pie 3 minutes or until topping is golden and sugar dissolves. Cool pie on wire rack; garnish with whipped cream. Makes 10 servings. 325 cals per serving.

SQUASH PIE: Prepare pie as in Sour-Cream Pumpkin Pie but, instead of pumpkin, use *2 cups mashed cooked butternut squash* or *one 12-ounce package frozen cooked winter squash*, thawed. If you like, pipe pie with whipped cream or serve whipped cream separately. Makes 10 servings. 206 cals per serving.

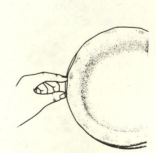
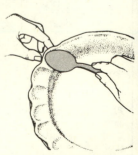

Forming a Spoon-Scalloped Edge: Form stand-up edge. Put thumb and index finger of one hand about 1¼ inches apart on outside of edge.

Pressing pastry to form scallops: With floured tablespoon, press against pastry to make large flat scallops. Pinch the points in between.

SLIPPED COCONUT-CUSTARD PIE

1 9-inch Baked Piecrust (p.310)
4 eggs
½ cup sugar
½ teaspoon salt
1 teaspoon vanilla extract
½ cup shredded coconut
2 cups hot milk

Softened butter or margarine
¼ teaspoon ground nutmeg
Whipped cream, berries, toasted coconut, or maple-blended syrup for garnish

1. Prepare Baked Piecrust, but trim pastry even with pan edge. For Quarter-Moon Edge: Roll out any trimmings, cut a long strip of pastry same width as pan edge and press down on to moistened pastry on rim. With the handle of a small teaspoon, press design of two semi-circles (one inside the other) around edge.

2. Preheat oven to 350°F. In medium bowl, with hand beater or wire whisk, beat eggs, sugar, salt, vanilla, and shredded coconut. Slowly pour milk into egg mixture, stirring rapidly to prevent lumping.

3. Butter a second 9-inch pie plate; set in shallow baking pan on oven rack. Pour egg mixture into pie plate; lightly sprinkle egg mixture with nutmeg. Pour enough hot water into baking pan to come half way up side of pie plate.

4. Bake 35 minutes or until knife inserted about 1 inch from edge comes out clean. Cool.

5. When custard is cool, loosen from side of pie plate with spatula; shake gently to loosen bottom.

6. Hold far edge of plate over far edge of pie crust; tilt custard gently; as it slips into crust, pull plate back quickly until custard rests in crust.

7. Let filling settle a few minutes. Serve topped with one or more of the suggested garnishes.

- Color index page 69
- Begin early in day
- 10 servings
- 184 cals per serving

DECORATING WITH WHIPPED CREAM

Whipped cream used to garnish pies should hold its shape, but do not over-whip.

Spoon whipped cream into pastry bag with medium star tube and pipe cream over chiffon or cream pies in a lattice-style decoration on top.

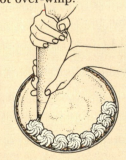

Pipe rosettes or stars around custard-type pies, covering any gaps where filling may have shrunk away from edge during baking.

BLACK SATIN PIE

Chocolate, oranges, and whipped cream are the American favorites that make this creamy pie a super dessert.

- Color index page 68
- Begin 5 hrs ahead or early in day
- 10 servings
- 265 cals per serving

Walnut Crust
¾ cup walnuts, finely chopped
¼ cup dried breadcrumbs
4 tablespoons butter or margarine, softened
3 tablespoons sugar

¼ teaspoon salt
3 tablespoons cornstarch
⅔ cup sugar
¼ teaspoon salt
2 cups milk
3 squares unsweetened chocolate, coarsely chopped

2 egg yolks
2 tablespoons orange-flavor liqueur
½ cup heavy or whipping cream
Crystalized violets for garnish

1 Preheat oven to 350°F. Prepare Walnut Crust: In 9-inch pie plate, mix walnuts, breadcrumbs, butter, sugar, and salt.

2 With hand, press walnut mixture evenly on bottom and up side of pie plate. Bake 15 minutes until golden brown. Cool on wire rack.

3 In heavy 3-quart saucepan, mix cornstarch, ⅔ cup sugar, and ¼ teaspoon salt. Stir in milk and chopped unsweetened chocolate.

4 Cook over medium heat until chocolate is melted and mixture thickens and boils; boil 1 minute, stirring constantly. Remove saucepan from heat.

5 In small bowl, with wire whisk or fork, beat egg yolks; stir in a small amount of hot chocolate mixture. Pour yolk mixture back into hot mixture, stirring rapidly.

6 Cook over low heat, 2 minutes until very thick, stirring constantly. Stir in the orange-flavor liqueur. Spread the filling evenly in the bottom of the cooled piecrust.

7 Place a piece of plastic wrap or waxed paper directly on surface of the filling to prevent a skin forming. Refrigerate the pie at least 3 hours or until well chilled. Place a small bowl and mixer beaters in refrigerator to chill. About 15 minutes before serving, in a bowl, with mixer at medium speed, beat heavy or whipping cream until soft peaks form; be careful not to over-beat the cream.

8 Spoon cream into pastry bag fitted with medium star tube. Pipe 4 lines of cream, 2 inches apart, over pie.

9 Pipe 4 more lines diagonally across first lines to create a lattice design. Garnish with crystalized violets.

Rich pies

BANANA CREAM PIE

Since bananas were first shipped from Cuba to New York in 1804, they've become an American favorite. Banana Cream Pie, made since the 1920s, is a luscious way to use this popular tropical fruit.

- Color index page 68
- Begin 4½ hrs ahead or early in day
- 10 servings
- 285 cals per serving

½ cup sugar
⅓ cup cornstarch
½ teaspoon salt
3 cups milk
2 egg yolks
1½ teaspoons vanilla extract

Butter or margarine
1 Graham-Cracker Crumb Crust (p.321) or 9-inch Baked Piecrust (p.310)

½ cup heavy or whipping cream
2 medium ripe bananas
¼ cup apple jelly

1 Prepare custard: In a 3-quart saucepan, stir sugar, cornstarch, and salt; stir in the milk until blended. Cook mixture over medium heat, stirring constantly, until the mixture thickens and boils; cook 1 minute, stirring often. Remove saucepan from heat. In small bowl, with wire whisk, beat the egg yolks; stir in small amount of the hot-milk mixture until it is well blended with the beaten egg yolks.

2 Slowly pour the yolk mixture back into the hot-milk mixture, stirring rapidly to prevent the sauce from lumping.

3 Return saucepan to heat; cook, stirring constantly, until mixture thickens and boils. Cook 1 minute; stir often.

4 Stir in vanilla extract and 1 tablespoon butter or margarine. Cover and refrigerate custard until cooled but not set, about 1 hour.

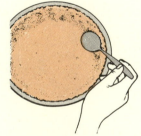

5 Meanwhile, prepare Graham-Cracker Crumb Crust or Baked Piecrust; cool on wire rack. Set aside until needed.

6 While custard is cooling, in small bowl, with mixer at medium speed, beat heavy or whipping cream until soft peaks form.

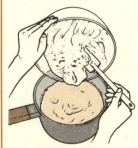

7 When custard is completely cool, with rubber spatula or wire whisk, gently fold the whipped cream into the custard.

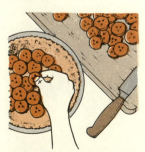

8 Thinly slice bananas. Line the crumb crust with half of the banana slices; top with custard mixture, then remaining banana slices.

9 In 1-quart saucepan over low heat, melt apple jelly. Brush top of pie with melted jelly. Refrigerate until pie is set, about 2 hours.

CHOCOLATE CREAM PIE

1 Vanilla- or Chocolate-Wafer Crumb Crust (p.327)
½ cup sugar
⅓ cup all-purpose flour
¼ teaspoon salt
2 cups milk
2 squares unsweetened chocolate, coarsely chopped

3 egg yolks
3 tablespoons butter or margarine
1 teaspoon vanilla extract
1 cup heavy or whipping cream

1. Prepare Vanilla- or Chocolate-Wafer Crumb Crust. In 2-quart saucepan with spoon, mix together sugar, flour, and salt; add the milk, stirring constantly.
2. Stir in chocolate and over low heat, cook mixture, stirring constantly, until chocolate is completely melted.
3. With wire whisk, beat until chocolate is blended; increase heat to medium; cook, stirring until mixture is thickened and boils (about 10 minutes); remove at once from heat.
4. In cup with wire whisk, beat egg yolks with small amount of hot chocolate mixture.
5. Slowly pour egg mixture into saucepan, stirring rapidly. Over low heat, cook, stirring until very thick (do not boil) and mixture mounds when dropped from spoon.
6. Remove from heat; stir in butter and vanilla, then pour into crumb crust. Cover surface with plastic wrap to prevent skin forming. Refrigerate until set, about 4 hours.
7. Just before serving, in small bowl with mixer at medium speed, beat cream until stiff peaks form; do not over-beat.
8. Discard plastic wrap on filling. Spread or pipe the whipped cream on top of pie to make an attractive top.

- Color index page 68
- Begin 5½ hrs ahead or early in day
- 10 servings
- 379 cals per serving

MERINGUE-TOPPED CHOCOLATE CREAM PIE: Prepare as Chocolate Cream Pie (above) but omit whipped cream. Do not cool pie. Top with *3-egg White Meringue Topping* (below); bake as directed. Cool, then refrigerate. 10 servings. 300 cals per serving.

3-EGG WHITE MERINGUE TOPPING: Preheat oven to 400°F. Have egg whites at room temperature. Be sure bowl and beaters are clean and free of any grease. In a small bowl with mixer at high speed, beat *3 egg whites* and *¼ teaspoon salt* until soft peaks form. At high speed, sprinkle in *½ cup sugar*, 2 tablespoons at a time, beating after each addition until sugar dissolves. Rub a bit of meringue between fingers; if it is smooth, sugar is dissolved. Whites should stand in stiff glossy peaks. With back of spoon, spread meringue over filling; seal to piecrust all around edge. Swirl up points to make attractive top. Bake 10 minutes or until golden. Cool the meringue-topped pie on a wire rack away from drafts.

CRUMB AND NUT CRUSTS

Crumb and nut crusts make a pleasant alternative to flaky pastry as a base for one-crust pies. They go especially well with light chiffon fillings. Unbaked crumb crusts are the quickest way to prepare a last minute dessert.

GRAHAM-CRACKER CRUMB CRUST: Place *18 graham crackers* in a strong bag and crush them finely with a wooden rolling pin. Preheat oven to 375°F. In bowl mix the graham-cracker crumbs, *¼ cup sugar*, and *⅓ cup melted butter* or *margarine*. With the back of a spoon, press the mixture to bottom and side of 9-inch pie plate, making small rim. Bake for 8 minutes; cool on wire rack. Fill as recipe directs. 1180 cals per 9-inch pie shell.

Crushing the crackers: Place the crackers in a strong bag and crush them finely with a rolling pin.

Lining the pie-plate: Using the back of a spoon, press the mixture to the bottom and side of a 9-inch pie plate.

GINGERSNAP OR PEANUT-BUTTER-COOKIE CRUMB CRUST: Prepare as above using about *24 gingersnaps* or *peanut-butter cookies* (1½ cups crumbs). 1360 cals per 9-inch pie shell.

VANILLA- OR CHOCOLATE-WAFER CRUMB CRUST: Prepare as above using about *35 vanilla* or *18 chocolate wafers* (1½ cups crumbs). 1340 cals per 9-inch pie shell.

CORN- OR WHEAT-FLAKE CRUMB CRUST: Prepare as above, using *1¼ cups corn-* or *wheat-flake crumbs*, *4 tablespoons butter* or *margarine*, melted, and *2 tablespoons sugar* (for 8-inch pie). For 9 inch pie, use *1½ cups crumbs*, *6 tablespoons butter* or *margarine*, melted, and *3 tablespoons sugar*. 1050 cals per 8-inch crumb crust, 1400 cals per 9-inch crumb crust.

UNBAKED CRUMB CRUST: Prepare as Graham-Cracker Crumb Crust (above) but do not make rim and do not bake. Chill well; fill as recipe directs or with any chilled filling. Refrigerate. 1180 cals per 9-inch pie shell.

WALNUT-PASTRY CRUST: Preheat oven to 400°F. In a 9-inch pie plate with fingers, mix *1 cup all-purpose flour*, *½ cup butter* or *margarine*, softened, *¼ cup confectioners' sugar*, and *¼ cup finely chopped walnuts* until soft and pliable. Press against bottom and side of pie plate. With fork, prick bottom of crust well. Bake 12 minutes; cool on wire rack. 1726 cals per 9-inch pie shell.

GROUND-NUT CRUST: Preheat oven to 400°F. In small bowl with spoon, mix *1½ cups finely ground Brazil nuts*, *walnuts*, *pecans*, *peanuts*, or *blanched almonds* with *3 tablespoons sugar* and *2 tablespoons butter* or *margarine*, softened. With back of spoon, press to bottom and side of 9-inch pie plate; do not spread on rim. Bake 8 minutes; cool on wire rack. 1648 cals per 9-inch pie shell.

- Color index page 69
- Begin early in day or day ahead
- 10 servings
- 270 cals per serving

BLACK-BOTTOM PIE

This pie first appeared in American cookbooks around 1900, and was appropriately named after its chocolate base.

1 Gingersnap Crumb Crust (left)	*2¼ teaspoons cornstarch*
2 squares unsweetened chocolate	*3 eggs, separated*
1 envelope unflavored gelatin	*1¼ cups milk*
Sugar	*1 teaspoon vanilla extract*
	1 tablespoon light rum
	½ cup heavy or whipping cream, whipped

1 Prepare Gingersnap Crumb Crust. In a saucepan over very low heat, melt the chocolate; set aside.

2 In a second small saucepan, stir gelatin with ¼ cup sugar and the cornstarch, until they are well mixed.

3 In small bowl, with fork, beat egg yolks with milk; stir into gelatin mixture. Cook over medium-low heat, stirring, until mixture is thickened and coats spoon. Remove from heat; divide in half. Into one half of mixture, stir melted chocolate and vanilla extract; with spoon, beat smooth. Refrigerate until mixture mounds when dropped from a spoon. Pour into crust; refrigerate. Refrigerate remaining custard.

4 Meanwhile, in small bowl, with mixer at high speed, beat the egg whites until soft peaks form; gradually sprinkle in ¼ cup sugar; beat until sugar is dissolved.

5 With rubber spatula, gently fold whites and rum into the chilled custard; pour as much custard mixture as crust will hold over the chilled chocolate mixture.

6 Refrigerate pie a few minutes. Pour rest of custard mixture on top. Refrigerate until set. Pipe or spoon whipped cream on top of pie.

Rich pies

LEMON MERINGUE PIE

Lemon custard pie was Calvin Coolidge's favorite and this Southern version has become an American classic.

- *Color index page 69*
- *Begin 4 hrs ahead or early in day*
- *10 servings*
- *346 cals per serving*

1 9-inch Baked Piecrust (p.310)
2 to 3 medium lemons
⅓ cup cornstarch
⅛ tablespoon salt
1¼ cups sugar
1½ cups water
4 eggs, separated
1 tablespoon butter or margarine
¼ teaspoon cream of tartar

1 Prepare Baked Piecrust with Fluted Edge (p.313). Grate peel from 1 lemon to make 1 tablespoon; squeeze juice from all lemons to make ½ cup. Set peel and juice aside. In 2-quart saucepan, stir cornstarch, salt and ¾ cup sugar. Stir in water; cook over medium heat, stirring constantly, until mixture is thickened and boils; boil 1 minute. Remove the saucepan from heat. Set aside until needed.

2 In small bowl with wire whisk or fork, beat yolks well; stir small amount of hot cornstarch mixture into the yolks.

3 Slowly pour the yolk mixture back into hot cornstarch mixture in the saucepan, stirring rapidly to prevent lumping.

4 Return saucepan to heat; cook, stirring constantly, until filling is thickened. (Do not boil, or it will curdle.)

5 Gradually stir in the lemon juice, lemon peel, and butter or margarine; pour the filling into the prepared piecrust; set aside to cool (about 10 minutes).

6 Meanwhile, preheat the oven to 400°F. In a small bowl with the mixer at high speed, beat the egg whites and the cream of tartar until soft peaks form.

7 At high speed, sprinkle in ½ cup sugar, 2 tablespoons at a time, beating after each addition until sugar dissolves and whites form stiff glossy peaks.

8 With spatula, spread the meringue over the filling to the edge of the crust. Swirl the meringue with the back of a spoon to make an attractive design on top.

9 Bake the pie 10 minutes or until golden. Remove from oven and cool on wire rack away from drafts. Store any left-over pie in the refrigerator.

USEFUL PASTRY TOOLS

Using the correct utensils can help make pastry-making easy and foolproof. Chilling the rolling pin helps make rolling the pastry easier.

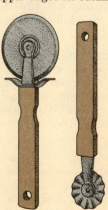

Pastry wheel: Both straight and ripple-edged for cutting dough.

Pastry blender: For cutting fats into dry ingredients; avoids excessive handling of pastry with warm hands.

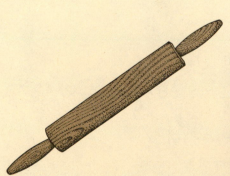

Rolling pin: With handles and ball bearings for rolling out dough.

Pastry scraper: Metal or plastic for scraping off any dough that sticks to work surface.

Pastry brush: For brushing on egg and milk glazes, and for brushing open fruit tarts with jelly glazes.

KEY-LIME PIE

- Color index page 69
- Begin 3 hrs ahead or early in day
- 8 servings
- 404 cals per serving

1 Graham-Cracker Crumb Crust (p.321)
1 14-ounce can sweetened condensed milk
½ cup lime juice, preferably extracted from Key limes*
2 egg yolks

1 cup heavy or whipping cream
Lime twists for garnish (p.100)

*Key limes are a variety grown exclusively in the Florida Keys.

1. Prepare Graham-Cracker Crumb Crust. In medium bowl, with wire whisk or fork, stir sweetened condensed milk with lime juice and egg yolks until mixture thickens; pour into crust. Refrigerate until well chilled and set.
2. Just before serving, in small bowl with mixer at medium speed, beat cream until stiff peaks form. Pipe or spread whipped cream on top of pie and decorate with lime twists.

ORANGE-CHIFFON PIE

- Color index page 69
- Begin early in day or day ahead
- 8 servings
- 415 cals per serving

1 Unbaked Crumb Crust (p.321)
1 envelope unflavored gelatin
¼ teaspoon salt
Sugar
3 eggs, separated

1 teaspoon grated orange peel
1 cup orange juice
2 tablespoons lemon juice
1½ cups heavy cream
Orange slices for garnish

1. Prepare Unbaked Crumb Crust. In 1-quart saucepan, stir gelatin with salt and ½ cup sugar until well mixed. In small bowl with wire whisk or hand beater, beat egg yolks with orange peel, orange juice, and lemon juice until mixed; stir into gelatin mixture.
2. Cook over medium-low heat, stirring constantly, until mixture is thickened and coats spoon; remove from heat. Refrigerate, stirring occasionally, until mixture mounds when dropped from spoon, about 45 minutes.
3. In large bowl with mixer at high speed, beat egg whites until soft peaks form; beating at high speed, gradually sprinkle in ¼ cup sugar; beat until sugar is completely dissolved. With wire whisk or rubber spatula, gently fold gelatin mixture into whites.
4. In small bowl with same beaters and with mixer at medium speed, beat ½ cup heavy cream until soft peaks form; fold into gelatin mixture. Spoon mixture into crust; refrigerate pie until set, about 30 minutes.
5. To serve, in small bowl with mixer at medium speed, beat remaining heavy cream with 2 tablespoons sugar until stiff peaks form.
6. Spoon or pipe whipped cream on pie; garnish with orange slices.

CRANBERRY-CHIFFON PIE: Prepare as above but omit salt, lemon juice, and orange slices. Reduce orange juice to 2 tablespoons, and add *1 cup cranberry juice*. To garnish, dip *24 whole cranberries* into *1 egg white*; coat with *sugar*; let dry on rack. Decorate pie with cranberries. 8 servings. 175 cals per serving.

GRASSHOPPER PIE

Named after the grasshopper cocktail, this creamy pie gets its delicate green color from the crème de menthe liqueur it contains.

- Color index page 69
- Begin 5 hrs ahead or early in day
- 10 servings
- 265 cals per serving

1 Chocolate-Wafer Crumb Crust (p.321)
½ cup water
⅛ teaspoon salt
3 eggs, separated, at room temperature
Sugar

1 envelope unflavored gelatin
¼ cup crème de menthe
½ cup cold coffee
1 cup heavy or whipping cream
Chocolate curls for garnish (p.330)

1 Prepare Chocolate-Wafer Crumb Crust. In a heavy 1-quart saucepan, beat the water, salt, egg yolks, and ¼ cup sugar until well mixed. Sprinkle gelatin evenly over egg yolk mixture; let stand 1 minute to soften gelatin slightly. Cook over low heat about 10 minutes, stirring constantly, until mixture thickens and coats a spoon. (Do not boil or the mixture will curdle.)

2 Remove saucepan from the heat; stir in the crème de menthe and the cold coffee.

3 Refrigerate mixture about 20 minutes, stirring occasionally, until the chilled mixture mounds slightly when dropped from a spoon.

4 In large bowl, with mixer at high speed, beat egg whites until soft peaks form; gradually sprinkle in ¼ cup sugar, beating until completely dissolved and the whites stand in stiff peaks.

5 In small bowl, with mixer at medium speed, beat cream to stiff peaks. With rubber spatula or wire whisk, fold cream and gelatin mixture into whites.

6 Spoon the mixture into the Chocolate-Wafer Crumb Crust. Refrigerate the pie for 3 hours, until it is set. Garnish with chocolate curls.

Rich pies

CHOCOLATE-PEANUT-BUTTER PIE

- Color index page 68
- Begin 3 hrs ahead or early in day
- 12 servings
- 280 cals per serving

Ever since Mr Reese of Hershey, PA produced a chocolate and peanut-butter candy in 1923, Americans of all ages have enjoyed this sweet and nutty combination.

1 Peanut-Butter-Cookie Crumb Crust (p. 333)
1½ cups milk
2½ teaspoons cornstarch
4 eggs, separated, at room temperature

Sugar
1 envelope unflavored gelatin
½ cup creamy peanut butter
1 square unsweetened chocolate, melted

½ cup heavy or whipping cream
Chopped peanuts, peanut-butter pieces, or chocolate curls for garnish

1 Prepare Peanut-Butter-Cookie Crumb Crust. In heavy 2-quart saucepan, with wire whisk, beat the milk, cornstarch, egg yolks, and ⅓ cup sugar until well blended. Sprinkle the unflavored gelatin evenly over the milk and egg-yolk mixture; let stand 1 minute to soften gelatin slightly. Cook over low heat, stirring the mixture constantly, until the mixture thickens and boils; boil for one minute, stirring occasionally.

2 Spoon 1 cup mixture into small bowl; stir in peanut butter until blended. Stir the melted chocolate into remaining mixture in saucepan.

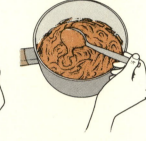

3 Refrigerate both mixtures until each mounds slightly when dropped from a spoon; then spoon chocolate mixture into crust.

4 To prepare peanut-butter mixture, in large bowl, with mixer at high speed, beat egg whites until soft peaks form.

5 Gradually sprinkle in ⅓ cup sugar, 2 table-spoons at a time, beating until sugar dissolves and whites stand in stiff peaks.

6 In small bowl with same beaters and with mixer at medium speed, beat ¼ cup heavy or whipping cream until stiff peaks form.

7 With rubber spatula or wire whisk, fold the chilled peanut-butter mixture and whipped heavy or whipping cream into the beaten egg whites.

8 Spoon the peanut-butter mixture evenly over the chocolate mixture in crumb crust. Refrigerate 2 hours or until the filling is set.

9 To serve, in small bowl, beat remaining ¼ cup heavy cream until soft peaks form. Garnish with cream and peanuts.

GEORGIA-PECAN TART WITH CREAM-CHEESE PASTRY

Cream-Cheese Pastry
1½ cups all-purpose flour
1 3-ounce package cream cheese, softened
½ cup butter or margarine, softened
2 tablespoons sugar

3 eggs
1 cup dark corn syrup
1 teaspoon vanilla extract
⅓ cup sugar
1 cup pecan halves
Whipped cream (optional)

Filling:
¼ cup of butter or margarine

1. Prepare Cream-Cheese Pastry: Into medium bowl, measure flour, cream cheese, butter, and sugar. With hand, knead mixture until blended. Pat pastry onto bottom and up side of 10-inch tart pan with removable bottom; refrigerate.
2. Preheat oven to 350°F. In 1-quart saucepan over low heat, melt remaining ¼ cup butter. In large bowl, with wire whisk or fork, beat eggs, corn syrup, vanilla extract, sugar, and melted butter until blended.
3. Arrange pecan halves on bottom of crust. Place tart pan on oven rack; carefully pour egg mixture over pecans. Bake tart 50 minutes or until knife inserted 1 inch from edge comes out clean. Cool tart in pan on wire rack.
4. To serve, carefully remove side of pan from tart; place tart on large plate. If you like, serve with whipped cream.

- Color index page 68
- Begin 3 hrs or day ahead
- 10 servings
- 435 cals per serving

SHOOFLY PIE

1 9-inch Unbaked Piecrust (p.310)
2 cups all-purpose flour
⅔ cup packed brown sugar
½ teaspoon ground cinnamon
¼ teaspoon ground ginger

¼ teaspoon ground nutmeg
¼ teaspoon salt
⅔ cup butter or margarine
¾ cup boiling water
½ cup molasses
¾ teaspoon baking soda

1. Prepare Unbaked Piecrust with a Pinched Edge (p.313). Preheat oven to 375°F.
2. In large bowl, combine flour, brown sugar, cinnamon, ginger, nutmeg, and salt. With pastry blender or 2 knives used scissors fashion, cut in butter until mixture resembles coarse crumbs. Set mixture aside.
3. In medium bowl, combine boiling water and molasses; stir in the soda.
4. Sprinkle ½ cup of the crumb mixture into piecrust; pour molasses mixture over crumbs. Sprinkle remaining crumbs evenly on top.
5. Bake pie 35 to 40 minutes until pie is set. Cool on wire rack. Serve at room temperature.

- Color index page 68
- Begin 3 hrs ahead or early in day
- 10 servings
- 448 cals per serving

CAKES COOKIES CANDIES

"If I knew you were coming, I'd have baked a cake, baked a cake . . . ."

© HOFFMAN, WATTS AND MERRILL

Cakes, cookies, and candies are truly all-American. Childhood memories always seem to revolve around beautifully frosted birthday cakes dotted with flickering candles, perfectly decorated Sugar Cookies and Gingerbread Men at Christmastime, and dipped Candy Apples for Halloween.

However, cake baking is a relatively recent invention. Before the 19th century, outdoor ovens and open-hearth fireplaces could produce breads, but not fine cakes; even fruitcakes were sometimes steamed like puddings to produce satisfactory results. Home baking advanced with the advent of stoves with enclosed ovens. As early as the 1740s, Benjamin Franklin had invented a heating stove which could heat a room to 50°F.! But baking was still uncertain as it was difficult to regulate the heat, measurements for ingredients were not standardized; and flours and butters varied greatly.

The introduction of English cookbooks and baking equipment, and the invention of baking powder in the mid-1800s, improved baking in general, and housewives began to prepare all kinds of cakes and cookies. In the 1880s, Garland manufactured a stove that had a warming oven as well as a baking oven. Baking was becoming more sophisticated, and a truly American form of baking was evolving.

As the country expanded and people moved westward, they took their traditions with them. The "stack cake," a traditional pioneer wedding cake, was made with various cake layers brought by each guest. Applesauce was spread between the layers and the cake was assembled at the celebration itself. The number of stacks and layers indicated the bride's popularity. Perhaps our Seven-Layer Chocolate Chiffon Cake evolved from this early cake.

European immigrants arrived during the 19th century bringing their traditional cake, cookie, and candy recipes with them. The English brought fruitcakes and sponges, the Germans came with butter-rich pound cakes, the Italians brought cheesecakes, and the Dutch brought their *koekje*, little cakes, which we now call cookies – an integral part of American baking.

Chocolate layer cakes became well known and creations like Devil's Food Cake and Sour-Cream Chocolate Torte remain as popular as ever. Angel-Food Cake, pound cakes, delicious cookies, and macaroons began to redefine American baking. Many immigrant groups brought fruit and spice cakes, like our Chunky Applesauce Cake and Gingerbread which are still favorites. But perhaps the most important influence of this period was that of the Scandinavians and Germans who introduced their coffeecakes and the tradition of a morning coffee break with neighbors. Coffeecakes are very much an American institution and cakes like our Sour-Cream Coffeecake are always popular.

A thermostatically controlled oven was introduced in 1915, and American tabletop ranges, fueled by gas, came into their own in the 1930s. By then, electric ranges, too, had appeared on the market. Cake and cookie baking became a fine art; school and church cake sales were social events, and the competition produced wonderful cakes and delicious cookies.

The advent of the packaged cake mix in the 1950s brought easy cake making into most households, but although they still have their uses, people are now going back to homemade cakes, and taking pride in making traditional and modern cakes and cookies, which represent a very original form of American baking.

Candy making is a pastime usually left for holidays, special occasions, or sometimes just a rainy day. Making fudge is probably one of a child's first experiences in the kitchen. Dipping apples into a candy coating for Candy Apples and breaking up Peanut Brittle are great fun for children.

With a wealth of native products, traditional ethnic specialties, and American ingenuity, our cakes, cookies, and candies have become famous at home and abroad.

White cakes

ANGEL-FOOD CAKE

1¼ cups confectioners' sugar
1 cup cake flour
1½ cups egg whites, at room temperature (12 to 14 egg whites)
1½ teaspoons cream of tartar
1½ teaspoons vanilla extract
¼ teaspoon salt
¼ teaspoon almond extract
1 cup sugar

1. Preheat oven to 375°F. In small bowl, stir confectioners' sugar and cake flour; set aside.
2. Add egg whites, cream of tartar, vanilla extract, salt, and almond extract to large bowl and, with mixer at high speed, beat until mixture is well blended.
3. Beating at high speed, sprinkle in sugar, 2 tablespoons at a time; beat just until sugar dissolves and whites form stiff peaks. Do not scrape bowl during beating.
4. With rubber spatula, gently fold in flour mixture, about ¼ at a time, just until flour disappears.
5. Pour mixture into ungreased 10-inch tube pan and with spatula, cut through batter to break any large air bubbles.
6. Bake 35 minutes or until top of cake springs back when lightly touched with finger. Any cracks on surface should look dry. If cake is not done, bake a few minutes longer and check again.
7. Invert cake in pan on funnel or bottle; cool. With spatula, loosen cake from pan; remove to plate. Use serrated knife for easier slicing.

Testing for doneness: The cake is cooked if it springs back when lightly pressed with fingertip.

Cooling the cake: Carefully invert the cake over a funnel or bottle until completely cool.

- Color index page 70
- Begin early in day
- 12 servings
- 166 cals per serving

LADY BALTIMORE CAKE: Prepare and cool *Lane Cake* (right), steps 1 to 4. Cut each cake layer horizontally in half. In small bowl, with wooden spoon, combine *½ cup candied cherries,* chopped, *⅓ cup dried figs,* chopped, *⅓ cup dark seedless raisins,* chopped, and *¼ cup chopped pecans*; set fruit mixture aside. Meanwhile, prepare *2 packages fluffy white-frosting mix* as label directs; gently stir fruit mixture into 3 cups of frosting; use this mixture to fill cake layers. With metal spatula, spread remaining frosting on top and side of cake. Makes 16 servings. 305 cals per serving.

LANE CAKE

Named after Emma Lane, a Southern cookbook author, this Southern Christmas cake is filled with coconut, fruit, and nuts.

6 egg whites, at room temperature
2 cups sugar
2¾ cups cake flour
1 cup milk
1 cup butter or margarine
3 teaspoons baking powder
1 teaspoon salt

1 teaspoon vanilla extract
Coconut Filling
8 egg yolks
1¼ cups sugar
½ cup butter
1 4-ounce can shredded coconut
1 cup pecan halves, chopped

- Color index page 70
- Begin early in day
- 16 servings
- 527 cals per serving

1 cup candied red cherries, chopped
1 cup dark seedless raisins
⅓ cup bourbon
Vanilla Frosting (p.344)

1 Preheat oven to 375°F. Grease two 9-inch round cake pans; line bottoms of cake pans with waxed paper; grease the waxed paper; set aside.

2 In large bowl beat whites until soft peaks form. Beating at high speed, gradually add 1 cup sugar. Continue beating until stiff peaks form.

3 In large bowl at low speed, mix flour, next 5 ingredients, and 1 cup sugar. At medium speed, beat 4 minutes; with rubber spatula, fold in whites.

4 Pour into pans; bake 35 minutes. Cool in pans on wire racks 10 minutes. Remove from pans and discard paper. Place on wire rack and cool completely.

5 Prepare Coconut Filling: In a large saucepan over medium heat, combine yolks, sugar, and butter. Cook, stirring, until thickened, about 5 minutes.

6 Remove saucepan from heat; stir in shredded coconut, chopped pecan halves, candied red cherries, seedless raisins, and bourbon. Set aside.

7 Prepare Vanilla Frosting; set aside. Cut each cake layer in half horizontally.

8 Place first layer on plate; spread with ⅓ filling. Repeat with remaining layers and filling.

9 With a palette knife, frost side and top of cake, making decorative swirls with the knife.

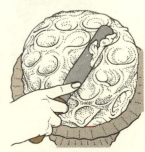

Yellow cakes

APRICOT JELLY ROLL

Jelly-roll cakes have been popular for over 100 years. We use apricot preserves, but any favorite jam or jelly would be delicious.

1 3½-ounce can sliced blanched almonds
½ cup all-purpose flour
1 teaspoon baking powder
¼ teaspoon salt

4 eggs, separated, at room temperature
Sugar
½ teaspoon almond extract
Confectioners' sugar

1 10- to 12-ounce jar apricot preserves
2 cups heavy or whipping cream

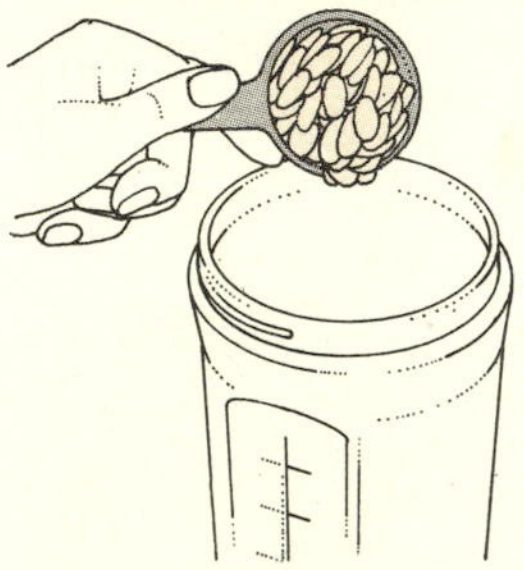

- Color index page 70
- Begin 2 hrs ahead
- 14 servings
- 318 cals per serving

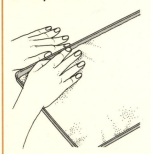

1 Preheat oven to 375°F. Grease 15½" by 10½" jelly-roll pan; line pan bottom and sides with waxed paper.

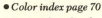

2 In blender at medium speed, blend ⅓ cup almonds until very fine; reserve remaining almonds.

3 In small bowl, mix the ground almonds, flour, baking powder, and salt; set aside. In another small bowl with mixer at high speed, beat egg whites until soft peaks form. Beating at high speed, gradually sprinkle in ⅓ cup sugar, beating until sugar is completely dissolved. (Whites should stand in stiff, glossy peaks.) Set aside while preparing yolk mixture.

4 In large bowl with same beaters and with mixer at high speed, beat egg yolks, almond extract, and ½ cup sugar until thick and lemon-colored. With rubber spatula, gently fold the flour mixture and the beaten egg whites into the egg-yolk mixture until thoroughly blended. With a palette knife, gently spread the batter evenly in the prepared pan. Bake 15 minutes or until top of cake springs back when lightly touched with finger.

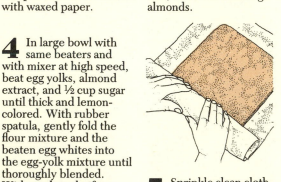

5 Sprinkle clean cloth towel with ⅓ cup confectioners' sugar. Immediately invert cake onto towel; peel off paper. Starting at narrow end, roll with towel, jelly-roll style. Cool on rack.

6 While the cake is cooling, press apricot preserves through fine strainer into bowl. In skillet over medium heat, toast remaining almonds, shaking skillet to brown. Remove from heat.

7 When cake is cool, carefully unroll; spread top evenly with strained apricot preserves. Starting at same narrow end, roll cake without towel. Place cake, seam side down, on platter.

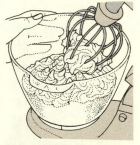

8 In large bowl with electric mixer at medium speed or hand rotary beater, beat heavy or whipping cream and ¼ cup confectioners' sugar until stiff peaks form.

9 Spoon the whipped cream into decorating bag with medium rosette tube. Pipe mixture in lengthwise rows on cake and over ends of cake. Arrange almonds to make a design. Chill.

PINEAPPLE UPSIDE-DOWN CAKE

1¾ cups packed brown sugar
½ cup butter or margarine
1 15½-ounce can pineapple chunks, drained

Maraschino cherries
Yellow Cake (p.338)
Whipped cream or vanilla ice cream to serve

1. Preheat oven to 375°F. In a 13" by 9" baking pan, place brown sugar and butter or margarine. Place pan in oven and heat until butter and sugar melt; stir to mix. Do not turn oven off.
2. Remove pan from oven. Arrange pineapple chunks in sugar mixture to form "flowers." Use 1 maraschino cherry for center of each; set aside.
3. Prepare Yellow Cake batter; carefully spoon over design in pan. Bake 35 to 40 minutes or until toothpick inserted in center comes out clean.
4. Cool cake in pan on wire rack 10 minutes, then loosen cake from side of pan. Place platter on top of pan and invert both; lift off pan. (If fruit sticks to pan, lift off with spatula and replace in design on cake.)
5. To serve, cut into 12 squares; serve with whipped cream or vanilla ice cream.

- Color index page 72
- Begin early in day
- 12 servings
- 535 cals per serving

BOSTON CREAM PIE

1 cup cake flour
¾ cup sugar
⅓ cup milk
6 tablespoons butter or margarine, softened
1½ teaspoons baking powder
1½ teaspoons vanilla extract

¼ teaspoon salt
¼ teaspoon baking soda
2 eggs
Creamy Custard Filling (p.344)
Chocolate Icing (p.344)

1. Preheat oven to 375°F. Grease one 9-inch round cake pan.
2. Into large bowl, measure first 9 ingredients. With mixer at low speed, beat ingredients just until mixed, constantly scraping bowl with rubber spatula. Increase speed to high; beat 2 minutes, occasionally scraping bowl.
3. Pour batter into pan. Bake 25 minutes or until toothpick inserted in center of cake comes out clean. Cool cake in pan on wire rack 10 minutes. Remove from pan; cool completely.
4. Prepare Creamy Custard Filling.
5. Prepare Chocolate Icing. With serrated knife, cut cake horizontally in half to form 2 layers. Place 1 cake layer on cake platter; spread evenly with cooled custard. Top with second cake layer, pressing down firmly. Frost top of cake with Chocolate Icing. Refrigerate until serving time.

- Color index page 70
- Begin 2½ hrs ahead
- 10 servings
- 327 cals per serving

Coffeecakes

SOUR-CREAM COFFEECAKE

- Color index page 71
- Begin 2¼ hrs ahead
- 14 servings
- 395 cals per serving

1 cup walnuts, chopped
1¼ teaspoons ground cinnamon
Sugar
3 cups all-purpose flour
¾ cup butter or margarine, softened
¼ cup milk
1½ teaspoons baking powder
1½ teaspoons baking soda
1 8-ounce container sour cream (1 cup)
3 eggs

1. Grease and flour 9″ by 3″ springform pan. In medium bowl, mix chopped walnuts, ground cinnamon, and ¾ cup sugar.
2. In large bowl with mixer at low speed, beat flour, butter or margarine, milk, baking powder, baking soda, sour cream, eggs, and 1¼ cups sugar just until blended.
3. Increase speed to medium; beat 2 minutes, occasionally scraping bowl with rubber spatula.
4. Preheat oven to 350°F. Spoon half of batter into prepared pan; sprinkle with half of nut mixture. Spread evenly with remaining batter; sprinkle remaining nut mixture on top.
5. Bake cake 60 minutes or until golden and toothpick inserted into center of cake comes out clean. Cool cake in pan on wire rack 10 minutes. Remove side of pan. Serve warm. Or, cool completely to serve later.

PECAN-CRUMB COFFEECAKES

- Color index page 71
- Begin 1½ hrs ahead
- 18 servings
- 329 cals per serving

¼ cup packed brown sugar
¾ teaspoon ground cinnamon
4 cups all-purpose flour
1 cup butter or margarine, softened
½ cup pecan halves, chopped
1½ cups sugar
⅔ cup quick-cooking or old-fashioned oats
1 tablespoon baking powder
1 teaspoon salt
4 eggs
1½ cups milk

1. In medium bowl with fork, stir brown sugar, cinnamon, and 1 cup flour. With pastry blender or two knives used scissor-fashion, cut ⅓ cup butter or margarine into flour mixture until mixture resembles large crumbs. Stir in the chopped pecans, then set aside.
2. Grease and flour two 8″ by 8″ baking pans. Preheat oven to 375°F.
3. In large bowl, mix sugar, oats, baking powder, salt, and 3 cups all-purpose flour. With pastry blender or 2 knives used scissor-fashion, cut in remaining ⅔ cup butter until mixture resembles coarse crumbs.
4. In small bowl with fork, beat eggs with milk until blended; stir into flour mixture just until flour is moistened. Spoon batter evenly into pans. Evenly sprinkle pecan mixture on top of the coffeecakes.
5. Bake 35 minutes or until toothpick inserted in centers comes out clean. Cool coffeecakes in pan on wire racks 10 minutes; remove from pans. Serve warm. Or, to serve later, wrap cakes with foil and reheat in 375°F oven 35 minutes.

POUND CAKE WITH COCONUT-ALMOND TOPPING

- Color index page 71
- Begin 2 hrs ahead
- 18 servings
- 381 cals per serving

Old-fashioned pound cakes contained one pound each of flour, butter, sugar, and eggs; our recipe reflects today's healthier lifestyle.

1¼ cups sugar
1 8-ounce package cream cheese, softened
1½ cups butter or margarine, softened
2¼ cups cake flour
2 teaspoons baking powder
4 eggs
Almond extract
½ cup packed light brown sugar
1 3½-ounce can flaked coconut
1 3½-ounce can sliced blanched almonds

1 Preheat oven to 350°F. Grease and flour 13″ by 9″ baking pan; set aside.

2 Into a large bowl, measure sugar, the cream cheese, and 1 cup butter or margarine.

3 With electric mixer at low speed, beat until sugar, cream cheese, and butter mixture is light and fluffy. Add the flour, baking powder, eggs, and 1¼ teaspoons almond extract; continue beating at low speed until the flour and egg mixture is completely blended into the cream cheese mixture, constantly scraping the side of the bowl with rubber spatula. Increase mixer speed to medium; beat 2 minutes longer, occasionally scraping bowl with spatula.

4 Pour the batter into prepared pan. Bake 25 to 30 minutes until a toothpick inserted in center comes out clean. Cool cake in pan on wire rack 10 minutes.

5 While cake is cooling, preheat the broiler if manufacturer directs. In heavy 2-quart saucepan over low heat, melt ½ cup butter or margarine; stir in the brown sugar, flaked coconut, sliced almonds, and ¾ teaspoon almond extract. Continue stirring until all ingredients are well mixed. Spoon the coconut-almond mixture evenly over top of cooled cake. Using a palette knife, spread coconut-almond mixture just to edge.

6 Broil 7 to 9 inches from source of heat (or at 450°F.) 1 minute or until topping is golden. Cool cake completely in pan on wire rack.

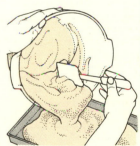

Chocolate cakes

SEVEN-LAYER CHOCOLATE CHIFFON CAKE

A truly American culinary invention, chiffon cake replaces solid shortening with salad oil and is beaten rather than creamed.

2 squares semisweet
   chocolate
2 cups cake flour
1 tablespoon baking
   powder
¾ teaspoon salt
Sugar
½ cup salad oil
½ cup water
6 eggs, separated, at
   room temperature
½ teaspoon cream of
   tartar
Chocolate-Cream Filling
   (p.344)

Easy Chocolate Curls
   (below)
1 cup heavy or whipping
   cream
2 tablespoons cocoa

- Color index page 70
- Begin 3 hrs ahead
- 16 servings
- 465 cals per serving
  without chocolate curls

1 In heavy 1-quart saucepan over low heat, heat semisweet-chocolate squares until melted and smooth, stirring occasionally.

2 Preheat oven to 350°F. Grease two 9-inch round cake pans; line bottoms of pans with waxed paper and grease the paper.

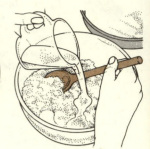

3 In bowl, mix flour, baking powder, salt, and 1½ cups sugar until blended; beat in oil, water, yolks, and chocolate until smooth.

4 In large bowl with mixer at high speed, beat whites and cream of tartar until stiff peaks form. Fold a large spoon of egg whites into chocolate mixture, then fold chocolate mixture into remaining egg whites.

5 Spoon ¾ cup batter into each pan. Bake 8 to 10 minutes until top of cake springs back when touched with finger. Cool cakes in pans on wire racks 10 minutes. With metal spatula, carefully loosen and remove cakes from pans; cool completely on wire racks. Repeat with remaining batter to make 5 more layers, washing, greasing, and lining cake pans with waxed paper each time. Meanwhile, prepare Chocolate-Cream Filling; set aside. Prepare Easy Chocolate Curls; cover and refrigerate until needed.

6 Assemble cake: Place 1 cake layer, rounded side up, on cake plate; spread with one-sixth Chocolate-Cream Filling; top with second cake layer, rounded side up. Repeat layering, ending with seventh cake.

7 In small bowl with mixer at medium speed, beat heavy or whipping cream, cocoa, and 1 tablespoon sugar until soft peaks form. Spread cocoa-cream over top and side of cake.

8 If you like, with four-tined fork, run fork vertically around the side of the cake to make an attractive design; garnish cake with Easy Chocolate Curls. Chill completely. To serve, cut into slices.

HOW TO MAKE CHOCOLATE GARNISHES

Easy chocolate garnishes made with semisweet chocolate can turn the simplest dessert or cake into a spectacular presentation, like our special Valentine's Devil's Food Cake, decorated with Chocolate Lace Hearts (p.128).

Chocolate Leaves: Rinse and pat dry lemon leaves. With pastry brush, spread layer of melted chocolate mixture on leaves using underside of leaf for more distinct design. Refrigerate until firm, about 30 minutes. Carefully peel off leaf.

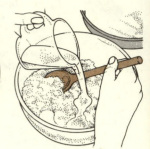

In double boiler over hot, *not* boiling, water, heat ½ 6-ounce package semisweet-chocolate pieces and 2 teaspoons shortening until melted and smooth, 5 minutes, stirring often.

Chocolate Lace Hearts: Draw heart on paper. Fill decorating bag, fitted with round tube, with melted chocolate. Place waxed paper over design;

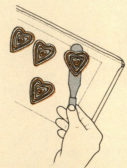

trace with chocolate. Move design and repeat. Chill until firm; carefully remove with metal spatula.

Easy Chocolate Curls: Warm chocolate squares to soften. Draw blade of vegetable peeler along smooth surface. Use toothpick to transfer curls.

DEVIL'S FOOD CAKE

2 cups cake flour
1½ cups sugar
1¼ cups buttermilk
½ cup shortening
3 eggs
3 squares unsweetened
    chocolate, melted
1½ teaspoons baking
    soda
1 teaspoon salt
1 teaspoon vanilla extract
½ teaspoon baking
    powder
Quick Fudge Frosting
    (below)

- Color index
  page 72
- Begin
  early in day
- 10 servings
- 517 cals
  per serving

1. Preheat oven to 350°F. Grease and flour two 9-inch round cake pans.
2. Into large bowl, measure all ingredients except frosting. With mixer at low speed, beat until well mixed, constantly scraping bowl with rubber spatula. Increase speed to high; beat 5 minutes, occasionally scraping bowl.
3. Pour batter into pans. Bake 25 to 30 minutes until toothpick inserted in center comes out clean. Cool on wire racks 10 minutes, remove from pans; cool completely. Prepare Quick Fudge Frosting. Fill and frost cake.

QUICK FUDGE FROSTING: In double boiler over hot, not boiling, water, melt *one 12-ounce package semisweet chocolate pieces* with *¼ cup shortening*. Stir in *3 cups confectioners' sugar* and *½ cup milk*; remove from heat. With spoon, beat until smooth. Frosts a 13" by 9" cake, tube cake or 24 cupcakes, or to fill and frost a 2-layer cake. 3672 cals.

CHOCOLATE CUPCAKES: Preheat oven to 350°F. Place liners in 24 3-inch muffin-pan cups or grease and flour cups. In a large bowl, combine *2 cups cake flour, 1¾ cups sugar, ¾ cup cocoa, 1¼ cups milk, ¾ cup shortening, 3 eggs, 1¼ teaspoons baking soda, 1 teaspoon salt, 1 teaspoon vanilla extract* and *½ teaspoon baking powder*. With mixer at low speed, beat until well mixed, constantly scraping bowl with rubber spatula. Spoon into muffin-pan cups, filling each half full. Bake 20 minutes or until a toothpick inserted in center comes out clean. Cool in pans on wire racks 10 minutes, then remove from pans and cool completely on racks. Prepare Quick Fudge Frosting (above) or Fluffy Boiled Frosting (below). Dip cupcakes into frosting and turn slightly to coat. Makes 24. 321 cals per cupcake.

FLUFFY BOILED FROSTING: In a 1-quart saucepan over medium heat, heat *1¼ cups sugar, ⅛ teaspoon cream of tartar, ⅛ teaspoon salt,* and *6 tablespoons water* to boiling. Set candy thermometer in place and boil, without stirring, until temperature reaches 260°F. or until a little mixture dropped in cold water forms a hard ball; remove from heat. In a small bowl with mixer at high speed, beat *3 egg whites*, at room temperature, until soft peaks form. Pour syrup in thin stream into whites, beating constantly, then add *1 teaspoon vanilla extract* and continue beating until mixture forms stiff peaks. 1008 cals.

CHOCOLATE SOUR-CREAM TORTE

2 cups all-purpose flour
1½ cups sugar
¾ 16-ounce container
    sour cream (1½ cups)
1 cup butter or
    margarine, softened
½ cup cocoa
1 tablespoon instant-
    coffee powder
1 teaspoon baking soda
1 teaspoon baking
    powder
1 teaspoon almond
    extract
2 eggs
Chocolate Sour-Cream
    Frosting (below)
1 square semisweet
    chocolate for garnish

- Color index
  page 70
- Begin
  3 hrs ahead
- 16 servings
- 400 cals
  per serving
  without
  garnish

1. Preheat oven to 350°F. Grease two 9-inch round cake pans.
2. In large bowl with mixer at low speed, beat first 10 ingredients until well blended, occasionally scraping bowl with rubber spatula.
3. Pour batter into prepared pans. Bake 35 to 40 minutes until toothpick inserted in center of cake comes out clean. Cool cake in pans on wire racks 10 minutes. Remove cakes from pans; cool completely on racks, about 1 hour.
4. When cake layers are cool, prepare Chocolate Sour-Cream Frosting. Quickly fill and frost side and top of cake with frosting.
5. To garnish cake, in heavy small saucepan over low heat, heat semisweet-chocolate square until melted and smooth, stirring frequently. Spoon melted chocolate into small decorating bag with small writing tube; pipe design on top of cake.
6. Before slicing, refrigerate cake until frosting is firm, about 30 minutes. Cut cake into 16 wedges. If you like, separate wedges slightly and place a small piece of waxed paper between cake wedges for easier serving later. Refrigerate cake until ready to serve.

Piping design: Using melted chocolate, pipe an attractive design on top of cake.

For easy serving: Place a small piece of waxed paper between each slice of cake.

CHOCOLATE SOUR-CREAM FROSTING: In heavy 1-quart saucepan over low heat, heat *one 8-ounce package semisweet-chocolate squares* and *1 tablespoon butter* or *margarine* until melted and smooth, stirring occasionally. Remove saucepan from heat. In small bowl with mixer at medium speed, beat melted chocolate mixture, *⅔ cup sour cream, ¼ cup confectioners' sugar,* and *¼ teaspoon salt* until smooth. 1817 cals.

Christmas Dinner

Christmas is the happiest and busiest time of the year for most of us. From the tiniest villages to the biggest cities, streets, stores, and houses are filled with bright lights and decorations. Preparations begin weeks before with shopping for gifts, sending cards, baking cookies, decorating the tree, and filling stockings. With all the excitement of wellwishers and children opening gifts in the morning, Christmas dinner is often in the afternoon.

We celebrate this happy day in grand style using our best dishes, silver, and other family heirlooms, all complemented by beautiful full-blown red roses. Our impressive centerpiece is a Standing Rib Roast with its trimmings. Start with an elegant Shrimp Cocktail and for a change, serve a sophisticated composed salad. Our Cranberry Swirl Cheesecake, garnished with Sugar-Frosted Cranberries and decorated with holly leaves and berries, provides the perfect ending to a glorious meal.

MENU

12 people

*

Shrimp Cocktail with Tangy Dip
(double quantity) page 89

*

*Standing Rib Roast
with Yorkshire Pudding*
page 176
Roasted Potato Fans
(double quantity) page 244
Broccoli with Butter-Almond Sauce
(double quantity) page 234
*Watercress, Pear, Endive,
and Walnut Salad*
(for 12) page 270
Pumpernickel-Rye Bread
page 358
Horseradish Sauce
page 385

*

Cranberry Swirl Cheesecake
Page 340
Chocolate Dipped Fruit
page 354

HOW TO SERVE A COMPOSED SALAD

A composed salad generally has fewer ingredients than a tossed salad and is carefully arranged on a plate. It can be served as a first course, appetizer, or, as a refresher between the main meal and the dessert; the combinations and variations are limited only by your imagination.

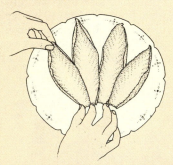

Arrange several leaves of Belgian endive on individual salad plates.

Place slices of unpeeled pear in the center of each leaf.

Add a sprig of watercress and several walnut halves.

Carefully pour dressing over salad so it does not disturb the arrangement.

Planning Ahead

2 days ahead:	Bake bread; freeze 2 loaves, store one in airtight container. Prepare Horseradish Sauce and Tangy Dip; cover and refrigerate.
Day ahead:	Prepare cheesecake but do not unmold or garnish; refrigerate. Wash salad ingredients; refrigerate.
Early in day:	Prepare shrimp for cocktail, but do not assemble; refrigerate. Dip fruits in chocolate; chill.
2 hours ahead:	Place rib roast and potatoes in oven. Frost cranberries; unmold cheesecake and garnish; keep refrigerated.
1 hour ahead:	Assemble salads and Shrimp Cocktail. Remove beef to rest; bake Yorkshire Pudding. Prepare broccoli. Slice bread and remove fruits and cheesecake from refrigerator.

New Year's Eve Supper

December 31st is the ideal time for a big party to celebrate the New Year. Choose a Southwestern-style buffet supper with a warming Tex-Mex menu starting with Guacamole, corn chips, crisp crudités, and tasty Quesados – avocado sandwiches. Garnish with chili flowers: make lengthwise slits quarter-inch from stem end and soak in cold water; the strips will open out. Serve a large bowl of Texas-Style Chili with accompaniments of shredded Monterey Jack cheese, chopped onions, chilies, a bowl of sour cream, and rice. Mexican-Style Meatballs and Chicken Tostadas provide equally flavorful choices. Placed in wooden bowls and painted dishes, they create a cheerful atmosphere. Finish with Baked Coffee Custards and Lemon-Lime Milk Sherbet to welcome the New Year.

Planning Ahead

Up to 2 days ahead:	Bake bread; wrap well. Make chili and meatballs; refrigerate. Make sherbet. Cut up crudités; wrap and refrigerate.
Early in day:	Make custards. Cook chicken for tostadas. Make Guacamole and Avocado Butter; cover.
2 hours ahead and just before serving:	Assemble crudités. Prepare Salsa Cruda, chili accompaniments, tostadas, and Quesados. Reheat bread, chili, and meatballs; cook rice.

MENU

18 people

✳

Guacamole and Tex-Mex Crudités
pages 91 and 94
Quesados
page 87

━━━━━

✳

Texas-Style Chili
(1½ quantity) page 182
Mexican-Style Meatballs
(triple quantity) page 183
Chicken Tostadas
(triple quantity) page 151
Chili-Cheese Corn Bread
(double quantity) page 367

━━━━━

✳

Lemon-Lime Milk Sherbet
(double quantity) page 306
Baked Coffee Custards
(double quantity) page 296

━━━━━

Cold Beer

New Year's Day Brunch

New Year's Day, the first day of the calendar year, is a national holiday and celebrated coast to coast. A long, late, leisurely brunch is the ideal way to begin the day, after the exuberant festivities of the night before. A brunch gives the hostess plenty of time for a bit of extra sleep, and some last minute preparations. We've chosen a refreshing California-style meal starting with fresh fruit juices, Blueberry Muffins, and Pecan-Crumb Coffeecakes. For the hungry ones, stacks of Country Brunch Pancakes, Breakfast Sausage Patties, and Party Creamy Eggs with a platter of delicious accompaniments, provide a variety of choices. Colorful tropical fruits surround a dish of Two-Melon Granita for a cooling finish.

Planning Ahead

2 days ahead:	Bake muffins and coffeecakes. Make and freeze granita. Soften to scoop; arrange scoops in bowl; refreeze.
Day ahead:	Prepare fresh juices. Make sausage patties and pancake batter; cover and refrigerate.
Early in day:	Slice fruits and arrange on plate; refrigerate until ready to serve. Fry bacon and sausage patties; keep warm in oven. Make Fig-Maple Syrup.
1 hour ahead:	Make pancakes; arrange with patties and keep warm in oven. Prepare mushrooms, avocados, and smoked salmon; begin cooking eggs; add bacon to accompaniments. Heat muffins if you like.

MENU

8 people

*

Fresh Fruit Juices
(orange, grapefruit, pineapple)

*

Country Brunch Pancakes
page 370
Breakfast Sausage Patties
page 213
Party Creamy Eggs
page 111
Blueberry Muffins
page 368

*

Pecan-Crumb Coffeecakes
page 329
Two-Melon Granita
page 306

*

Tropical Fruits

*

Coffee

PREPARING TROPICAL FRUITS

Many new and exciting fruits from exotic places are available today. They provide plenty of color, texture, flavor, and variety. We have chosen to use them with some of California's finest grapes and strawberries to provide an edible centerpiece for our brunch.

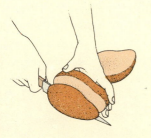

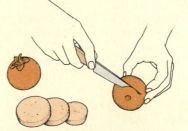

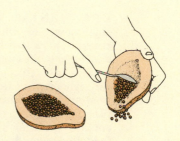

Mangoes are oval or round with a yellow or bright orange, sometimes speckled skin. With sharp knife, cut a lengthwise slice from each side of the long flat seed as close to seed as possible; set aside section containing seed.

Peel the skin from cut off pieces and slice lengthwise. Cut the skin from the reserved seed section and carefully slice pieces from seed section.

Persimmons, either Oriental or homegrown, are a firm, plump fruit with the stem cap attached. When ripe, remove cap; cut crosswise in slices to eat pulp. Or, place stem end down on a plate; cut gashes through the top skin so that the pulp can be eaten with a spoon.

Papayas are a greenish-yellow to almost yellow fruit with golden or pink flesh. With a sharp knife, cut in half lengthwise, scrape out seeds, peel, and cut up or slice.

Kiwifruit has bright green flesh with tiny black seeds. With sharp knife, peel off skin; cut in wedges or slices. Or cut unpeeled fruit lengthwise in half to eat with spoon.

Special occasion cakes

- Color index page 71
- 3 hrs ahead or early in day
- 32 servings
- 340 cals per serving

4TH OF JULY CAKE

Yellow Cake
2¼ cups cake flour
1½ cups sugar
¾ cup shortening
¾ cup milk
3 eggs
2½ teaspoons baking powder
1 teaspoon salt
1 teaspoon vanilla extract
½ teaspoon almond extract

3 pints strawberries, hulled
4 cups heavy or whipping cream
½ cup confectioners' sugar
2 teaspoons vanilla extract
¼ teaspoon salt
1 cup blueberries
½ cup strawberry jelly

1. Preheat oven to 375°F. Grease and flour a 13" by 9" baking pan. Prepare Yellow Cake: In a large bowl, measure the cake flour, sugar, shortening, ¾ cup milk, eggs, baking powder, salt, and vanilla and almond extracts. With mixer at low speed, beat until well mixed, constantly scraping bowl with rubber spatula. Increase speed to medium; beat 5 minutes longer.

2. Place batter in pan; bake about 40 minutes or until toothpick inserted in center comes out clean. Cool cake in pan on wire rack 15 minutes. Loosen edges of cake; invert cake onto rack, remove pan. Leave cake to cool completely.

3. Slice 1 pint strawberries; cut each of remaining strawberries in half; set aside.

4. In large bowl, with mixer at medium speed, beat cream, confectioners' sugar, vanilla extract, and salt until soft peaks form, occasionally scraping bowl with rubber spatula.

5. Invert cooled cake on work surface. With large serrated knife, split cake horizontally.

6. Place top half of cake cut side up, on platter; with metal spatula, spread with about 2 cups whipped-cream mixture. Top with sliced strawberries, then with bottom half of cake, cut side down; spread about 4 cups of the remaining whipped cream on sides and top of cake to make a smooth surface.

7. Arrange blueberries and halved strawberries on cake to resemble American flag. Over medium heat, melt strawberry jelly. Carefully brush over berries to glaze fruit.

8. Spoon remaining 2 cups whipped-cream mixture into decorating bag with medium star tube; pipe stars separating blueberries and strawberries. Pipe stars around top and bottom edge of cake. Refrigerate until ready to serve.

ORNAMENTAL COOKIE FROSTING: In small bowl with mixer at low speed, beat *2½ cups confectioners' sugar, ¼ teaspoon cream of tartar,* and *2 egg whites* until blended. Increase speed to high; beat mixture until so stiff that a knife drawn through mixture leaves a clean-cut path. Spoon frosting into decorating bag with small writing tube for decorating or writing messages on cakes, cookies, or other baked goods. Tint with natural food colorings, if you like.

HOW TO DECORATE WITH FROSTING

With a decorating bag fitted with a coupler and a selection of tubes and flower nails, you can make a wide range of frosting shapes and designs. The consistency of the frosting used is very important: use a stiff frosting, such as Butter-Cream Frosting (p. 344), for flowers; use medium-stiff, such as Fluffy Boiled Frosting (p. 331), for borders; and a thinner icing, such as Ornamental Cookie Frosting (left), for writing. Our instructions are for right-handed cooks. If you are left-handed, read "left" for "right" and vice versa.

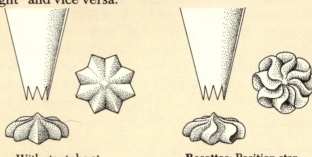

Stars: With star tube at 90° and almost touching surface, squeeze, then lift slightly, keeping tip in icing. Stop pressure and lift tube.

Rosettes: Position star tube as for star, but as you squeeze, move tube up and to left in a circular motion. Stop pressure and lift tube away.

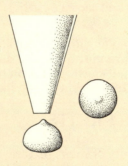

Dots: With round tube at 90° and almost touching surface, squeeze to form dot, then lift slightly keeping tip in icing. Stop pressure and lift tube.

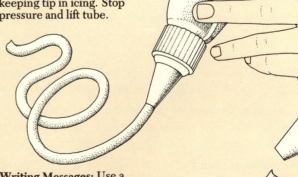

Writing Messages: Use a round tube and thinned icing, such as Ornamental Cookie Frosting (left). With tube at 45°, touch surface to secure icing, then slightly lift tube as it moves to form letters.

Use even pressure and guide tube with your entire arm. To finish a letter or word, just stop pressure and lift tube.

MOTHER'S DAY CAKE

Treat Mom to this lovely bonnet cake that is guaranteed to make her day special. It's surprisingly easy to make. We've used yellow roses but you can use any favorite flowers.

Yellow Cake (p.338)
2 medium lemons
4 cups confectioners'
sugar
½ cup butter or
margarine, softened
⅛ teaspoon salt
Yellow food coloring
Yellow rose buds, baby's
breath, and yellow
ribbons, to garnish

- *Color index page 71*
- *Begin 3 hours ahead or early in day*
- *16 servings*
- *360 cals per serving*

1 Preheat oven to 350°F. Generously grease and flour 12-inch round pizza pan with at least a ¾ inch-high rim (to bake hat brim). Grease 1¼-quart heat-safe bowl (to bake hat's crown). Prepare Yellow Cake: Place 3½ cups batter in greased bowl; spread remaining batter in pizza pan. Bake batter in pizza pan about 15 minutes or until a toothpick inserted in center of cake comes out clean. Cool cake in pan on wire rack 10 minutes. Loosen and invert onto rack; cool completely.

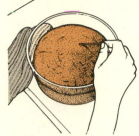

2 Bake batter in bowl about 50 minutes or until toothpick inserted in center of cake comes out clean. Cool cake in bowl on wire rack 10 minutes. Loosen and invert onto rack; cool completely.

3 Meanwhile, from lemons, grate 1½ teaspoons peel and squeeze 5 tablespoons juice. Place lemon peel and juice in large bowl; add confectioners' sugar, butter, and salt. At low speed, beat until smooth.

4 Spoon about ¼ cup icing into small bowl; stir in enough yellow food coloring to tint icing a pale yellow color. Cover both bowls with plastic wrap to prevent icing from drying out.

5 Assemble cake: Place cake brim on flat cake plate or tray. With metal spatula, spread 1 cup white icing on cake brim, occasionally dipping spatula into bowl of hot water to smooth out icing.

6 Place cake crown on center of cake brim (if bottom of cake crown is very rounded, with sharp knife, cut off thin slice to make flat). With metal spatula, spread 1¼ cups white icing on cake crown.

7 Spoon remaining white icing into small decorating bag with petal tube; pipe ruffle around edge of cake brim. With yellow ribbon, tie bow and attach to straight pin or cocktail stick.

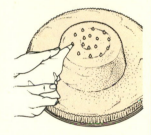

8 Spoon yellow icing into small decorating bag with small writing tube; pipe dots over cake crown to make a pretty design. Attach bow to the base of crown. Garnish with flowers.

HOW TO MAKE ROSES AND LEAVES

Making roses and leaves from frosting is easier than you think. Follow our simple directions.

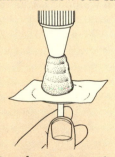

To make a rose: Attach 2-inch square of waxed paper to flat-head flower nail with dab of frosting; hold nail between thumb and forefinger of left hand. With round tube at 90°, pipe mound of icing. Now use nail as turntable, turning nail to left as you form petals to right.

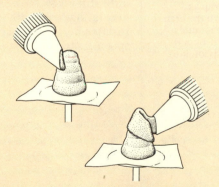

With petal tube at 45°, touch wide end to just below top of mound with narrow end straight up; turn nail to left as you pipe band of icing up, around, and down to starting point to make bud.

Touch wide end to base, narrow end up; move tube up and down in arc. Make two more petals. With narrow end pointing out a little, pipe row of 4 petals under the first row.

With narrow end of tube pointing out, pipe final row of 5 to 7 petals under previous row. Slip finished rose off nail; let dry.

To make a plain leaf: Hold leaf tube at 45°. Squeeze until icing fans out, then relax pressure and draw leaf to a point. Stop pressure and pull tube away.

To make a stand-up leaf: Hold leaf tube at 90°. Squeeze until icing fans out, then relax pressure as you raise tube, drawing leaf up to a point. Stop pressure and lift tube.

Cheesecakes

CRANBERRY SWIRL CHEESECAKE

About 1900, rich cream-cheese-based cakes, often known as "New York Cheesecake," became popular. These cakes originated in New York's Italian and Jewish neighborhoods.

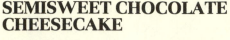

- Color index page 72
- Begin early in day
- 16 servings
- 380 cals per serving

5 eggs
3 envelopes unflavored gelatin
Water
1 medium orange
4 8-ounce packages cream cheese, softened

1 teaspoon vanilla extract
Sugar
1¾ cups cranberries
1½ cups finely crushed vanilla wafers (about 40 cookies)

4 tablespoons butter or margarine, softened
Small holly leaves or other nontoxic leaves for garnish
Sugar-Frosted cranberries (p.294)

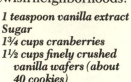

1 Separate the eggs, placing egg yolks in large mixing bowl and whites in small bowl.

2 In 1-quart saucepan, evenly sprinkle the unflavored gelatin over 2 cups cold water. Gently cook over medium heat until gelatin is completely dissolved and no granules remain, stirring frequently with a spoon. Remove the saucepan from the heat, then set aside for gelatin to cool slightly.

3 From orange, grate 1 tablespoon peel; cut in half and squeeze 2 tablespoons juice.

4 To large bowl with egg yolks, add cream cheese, vanilla, orange juice and peel, and 1 cup sugar; at low speed, beat until blended. Gradually beat in 1¾ cups gelatin. Increase speed to medium; beat until smooth, scraping bowl.

5 With mixer at high speed, beat egg whites in bowl until stiff peaks form. With rubber spatula, fold whites into cheese mixture. Cover with plastic wrap; refrigerate until mixture mounds slightly when dropped from a spoon.

6 Meanwhile, in 2-quart saucepan over high heat, cook ¾ cup sugar, 2 tablespoons water, and the cranberries 5 minutes or until cranberry skins pop, stirring occasionally with a long-handled wooden spoon; stir in remaining ¼ cup gelatin mixture. In an electric blender at medium speed, blend the cranberry mixture until smooth; pour mixture into small bowl; cover with plastic wrap and refrigerate until the cranberry mixture mounds slightly when dropped from a metal spoon into the bowl.

7 In 10" by 3" springform pan, with hand, mix crushed vanilla wafers and butter or margarine; firmly press onto the bottom of the pan.

8 Alternately spoon cheese and cranberry mixtures into pan. With knife, cut through to make swirl. Cover; refrigerate until set.

9 Prepare frosted cranberries; set aside. Carefully remove side of pan from cheesecake. Garnish with cranberries and leaves.

SEMISWEET CHOCOLATE CHEESECAKE

1 cup walnuts, minced
½ cup all-purpose flour
6 tablespoons butter or margarine, softened
Sugar
1 8-ounce package semisweet-chocolate squares
4 8-ounce packages cream cheese, softened

⅓ cup milk
½ teaspoon vanilla extract
3 eggs
⅓ cup heavy or whipping cream
2 squares semisweet chocolate, coarsely grated for garnish

1. In small bowl with hands, knead walnuts, flour, butter or margarine, and ¼ cup sugar until blended. Wrap dough with plastic wrap and refrigerate 30 minutes or until easy to handle.
2. Preheat oven to 400°F. Press one-third of dough onto bottom of 9" by 3" springform pan; keep remaining dough refrigerated. Bake bottom crust 8 minutes or until golden. Cool crust in pan on wire rack while preparing filling. Turn oven control to 475°F.
3. In 2-quart saucepan over low heat, heat 8 squares semisweet chocolate until melted and smooth, stirring occasionally.
4. In large bowl with mixer at low speed, beat cream cheese just until smooth. Add melted chocolate, milk, vanilla, eggs, and ¾ cup sugar; beat until blended. Increase speed to medium; beat 3 minutes, scraping bowl.
5. Press remaining dough around side of pan to within 1 inch of top. Pour cream-cheese mixture into pan; bake 12 minutes. Turn oven control to 300°F.; bake 35 minutes longer. Turn oven control off; leave cheesecake in oven 30 minutes. Cool cake in pan on wire rack. Cover with plastic wrap or aluminum foil and refrigerate at least 4 hours or until well chilled.
6. To serve, remove cake from springform pan; place on plate. In small bowl with mixer at medium speed, beat heavy or whipping cream until stiff peaks form. Spoon whipped cream into decorating bag with medium star tube. Pipe rosettes on top of cake to make a pretty design; spoon grated chocolate onto center.

Making bottom crust: Press dough to cover bottom of pan.

Garnishing top: Use decorating bag to pipe whipped cream rosettes.

- Color index page 72
- Begin early in day
- 16 servings
- 480 cals per serving

Fruit, spice, and nut cakes

LIGHT AND CREAMY CHEESECAKE

- Color index page 72
- Begin early in day
- 16 servings
- 325 cals per serving

1 16-ounce container creamed cottage cheese
2 8-ounce packages cream cheese, softened
1½ cups sugar
1 16-ounce container sour cream (2 cups)
4 eggs, slightly beaten
4 tablespoons butter or margarine, melted

3 tablespoons all-purpose flour
3 tablespoons cornstarch
1½ teaspoons almond extract
½ teaspoon salt
Lemon and Lime Twists (p.100) for garnish

1. Preheat oven to 325°F. Grease 10″ by 2½″ springform pan.
2. Press cottage cheese through fine strainer. In large bowl, with mixer at low speed, beat cottage cheese, cream cheese, and sugar just until blended, scraping bowl with rubber spatula. Beat in sour cream and next 6 ingredients until blended, occasionally scraping bowl.
3. Spoon into prepared springform pan. Bake cheesecake 1 hour. Turn oven control off; leave cheesecake in oven 1 hour. Remove from oven; cool on wire rack. Cover; refrigerate at least 4 hours. To serve, remove side of pan; garnish.

MANHATTAN-STYLE CHEESECAKE

- Color index page 72
- Begin early in day
- 16 servings
- 360 cals per serving

⅔ cup butter or margarine, softened
All-purpose flour
Sugar
2 egg yolks
Grated peel of 1 lemon
3 8-ounce packages cream cheese, softened

2 tablespoons milk
3 eggs
2 large kiwifruit
½ pint strawberries
2 tablespoons apple jelly

1. In small bowl with mixer at low speed, beat butter, 1 cup flour, 3 tablespoons sugar, 1 egg yolk, and ½ of lemon peel until mixed. Shape into ball; wrap and refrigerate 1 hour.
2. Preheat oven to 400°F. Press ⅓ of dough onto bottom of 10″ by 3″ springform pan. Bake 8 minutes; cool. Turn oven control to 475°F.
3. Meanwhile, in large bowl with mixer at medium speed, beat cream cheese just until smooth; slowly beat in 1 cup sugar. With mixer at low speed, beat in 2 tablespoons flour, milk, eggs, 1 egg yolk, and remaining peel; at medium speed, beat 5 minutes, scraping bowl.
4. Press remaining dough around side of pan to within 1¾ inches of top; do not bake. Pour cream-cheese mixture into pan; bake 10 minutes. Turn oven control to 300°F; bake 20 minutes.
5. Turn off oven; let cheesecake remain in oven 20 minutes. Remove; cool cake in pan on wire rack; refrigerate until chilled, about 2 hours.
6. To serve, peel and thinly slice kiwifruit, cut each strawberry in half, and arrange on top. In small saucepan over low heat, melt apple jelly. With pastry brush lightly brush fruit with jelly.

STRAWBERRY SHORTCAKE

"Shortcake" is a flaky, baking powder biscuit; layered with fresh strawberries and cream, it is one of America's most popular cakes.

- Color index page 70
- Begin 45 mins ahead
- 10 servings
- 329 cals per serving

2 cups all-purpose flour
2 teaspoons baking powder
1 teaspoon salt
Sugar
⅓ cup shortening
⅔ cup milk
2 pints strawberries
3 tablespoons butter or margarine, softened
1 cup heavy or whipping cream, whipped

1 Preheat oven to 425°F. Grease 8-inch round cake pan. In bowl with a fork, mix flour, baking powder, salt, and 2 tablespoons sugar. With a pastry blender or with two knives used scissor-fashion, cut in shortening until mixture resembles coarse crumbs. Add milk; with fork, stir until mixture forms soft dough.

2 On lightly floured surface with floured hands, knead dough 10 times. Pat dough evenly into pan. Bake 15 minutes or until golden.

3 Meanwhile, wash strawberries. Reserve four whole strawberries for garnish; hull and halve or quarter remaining strawberries.

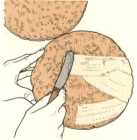

4 In medium bowl with rubber spatula, toss cut-up strawberries with ½ cup sugar until sugar dissolves.

5 Invert shortcake on work surface. With long serrated knife, split horizontally; spread cut surfaces with butter.

6 Place bottom half of shortcake, cut side up, on a dessert platter; spread with half of cream; top with half of strawberry mixture; use spatula to gently spread strawberry mixture to edge of shortcake half. Arrange top cake half, cut side down, on top of the strawberry mixture. Spoon remaining strawberry mixture over top of cake; do not spread strawberry mixture too near the edge, as mixture may run over.

7 Spoon ¾ remaining cream over strawberry mixture. Garnish with reserved whole strawberries and cream.

Fruit, spice, and nut cakes

CHOCOLATE FRUITCAKE

English settlers in the South brought their traditional Christmas fruitcakes with them; we have added chocolate for extra richness.

3 6-ounce cans pecan halves (6 cups)
1 8-ounce container red candied cherries (1 cup)
1 cup golden raisins
1 cup dark seedless raisins
¼ cup dry sherry or orange juice

1 4-ounce container diced candied citron (½ cup)
All-purpose flour
1¼ cups sugar
1 cup water
¾ cup butter or margarine, softened
1½ teaspoons baking soda
1 teaspoon vanilla extract

½ teaspoon baking powder
½ teaspoon salt
4 squares unsweetened chocolate, melted
3 eggs
¼ cup light corn syrup

- Color index page 71
- Begin up to 1 month ahead
- 32 servings
- 302 cals per serving

1 Line 10-inch tube pan with foil; press out wrinkles as much as possible so cake surface will come out smooth.

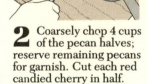

2 Coarsely chop 4 cups of the pecan halves; reserve remaining pecans for garnish. Cut each red candied cherry in half.

3 In a large bowl, gently combine the chopped pecans, red-cherry halves, golden and dark seedless raisins, dry sherry or orange juice, and diced candied citron; set aside and let stand 30 minutes until all the sherry is absorbed, gently stirring occasionally. Stir in ¼ cup flour until the fruit and nuts are evenly coated. (This prevents fruit and nuts from sinking to the bottom of the cake during baking.)

4 In another bowl with mixer at low speed, beat sugar, next 8 ingredients, and 2 cups flour, scraping bowl with rubber spatula. Increase speed to high; beat 3 minutes.

5 Preheat oven to 300°F. Stir fruit mixture into batter until mixed. Spoon batter into prepared tube pan, packing down batter evenly to eliminate air pockets. Bake fruitcake 1¾ to 2 hours, until toothpick inserted in center of cake comes out clean. Remove cake from oven but do not turn oven off. Cool cake in tube pan on wire rack; remove fruitcake from pan and carefully peel off the aluminum foil lining.

6 Meanwhile, place remaining pecan halves in 9" by 9" baking pan. In oven, toast pecans until lightly browned, stirring nuts occasionally. Set aside; cool.

7 In small saucepan over medium heat, heat the corn syrup to boiling; boil 1 minute; remove from heat.

8 With pastry brush, brush top of fruitcake with syrup. Arrange pecan halves on top of cake to cover completely.

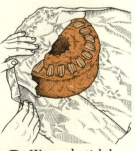

9 Wrap cake tightly with foil or plastic wrap. Refrigerate to use up within 1 month. To serve, cut into slices.

GINGERBREAD RING WITH MAPLE CREAM

3 cups all-purpose flour
1½ cups light corn syrup
1 cup buttermilk
¾ cup butter or margarine, softened
½ cup packed light brown sugar
1½ teaspoons baking soda
1½ teaspoons ground ginger
1½ teaspoons ground cinnamon

½ teaspoon ground allspice
½ teaspoon salt
1 egg
½ cup golden raisins
1 tablespoon sugar
1 cup heavy or whipping cream
2 tablespoons maple syrup or maple-flavor syrup

1. Preheat oven to 325°F. Grease and flour 10-inch Bundt pan or tube pan.
2. Into large bowl, measure first 11 ingredients. With electric mixer at low speed, beat ingredients just until mixed, constantly scraping bowl with rubber spatula.
3. Increase speed to medium; beat 1 minute, occasionally scraping bowl. Stir in raisins.
4. Spoon batter into pan. Bake 1¼ hours or until toothpick inserted in center comes out clean.
5. Cool gingerbread in pan on wire rack 10 minutes; remove from pan. Sprinkle gingerbread with sugar; let cool completely on wire rack.
6. To serve, in small bowl with mixer at medium speed, beat heavy or whipping cream and maple syrup until soft peaks form. Place gingerbread on cake plate; spoon maple cream into center.

- Color index page 70
- Begin 3 hrs ahead
- 16 servings
- 325 cals per serving

OLD-FASHIONED SPICE CAKE

3 cups all-purpose flour
2 cups packed brown sugar
1½ 8-ounce containers sour cream (1½ cups)
¾ cup butter or margarine, softened
1 tablespoon ground cinnamon
1½ teaspoons baking powder

1½ teaspoons ground cardamom
¾ teaspoon baking soda
½ teaspoon salt
½ teaspoon vanilla extract
⅛ teaspoon ground ginger
3 eggs
Confectioners' sugar for garnish

1. Preheat oven to 350°F. Grease and flour 10-inch Bundt pan or tube pan.
2. Into large bowl, measure all ingredients. With mixer at low speed, beat just until blended, constantly scraping bowl with rubber spatula. Increase speed to high; beat 2 minutes.
3. Spoon into pan. Bake 55 to 60 minutes, until toothpick inserted in center comes out clean. Cool on wire rack 10 minutes; remove from pan; cool on rack. Sprinkle with confectioners' sugar.

- Color index page 71
- Begin 4 hrs ahead
- 16 servings
- 326 cals per serving

CARROT CAKE WITH CREAM-CHEESE FROSTING

- Color index page 72
- Begin 3 hrs ahead or early in day
- 12 servings
- 708 cals per serving

4 eggs
1½ cups salad oil
1 cup sugar
2 cups all-purpose flour
2 teaspoons baking soda
2 teaspoons ground cinnamon
1 teaspoon salt
2 cups shredded carrots

1 cup dark seedless raisins
½ cup finely chopped walnuts
1 teaspoon vanilla extract
Cream-Cheese Frosting (below)
Chopped walnuts for garnish

1. Preheat oven to 350°F. Grease and flour two 9-inch round cake pans.
2. In large bowl, with mixer at medium speed, beat eggs, oil, and sugar. Reduce speed to low; beat in flour, baking soda, cinnamon, and salt.
3. With spoon, stir in carrots, raisins, walnuts, and vanilla. Pour batter into pans. Bake 35 minutes, or until toothpick inserted into center comes out clean. Cool layers in pans on wire racks 10 minutes. Remove from pans; cool completely on racks.
4. When layers are cool, prepare Cream-Cheese Frosting; use to fill and frost layers. To garnish, pat chopped walnuts onto side of cake. Keep cake refrigerated until ready to serve.
CREAM-CHEESE FROSTING: In small bowl, with mixer at low speed, beat *two 3-ounce packages cream cheese*, softened, with *1 tablespoon milk* and *1 teaspoon vanilla extract* just until smooth. Gradually beat in *one 16-ounce package confectioners' sugar*. 2400 cals.

CHUNKY APPLE CAKE

- Color index page 71
- Begin 4 hrs ahead
- 16 servings
- 435 cals per serving

1 large cooking apple (about ½ pound)
3 cups all-purpose flour
2 cups sugar
1 cup salad oil
⅓ cup orange juice
1 teaspoon baking soda
1 teaspoon ground cinnamon
1 teaspoon vanilla extract

¼ teaspoon salt
3 eggs
1½ cups walnuts, coarsely chopped
1 3½- to 4-ounce can flaked or shredded coconut (about 1⅓ cups)

1. Preheat oven to 350°F. Grease and flour 10-inch tube pan. Peel and dice apple.
2. In large bowl, with mixer at low speed, beat flour and next 8 ingredients just until blended, constantly scraping bowl with rubber spatula. Increase speed to high; beat 2 minutes, occasionally scraping bowl with rubber spatula.
3. Stir in diced apple, 1 cup chopped walnuts, and half of coconut. Spoon batter into pan. Gently pat the remaining walnuts and coconut on top of the cake.
4. Bake cake 25 minutes, then cover cake quickly with a tent of foil; bake 1 hour longer or until top of cake is golden and toothpick inserted in center of cake comes out clean. Cool cake in pan on wire rack 10 minutes; remove cake from pan; cool completely on rack.

PEANUT-BUTTER CUPCAKES

- Color index page 72
- Begin 2 hrs ahead
- 24 cupcakes
- 145 cals per serving

1¾ cups all-purpose flour
1 cup milk
¾ cup sugar
½ cup chunky or creamy peanut butter
4 tablespoons butter or margarine, softened

1 tablespoon baking powder
¾ teaspoon vanilla extract
½ teaspoon salt
2 eggs
⅔ cup milk-chocolate pieces

1. Preheat oven to 350°F. Grease twenty-four 2½-inch muffin-pan cups.
2. Into large bowl, measure all ingredients except chocolate pieces. With mixer at low speed, beat ingredients just until blended. Increase speed to high; beat 2 minutes.
3. Spoon batter into muffin-pan cups. Top each cupcake with some milk-chocolate pieces. Bake 18 to 20 minutes, until toothpick inserted in center of 1 cupcake comes out clean. Cool cupcakes in pans on wire racks 10 minutes; remove from pans and cool completely on rack.

HOW TO MAKE FROG CUPCAKES

Cupcakes can be decorated in many ways but this idea is a real novelty and would make a great children's party favor. Make 24 Chocolate Cupcakes (p.331) but omit frosting.

Remove 12 cupcakes from baking cups; leave the rest in their baking cups; slice off rounded tops from all cupcakes so they are even. (Reserve cupcake tops for use another day. Sandwich together one cut cupcake on top of one cupcake still in baking cup, cut sides together. With a

pointed, serrated knife, cut a wedge from the top cupcake of each pair, to form frog's mouth. To decorate, prepare half quantity "Seven Minute" Frosting (p.344). Spoon about ⅓ cup "Seven Minute" Frosting into a bowl; cover with plastic wrap; set aside.

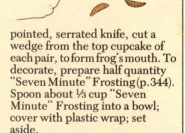

Tint the remaining frosting with green food coloring. Cover each frog cupcake with green frosting; leave mouths unfrosted. Smooth frosting with metal spatula.

Spoon reserved white frosting into decorating bag with small writing tube; use to pipe dots onto each frog cupcake, for eyes. Press a semi-sweet chocolate mini piece into center of each eye.

Frostings and fillings

CHOCOLATE ICING

● Begin 15 mins ahead

2 squares semisweet chocolate	½ cup confectioners' sugar
1 tablespoon butter or margarine	2 to 3 tablespoons milk

1. In heavy 1-quart saucepan over low heat, melt chocolate and butter; remove from heat.
2. With wire whisk or fork, beat in confectioners' sugar and milk until smooth and easy spreading consistency. Makes enough to ice one 9-inch single layer cake. 581 cals.

CHOCOLATE-CREAM FILLING

● Begin 1½ hrs ahead

1½ cups heavy or whipping cream	4 tablespoons butter or margarine
1 8-ounce package semisweet-chocolate squares	

1. In 2-quart saucepan over medium heat, heat all ingredients until smooth and boiling, stirring.
2. Pour into large bowl; cover and refrigerate until chilled, about 1 hour. With mixer at high speed, beat until fluffy. 2881 cals.

BUTTER-CREAM FROSTING

● Begin 20 mins ahead

1 16-ounce package confectioners' sugar (4 cups)	3 to 4 tablespoons milk
6 tablespoons butter or margarine, softened	1½ teaspoons vanilla extract
	½ teaspoon salt

In a large bowl with a spoon or mixer at medium speed, beat all ingredients until very smooth, adding more milk if necessary to make a good spreading consistency. 2628 cals.
MOCHA-BUTTER-CREAM FROSTING: Prepare as above but add ½ cup cocoa; substitute ½ cup hot coffee for the milk and reduce vanilla extract to ½ teaspoon. 2742 cals.

FRESH LEMON FILLING

● Begin 45 mins ahead

½ cup water	¼ cup lemon juice
¼ cup sugar	4 teaspoons cornstarch
1 tablespoon grated lemon peel	¼ teaspoon salt
	1 tablespoon butter

1. In 1-quart saucepan over medium heat, stir all ingredients except butter until blended. Cook until very thick and boiling briskly, stirring.
2. Reduce heat; simmer 1 minute, stirring occasionally. Remove from heat; stir in butter. Cool mixture at room temperature. 357 cals.

"SEVEN-MINUTE" FROSTING

● Begin 35 mins ahead

1½ cups sugar	1 tablespoon light corn syrup
½ cup water (for crusty surface use ⅓ cup)	1 teaspoon vanilla extract
2 egg whites	½ teaspoon salt

1. In top of a double boiler with mixer at high speed, beat all the ingredients about 1 minute.
2. Place over rapid boiling water; beat at high speed until mixture forms soft peaks (this may take longer than 7 minutes). Pour into a large bowl; beat until thick enough to spread. 1236 cals.

CHOCOLATE-WALNUT FILLING

● Begin 30 mins ahead

1 cup evaporated milk, undiluted	2 squares semisweet chocolate
½ cup packed brown sugar	3 egg yolks, lightly beaten
½ cup butter or margarine	1 8-ounce can walnuts
	1 teaspoon vanilla extract

1. In a 3-quart saucepan over medium heat, heat evaporated milk, brown sugar, butter or margarine, chocolate, and egg yolks, stirring frequently, about 10 minutes. With wooden spoon, stir in the walnuts and the vanilla extract until the mixture is well mixed.
2. Remove saucepan from heat. Cool filling slightly until thick enough to spread, stirring occasionally. 3165 cals.

VANILLA FROSTING

● Begin 45 mins ahead

1½ cups sugar	½ teaspoon salt
1 tablespoon light corn syrup	2 egg whites
⅓ cup water	1 teaspoon vanilla extract

1. In saucepan over medium heat, heat first 4 ingredients to boiling. Boil, without stirring, to 240°F. on candy thermometer; remove from heat.
2. With mixer at high speed, beat egg whites until soft peaks form. Pour syrup in thin stream into whites, beating. Add vanilla extract; continue beating until thick. 1236 cals.

CREAMY CUSTARD FILLING

● Begin 35 mins ahead

2 cups milk	¼ teaspoon salt
¼ cup sugar	2 egg yolks
3 tablespoons cornstarch	1 teaspoon vanilla extract

1. In heavy 2-quart saucepan, stir together all ingredients except vanilla extract until blended.
2. Over medium low heat, cook until mixture thickens and boils, about 20 minutes. Boil 1 minute. Remove from heat; stir in vanilla. Cover and refrigerate about 30 minutes. 736 cals.

Unless otherwise indicated, each of these frostings makes enough to frost one 13″ by 9″ cake, a tube cake or 24 cupcakes, or to fill and frost a 2-layer cake.

Each of the filling recipes makes enough filling for a 2-layer cake. Cover with plastic wrap and keep the filling at room temperature until ready to use.

Brownies

CHOCOLATE CHUNK BROWNIES

- Color index page 72
- Begin 2 hrs ahead
- 12 brownies
- 420 cals per brownie

1 cup butter or margarine
5 squares unsweetened chocolate
2 cups sugar
4 eggs
1½ cups all-purpose flour
1 teaspoon vanilla extract
½ teaspoon salt
½ 12-ounce package semisweet-chocolate chunks

1. Preheat oven to 350°F. Grease 13" by 9" baking pan. In heavy 3-quart saucepan over low heat, melt butter and 4 squares chocolate, stirring. Remove from heat; stir in sugar. Cool slightly.
2. Add eggs, one at a time, beating well. Stir in flour, vanilla, and salt. Spread in baking pan.
3. Sprinkle batter with semisweet-chocolate chunks. Bake 40 minutes, until toothpick inserted in center comes out clean. Cool in pan on rack.
4. Prepare topping: In 1-quart pan over low heat, melt remaining chocolate. With spoon, drizzle chocolate over brownies; cut into squares.

BLONDIES

- Color index page 72
- Begin 2½ hrs ahead
- 15 brownies
- 285 cals per serving

½ cup butter or margarine
1½ cups packed light brown sugar
2 eggs
1½ cups all-purpose flour
½ teaspoon salt
2 teaspoons baking powder
1 teaspoon vanilla extract
1 6-ounce package semi-sweet-chocolate pieces
¾ cup walnuts, chopped

1. Preheat oven to 350°F. Grease 13" by 9" baking pan. In 4-quart pan over low heat, melt butter. Remove from heat; stir in sugar and eggs.
2. Beat until blended; stir in next 4 ingredients; fold in chocolate. Spread into pan. Sprinkle walnuts over; bake 30 minutes, until toothpick inserted in center comes out clean. Cool on wire rack. Cut into 15 squares.

MARBLE BROWNIES

- Color index page 72
- Begin 3 hrs ahead
- 16 brownies
- 220 cals per serving

6 squares semisweet chocolate
½ cup butter or margarine
½ cup all-purpose flour
½ teaspoon salt
¼ teaspoon baking soda
3 eggs
Sugar
1 8-ounce package cream cheese, softened
¼ teaspoon maple extract

1. Grease 8" by 8" baking dish. In saucepan over low heat, melt chocolate and butter.
2. Remove from heat; stir in flour, salt, baking soda, 2 eggs, and ½ cup sugar until blended. Pour into dish; set aside.
3. Preheat oven to 325°F. In small bowl, with mixer at medium speed, beat cream cheese, maple extract, ¼ cup sugar, and 1 egg until smooth, occasionally scraping bowl with rubber spatula. Spoon over batter; with spatula, cut and twist through batter to obtain a marbled effect.
4. Bake 40 minutes, until toothpick inserted in center comes out clean. Cool on wire rack; cut.

CHOCOLATE-MINT BROWNIES

- Color index page 72
- Begin 1½ hrs ahead
- 25 brownies
- 145 cals per serving

This popular American snack gets its name from the dark chocolate color; peppermint wafers make these extra moist and chewy.

½ cup butter or margarine, softened
¾ cup sugar
1 cup all-purpose flour
⅓ cup cocoa
¼ cup dark corn syrup
½ teaspoon baking powder
¼ teaspoon salt
2 eggs
1 6-ounce package semi-sweet-chocolate pieces
¾ cup walnuts, chopped
1 6-ounce box chocolate-coated peppermint-cream wafers
½ cup confectioners' sugar
2 teaspoons water

1 Preheat oven to 350°F. Grease 9" by 9" baking pan. In small bowl with mixer at high speed, beat butter and sugar until light and fluffy. Reduce speed to low; add next 6 ingredients. Beat until well mixed, occasionally scraping bowl with rubber spatula. Stir in chocolate pieces and nuts. Spread batter evenly into prepared pan; bake brownies 25 minutes.

2 Remove from oven; evenly arrange chocolate-coated wafers on top. Return to oven.

3 Bake 5 minutes or until a toothpick inserted in center of cake comes out clean.

4 Remove pan from oven; cool brownies in pan on wire rack. Meanwhile, in small bowl with spoon, mix confectioners' sugar and water until icing is smooth. Drizzle the icing over brownies in pan. When the icing is dry, with sharp knife, cut brownies into 25 equal squares. Cover with plastic wrap or aluminum foil and refrigerate or store in tightly covered container.

BUTTERSCOTCH BROWNIES

- Color index page 72
- Begin 1½ hrs ahead
- 16 brownies
- 220 cals per serving

1 cup packed light brown sugar
¾ cup all-purpose flour
¼ cup shortening
1 teaspoon baking powder
¼ teaspoon salt
¼ teaspoon vanilla extract
1 egg
½ cup walnuts, chopped
½ cup peanut-butter-flavor pieces

1. Preheat oven to 350°F. Grease 8" by 8" baking pan; set aside. Into large bowl, measure first 7 ingredients; with mixer at low speed, blend, occasionally scraping bowl with rubber spatula.
2. With spoon, stir in nuts and peanut-butter-flavor pieces. Evenly spread in baking pan.
3. Bake 25 minutes, until toothpick inserted in center comes out clean; cool on wire rack. Cut into 16 squares. Cover; use up within 1 week.

Chocolate cookies

CHOCOLATE THUMBPRINTS

These chocolate-filled sugar cookies get their name from the indentations made with the thumb before the cookie is baked.

- *Color index page 74*
- *Begin 2 hrs ahead*
- *36 cookies*
- *110 cals per serving*

1 6-ounce package semisweet-chocolate pieces (1 cup)
1¼ cups all-purpose flour
½ cup butter or margarine, softened
¼ cup sugar

½ teaspoon vanilla extract
¼ teaspoon salt
1 egg, separated
1 14-ounce can walnuts (1 cup), chopped

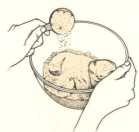

1 In small saucepan over low heat, melt ¼ cup semisweet-chocolate pieces. Remove the saucepan from heat; set aside to cool slightly.

2 In small bowl, measure flour, butter or margarine, sugar, vanilla extract, salt, egg yolk, and the melted chocolate.

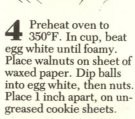

3 With mixer at low speed, beat ingredients until blended, constantly scraping bowl with rubber spatula. Increase speed to medium; beat 1 minute. Shape into ¾-inch balls.

4 Preheat oven to 350°F. In cup, beat egg white until foamy. Place walnuts on sheet of waxed paper. Dip balls into egg white, then nuts. Place 1 inch apart, on ungreased cookie sheets.

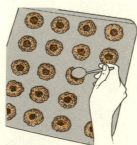

5 Press thumb into center of each ball to make a ½-inch-deep indentation. Bake cookies about 15 minutes or until set. Remove the cookie sheet from the oven.

6 Quickly fill indentations with remaining chocolate pieces, smoothing with tip of spoon as they melt. Cool on wire rack; store in tightly-covered container.

CHOCOLATE-CHIP COOKIES

- *Color index page 74*
- *Begin 2½ hrs ahead*
- *48 cookies*
- *65 cals per cookie*

1¼ cups all-purpose flour
½ cup packed light brown sugar
½ cup butter, softened
¼ cup sugar
1 egg
1 teaspoon vanilla extract

½ teaspoon baking soda
½ teaspoon salt
1 6-ounce package semisweet-chocolate pieces (1 cup)
½ cup chopped walnuts

1. Preheat oven to 375°F. Grease cookie sheets. Into large bowl, measure all ingredients except chocolate pieces and chopped walnuts.
2. With mixer at medium speed, beat until mixed, scraping bowl. Add chocolate pieces and chopped walnuts; stir well.
3. Drop by rounded teaspoonfuls, 2 inches apart, on sheets. Bake 10 to 12 minutes, until lightly browned. With pancake turner or spatula, remove cookies to wire racks; cool completely. Store in a tightly-covered container.

CHOCOLATE-CHIP-WALNUT COOKIES:
Preheat oven to 350°F. Into a large bowl, measure *1 cup all-purpose flour*, *1 cup sugar*, *½ cup butter* or *margarine*, softened, *1 teaspoon vanilla extract*, *⅛ teaspoon salt*, *2 eggs*, and *2 squares unsweetened chocolate*, melted. With mixer at low speed, beat ingredients until blended, occasionally scraping bowl with rubber spatula. With spoon, stir in *one 6-ounce package semisweet-chocolate pieces (1 cup)* and *¾ cup walnuts*, coarsely broken. Drop chocolate mixture by heaping tablespoonfuls, 2 inches apart, onto cookie sheet. Measure out *1 cup walnuts*, coarsely broken; set aside. Spread each cookie into a 2-inch round; top with some of the remaining walnuts. Bake 12 minutes. With pancake turner, remove cookies to wire rack to cool. Repeat until all dough and walnuts are used. Store cookies, tightly covered; use up within 2 weeks. Makes about 30 cookies. About 160 cals per cookie.

CHOCOLATE CRACKLETOPS

- *Color index page 74*
- *Begin early in day*
- *48 cookies*
- *57 cals per cookie*

2 cups finely ground pecans
3 squares unsweetened chocolate, grated
1 cup sugar
2 eggs
¼ cup dried bread crumbs

2 tablespoons all-purpose flour
½ teaspoon ground cinnamon
½ teaspoon ground cloves
Confectioners' sugar

1. Preheat oven to 325°F. Grease cookie sheets.
2. Into large bowl, measure all ingredients except confectioners' sugar. With mixer at medium speed, beat until well mixed, occasionally scraping bowl with rubber spatula.
3. Sprinkle confectioners' sugar onto waxed paper. With hands, shape dough into 1-inch balls; roll in sugar; place 1 inch apart on cookie sheet. Bake 12 to 15 minutes (they'll be soft with crackled tops). With pancake turner, immediately remove cookies to wire racks; cool completely. Store in a tightly-covered container.

Spice cookies

SNICKERDOODLES

2⅔ cups all-purpose flour
1 cup butter or
   margarine, softened
2 teaspoons cream of
   tartar
1 teaspoon baking soda
½ teaspoon salt

½ teaspoon vanilla
   extract
2 eggs
Sugar
2 teaspoons ground
   cinnamon

- Color index
  page 73
- Begin
  4 hrs ahead
- 36 cookies
- 135 cals
  per cookie

1. Into large bowl, measure first 7 ingredients and 1¼ cups sugar. With mixer at low speed, beat until blended, occasionally scraping bowl with rubber spatula.
2. Shape dough into a ball; wrap with plastic wrap. Refrigerate 2 hours, until easy to handle.
3. Preheat oven to 400°F. In small bowl, mix cinnamon with 2 tablespoons sugar. With hands, shape dough into 1½-inch balls. Roll dough balls in cinnamon mixture to coat lightly.
4. Place dough balls, about 2 inches apart, on ungreased large cookie sheets. With dull edge of knife, mark each cookie several times if you like. Bake 10 to 12 minutes until lightly browned. Remove to wire racks to cool.

MOLASSES SPIRALS

1⅔ cups all-purpose flour
⅓ cup sugar
⅓ cup shortening
⅓ cup molasses
2 tablespoons cider
   vinegar
½ teaspoon baking soda
¼ teaspoon ground
   cinnamon

¼ teaspoon ground
   ginger
⅛ teaspoon ground
   allspice
⅛ teaspoon salt
1 egg

- Color index
  page 73
- Begin
  2 hrs
  or up to
  1 wk
  ahead
- 36 cookies
- 60 cals
  per cookie

1. Into large bowl, measure all ingredients. With mixer at low speed, beat until blended, occasionally scraping bowl with rubber spatula.
2. Preheat oven to 350°F. Grease large cookie sheets. Spoon dough into decorating bag with ¼-inch writing tube.
3. For each cookie, pipe some dough in a continuous spiral beginning with a 2-inch circle and narrowing the spiral to a point in the center, about 2 inches apart.
4. Bake 8 to 10 minutes, until golden brown. Remove cookies to wire racks; cool.

Filling decorating bag: Spoon the dough into decorating bag fitted with writing tube.

Piping cookies: Pipe in a continuous spiral from outside to center.

MORAVIAN GINGER COOKIES

The Moravians, as well as other Pennsylvania Dutch sects, were quick to use the ginger and other spices brought to the bustling port of Philadelphia in the 18th century.

4 tablespoons butter or
   margarine, softened
¼ cup packed dark
   brown sugar
2 tablespoons molasses
1¼ cups all-purpose flour
1 teaspoon grated lemon
   peel

¾ teaspoon ground
   ginger
½ teaspoon baking soda
½ teaspoon ground
   cinnamon
¼ teaspoon ground
   cloves
Sugar

- Color index
  page 73
- Begin
  4 hrs
  or up to
  1 wk
  ahead
- 32 cookies
- 50 cals per
  cookie

1 Into 2-quart saucepan, measure butter, sugar, and molasses; cook over medium heat, until sugar dissolves and butter melts, stirring mixture occasionally.

2 Remove from heat; stir in flour and remaining ingredients except sugar until well blended. Spoon onto waxed paper; cover and refrigerate 2 hours, until firm enough to roll.

3 Preheat oven to 350°F. Grease cookie sheet. On floured surface with floured rolling pin, roll half of dough into a 10″ by 10″ square.

4 With pastry wheel or knife, cut the dough into 2½″ by 2½″ squares. Place the dough squares about 1 inch apart on greased cookie sheet.

5 With fork, gently prick squares in many places to make a design. Lightly sprinkle with sugar; bake about 7 minutes.

6 With pancake turner or metal spatula, remove cookies to wire racks to cool; repeat with remaining dough.

Sugar cookies

STRAWBERRY JAM DANDIES

This delicious sandwich cookie is flavored with ground almonds, layered with lemon icing, then filled with strawberry preserves.

- Color index page 73
- Begin 3 hrs ahead
- 20 cookies
- 175 cals per cookie

1 4½-ounce can blanched whole almonds, very finely ground
1½ cups all-purpose flour
¾ cup butter or margarine, softened
½ teaspoon almond extract
⅛ teaspoon salt
1 egg
Confectioners' sugar
1 tablespoon lemon juice
3 tablespoons strawberry preserves

1 Into a large bowl, measure the almonds, flour, butter, almond extract, salt, egg, and ½ cup confectioners' sugar. With mixer at low speed, beat ingredients until well blended, occasionally scraping bowl with rubber spatula. Shape into a ball; wrap and refrigerate 2 hours or until dough is firm enough to handle. (Or, place in freezer 40 minutes until firm enough to handle.)

2 Preheat oven to 375°F. Grease two large cookie sheets. On lightly floured surface with rolling pin, roll half of dough into 12" by 9" rectangle; keep remaining dough refrigerated. Cut lengthwise into 3 strips; then cut each strip crosswise into 6 pieces to make eighteen 3" by 2" rectangles. With floured ¾-inch-round cookie cutter, cut out centers from half of rectangles.

3 With pancake turner, place rectangles on cookie sheet, ½ inch apart. Bake 10 minutes or until golden. Remove cookies to wire racks to cool completely. Repeat with the remaining dough and any trimmings.

4 In small bowl, stir lemon juice and ½ cup confectioners' sugar until smooth. Spread thin layer of icing on cookies without cut-out centers; top each with a cookie with cut-out center, top side up, pressing gently.

5 Fill each of the cut-out centers with scant ½ teaspoon strawberry preserves, gently smoothing to edge of the centers.

6 Store in tightly-covered container to use up within 2 days. Just before serving, lightly sprinkle cookies with confectioners' sugar.

SPRITZ

3 cups all-purpose flour
1½ cups butter or margarine, softened
¾ cup sugar
¼ cup orange juice
1 egg

- Color index page 73
- Begin 2 hrs or up to 1 wk ahead
- 98 cookies
- 40 cals per cookie

1. Into large bowl, measure all ingredients. With mixer at low speed, beat until blended, scraping bowl with rubber spatula. Preheat oven to 375°F.
2. Using cookie press, fitted with bar-plate tip, press dough in strips, 1 inch apart, for length of ungreased cookie sheet.
3. Bake 8 minutes, until light golden.
4. Immediately cut each strip crosswise into 2½-inch cookies. With metal spatula, remove to wire racks to cool; repeat with remaining dough.

SUGAR COOKIES

3¼ cups all-purpose flour
1½ cups sugar
⅔ cup shortening
2 eggs
2½ teaspoons baking powder
2 tablespoons milk
1 teaspoon vanilla extract
½ teaspoon salt
Heavy or whipping cream
Nonpareils or other toppings, to garnish

- Color index page 73
- Begin 6 hrs ahead
- 72 cookies
- 79 cals per cookie

1. Into large bowl, measure first 8 ingredients. With mixer at medium speed, beat until well mixed, occasionally scraping bowl.
2. Shape into ball; wrap; refrigerate 3 hours, until easy to handle. Preheat oven to 400°F.
3. Grease cookie sheets. On floured surface, roll half of dough; refrigerate rest. For crisp cookies, roll paper thin; for soft cookies, roll ¼-inch thick.
4. With floured cookie cutters, cut dough into shapes; reroll trimmings and cut more shapes.
5. Place ½ inch apart on cookie sheets. Brush tops with cream; sprinkle with choice of toppings; bake 8 minutes or until very light brown. With pancake turner remove to racks; cool.

DUTCH BUTTER COOKIES

2½ cups all-purpose flour
1 cup sugar
1 cup butter, softened
1½ teaspoons baking powder
1 teaspoon vanilla extract
½ teaspoon salt
1 egg
1 egg yolk
2 tablespoons water
¼ cup chopped candied ginger

- Color index page 73
- Begin 3½ hrs or up to 1 wk ahead
- 72 cookies
- 54 cals per cookie

1. Into large bowl, measure first 7 ingredients. With mixer at low speed, beat until blended.
2. With hands, on waxed paper, roll into three 6-inch-long rolls. Flatten each slightly to shape into a bar. Wrap; refrigerate 2 hours or up to 1 week.
3. Preheat oven to 350°F. Grease cookie sheets. In cup with fork, beat yolk with water. Slice one roll of dough at a time crosswise into ¼-inch-thick slices. Place, 1 inch apart, on cookie sheets. Brush each cookie with egg-yolk mixture and press chopped ginger into tops.
4. Bake 10 minutes, until lightly browned. With spatula remove to wire racks to cool.

PECAN CRUNCH

2 cups all-purpose flour
1 cup packed light brown sugar
1 cup butter or margarine, softened
1 egg
1 teaspoon vanilla extract

1 6-ounce package semi-sweet-chocolate pieces
1½ cups pecans, toasted and chopped

- Color index page 73
- Begin 2 hrs or up to 1 wk ahead
- 72 bars
- 75 cals per bar

1. Into large bowl, measure first 5 ingredients. With hand, knead dough until well blended and it holds together.
2. Preheat oven to 350°F. Pat dough evenly into 15½" by 10½" jelly-roll pan. Bake 25 minutes.
3. In small saucepan over low heat, melt chocolate, stirring frequently; set aside.
4. Remove pan from oven; pour chocolate over baked layer; with spatula, evenly spread over; sprinkle with pecans. Cool on wire rack.
5. When cool, cut lengthwise into 6 strips, cut each strip crosswise into 12 pieces. Store in tightly-covered container; use up within 1 week.

APRICOT MERINGUE STRIPS

½ cup all-purpose flour
4 tablespoons butter or margarine, softened
½ teaspoon vanilla extract
⅛ teaspoon salt

1 egg, separated
Confectioners' sugar
⅓ cup walnuts, finely chopped
⅓ cup apricot preserves

- Color index page 73
- Begin 2 hrs or up to 3 days ahead
- 16 cookies
- 95 cals per cookie

1. Preheat oven to 350°F. Into small bowl, measure first 4 ingredients, egg yolk, and ¼ cup confectioners' sugar.
2. With mixer at low speed, beat until blended, occasionally scraping bowl with rubber spatula. Evenly spread mixture onto bottom of ungreased 8" by 8" baking pan; bake 10 minutes.
3. Meanwhile, in another small bowl with mixer at high speed, beat white until soft peaks form.
4. Beating at high speed, gradually beat in ¼ cup confectioners' sugar until stiff, glossy peaks form; fold in nuts.
5. Remove from oven. Spread apricot preserves over baked layer; top with meringue. Bake 20 minutes, until lightly browned.
6. Cool on wire rack 15 minutes; cut into 4" by 1" fingers; cool completely.

Making meringue: Gradually beat in confectioners' sugar until stiff, glossy peaks form.

Topping cookies: Evenly spread apricot preserves over cooked base, then top with meringue.

CRUNCHY SNACK BARS

These easy-to-make, crunchy bar cookies use condensed milk, which was invented in 1856 to eliminate milk-based diseases.

1 12-ounce package semisweet-chocolate pieces (2 cups)
1 14-ounce can sweetened condensed milk (1¾ cups)
Butter or margarine, softened
2 cups pecans or walnuts, chopped

Vanilla extract
3 cups all-purpose flour
1¾ cups packed light-brown sugar
1½ teaspoons baking soda
¾ teaspoon salt
3 eggs
2 cups quick-cooking oats, uncooked

- Color index page 73
- Begin 3 hrs ahead or early in day
- 48 bars
- 215 cals per bar

1 In double boiler over hot, not boiling, water, heat chocolate pieces, sweetened condensed milk, and 3 tablespoons butter or margarine, stirring occasionally, until chocolate is melted and mixture is smooth. Stir in ¾ cup chopped nuts and 1 teaspoon vanilla; remove from heat; keep mixture warm. Preheat oven to 350°F. Grease 13" by 9" baking pan.

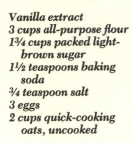

2 Into large bowl, measure flour, sugar, baking soda, salt, eggs, 1 cup butter, and 1 tablespoon vanilla.

3 With mixer at low speed, beat until mixed, scraping bowl. Increase speed to medium; beat 3 minutes. Stir in oats and rest of nuts.

4 Pat half of dough onto bottom of pan. Spread chocolate over dough; drop remaining dough by teaspoonfuls to cover chocolate mixture.

5 Bake 45 minutes or until top is firm when lightly touched. Cool completely in pan on wire rack.

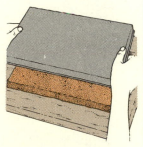

6 When cold, invert onto cutting board. Cut crosswise into 12 strips; cut each into 4 pieces. Store in tightly-covered container.

Nut and grain cookies

PEANUT-CHOCO NUGGETS

Half of America's peanut crop goes into peanut butter. We've combined it with chocolate to fill this super-rich cookie.

Chocolate Filling
1 6-ounce package semisweet-chocolate pieces
¾ cup creamy peanut butter
½ cup cocoa

½ cup peanuts, finely chopped
½ cup confectioners' sugar

Cookie-Shell Dough
3 cups all-purpose flour

- Color index page 74
- Begin 3 hrs or up to 1 week ahead
- 50 cookies
- 130 cals per cookie

1¼ cups butter or margarine, softened
1 tablespoon vanilla extract
Confectioners' sugar

1 Prepare Chocolate Filling: In heavy 2-quart saucepan over low heat, heat chocolate pieces until melted and smooth, stirring often.

2 Remove saucepan from heat; with wooden spoon stir in peanut butter, cocoa, peanuts, and confectioners' sugar until blended.

3 Drop by teaspoonfuls onto ungreased cookie sheet. With fingers, smooth and shape into mounds. Cover; refrigerate 30 minutes.

4 Meanwhile, prepare Cookie-Shell Dough: In large bowl with hand, quickly knead the flour, butter, vanilla, and 1 cup confectioners' sugar until blended and stiff.

5 With hands, gently shape stiff dough into a 25-inch-long log. With sharp knife, carefully cut the log into 50 ½-inch slices. Preheat the oven to 400°F.

6 Place a mound of Chocolate Filling on a slice of Cookie-Shell Dough; shape the dough around filling to cover completely, pinching the edges to seal.

7 Shape cookie into a 2-inch-long log; place on ungreased cookie sheets. Repeat with remaining chocolate filling and dough.

8 Bake 10 to 12 minutes, until golden. With pancake turner, remove to wire racks; cool. Onto waxed paper, measure ½ cup sugar.

9 When cold, roll cookies in the confectioners' sugar to coat completely. Store in tightly-covered container to use up within 1 week.

PEANUT BUTTER CANDY TOPS

2¾ cups all-purpose flour
1 cup packed brown sugar
1 cup chunky peanut butter
1 cup butter or margarine, softened
1½ teaspoons baking soda

¾ cup sugar
1 teaspoon salt
1 teaspoon vanilla extract
2 eggs
1 8-ounce package nonmelting chocolate-covered candies (1 cup)

1. Preheat oven to 350°F. Into large bowl, measure all ingredients except candies. With mixer at low speed, beat until well blended, occasionally scraping bowl with rubber spatula.
2. Shape dough into 1-inch balls. Place balls, about 2 inches apart, on ungreased cookie sheets. Bake 12 minutes, until lightly browned.
3. Remove from oven; quickly press 3 or 4 candies into tops; return to oven; bake 3 minutes.
4. With pancake turner, carefully remove cookies to wire racks; cool.

- Color index page 74
- Begin 2 hrs or up to 1 week ahead
- 84 cookies
- 84 cals per cookie

ALMOND LACE ROLLS

⅔ cup blanched almonds, ground
½ cup sugar
½ cup butter
2 tablespoons milk

1 tablespoon all-purpose flour
Confectioners' sugar

1. Preheat oven to 350°F. Grease and flour large cookie sheet. Into large skillet, measure all ingredients except confectioners' sugar.
2. Cook over low heat, stirring, until butter melts and mixture is blended. Keeping over very low heat, drop 4 heaping teaspoonfuls, 2 inches apart, onto cookie sheet; bake 5 minutes.
3. With metal spatula, quickly remove cookies, one by one, and immediately roll around wooden spoon handle.
4. Cool; repeat until all batter is used, greasing and flouring cookie sheet each time. To serve, dust with confectioners' sugar.

Cooking batter: Cook mixture in large skillet over low heat.

Shaping rolls: One by one, roll around wooden spoon handle.

- Color index page 73
- Begin early in day
- 30 cookies
- 64 cals per cookie

MACADAMIA MELTAWAYS

2 7½-ounce jars macadamia nuts
2 cups all-purpose flour
1 cup butter or margarine, softened
¼ cup confectioners' sugar
1 teaspoon almond extract

- Color index page 74
- Begin 2 hrs or up to 1 wk ahead
- 60 cookies
- 95 cals per cookie

1. In blender at medium speed, blend 1 cup nuts until finely ground; place in large bowl. Reserve remaining nuts for tops.
2. Into bowl with ground nuts, measure remaining ingredients. Knead until blended and dough holds together. Preheat oven to 350°F.
3. With hands, shape scant tablespoonfuls of dough into balls. Place 1 inch apart on ungreased cookie sheets; press reserved nuts into tops.
4. Bake 12 to 15 minutes, until lightly browned. Remove to wire racks; cool.

FILBERT COOKIE RAFTS

½ cup filberts
Sugar
1¼ cups all-purpose flour
½ cup butter or margarine, softened
½ teaspoon vanilla extract
⅛ teaspoon salt

- Color index page 74
- Begin 1½ hrs or up to 2 wks ahead
- 32 cookies
- 63 cals per cookie

1. In blender at medium speed, blend filberts and 2 tablespoons sugar until very finely ground.
2. Into medium bowl, measure remaining ingredients, 2 tablespoons sugar, and ground filberts. Knead until blended and dough holds together.
3. Preheat oven to 325°F. On waxed paper with floured rolling pin, roll out half dough into a 6″ by 6″ square. Cut into sixteen 1½″ by 1½″ squares.
4. With metal spatula, place on ungreased cookie sheet. With dull edge of knife, lightly mark each with three parallel lines. Bake 12 to 15 minutes, until lightly browned. Remove to wire racks; cool. Repeat with remaining dough.

OATMEAL COOKIES

1 cup all-purpose flour
1 cup shortening
¾ cup packed light brown sugar
½ cup sugar
3 tablespoons water
1 teaspoon ground allspice
¾ teaspoon vanilla extract
½ teaspoon salt
1 egg
3 cups quick-cooking oats, uncooked
¾ cup walnuts, chopped
½ cup dark seedless raisins

- Color index page 73
- Begin 2 hrs or up to 2 wks ahead
- 36 cookies
- 126 cals per cookie

1. Preheat oven to 375°F. Grease large cookie sheet. In large bowl, measure first 9 ingredients. With mixer at low speed, beat until well blended, scraping bowl with rubber spatula. With spoon, stir in oats, walnuts, and raisins.
2. Drop dough by heaping tablespoonfuls, 2 inches apart, onto cookie sheet; bake 12 minutes.
3. With metal spatula, remove cookies to wire racks to cool. Repeat until all dough is used, greasing cookie sheet each time.

POPPY-SEED PINWHEELS

½ cup sugar
Butter or margarine
1¾ cups all-purpose flour
½ teaspoon vanilla extract
¼ teaspoon salt
1 egg
½ cup poppy seeds
½ cup walnuts, finely ground
¼ cup honey
¾ teaspoon grated orange peel
¼ teaspoon ground cinnamon

- Color index page 74
- Begin early in day
- 60 cookies
- 55 cals per cookie

1. In large bowl with mixer at high speed, beat sugar and ½ cup butter until light and fluffy. Add flour, vanilla, salt, and egg; at low speed, beat until blended, occasionally scraping bowl with spatula.
2. Shape into ball; wrap and refrigerate 1 hour, until firm enough to handle.
3. Meanwhile, in bowl, stir remaining ingredients, and 4 tablespoons butter until mixed.
4. On waxed paper, roll half of dough into 10″ by 8″ rectangle; spread with half poppy-seed mixture. Starting at narrow side, roll jelly-roll fashion; wrap and refrigerate 1 hour, until firm. Repeat with remaining dough and filling.
5. Preheat oven to 375°F. Slice one roll crosswise into ¼-inch-thick slices; place ½ inch apart on ungreased cookie sheets; bake 10 to 12 minutes, until lightly browned. Cool on wire rack; repeat with remaining roll.

Rolling pinwheels: Starting on narrow side, carefully roll up dough and filling jelly-roll style.

Slicing pinwheels: Carefully slice roll into ¼-inch slices; place on ungreased cookie sheet.

COCONUT MACAROONS

3 egg whites, at room temperature
½ cup sugar
1 teaspoon vanilla extract
½ teaspoon salt
2 cups flaked coconut
⅓ cup all-purpose flour

- Color index page 74
- Begin 2 hrs or up to 3 days ahead
- 30 cookies
- 38 cals per cookie

1. Preheat oven to 325°F. Lightly grease two cookie sheets.
2. In small bowl with mixer at high speed, beat whites until soft peaks form. At high speed, beat in sugar, 2 tablespoons at a time, beating well after each addition until completely dissolved. Beat in vanilla and salt; whites should stand in stiff, glossy peaks. With rubber spatula, gently fold in coconut and flour.
3. Drop by heaping teaspoonfuls, 1 inch apart, onto cookie sheets; bake 20 minutes, until lightly browned. With metal spatula, carefully remove cookies to wire racks; cool.

Christmas cookies

CHRISTMAS TREE COOKIES

Making sugar cookies is a traditional holiday pastime. Use them as festive Christmas tree ornaments by making a small hole in the top of the cookie before baking; use ribbon to tie onto the branches.

2½ cups all-purpose flour
1 cup sugar
1 cup butter or margarine, softened
1½ teaspoons baking powder

½ teaspoon salt
½ teaspoon almond extract
1 egg

● Color index page 74
● Begin 3½ hrs or up to 1 wk ahead
● 72 cookies
● 55 cals per cookie

About ¼ cup green sugar crystals
1 1½-ounce container confetti decors

1 Into a large bowl, measure all-purpose flour, sugar, butter or margarine, baking powder, salt, almond extract, and egg. With electric mixer at low speed, beat the ingredients until well blended, occasionally scraping the bowl with rubber spatula; dough may be crumbly. With hand, gently knead the dough until the mixture holds together.

2 Reserve ⅓ cup dough; wrap in plastic wrap or aluminum foil and refrigerate. With hands, roll remaining dough into three 6-inch-long rolls.

3 Roll in sugar crystals to coat. Form each roll into triangle-shaped log by pressing to flatten bottom, then pinching sides together to form a point.

4 Wrap each log in plastic wrap and refrigerate 2 hours or until the dough is firm enough to slice (refrigerate up to 1 week).

5 Preheat oven to 350°F. Slice one log crosswise into ¼-inch-thick slices; place slices, 1-inch apart, on large ungreased cookie sheet.

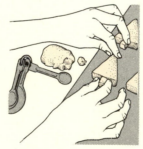

6 For each cookie, with fingers, shape ¼ teaspoon reserved dough to resemble tree trunk; carefully attach to bottom of each slice.

7 Lightly sprinkle each cookie with some confetti decors. Bake the cookies 10 to 12 minutes or until lightly browned.

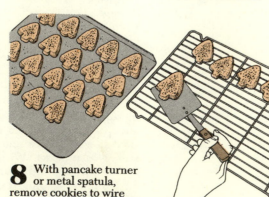

8 With pancake turner or metal spatula, remove cookies to wire racks to cool. Repeat with remaining logs and confetti decors.

FROSTED SNOWMEN

2 cups all-purpose flour
1 cup sugar
½ cup shortening
⅓ cup honey
1 teaspoon baking soda
¾ teaspoon salt
2 eggs
2 cups quick-cooking oats, uncooked

½ cup walnuts, finely chopped
2 cups confectioners' sugar
¼ teaspoon cream of tartar
2 egg whites
Decorations: chocolate, cinnamon, and silver decors, sugar crystals

1. Into large bowl, measure first 7 ingredients. With mixer at low speed, beat until blended. With wooden spoon, stir in oats and walnuts.
2. Preheat oven to 375°F. With floured hands, shape mixture into thirty-six 1-inch balls and thirty-six ¾-inch balls. Place 1-inch balls, 2½ inches apart, on ungreased cookie sheets; then place ¾-inch balls ½ inch above 1-inch balls.
3. Bake 10 to 12 minutes, until golden. With metal spatula, remove to wire racks to cool.
4. Prepare frosting: In medium bowl with mixer at low speed, beat confectioners' sugar, cream of tartar, and egg whites until blended. Increase speed to high and beat 1 minute.
5. Dip front of each into frosting to cover. Place frosted-side up, on wire racks; decorate quickly. Let frosting dry, about 1 hour.

● Color index page 74
● Begin 2½ hrs or up to 1 wk ahead
● 36 cookies
● 135 cals per cookie

JOLLY SANTAS

2½ cups all-purpose flour
¾ cup butter, softened
⅔ cup sugar
2 tablespoons milk
1 teaspoon baking powder
½ teaspoon salt

1 teaspoon almond extract
2 eggs
Ornamental Cookie Frosting (p.338)
About 2 tablespoons dried currants

1. Into large bowl, measure all ingredients except Ornamental Cookie Frosting and currants. With mixer at low speed, beat until blended, scraping bowl with rubber spatula. Shape into a ball; wrap and refrigerate 3 hours.
2. Preheat oven to 350°F. Grease large cookie sheet. On lightly floured surface with floured rolling pin, roll one-third of the dough ⅛-inch thick, keeping remaining dough refrigerated. With floured 3-inch round cookie cutter, cut into rounds. Place on cookie sheet, 1 inch apart.
3. Bake 12 minutes, until lightly browned. With metal spatula, immediately remove cookies to wire racks; cool. Repeat with remaining dough.
4. Prepare Ornamental Cookie Frosting. Decorate cookies: With frosting, attach 2 currants on each for eyes, decorate with red and white frostings to make "Santa faces." Let frosting dry.

● Color index page 74
● Begin 5 hrs or up to 1 wk ahead
● 42 cookies
● 100 cals per cookie

COOKIE CHALETS

- *Color index page 74*
- *Begin 3 hrs or up to 1 wk ahead*
- *24 cookies*
- *125 cals per cookie*

These tiny houses, baked from a spiced cookie dough, are fun to decorate. Cover them with almond roofs and build red-hot cinnamon doors.

2¼ cups all-purpose flour
½ cup sugar
½ cup shortening
½ cup light molasses
1½ teaspoons ground cinnamon
1 teaspoon baking powder
1 teaspoon ground ginger

½ teaspoon baking soda
½ teaspoon ground cloves
½ teaspoon salt
¼ teaspoon ground nutmeg
1 egg
Sliced blanched almonds for decoration
Cinnamon red-hot candies for decoration

1 Into large bowl, measure all the ingredients except almonds and candies. With mixer at low speed, beat ingredients until well blended, occasionally scraping bowl with rubber spatula. Shape the dough into a ball; wrap with plastic wrap or foil and refrigerate 1 hour or until dough is firm enough to handle. (Or, place dough in freezer 30 minutes.)

2 Meanwhile, from cardboard, with scissors, cut a 2½" by 1½" house-shaped pattern.

3 On lightly floured surface with lightly floured rolling pin, gently roll out half of dough to ⅛-inch thick.

4 Using pattern, cut as many cookie houses as possible. With pancake turner, place cookies on ungreased cookie sheet, about ½ inch apart.

5 Preheat oven to 350°F. Lightly press almonds along top of each cookie to resemble a roof.

6 Press cinnamon red-hot candies into each cookie to resemble a door. Bake cookies 5 to 6 minutes or until set (do not overbake or candies will melt). With pancake turner or metal spatula, remove cookies to wire racks to cool. Repeat with the remaining dough, trimmings, almonds, and candies. Store cookies in tightly-covered container to use up within 1 week.

GINGERBREAD MEN

- *Color index page 74*
- *Begin 3 hrs or up to 1 wk ahead*
- *24 cookies*
- *140 cals per cookie*

These Pennsylvania Dutch spice cookies are Christmastime favorites; decorating them is always fun for the children.

2¼ cups all-purpose flour
½ cup sugar
½ cup shortening
½ cup light molasses
1½ teaspoons ground cinnamon
1 teaspoon baking powder

1 teaspoon ground ginger
1 teaspoon ground cloves
½ teaspoon baking soda
½ teaspoon salt
1 egg
½ quantity Ornamental Cookie Frosting (p.338)

1 Preheat oven to 350°F. Into large bowl, measure all the ingredients except Ornamental Cookie Frosting. With mixer at low speed, beat the ingredients until well mixed, occasionally scraping the bowl with rubber spatula. Shape dough into a ball; wrap with plastic wrap and refrigerate 1 hour or until dough is firm enough to handle. (Or, place in the freezer 30 minutes.)

2 On lightly floured surface with lightly floured rolling pin, roll dough ¼-inch thick.

3 With 4½-inch-long gingerbread man cookie cutter, cut out as many cookies as possible.

4 With metal spatula, place cookies, about ½ inch apart, on ungreased cookie sheets.

5 Re-roll trimmings and cut again. Bake cookies 8 minutes or until browned. With pancake turner, remove cookies to wire racks to cool. When the cookies are cooled, prepare the Ornamental Cookie Frosting.

6 With frosting in waxed paper cone or decorating bag fitted with small writing tube, decorate cookies. Leave frosting to dry. Store cookies in tightly-covered container to use within 1 week.

Candies

PEANUT BRITTLE

Peanut brittle, one of America's most well-known candies, became very popular at the end of the 19th century.

- *Color index page 74*
- *Begin 1 hr or up to 1 wk ahead*
- *1 pound*
- *146 cals per ounce*

1 cup sugar
½ cup light corn syrup
¼ cup water
¼ teaspoon salt

1 cup shelled raw peanuts
2 tablespoons butter or margarine, softened
1 teaspoon baking soda

1 Grease large cookie sheet. In heavy 2-quart saucepan over medium heat, heat first 4 ingredients to boiling, stirring until the sugar is dissolved; stir in nuts. Carefully set a candy thermometer in place and continue cooking, stirring frequently, until temperature reaches 300°F. or hard-crack stage (when a small amount of mixture dropped into a bowl of very cold water separates into hard and brittle threads), 20 minutes.

2 Remove saucepan from heat; immediately stir in the butter or margarine and baking soda; pour the hot mixture at once onto prepared cookie sheet.

3 With two forks, lift and pull the peanut mixture into a rectangle about 14″ by 12″; set aside to cool completely.

4 With hands, snap candy into small pieces. Store in tightly-covered container to use up within 1 week.

HOW TO DIP FRUIT

Chocolate-dipped fruit can be used to decorate cakes and desserts or served on their own with coffee.

Insert a wooden skewer into a non-juicy fresh fruit or candied fruit. Dip half of it into melted semisweet chocolate.

Slide fruit off skewer onto pan lined with waxed paper. Use strawberries, grapes, orange sections, dried apricots, and prunes or other seasonal fruits.

CHOCOLATE FUDGE

- *Color index page 74*
- *Begin 2½ hrs ahead*
- *32 pieces*
- *122 cals per piece*

3 cups sugar
1 cup milk
2 tablespoons light corn syrup
2 squares unsweetened chocolate

3 tablespoons butter or margarine
1 teaspoon vanilla extract
1 cup chopped walnuts or pecans

1. In large saucepan over medium heat, heat sugar, milk, corn syrup, and unsweetened chocolate squares to boiling, stirring constantly.
2. Set candy thermometer in place and continue cooking, stirring occasionally, until temperature reaches 238°F., or until a small amount of mixture dropped into very cold water forms a soft ball.
3. Remove from heat; immediately add butter or margarine and vanilla extract.
4. Cool mixture, without stirring, to 110°F., or until outside of saucepan feels lukewarm to hand. Meanwhile, butter 8″ by 8″ baking pan.
5. With spoon, beat until mixture becomes thick and begins to lose its gloss. Quickly stir in nuts; pour into pan. (Don't scrape saucepan; mixture on side may be sugary.) Cool in pan; when cold, cut into 32 squares.

PEANUT BUTTER FUDGE: Prepare as above but use *¼ cup creamy peanut butter* for butter and substitute *1 cup chopped salted peanuts* for walnuts. Makes 32 pieces. 160 cals per piece.

CHOCOLATE-MARSHMALLOW FUDGE: Prepare as above but stir in *1 cup miniature marshmallows* just before pouring mixture into pan. Makes 32 pieces. 126 cals per piece.

CANDY APPLES

- *Color index page 74*
- *Begin early in day*
- *8 apples*
- *416 cals per apple*

8 small Red Delicious apples
8 wooden ice-cream-bar sticks
3 cups sugar

½ cup light corn syrup
¼ cup red-hot candies
½ teaspoon red food color
1 cup water

1. *Early in day:* Wash and thoroughly dry apples; carefully insert a wooden stick part way through stem end of each. Grease large cookie sheet; set aside.
2. In medium saucepan over medium heat, heat remaining ingredients to boiling, stirring frequently until sugar and candies are dissolved.
3. Set candy thermometer in place and continue cooking, without stirring, until temperature reaches 290°F. or until a small amount of mixture dropped into very cold water separates into thin, hard threads, about 20 minutes.
4. Immediately remove syrup from heat and dip in apples: Tip saucepan and swirl each apple in mixture to coat evenly; lift out apple and swirl over saucepan a few more seconds to catch drips. Place apples on greased cookie sheet to cool. Work quickly before syrup hardens; if it does harden, place over very low heat to soften. Cool apples for at least 1 hour before serving.

BREADS

"And the best bread was of my mother's own making — the best in all the land."

HENRY JAMES

American Indians had long been using cornmeal to make their flatbreads by the time the earliest settlers arrived in the New World. The Plymouth colonists planted wheat and rye seeds brought from Europe; these first crops saved them from starvation. They began combining cornmeal with other flours such as wheat, rye, barley, and oatmeal. Later they obtained yeast from beer brewers and produced a risen bread more like the loaves we know today.

The expansion of farming toward the Western frontiers was advanced by the mechanization of wheat production and the patent of the reaper by Cyrus McCormick. After the Civil War, more and more bakeries were established producing purer, whiter, and more refined bread. This white bread quickly gained popularity and came to be seen as something of a status symbol. Wheat was planted throughout the Midwest, from Minnesota and Wisconsin to Iowa and Kansas. America's "wheat belt" was soon to become the world's greatest producer of grain.

During the years of the great European immigration, the varieties of breads and baked goods increased enormously. Rye flour had been used since the early days of the Massachusetts Bay Colony, but the Scan-dinavians in the Midwest used it in breads such as their Limpa, and the Germans continued using it in their dark moist Pumpernickel Rye Bread. As each ethnic group arrived bringing favorite recipes, they adapted them to their new home, sometimes using new ingredients.

Old English rock cakes evolved into muffins such as sweet moist Blueberry Muffins; waffles came from the Dutch and became very popular as a breakfast food and snack; griddle cakes were mainstays of almost all our ancestors, as they could be cooked wherever there was a griddle or pan. Sourdough, a bread made using an ancient system based on a natural "starter," rather than yeast, was brought to America with the first settlers. It is still associated with the West, especially San Francisco. Blintzes, common on delicatessen menus, were brought by Jewish immigrants, and dough-nuts were standard fare of the Pennsylvania Dutch. Another important bread-based dish in America is pizza, originally brought by Italian immigrants from Naples.

The invention of the "sandwich" loaf in 1920 probably revolutionized the American diet. Nowadays, sandwiches, the classic all-American lunch, are often made with a variety of delicious home-baked breads.

HOW TO KNEAD BREAD

Kneading should be done on a lightly floured surface, a board or counter top; add a little more flour if the dough remains sticky. Knead 8 to 10 minutes until smooth and elastic; it should have tiny air bubbles under the surface.

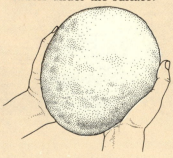

Turn the dough on to a lightly floured board or counter top. With lightly floured hands, shape the dough into a ball and fold it toward you.

With the heels of hands, using a rolling motion, push it away. Give dough a quarter of a turn.

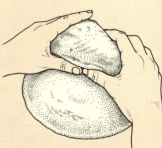

Knead 8 to 10 minutes; dough should no longer stick and will be ready for second rising or shaping as recipe directs.

Grain breads

WHITE BREAD

3 tablespoons sugar
2 teaspoons salt
1 package active dry yeast

5½ to 6½ cups all-
purpose flour
2 cups milk
Butter or margarine

1. In large bowl, combine sugar, salt, yeast, and 2 cups flour. In 2-quart saucepan over low heat, heat milk and 3 tablespoons butter until warm (120° to 130°F.). (Butter does not need to melt.)
2. With mixer at low speed, gradually beat liquid into dry ingredients, until just blended. Increase speed to medium; beat 2 minutes, scraping bowl.
3. Beat in ¾ cup flour or enough to make a thick batter; continue beating 2 minutes, scraping bowl often. With spoon, stir in enough flour (about 3 cups) to make soft dough.
4. On floured surface, knead dough until elastic, about 10 minutes. Shape into ball; turn over in greased bowl to grease top. Cover; let rise until doubled, about 1 hour (below).
5. Punch down dough by pushing fist into center and pulling in edges. Transfer to a lightly floured surface; cut in half; cover with bowl; let dough rest 15 minutes.
6. Grease two 9″ by 5″ loaf pans. With lightly floured rolling pin roll each dough half into 12″ by 8″ rectangle. Starting at narrow end, roll dough up tightly; pinch edges to seal. Seal ends by pressing with sides of hands; fold under. Place, seam side down, in loaf pan.
7. Cover with towel; let dough rise in a warm place, away from draft, until doubled, 1 hour.
8. Preheat oven to 400°F. If you like, brush loaves with 2 tablespoons melted butter. Bake 25 to 30 minutes; test for doneness (p.360). Remove from pans; cool on a wire rack.

 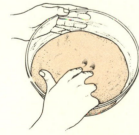

Greasing the dough:
Grease large bowl; place dough in the bowl and turn the dough over so top is greased.

Checking the dough has risen: Press two fingers lightly into dough; if fingers leave two dents, the dough has risen.

- Color index page 75
- Begin 4 hrs ahead
- 2 loaves
- 1608 cals per loaf

LETTING THE DOUGH RISE: Place the dough in large greased bowl, turning over so top of dough is greased. Cover dough with clean towel and let rise in warm place (80° to 85°F.), away from drafts, until doubled, about 1 to 2 hours. (Dough is doubled when two fingers pressed lightly into dough leave a dent; if dent fills in quickly, leave dough a little longer.)

CRUSTY WHOLE-WHEAT OATMEAL BREAD

In the mid-19th century, the Shakers were advocating greater use of the whole grain in making flour as they felt it prevented indigestion. Here we combine whole-wheat flour with oats to create a hearty, tasty loaf.

2 cups all-purpose flour
2 teaspoons salt
2 packages active dry yeast
3 cups water
⅓ cup molasses

6 tablespoons butter or margarine
3 cups plus 2 tablespoons quick-cooking or old-fashioned oats, uncooked

About 4½ cups whole-wheat flour
1 egg

- Color index page 75
- Begin 3½ hrs ahead or early in day
- 1 large loaf
- 4968 cals per loaf

1 In large bowl, combine all-purpose flour, salt, and yeast. In 2-quart saucepan over low heat, heat water, molasses, butter, and 3 cups oats until very warm (120° to 130°F.). (Butter does not need to melt completely.) With mixer at low speed, gradually beat oat mixture into dry ingredients just until blended. Increase speed to medium; beat 2 minutes, occasionally scraping bowl with rubber spatula.

2 Beat in 1 cup whole-wheat flour to make a thick batter; continue beating 2 minutes, occasionally scraping bowl.

3 With wooden spoon, stir in 3 cups whole-wheat flour to make a soft dough.

4 Turn dough onto a lightly floured surface. With floured hands, knead until smooth and elastic, about 10 minutes, working in about ½ cup whole-wheat flour (dough should not be sticky).

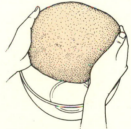

5 Shape dough into ball and place in a greased large bowl, turning dough over so that top is greased. Cover and let rise in warm place until doubled in size, about 1 hour (left).

6 Grease large cookie sheet. Punch down dough. Shape into a ball; place on cookie sheet. Cover dough with towel and let rise in warm place until doubled in size, about 40 minutes.

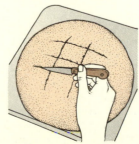

7 Preheat oven to 350°F. With knife, cut 5 slashes on top of loaf. In cup with fork, beat egg.

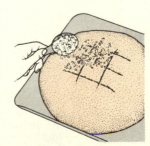

8 With pastry brush, brush bread with beaten egg; sprinkle with 2 tablespoons oats.

9 Bake 1 hour. Remove bread from cookie sheet and place on wire rack to cool.

Grain breads

PUMPERNICKEL-RYE BREAD

Rye flour has been used since the days of the Massachusetts Bay Colony, but it was German immigrants who brought us the recipe for pumpernickel bread.

- *Color index page 75*
- *Begin 6½ hrs ahead*
- *3 loaves*
- *1736 cals per loaf*

5 cups rye flour
4 to 5 cups all-purpose flour
1 tablespoon salt
2 packages active dry yeast

2 12-ounce cans beer
1 cup light molasses
⅓ cup butter or margarine
1 tablespoon caraway seeds

1 In large bowl, combine 3 cups rye and 1 cup all-purpose flour, salt, and yeast. In medium saucepan over low heat, heat the beer, the molasses, and the butter until very warm (120° to 130°F.). (Butter or margarine does not need to melt completely.) With the mixer at low speed, gradually pour the liquid ingredients into the dry ingredients. Increase the speed of the mixer to medium; beat 2 more minutes, occasionally scraping side of bowl with rubber spatula.

2 Beat in 2 cups rye flour or enough to make a thick batter; continue beating 2 minutes. With spoon, stir in caraway seeds and about 2½ cups all-purpose flour to make a soft dough.

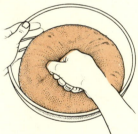

3 Turn dough onto well-floured surface and knead until smooth and elastic, about 10 minutes. Shape into ball, place in bowl; cover; let rise 1 to 2 hours (p.357).

4 Punch down dough by pushing down the center of dough with fist, then pushing edges into center. Turn dough over; let rise again until doubled, about 1½ hours.

5 Again, punch down dough; turn onto lightly floured surface; cut into three pieces; shape into three balls.

6 Place the balls, about 5 inches apart, on greased cookie sheets. Cover the dough and let rise in a warm place until doubled, about 1 hour. Preheat the oven to 350°F. Bake the loaves 50 to 60 minutes until the loaves sound hollow when lightly tapped with the fingers. Remove the loaves from the cookie sheets immediately; place the loaves on wire racks and leave them to cool completely.

QUICK-AND-EASY ANADAMA BREAD

- *Color index page 75*
- *Begin 2½ hrs ahead or early in day*
- *1 loaf*
- *2000 cals*

⅓ cup cornmeal
1 teaspoon salt
1 package active dry yeast
3 cups all-purpose flour
1 cup water

¼ cup light molasses
3 tablespoons butter or margarine
1 egg

1. In large bowl, combine cornmeal, salt, yeast, and 1 cup flour. In 1-quart saucepan over low heat, heat water, molasses, and butter until warm (120° to 130°F.). (Butter does not need to melt.) Grease 2-quart soufflé dish or casserole.
2. With mixer at low speed, gradually beat liquid into dry ingredients just until blended. Increase speed to medium; beat 2 minutes, occasionally scraping bowl with rubber spatula.
3. Beat in egg and 1 cup flour to make a thick batter; continue beating 2 minutes, scraping bowl often. With wooden spoon, stir in remaining 1 cup flour to make a soft dough.
4. Place dough in soufflé dish. Cover with towel and let rise in warm place (80° to 85°F.), until doubled, about 1 hour (p.357).
5. Preheat oven to 375°F. Bake bread 30 to 35 minutes until browned and loaf sounds hollow when lightly tapped with fingers.
6. Remove loaf from soufflé dish; cool on wire rack about 30 minutes for easier slicing. Serve bread warm, or cool completely to serve later.

SALLY LUNN

- *Color index page 75*
- *Begin 3½ hrs ahead*
- *1 loaf*
- *2315 cals*

3¼ cups all-purpose flour
3 tablespoons sugar
1¼ teaspoons salt
1 package active dried yeast

1 cup milk
3 tablespoons butter or margarine
2 eggs

1. In large bowl combine 1¼ cups flour, sugar, salt, and yeast. In medium saucepan over low heat, heat milk and butter or margarine until very warm (120° to 130°F.). (Butter or margarine does not need to melt.)
2. With mixer at low speed, gradually pour liquid into dry ingredients. Increase speed to medium; beat 2 minutes, occasionally scraping bowl with rubber spatula.
3. Beat in eggs and ¾ cup flour or enough to make a thick batter; continue beating 2 minutes, occasionally scraping bowl. With spoon, stir in the remaining 1¼ cups flour.
4. Cover bowl with towel; let dough rise in warm place (80° to 85°F.), about 1 hour (p.357).
5. Grease and flour well 10-inch tube pan. With spoon, stir down dough. Spoon dough into tube pan; with well-floured hands, pat dough evenly in pan. Cover with towel; let rise in warm place, about 1 hour.
6. Preheat oven to 300°F. Bake bread 40 minutes or until golden and bread sounds hollow when lightly tapped with fingers. With spatula, loosen bread from sides and center of pan and cool on wire rack.

SOURDOUGH BREAD

Sourdough Starter
2 cups all-purpose flour
1 package active dry yeast
2 cups warm water
Dough
2 tablespoons sugar
1 tablespoon salt
1 teaspoon baking soda
Water
6 to 8 cups all-purpose flour
3 tablespoons butter or margarine, melted

1. *4 days ahead:* Prepare Sourdough Starter: In large bowl, combine flour and yeast; stir in water; beat until smooth. Cover with waxed paper. Let stand 48 hours in a warm place, stirring occasionally. If it does not rise, form bubbles, and separate, start again. Stir well before using it.

2. *Day before serving:* In large bowl with mixer at medium speed, beat well sugar, salt, soda, 2 cups warm water, 1 cup Starter and 3 cups flour. Cover bowl with towel and let batter rise at room temperature, away from draft, at least 18 hours.

3. *About 4½ hours before serving:* Stir in 3½ to 4 cups flour to make a soft dough. On floured surface knead the dough until smooth and elastic, 8 to 10 minutes. Cut dough in half; shape into 2 flat, round loaves, measuring about 7 inches in diameter. Place on well-greased cookie sheets; cover with towels and let rise in a warm place about 2 hours (p.357).

4. Preheat oven to 400°F. Brush loaves with water; with a sharp knife, cut 3 to 5 criss-cross slashes across top of each loaf.

5. Bake 45 to 50 minutes until loaves are golden and sound hollow when tapped. Remove to racks; brush with melted butter.

 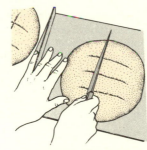

Making Starter: Stir water into flour-yeast mixture; beat until smooth; cover with waxed paper.

Slashing the loaves: After brushing with water, slash top of each loaf 3 to 5 times.

- Color index page 75
- Begin 4 days ahead
- 2 loaves
- 2051 cals per loaf

TO REPLENISH STARTER: If you plan to make Sourdough Bread regularly (at least once a week), the remaining Starter may be replenished if there is at least 1 cup of it left. Combine 1 cup all-purpose flour with 1 cup warm water and beat until smoothly blended. Stir into remaining Starter. Leave at room temperature a few hours until the mixture begins to bubble. Cover the bowl loosely; refrigerate the replenished Starter until needed.

Sweet yeast breads

RAISIN-ALMOND BRAID

A sweet yeast dough filled with plump California raisins is one of America's favorite breads. It is still the specialty for toast at the Palace Hotel in San Francisco.

⅔ cup sugar
1 teaspoon salt
2 packages active dry yeast
7½ to 8 cups all-purpose flour

1½ cups milk
3 eggs
¾ cup dark seedless raisins
½ cup sliced blanched almonds

- Color index page 75
- Begin 4½ hrs ahead
- 1 loaf
- 7471 cals per loaf

  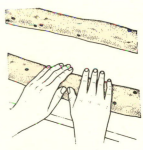

1 In large bowl, combine sugar, salt, yeast, and 2 cups flour. In 2-quart saucepan over low heat, heat milk, water, and butter until very warm (120° to 130°F.).

2 With mixer at low speed, gradually beat liquid into dry ingredients. Increase speed to medium; beat 2 minutes more, occasionally scraping bowl.

3 Beat in 2 eggs and 2 cups flour; continue beating 2 minutes, occasionally scraping bowl with rubber spatula.

4 With spoon, stir in raisins, ¼ cup almonds, and enough flour (about 3 cups) to make a soft dough.

5 Turn the dough onto a lightly floured surface; knead the dough until smooth and elastic, about 10 minutes. Shape into a ball. Place dough in large greased bowl and turn over to grease the top. Cover; let rise in warm place until dough is doubled, about 1½ hours (p.357). Punch down dough. On lightly floured surface divide the dough into 3 pieces. Cover; let dough rest 15 minutes.

6 Grease 9-inch springform pan. With floured hands, roll each piece of dough into a roll 22 inches long.

7 Place the rolls side by side and braid, pinching the ends to seal them well. Coil the braid into the pan.

8 Beat remaining egg; brush egg over coil and sprinkle with ¼ cup almonds. Cover and let the dough rise in a warm place, about ¾ hour until doubled in size.

9 Preheat oven to 350°F. Bake 1 to 1¼ hours or until bread sounds hollow when tapped. Cool in pan about 10 minutes. Remove from pan; cool on wire rack.

Sweet yeast breads

CARDAMOM CHRISTMAS WREATH

This cardamom-scented loaf may have been brought to the Midwest by Scandinavian immigrants. Our ribbon-wrapped wreath makes a beautiful presentation or gift.

1 cup sugar
1 teaspoon salt
1 teaspoon ground cardamom
2 packages active dry yeast
About 7 cups all-purpose flour

1 cup butter or margarine
Milk
3 eggs
1 tablespoon grated lemon peel

- *Color index page 75*
- *Begin 4½ hrs ahead*
- *1 wreath*
- *6360 cals*

½ teaspoon almond extract
About 1 yard decorative ribbon

1 In large bowl, combine first 4 ingredients and 2 cups flour. In 1-quart saucepan over low heat, heat butter and 1½ cups milk until very warm (120° to 130°F.). With mixer at low speed, beat liquid into dry ingredients until just blended. At medium speed, beat 2 minutes. Reserve 1 egg white. Beat in remaining eggs, lemon peel, almond extract, and 2 cups flour; beat 2 minutes longer. Stir in about 2½ cups flour to make a soft dough.

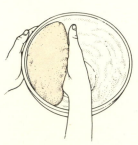

2 On floured surface, knead dough about 10 minutes, adding more flour if needed. Shape into ball; place in large greased bowl, turning to grease the top.

3 Cover dough; let rise about 1 hour (p.357). Punch down. Turn onto lightly floured surface; cover with clean towel; let rest 15 minutes. Lightly grease a large cookie sheet and the outside of 2-quart, straight-sided, oven-safe bowl. Invert the bowl; place in center of cookie sheet. In small bowl, combine the reserved egg white and 1 tablespoon milk; set aside. Cut off about ½ cup of dough; set this aside.

4 With rolling pin, roll dough into 30″ by 10″ rectangle. From 30-inch side, with floured hands, roll jelly-roll fashion into rope; twist slightly.

5 Wrap the rope around the outside of the greased bowl on sheet; press ends of rope together to seal and tuck them under.

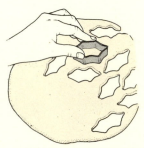

6 Roll reserved dough ⅛-inch thick. With floured 2½-inch leaf-shaped cookie cutter, cut about 15 leaves. Shape scraps into ¼-inch balls.

7 Brush some egg-white mixture on back of leaves and balls. Place 3 leaves together and top with three balls.

8 Decorate wreath with leaves and balls; let rise in warm place, about 45 minutes. Preheat oven to 350°F.

9 Brush wreath with remaining egg-white mixture. Bake 1 hour. Remove bowl; cool on wire rack. Tie with ribbon.

LIMPA BREAD

2 cups rye flour
About 4 cups all-purpose flour
2 packages active dry yeast
¼ cup sugar
1 tablespoon salt

2 cups milk
2 tablespoons molasses
2 tablespoons butter or margarine
2 teaspoons anise seed
1 egg white

1. In medium bowl, combine rye flour and 3½ cups all-purpose flour. In large bowl, combine yeast, sugar, salt, and 1½ cups flour mixture. In 2-quart saucepan, stir milk, molasses, butter, and anise seed; over low heat, heat until very warm (120° to 130°F.).

2. With mixer at low speed, gradually beat liquid mixture into yeast mixture until just blended. Increase speed to medium; beat 2 minutes, occasionally scraping bowl with rubber spatula. Gradually beat in 1 cup flour mixture or enough to make a thick batter. Continue beating 2 minutes, occasionally scraping bowl with rubber spatula. Stir in enough additional flour mixture (about 2½ cups) to make a soft dough.

3. Lightly sprinkle work surface with all-purpose flour; turn dough onto surface; with floured hands, knead dough about 10 minutes, until smooth and elastic, working in remaining flour mixture while kneading. Shape dough into ball and place in greased large bowl, turning dough over to grease top. Cover with towel; let rise in warm place about 1½ hours (p.357).

4. Punch down dough; turn onto lightly floured surface; cut in half. Cover with towel and let rest 15 minutes. Grease large cookie sheet.

5. Shape each dough half into about 12″ by 4″ oval, tapering ends. Place ovals, 3 inches apart, on cookie sheet. Cover with towel; let rise in warm place until doubled, about 1 hour.

6. Preheat oven to 375°F. Brush ovals with egg white; bake 35 minutes or until loaves sound hollow when lightly tapped with fingers. Remove from cookie sheet; cool on wire rack.

- *Color index page 75*
- *Begin 4½ hrs or up to 3 days ahead*
- *2 loaves*
- *1707 cals per loaf*

TESTING FOR DONENESS

Begin testing bread for doneness after the minimum time specified in the recipe.

Bread is done if it sounds hollow when tapped lightly with fingertips and is well browned on top. Remove from pan so bottom does not become soggy; cool on wire rack away from drafts.

Rolls and buns

PARKER HOUSE ROLLS

Created at the Parker House Hotel in Boston, these favorite American rolls are famous for the crease or "pocket" across each one.

½ cup sugar
2 teaspoons salt
2 packages active dry
*   yeast*
About 6½ cups all-
*   purpose flour*
2 cups water
1 cup butter or margarine
1 egg

● *Color index page 76*
● *Begin 3½ hrs ahead*
  or early in day
● *3 dozen rolls*
● *148 cals per roll*

1 In large bowl, combine sugar, salt, yeast, and 2¼ cups flour. In 2-quart saucepan over low heat, heat water and ½ cup butter until very warm (120° to 130°F.).

2 With mixer at low speed, gradually beat liquid into dry ingredients just until blended; beat in egg. Increase speed to medium; beat 2 minutes, occasionally scraping bowl.

3 Beat in 1 cup flour to make a thick batter; continue beating 2 minutes, scraping the bowl often. With wooden spoon, stir in 2¾ cups all-purpose flour to make a soft dough.

4 Turn dough onto well-floured surface and knead about 10 minutes, working in more flour (about ½ cup). Shape the dough into a ball; place in large, greased bowl; turn to grease top; cover; let rise about 1 hour (p.357). Punch down. Turn onto lightly floured surface; cover with bowl and let rest for about 15 minutes for easier shaping. Meanwhile, grease 17¼" by 11½" roasting pan. In small saucepan over low heat, melt the remaining ½ cup butter.

5 On lightly floured surface with floured rolling pin, roll dough ½-inch thick. With floured 3-inch round cookie cutter, cut the dough into rounds.

6 With dull edge of knife, make a crease across center of each dough round. Brush rounds lightly with some melted butter; fold in half along crease.

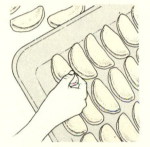

7 Arrange folded dough in rows in pan, each nearly touching the other. Knead trimmings together; reroll and cut until all dough is used, making 36 rolls.

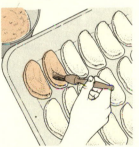

8 Brush tops of rolls with remaining melted butter. Cover the pan with towel; let the rolls rise, about 40 minutes. Meanwhile, preheat the oven to 425°F.

9 Bake 18 to 20 minutes until browned. Serve warm. Or, to serve later, wrap with foil in one layer. Just before serving, reheat in 375°F. oven 10 minutes.

HOW TO FORM ROLLS

Using Parker House Roll dough (above), shape as shown below. Cover, let rise until doubled, and bake as directed above.

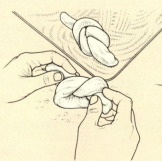

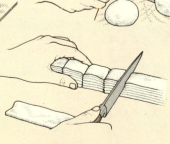

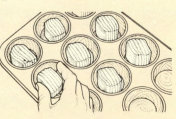

Posies: Shape dough into 2-inch balls. Flatten onto greased cookie sheet. Snip edges of each. Brush with milk; sprinkle with poppy seeds.

Knots: Divide dough into 12 or more equal pieces. Roll into 6-inch-long ropes.

Tie each rope into a knot. Arrange on greased cookie sheet. Brush with melted butter.

Fan tails: Roll dough into ⅛-inch-thick rectangle. Brush with melted butter. Cut into 1½-inch-wide strips.

Stack 6 or 7 strips together; cut into 1½-inch-pieces. Place cut side up in greased 2½ or 3-inch muffin-pan cups.

Rolls and buns

STICKY BUNS

Philadelphia was famous for these sticky buns, an old specialty of the Pennsylvania Dutch. These fruit-and-nut-filled yeast cakes, covered with a sticky butter-syrup coating, are delicious served warm.

1/3 cup sugar
1 teaspoon salt
1 package active dry yeast
About 5½ cups all-purpose flour.

1½ cups water
1 cup butter or margarine
1 egg
1 cup packed dark brown sugar
½ cup dark corn syrup

1 cup pecan halves, chopped
½ cup dark seedless raisins or currants
1 teaspoon ground cinnamon

- *Color index page 77*
- *Begin 4 hrs or day ahead*
- *15 buns*
- *456 cals per bun*

1 In large bowl, combine sugar, salt, yeast, and 2 cups flour. In 1-quart saucepan over low heat, heat water and ½ cup butter until warm (120° to 130°F.).

2 With mixer at low speed, gradually beat liquid into dry ingredients just until blended. Increase speed to medium; beat 2 minutes, occasionally scraping bowl with rubber spatula. Beat in egg and 1 cup flour to make a thick batter; continue beating 2 minutes, scraping bowl often. With wooden spoon, stir in 2¼ cups flour to make a soft dough. Turn onto well-floured surface.

3 Knead dough until smooth and elastic, about 10 minutes, working in more flour, (about ¼ cup). Shape into ball; cover and let rise about 1 hour (p.357).

4 In 1-quart saucepan over medium heat, heat brown sugar, corn syrup, and ½ cup butter to boiling; reduce heat to low; cook 3 minutes.

5 Measure ½ cup mixture into small bowl; stir in pecans, raisins, and cinnamon; set the mixture aside.

6 Spread remaining mixture into 13" by 9" baking pan. Punch down dough. Turn onto floured surface; cover; let rest 15 minutes.

7 On lightly floured surface with floured rolling pin, roll dough into a 15" by 12" rectangle. Sprinkle with pecan-raisin mixture.

8 Starting with long side, tightly roll dough, jelly-roll fashion; pinch seam to seal. Place seam side down; cut crosswise in 15 slices.

9 Place slices cut side down in baking pan. Cover with towel; let rise in warm place until doubled, about 45 minutes. Preheat oven to 375°F. Bake buns 30 minutes. Invert pan onto platter and allow syrup to drip on buns; remove the pan. Serve warm. Or, to serve later, invert buns onto foil; wrap with foil. Just before serving, reheat the buns in 375° oven and bake 15 to 20 minutes.

PECAN-CINNAMON BUNS

½ teaspoon salt
1 package active dry yeast
Sugar
About 3 cups all-purpose flour
2/3 cup milk
Butter or margarine
1 egg

1 6-ounce can pecan halves (2 cups)
1 cup packed brown sugar
6 tablespoons maple or maple-flavor syrup
1 teaspoon ground cinnamon

1. In large bowl, combine salt, yeast, ¼ cup sugar, and 1 cup flour. In 1-quart saucepan over low heat, heat milk and 4 tablespoons butter until very warm (120° to 130°F.). Butter does not need to melt completely.

2. With electric mixer at low speed, gradually beat the liquid ingredients into the dry ingredients just until they are blended. Increase the speed to medium; beat 2 minutes, occasionally scraping the bowl with a rubber spatula. Beat in the egg and ½ cup flour to make a thick batter; continue beating the batter 2 minutes, scraping the bowl often, to be sure all flour is mixed in. With a wooden spoon, stir in 1¼ cups flour to make a soft dough.

3. Turn dough onto lightly floured surface and knead until smooth and elastic, about 10 minutes, working in more flour (about ¼ cup) while kneading. Shape into ball; place in large greased bowl, turning to grease top. Cover; let rise, about 1 hour (p.357).

4. Punch down dough. Turn onto lightly floured surface; cover; let rest 15 minutes.

5. Meanwhile, reserve half of pecans; chop remaining pecans; set aside. In 1-quart saucepan over medium heat, melt ½ cup butter. Remove pan from heat; stir in brown sugar and maple syrup until smooth.

6. Evenly spread mixture in 13" by 9" baking pan. Scatter reserved pecan halves on sugar mixture; set aside. In small bowl, mix cinnamon, 2 tablespoons sugar, and chopped pecans.

7. With floured rolling pin, roll dough into 12" by 12" square. With metal spatula, spread dough with 3 tablespoons softened butter; sprinkle with cinnamon mixture.

8. From one edge, roll dough tightly jelly-roll fashion; pinch seam to seal. Turn the seam side down and cut crosswise into 12 pieces. Place pieces in baking pan. Cover; let rise in warm place until doubled, about 45 minutes.

9. Preheat oven to 375°F. Bake buns about 20 minutes or until lightly browned. Remove pan to wire rack; let cool 10 minutes (no longer) so syrup will remain on buns when pan is inverted.

10. Invert pan onto large platter or tray. Let pan remain on buns about 1 minute to allow syrup to drip onto buns; remove pan. Serve warm.

- *Color index page 77*
- *Begin 4½ hrs ahead*
- *12 buns*
- *475 cals per bun*

WALNUT-CINNAMON BUNS Prepare buns as for Pecan-Cinnamon Buns above, but omit pecans and add 2 cups walnut halves.

Biscuits

BUTTERMILK BISCUITS

2 cups all-purpose flour
2 teaspoons baking powder
¼ teaspon baking soda
1 teaspoon salt
¼ cup shortening
¾ cup buttermilk

- Color index page 76
- Begin 35 mins ahead
- 18 biscuits
- 81 cals per biscuit

1. Preheat oven to 450°F. In large bowl with fork, mix flour, baking powder, baking soda, and salt. With pastry blender, cut in shortening until mixture resembles coarse crumbs.
2. Add the buttermilk and using a fork, mix just until the mixture forms a soft dough that leaves the side of the bowl.
3. Turn onto lightly floured surface; knead 6 to 8 strokes to mix dough thoroughly.
4. Roll out the dough, ½-inch thick for high, fluffy biscuits, ¼-inch thick if you are going to make thin, crusty ones.
5. With floured 2-inch biscuit cutter, cut the biscuits, using a straight downward motion. Do not twist the cutter.
6. Place biscuits on ungreased cookie sheet, 1 inch apart for the crusty biscuits, and nearly touching for the soft-sided ones.
7. Press the dough trimmings together (don't knead); reroll and cut until all the dough is used. Bake the biscuits 12 to 15 minutes until they are golden.

PLAIN BISCUITS: Prepare as Buttermilk Biscuits (above) but use *milk* in place of buttermilk; increase the baking powder to 1 tablespoon and omit the baking soda. Bake as above. Makes 18 biscuits. 84 cals per biscuit.

FRUITED DROP BISCUITS: Prepare as Buttermilk biscuits (above) but use *1 cup milk* in place of buttermilk and add *¼ cup sugar* and *½ teaspoon ground cinnamon* to flour mixture. Add *one 8¾-ounce can fruit cocktail*, well drained, with the milk. With fork, stir dough until completely mixed; do not knead it. Onto ungreased cookie sheet, drop heaping tablespoonfuls of mixture 1 inch apart. Bake as directed. Makes 20 biscuits. 96 cals per biscuit.

VERMONT BISCUITS

2 cups all-purpose flour
1 tablespoon baking powder
1 tablespoon sugar
½ teaspoon salt
⅓ cup shortening
1 cup milk
¼ pound extra-sharp Cheddar cheese, shredded (1 cup)

- Color index page 76
- Begin 20 mins ahead
- 8 biscuits
- 270 cals per biscuit

1. Preheat oven to 450°F. In medium bowl, mix flour, baking powder, sugar, and salt. With pastry blender or two knives used scissor-fashion, cut in shortening until mixture resembles coarse crumbs.
2. With fork stir in the milk and the cheese just until the mixture forms a soft dough and leaves the side of the bowl.
3. Drop dough by ⅓ cupfuls, about 1 inch apart, onto ungreased large cookie sheet. Bake 10 to 12 minutes until golden.

SOUR CREAM BISCUITS

Before baking powder, biscuits were made with sour milk or buttermilk for leavening. We use sour cream for a distinctive flavor.

- Color index page 76
- Begin 45 mins ahead
- 20 biscuits
- 189 cals per biscuit

4 cups all-purpose flour
2 tablespoons baking powder
2 teaspoons salt
2 teaspoons sugar
½ teaspoon baking soda
1 16-ounce container sour cream (2 cups)
½ cup shortening

1 Preheat oven to 425°F. In a large bowl, mix flour, baking powder, salt, sugar, and baking soda.

2 With pastry blender or 2 knives used scissor-fashion, cut in sour cream and shortening until mixture resembles coarse crumbs. Turn the dough onto a lightly floured surface; knead 6 to 8 strokes to mix thoroughly (if dough is dry add a little water, a teaspoon at a time, while kneading). With a lightly floured rolling pin, roll the dough ½-inch thick.

3 With floured 2½-inch round cookie cutter, cut out biscuits. With a metal spatula place the biscuits on an ungreased cookie sheet, 1 inch apart.

4 Press trimmings together; roll and cut as above until all the dough is used. Bake 10 to 15 minutes until biscuits are golden.

KENTUCKY HAM BISCUITS

- Color index page 76
- Begin 35 mins ahead
- 12 biscuits
- 165 cals per biscuit

2 cups all-purpose flour
2 tablespoons sugar
1 tablespoon baking powder
1 teaspoon salt
¼ cup shortening
1 cup milk
2 tablespoons chopped parsley
1 4-ounce package sliced cooked ham, diced

1. Preheat oven to 450°F. In large bowl with fork, mix flour, sugar, baking powder, and salt. With pastry blender or two knives used scissor-fashion, cut in shortening until mixture resembles coarse crumbs.
2. Add milk, parsley, and ham; with fork, stir dough until just mixed.
3. Onto ungreased cookie sheet, drop dough by ¼ cupfuls, 1 inch apart, to make 12 biscuits. Bake 15 minutes or until golden. Serve warm.

Biscuits

Quick breads

BEATEN BISCUITS

- Color index page 76
- Begin 1½ hrs ahead
- 15 biscuits
- 96 cals per biscuit

Before the Civil War, beaten biscuits were a specialty of the deep South. If you like, use a food processor to save time and energy.

2 cups all-purpose flour
1½ teaspoons sugar
1 teaspoon baking powder
½ teaspoon salt
¼ cup lard
¼ cup milk
2 to 3 tablespoons cold water

1 In medium bowl, combine flour, sugar, baking powder, and salt. With pastry blender, cut in lard until mixture resembles coarse bread crumbs.

2 With fork, stir in milk and enough water until dough forms a ball. On floured board, knead until smooth and elastic, about 10 minutes.

3 With meat mallet, pound dough until slightly blistered and very elastic about 25 minutes. Preheat oven to 400°F. Grease large cookie sheet.

4 Roll dough ½ inch thick; with floured 2-inch biscuit cutter, cut out dough. Place biscuits, 1 inch apart, on cookie sheet. With fork pierce each biscuit twice in 2 parallel rows. Bake 25 minutes or until golden. Biscuits will be as firm as crackers. Serve warm. (To make in food processor, combine dry ingredients with knife blade attached; cut in lard; add milk and water to form a ball; process until blistered, about 5 minutes.)

GIANT POPOVERS

- Color index page 77
- Begin 1½ hrs ahead
- 8 popovers
- 285 cals per popover

6 tablespoons butter or margarine
6 eggs
2 cups milk
2 cups all-purpose flour
1 teaspoon salt

1. In small saucepan over low heat, melt butter. Grease well eight deep 7-ounce pottery custard cups. Set custard cups in jelly-roll pan for easier handling. Preheat oven to 375°F.
2. In large bowl, with mixer at low speed, beat eggs until frothy; beat in milk and butter until blended. Beat in flour and salt until batter is smooth.
3. Fill each custard cup three-quarters full with batter. Bake 1 hour; then quickly make small slit in top of each popover to let out steam; bake 10 minutes longer. Immediately remove popovers from cups. Serve piping hot.

BOSTON BROWN BREAD

- Color index page 76
- Begin 2½ hrs ahead
- 2 loaves
- 1229 cals per loaf

This colonial staple was traditionally eaten with Boston baked beans. Steamed in coffee cans, it has a character all its own.

1 cup whole-wheat flour
1 cup rye flour
1 cup cornmeal
1½ teaspoons baking soda
1½ teaspoons salt
2 cups buttermilk
¾ cup dark molasses
1 cup dark seedless raisins

1 Grease and flour two tall 1-pound coffee cans and cut foil to use as lids; grease. (Or, grease and flour a 2-quart mold and its lid.)

2 Into large bowl, measure all ingredients; with wire whisk or spoon, stir until well mixed. Pour the batter into the cans.

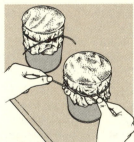

3 Cover with foil and tie foil to can with string. Place cans on rack in deep kettle; add boiling water to come halfway up sides of the coffee cans.

4 Cover kettle. Over low heat, simmer 3 hours or until toothpick inserted in center of bread comes out almost clean. Invert cans onto wire rack to cool.

DATE-NUT BREAD

- Color index page 76
- Begin 2 hrs ahead
- 1 loaf
- 3317 cals

1 8-ounce package pitted dates, chopped (1¾ cups)
1¼ cups boiling water
2¼ cups all-purpose flour
1 cup walnuts, chopped
¾ cup packed light brown sugar
1 teaspoon baking soda
½ teaspoon salt
1 egg, slightly beaten
2 tablespoons salad oil

1. In bowl combine dates and boiling water; let stand 15 minutes. Grease and flour 9" by 5" loaf pan; preheat oven to 350°F.
2. In large bowl with fork, mix flour and next 4 ingredients. Stir in egg, oil, and date mixture.
3. Spoon mixture evenly into loaf pan. Bake 65 minutes or until toothpick inserted in center comes out clean. Cool in pan on rack 10 minutes; remove from pan. Serve warm or cold.

PEANUT-BUTTER BREAD

- Color index page 76
- Begin day ahead
- 1 loaf
- 3206 cals

¾ cup peanut butter
¼ cup butter or
   margarine, softened
2 cups all-purpose flour
½ cup sugar
2 teaspoons baking
   powder
1 teaspoon salt
1¼ cups milk
1 tablespoon grated
   orange peel
1 egg, beaten

1. Preheat oven to 375°F. Grease 9″ by 5″ loaf pan. In small bowl, with fork, beat peanut butter and butter until light and fluffy.
2. In medium bowl with fork, mix flour, sugar, baking powder and salt; add peanut-butter mixture; mix until mixture resembles coarse crumbs.
3. Add milk and orange peel to beaten egg. Stir into flour mixture. Pour mixture into pan; bake 1 hour. Cool in pan on wire rack 10 minutes; remove from pan; cool completely on rack.

PUMPKIN BREAD

- Color index page 76
- Begin 2½ hrs ahead
- 2 loaves
- 2771 cals per loaf

3 cups all-purpose flour
1½ cups sugar
1½ teaspoons ground
   cinnamon
1 teaspoon baking soda
1 teaspoon salt
¾ teaspoon ground
   nutmeg
¾ teaspoon ground
   cloves
½ teaspoon baking
   powder
3 eggs
1 16-ounce can pumpkin
1 cup salad oil
1 cup golden or dark
   seedless raisins
½ cup walnuts, chopped

1. Preheat oven to 350°F. Grease two 8½″ by 4½″ loaf pans. In large bowl with fork, mix first 8 ingredients.
2. In medium bowl with fork, beat eggs, pumpkin, and salad oil until blended; stir into flour mixture just until flour is moistened. Stir in raisins and walnuts. Spoon evenly into loaf pans.
3. Bake 1 hour 15 minutes or until toothpick inserted comes out clean. Cool in pans on rack 10 minutes; remove from pans; cool on rack.

CHEESE QUICK BREAD

- Color index page 76
- Begin day ahead
- 1 loaf
- 2143 cals

2 cups all-purpose flour
2 teaspoons baking
   powder
2 teaspoons dry mustard
1 teaspoon salt
4 ounces shredded
   Cheddar cheese (1 cup)
¼ cup butter or
   margarine
1 cup milk
2 eggs

1. Preheat oven to 375°F. Grease 9″ by 5″ loaf pan. In large bowl, with fork, mix flour with next 4 ingredients.
2. In small saucepan over medium heat, melt butter; stir in milk, then eggs. With hand beater, beat mixture just until blended; add all at once to flour mixture; stir just until moistened.
3. Pour into pan. Bake 1 hour or until toothpick inserted in center comes out clean. Cool in pan on wire rack 10 minutes; remove from pan and cool completely on rack.

CRANBERRY-RAISIN BREAD

Cranberries, long cultivated by the New England Indians, add color and zest to this "quick bread" – a bread made without yeast

- Color index page 76
- Begin 4 hrs ahead
- 2 loaves
- 1837 cals per loaf

3 large oranges
4 cups all-purpose flour
1¾ cups sugar
1 tablespoon baking
   powder
1½ teaspoons salt
1 teaspoon baking soda
½ cup butter or
   margarine
2 eggs
2 cups fresh or frozen
   cranberries, coarsely
   chopped
1 cup dark seedless
   raisins

1 Preheat oven to 350°F. Grease and flour two 8½″ by 4½″ loaf pans. From oranges, grate 1 tablespoon peel and squeeze 1½ cups juice; set aside.

2 In large bowl, mix flour and next 4 ingredients. With pastry blender or two knives used scissor-fashion, cut in butter until mixture resembles coarse crumbs.

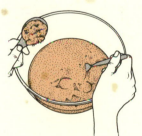

3 In medium bowl with fork, beat eggs, orange juice, and orange peel; stir into flour mixture just until flour is moistened.

4 Gently fold cranberries and raisins into the batter. Spoon the batter evenly into the greased loaf pans.

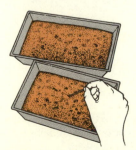

5 Bake 1 hour and 10 minutes or until toothpick inserted in the center of the the bread comes out clean.

6 Cool breads in pans on wire rack 10 minutes; remove bread from pans. Cool breads completely on the rack.

Quick breads

10/14/06

BANANA BREAD

During the 1960s and 1970s this cake-like bread, made with America's favorite fruit, the banana, became extremely popular.

- *Color index page 76*
- *Begin day ahead*
- *1 loaf*
- *2606 cals*

1¾ cups all-purpose flour
⅔ cup sugar
1 teaspoon baking powder
½ teaspoon salt
¼ teaspoon baking soda

½ cup shortening
1 cup mashed bananas (about 2 very ripe medium bananas)
2 eggs, slightly beaten

 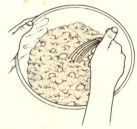

1 Preheat oven to 350°F. Grease and flour 9″ by 5″ loaf pan. In large bowl, with fork, mix first 5 ingredients.

2 With pastry blender or 2 knives used scissor-fashion, cut in shortening until mixture resembles coarse crumbs.

3 With fork, stir in bananas and eggs just until blended; spread batter evenly in pan.

4 Bake 55 minutes to 1 hour until toothpick inserted in center of bread comes out clean.

5 Cool in pan on wire rack 10 minutes; remove from pan and cool completely on rack.

BANANA-CRANBERRY: Prepare as above but add *1 cup cranberries*, coarsely chopped, with bananas.
BANANA-DATE: Prepare as above but add *½ cup chopped, pitted dates* with bananas.
BANANA-NUT: Prepare as above but add *½ cup coarsely chopped pecans*, *almonds* or *walnuts* with bananas.

Corn breads

BACON CORN BREAD

The American Indians used only cornmeal for their breads. Today, cornmeal is mixed with all-purpose flour for better texture.

- *Color index page 76*
- *Begin 1 hr ahead or early in day*
- *12 servings*
- *190 cals per serving*

1 8-ounce package sliced bacon
1 cup all-purpose flour
1 cup cornmeal
2 tablespoons sugar
4 teaspoons baking powder

½ teaspoon salt
1 8½- to 8¾-ounce can cream-style golden corn
½ cup milk
1 egg

1 In 10-inch skillet over medium-low heat, cook bacon until browned; remove to paper towels. Crumble; set aside. Reserve ¼ cup bacon drippings.

2 Preheat oven to 425°F. Grease 9″ by 9″ baking pan. In medium bowl, mix next 5 ingredients. In small bowl, beat corn, milk, egg, and reserved bacon drippings.

3 Stir corn mixture into flour mixture just until flour is moistened (batter will be lumpy). With rubber spatula fold in bacon. Spread batter evenly in pan.

4 Bake 15 to 20 minutes until toothpick inserted in center comes out clean. Cut into 12 pieces; serve warm. Or cool in pan on wire rack to serve later.

SPOON BREAD

- *Color index page 77*
- *Begin 1½ hrs ahead*
- *8 side-dish servings*
- *169 cals per serving*

Water
2 cups cornmeal
2 teaspoons baking powder
1½ teaspoons salt

1½ teaspoons baking soda
2 cups milk
2 eggs

1. In bowl, mix 1 cup water with next 4 ingredients. In 3-quart saucepan over high heat, heat 1 cup water to boiling; reduce heat to low; stir in cornmeal mixture; cook, stirring, until thick. Remove from heat. Preheat oven to 350°F.
2. Grease 2-quart casserole. Into cornmeal mixture, gradually add milk, then eggs; beat until smooth. Pour into casserole. Bake 1 hour until set.

GOLDEN CORN STICKS

- Color index page 77
- Begin 35 mins ahead
- 14 sticks
- 121 cals per stick

Salad oil
1 cup all-purpose flour
¾ cup cornmeal
2 to 4 tablespoons sugar
1 tablespoon baking powder
1 teaspoon salt
1 egg
⅔ cup milk
⅓ cup butter or margarine, melted

1. Preheat oven to 425°F. Grease 14 corn-stick molds very well with salad oil. In medium bowl, with fork, mix flour, cornmeal, sugar, baking powder, and salt.

2. In a small bowl, with a fork, beat together the egg, milk, and butter. Pour this mixture all at once into the flour mixture, stirring just until the flour is moistened.

3. Spoon the batter into the corn-stick molds, filling each mold three-fourths full. Bake the corn sticks 15 to 20 minutes. Cool 10 minutes; serve warm. Or, if you like, leave on rack to cool completely. Reheat if desired.

Greasing the corn-stick molds: Grease 14 corn-stick molds very well with salad oil.

Filling the corn-stick molds: Fill the molds three-fourths full to avoid overflowing.

CORN-BREAD RING: Grease a 5½-cup ring mold. Prepare as above but spoon batter into ring mold. Bake about 25 minutes; invert from mold onto serving platter. Slice and serve as bread or fill center with *creamed ham, chicken, shrimp,* or *favorite curry mixture* and serve as main dish for 8. Makes 1 corn-bread ring. 385 cals per serving.

CORN MUFFINS: Grease twelve 2½-inch muffin-pan cups. Prepare as above; spoon into cups, filling each two-thirds full. Bake about 20 minutes. Makes 12 muffins. 449 cals per muffin.

DEVILED-HAM CORN BREAD: Prepare as above but stir *one 2½-ounce can deviled ham* into egg mixture before adding to flour mixture. Pour batter into greased 8" by 8" baking pan. Bake 25 minutes. Cut into squares. Makes 9 servings. 610 cals per serving.

CORN-BREAD SHORTCAKE: Split squares of hot corn bread. Spoon *chicken à la king* or *creamed ham, turkey* or *shrimp* between halves and on top of squares. Makes 9 servings. 599 cals per serving.

GOLDEN CORN BREAD: Prepare as above, but pour batter into greased 8" by 8" baking pan. Bake 25 minutes. Cut into squares. Makes 9 servings. 598 cals per serving.

CHILI-CHEESE CORN BREAD

Cornbread recipes vary from region to region and family to family. This Tex-Mex version uses chilies and chorizos.

- Color index page 76
- Begin 1¼ hrs ahead
- 14 side-dish servings
- 385 cals per serving

½ pound chorizos (Spanish sausage) or pepperoni
2 cups all-purpose flour
1½ cups yellow cornmeal
⅓ cup sugar
2 tablespoons baking powder
1½ teaspoons salt
2 eggs
1 cup milk
½ cup salad oil
½ cup sour cream
6 ounces Cheddar cheese, shredded (1½ cups)
1 4-ounce can chopped green chilies, drained

1 Remove casing and chop chorizos. In 10-inch skillet over medium-low heat, cook chorizos until lightly browned, stirring occasionally. If pepperoni is used, chop but omit cooking.

2 With slotted spoon, remove chorizos to paper towels to drain. Preheat oven to 375°F. Grease two 9" by 5" loaf pans.

3 Into large bowl, measure flour, cornmeal, sugar, baking powder, and salt.

4 In medium bowl with wire whisk or fork, beat eggs, milk, salad oil, and sour cream until smooth. With fork, stir the egg mixture into the flour mixture just until blended. Stir in the chorizos, cheese, and green chilies. Spoon the batter into the prepared pans. Bake 45 minutes or until bread is golden and toothpick inserted in center comes out clean.

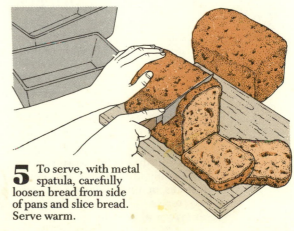

5 To serve, with metal spatula, carefully loosen bread from side of pans and slice bread. Serve warm.

Muffins

BLUEBERRY MUFFINS

- Color index page 77
- Begin 40 mins ahead or early in day
- 6 muffins
- 296 cals per muffin

Muffins, often buttered and toasted, are served for breakfast or as a mid-morning snack; fresh or frozen blueberries add color and flavor.

1¾ cups all-purpose flour
⅔ cup sugar
1 tablespoon baking powder
¾ teaspoon salt
6 tablespoons butter or margarine
1 egg

½ cup milk
1 teaspoon grated lemon peel
½ teaspoon vanilla extract
1 cup fresh or frozen blueberries

1 Preheat oven to 400°F. Grease six 3" by 1½" muffin-pan cups. In bowl, mix flour, sugar, baking powder, and salt.

2 With pastry blender or 2 knives used scissor-fashion, cut in butter until mixture resembles fine crumbs.

3 In small bowl, beat egg, milk, lemon peel, and vanilla extract until blended.

4 Stir egg mixture into flour mixture just until flour is moistened (batter will be lumpy). Fold blueberries into batter. Spoon batter into muffin-pan cups. Bake 20 to 25 minutes until golden and toothpick inserted in center comes out clean. Immediately remove muffins from pan; serve warm. Or cool muffins on wire rack to serve later; reheat if desired.

MAPLE-BRAN MUFFINS

- Color index page 77
- Begin 1 hr ahead
- 9 muffins
- 205 cals per muffin

2½ cups bran flakes, crushed
1¼ cups all-purpose flour
1 teaspoon baking soda
¼ teaspoon salt

1 egg
¾ cup buttermilk
⅓ cup maple syrup or maple-flavor syrup
¼ cup salad oil

1. Grease nine 2½" by 1¼" muffin-pan cups. Preheat oven to 350°F. In large bowl with fork, mix first 4 ingredients.
2. In small bowl with fork, beat egg, buttermilk, maple syrup, and salad oil until blended. Stir egg mixture into flour mixture just until moistened.
3. Spoon into muffin-pan cups. Bake for 25 minutes or until lightly browned and toothpick inserted in center comes out clean. Immediately remove muffins from pan.

APPLE-MOLASSES MUFFINS

- Color index page 77
- Begin 1 hr or day ahead
- 18 muffins
- 271 cals per muffin

4 cups all-purpose flour
¾ cup molasses
½ cup packed brown sugar
½ cup butter or margarine, softened
⅓ cup milk
2 teaspoons baking soda
2 teaspoons ground cinnamon

1 teaspoon ground allspice
1 teaspoon salt
2 eggs
3 large red cooking apples (1¾ pounds), peeled and diced
¾ cup walnuts, chopped

1. Preheat oven to 375°F. Grease and flour 18 3-inch muffin-pan cups. Into large bowl, measure all ingredients except apples and walnuts; with mixer at low speed, beat until blended, constantly scraping bowl. Stir in apples and walnuts.
2. Spoon batter into muffin-pan cups to come almost to the top. Bake 25 minutes or until toothpick inserted in center comes out clean.
3. Cool muffins in pans on wire racks 10 minutes; remove from pans. Serve muffins warm. Or, to serve later, cool muffins on wire racks; wrap muffins in single layer with foil. Just before serving, reheat wrapped muffins in preheated 375°F oven 10 minutes or until warm.

ZUCCHINI-OATMEAL MUFFINS

- Color index page 77
- Begin 45 mins ahead or earlier in day
- 12 muffins
- 120 cals per muffin

2½ cups all-purpose flour
1½ cups sugar
½ cup quick-cooking oats, uncooked
1 tablespoon baking powder
1 teaspoon salt
1 teaspoon ground cinnamon

1 3-ounce can pecans (1 cup), chopped
4 eggs
1 medium zucchini (about 10 ounces), unpeeled and finely shredded
¾ cup salad oil

1. Preheat oven to 400°F. Grease twelve 3" by 1½" muffin-pan cups. In large bowl, mix first 7 ingredients. In medium bowl, beat eggs slightly; stir in zucchini and salad oil. Stir egg mixture into flour mixture just until flour is moistened (batter will be lumpy).
2. Spoon batter into muffin-pan cups. Bake 25 minutes or until golden and toothpick inserted in center of muffin comes out clean. Immediately remove muffins from pan; serve warm. Or cool on wire rack to serve later; reheat if desired.

Filling muffin-pan cups: Fill each muffin-pan cup with batter. Wipe away any spills.

Testing for doneness: Muffins are done when toothpick inserted comes out clean.

Doughnuts

APPLE-CINNAMON FUNNEL CAKES

- Color index page 77
- Begin 30 mins ahead
- 7 funnel cakes
- 150 cals per cake

Salad oil
1¼ cups all-purpose flour
¾ cup apple cider or apple juice
1 teaspoon baking powder
1 teaspoon almond extract
⅛ teaspoon salt
1 egg
Ground cinnamon
2 tablespoons confectioners' sugar

1. In 12-inch skillet over medium heat, heat about ¾-inch salad oil to about 325°F. on deep-fat thermometer (or, heat the salad oil in an electric skillet set at 325°F.).
2. Meanwhile, in medium bowl with wire whisk or fork, mix the flour, apple cider or apple juice, baking powder, almond extract, salt, egg, and ½ teaspoon ground cinnamon to make a batter.
3. Holding a narrow-spouted funnel (½-inch spout) or teapot, close the spout with a finger; pour ¼ cup batter into the funnel. Over the hot oil in the skillet, carefully remove finger to let the batter run out in a stream, while making a spiral about 6 inches in diameter.
4. Fry 3 to 5 minutes until golden brown, turning once with tongs, Drain well on paper towels. Repeat with remaining batter, stirring well before pouring.
5. In a small bowl, mix confectioners' sugar and ¼ teaspoon cinnamon. Sprinkle cakes with the cinnamon-sugar mixture; arrange on a large platter and serve warm.

NEW ORLEAN BEIGNETS

- Color index page 77
- Begin 1 hr ahead
- 12 servings
- 132 cals per serving

Raspberry Sauce (p.290)
1 cup water
½ cup butter or margarine
1 teaspoon sugar
¼ teaspoon salt
1 cup all-purpose flour
1 teaspoon vanilla extract
4 eggs
Salad oil
¼ cup confectioners' sugar

1. Prepare Raspberry Sauce; set aside.
2. In 2-quart saucepan over medium heat, heat water, butter or margarine, sugar, and salt until butter or margarine is melted and mixture boils; remove saucepan from heat.
3. With wooden spoon, vigorously stir in flour all at once until mixture forms a ball and leaves side of pan. Beat in vanilla and eggs until mixture is smooth and satiny.
4. Meanwhile, in 12-inch skillet over medium heat, heat 1 inch salad oil to 375°F. on deep-fat thermometer (or, heat oil in electric skillet set at 375°F.). Drop the dough by rounded tablespoonfuls into the hot oil and fry the beignets, a few at a time, until they are golden, about 5 minutes. (Each beignet will puff up to about 2 inches in diameter when done.) Drain the beignets on paper towels; keep warm.
5. To serve, sprinkle warm beignets with confectioners' sugar; arrange on large platter. Serve with Raspberry Sauce.

NUTMEG-SUGAR DOUGHNUTS

The Pennsylvania Dutch were the first to make holes in doughnuts which were brought to America by settlers in the early 17th century.

- Color index page 77
- Begin 2½ hrs ahead
- 2 dozen doughnuts
- 149 cals per doughnut

3 cups all-purpose flour
1 cup sugar
¾ cup buttermilk
2 eggs
2 tablespoons shortening
2 teaspoons baking powder
1 teaspoon baking soda
1 teaspoon salt
½ teaspoon ground nutmeg
Salad oil

Nutmeg Sugar
1 cup sugar
¾ teaspoon ground nutmeg

1 Into large bowl, measure 1½ cups flour and remaining ingredients except salad oil and Nutmeg Sugar; with mixer at low speed, beat just until smooth, constantly scraping bowl.

2 At medium speed, beat 1 minute, constantly scraping bowl. Stir in remaining flour to make soft dough. Refrigerate at least 1 hour to make it easier to handle.

3 On well-floured surface with floured rolling pin, roll dough ½-inch thick.

4 With floured doughnut cutter, cut out doughnuts. Reroll and cut trimmings until all the dough is used.

5 In deep-fat fryer, heat 3 or 4 inches salad oil to 370°F. Fry 4 or 5 rings at a time. Turn with a metal spatula as the rings rise to the surface, then turn the rings often until golden brown. Lift them from fat with slotted spoon and drain them on paper towels. Prepare the Nutmeg Sugar: In a paper bag, combine sugar and ground nutmeg.

6 Shake warm doughnuts in mixture to coat well. Serve warm.

Pancakes and waffles

SILVER DOLLAR PANCAKES

Pancakes are an American passion, and Silver Dollar pancakes, named for the coin they resemble, are one of the most popular.

- *Color index page 78*
- *Begin 30 mins ahead*
- *24 2-inch pancakes*
- *51 cals per pancake*

1¼ cups all-purpose flour	1 egg, slightly beaten
2 tablespoons sugar	Butter or margarine
2 teaspoons baking powder	Maple or maple-flavored syrup, honey,
¾ teaspoon salt	preserves, marmalade,
Salad oil	apple butter as desired
1⅓ cups milk	

1 In large bowl, with fork, mix the first 4 ingredients; add 3 tablespoons salad oil, the milk, and the egg and stir just until the flour is moistened.

2 Preheat electric griddle or skillet as manufacturer directs. Unless using griddle with non-stick finish, brush griddle lightly with salad oil.

3 Pour batter by measuring tablespoonfuls onto hot griddle to make small pancakes; cook until bubbly and bubbles burst; the edges will look dry.

4 With pancake turner or metal spatula, turn the pancakes and cook until the underside is golden; place on heated platter; keep the pancakes warm in the oven. Repeat until all the batter is used, brushing the griddle with more salad oil, if necessary. Serve the warm pancakes with butter or margarine and syrup or other toppings as desired. If you like, melt the butter to serve with pancakes.

BUCKWHEAT: Prepare as above but substitute *½ cup buckwheat flour* for ½ cup all-purpose flour. Makes 12 4-inch pancakes. 98 cals each.

BLUEBERRY: Use *1 cup milk* and prepare pancakes as above but add *½ cup blueberries* to batter; pour batter by scant ¼ cupfuls onto hot griddle. Or, sprinkle poured pancakes with blueberries. Makes 8 4-inch pancakes. 153 cals each.

PLAIN: Prepare as above but pour batter by scant ¼ cupfuls onto hot griddle. Makes 12 4-inch pancakes. 102 cals each.

OTHERS: To pancake or waffle batter, add drained *canned whole-kernel corn*, drained *canned crushed pineapple*, *chopped nuts*, *flaked coconut*, *raisins*, or *fresh fruit*, as desired.

COUNTRY BRUNCH PANCAKES

- *Color index page 78*
- *Begin 45 mins ahead*
- *6 servings*
- *605 cals per serving*

Fig-Maple Syrup (below)	½ cup milk
2 cups all-purpose flour	1 8-ounce container
3 tablespoons sugar	creamed cottage cheese
4 teaspoons baking powder	(1 cup);
1 teaspoon salt	3 eggs, slightly beaten
½ teaspoon baking soda	2 tablespoons lemon juice
	Salad oil

1. Prepare Fig-Maple Syrup; keep warm.
2. In large bowl, mix flour and next 4 ingredients. Add milk, cottage cheese, eggs, and lemon juice; stir just until flour is moistened.
3. Heat griddle or skillet over medium heat until drop of water sizzles (or use electric griddle or skillet); brush lightly with salad oil. Pour batter by scant ¼ cupfuls onto hot griddle, making a few pancakes at a time; cook until tops are bubbly and bubbles burst; edges will look dry. With pancake turner, turn and cook the pancakes until the undersides are golden; place on warm platter; keep pancakes warm.
4. Repeat until batter is used, brushing griddle with more salad oil if necessary. Serve with Fig-Maple Syrup.

FIG-MAPLE SYRUP: In 1-quart saucepan over high heat, heat *1½ cups maple* or *maple-flavor syrup*, *½ cup dried figs*, finely chopped, *4 tablespoons butter* or *margarine*, and *1 teaspoon grated lemon peel* to boiling; reduce heat to low and simmer 3 to 4 minutes, keep warm.

RICE FRITTERS (CALAS)

- *Color index page 78*
- *Begin 1½ hrs ahead*
- *Makes 30 rice fritters*
- *57 cals each*

2½ cups cold cooked regular long-grain rice	¼ teaspoon ground nutmeg
¾ cup all-purpose flour	1 package active dry yeast
¼ cup sugar	3 eggs
2 teaspoons grated lemon peel	Salad oil
¼ teaspoon salt	Confectioner's sugar
	Praline Syrup (optional)

1. In large bowl with mixer at medium speed, beat rice, flour, sugar, lemon peel, salt, nutmeg, yeast, and eggs until well mixed.
2. Cover bowl with towel; let stand in warm place (80° to 85°F.), away from drafts, 1 hour. (Batter will become thick and foamy.)
3. In 4-quart saucepan, heat about 2 inches salad oil to 370°F. on deep-fat thermometer. Drop batter, by level measuring tablespoonfuls into hot oil. Fry about 6 at a time, turning once, until lightly browned. Drain on paper towels. Sprinkle with confectioners' sugar; serve warm. If you like, serve with Praline syrup.

PRALINE SYRUP: In 1-quart saucepan over medium heat, stir *1 cup packed brown sugar*, *½ cup light corn syrup*, *2 tablespoons water*, *1 tablespoon butter* or *margarine*, and *⅛ teaspoon salt* until the sugar dissolves. Stir in *½ cup pecan halves*, finely chopped. Makes 2 cups. 59 cals per tablespoon.

Crêpes

BUTTERMILK-PECAN WAFFLES

1¾ cups all-purpose flour
1 teaspoon baking powder
1 teaspoon baking soda
½ teaspoon salt
1 tablespoon sugar
2 cups buttermilk
⅓ cup salad oil
2 eggs
3-ounces pecans (1 cup), coarsely chopped
Butter or margarine
Maple or maple-flavor syrup

1. Preheat waffle baker as manufacturer directs. In large bowl, mix flour, baking powder, baking soda, salt, and sugar; add buttermilk, salad oil, eggs, and pecans; beat until well blended.
2. When waffle baker is ready to use, pour the batter into the center of the lower half until it spreads to about 1 inch from the edges. Cover and bake as manufacturer directs; do not lift the cover during baking.
3. When waffle is done, lift cover; loosen waffle with fork; serve at once with butter or margarine and syrup. Reheat baker before pouring in next waffle; stir batter each time before pouring to distribute nuts. If batter becomes too thick while standing, stir in a little more buttermilk until batter has good pouring consistency.

- Color index page 78
- Begin 30 mins ahead
- 5 waffles
- 530 cals each

PLAIN BUTTERMILK WAFFLES: Prepare as above but omit sugar and pecans. 355 cals each.

FRENCH TOAST

At home and in restaurants, French toast is a popular breakfast dish made from bread dipped in an egg-and-milk mixture; fried in butter; served with syrup or sugar.

Dip a slice of white bread into a batter made from 2 eggs, ¼ cup milk, 1 tablespoon sugar, and dash of salt.

Coat well and lightly fry in butter until browned on both sides.

Try adding flavorings to batter such as ground cinnamon or nutmeg, vanilla or almond extract, grated orange or lemon peel; serve with a variety of syrups, honey, jams and preserves.

STRAWBERRY BLINTZES

Blintzes, a Jewish American specialty, are made by filling crêpes with a cheese mixture, then folding and frying them. Toppings range from a dusting of confectioners' sugar to our delicious Brandied-Strawberry Sauce.

Crêpes
⅔ cup all-purpose flour
½ teaspoon salt
3 eggs
1½ cups milk
2 tablespoons butter or margarine, melted

Filling
1 8-ounce container creamed cottage cheese (1 cup)
1 3-ounce package cream cheese, softened
¼ cup sugar

½ teaspoon vanilla extract
Brandied-Strawberry Sauce (p.306)

- Color index page 78
- Begin early in day or up to 2 months ahead
- 12 blintzes
- 156 cals per blintz

1 Prepare Crêpes: In medium bowl, with wire whisk or hand beater, beat flour, salt, and eggs until smooth.

2 Slowly beat in milk and 1½ tablespoons melted butter. Cover refrigerate 2 hours. Prepare Brandied-Strawberry Sauce.

3 Brush bottom and side of 7-inch skillet generously with melted butter. Over low heat, heat skillet; pour in scant ¼ cup batter.

4 Tip pan to coat bottom with batter. Over low heat, cook until top is set and underside browned, about 3 minutes.

5 With metal spatula turn crêpe and cook other side until golden, about 1 minute. Slip crêpe onto waxed paper.

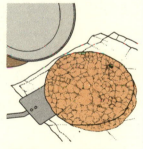

6 Repeat until all batter is used, stacking with waxed paper between crêpes. (Wrap in foil and refrigerate if not using immediately.)

7 In small bowl, with mixer at medium speed, beat cottage cheese, cream cheese, sugar, and vanilla extract.

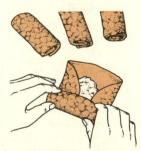

8 Spread a spoonful of mixture along center of each crêpe; fold two sides towards middle; roll up in opposite direction.

9 In large skillet over medium heat, in 2 tablespoons hot butter, cook until golden. Serve with the sauce.

Sandwiches

An American Meal – The Sandwich

By the 1920s, when soft white bread, the sandwich loaf, became available, the sandwich quickly gained in popularity. Although it has come to symbolize the American lunch, credit for inventing the sandwich is given to England's Fourth Earl of Sandwich, who used to order bread-and-meat dishes so he could eat with his hands at gambling sessions and never leave the table.

While sandwiches are still made with presliced bread, new "containers," such as rolls, pita breads, tortillas, pizzas, croissants, flatbreads, and crêpes, are being used to sandwich new combinations, and old favorites are sometimes combined with cheese and melted. Many American sandwiches derived from ethnic specialties and still maintain these associations.

THE DELUXE STEAK SANDWICH

Steak, one of America's favorite beef cuts, is eaten in many forms; in a sandwich of toasted French bread it makes a hearty lunch.

HAM 'N' SWISS CROISSANT

The croissant, a buttery, flaky, French breakfast roll, has become a sophisticated container for traditional sandwich fillings.

Cut *one croissant* horizontally in half; place, cut sides up, on cookie sheet. Arrange *slices of Swiss cheese* on top half folding to fit if necessary. Broil 30 seconds or until cheese is slightly melted and bottom half of croissant is lightly toasted. Spread bottom half with *Dijon mustard*; top with *lettuce leaf* and one *ham slice*, cutting to fit if necessary. Cover with top half and serve with *Oranges and tomatoes Vinaigrette* (p.276) or *Crudités* with *Oriental Onion Dip* (p.95).

Under the broiler, toast a split *6-inch piece of French bread*; keep warm. Spread bottom piece with *mustard* and arrange *thin slices of London Broil* or *pan-fried top round steaks* on it. Cover with *sautéed onion rings* and top of French bread. Serve with *French Fries*.

DELI SPECIALS

World famous New York deli-style sandwiches like the special pan-fried Reuben and over-stuffed bagels are meals in themselves.

THE RIBBON SANDWICH

Delicate sandwiches make easy finger food at any party; this attractive presentation can be done ahead and refrigerated.

Trim crust from *one 1-pound loaf unsliced white bread*; cut horizontally into 6 equal slices. Thinly spread bottom slice with *cream-cheese-chive mixture*. Place second slice over first, spread with *devilled ham spread*. Spread third slice with *cream-cheese-chive mixture* and place cream-cheese side down on top of second slice. Wrap in plastic wrap or foil; repeat with remaining slices of bread. Refrigerate loaves until well chilled; cut into ½-inch thick slices; cut each of these crosswise in half and arrange on a serving platter. Garnish with *watercress* and *Lemon Twists* (p.100).

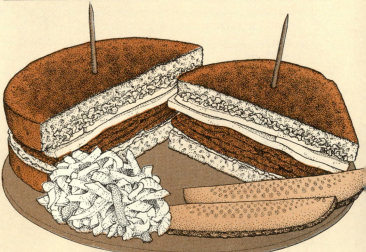

Reuben: Spread *2 slices rye bread* with *Russian Dressing*. Arrange *thin slices of corned beef* and *Swiss cheese* on 1 slice; top with *sauerkraut*, well drained. Cover with second slice of bread. Lightly *butter* outside of bread and pan fry until golden on both sides. Cut in half, secure with cocktail sticks; serve with *coleslaw* and *Dill Pickles* (p.377).
Bagel: Fill a *sliced bagel* with *lettuce leaves* and favorite deli filling such as *chopped chicken liver* and *sliced onions* or *hot pastrami* and *mustard*. Serve with *Dill Pickles* (p.377).

CALIFORNIA OPEN SANDWICH

The open sandwich, originally a Scandinavian idea, is now enjoyed all over America. Use a firm bread like rye as a base.

Spread *1 large slice rye bread*, buttered, with *Green Mayonnaise Dressing* (p.385); top with *flaked crab meat* and garnish with *Lemon Twists* (p.100) and *watercress sprigs*.

THE COUNTRY CLUB SANDWICH

This favorite lunch-time sandwich is found all over America; it is traditionally made with three slices of buttered toast.

Top *one slice of toast* with *crisp lettuce* and *several slices of chicken breast*. Cover with *second slice of toast* and spread it with *mayonnaise*; add *slices of tomato* and *2 slices crisp bacon*. Cover with remaining toast, buttered side down. Cut into 4 triangles and secure each with cocktail sticks; serve with *Bread-and-Butter Pickles* (p.377) and *potato chips*.

OUR AMERICAN HERO

Heros are a national institution. These combination sandwiches known as submarines in New York, hoagies or grinders in Philadelphia, wedges in Italian neighbourhoods, and po'boys in New Orleans, can be made to measure up to 14 feet long!

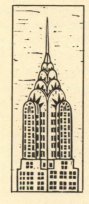

THE TRADITIONALS

Although fillings and combinations have become as varied as our diverse American heritage, certain sandwich fillings are universally popular across America. Peanut butter and jelly is still a favorite lunch-box filler; creamy egg salad on cracked wheat bread and traditional tuna salad are always number one lunch-counter specials. The simple B.L.T. – bacon, lettuce, and tomato – with crisp bacon and cool mayonnaise is now a household word.

CHILI DOGS

Frankfurters, first sold at the 1904 St. Louis World Fair, are now sold in many lengths with many toppings; try our zesty Chili Dog!

Place *one boiled* or *pan-fried frankfurter* on a *split hot-dog bun*, lightly toasted; top with *hot Chili Con Carne* (p.182), sprinkle with *chopped onions* and *shredded Cheddar cheese*.

For a super-size hero, split *one loaf of Italian bread* lengthwise; brush cut surface with *olive oil*. Fill with a choice of *sliced Italian meats*, such as salami, proscuitto, sliced ham, or mortadella; then lay *slices of provolone* or other cheese on top; add *tomato slices*, *shredded lettuce*, *sliced onions*, *sliced pitted ripe olives*, and *coarsely chopped fresh parsley*. Sprinkle with *Italian-style salad dressing*. For a roast beef wedge, split *bread* as above; spread cut surfaces with *mustard* and *mayonnaise*. Fill with *thinly sliced rare roast beef*.

Pizza

EXTRA-CHEESE PIZZA WITH BASIL

- Color index page 78
- Begin 40 mins ahead
- 6 servings
- 425 cals per serving

Pizza became popular in the U.S. when soldiers who were stationed in Italy returned. Now it is considered more American than Italian!

Basic Pizza Dough
1 package active dry yeast or fast-rising yeast
Water
2 cups all-purpose flour
Salt
Salad oil
1 tablespoon corn meal

1¼ pounds mozzarella cheese shredded (5 cups)
½ 7-ounce jar roasted sweet red peppers, drained and cut in strips
Fresh basil

1 Preheat oven to 425°F. Prepare Basic Pizza Dough: Dissolve yeast in ¾ cup very warm water (105° to 115°F.).

2 In large bowl, blend flour, ½ teaspoon salt, and yeast mixture. Cover with waxed paper; let dough rest 5 minutes.

3 Lightly brush 12- to 14-inch pizza pan with salad oil; sprinkle with cornmeal. Pat dough onto bottom of pan.

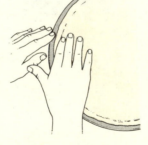

4 Shape dough into ½-inch-high rim at edge of pan; sprinkle mozzarella cheese over the pizza dough.

5 Bake pizza on bottom rack of oven 15 minutes. Remove from oven. Arrange pepper on cheese, spoke fashion, radiating from center.

6 Arrange basil leaves on both sides of red pepper strips. Return pizza to oven; bake 10 minutes longer or until crust is golden and crisp.

DEEP-DISH CHICAGO PIZZA

- Color index page 78
- Begin 1 hr ahead
- 8 servings
- 530 cals per serving

1 pound hot Italian-sausage links
Water
1 13¾-ounce package hot-roll mix
1 15-ounce jar spaghetti sauce
2 tablespoons chopped parsley
2 teaspoons sugar

½ teaspoon basil
¼ teaspoon oregano leaves
¼ teaspoon pepper
1 8-ounce package mozzarella cheese coarsely shredded
3 tablespoons grated Parmesan cheese

1. In 10-inch skillet over medium heat, heat sausages and ¼ cup water to boiling. Cover and simmer 5 minutes. Remove cover; continue cooking, turning sausages frequently, until sausages are well browned, about 20 minutes.

2. Remove sausages to paper towels to drain. With knife, cut the sausages diagonally into ¼-inch-thick slices; place the sausage slices in a bowl. Preheat oven to 400°F.

3. Grease 13" by 9" baking dish. Prepare hot-roll mix as label directs but use 1 cup water and omit egg; do not let dough rise. Pat the dough onto the bottom and halfway up the sides of the baking dish to make a stand-up edge.

4. In medium bowl, mix spaghetti sauce, next 5 ingredients, and sliced sausage. Sprinkle half of mozzarella over the dough in the baking dish; top with spaghetti-sauce mixture, Parmesan cheese, and remaining mozzarella.

5. Bake the pizza on the bottom rack of the oven 25 minutes or until the topping is hot and bubbly and the crust is browned and crisp.

AVOCADO-TOMATO PIZZA

- Color index page 78
- Begin 45 mins ahead
- 6 servings
- 430 cals per serving

Basic Pizza Dough (left)
1 10-ounce package sharp Cheddar cheese, shredded (2½ cups)
1 small avocado
1 medium tomato
1 tablespoon cider vinegar

½ 8¾- to 10½-ounce can red kidney beans, drained
2 tablespoons chopped parsley

1. Preheat oven to 425°F. Prepare Basic Pizza Dough (steps 1 to 3). Shape dough into ½-inch-high rim at edge of pizza pan.

2. Sprinkle Cheddar cheese over the dough. Place the pizza on the bottom rack of the oven and bake 15 minutes.

3. Meanwhile peel, pit, and cut the avocado into ½-inch pieces; chop the tomato. In a bowl, mix the avocado, tomato, and vinegar. In small bowl mix kidney beans and parsley.

4. Remove the pizza from the oven. Drain the avocado mixture well. Arrange the bean mixture on the center of the pizza. Spoon the avocado mixture around the bean mixture, leaving a 1-inch border of cheese around the edge.

5. Return the pizza to the oven; bake about 10 minutes longer or until the topping is hot and the crust is browned and crisp. If you like, transfer the pizza to a large, warmed serving platter.

PICKLES PRESERVES RELISHES

"You ought to have seen what I saw on my way . . .
Blueberries as big as the end of your thumb,
Real sky-blue, and heavy and ready to drum
In the cavernous pail of the first one to come!"

ROBERT FROST "Blueberries"

In early colonial America, the storage and preservation of all food was a matter of survival, especially in the colder climates. Various methods of salting and drying were used for meats and fish. Produce such as potatoes, cabbage, squash, and root vegetables was stored in special "root cellars," dug out and provided with adequate ventilation. Old letters refer to these methods of food preservation, but there are very few recipes from the time, as each family stored their own food in their own way.

It is probably the Pennsylvania Dutch more than any other ethnic group who have influenced preserving food in America. These early German farmers, fleeing from religious persecution, cherished their food, because in many cases their European enemies had destroyed their crops and orchards to drive them away. Settling in southeast Pennsylvania, they farmed the fertile lands and built houses with large kitchens to serve as food preparation centers.

The general availability of sugar made the preserving of jams, jellies, pickles, and relishes an art in these early kitchens. They developed recipes and techniques for canning beautiful fruits and vegetables and are famous for their fruit butters, like our Apricot Butter. The combination of flavors and spices in their relishes and sauces is still renowned, and some Pennsylvania Dutch say no meal is complete without seven sweet and seven sour condiments. It was also in Pennsylvania that Henry J. Heinz, still the most well-known name in relishes and condiments, began selling his "57 Varieties."

In the South, the spice trade was bringing exotic ingredients and recipes through American seaports like Charleston and along with these dishes came the taste for chutneys, pickles, and preserved fruits. A plate of Pickled Peaches and Apricots or Spicy Watermelon Pickles might still accompany a meal in the South today.

In the late 19th century, the introduction of canning jars encouraged more people to "put up" home-grown fruits and vegetables. But in the early 1900s, commercial canning was becoming big business and the industry was refining instructions and techniques for the home canner.

With the advent of the freezer, home canning declined, but more recently there has been a renewed interest in the art of preserving. As the homemaker looks for good ways of making use of excess garden produce or local farmstand products, making preserves like our Grape Jelly, Strawberry Jam and Red Pepper Freezer Jelly, the old-fashioned ideas of food preservation are reappearing. Surely there is nothing so satisfying as seeing neat rows of your own clear shimmering jellies, thick fruit jams and butters, and colorful pickles and relishes displayed in the family kitchen or pantry.

EQUIPMENT FOR HOME PRESERVING

Before starting to prepare food to be preserved, make sure that you are using the right kind of equipment and that it is in good working order.

Canner

Rack

Jar Lifter or Tongs

Metal Spoon

Canning Jars and Lids

Paraffin and Can for Melting

Jelly Glasses

Pickles

BREAD-AND-BUTTER PICKLES

16 cups sliced cucumbers, about ¼-inch thick (about 4 pounds)
6 cups thinly sliced onions
½ cup salt
Water
5 cups sugar
5 cups cider vinegar
1½ teaspoons turmeric
1½ teaspoons celery seeds
1½ teaspoons mustard seeds
6 1-pint canning jars and caps

1. In 8-quart container, mix well the cucumbers, onions, and salt. Cover with cold water and 3 trays ice cubes; let stand 3 hours. Drain the vegetables; rinse them well and drain again; set vegetables aside.

2. In 8-quart Dutch oven, mix the sugar with the cider vinegar, turmeric, celery seeds, and mustard seeds; over high heat, heat the mixture to boiling. Reduce the heat; simmer, uncovered, 30 minutes or until the mixture is syrupy; stir the mixture often.

3. Meanwhile, prepare jars and caps for processing (p.382). Add the cucumbers and onions to the syrup. Over high heat, heat almost to boiling, stirring occasionally; do not boil. Ladle hot mixture into hot jars, to ¼ inch from top; wipe tops and threads of jars with damp cloth; close jars. Process jars in boiling-water bath (p.382) 10 minutes. Cool at least 12 hours. Test seal (p.382). Store in cool, dark, dry place.

- Color index page 79
- Begin day ahead
- 6 pints
- 35 cals per ¼ cup

SUNCHOKE PICKLES

1 medium onion, thinly sliced
1 cup water
1 cup white vinegar
½ cup sugar
½ teaspoon salt
½ teaspoon mustard seeds
½ teaspoon dry mustard
⅛ teaspoon celery seeds
⅛ teaspoon crushed red pepper
2 pounds sunchokes (Jerusalem artichokes)

1. In 2-quart saucepan, combine sliced onion, water, white vinegar, sugar, salt, mustard seeds, dry mustard, celery seeds, and crushed red pepper; set aside.

2. Peel sunchokes; cut into thin slices. Add sliced sunchokes to mixture in saucepan as soon as they are sliced. (Sunchokes will darken upon exposure to air after peeling.)

3. Over high heat, heat the sunchoke mixture to boiling. Reduce the heat to low; simmer, uncovered, about 15 minutes or until the sunchokes are tender-crisp, stirring the sunchoke mixture occasionally.

4. Pour the sunchokes and their liquid into a medium bowl. Cover and refrigerate until well chilled. Store in refrigerator up to 1 week. Serve with hamburgers, roast poultry, pork, or beef.

- Color index page 79
- Begin 4 hrs or 1 wk ahead
- 4 cups
- 40 cals per ¼ cup

DILL PICKLES

This all-time favorite pickle, often stored in crocks or barrels, is a traditional accompaniment to delicatessen-style sandwiches. Try making your own.

About 20 small cucumbers, each about 3 to 3½ inches long (about 4¼ pounds)
4 medium garlic cloves
1 medium bunch fresh dill (about 16 large sprigs)
¼ cup mixed pickling spice
2 teaspoons dill seeds
¼ teaspoon crushed red pepper

- Color index page 79
- Begin 5 to 8 days ahead
- 20 pickles
- 15 cals per pickle

2 quarts water
½ cup white vinegar
½ cup noniodized salt
2 tablespoons sugar

1 Wash cucumbers thoroughly under running cold water to remove any sand and grit; drain. With flat side of knife, and on a cutting board, crush each of the garlic cloves slightly.

2 In bottom of 2-gallon crock or wide-mouth jar, place 2 garlic cloves, half of fresh dill, half of mixed pickling spice, half of dill seeds, and half of crushed red pepper.

3 Pack cucumbers into crock to 3 inches from top of crock. Add remaining garlic, pickling spice, dill seeds, and crushed red pepper. Top with layer of remaining fresh dill.

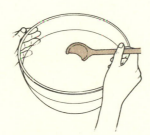

4 In large bowl, mix water, vinegar, salt, and sugar until salt and sugar dissolve.

5 Pour saltwater brine into crock or jar to completely cover the cucumbers.

6 Cover cucumbers with clean heavy plate or something similar to hold them under brine.

7 Place crock on stainproof surface (brine may overflow as pickles ferment). Keep at 70°F. 3 to 5 days for half sour, 8 days for very sour.

8 Check pickles every day and remove any scum that forms over the top. (The development of some cloudiness in the brine is also typical.)

9 When pickles have reached the degree of sourness you like, they can be stored in the refrigerator to be used up within 1 month. To store the dill pickles in the refrigerator, remove them from the crock, reserving the brine. Pack the pickles in jars. Strain the brine and pour over the pickles to completely cover them. (Do not leave the pickles at room temperature after fermentation is complete or they may spoil.)

Pickles

PICKLED VEGETABLE MEDLEY

This colorful vegetable mix, preserved in a zesty brine, makes a perfect accompaniment to barbecued meats in summer, or a cheerful addition to the table any time of the year.

- *Color index page 79*
- *Begin day ahead*
- *6 pints*
- *30 cals per ¼ cup*

4 medium carrots
4 medium celery stalks
3 large cucumbers
3 medium red peppers
2 medium onions
1 medium head broccoli

4 quarts water
1 cup salt
6 1-pint canning jars and caps
6½ cups white vinegar

2 cups sugar
2 tablespoons mustard seeds
½ teaspoon crushed red pepper

1 Cut the carrots and celery into ½-inch-long pieces. If you like, peel cucumbers, leaving a few strips of skin on them for color; cut into ½-inch-thick slices.

2 Cut red peppers into ¼-inch-wide strips. Cut onions into ¼-inch-thick slices. Cut broccoli into bite-sized flowerets.

3 In 10-quart enamel, stainless steel, or glass container, stir water and salt until salt dissolves. Add vegetables and cover; let stand in cool place about 6 hours.

4 Meanwhile, prepare jars and caps for processing (p.382). Drain vegetables; rinse with running cold water; drain again thoroughly.

5 In 8-quart saucepot or Dutch oven over high heat, heat vinegar, sugar, mustard seeds, and crushed red pepper to boiling; stir occasionally.

6 Reduce heat to medium; cover; cook 5 minutes. Add vegetables; heat to boiling. Reduce heat to low; cover; simmer 5 minutes; stir often.

7 With slotted spoon, spoon vegetables into hot jars to ¼ inch from top. Add hot vinegar mixture to ¼ inch from top. (Simmer while filling jars.)

8 With small spatula, carefully remove any air bubbles between the vegetables and the jar. Close the jars as manufacturer directs.

9 Process jars in boiling-water bath (p.382) 15 minutes. With jar lifter or tongs, remove jars from canner; set jars, several inches apart, on wire racks. Complete seal on jars with glass or zinc caps as manufacturer directs. Do not tighten screw bands. Cool at least 12 hours. Now, test seal (p.382). Store unsealed jars in refrigerator to use within one month. Store sealed jars in cool, dark, dry place; use up pickles within one year.

SPICY WATERMELON PICKLES

Rind from 1 medium watermelon
½ cup noniodized salt
Water
9 3-inch cinnamon sticks
1 tablespoon whole cloves

Small square cheesecloth
4 cups sugar
2 cups white vinegar
5 1-pint canning jars and caps

1. Trim and discard dark-green skin from rind; cut rind into 1-inch pieces (about 14 cups).
2. In large bowl, dissolve salt in 6 cups water; add rind and water to cover; cover and refrigerate.
3. *Next day:* Drain rind; rinse in running cold water and drain again.
4. In 10-quart kettle, cover rind with cold water. Over high heat, heat to boiling; reduce heat to low; simmer 30 minutes; drain.
5. Tie spices in cheesecloth. In same kettle, combine sugar, vinegar, 2 cups water, spice bag, and rind. Heat to boiling. Reduce heat; cover; simmer 1 hour, stir often; remove from heat. Prepare jars and caps for processing (p.382).
6. Discard spice bag. Ladle hot mixture into jars, to ¼ inch from top; close jars. Process jars in boiling-water bath (p.382) 10 minutes; cool; test seal (p.382).

- *Color index page 79*
- *Begin day ahead*
- *5 pints*
- *55 cals per ¼ cup*

PICKLED BEETS

2 tablespoons sugar
¾ teaspoon salt
½ teaspoon dry mustard
⅛ teaspoon ground cloves

⅓ cup cider vinegar
⅓ cup water
1 16-ounce can sliced beets, drained
1 medium onion, sliced

1. In medium bowl, mix the first 4 ingredients; stir in vinegar, water, beets, and onion.
2. Cover and refrigerate, stirring occasionally. Serve with pork or beef.

- *Color index page 79*
- *Begin early in day*
- *3¾ cups*
- *18 cals per ¼ cup*

SPICED PRUNES

Water
1 pound pitted large prunes
1 cup sugar

1 cup cider vinegar
1 teaspoon ground cinnamon
1 teaspoon ground cloves

1. In 2-quart saucepan over high heat, in water to cover, heat prunes to boiling; reduce heat to low; cover and simmer 10 minutes; drain.
2. In same saucepan over high heat, heat to boiling remaining ingredients with 1 cup water; boil the mixture 1 minute.
3. Add prunes and heat to boiling. Cover and refrigerate for up to 2 weeks.

- *Color index page 79*
- *Begin day or up to 2 wks ahead*
- *3 cups*
- *162 cals per ¼ cup*

Preserves

PICKLED PEACHES AND APRICOTS

- Color index page 79
- Begin day ahead
- 6 pints
- 58 cals per ¼ cup

4 pounds medium peaches	2½ cups sugar
5 3-inch cinnamon sticks	2 cups cider vinegar
2 teaspoons whole cloves	6 1-pint canning jars and caps
Small square cheesecloth	
1½ pounds apricots, unpeeled	

1. Peel peaches and cut in half; remove pits.
2. Place peaches in 8-quart kettle or Dutch oven. Cover with boiling water; cook over high heat 3 minutes; (do not boil).
3. With slotted spoon, remove peaches to large bowl. Drain all but 1 cup liquid from kettle. Tie spices in cheesecloth.
4. In same kettle over high heat, heat apricots, spice bag, sugar, vinegar, and 1 cup liquid to boiling; boil 5 minutes. Pour mixture over peaches. Let stand overnight.
5. *Next day:* Prepare jars and caps for processing (p.382). Remove skins from apricots. In 8-quart kettle over high heat, heat the peaches and the apricots, and liquid to boiling.
6. Discard the spice bag. Place the fruit in hot jars; ladle hot syrup over fruit, to ¼ inch from top of jar. Close jars as manufacturer directs. Process jars in boiling-water bath (p.382) 15 minutes. Cool at least 12 hours. Test seal (p.382).

SPICED CRAB APPLES

- Color index page 79
- Begin day ahead
- 8 pints
- 107 cals per ¼ cup

8 pounds crab apples	Small square cheesecloth
7 3-inch cinnamon sticks	8½ cups sugar
2 tablespoons whole cloves	3 cups cider vinegar
2 tablespoons whole allspice	2 cups water
	8 1-pint canning jars and caps

1. Leave stems on crab apples; scrape out any hard bits in blossom ends. Run a skewer through each apple (to help prevent bursting). To make a spice bag, tie cinnamon sticks, whole cloves, and whole allspice in cheesecloth.
2. In 10-quart kettle or Dutch oven over high heat, heat sugar, vinegar, water, and bag of spices to boiling. Reduce heat to medium; cover kettle tightly and cook 5 minutes.
3. Add the apples; heat to boiling; cover, then simmer 10 minutes or until the apples are tender. Remove kettle or Dutch oven from heat; let apple mixture stand overnight.
4. Prepare jars and caps for processing (p.382). Drain apples, reserving syrup; discard the spice bag. In heavy saucepan, over high heat, heat syrup to boiling.
5. Place apples in hot jars; ladle hot syrup over them, to ¼ inch from top of jar. Close jars as manufacturer directs. Process jars in boiling-water bath (p.382) 15 minutes. Cool; test seal (p.382). Store in a cool, dark, dry, place. Flavors will blend and mellow if allowed to stand several weeks before eating.

APRICOT BUTTER

Colonial Americans made fruit "butters" from very ripe fruit; if no sugar or honey was available, the natural sweetness was enough.

- Color index page 80
- Begin 45 mins or up to 1 wk ahead
- 1½ cups
- 35 cals per tablespoon

1 8-ounce package dried apricot halves	¼ cup sugar
1 6-ounce can unsweetened pineapple juice (¾ cup)	1½ cups water

1 In 3-quart saucepan over high heat, heat all ingredients to boiling. Reduce heat to low and cover; simmer 25 minutes or until the fruit is very tender; stir occasionally.

2 Remove cover and continue to cook 10 minutes longer or until liquid is absorbed and mixture is thick, stirring often to prevent fruit mixture from burning.

3 Press fruit mixture through food mill or coarse sieve into a large mixing bowl.

4 Spoon into containers with tightly fitting lids; refrigerate. Serve as jam or jelly.

PEACH BUTTER: Prepare as for Apricot Butter above, but substitute *one 8-ounce package dried peach halves* for dried apricot halves and *¾ cup orange juice* for pineapple juice. Makes about 1½ cups. 30 cals per tablespoon.

CHUNKY APPLESAUCE

- Color index page 79
- Begin 2 hrs ahead
- 3 cups
- 58 cals per ¼ cup

6 medium cooking apples	1 teaspoon lemon juice
½ cup water	Dash ground cinnamon
⅓ cup sugar	

1. Peel and core apples; Remove any seeds. Cut up apples. In 3-quart saucepan over high heat, heat apples and water to boiling. Reduce heat to low; cover and simmer 8 to 10 minutes, stirring occasionally until apples are tender.
2. Stir in sugar, lemon juice, and cinnamon. Cover and refrigerate until ready to serve.

Preserves

CRAN-APPLE JELLY

Jelly is made by boiling fruit juice and sugar, usually with additional fruit pectin. Try a spoonful of this tasty combination in meat sauces and gravies for extra zest.

9 green medium cooking apples (3 pounds)
3 cups water
Cheesecloth
About 2 cups cranberry-juice cocktail
8 8-ounce jelly glasses and lids or other 8-ounce heat-safe glasses

Paraffin
1 3½-inch cinnamon stick
String
½ teaspoon whole allspice

1 tablespoon lemon juice
1 1¾-ounce package powdered fruit pectin
5 cups sugar

- *Color index page 79*
- *Begin day ahead*
- *Eight 8-ounce glasses*
- *40 cals per tablespoon*

1 With small, sharp knife on a cutting board, remove and discard stem and blossom end of apples (do not core or peel the apples). Cut the apples into bite-sized pieces. In 5-quart Dutch oven or saucepot over high heat, heat the apple pieces and the water to boiling. Reduce heat to low; cover Dutch oven and simmer the apples 25 minutes until they are very tender.

2 Use four layers of damp cheesecloth to completely line the inside of a colander or a very large strainer.

3 Over large bowl, pour apple mixture into colander; let stand until the juice drains into bowl, at least 3 hours.

4 Add enough cranberry juice to apple juice to make 3½ cups. Set aside. (Do not squeeze mixture in cheesecloth, or jelly may be cloudy.)

5 Prepare eight 8-ounce glasses and lids for making jelly, and melt paraffin (p.382). Break the cinnamon stick into small pieces.

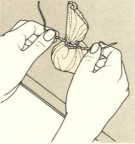

6 Tie cinnamon pieces and the allspice in cheesecloth bag. Place in 8-quart Dutch oven with apple, cranberry, lemon juice, and pectin.

7 Over high heat, heat to boiling, stirring often; immediately add sugar and, stirring, heat to a full rolling boil.

8 Boil for 1 minute. Discard spice bag. Remove from heat; with spoon skim off foam.

9 Immediately ladle jelly into glasses to ½ inch from the top. Quickly add hot paraffin. Spread to ⅛-inch thick layer with tip of spoon so it touches side of glass all around. Prick any air bubbles in paraffin. When cool, cover glasses with lids. Store opened jelly in refrigerator. Store unopened jelly in cool, dark, dry place to use up within 1 year.

GRAPE JELLY

4 8-ounce jelly glasses and lids or other 8-ounce heat-safe glasses
Paraffin
2 cups unsweetened bottled grape juice

1 cup water
1 1¾-ounce packaged powdered fruit pectin
3½ cups sugar

1. Prepare glasses and lids for making jelly (p.382). Melt paraffin (p.382).
2. In 6-quart Dutch oven or heavy saucepot, mix grape juice, water, and fruit pectin. Over high heat, heat mixture to boiling, stirring constantly. Immediately stir in sugar. Stirring constantly, heat until mixture comes to a full rolling boil; boil 1 minute. Remove Dutch oven from heat. With spoon, skim off foam.
3. Immediately ladle mixture into glasses to ½ inch from top and seal with paraffin (p.382). When cool, cover glasses with lids.

- *Color index page 79*
- *Begin early in day*
- *Four 8-ounce glasses*
- *50 cals per tablespoon*

RED-PEPPER FREEZER JELLY

6 large hot red chilies
4 large sweet red peppers
2 cups white wine vinegar
5 whole allspice
6 8-ounce freezer-safe, dishwasher-safe containers with tight-fitting lids

Cheesecloth
4 cups sugar
½ teaspoon salt
1 1¾-ounce package powdered fruit pectin
¾ cup water

1. Finely chop chilies and peppers; do not discard chili seeds. In 4-quart saucepan over high heat, heat chilies, peppers, vinegar, and allspice to boiling. Reduce heat to low; cover; simmer 30 minutes until tender. Wash containers and lids in hot, soapy water; rinse. Slowly pour boiling water inside and out of freezer-safe containers or glasses and lids; invert on clean towel, away from drafts, to drain dry. Or, wash them in dishwasher, set for the rinse cycle, with very hot water (150° or higher) and leave in dishwasher until you are ready to fill them.
2. Line large strainer with 4 layers of damp cheesecloth; place in 8-quart mixing bowl. Pour chili mixture into strainer; let the mixture stand until 2¼ cups juice drain into cup, about 2½ hours. (Amount of juice may vary; add water to make 2¼ cups.) Do not squeeze cheesecloth or jelly may be cloudy. Stir sugar and salt into juice; let stand 10 minutes.
3. In saucepan, heat pectin and water to boiling, stirring; pour into juice; stir 3 minutes (no less); a few sugar crystals may remain. Pour into containers to ½ inch from top; cover. Stand at room temperature 24 hours. Freeze to use in 1 year, or refrigerate to use in 3 weeks.

- *Color index page 79*
- *Begin day ahead*
- *Six 8-ounce containers*
- *35 cals per tablespoon*

BLUEBERRY JAM

- Color index page 80
- Begin early in day
- 9 ½-pint jars
- 40 cals per tablespoon

9 ½-pint canning jars and caps
About 3 pints blueberries
7 cups sugar
2 tablespoons lemon juice
1 6-ounce package liquid fruit pectin

1. Prepare jars and caps for processing (p.382).
2. With potato masher, thoroughly crush blueberries to make 4 cups. In 8-quart saucepot or Dutch oven, mix well the blueberries, sugar, and lemon juice.
3. Over high heat, heat mixture to boiling, stirring constantly; boil rapidly 1 minute, stirring the mixture constantly.
4. Remove from heat; stir in fruit pectin. With spoon, skim off foam. Immediately ladle mixture into hot jars to ¼ inch from top (keep mixture simmering while filling jars). Close jars as manufacturer directs.
5. Process the jars in boiling-water bath (p.382) 5 minutes; cool the jars and test seal (p.382) to be sure it is airtight.

PEACH PRESERVES

- Color index page 80
- Begin early in the day
- 8 ½-pint jars
- 37 cals per tablespoon

12 firm very large peaches (about 6 pounds)
5 cups sugar
½ cup lemon juice
2 teaspoons salt
8 ½-pint canning jars and caps

1. With small, sharp knife, peel, pit, and cut peaches into thin slices.
2. In 8-quart Dutch oven or heavy saucepot over medium-high heat, heat peaches, sugar, lemon juice, and salt to boiling, stirring frequently. Reduce heat to medium-low; gently simmer, uncovered, stirring frequently with wooden spoon, about 1 hour or until the fruit is translucent and the syrup thickens slightly.
3. Meanwhile, prepare jars and caps for processing (p. 382).
4. With large metal spoon, skim off foam from preserves, if necessary. Immediately ladle hot peach mixture into hot jars to ¼ inch from top (keep mixture simmering while filling jars). Close jars as manufacturer directs. Process jars in boiling-water bath (p.382) 15 minutes; cool jars and test seal (p.382).

Skimming foam: Use a metal spoon to skim off any foam from the surface of the preserve mixture.

Filling the jars: Ladle the hot peach mixture into jars to ¼ inch from the top.

STRAWBERRY JAM

Jams have a thicker texture than jellies and contain the fruit as well as the juice. Take advantage of beautiful berries in season and make this luscious jam.

- Color index page 80
- Begin early in day
- 8 ½-pint jars
- 45 cals per tablespoon

8 ½-pint canning jars and caps
About 2-quarts fully ripened strawberries
7 cups sugar
¼ cup lemon juice
½ 6-ounce package liquid fruit pectin

1 Prepare jars and caps for processing (p.382). Hull the strawberries. With potato masher, crush strawberries well, one layer at a time, to make 3¾ cups crushed fruit.

2 In 8-quart saucepot or Dutch oven, mix well strawberries, sugar, and lemon juice. Over high heat, heat mixture to boiling, stirring constantly; boil rapidly 1 minute, stirring.

3 Remove from heat; stir in fruit pectin. With metal spoon, skim off foam. Immediately ladle mixture into hot jars to ¼ inch from top and keep mixture simmering while filling the jars.

4 Close jars as manufacturer directs. Process jars in boiling-water bath (p.382) 5 minutes; cool jars and test seal (p.382). Store in cool, dark, dry place for up to 1 year.

SWEET-CHERRY JAM: Prepare as above, but for strawberries, substitute about *3 pounds Bing* or *other sweet cherries*. Remove the stems and seeds from the cherries; with small, sharp knife on cutting board, finely chop enough cherries to make 3½ cups fruit. Use *one 6-ounce package liquid fruit pectin*. Makes about nine ½-pint jars. 35 cals per tablespoon.

SOUR-CHERRY JAM: Prepare as Strawberry Jam above, but for strawberries, substitute *3 pounds sour cherries*. Remove the stems and the seeds from the cherries; with a small, sharp knife, finely chop enough cherries to make 4 cups. Omit the lemon juice. Use *one 6-ounce package liquid pectin*. Makes about nine ½-pint jars. 34 cals per tablespoon.

Preserves

HOW TO PREPARE FOR HOME PRESERVING

Home canning is the traditional way to preserve seasonal fruits and vegetables. Foods are preserved by heating them hot enough and long enough to destroy harmful organisms and stop enzyme action.

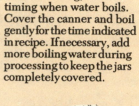

Heat to boiling; start timing when water boils. Cover the canner and boil gently for the time indicated in recipe. If necessary, add more boiling water during processing to keep the jars completely covered.

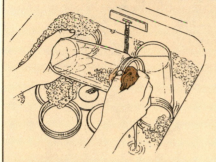

To Prepare Jars and Caps For Processing: Check there are no nicks, cracks, or sharp edges. Wash all pieces in hot soapy water; rinse. Metal lids with sealing compound may need boiling; check manufacturer's directions. Leave in hot water until ready to use; if using rubber rings, keep them wet until used so that they are pliable and stretch easily.

After filling, run a narrow rubber spatula between food and side of jar to remove any air bubbles; metal utensils may chip or cause jar to crack. Wipe jar rim (and threads) clean; cover with cap or lid.

To Process Jars In Boiling-Water Bath: Place rack on bottom of canner; fill half full with hot water. Over high heat, heat to full boiling. Place filled jars in canner so water can circulate freely; add additional boiling water if needed, to come to 1 to 2 inches over jars (do not pour water directly on jars).

With tongs or jar lifter, remove jars from canner; seal caps as manufacturer directs. Cool jars, top side up, on a wooden board or folded towels, away from drafts. Set jars 2 or 3 inches apart so air can circulate.

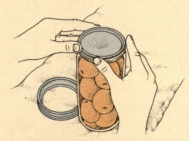

To Test Seal: When jars are cool, at least 12 hours after processing, test seal. If using 2-piece caps, carefully remove the screw band; if center of lid has slight dip and will not move, jar is sealed.

If center can be pushed down and stays down, seal is questionable; hold jar over a padded surface (to avoid breakage) and carefully lift lid by edges.

If lid comes off, use the food promptly; if not, jar is sealed. Store jars without replacing screw bands.

Test jars with rubber rings by turning them partly over; if there is no leakage or bubbles rising from lid through contents, jar is sealed.

HOW TO PREPARE FOR MAKING JELLY

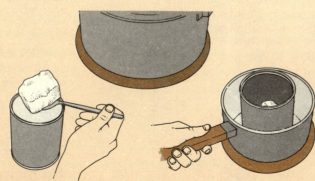

Sterilizing Glasses and Jars: Boil 10 minutes in enough water to cover. Prepare lids and screw bands as manufacturer directs. Prepare jelly as recipe directs.

To Melt Paraffin: Place paraffin in small, clean metal can and set in saucepan filled with 1 inch water.

Over medium heat, heat, uncovered, until paraffin melts (never melt paraffin over direct heat; it catches fire easily). Keep hot.

To Seal Jelly Glasses With Paraffin: Pour hot mixture into hot glasses to ½ inch from top. Cover with ⅛-inch-thick layer of melted paraffin, making sure paraffin touches the glass at all points to seal. Prick any bubbles.

Relishes

GREEN-TOMATO CHOW CHOW

Chow chow, a delicious relish made from any combination of mixed pickled vegetables, is the perfect way to use up the odds and ends from the garden at the end of the summer.

12 medium green
   tomatoes (about 5
   pounds)
2 pounds green beans
4 medium red peppers
4 medium onions
4 quarts water
1 cup salt

6 1-pint canning jars and
   caps
2½ cups white vinegar
1½ cups sugar
1 tablespoon minced,
   peeled gingerroot or
   ¾ teaspoon ground
   ginger

- Color index page 80
- Begin day ahead
- 6 pints
- 9 cals per tablespoon.

1 tablespoon dry mustard
1 tablespoon mustard
   seeds
1 teaspoon turmeric

1 Cut and discard stem ends from tomatoes; cut into chunks; cut green beans into 2-inch pieces; cut peppers into chunks; cut onions into wedges.

2 In 10-quart enamel, stainless steel, or glass container, stir water and salt until salt is dissolved. Add vegetables; cover and let stand in a cool place about 6 hours.

3 Prepare jars and caps for processing (p.382). Leave jars and caps in hot water until ready to use. Wet rubber rings before using to make them more pliable.

4 Drain vegetables; rinse with running cold water; drain thoroughly. In 8-quart sauce-pot or Dutch oven over high heat, heat vinegar, sugar, ginger, dry mustard, mustard seeds, and turmeric to boiling, stirring the mixture occasionally. Reduce heat to medium; cover and cook 5 minutes. Add vegetables; heat to boiling. Reduce heat to low; cover; simmer 10 minutes longer, stirring the vegetables occasionally.

5 With slotted spoon, spoon the hot vegetables into the hot jars, to ¼ inch from top of each jar.

6 Immediately ladle hot vinegar mixture over the vegetables in the jars to within ¼ inch of top of jar.

7 With small spatula, carefully remove any air bubbles between vegetables and jar. Close jars as manufacturer directs.

8 Process jars in boiling-water bath (p.382) 10 minutes. With jar lifter or tongs, remove jars from canner.

9 Set the jars, several inches apart, on wire racks. Complete the seal on jars with glass or zinc caps as manufacturer directs. Do not tighten the screw bands. Cool at least 12 hours. Now, test seal (p.382). Store unsealed jars in refrigerator to use within one month. Store sealed jars in cool, dark, dry place to use within one year. Serve as an accompaniment to roasted or barbecued meats.

AMERICAN HEIRLOOM CHUTNEY

2 large cooking apples,
   diced
2 medium onions, diced
1 medium green or red
   pepper, cut into
   ½-inch pieces
1 garlic clove, crushed
¾ cup white vinegar
¾ cup sugar
½ cup water

1 12-ounce package pitted
   prunes, each cut in half
1 tablespoon peeled,
   grated gingerroot
2 teaspoons mustard
   seeds
½ teaspoon salt
½ teaspoon crushed red
   pepper

1. In 3-quart saucepan over medium-high heat, heat apples, onions, pepper, garlic, vinegar, sugar, and water to boiling. Reduce heat to low; simmer, uncovered, 15 minutes or until vegetables are tender, stirring occasionally.
2. Add prunes and remaining ingredients; continue cooking until mixture thickens slightly and becomes syrupy, about 35 minutes. Store in jars in refrigerator to use within 2 weeks.

- Color index page 80
- Begin day ahead
  or up to 2 wks ahead
- 4 cups
- 30 cals per tablespoon

CRANBERRY SAUCE

1 cup sugar
1 cup water

1 12-ounce package
   cranberries

In 2-quart saucepan over medium heat, heat sugar and water to boiling. Add cranberries and return to the boil. Reduce heat to low; cover and simmer 7 minutes or until berries pop.

- Color index page 80
- Begin 20 mins ahead
- 2¼ cups
- 22 cals per tablespoon

CRANBERRY-APPLE RELISH

2 medium oranges
1 lemon
2 cooking apples

4 cups cranberries
2½ cups sugar

1. Cut unpeeled oranges and lemon into quarters; remove seeds; core apples; do not peel.
2. Put first 4 ingredients through food grinder using medium blade. Stir in sugar. Cover, refrigerate. Serve within several days.

- Color index page 80
- Begin early in day
- 6¾ cups
- 23 cals per tablespoon

CRANBERRY-TANGERINE: Omit lemon and apples. For oranges, substitute 3 large tangerines; remove seeds and membranes; use peel; prepare as above. Makes 4 cups. 23 cals per tablespoon.

CRANBERRY-PINEAPPLE: Omit oranges and apples. Grind lemon with cranberries as above. With sugar, stir one 8¼-ounce can crushed pineapple, undrained. Makes 4 cups. 20 cals per tablespoon.

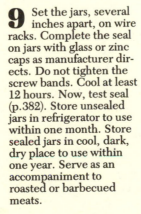

Relishes

CUCUMBER-MINT RELISH

- Color index page 80
- Begin day or up to 1 week ahead
- 5¼ cups
- 20 cals per tablespoon

3 medium cucumbers; peeled
½ cup water
⅔ cup white vinegar
1 tablespoon sugar
⅓ cup chopped fresh mint
1 teaspoon salt
¼ teaspoon pepper

1. Cut cucumbers in half lengthwise, then crosswise into ¼-inch-thick slices. Place in bowl with remaining ingredients; toss with fork.
2. Cover and refrigerate. Store in refrigerator up to 1 week. Serve with hot or cold foods.

SWEET-AND-SOUR RELISH

- Color index page 80
- Begin early in day or up to 2 wks ahead
- 5½ cups
- 15 cals per tablespoon

9 medium onions (about 3 pounds)
1 medium green pepper
1 medium red pepper
2 bay leaves
8 whole cloves
½ teaspoon whole peppercorns
½ teaspoon crushed red pepper
Cheesecloth
String
¾ cup light corn syrup
½ cup sugar
½ cup white vinegar
1½ teaspoons salt
1½ teaspoons dry mustard
½ teaspoon celery seeds

1. Thinly slice onions. Cut peppers in strips.
2. Break bay leaves into several pieces. Wrap bay leaves, cloves, peppercorns, and crushed red pepper in piece of double-thickness cheesecloth. Tie spice bag with string.
3. In 5-quart saucepot over medium heat, heat corn syrup, sugar, vinegar, salt, dry mustard, celery seeds, and spice bag to boiling, stirring occasionally. Reduce heat to low; simmer, uncovered, 5 minutes, stirring occasionally.
4. Stir in onions and peppers; over high heat, heat to boiling. Reduce heat to low; cover and simmer 15 minutes or until tender. Discard spice bag. Store in tightly covered jars in refrigerator to use up within 2 weeks.

PEPPER-PEAR RELISH

- Color index page 80
- Begin day ahead
- 5 pints
- 20 cals per tablespoon

10 large pears (about 5 pounds)
5 medium red peppers
5 medium green peppers
2 cups cider vinegar
2 cups packed dark-brown sugar
2 tablespoons salt
2 tablespoons minced peeled gingerroot
1 tablespoon mustard seeds
5 1-pint canning jars and caps

1. Peel, core, and cut pears into ½-inch chunks. Remove seeds and membrane from peppers; dice.
2. In 8-quart Dutch oven or heavy saucepot over high heat, heat all relish ingredients to boiling, stirring. Reduce heat to low; cover and simmer 40 minutes, stirring occasionally; remove cover and simmer 30 minutes, stirring frequently.
3. Meanwhile, prepare jars and caps for processing (p.382). Ladle relish into hot jars to ¼ inch from top. Close jars as manufacturer directs. Process in boiling-water bath (p.382) 20 minutes; cool; test seal (p.382).

PICCALILLI

The Shakers gave this colorful relish its lively name; use it to garnish hamburgers, hot dogs or any cold meat.

- Color index page 80
- Begin early in day
- 6 pints
- 14 cals per tablespoon

2½ pounds green tomatoes
6 cups cider vinegar
6 medium green peppers
6 medium red peppers
4 medium onions
Water
6 1-pint canning jars and caps
3½ cups sugar
¼ cup mustard seeds
¼ cup salt
2 tablespoon celery seeds
2 teaspoons ground allspice
1 teaspoon ground cinnamon

1 Cut enough tomatoes into quarters (or eighths, if large) to make 8 cups. Put 1 cup vinegar and one-fourth of tomatoes into blender container; cover; blender-chop.

2 Pour chopped tomatoes with vinegar into 10-quart kettle or Dutch oven. Repeat three more times until 4 cups vinegar have been used and all tomatoes have been chopped.

3 With small knife, cut peppers into eighths; remove seeds and membranes.

4 Peel onions; cut into sixths. Blender-chop peppers and onions with water to cover; drain.

5 Add pepper and onions to tomatoes. Over high heat, heat to boiling; reduce heat to medium; boil, uncovered, 30 minutes, stirring often. Drain vegetables and discard liquid. Meanwhile prepare jars and caps for processing (p.382). Into the drained vegetables, stir remaining 2 cups vinegar and rest of ingredients. Over high heat, heat to boiling; reduce heat to medium and simmer 3 minutes.

6 Ladle into jars to ½ inch from top; close as manufacturer directs. Process in boiling-water bath (p.382) 5 minutes. Cool; test seal (p.382).

TANGY CORN RELISH

Making corn relish was one of the ways the Pennsylvania Dutch preserved abundant crops of this native American plant.

- Color index page 80
- Begin day ahead
- 5 pints
- 15 cals per tablespoon

12 ears corn, husks and silk removed
3 cups cider vinegar
2 medium green peppers, diced (about 1½ cups)
2 medium red peppers, diced (about 1½ cups)
2 medium tomatoes, diced (about 1½ cups)

2 medium onions, diced (about 1 cup)
1½ cups sugar
4½ teaspoons salt
1 teaspoon celery seeds
1 teaspoon dry mustard
1 teaspoon turmeric
5 1-pint canning jars and caps

1 With small, sharp knife on a cutting board, carefully cut the kernels from the ears of corn to make about 8 cups kernels.

2 In 5-quart saucepot over high heat, heat corn and remaining ingredients to boiling. Reduce heat to low; simmer 20 minutes, stir occasionally.

3 Meanwhile, prepare jars and caps for processing (p.382). Leave jars and caps in hot water until ready to use. Wet the rubber rings before using them to make them more pliable.

4 Immediately ladle hot corn mixture into hot jars to within ¼ inch from top of jar. (Keep the mixture simmering while filling jars.) Close jars as manufacturer directs.

5 Process the jars in boiling-water bath (p.382) 15 minutes.

6 With jar lifter or tongs, remove jars from canner; set jars, several inches apart, on wire racks. Complete seal on jars with glass or zinc caps as manufacturer directs. Do not tighten screw bands. Cool at least 12 hours. Now test seal (p.382). Store unsealed jars in refrigerator; store sealed jars in cool, dark, dry place to use within one year.

Sauces

SAUCES

Sauces add a special touch to many dishes. Serve with egg, seafood, vegetable, meat, and poultry preparations.

HOLLANDAISE SAUCE: Add *3 egg yolks* and *2 tablespoons lemon juice* to double-boiler top. With wire whisk or slotted spoon, beat until well mixed. Place double-boiler top over bottom containing hot, not boiling water. Add *2 tablespoons butter* to the egg yolk mixture and cook, beating constantly, until the butter is completely melted. Add *another 2 tablespoons butter*, beating constantly; repeat with an additional *4 tablespoons butter*, beating until mixture thickens and is heated through. Remove from heat; stir in *¼ teaspoon salt*. Keep warm. Serve on hot cooked artichoke hearts, asparagus, broccoli, seafood, or poached eggs. Makes ⅔ cup. 90 cals per tablespoon.

GREEN MAYONNAISE DRESSING: In covered blender container at medium speed, blend *2 cups mayonnaise, ⅓ cup chopped parsley, 4 teaspoons tarragon vinegar, ½ teaspoon tarragon,* and *2 green onions*, cut up, until smooth, occasionally stopping blender and scraping side. Refrigerate. Serve on fish. Makes 2 cups. 93 cals per tablespoon.

TARTAR SAUCE: In small bowl with fork, stir together *1 cup mayonnaise, 2 tablespoons minced parsley, 1 to 2 tablespoons minced dill pickle, 1 to 2 tablespoons minced onion, 1 tablespoon bottled capers,* and *1 tablespoon minced pimento-stuffed olives* (optional) until well mixed. Makes 1½ cups. 68 cals per tablespoon.

SPICY RED-PEPPER SAUCE: In small bowl with fork, stir together *½ 7-ounce jar roasted sweet red peppers*, drained and finely chopped, *2 tablespoons catchup, ½ teaspoon sugar,* and *¼ teaspoon hot pepper sauce*, until well mixed. Makes ½ cup. 8 cals per tablespoon.

SHRIMP-OLIVE SAUCE: In 1-quart saucepan over medium heat, heat *one 8-ounce can tomato sauce, ½ pound shelled, deveined small shrimp*, cooked, *½ cup sliced pimento-stuffed olives,* and *⅓ cup white wine*, stirring. Serve hot. Makes 1⅔ cups. 63 cals per tablespoon.

HORSERADISH SAUCE: In small bowl with spoon, combine *⅓ cup mayonnaise* with *¼ cup minced dill pickles*, and *2 tablespoons horseradish*. Stir in *1 tablespoon milk* and *⅛ teaspoon pepper*, and blend well. Cover and refrigerate until ready to serve. Makes ¾ cup. 47 cals per tablespoon.

CREAMY COCKTAIL SAUCE: In small bowl with spoon, combine *⅓ cup chili sauce, ⅓ cup catchup, 2 teaspoons horseradish, 1½ teaspoons lemon juice,* and *2 tablespoons mayonnaise*. Cover; refrigerate. Serve with seafood. Makes 1 cup. 26 cals per tablespoon.

YOGURT-WATERCRESS SAUCE: Peel *1 small cucumber*. Cut cucumber lengthwise in half; with spoon, remove seeds; chop cucumber. In small bowl, toss cucumber with *½ teaspoon salt*; cover and let stand at room temperature about 15 minutes. Meanwhile, in blender at medium speed or in food processor with knife blade attached, blend *one 8-ounce container plain yogurt, ½ cup mayonnaise, ¼ cup loosely-packed watercress leaves,* and *1 medium green onion*, cut up, just until green onion and watercress are finely chopped. Drain cucumber: tip bowl over sink, pressing cucumber with hand to drain as much liquid as possible, pat dry with paper towels. Place yogurt mixture in small bowl; stir in cucumber. Makes 2 cups. 30 cals per tablespoon.

THE INDEX

Italic numbers indicate recipes with step-by-step illustrations

A

Accompaniments
  for soup 97
Acorn squash
  skillet-baked 245
  stuffed 245
  with cranberry pot roast
    179
Alaskan ice-cream
  snowball 303
Almond-curry sauce 206
Almond lace rolls 350
American heirloom chutney
  383
American hero 373
Anadama bread, quick-and-
  easy 358
Anchovy sauce 265
Angel-food cake 327
Angel's hair pasta with
  feta 260
Angels on horseback 125
APPETIZER(S) 83–94
  cold 89–94
    avocado salad, first course
      91
    cashews with chili 92
    cheese-stuffed bread *93*
    country pâté loaf *91*
    crab claws with spicy red
      pepper dip 89
    crudités, arranging festive
      94
    deviled eggs and variations
      90
    dips
      chili-cheese 94
      hot tuna 94
      oriental onion 94
    fresh fruit in orange cups
      90
    guacamole 91
    guacamole-filled tomatoes
      91
    herbed goat cheese with sun-
      dried tomatoes 92

  hot pepper pecans 92
  Liptauer cheese 92
  marinated mussels on the half
    shell 89
  shrimp cocktail with tangy
    dip 89
  spreads
    blue cheese 92
    Cheddar cheese 92
    Vermont Cheddar sticks *93*
  hot 85–88
    Brie and smoked salmon tortilla
      triangles 86
    Cheddar-cheese fondue 88
    chicken wing(s)
      appetizers, baked 85
      Buffalo-style *85*
      oven-fried 85
      saucy 85
    cocktail meatballs 86
    fried artichoke hearts and
      zucchini 88
    ham and cheese cups 86
    "oven-fried" artichoke hearts
      and zucchini 88
    pig-in-a-blanket 87
    quesados 87
    sausage-Muenster melts 86
    stuffed mushrooms 88
Apple(s)
  and bananas in caramel
    sauce 292
  and pork grill 193
  baked, New England 287
  brown Betty 287
  cake, chunky 343
  candy 354
  chevrons 291
  crab, spiced 379
  dumplings, how to make
    311
  funnel cakes, -cinnamon
    369
  -glazed
    beef brisket 217
    franks and cabbage *212*
    pork tenderloin *191*
  jelly, cran- *380*
  muffins, -molasses 368
  pandowdy 287
  pie

  -custard *311*
  deep-dish- 312
  old-fashioned pear- *312*
  open-face- 311
  sugar-frosted *309*
  relish, cranberry- 383
  rings, how to make spiced-
    290
  sauce
    chunky- *379*
    cran- wine 206
  snow *288*
  stuffing, -herb 170
  varieties, best ways to
    use 288
Apricot(s)
  and pickled peaches 379
  butter 379
  jelly roll 328
  -maple glazed ham
    202
  meringue strips 349
Artichoke (s)
  and chicken cutlets 158
  bottoms, how to prepare
    229
  hearts and zucchini,
    fried 88
  hearts and zucchini, "oven-
    fried" 88
  quiche, no-crust 114
  soup, creamy California 98
  stuffed, Monterey 229
  with mustard sauce *229*
Asparagus
  and cherry tomatoes *230*
  California braised, and
    celery 230
  lemon-buttered 177
  quiche *114*
Avocado(s)
  and grapefruit with honey
    and yogurt 283
  butter 151
  guacamole and variation 91
  salad, first course 91
  seasoned 111
  -tomato pizza 374
  tropical chicken-potato salad
    with -and papaya 280
  veal chops with *209*

B

Bacon
  and chicken salad 280
  cornbread *366*
  -fried brown rice 266
  liver and onions, pan-fried
    211
  -rice stuffing 164
  spinach, and mushroom
    salad *271*
  with chicken livers, onions,
    and apple 168
  -wrapped chicken-mushroom
    kabobs *222*
  -wrapped tomatoes, broiled
    247
Bagel 372
Baked
  Alaska *301*
  candied sweet potatoes *246*
  cauliflower in cheese sauce 235
  chicken wing appetizers 85
  cod with grapefruit 136
  coffee custards 296
  crispy chicken thighs 155
  Indian pudding *298*
  lamb shanks and beans
    207
  macaroni and cheese 259
  onions 238
  sole with lemon sauce 142
  stuffed pork chops 191
  Swiss steak 174
Banana(s)
  and apples in caramel
    sauce 292
  bread and variations *366*
  coconut Betty 287
  cream pie 320
  split, Brooklyn 302
BARBECUE(D) 215–226
  apricot chicken 221
  bass fillets, grilled, with mushroom
    stuffing 224
  beef and vegetable kabobs with
    peanut sauce *220*

beef brisket, apple-glazed 217
chicken-mushroom kabobs, bacon-wrapped 222
chicken, old-west 221
chicken, sugar-smoked *221*
Cornish hens with sweet-and-sour sauce 222
corn-on-the-cob, how to- 225
desserts, quick- 226
duckling, savory grilled *222*
equipment 216
fish fillets in corn husks *223*
fish packs, how to prepare 224
fish steaks, grilled, with chili butter *223*
fruit, grilled curried 226
kabobs, preparing 220
lamb, lemon-marinated grilled *218*
marinades
  ginger 223
  Mexicali 223
  soy-sesame 223
pork chops with tangy pear sauce 220
pork tenderloins, maple-glazed 218
ribs, Texas country *219*
sauces
  cranberry-honey 226
  East Indies 226
  fiery chili 226
  green-onion-soy 226
  peanut-ginger 226
  peppery hot 226
  rosemary-butter 226
  tangy beer 226
sirloin steaks with fresh-pepper relish 217
spareribs, Tex-Mex 219
spareribs with peach sauce 219
steak with anchovy butter 217
trout, grilled, with summer-vegetable stuffing *224*
veal breast, plum-glazed 218
vegetable kabobs 225
Barley
beef, and vegetable *102*
-walnut salad 275
Batter-fried stuffed chilies 240
Bavarian
pineapple-orange 294
Bean(s)
and baked lamb shanks 207
and pepper salad 274
Boston baked *232*
island pork and 233
ranch-style 233
tacos, prairie- 233
three- and cheese salad 274
Bean(s), black
and rice 232
soup *100*

Bean(s), black-eyed
hoppin' John 232
Bean(s), green
and onion casserole 231
and wax, with blue-cheese sauce *231*
and wax, with mustard sauce 274
Bean(s), kidney
red- and rice 232
zesty Mexican eggs and 109
Bean(s), Lima
buttered-crumb 231
Bean(s), navy
chunky lamb and -soup *101*
Vermont pork and 193
Bean(s), wax
and green, with mustard sauce 274
and whole green beans, with blue-cheese sauce *231*
Beaten biscuits *364*
Beef 173–187
and oyster pie 181
and vegetable kabobs with peanut sauce 220
barley, and vegetables *102*
enchiladas *181*
ground
  chili con carne 182
  chili, Texas-style 182
  corn-pone casserole 185
  hamburgers 186–187
  meat and potato loaf *184*
  meatballs, hearty 183
  meatballs, Mexican-style 183
  meat loaf, old-fashioned 184
  meat-loaf roll with spinach stuffing 184
  pasties, Michigan-style *182*
  Salisbury steaks with onions and peppers 185
  stuffed cabbage rolls *183*
pot roast(s)
  corned beef hash 179
  corned beef with cabbage and carrots 178
  cranberry, with acorn squash *179*
  New England boiled dinner 179
  red flannel hash 179
  spicy beef brisket 178
  Yankee *178*
roast(s)
  favorite rib-eye *177*
  how to carve 177
  standing rib, with Yorkshire pudding 176
steak(s)
  baked Swiss 174
  celebration filet mignon 173
  chicken-fried, with cream gravy *173*
  Diane *175*
  lemon-pepper 173
  London broil 175
  party -teriyaki *174*

sherried cubed 174
stuffed beef roll *176*
with mustard butter 173
with red-wine sauce 175
stew
  enchiladas *181*
  in beer *180*
  old-country short-rib dinner 180
  pressure-cooked 180
Beer-batter chicken rolls 156
Beer-batter-fried shrimp 124
Beet(s)
and vegetable soup *102*
Harvard 234
pickled 378
salad, jeweled 277
Beignets, New Orleans 369
Best sparkling lemonade 192
Big Apple bagel burger 186
Biscuits
beaten *364*
buttermilk 363
fruited drop 363
Kentucky ham 363
plain 363
sour cream *363*
Vermont 363
Bittersweet chocolate dessert sauce 290
Black beans see Bean(s)
Blackberry pie with cobbler crust 314
Black-bottom pie *321*
Black-eyed beans see Bean(s)
Black satin pie 319
Blender mayonnaise 284
Blintzes
strawberry *371*
Blondies 345
Blueberry(ies)
jam 381
muffins *368*
pancakes 370
pie with cobbler crust 314
Blue-cheese
burgers *185*
dressing, creamy 284
spread 92
Boston baked beans 232
Boston brown bread 364
Boston cream pie 328
Bouquet garni, how to make 208
Brandied-strawberry sauce 306
Brandy hard sauce 315
Bran muffins, maple- 368
BREAD(S) 355–374
biscuit(s) 363–364
  beaten *364*
  buttermilk 363
  fruited drop 363
  giant popovers 364

Kentucky ham 363
plain 363
sour cream *363*
Vermont 363
quick bread(s) 364–371
  banana 366
  banana-cranberry 366
  banana-date 366
  banana-nut 366
  beignets, New Orleans 369
  blintzes, strawberry *371*
  Boston brown *364*
  cheese 365
  corn bread
    bacon 366
    chili-cheese 367
    deviled-ham 367
    golden 367
    ring 367
    shortcake 367
  corn sticks, golden 367
  cranberry-raisin 365
  date-nut 364
  doughnuts, nutmeg-sugar 369
  French toast 371
  funnel cakes, apple-cinnamon 369
  muffins
    apple-molasses 368
    blueberry *368*
    corn 367
    maple-bran 368
    zucchini-oatmeal 368
  pancakes
    blueberry 370
    buckwheat 370
    country brunch 370
    plain 370
    silver dollar *370*
  pumpkin 365
  peanut-butter 365
  rice-fritters (calas) 370
  spoon 366
  waffles
    buttermilk-pecan 371
    plain buttermilk 371
sandwich(es) 372–373
  American hero 373
  California open 373
  chili dogs 373
  deli specials 372
  deluxe steak 372
  ham 'n' Swiss croissant 372
  ribbon 372
yeast bread(s) 357–362
  anadama, quick-and-easy 358
  braid, raisin-almond *359*
  buns
    pecan-cinnamon 362
    sticky *362*
    walnut-cinnamon 362
  cardamom Christmas wreath *360*
  dough
    kneading 356
    letting rise 357
    testing for doneness 360

Limpa 360
pizza
    avocado-tomato 374
    deep-dish Chicago 374
    extra-cheese, with basil
        374
    pumpernickel-rye 358
    rolls
        how to form 361
        Parker House 361
    Sally Lunn 358
    sourdough 359
    white 357
    whole-wheat oatmeal, crusty
        357
Bread stuffing
    moist 170
    rye 166
Bread-and-butter pickles
    377
Breaded lamb shoulder
    chops 205
Breakfast, All-American
    108
Breakfast sausage patties
    213
Breast of duckling with
    green peppercorns 165
Brie and smoked salmon
    tortilla triangles 86
Brisket
    apple-glazed 217
    spicy 178
Broccoli
    quiche with whole-wheat
        crust 114
    with butter-almond sauce
        234
    with sour-cream sauce 234
Broiled cod steaks Montauk
    136
Broiled halibut steaks with
    lemon-dill sauce 139
Broiled leeks, sweet peppers
    and mushrooms 255
Broiler-fryer see Chicken
Brooklyn banana split 302
Brown rice
    bacon fried 266
    plain boiled 266
Brownies
    butterscotch 345
    chocolate chunk 345
    chocolate-mint 345
    marble 345
Brunswick stew 154
Buckwheat pancakes 370
Buffalo-style chicken wings
    85
Buns
    pecan-cinnamon 362
    sticky 362
    walnut-cinnamon 362
Butter(s)
    chili 243
    chive 243
    dill 243
Butter-cream frosting
    344
Buttered-crumb Lima
    beans 231
Buttered raisin sauce 195
Buttermilk biscuits 363

Buttermilk-pecan waffles 371
Butternut squash, maple 245
Butter sauce for vegetables 256
Butterscotch brownies 345

C

Cabbage
    for slaws 272
    red, with Polish sausage 213
    rolls, stuffed 183
    sautéed 178
    with corned beef and carrots 178
CAKE(S) 325–343
    angel-food 327
    apricot jelly roll 328
    Boston cream pie 328
    carrot, with cream-cheese
        frosting 343
    cheesecake
        cranberry swirl 340
        light and creamy 341
        Manhattan-style 341
        semisweet chocolate 340
    chiffon, seven-layer chocolate 330
    chocolate garnishes, how to
        make 330
    chunky apple 343
    coffeecake, sour-cream 329
    coffeecakes, pecan-crumb 329
    cupcakes, chocolate 331
    cupcakes, peanut-butter 343
    devil's food 331
    filling(s) 344
    4th of July 338
    frosting
        decorating with 338
        making roses and leaves 339
        see also Frosting(s)
    fruitcake, chocolate 342
    gingerbread ring with maple
        cream 342
    Lady Baltimore 327
    Lane 327
    Mother's day 339
        variation 133
    old-fashioned spice 342
    pineapple upside-down 328
    pound, with coconut-almond
        topping 329
    shortcake, strawberry 341
    torte, chocolate sour-cream 331
    Valentine's devil's food 128
Calf's liver
    pan-fried, bacon, and onions 211
California braised asparagus
    and celery 230

California duck roast 165
California goat's cheese burger
    186
California open sandwich
    373
California quiche 114
California salad 271
California-style marinated
    halibut 139
California veal cutlets 210
Camp-stove stew 213
CANDY(IES) 354
    apples 354
    chocolate fudge 354
    chocolate-marshmallow
        fudge 354
    peanut brittle 354
    peanut butter fudge 354
Cannelloni 262
Capon
    stuffed, with cranberry-poached
        pears 147
Cardamom Christmas
    wreath 360
Carnival mashed potatoes
    243
Carrot(s)
    and grapes 234
    cake with cream-cheese frosting
        343
    curl 100
    fruited 235
    glazed 234
    orange baby 178
    with corned beef and cabbage
        178
Carving
    fish 140
    roast beef 177
    turkey 161
Cashews with chili 92
Casserole(s)
    corn-pone 185
    egg-and-spinach 110
    Louisiana chicken 154
    San Francisco seafood
        126
    tuna-noodle 144
Cauliflower
    baked, in cheese sauce
        235
    Parmesan 235
Celebration filet mignon
    173
Celery
    California braised asparagus
        and 230
Cheddared onions 239
CHEESE 114–116
    and herb soufflé 116
    baked macaroni and 259
    Brie and smoked salmon tortilla
        triangles 86
    corn bread, chili- 367
    decorating 84
    dip, chili- 94
    dressing, creamy ginger-
        284
    feta, angel's hair pasta with
        260
    fondue, Cheddar- 88
    Georgia-pecan tart with cream-
        pastry 324

goat- herbed, with sun-dried
        tomatoes 92
    golden buck 115
    ham and cups 86
    lasagna, Monterey 264
    Liptauer 92
    manicotti, -filled 263
    pizza, extra-, with basil 374
    quiche
        asparagus 114
        broccoli- with whole-wheat
            crust 114
        California 114
        no-crust artichoke 114
        spinach 114
    quick bread 365
    salad, three-bean and- 274
    sauce, Parmesan- 262
    sausage-Muenster melts 86
    soufflé, wild rice and
        chicken 116
    spread(s)
        blue 92
        Cheddar 92
        how to serve 92
        -stuffed bread 93
        tortilla bake 115
    veal cutlets, ham and -stuffed
        210
    Vermont Cheddar sticks
        93
    Welsh rabbit 115
Cheesecake(s)
    cranberry swirl 340
    light and creamy 341
    Manhattan-style 341
    semisweet chocolate 340
Cheesy tortilla bake 115
Cherry(ies)
    jam, sour 381
    jam, sweet 381
    jubilee 302
    -streusel pie 315
Chestnut
    and veal ragout 211
    cream mousse 299
    stuffing 169
Chicago pizza burger
    186
Chicken 147–159
    à la king 158
    and bacon salad 280
    and corn soup, Pennsylvania
        Dutch 104
    and oyster gumbo 150
    and pasta salad, party
        281
    and pork stew 199
    and rice soup 105
    and wild rice soufflé 116
    barbecued apricot- 221
    breasts in a pecan crust
        156
    Brunswick stew 154
    burritos 157
    cacciatore 150
    casserole, Louisiana 154
    chilled orange- 156
    country captain 152
    croquettes 158
    cutlets and artichokes 158
    cutlets with sun-dried tomatoes
        and Mozzarella 158

farmhouse 149
fricassee with dumplings *150*
Havana *152*
jambalaya 153
legs, deviled 155
legs, shrimp-stuffed *155*
-liver and mushroom ragout 168
livers with bacon, onions, and apple 168
-mushroom kabobs, bacon-wrapped 222
Napa Valley 152
old-west barbecued 221
paprika broiled 149
party stuffed 148
pie, deep-dish- 154
-potato salad, tropical, with avocado and papaya *280*
quarters, stuffed, with cherry tomatoes *153*
Rock Cornish hens
  peasant-style *159*
  with sweet-and-sour sauce 222
  with wild-rice stuffing 159
rolls, beer-batter- *156*
soup, -escarole 104
southern-fried 149
stuffed capon with cranberry-poached pears 147
sugar-smoked *221*
thighs, baked crispy 155
-tomato cups, curried 280
tostadas *151*
wings
  appetizers, baked 85
  Buffalo-style *85*
  oven-fried 85
  saucy 85
  Yucatan 151
Chicken-fried steak with cream gravy *173*
Chicken liver(s)
  and mushroom ragout 168
  with bacon, onions, and apple 168
Chiffon cake, seven-layer chocolate *330*
Chiffon pie
  cranberry- 323
  orange- 323
Chili(es)
  batter-fried stuffed *240*
  butter 243
  -cheese corn bread *367*
  cheese dip 94
  con carne 182
  dogs 373
  flowers, how to make 334
  how to prepare 240
  Texas-style 182
  Tex-Mex -burger 187
Chilled cucumber soup 99
Chilled lemony mushrooms 238
Chilled orange chicken 156
Chilled salmon steak with marinated cucumber *141*
Chilled seafood risotto 127
Chilled watercress soup 99
Chive butter 243

Chocolate
cheesecake, semisweet 340
chiffon cake, seven-layer *330*
-chip cookies 346
-chip walnut cookies 346
chunk brownies 345
crackletops 346
-cream filling 344
cream pie 320
cream pie, meringue-topped 320
cupcakes 331
dessert sauce, bittersweet- 290
fruitcake 342
fudge 354
fudge-swirl ice cream *304*
garnishes, how to make 330
icing 344
-marshmallow fudge 354
-marshmallow sauce 306
-mint brownies *345*
mousse, marbled 299
-peanut-butter pie *324*
peanut-choco nuggets *350*
pudding *297*
sour-cream frosting 331
sour-cream torte 331
thumbprints *346*
-wafer crumb crust 321
-walnut filling 344
Chop suey *192*
Christmas cookies
Christmas tree cookies 352
cookie chalets *353*
cookie ornaments, how to make 253
frosted snowmen 352
gingerbread men *353*
how to wrap 253
jolly Santas 352
Christmas Dinner (menu) 332
Christmas Eve Party (menu) 261
Christmas tree cookies *352*
Christmas wreath, cardamom *360*
Chunky apple cake 343
Chunky applesauce 379
Chunky lamb and bean soup *101*
Cinnamon
buns, pecan- *362*
buns, walnut- 362
funnel cakes, apple- 369
Clam(s)
and mussels fra diavolo 126
-bake, family *119*
chowder, Manhattan 106
chowder, New England *106*
fritters 119
linguine with white clam sauce 260
soft-shell, steamed 119
Classic bacon cheeseburger 187
Classic French dressing 284
Classic tossed green salad 271
Cobbler
blackberry pie with -crust 314
blueberry pie with -crust 314
cranberry-pear- *289*
Cocktail corn garnish 160
Cocktail meatballs 86

Coconut(s)
banana Betty 287
macaroons 351
-pineapple tapioca 295
slipped -custard 319
Cod
baked, with grapefruit 136
broiled steaks Montauk 136
crisp fish cakes and variation *137*
fried fish and hush puppies *136*
San Francisco seafood casserole *126*
scampi-style fish *137*
Codfish balls 137
Coffee
baked custards *296*
Coffeecake(s)
pecan-crumb 329
sour-cream 329
Cold chiffon sauce 250
Coleslaw
deluxe 272
golden slaw 272
summer squash and pepper slaw 272
Collard greens
ham hocks and *203*
Confetti rice mold 282
Cool lemon soufflés 300
COOKIE(S) 345–353
almond lace rolls 350
apricot meringue strips 349
blondies 345
brownies
  butterscotch 345
  chocolate chunk 345
  chocolate-mint *345*
  marble 345
chalets *353*
chocolate-chip 346
chocolate-chip walnut 346
chocolate crackletops 346
chocolate thumbprints *346*
Christmas tree 352
coconut macaroons 351
crunchy snack bars 349
Dutch butter 348
filbert -rafts 351
frosted snowmen 352
gingerbread men 353
Jack O'Lantern 256
jolly Santas 352
macadamia meltaways 351
molasses spirals 347
Moravian ginger *347*
oatmeal 351
ornaments, how to make 253
peanut butter candy tops 350
peanut-choco nuggets *350*
pecan crunch 349
poppy-seed pinwheels 351
snickerdoodles 347
spritz 348
strawberry jam dandies 348
  variation: heart-shaped 128
sugar 348

Corn
chowder 97
cocktail- garnish 160
fritters 236
muffins 367
-on-the-cob, how to barbecue 225
-pone casserole 185
pudding, custard- 236
relish, tangy *385*
salad, festive 275
skillet 236
soup, Pennsylvania Dutch chicken and *104*
sweet- with herb butter 236
Corn-bread
and sausage stuffing *169*
bacon 366
chili-cheese 367
deviled-ham 367
golden 367
golden sticks 367
muffins 367
ring 367
shortcake 367
spoon bread 366
Corned beef
hash 179
hash and eggs 110
with cabbage and carrots 178
Corn-flake crumb crust 321
Cornish hens with sweet-and-sour sauce 222
Country brunch pancakes 370
Country captain 152
Country egg bake 109
Country ham with four sauces 195
Country pâté loaf *91*
Country ribs with red chili sauce *194*
Country-style pork shoulder roast 188
Country turkey hash 163
Crab
cakes 121
claws with spicy red-pepper dip 89
fresh cooked *120*
imperial 121
Louis 279
pan-fried soft-shell 120
Cran-apple jelly *380*
Cranberry(ies)
-apple jelly *380*
-apple relish 383
-apple wine sauce 206
banana bread 366
-chiffon pie 323
-honey barbecue sauce 226
-pear cobbler *289*
-pear wine sauce 206
-pineapple relish 383
-poached pears 147
pot roast with acorn squash *179*
-raisin bread *365*
relish, how to make 160
sauce 383
swirl cheesecake *340*
-tangerine relish 383
-wine mold *293*
-wine sauce 195

Crayfish étouffée *121*
Cream-cheese frosting 343
Creamed onions 239
Cream of fresh tomato soup 98
Cream of mushroom soup 98
Cream of peanut soup 102
Cream pie
  Boston 328
Creamy blue-cheese dressing 284
Creamy California artichoke soup 98
Creamy cappelletti *262*
Creamy cocktail sauce 385
Creamy custard filling 344
Creamy ginger-cheese dressing 284
Creamy mushroom gravy 166
Creamy potato and vegetable salad 273
Creamy sole fillets *142*
Crème brûlée with tropical fruits 297
Creole sauce 112
Creole turkey soup *105*
Crêpe(s)
  Dolly Madison ice-cream- 303
  strawberry blintzes *371*
Crisp fish cakes *137*
Croquettes
  salmon- with dill sauce 141
Croutons 103
Crudités
  arranging festive 94
Crumb crust(s)
  corn- or wheat-flake 321
  gingersnap or peanut-butter 321
  graham-cracker 321
  unbaked 321
  vanilla- or chocolate-wafer 321
Crunchy snack bars *349*
Crusty whole-wheat oatmeal bread *357*
Cucumber(s)
  chilled salmon steak with marinated- *141*
  in dilled yogurt 276
  in sour cream 276
  -mint relish 384
  salad, molded 277
  soup, chilled 99
Cupcakes
  chocolate 331
  frog-, how to make 343
  peanut-butter 343
Currant-glazed ham steak 203
Currant-orange sauce 206
Curry(ied)
  chicken tomato cups 280
  fruit, grilled 226
  sauce, almond- 206
  turkey with apples and peanuts 163
Custards
  baked coffee *296*
  corn pudding 236
  filling, creamy 344
  peaches in strawberry and -sauce 290
  pie, apple- *311*
  sauce 290

slipped coconut- 319
velvety- with banana sauce 296

D

Date(s)
  banana- bread 366
  -nut bread 364
  persimmon- pudding 298
Decorating
  cheese 84
  with frosting 338
  with vegetables 230
  with whipped cream 319
Deep-dish apple pie 312
Deep-dish Chicago pizza 374
Deep-dish chicken pie 154
Deep-dish plum pie 312
Delmonico potatoes 244
Deluxe coleslaw 272
Deluxe layered chef's salad 278
Deluxe steak sandwich 372
DESSERT(S) 285–306
  apple brown Betty 287
  apple pandowdy *287*
  apple varieties, best ways to use 288
  baked coffee custards *296*
  baked Indian pudding *298*
  banana coconut Betty 287
  bananas and apples in caramel sauce 292
  bittersweet chocolate dessert sauce 290
  chestnut cream mousse 299
  chocolate pudding *297*
  coconut-pineapple tapioca 295
  cool lemon soufflés 300
  cranberry-pear cobbler 289
  cranberry-wine mold 293
  crème brûlée with tropical fruits 297
  custard sauce 290
  eggnog charlotte russe 295
  fig flowers 296
  foamy hard sauce 298
  fruit, how to present fresh 291
  fruits, sugar-frosted 294
  gingered crème brûlée 297
  grape clusters in shimmering lemon-cheese gel *294*
  grilled pineapple wedges 292
  ice cream(s) 301–306
    Alaskan -snowball 303

    baked Alaska 301
    Brooklyn banana split 302
    cherries jubilee 302
    chocolate fudge-swirl *304*
    Dolly Madison -crêpes 303
    Georgia peach mebla 302
    how to ripple 304
    Johnny Appleseed à la mode 303
    lemon-lime milk sherbet *306*
    liberty -cones 303
    old-fashioned hot-fudge sundae 303
    Philadelphia -soda 302
    -pies, how to make 305
    rainbow- torte *305*
    -sandwiches, how to make 301
    San Francisco strawberry parfait 303
    sauces for 306
    two-melon granita 306
  maple bread pudding 298
  marbled chocolate mousse 299
  molded strawberries 'n' cream *300*
  New England baked apples 287
  peaches in strawberry and custard sauce 290
  persimmon-date pudding 298
  pineapple-orange Bavarian 294
  quick barbecue- 226
  range-top rice pudding with fresh fruit 295
  raspberry sauce 290
  red-white-and-blueberry mold 293
  snow apples *288*
  spiced apple rings, how to make 290
  spiced pears with chocolate sauce *291*
  springtime rhubarb refresher 291
  strawberry purée 290
  strawberry rhubarb grunt 289
  summer fruits in apple-wine gelatin 293
  velvety custard with banana sauce 296
  whips and other fruit purées, how to make 292
Deviled chicken legs 155
Deviled eggs 90
Deviled-ham corn bread 367
Devil's food cake 337
  variation: Valentine's 128
Dill
  butter 243
  pickles 377
  vegetables and 254
Dip(s)
  chili-cheese 94
  oriental onion 94
  spicy red pepper 89
  tangy 89
Dolly Madison ice-cream crêpes 303
Doughnut(s)
  apple-cinnamon funnel cakes 369

  New Orleans beignets 369
  nutmeg-sugar *369*
Down-home peach pie *313*
Duchess potatoes *244*
Duckling(s)
  breast, with green pepper-corns *165*
  roast *164*
  roast, California 165
  savory grilled *222*
Dumplings
  chicken fricassee with *150*
Dutch butter cookies 348

E

Easter Lunch (menu) 130
East Indies sauce 226
EGG(S) 107–113
  -and-spinach casserole *110*
  -bake, country 109
  Benedict *109*
  corned beef hash and 110
  deviled- and variations 90
  ham-and-onion frittata 112
  marbled 113
  omelet
    rolled mushroom 113
    shrimp-Creole *112*
  party creamy 111
  pickled 113
  ranch-style *111*
  skillet peppers and 112
  spiced 113
  tomato-sausage scramble 110
  western scrambled 110
  zesty Mexican- and beans 109
Eggnog 253
Eggnog charlotte russe 295
  variation: Valentine's 128
Eggplant
  Parmigiana 237
  sauce, spicy- with linguine 260
Enchiladas
  beef *181*
Endive
  skillet braised- and radicchio 256
Equipment
  barbecues 216
  home preserving 376
  pastry-making 322
Escarole
  chicken- soup 104
Extra-cheese pizza with basil 374

F

Family clambake *119*
Farmhouse chicken 149
Favorite rib-eye roast *177*
Festive corn salad 275
Fettuccine Alfredo 255
Fiery chili barbecue sauce 226
Fig flowers 296
Fig-maple syrup 370
Filbert cookie rafts 351
Filling(s)
  chocolate-cream 344
  chocolate-walnut 344
  creamy custard 344
  fresh lemon 344
Fine herbs 256
First course avocado salad 91
FISH 117–144
  barbecue -packs, how to prepare 224
  bass fillets, grilled, with mushroom stuffing 224
  bluefish, oven-baked *134*
  -cakes, crisp *137*
  catfish, fried *135*
  cod
    baked, with grapefruit 136
    -fish balls 137
    steaks, broiled Montauk 136
  fillets
    in corn husks *223*
    sautéed, with walnut coating 142
  flounder
    spinach-stuffed 138
    with green-chili sauce 138
  fried, and hush puppies *136*
  halibut
    California-style marinated 139
    steaks, broiled, with lemon-dill sauce *139*
    steaks, Hawaiian 139
  red snapper
    Creole 140
    with lime butter *140*
  roe, sautéed 136
  salmon
    croquettes with dill sauce 141
    mousse 141
    steak, chilled, with marinated cucumber *141*
  scampi-style *137*
  sea bass
    oven-steamed 134
    stuffed baked 134
  shrimp-filled fillets *138*
  sole
    baked, with lemon sauce 142
    fillets, creamy *142*
  steaks, grilled, with chili butter 223

swordfish
  stir-fried 143
  with herb butter 143
trout
  grilled, with summer-vegetable stuffing *224*
  pan-fried, with vegetable stuffing 143
tuna
  bake, fresh 144
  -noodle casserole 144
  pâté, molded *144*
  whole, how to serve 140
Flaky pastry *310*
Florida surf 'n' turf burger 187
Flounder
  shrimp-filled fillets *138*
  spinach-stuffed 138
  with green-chili sauce 138
Fluffy boiled frosting 331
Foamy hard sauce 298
Four-cheese sauce 265
4th of July Barbecue (menu) 198
4th of July cake 338
Frankfurter(s)
  and lentil soup 101
French dressing, classic 284
French-fried onion rings 238
French toast 371
Fresh cooked crab *120*
Fresh fruit in orange cups *90*
Fresh lemon filling 344
Fresh tongue with sweet-and-sour tomato sauce *214*
Fresh tuna bake 144
Fried artichoke hearts and zucchini 88
Fried catfish *135*
Fried fish and hush puppies *136*
Fritters
  clam 119
  corn 236
  rice 370
Frog cupcakes 343
Frosted snowmen 352
Frosting(s)
  butter-cream 344
  chocolate icing 344
  chocolate sour-cream 337
  cream-cheese 343
  decorating with 338
  fluffy boiled 331
  mocha-butter-cream 344
  ornamental cookie 338
  quick fudge 331
  roses and leaves, how to make 339
  "seven-minute" 344
  vanilla 344
Fruit(s)
  and rice ring 265
  fresh, how to present 291
  grilled, curried 226
  sugar-frosted 294
  summer- in apple-wine gelatin 293
  tarts, arranging 316
  tropical, preparing 337

  whips and other fruit purées, how to make 292
  see also specific varieties
Fruited carrots 235
Fruited drop biscuits 363
Fruit salads
  fresh, in orange cups 90
  in melon baskets 283
  luncheon salad 283
Fudge sauce 304

G

Game
  pheasant in cream *168*
  quail with mushrooms 167
  roast wild duck with spiced apples 167
Garnish(es)
  chocolate 330
  cocktail corn 160
  lemon 135
Gazpacho 100
Georgia peach melba 302
Georgia-pecan tart with cream-cheese pastry 324
Giant popovers 364
Giblet gravy
  for duckling 164
  for stuffed capon 147
  for turkey *161*
Ginger
  cookies, Moravian *347*
  marinade 223
Gingerbread men *353*
Gingerbread ring with maple cream 342
Gingered crème brûlée 297
Gingersnap crumb crust 321
Glazed carrots 234
Glazed ham
  apricot-maple 202
  currant-glazed ham steak 203
  glazed sliced ham 202
  peach-glazed Canadian bacon 203
  plum-glazed baked ham 202
Glazed onions 239
Glaze(s)
  for fruit tarts 317
  for poultry
    honey-barbecue 164
    mustard 164
    quince 164
    wine-jelly 164
Golden buck 115
Golden corn bread 367
Golden corn sticks 367

Golden glazed pork chops 189
Golden rice 268
Golden slaw 272
Golden veal chops 209
Goose
  roast stuffed, with candied oranges *166*
  roast, with chestnut stuffing, sausage, and apples 167
Grape clusters in shimmering lemon-cheese gel *294*
Grapefruit
  and avocado with honey and yogurt 283
Grape(s)
  and carrots *234*
  jelly 380
Grasshopper pie 323
Gravy
  creamy mushroom 166
  giblet-, for duckling 164
  giblet-, for stuffed capon 147
  how to prepare 190
  turkey giblet- 161
Green and wax beans with mustard sauce 274
Green bean(s)
  and onion casserole 231
  see also Bean(s)
Green goddess dressing 284
Green mayonnaise dressing 385
Green-onion-soy sauce 226
Green-tomato chow chow 383
Grilled bass fillets with mushroom stuffing 224
Grilled curried fruit 226
Grilled fish steaks with chili butter 223
Grilled pineapple wedges 292
Grilled trout with summer-vegetable stuffing 224
Ground beef *see Beef, ground*
Ground-nut crust 321
Guacamole 91
Guacamole-filled tomatoes 91
Guard of honor 133
Gumbo
  chicken and oyster 150
  Louisiana 106

H

Halibut
  California-style marinated 139
  steaks, broiled, with lemon-dill sauce *139*
  steaks, Hawaiian 139

Halloween Party Buffet (menu) 248
Ham
  and cheese cups 86
  and cheese stuffed veal cutlets 210
  and grits with red-eye gravy 195
  and onion frittata 112
  apricot-maple glazed 202
  country- with four sauces 195
  deviled- corn bread 367
  glazed sliced 202
  hocks and collard greens 203
  Kentucky- biscuits 363
  Luau kabobs 202
  'n' Swiss croissant 372
  peach-glazed Canadian bacon 203
  plum-glazed baked 202
  steak, currant-glazed 203
  whole, clove-studded 130
Hamburger(s)
  Big Apple bagel burger 186
  blue-cheese burgers 185
  California goat's cheese burger 186
  Chicago pizza burger 186
  classic bacon cheeseburger 187
  Florida surf 'n' turf burger 187
  Louisiana Creole burger 187
  San Francisco burger 187
  sloppy Joe 186
  Tex-Mex chili burger 187
Hangtown fry 123
Hard sauce
  brandy 315
  foamy 298
Harvard beets 234
Hash
  corned beef 179
  red flannel 179
  roast beef 176
Hash brown potatoes 242
Hawaiian halibut steaks 139
Heart-shaped strawberry jam dandies 128
Hearty meatballs 183
Hearty split pea soup 103
Hearty stuffed peppers 241
Herb(s) (ed)
  and cheese soufflé 116
  apple- stuffing 170
  goat cheese with sun-dried tomatoes 92
  orange rice 266
  sautéed, mushrooms 177
Hollandaise sauce 385
Home-fried potatoes 242
Homemade pasta dough 261
Honey-barbecue glaze 164
Honey-mustard sauce 195
Hoppin' John 232
Horseradish sauce 385
Hot butterscotch sauce 306
Hot pepper pecans 92
Hot tuna dip 94

Hush puppies
  fried fish and 136

I

Ice cream(s) 301–306
  Alaskan- snowball 303
  baked Alaska 301
  Brooklyn banana split 302
  cherries jubilee 302
  chocolate fudge-swirl 304
  Dolly Madison -crêpes 303
  Georgia peach melba 302
  how to ripple 304
  Johnny Appleseed à la mode 303
  lemon-lime milk sherbet 306
  liberty -cones 303
  old-fashioned hot-fudge sundae 303
  Philadelphia -soda 302
  -pie, how to make 305
  rainbow -torte 305
  -sandwiches, how to make 301
  San Francisco strawberry parfait 303
  two-melon granita 306
Ice-cream sauce(s)
  brandied-strawberry 306
  chocolate-marshmallow 306
  hot butterscotch 306
  melba 306
Island pork and beans 233
Italian sausages and peppers 212
Italian-style rice 267

J

Jack O'Lantern cookies 248
Jam
  blueberry 381

  sour-cherry 381
  strawberry 381
  sweet-cherry 381
  see also Preserves
Jambalaya chicken 153
Jelly
  cran-apple 380
  grape 380
  red-pepper freezer 380
  see also Preserves
Jelly roll, apricot 328
Jeweled beet salad 277
Johnny Appleseed à la mode 303
Jolly Santas 352
Julienne leeks 100
Jumbo ravioli with Swiss chard 263

K

Kabob(s)
  beef and vegetable- with peanut sauce 220
  Luau 202
  scallop 124
  shish 207
  tips on preparing 220
  vegetable 225
Kentucky ham biscuits 363
Key-lime pie 323
Kidney bean(s) see Bean(s)
Kielbasa with sauerkraut 212
Knackwurst sauerbraten 213
Kneading dough 356

L

Labor Day Clambake (menu) 201
Lady Baltimore cake 327
Lamb 204–207

  and bean soup, chunky 101
  guard of honor 133
  how to carve a leg 204
  lemon-marinated grilled 218
  Mulligan stew 207
  noisettes 206
  rack, with parsley crust 205
  roast leg 204
  shanks, baked, and beans 207
  shish kabob 207
  shoulder chops, breaded 205
  spring- with green vegetables 205
  stuffed shoulder 204
Lane cake 327
Lasagna 264
  Monterey cheese 264
  vegetable 264
Lattice-topped raisin pie 315
Leek(s)
  broiled-, sweet peppers, and mushrooms 255
  julienne 100
  vichyssoise 99
  with party potatoes 243
  -wrapped shrimp with cheese filling 125
Lemon(s)
  butter 256
  -buttered asparagus 177
  -buttered vegetables 254
  filling, fresh 344
  garnishes 135
  lime milk sherbet 306
  marinated grilled lamb 218
  meringue pie 322
  mushrooms, chilled 238
  -pepper steak 173
  soufflés, cool 300
  twist 100
  vinaigrette 210
Lemonade, best sparkling 196
Lentil(s)
  and frankfurter soup 101
Liberty ice-cream cones 303
Light and creamy cheesecake 341
Lima bean(s) see Bean(s)
Lime(s)
  garnishes 135
  milk sherbet, lemon- 306
  pie, Key- 323
Limpa bread 360
Linguine
  with red mussel sauce 260
  with spicy eggplant sauce 260
  with white clam sauce 260
Liptauer cheese 92
Liver
  and onions 211
  pan-fried, bacon, and onions 211
Lobster
  à l'Americaine 122
  how to eat 201
  salad 279
  skillet seafood Newburg 126
  thermidor 122
London broil 175
Louisiana chicken casserole 154

Louisiana creole burger 187
Louisiana gumbo 106
Luau kabobs 202

M

Macadamia meltaways 351
Macaroni
  baked, and cheese 259
Macaroons, coconut 351
Manhattan clam chowder
  106
Manhattan-style cheesecake
  341
Manicotti, cheese-filled 263
Maple-bran muffins 368
Maple bread pudding 298
Maple butternut squash 245
Maple-glazed pork tenderloins
  218
Marble brownies 345
Marbled chocolate mousse
  299
Marbled eggs 113
Marinades, barbecue
  ginger 223
  Mexicali 223
  soy-sesame 223
Marinara sauce 265
Marinated garden vegetables
  276
Marinated mussels on the half
  shell 89
Marsala wine
  turkey cutlets Marsala
  162
Marshmallow
  chocolate- sauce 306
Mayonnaise
  blender 284
  green- dressing 385
  mustard dill 89
MEAT 171–214
  see Beef; Lamb; Pork; Variety
  Meat(s); Veal
Meatballs
  cocktail 86
  hearty 183
  Mexican-style 183
  spaghetti and 253
Meat loaf(ves)
  meat and potato 184
  old-fashioned 184
  roll with spinach stuffing
  184
Meat sauce 265
Melba sauce 306

Melon(s)
  baskets, fruit in 283
  granita, two- 306
  steps 291
Memorial Day Picnic (menu)
  196
Menus for special occasions
  Christmas dinner 332
  Christmas Eve party 253
  Easter lunch 130
  4th of July barbecue 194
  Labor Day clambake 197
  Halloween party buffet
  248
  Memorial Day picnic 196
  Mother's Day lunch 133
  New Year's Day brunch 337
  New Year's Eve supper
  334
  Thanksgiving Day 250
  Valentine's Day party 128
Meringue(s)
  pie, lemon- 322
  strips, apricot- 255
  -topped chocolate-cream pie
  320
  topping, 3-egg white 320
Mexicali marinade 223
Mexican-style meatballs 183
Michigan-style pasties 182
Mince pie 315
Minestrone 101
Mint
  brownies, chocolate- 345
  -lime dressing 284
  relish, cucumber- 384
Minted peas 239
Mocha-butter-cream frosting
  344
Moist bread stuffing 170
Molasses
  muffins, apple- 368
  spirals 347
Molded cucumber salad 277
Molded desserts
  cranberry-wine mold 293
  eggnog charlotte russe 295
  grape clusters in shimmering
  lemon-cheese gel 294
  molded strawberries 'n' cream
  300
  pineapple-orange Bavarian
  294
  red-white-and-blueberry mold
  293
  summer fruits in apple-wine
  gelatin 293
Molded tuna pâté 144
Monterey cheese lasagna
  264
Moravian ginger cookies
  347
Mornay sauce 250
Mother's Day cake 339
  variation 133
Mother's Day Lunch (menu)
  133
Mousse
  chestnut cream 299
  marbled chocolate 299
  salmon 141
Muffin(s)
  apple-molasses 368

  blueberry 368
  maple-bran 368
Mulligan stew 207
Mulligatawny 104
Mushroom(s)
  and chicken-liver ragout 168
  -and-pepper topping 185
  and wild-rice stuffing 159
  broiled leeks, sweet peppers,
  and 255
  chicken- kabobs, bacon-wrapped
  222
  chilled lemony 238
  omelet, rolled- 113
  pinwheel 100
  sautéed herbed 177
  soup, cream of- 98
  spinach, bacon salad and 271
  stir-fried 238
  stuffed 88
  -stuffed breast of veal 208
  wild rice with peas, and 268
  with veal chops 209
Mussel(s)
  and clams fra diavolo 126
  linguine with red- sauce 260
  marinated- on the half shell 89
  San Francisco seafood casserole 126
Mustard glaze 164

N

Navy bean(s) see Bean(s)
New England baked apples
  287
New England boiled dinner
  179
New England clam chowder
  106
New Orleans beignets 369
New potatoes with lemon and
  chives 243
New Year's Day Brunch (menu)
  337
New Year's Eve Supper (menu)
  334
No-crust artichoke quiche 114
Noodle(s)
  tuna- casserole 144
Nut crust(s)
  ground-nut 321
  walnut-pastry 321
Nutmeg-sugar doughnuts
  369
Nut(s)
  banana- bread 366
  date- bread 364

Nutty brown-rice stuffing
  169

O

Oatmeal
  bread, crusty whole-wheat 357
  cookies 351
  muffins, zucchini- 368
Old-country short-rib dinner
  180
Old-fashioned creamed turkey
  with biscuits 163
Old-fashioned hot-fudge sundae
  303
Old-fashioned meat loaf 184
Old-fashioned pear-apple pie
  312
Old-fashioned potato salad 273
Old-fashioned spice cake 342
Old-west barbecued chicken 221
Onion(s)
  and green bean casserole 231
  and-ham frittata 112
  baked 238
  Cheddared 239
  creamed 239
  dip, oriental 94
  glazed 239
  peas with green 239
  rings, French-fried 238
  soup gratiné 97
  topping, sautéed- 185
Open-face apple pie 311
Orange(s)
  and tomatoes vinaigrette
  276
  -baby carrots 178
  Bavarian, pineapple- 294
  -chiffon pie 323
  -cups, fresh fruit in 90
  rice, herbed- 266
  sauce, currant- 206
Oriental onion dip 94
Ornamental cookie frosting
  338
Oven-baked bluefish 134
Oven-barbecued spareribs 194
"Oven-fried" artichoke hearts
  and zucchini 88
Oven-fried chicken wings 85
Oven-steamed sea bass 134
Oyster(s)
  and beef pie 181
  and chicken gumbo 150
  hangtown fry 123
  on half shell 123

Rockefeller *123*
scalloped 123
soup 106
stuffing 170

P

Pancake(s)
blueberry 370
buckwheat 370
country brunch 370
plain 370
silver dollar *370*
Pan-fried cherry tomatoes 247
Pan-fried liver, bacon, and onions 211
Pan-fried scallops 124
Pan-fried soft-shell crabs *120*
Pan-fried trout with vegetable stuffing 143
Papaya
tropical chicken-potato salad with -and avocado *280*
Paprika broiled chicken 149
Parfait, San Francisco strawberry 303
Parker House rolls *361*
Parmesan-cheese sauce 262
Parsley
rack of lamb with -crust *205*
Party chicken-and-pasta salad 281
Party creamy eggs 111
Party paella *127*
Party pizza 248
Party potatoes with leeks 243
Party steak teriyaki *174*
Party stuffed chicken 148
PASTA 257–265
angel's hair, with feta 260
cannelloni 262
cappelletti, creamy *262*
fetuccine Alfredo 261
homemade dough 261
lasagna 264
    Monterey cheese 264
    vegetable *264*
linguine
    with red mussel sauce 260
    with spicy eggplant sauce 260
    with white clam sauce 260
macaroni, baked, and cheese 259
manicotti, cheese-filled *263*
ravioli, jumbo, with Swiss chard 263

salad, party chicken-and- *281*
salad, picnic-, for a crowd *282*
spaghetti and meatballs 259
spaghetti sauce 259
tortellini pesto platter 282
ziti with hearty home-style meat sauce 261
Pasta sauce(s)
anchovy 265
four-cheese 265
marinara 265
meat 265
pesto 265
spinach 265
walnut 265
Pasties, Michigan-style *182*
Pastry
baked piecrust 310
decorating with 309
decorative pie edges 313
egg glaze 312
flaky *310*
rolling out 310
tart shell *316*
three-berry 316
unbaked piecrust 310
useful tools 322
Pâté
country loaf *91*
molded tuna *144*
Peach(es)
butter 379
-glazed Canadian bacon 203
in strawberry and custard sauce *290*
melba, Georgia 302
pickled, and apricots 379
pie, down-home *313*
preserves 381
Peanut(s)
brittle *354*
-choco nuggets *350*
-ginger barbecue sauce 226
soup, cream of 102
Peanut-butter
bread 365
candy tops 350
-cookie crumb crust 321
cupcakes 343
fudge 354
pie, chocolate- *324*
Pear(s)
cobbler, cranberry- *289*
cranberry-poached 147
pie, old-fashioned -apple *312*
relish, pepper- 384
sauce, cranberry- wine 206
spiced, with chocolate sauce *291*
Pea(s)
minted 239
sugar snap, stir-fried 239
wild rice with mushrooms and 268
with green onions 239
Peasant-style Cornish hens *159*
Pecan(s)
buns, -cinnamon 362
chicken breasts in a -crust 156

coffeecakes, -crumb 329
crunch 349
hot pepper 92
pumpkin pie, -crunch 318
stuffing 160
tart, Georgia-, with cream-cheese pastry 324
waffles, buttermilk- 371
Pennsylvania Dutch chicken and corn soup *104*
Pepper(s)
hearty stuffed 241
jelly, red- freezer 380
ratatouille in roasted 241
relish, -pear 384
salad, bean and 274
sauce, spicy red- 385
skillet- and eggs 112
slaw, summer squash and 272
sweet-, broiled leeks, and mushrooms 255
topping, mushroom-and- 185
Peppery hot sauce 226
Persimmon-date pudding 298
Pesto 265
Pheasant in cream *168*
Philadelphia ice-cream soda 302
Philadelphia pepper pot 102
Piccalilli *384*
PICKLE(S) 375–379
beets 378
bread-and-butter 377
dill 377
peaches and apricots 379
spiced crab apples 379
spiced prunes 378
spicy watermelon 378
sunchoke 377
vegetable medley 378
Pickled eggs 113
Picnic(s)
packing food for 196
-pasta salad for a crowd 282
Memorial Day 196
PIE(S) 307–330
apple-custard *311*
apple dumplings 311
banana cream *320*
beef and oyster 181
blackberry, with cobbler crust 314
black-bottom 321
black satin *319*
blueberry, with cobbler crust 314
cherry-streusel 315
chocolate cream 320
chocolate-peanut-butter *324*
cranberry-chiffon 323
deep-dish apple 312
deep-dish chicken 154
deep-dish plum 312
down-home peach *313*
fruit tarts, arranging 316
Georgia-pecan tart with cream-cheese pastry 324

grasshopper *323*
Key-lime 323
lattice-topped raisin *315*
lemon meringue 322
meringue-topped chocolate cream 320
mince 315
old-fashioned pear-apple *312*
open-face apple 311
orange-chiffon 323
pecan-crunch pumpkin 318
raspberry tart royale *317*
shoofly 324
slipped coconut-custard 319
sour-cream pumpkin 318
squash 318
strawberry-rhubarb *314*
streusel topping 315
sugar-frosted apple 309
summer tarts and tartlets, how to make 317
sweet-potato, with walnut-crunch topping 318
Piecrust(s)
crumb and nut crusts 321
decorating with pastry 309
decorative edges 313
flaky pastry *310*
tart shell *316*
three-berry pastry 316
unbaked 310
Pig-in-a-blanket *87*
Pineapple(s)
Bavarian, -orange 294
-glazed spareribs 194
relish, cranberry- 383
tapioca, coconut- 295
upside-down cake 328
wedges, grilled *292*
Pizza
avocado-tomato 374
deep-dish Chicago 374
extra-cheese, with basil *374*
party 248
Plain biscuits 363
Plain buttermilk waffles 371
Plain pancakes 370
Planked steak, how to present 217
Plum(s)
-glazed baked ham 202
-glazed veal breast 218
pie, deep-dish- *312*
Polish sausage with red cabbage 213
Popovers, giant 364
Poppy-seed
dressing 284
pinwheels 351
Pork 188–203
and apple grill 193
and beans, Vermont 193
and chicken stew *193*
chops and steaks
    -and-sauerkraut supper 191
    baked stuffed 191
    barbecued, with tangy pear sauce 220
    chop suey *192*
    Creole-style 190

golden glazed 189
loin, with prune stuffing 190
with creamy gravy 189
fried rice 267
hocks and potatoes 192
island- and beans 233
roasts
crown, with cran-apple stuffing 188
loin, with gravy 189
shoulder, country-style 188
spareribs
country, with red chili sauce 194
oven-barbecued 194
pineapple-glazed 194
Texas country 219
Tex-Mex barbecued 219
with peach sauce 219
tenderloin
apple-glazed 191
maple-glazed 218
Potato(es)
carnival mashed 243
Delmonico 244
duchess 244
hash brown 242
home-fried 242
loaf, meat and- 184
new- with lemon and chives 243
party- with leeks 243
roasted fans 244
salad, creamy- and vegetable 273
salad, old-fashioned 273
salad, tangy hot 273
salad, tropical chicken-, with avocado and papaya 280
salad, -tuna 279
twice-baked 242
Pot-roast(s)
cranberry, with acorn squash 179
Yankee 178
POULTRY 145–170
boning and stuffing 148
calculating stuffing quantities 170
carving turkey 161
glazes 164
stuffings 169–170
see also Chicken; Duckling; Game; Goose; Turkey
Pound cake with coconut-almond topping 329
Prairie bean tacos 233
Praline sauce 195
Praline syrup 370
PRESERVES 379–382
apricot butter 379
blueberry jam 381
chunky applesauce 379
cran-apple jelly 380
equipment for home preserving 376
grape jelly 380
peach butter 379
peach preserves 381
preparing for home preserving 382
red-pepper freezer jelly 380
sour-cherry jam 381
strawberry jam 381

sweet-cherry jam 381
Pressure-cooked beef stew 180
Pudding(s)
baked Indian 298
chocolate 297
persimmon-date 298
range-top rice, with fresh fruit 295
Yorkshire 176
Pumpernickel-rye bread 358
Pumpkin
bisque, velvety 97
bread 365
pie, pecan-crunch 318
pie, sour-cream 318
Prunes, spiced 378
Purée(s)
fruit, how to make 292
strawberry 290
vegetable, how to make 255

Q

Quail with mushrooms 167
Quesados 87
Quick-and-easy anadama bread 358
Quick barbecue desserts 226
Quick fudge frosting 337
Quince glaze 164

R

Rack of lamb with parsley crust 205
Radicchio
and endive, skillet braised 256
Rainbow ice-cream torte 305
Raisin(s)
braid, -almond 359
bread, cranberry- 365
pie, lattice-topped 315
Ranch-style beans 233
Ranch-style eggs 111

Range-top rice pudding with fresh fruit 295
Raspberry sauce 290
Raspberry tart royale 317
Ratatouille in roasted peppers 241
Ravioli
fillings
cheese 263
meat 263
spinach 263
jumbo, with Swiss chard 263
Red beans and rice 232
Red flannel hash 179
Red-pepper freezer jelly 380
Red snapper
Creole 140
with lime butter 140
Red-white-and-blueberry mold 293
RELISHES 383–385
American heirloom chutney 383
cranberry 160
cranberry-apple 383
cranberry-pineapple 383
cranberry sauce 383
cranberry-tangerine 383
cucumber-mint 384
green-tomato chow chow 383
pepper-pear 384
piccalilli 384
sweet-and-sour 384
tangy corn 385
Reuben 372
Rhubarb
grunt, strawberry- 289
pie, strawberry- 314
refresher, springtime- 291
Ribbon sandwich 372
Ribs *see Spareribs*
RICE 265–268
and fruit ring 265
and red beans 232
brown, bacon-fried 266
fritters 370
golden 268
herbed orange 266
Italian-style 267
mold, confetti 282
mold, supper 266
pork fried 267
pudding, range-top, with fresh fruit 295
soufflé, wild- and chicken 116
soup, chicken and 105
stuffing, bacon- 164
stuffing, nutty brown- 169
stuffing, sausage- 169
summer-garden 268
supper mold 266
Tex-Mex style 267
wild- with peas and mushrooms 268
zucchini with -filling 246
Risotto, chilled seafood 127
Roast(s)
beef hash 176
duckling 164

goose with chestnut stuffing, sausage, and apples 167
leg of lamb 204
stuffed goose with candied oranges 166
turkey with pecan stuffing 160
wild duck with spiced apples 167
Roasted potato fans 244
Roasted vegetable mélange 254
Rock Cornish hens with wild-rice stuffing 159
Rolled mushroom omelet 113
Rolls, Parker House 361
Rosemary-butter sauce 226
Russian dressing 284
Rye
bread, pumpernickel- 358
Rye-bread stuffing 166

S

SALAD(S) 269–284
avocado and grapefruit with honey and yogurt 283
avocado, first course 91
barley-walnut 275
bean and pepper 274
beans, green and wax, with mustard sauce 274
beet, jeweled 277
Caesar 271
California 271
chef's, deluxe layered 278
chef's, presenting 278
chicken and bacon 280
chicken-and-pasta, party 281
chicken-potato, tropical, with avocado and papaya 280
chicken tomato cups, curried 280
coleslaw, deluxe 272
combinations 270
composed, how to serve 332
corn-, festive 275
crab Louis 279
cucumber-, molded 277
cucumbers in dilled yogurt 276
cucumbers in sour cream 276
fruit in melon baskets 283
fruit luncheon 283
gelatin-, how to mold and present 277
green-, classic tossed 271
lobster 279
mold, confetti rice 282
picnic pasta- for a crowd 282
potato and vegetable-, creamy 273

potato-, old-fashioned 273
potato-, tangy hot 273
potato-tuna 279
salmagundi 278
shells 281
shrimp 279
slaw, golden 272
slaw, summer squash and
    pepper 272
spinach, mushroom, and bacon
    271
Texas caviar 274
three-bean and cheese 274
tomatoes, sliced, with lemon
    dressing 276
tortellini pesto platter 282
vegetables, marinated garden
    276
vinaigrette, oranges and
    tomatoes 276
Waldorf 283
Salad dressing(s)
    blender mayonnaise 284
    classic French 284
    creamy blue-cheese 284
    creamy ginger-cheese 284
    green goddess 284
    honey-caraway 284
    mint-lime 284
    poppy-seed 284
    Russian 284
    Thousand Island 284
Salisbury steaks with onions
    and peppers 185
Sally Lunn 358
Salmagundi 278
Salmon
    croquettes with dill sauce 141
    mousse 141
    smoked and Brie, tortilla
        triangles 86
    steak, chilled, with marinated
        cucumber 141
Salsa cruda 151
Sandwich(es)
    American hero 373
    California open 373
    chili dogs 373
    country club 373
    deli specials 372
    deluxe steak 372
    ham 'n' Swiss croissant
        372
    ribbon 372
    traditionals 373
San Francisco burger 187
San Francisco seafood casserole
    126
San Francisco strawberry parfait
    303
Sauce(s)
    almond-curry 206
    barbecue, sauces for
        cranberry-honey 226
        East Indies 226
        fiery chili 226
        green-onion-soy 226
        peanut-ginger 226
        peppery hot 226
        rosemary-butter 226
        tangy beer 226
    buttered raisin 195
    cran-apple wine 206

cranberry-pear wine 206
cranberry-wine 195
creamy cocktail 385
Creole 112
currant-orange 206
dessert, sauces for
    bittersweet chocolate
        290
    brandy hard 315
    custard 290
    foamy hard 298
    fudge 304
    raspberry 290
green mayonnaise 385
hollandaise 385
honey-mustard 195
horseradish 385
ice cream, sauces for
    brandied-strawberry 306
    chocolate-marshmallow
        306
    hot butterscotch 306
    Melba 306
pasta, sauces for
    anchovy 265
    four-cheese 265
    marinara 265
    meat 265
    Parmesan-cheese 262
    pesto 265
    spaghetti 259
    spinach 265
    walnut 265
praline 195
salsa cruda 151
shrimp-olive 385
spicy red-pepper 385
tartar 385
thick white 113
vegetables, sauces for
    butter 256
    cold chiffon 256
    fine herbs 256
    lemon butter 256
    mornay 256
    sour-cream mustard 256
    yogurt-watercress 385
Saucy chicken wings 85
Sauerkraut
    pork-and- supper 191
    with kielbasa 212
Sausage(s)
    and corn-bread stuffing 169
    apple-glazed franks and cabbage
        212
    camp-stove stew 213
    Italian- and peppers 212
    kielbasa with sauerkraut 212
    knackwurst sauerbraten 213
    -Muenster melts 86
    patties, breakfast- 213
    pig in a blanket 87
    Polish, with red cabbage 213
    -rice stuffing 169
Sautéed cabbage 178
Sautéed fish fillets with walnut
    coating 142
Sautéed herbed mushrooms
    177
Sautéed-onion topping 185
Sautéed roe 136
Savory grilled duckling 222
Scallion pompom 100

Scalloped oysters 123
Scallop(s)
    kabobs 124
    pan-fried 124
Scampi-style fish 137
Sea bass
    oven-steamed 134
    stuffed baked 134
Seafood
    casserole, San Francisco 126
    risotto, chilled 127
    skillet -Newburg 126
Seasoned avocados 111
Semisweet chocolate cheesecake
    340
Seven-layer chocolate chiffon
    cake 330
"Seven-minute" frosting 344
SHELLFISH 119–127
    angels on horseback 125
    clam(s)
        family -bake 119
        fritters 119
        steamed soft-shell 119
    crab(s)
        cakes 121
        fresh cooked 120
        imperial 121
        pan-fried soft-shell 120
    crayfish étouffée 121
    hangtown fry 123
    lobster
        à l'Americaine 122
        thermidor 122
    mussels and clams fra diavolo
        126
    oyster(s)
        on half-shell 123
        Rockefeller 123
        scalloped 123
    party paella 127
    scallop(s)
        kabobs 124
        pan-fried 124
    seafood
        casserole, San Francisco
            126
        risotto, chilled 127
        skillet -Newburg 126
    shrimp
        beer-batter-fried 124
        Jambalaya 125
        leek-wrapped, with cheese
            filling 125
Sherried cubed steaks 174
Shish kabob 207
Shoofly pie 324
Shrimp
    angels on horseback 125
    beer-batter-fried 124
    cocktail with tangy dip 89
    Creole omelet 112
    -filled fillets 138
    how to peel 332
    Jambalaya 125
    leek-wrapped, with cheese
        filling 125
    -olive sauce 385
    San Francisco seafood casserole
        126
    salad 279
    skillet seafood Newburg 126
    -stuffed chicken legs 155

Silver dollar pancakes 370
Sirloin steaks with fresh-pepper
    relish 217
Skillet-baked acorn squash
    245
Skillet braised endive and
    radicchio 256
Skillet corn 236
Skillet peppers and eggs 112
Skillet seafood Newburg 126
Sliced tomatoes with lemon
    dressing 276
Slipped coconut-custard 319
Sloppy Joe 186
Snickerdoodles 347
Snow apples 288
Sole
    baked, with lemon sauce 142
    fillets, creamy 142
    sautéed fish fillets with walnut
        coating 142
Soufflé(s)
    herb and cheese 116
    wild rice and chicken 116
SOUP(S) 95–106
    accompaniments for 97
    chicken and turkey soups
        104–105
        chicken and rice 105
        chicken-escarole 104
        Creole turkey 105
        mulligatawny 104
        Pensylvania Dutch chicken and
            corn 104
    croutons, how to prepare
        103
    fish soups 106
        Louisiana gumbo 106
        Manhattan clam chowder 106
        New England clam chowder
            106
        oyster 106
    garnishes 100
    hearty soups 100–103
        barley, beef, and vegetable
            102
        beet and vegetable 102
        black bean 100
        chunky lamb and bean 101
        cream of peanut 102
        hearty split pea 103
        lentil and frankfurter 101
        minestrone 101
        Philadelphia pepper pot
            102
    vegetable soups 97–100
        chilled cucumber 99
        chilled watercress 99
        corn chowder 97
        cream of fresh tomato 98
        cream of mushroom 98
        creamy California artichoke
            98
        gazpacho 100
        onion soup gratiné 97
        velvety pumpkin bisque 97
        vichyssoise 99
Sour-cherry jam 381
Sour cream biscuits 363
Sour-cream coffeecake 329
Sour-cream mustard sauce
    256
Sour-cream pumpkin pie 318

Sourdough bread 359
Southern cooking 237
Southern-fried chicken *149*
Soy-sesame marinade 223
Spaghetti
  and meatballs 259
  sauce 259
Spaghetti squash with spicy
  meat sauce *245*
Spareribs
  country, Texas *219*
  country, with red chili sauce
    194
  oven-barbecued *194*
  pineapple-glazed *194*
  Tex-Mex barbecued *219*
  with peach sauce *219*
Special occasion menus
  Christmas dinner 332
  Christmas Eve party 253
  Easter lunch 130
  4th of July barbecue 198
  Labor Day clambake 201
  Halloween party buffet 248
  Memorial Day picnic 196
  Mother's Day lunch 133
  New Year's Day brunch 337
  New Year's Eve supper 334
  Thanksgiving Day 250
  Valentine's Day party 128
Spice cake, old-fashioned
  342
Spiced apple rings, how to
  make 290
Spiced crab apples 379
Spiced eggs 113
Spiced pears with chocolate
  sauce *291*
Spiced prunes 378
Spicy beef brisket 178
Spicy red-pepper sauce 385
Spicy veal round roast 208
Spicy watermelon pickles
  378
Spinach
  casserole, egg-and- *110*
  flounder, -stuffed 138
  meat-loaf roll with -stuffing
    184
  quiche 114
  salad, mushroom, bacon,
    and 271
  sauce 265
  stuffing 159
Split pea(s)
  soup, hearty *103*
Spoon bread 366
Spring lamb with green
  vegetables 205
Springtime rhubarb refresher
  291
Spritz 348
Squash
  acorn-, skillet-baked 245
  acorn-, stuffed 245
  cranberry pot roast with
    acorn- *179*
  maple butternut- 245
  pie 318
  spaghetti, with spicy meat
    sauce *245*
  summer- and pepper slaw 272
  anding rib roast 176

Steak(s)
  Diane *175*
  planked, how to present 217
  sirloin, with fresh-pepper relish
    217
  with anchovy butter 217
  with mustard butter *173*
  see also Beef
Steamed soft-shell clams 119
Stew(s)(ed)
  beef, pressure-cooked 180
  Brunswick 154
  camp-stove 213
  Mulligan 207
  pork and chicken 193
  tomatoes, fresh 247
  venison 214
Sticky buns 362
Stir-fried mushrooms 238
Stir-fried sugar snap peas
  239
Stir-fried sword fish 143
Strawberry(ies)
  blintzes *371*
  fans 291
  grunt, -rhubarb *289*
  jam *381*
  jam dandies *348*
    variation: heart-shaped 128
  molded- 'n' cream *300*
  peaches in- and custard
    sauce *290*
  pie, -rhubarb *314*
  preparing 314
  purée 290
  sauce, brandied- *306*
  shortcake *341*
Streusel topping 315
Stuffed acorn squash 245
Stuffed artichokes Monterey 229
Stuffed baked sea bass 134
Stuffed beef roll *176*
Stuffed cabbage rolls *183*
Stuffed capon with cranberry-
  poached pears *147*
Stuffed chicken quarters with
  cherry tomatoes *153*
Stuffed mushrooms 88
Stuffed shoulder of lamb 204
Stuffing(s)
  apple-herb *170*
  bacon-rice 164
  calculating quantities 170
  chestnut 169
  moist bread 170
  nutty brown-rice 169
  oyster 170
  pecan 160
  rye-bread 166
  sausage and corn-bread 169
  sausage-rice 169
  spinach 159
  vegetable-rice 147
  wild-rice-and-mushroom 159
Succotash 231
Sugar cookies 348
Sugar-frosted apple pie *309*
Sugar-smoked chicken 221
Summer fruits in apple-wine
  gelatin 293
Summer-garden rice *268*
Summer squash and pepper
  slaw 272

Sunchoke pickles 377
Sundae(s)
  old-fashioned hot fudge 303
Sweet-and-sour
  Cornish hens with -sauce 222
  fresh tongue with -tomato
    sauce *214*
  relish 384
Sweet-cherry jam 381
Sweet corn with herb butter
  236
Sweet potato(es)
  baked candied *246*
  pie with walnut-crunch
    topping *318*
Swiss chard
  jumbo ravioli with 263
Swordfish
  stir-fried 143
  with herb butter 143

T

Tangerine(s)
  relish, cranberry- 383
Tangy beer sauce 226
Tangy corn relish 385
Tangy hot potato salad 273
Tapioca
  coconut-pineapple 295
Tartar sauce 385
Tart(s)
  arranging fruit 316
  summer- and tartlets, how
    to make 317
  shell 316
Texas caviar 274
Texas country ribs *219*
Texas-style chili 182
Tex-Mex barbecued spareribs 219
Tex-Mex chili burger 187
Tex-Mex style rice *267*
Thanksgiving Day (menu) 250
Thick white sauce 113
Three-berry pastry 316
Thousand Island dressing 284
Three-bean and cheese
  salad 274
Toast
  French 371
Tomato(es)
  asparagus and cherry *230*
  bacon-wrapped broiled 247
  cherry, pan-fried 247
  chicken -cups, curried 280
  chicken quarters, stuffed, with
    cherry *153*

chow chow, green- *383*
goat cheese, herbed, with
  sun-dried 92
guacamole-filled 91
pizza, avocado- 374
-sausage scramble 110
sliced, with lemon dressing
  276
soup, cream of fresh 98
stewed fresh 247
tongue, fresh with sweet-and-
  sour-sauce *214*
vinaigrette, oranges and 276
Tongue
  fresh, with sweet-and-sour
    tomato sauce *214*
Torte, chocolate sour-cream
  331
Tortellini pesto platter 282
Tortilla(s)
  bake, cheesy *115*
  chicken burritos *157*
  quesados 87
  steaming and folding 157
  triangles, Brie and smoked
    salmon 86
Tropical chicken-potato salad
  with avocado and papaya
  280
Tropical fruit, preparing 337
Trout
  pan-fried, with vegetable
    stuffing 143
Tuna
  bake, fresh 144
  casserole, -noodle 144
  dip, hot 94
  pâté, molded *144*
  salad, potato- *279*
Turkey
  curried, with apples and
    peanuts 163
  cutlets Marsala *162*
  giblet gravy *161*
  hash, country 163
  Maryland *162*
  old-fashioned creamed, with
    biscuits 163
  roast, with pecan stuffing *160*
  soup, Creole *105*
Twice-baked potatoes 242
Two-melon granita 306

U

Unbaked crumb crust 321
Unbaked piecrust 310

V

Valentine's Day Party (menu) 128
Valentine's devil's food cake 128
Vanilla crumb crust 321
Vanilla frosting 344
Variety meat(s) 211–214
  apple-glazed franks and cabbage 212
  breakfast sausage patties 213
  camp-stove stew 213
  fresh tongue with sweet-and-sour sauce 214
  Italian sausages and peppers 212
  kielbasa with sauerkraut 212
  knackwurst sauerbraten 213
  liver and onions 211
  pan-fried liver, bacon, and onions 211
  Polish sausage with red cabbage 213
  venison steaks with wine sauce 214
  venison stew 214
Veal 208–211
  breast, mushroom-stuffed 208
  breast, plum-glazed 218
  chops, golden 209
  chops with avocado 209
  chops with mushrooms 209
  cutlets, California 210
  cutlets, ham and cheese-stuffed 210
  Parmigiana 210
  ragout, -and-chestnut 211
  round roast, spicy 208
VEGETABLE(S) 227–256
  artichoke(s)
    bottoms, how to prepare 229
    stuffed Monterey 229
    with mustard sauce 229
  asparagus
    and cherry tomatoes 230
    California braised, and celery 230
  barbecuing corn-on-the-cob and other 225
  barley, beef, and 102
  bean(s)
    black- and rice 232
    Boston baked 232
    buttered-crumb Lima 231
    casserole, green- and onion 231
    hoppin' John 232
    island pork and 233
    prairie- tacos 233
    ranch-style 233
    red- and rice 232
    succotash 231
    whole green and wax, with blue-cheese sauce 231
  beef and vegetable kabobs with peanut sauce 220

beet(s)
  and vegetable soup 102
  Harvard 234
broccoli
  with butter-almond sauce 234
  with sour-cream sauce 234
carrot(s)
  and grapes 234
  fruited 235
  glazed 234
cauliflower
  baked, in cheese sauce 235
  Parmesan 235
chilies, how to prepare 240
corn
  fritters 236
  pudding, custard- 236
  skillet 236
  sweet- with herb butter 236
  decorating with 230
eggplant Parmigiana 237
kabobs 225
lasagna 264
marinated garden vegetables 276
mixed vegetables
  and dill 254
  bouquet 255
  broiled leeks, sweet peppers, and mushrooms 255
  lemon-buttered 248
  roasted mélange 248
  skillet braised endive and radicchio 256
mushroom(s)
  chilled lemony 238
  stir-fried 238
onion(s)
  baked 238
  Cheddared 239
  creamed 239
  French-fried rings 238
  glazed 239
pea(s)
  minted 239
  stir-fried sugar snap 239
  with green onions 239
pepper(s)
  batter-fried stuffed chilies 240
  hearty stuffed 241
  ratatouille in roasted 241
potato(es)
  and vegetable salad, creamy- 273
  carnival mashed 243
  Delmonico 244
  duchess 244
  fans, roasted 244
  hash brown 242
  home-fried 242
  new- with lemon and chives 243
  party- with leeks 243
  twice-baked 242
purées, how to make 255

-rice stuffing 147
salad, creamy potato and- 273
sauces for vegetables
  butter 256
  cold chiffon 256
  fine herbs 256
  lemon butter 256
  mornay 256
  sour-cream mustard 256
squash
  maple butternut 245
  skillet-baked acorn 245
  spaghetti, with spicy meat sauce 245
  stuffed acorn 245
  zucchini with rice filling 246
sweet potatoes, baked candied 246
tomato(es)
  bacon-wrapped broiled 247
  pan-fried cherry 247
  stewed fresh 247
Velvety custard with banana sauce 296
Velvety pumpkin bisque 97
Venison
  steaks with wine sauce 214
  stew 214
Vermont biscuits 363
Vermont Cheddar sticks 93
Vermont pork and beans 193
Vichyssoise 99
Vinaigrette
  lemony 210
  oranges and tomatoes 276

Watercress
  sauce, yogurt- 385
  soup, chilled 99
Watermelon
  pickles, spicy 378
Wax bean(s) see Bean(s)
Welsh rabbit 115
Western scrambled eggs 110
Wheat-flake crumb crust 321
Whipped cream
  decorating with 319
White bread 357
White meringue topping 320
Whole-wheat
  bread, crusty oatmeal 357
Wild-rice
  and chicken soufflé 116
  and mushroom stuffing 159
  with peas and mushrooms 268
Wine-jelly glaze 164

Y

Yankee pot roast 178
Yogurt-watercress sauce 385
Yorkshire pudding 176

W

Waldorf salad 283
Walnut(s)
  buns, -cinnamon 362
  cookies, chocolate-chip- 346
  crust, -pastry 321
  filling, chocolate- 344
  salad, barley- 275
  sauce 265
  sweet-potato pie with -crunch topping 318

Z

Zesty Mexican eggs and beans 109
Ziti with hearty home-style meat sauce 261
Zucchini
  and artichoke hearts, fried 88
  and artichoke hearts, "oven-fried" 88
  -oatmeal muffins 368
  with rice filling 246

ACKNOWLEDGMENTS

Photographers:

Martin Brigdale
Clive Streeter
Grant Symon
Andrew Whittuck

Home Economists:

Jacki Baxter
Allyson Birch
Clare Gordon-Smith
Mary Luther
Bonnie Rabert
Jane Suthering
Michelle Thomson
Steven Wheeler

Stylists:

Bobby Baker
Liz Hippisley
Penny Markham
Sue Russell
Sarah Wiley
Alison Williams

Artists:

Nancy Anderson
David Ashby
Lindsay Blow
Kuo Kang Chen
Will Giles
Tony Graham
Robert Kettell
Coral Mula
Gilly Newman
Howard Pemberton
Richard Phipps
Sandra Pond
Jim Robins
Lorna Turpin